# HSE and Environment Agency Prosecutions: The New Climate

# HSE and Environment Agency Prosecution: The New Climate

Charlotte Waters
Mike Appleby
Louise Smail

Bloomsbury Professional

LONDON · DUBLIN · EDINBURGH · NEW YORK · NEW DELHI · SYDNEY

**BLOOMSBURY PROFESSIONAL**
Bloomsbury Publishing Plc
41–43 Boltro Road, Haywards Heath, RH16 1BJ, UK

**BLOOMSBURY** and the Diana logo are trademarks
of Bloomsbury Publishing Plc

First published in Great Britain 2019

Copyright © Bloomsbury Professional, 2019

All rights reserved. No part of this publication may be reproduced or transmitted in any form or by any means, electronic or mechanical, including photocopying, recording, or any information storage or retrieval system, without prior permission in writing from the publishers.

While every care has been taken to ensure the accuracy of this work, no responsibility for loss or damage occasioned to any person acting or refraining from action as a result of any statement in it can be accepted by the authors, editors or publishers.

All UK Government legislation and other public sector information used in the work is Crown Copyright ©. All House of Lords and House of Commons information used in the work is Parliamentary Copyright ©. This information is reused under the terms of the Open Government Licence v3.0 (http://www.nationalarchives.gov.uk/doc/open-government-licence/version/3) except where otherwise stated.

All Eur-lex material used in the work is © European Union, http://eur-lex.europa.eu/, 1998-2019.

Contains public sector information published by the Health and Safety Executive and licensed under the Open Government Licence.

British Library Cataloguing-in-Publication Data

A catalogue record for this book is available from the British Library.

ISBN:  PB:     978-1-52650-322-0
       ePDF:   978-1-52650-324-4
       ePub:   978-1-52650-323-7

Typeset by Evolution Design & Digital Ltd (Kent)
Printed and bound by CPI Group (UK) Ltd, Croydon, CR0 4YY

To find out more about our authors and books visit www.bloomsburyprofessional.com. Here you will find extracts, author information, details of forthcoming events and the option to sign up for our newsletters

# Foreword

Mike Appleby, Charlotte Waters and Louise Smail have produced a practical work that for the first time has sought to synthesize critical aspects of health and safety law and environmental law as it affects corporations and those who manage them.

Regulatory environmental law is concerned ultimately with safeguarding important features which contribute to the wellbeing of society. Health and safety law protects workers and the wider public alike. Whilst there have been offences associated with breaches of both aspects for very many decades, if not longer, there was a time when the criminal aspects of breaches of the law in these areas were treated as of much less significance than the civil aspects. Prosecutions were relatively few and far between and the penalties imposed by the courts were rarely substantial, in the sense of having a tangible impact on the businesses in question.

Public tolerance changed and so too did the approach of the courts. Fines increased and penalties were eventually subject to Sentencing Guidelines which cemented the change in approach that had for some time been in the making.

Most businesses are responsible and take their duties seriously. But the combination of exposure to increased financial penalties coupled with the reputational damage which can attach to regulatory breaches and the impact on securing contracts, has led to an increase in the determination of corporate entities to avoid breaches. At the same time the potential criminal liability of directors, senior managers and others directly responsible for transgressions has come to the fore. This accessible book, useful to lawyers and non-lawyers alike, provides guidance to help organisations manage risk not only for their own benefit, but for the benefit of others. It provides a handy reference for many aspects of environmental and health and safety regulatory law. It also touches on questions that may arise in public inquiries and inquests.

This valuable work thus provides organisations with an insight into how to manage risk in two important regulatory environments. The proper management of risk is likely to prevent accidents and injury and broader environmental mishaps. It will avoid harm to individuals and the public and at the same time protect the organisation and those who run it. The interests are entirely coincident.

Forewarned is forearmed.

The Right Honourable the Lord Burnett of Maldon
Lord Chief Justice of England and Wales
28 February 2019

# Preface

Corporate governance, the system of rules, practices and processes by which organisations are directed and controlled, has increasingly come under the media's spotlight. It has also risen up the Government's agenda.

Two highly critical reports were published in 2016 where Parliament found serious failings in corporate governance of two household names in the retail sector. The first was a joint report by the Work and Pensions and the Business, Innovation and Skills Committees concerning the sale and acquisition of BHS and its treatment of its pension fund, and the second report, by the Business, Innovation and Skills Committee, regarding the employment practices of Sports Direct. The Government is now considering reform.

The last 20 years or so has seen a growth in the prominence of health and safety and environmental duties. There is now a public expectation that when investigating authorities find serious failings, criminal prosecution should follow.

It is not that long ago that convicted organisations would receive quite modest fines for health and safety and environmental offences. However this is no longer the case. There has been a sea change in sentencing with the introduction in 2014 of the *Environmental Offences: Definitive Guideline* and in 2016 the *Health and Safety Offences, Corporate Manslaughter and Food Safety and Hygiene Offences: Definitive Guideline*.

In 2017 Thames Water was given a record fine of £20.3m after significant leaks of untreated sewage into the Thames and surrounding land. The leaks, which were over a long period of time, had a serious impact on residents, farmers, and wildlife. The previous year Thames Water had been fined £1m for repeated leaks into the Grand Union canal in Hertfordshire and £380,000 following a sewage leak in an area in the Chilterns.

£1m plus fines are no longer reserved for health and safety cases involving fatalities. The Sentencing Guideline points out these offences are concerned with failures to manage health and safety risk and do not require proof of harm, stating that the offence 'is in creating the risk of harm'. In 2016 Alton Towers operator Merlin Attractions was fined £5m for an admitted health and safety breach in relation to the 2015 crash on its Smiler rollercoaster. Sixteen people were injured including two teenage girls who had leg amputations.

The Court of Appeal has made clear that large fines are here to stay. In *R v Whirlpool* [2017] EWCA Crim 2186 the court warned:

*Preface*

'Large commercial entities in many areas of business are vulnerable to very substantial financial penalties for regulatory failings. The same is true for breaches of health and safety or environmental law in appropriate cases.'

Just as significant as the substantial fines that can be imposed upon organisations is the increase in prosecutions of directors and senior managers for offences under s 37 of the Health and Safety at Work etc Act 1974 where it is alleged that corporate failure was due to the consent or connivance of the defendant or attributable to their neglect. If convicted in the Crown Court a custodial sentence of up to two years can be imposed. The Sentencing Guideline states that where culpability is medium and the seriousness of harm risked is death or physical or mental impairment resulting in lifelong care, the starting point for sentence is six months imprisonment. In addition there has also been an increase in the number of disqualification orders made against convicted directors under the Company Directors Disqualification Act 1986.

Although health and safety law and environmental law is covered by different legislation and investigated by different regulatory authorities, many of the issues involved are the same or at the very least similar. The aim of this book is to bring together, it is believed for the first time, a book that gives guidance in both areas. It is divided into four parts:

**Part 1 Managing Risk:** including corporate governance, directors' duties and business continuity (ie planning to deal with major disruption);

**Part 2 The Law:** an overview of the offences – health and safety, manslaughter (individual and corporate), fire offences and environmental offences (including pollution and illegal waste disposal);

**Part 3 Enforcement and Sentencing:** including responding to a criminal investigation and an introduction to the prosecution process; and

**Part 4 Inquests and Claims:** an overview of inquests (and public inquiries), civil claims and insurance.

The Appendix contains summaries of the cases referred to in the text.

This book is not just intended as a reference work for lawyers but is aimed at directors and those in senior and middle management of organisations that are responsible for managing health and safety and environmental risks.

The law is stated as at 1 February 2019.

Mark Scoggins
Fisher Scoggins Waters LLP
March 2019

# About the Authors

Fisher Scoggins Waters LLP is a London based firm founded in 2002 by Alan Fisher, Mark Scoggins and Charlotte Waters. It has acted in many high profile cases ranging from representing Balfour Beatty when the company was acquitted in 2005 on all corporate manslaughter charges following the Hatfield train derailment (and its successful appeal against sentence for an admitted health and safety breach) to the judicial review in 2017 on behalf of the facilities management company OCS of HSE's Fee for Intervention scheme which led to an amended dispute process.

Its lawyers are construction, engineering and manufacturing litigators specialising in disputes and disasters. The firm's clients are from construction, engineering, utility and manufacturing companies, architects, surveyors, ports, facilities management, insurance companies, fire services, police forces, local authorities and schools and colleges.

In the *Legal 500 2018–2019* the firm is described as 'an excellent niche firm with a good reputation in the field [of health and safety]', Fisher Scoggins Waters LLP 'offers a complete service to companies and individuals alike' and 'really puts in the effort to get to know its clients and their business environments'. In *Chambers and Partners* the directory says: 'Respected team noted for its extensive expertise handling the full gamut of health and safety issues. Capable of assisting clients on criminal, civil and commercial proceedings in court as well as carrying out audits and reviews regarding regulatory compliance'.

**Mark Scoggins** is a Solicitor Advocate with full Higher Rights of Audience in all courts and in all proceedings.

His principal practice is the defence of organisations and individuals in the construction, chemical, transport, waste and water sectors in regulatory and civil cases, particularly health and safety, corporate manslaughter and environmental.

A graduate of Cambridge University, he has been based in the City of London since his call to the Bar in 1983.

Mark has been recommended in the *Legal 500* and *Chambers* since 1999. He is recommended in the *Legal 500 2018–2019* for health and safety where he is as 'a true battle-hardened campaigner and fully dedicated to his clients', and in *Chambers and Partners 2019* where it says Mark has an extensive health and safety practice handling cases following major injuries and fatalities. He often defends clients from prosecutions brought by the police and the HSE.

*About the Authors*

Mark appeared for the British Shooting Sports Council in the public inquiry arising out of the Dunblane school shootings. His notable cases include defence of Balfour Beatty in the Health and Safety Executive prosecution over the Heathrow Express tunnel collapse of 1994, and representation of Thames Trains at the public inquiry into the October 1999 collision near Ladbroke Grove before Lord Cullen. Among his other health and safety, regulatory and environmental work are cases arising from construction, pipelines, waste reclamation, fish farming, flooding, pollution, drinking water contamination, asbestos removal, electrocution, confined spaces and EU public procurement.

In a five-week trial ending in June 2003 Mark led the successful Old Bailey defence of Metropolitan Police Commissioner Sir John Stevens and his predecessor Lord Condon on all ten charges brought against them by the HSE arising out of roof falls suffered by patrolling police officers.

He was appointed by Balfour Beatty on the October 2000 derailment at Hatfield. In July 2005, and after a six-month trial, Mark (along with Mike Appleby and Charlotte Waters) helped win the acquittal of its railway arm on all corporate manslaughter charges it faced arising out of that incident, and in 2006 succeeded on its appeal against sentence for admitted health and safety failings.

Mark represented the Metropolitan Police in the health and safety prosecution against the service over the fatal shooting of Jean Charles de Menezes at Stockwell station in July 2005.

**Charlotte Waters** is the Managing Partner of Fisher Scoggins Waters LLP and specialises in construction, engineering and manufacturing disputes. Charlotte is an accredited Mediator and is a Solicitor-Advocate with full Higher Rights of Audience in all courts in all proceedings. She specialises in incident response following construction and engineering disasters and is a key member of the firm's major incident response team. Charlotte acts for contractors, subcontractors, employers, architects, engineers, quantity surveyors, insurers and manufacturers in complex major property damage claims arising out of construction and design defects, fire, flood, theft, impact and subsidence. Charlotte has worked on many high profile cases such as the Ladbroke Grove Rail Crash, the Hatfield Rail Crash, and the health and safety prosecution which followed the shooting of Jean Charles de Menezes at Stockwell station in July 2005. An honorary legal adviser to the ICPEM – Institute of Civil Protection and Emergency Management; a contributing author to the Lexis PSL on Construction, Member of the Oil, Petrochemical and Energy Risks Association and the Association for Petroleum and Explosives Administration.

**Mike Appleby** is a partner at Fisher Scoggins Waters LLP. He defends directors, senior individuals and companies facing investigation or prosecution for health and safety offences or manslaughter arising from work-related incidents.

Mike is ranked as a star individual for health and safety in *Chambers and Partners 2019*. The directory quotes clients as saying his knowledge of health and safety law 'is second to none' and that he provides 'excellent legal representation' along with 'commercial awareness, strategies and tactics'. The

*Legal 500 2018–2019* ranks him as a leading individual in the field of health and safety describing him as 'a real tactical genius' and 'master mind against the HSE'.

Mike began his career as a trade union lawyer. In 1998 he secured the acquittal of the train driver involved in the Watford train crash, prosecuted for a single count of gross negligence manslaughter. In the following year he secured the acquittal of the train driver involved in the Southall train crash who was prosecuted for gross negligence manslaughter and breaching s 7 of the Health and Safety at Work etc Act 1974. He then represented the drivers' union ASLEF in the public inquiries into the Southall train crash before Professor Uff and the Ladbroke Grove train crash before Lord Cullen.

Mike joined Fisher Scoggins Waters in 2003 and with Mark Scoggins and Charlotte Waters he represented the rail maintenance arm of Balfour Beatty in relation to the Hatfield train derailment prosecution and subsequent appeal.

Mike represented the managing director G in one of the leading appellate cases upon directors' health and safety duties *R v P Ltd and G* [2008] ICR 96, CA. G was acquitted of a charge of breaching s 37 of the Health and Safety at Work etc Act 1974. A preliminary issue went before the Court of Appeal in respect of the interpretation of s 37, particularly in regard to 'attributable neglect'.

In 2013 he acted for an engineering company that was acquitted of corporate manslaughter. The prosecution related to the collapse of a crane that killed a seaman. The company had been contracted to undertake thorough examinations of the lifting equipment.

In 2017 Mike represented the facilities management company OCS Group (UK) Limited in its successful judicial review of HSE's Fee for Intervention scheme (FFI) which led to HSE introducing an amended dispute process later that year.

Mike frequently writes and lectures on health and safety issues. For over ten years he wrote a regular column for health and safety magazine *SHP*. He is the author of the Transport chapter of *Corporate Liability: Work Related Deaths and Criminal Prosecutions* (Bloomsbury Professional, 3rd edn, 2014).

Mike lecturers at Loughborough University on the Postgraduate Diploma Course in Health and Safety Management, on IET's Electrical Safety Management course and at City University of London on its MSc Temporary Works and Construction Method Engineering.

Mike is a member of the Health and Safety Advisory Group for the Royal Institution of Chartered Surveyors (RICS) and is one of the contributors to its publication *Surveying Safely* (2nd edn, 2019).

**Louise Smail** is a specialist risk and safety consultant with Fisher Scoggins Waters with many years experience dealing with corporate governance. Previously, Louise has worked as principal consultant and director of two international consulting groups. Louise offers clients assistance with the preparation and validation of risk management plans with the aim of ensuring clients have

*About the Authors*

the highest standards in public safety. Louise has extensive experience in the fields of risk management, organisational resilience, and health, safety and environment law with a wide range of organisations, including local government, emergency services, the Cabinet Office, process and chemical industries, utilities, waste and construction. Louise gave expert evidence to the Ladbroke Grove Rail Public Inquiry.

Louise provides advice on environmental risk management including: contaminated land; writing reports; and negotiating with land owners and lease holders. Louise writes extensively and lectures risk management and health, safety and environmental issues.

Louise is a member of the British Computer Society – Chartered Information Technology Practitioner and is a charted member of the Institute of Occupational Safety and Health (CMIOSH).

Louise is the editor and contributor to the book *Corporate Liability: Work related Deaths and Criminal Prosecutions* (3rd edn, 2014). A fourth edition is planned for early 2020. Louise is author of *Waste Regulation Law 2016*.

# Contents

| | |
|---|---|
| *Foreword* | *v* |
| *Preface* | *vii* |
| *About the Authors* | *ix* |
| *Table of Statutes* | *xxv* |
| *Table of Statutory Instruments* | *xxix* |
| *Table of EC/EU Legislation* | *xxxiii* |
| *Table of Cases* | *xxxv* |

## Part 1 Managing Risk

| | | |
|---|---|---|
| 1 | **Corporate Governance, Directors' Duties** | 3 |
| | Introduction | 3 |
| | History of corporate governance | 5 |
| | UK Corporate Governance Code | 8 |
| |     Board leadership and company purpose | 8 |
| |     Division of responsibilities | 9 |
| |     Composition, succession and evaluation | 9 |
| |     Audit, risk and internal control | 10 |
| |     Remuneration | 10 |
| | Application of the latest Corporate Governance Report | 10 |
| | Key highlights of the Corporate Governance Code 2018 | 12 |
| |     Guidance on the effectiveness of boards | 14 |
| |     G20/OECD Principle of Corporate Governance | 14 |
| | | |
| 2 | **Risk Management** | 17 |
| | Introduction | 18 |
| | Controlling risks in the workplace | 18 |
| | Legislation | 18 |
| |     Health and Safety at Work etc Act 1974 | 18 |
| |     Management of Health and Safety at Work Regulations 1999 | 19 |
| |     Workplace (Health, Safety and Welfare) Regulations 1992 | 19 |
| |     Other legislation | 20 |
| |     Legislation with specific requirements | 21 |
| | Prosecutions for a lack of a risk management system | 21 |
| |     *Goldscheider v Royal Opera House Covent Garden Foundation* | 21 |
| |     *Cundall v Leeds City Council* | 22 |
| |     *Kennedy v Cordia (Services) LLP* | 22 |

*Contents*

|  |  |  |
|---|---|---|
| Risk assessment | | 22 |
|     Definition of a hazard | | 23 |
|     Definition of a risk | | 23 |
| Five steps to risk assessment | | 23 |
|     Step 1: Identify the hazards | | 23 |
|     Step 2: Decide who might be harmed and how | | 24 |
|     Step 3: Evaluate the risks | | 24 |
|     Step 4: Record the significant findings | | 27 |
|     Step 5: Review the risk assessment and update if necessary | | 28 |
| Safety auditing | | 28 |
|     Internal v external audits | | 28 |
| Certification audits | | 29 |
|     External certification | | 30 |
|     ISO 45001 Occupational Health and Safety | | 30 |

**3 Business Continuity** — 33

Introduction — 34
Business continuity plan — 34
Business continuity management — 35
Business impact analysis — 36
    Step 1 – identify key products and services — 36
    Step 2 – maximum time the organisation can manage — 36
    Step 3 – recovery time — 37
    Step 4 – critical activities — 37
    Step 5 – quantify the resources — 37
Creating a business continuity plan — 37
    Assessment of the current situation — 37
    Security — 37
    Fire — 38
    Services — 38
    Insurance — 38
    Salvage — 39
    Planning — 39
Communications — 42
    Relations with the public — 43
    Liaison with emergency services — 43
    Other issues to consider — 43
Revision of plans after the event — 44

## Part 2 The Law

**4 Manslaughter and Health and Safety Offences** — 47

Corporate manslaughter — 48
    Introduction — 48
    The offence — 49
    The organisation — 50
    Causation — 52

|  |  |  |
|---|---|---|
| | Relevant duty of care | 52 |
| | The gross breach | 53 |
| | Foreseeability | 53 |
| | Senior management | 54 |
| | Jurisdiction | 54 |
| | Exclusions | 54 |
| | Investigation | 55 |
| | Gross negligence manslaughter | 55 |
| | The offence | 55 |
| | Duty of care | 57 |
| | Grossness of the breach | 60 |
| | Health and Safety at Work etc Act 1974 Offences | 60 |
| | Employers | 60 |
| | Employees | 70 |
| 5 | **Health and Safety Enforcement Notices, Fee for Intervention (FFI) and Cautions** | 73 |
| | Health and safety enforcement notices | 73 |
| | Improvement notices | 74 |
| | Prohibition notices | 74 |
| | Appeals | 75 |
| | The process | 75 |
| | Costs | 76 |
| | Why appeal? | 77 |
| | Fee for intervention (FFI) | 77 |
| | What is FFI? | 77 |
| | Challenging an FFI invoice | 79 |
| | Why raise a query/dispute? | 81 |
| | Cautions | 82 |
| 6 | **Environmental Offences** | 83 |
| | Environmental offences | 84 |
| | Strict liability | 85 |
| | Waste | 85 |
| | What is waste? | 85 |
| | Waste offences | 85 |
| | Penalties | 86 |
| | Unlawful deposit of controlled waste | 86 |
| | Waste carriers brokers registration | 86 |
| | Examples of penalties | 87 |
| | EPA 1990, s 157 – Offences by bodies corporate | 87 |
| | Fly-tipping | 88 |
| | Penalties | 88 |
| | Examples of prosecutions | 88 |
| | Fixed penalty notices | 89 |
| | Packaging waste | 89 |
| | Definition of packaging | 90 |
| | Obligated packing producer | 90 |

*Contents*

|   |   |   |
|---|---|---|
| | Definition of handling | 90 |
| | Activity list: definition/description | 90 |
| | Registration | 91 |
| Batteries | | 91 |
| | Penalties | 92 |
| | Example of a prosecution | 92 |
| WEEE Regulations | | 92 |
| Water offences | | 93 |
| | In England and Wales | 93 |
| | Anti-pollution works notice under the Water Resources Act 1991 | 94 |
| | In Scotland and Northern Ireland | 94 |
| | Examples of penalties | 95 |
| Noise nuisance | | 95 |
| | Penalties for not complying with a noise abatement notice | 96 |
| | Criminal behaviour orders for noise pollution | 96 |
| Statutory nuisance | | 97 |
| | An abatement notice | 97 |
| | Penalties for not complying with an abatement notice | 97 |
| | Appeals | 98 |
| | Examples of abatement notices and appeal | 98 |
| | Restrictions on use of public sewers | 99 |
| Wildlife crime | | 99 |
| | Examples of wildlife crime | 99 |
| | Examples of prosecutions | 100 |

**7 Environmental Notices and Sanctions** — 101

| | |
|---|---|
| Environmental notices and sanctions | 102 |
| Injunctions | 102 |
| Warnings | 103 |
| Formal caution | 103 |
| Enforcement notice | 103 |
| Criminal sanctions | 104 |
|     Fixed penalty notices (FPNs) | 104 |
|     Formal caution | 104 |
|     Prosecution | 105 |
| Orders imposed by the court ancillary to prosecution | 105 |
|     Disqualification of directors | 105 |
|     Confiscation of assets – Proceeds of Crime Act 2002 | 106 |
|     Criminal behaviour orders | 107 |
|     Forfeiture of equipment used to commit the offence | 107 |
|     Compensation | 108 |
|     Vehicle seizure | 108 |
| Regulatory Enforcement and Sanctions Act 2008 | 109 |
|     Fixed monetary penalties (FMPs) | 109 |
|     Variable monetary penalties (VMPs) | 109 |
|     Compliance notices | 110 |
|     Restoration notices | 111 |

|   |   |
|---|---|
| Stop notices | 111 |
| Suspension notice | 112 |
| Enforcement undertakings (EUs) | 113 |
| Non-compliance penalties | 113 |
| VMP, FMP or other monetary penalty | 113 |
| Enforcement undertakings | 114 |
| Restoration notice or compliance notice imposed without VMP | 114 |
| Non-compliance penalty notice (NCP) | 114 |
| Restoration notice or compliance notice imposed with a VMP or a third party undertaking accepted by the regulator | 114 |
| Stop notices | 115 |
| Other options | 115 |
| Enforcement cost recovery notices | 115 |
| Application of NCPs | 115 |
| Climate change regimes | 116 |
| Appeals | 116 |
| Environment tribunal | 116 |
| Who sits on the tribunal? | 116 |
| What can be appealed against? | 116 |
| Grounds of appeal | 117 |
| Tribunals powers | 118 |
| **8 Fire Safety Offences and Notices** | **119** |
| Introduction | 120 |
| Legislation | 120 |
| England and Wales | 121 |
| Scotland | 122 |
| Northern Ireland | 122 |
| Fire certificates | 122 |
| Requirements of the Regulatory Reform (Fire Safety) Order 2005 | 123 |
| Fire risk assessment | 124 |
| Fire extinguishers | 124 |
| Fire safety signs | 125 |
| Fire alarm systems | 125 |
| Emergency lighting | 126 |
| Fire safety training | 126 |
| Enforcement | 127 |
| Fire and Rescue Service | 127 |
| Local authority | 128 |
| Health and Safety Executive | 128 |
| Crown Fire Inspectors | 129 |
| Fire inspections | 129 |
| Public register of notices | 130 |
| Public register | 130 |
| Enforcement options for England, Wales and Scotland | 131 |
| Notices | 131 |

*Contents*

|  |  |
|---|---|
| Prosecution | 135 |
| Factors which affect choice of enforcement action | 135 |
| Examples of prosecutions | 136 |
| Companies | 136 |
| Individual fire safety prosecutions | 136 |
| Responsible person prosecution | 137 |
| Appeals | 137 |
| England and Wales | 137 |
| Scotland | 138 |
| Northern Ireland | 138 |
| Determinations | 139 |
| England and Wales | 139 |
| Scotland | 140 |

# Part 3 Enforcement and Sentencing

| 9 | **Enforcement Agencies and Enforcement Policies** | **145** |
|---|---|---|
|  | Health and safety enforcement | 146 |
|  | How the HSE and LAs work together | 146 |
|  | HELA (Health and Safety Executive/Local Authorities Enforcement Liaison Committee) | 146 |
|  | Health and Safety Executive (HSE) | 146 |
|  | Local Authority (LA) | 147 |
|  | Office of the Rail Regulator (ORR) | 149 |
|  | Office of Nuclear Regulations (ONR) | 150 |
|  | Health and Safety Executive Northern Ireland (HSENI) | 151 |
|  | Other enforcing authorities | 152 |
|  | Environmental enforcement | 153 |
|  | Environment Agency | 153 |
|  | Scottish Environment Protection Agency (SEPA) | 155 |
|  | Natural Resources Wales (NRW) | 155 |
|  | Northern Ireland Environment Agency (NIEA) | 157 |
|  | Local authorities | 158 |
| 10 | **RIDDOR and Internal Investigations** | **159** |
|  | RIDDOR (Reporting Injuries, Diseases and Dangerous Occurrences Regulations) and Incident Investigation | 160 |
|  | Purpose of a RIDDOR report | 160 |
|  | Who makes the report? | 161 |
|  | Why reports must be made | 162 |
|  | What must be reported? | 162 |
|  | How to make a RIDDOR report | 168 |
|  | Insurance | 168 |
|  | Failure to report | 169 |
|  | Over reporting | 169 |
|  | Records that need to be kept | 169 |
|  | HSE investigation | 170 |

xviii

|  |  | Mandatory investigations | 170 |
|---|---|---|---|
|  |  | Records that need to be kept | 172 |
|  |  | When does an incident need to be reported? | 172 |
|  |  | Exemptions | 172 |
|  |  | How long must RIDDOR records be kept? | 173 |
|  | Carrying out internal investigations | | 173 |
|  |  | Incident | 173 |
|  |  | Reasons to investigate a workplace incident: | 173 |
|  |  | What to investigate and who investigates | 174 |
|  |  | Should the immediate supervisor be on the team? | 174 |
|  |  | The decision to investigate | 175 |
|  |  | The investigation | 175 |
|  |  | Gathering information | 175 |
|  |  | Information analysis | 175 |
|  |  | Recommendations | 176 |
| 11 | **Responding to a Criminal Investigation** | | **177** |
|  | When an incident occurs | | 178 |
|  | Investigators' powers | | 180 |
|  | Fatal incidents: Work-related Deaths – A Protocol for Liaison | | 180 |
|  | Code for Crown Prosecutors | | 181 |
|  |  | The evidential test | 181 |
|  |  | The public interest test | 182 |
|  | Protocol – co-ordinating the response | | 183 |
|  | 1 | Inform insurers of the incident | 183 |
|  | 2 | Do not delay in obtaining legal advice | 183 |
|  | 3 | Appoint one person as contact with the investigating authority | 183 |
|  | 4 | Do not assume the organisation only is being investigated | 184 |
|  | 5 | Ensure individuals understand their legal rights in respect to interviews | 184 |
|  | 6 | Nominate someone to speak on behalf of the organisation | 184 |
|  | 7 | Identify early on an internal advisory team to assist in the criminal/civil defence | 184 |
|  | 8 | Do not allow investigating authorities to exceed their authority | 185 |
|  | 9 | Make a record of potential witnesses/collect evidence of the scene | 185 |
|  | 10 | Do not rush to provide an internal investigation report | 185 |
|  | 11 | Do not ignore other associated legal proceedings | 185 |
|  | 12 | RIDDOR (health and safety incidents) | 185 |
|  | 13 | Experts | 186 |
|  | 14 | Do not ignore the media | 186 |
|  | Power of arrest | | 186 |

*Contents*

|  |  |
|---|---|
| Conflicts of interest – interviews | 187 |
| Interviews under caution | 189 |
|     When do interviews under caution take place? | 189 |
|     Adverse inference | 190 |
|     Option for interviews under caution | 191 |
|     'No comment' interviews | 191 |
|     Full interview | 192 |
|     Prepared statement | 193 |
|     Interviews under caution of organisations | 193 |
| Voluntary witness statements | 194 |
| Compelled interviews of witnesses | 195 |
| Legal professional privilege | 195 |
| Internal accident/incident investigation report | 198 |
| Obtaining documentary and other evidence – the powers' of the investigators | 199 |
|     Powers of the police | 199 |
|     Health and safety investigations | 201 |
|     Environment investigations | 202 |
| Freedom of Information Act 2000 | 204 |

| | | |
|---|---|---|
| **12** | **Prosecution – the Court Process** | **207** |
| | Criminal Procedure Rules | 208 |
| | Magistrates' court | 209 |
| | Crown Court | 210 |
| | Types of offences and where they are heard | 210 |
| |     Summary offences | 211 |
| |     Either way offences | 211 |
| |     Indictable offences | 213 |
| | The start of proceedings | 213 |
| | Case management | 215 |
| |     Transforming summary justice/better case management | 215 |
| |     Preparation for trial form – magistrates' court | 216 |
| |     Plea and trial preparation hearing (PTPH) and form – the Crown Court | 217 |
| |     Statements made in case management forms | 219 |
| |     Entering a plea – corporate body | 220 |
| |     Bail | 220 |
| | Disclosure and defence statement | 220 |
| |     Unused material | 220 |
| |     Duty of the investigator and disclosure officer | 220 |
| |     Disclosure test | 221 |
| |     The stages of disclosure | 221 |
| | Defence statement | 222 |
| |     Third party disclosure | 223 |
| | Expert evidence | 223 |
| | Hearsay evidence | 228 |
| | Bad character | 228 |

|  |  |  |
|---|---|---|
|  | Dismissal | 229 |
|  | Abuse of process | 230 |
|  | Trial | 232 |
|  | Burden of proof | 232 |
|  | Trial file/jury bundle | 232 |
|  | Witnesses giving evidence | 232 |
|  | Reading witness statements | 233 |
|  | Admissions | 233 |
|  | Points of law | 234 |
|  | Start of the trial | 234 |
|  | Prosecution case | 235 |
|  | No case to answer | 235 |
|  | Defence case | 236 |
|  | Closing addresses | 236 |
|  | Judge's summing up | 236 |
|  | Verdict | 236 |
|  | Sentencing | 237 |
|  | Sentencing hearing | 237 |
|  | Newton hearings | 238 |
|  | Confiscation (environmental prosecutions) | 239 |
|  | Costs | 239 |
|  | Defendant's costs order | 239 |
|  | Order that the defendant pay the prosecution costs | 240 |
|  | Appeals | 241 |
|  | Appeals from the magistrates' court | 241 |
|  | Appeals from the Crown Court | 242 |
| 13 | **Sentencing** | **243** |
|  | Introduction | 244 |
|  | The purposes of sentencing | 244 |
|  | Sentencing guidelines | 245 |
|  | Setting a fine | 247 |
|  | Health and Safety Offences, Corporate Manslaughter and Food Safety and Hygiene Offences – Definitive Guideline | 250 |
|  | Health and safety offences – organisations | 250 |
|  | Health and safety offences – individuals | 258 |
|  | Corporate manslaughter | 261 |
|  | Manslaughter – Definitive Guideline | 272 |
|  | Gross negligence manslaughter | 272 |
|  | Fire safety | 274 |
|  | Environmental Offences – Definitive Guideline | 275 |
|  | Structure ranges and starting points | 275 |
|  | Guidelines for offenders that are organisations | 275 |
|  | Guidelines for offenders that are individuals | 283 |
|  | Reduction in Sentence for Guilty Plea – Definitive Guideline | 288 |
|  | Offences Taken into Consideration and Totality – Definitive Guideline | 290 |

## Part 4 Inquests and Claims

| | | |
|---|---|---|
| **14** | **Coroners' Inquests and Public Inquiry** | **295** |
| | Introduction | 296 |
| | Coroners' inquests | 296 |
| |     Coroner areas | 297 |
| |     Eligibility and qualifications | 298 |
| |     Coroners' officer | 298 |
| | Calling an inquest | 299 |
| |     A coroner's duty to investigate | 299 |
| |     Duty to hold an inquest | 299 |
| |     Timing of an inquest | 299 |
| | Evidence | 300 |
| |     Coroner's powers in relation to evidence | 300 |
| |     Disclosure | 300 |
| |     Disclosure by coroners to interested persons | 300 |
| |     Interested persons | 300 |
| |     Restrictions on disclosure | 301 |
| | The inquest hearing | 301 |
| |     Witness evidence | 302 |
| |     Self-incrimination | 302 |
| | When is a jury required? | 303 |
| |     The jury | 303 |
| | Duty to suspend or adjourn an inquest | 304 |
| | Determinations and findings of an inquest | 304 |
| |     Summing up | 305 |
| |     Conclusions | 305 |
| |     Standard of proof | 307 |
| | Investigations lasting more than a year | 308 |
| | Reports to prevent further deaths | 309 |
| | Post-mortem examinations | 310 |
| | Conflicts of interest – insured and insurer at inquests | 311 |
| | Conflicts of interest – insured and insurer – inquest disclosure | 312 |
| | Public inquiry | 312 |
| |     Scope of any public inquiry | 313 |
| |     Power to establish a public inquiry | 313 |
| |     There is to be no determination of liability | 313 |
| |     Composition of the inquiry panel | 313 |
| |     Setting-up date and terms of reference | 314 |
| |     Requirement of impartiality | 314 |
| |     Assessors | 315 |
| |     Power to suspend inquiry | 315 |
| |     End of inquiry | 315 |
| |     Power to convert another inquiry into inquiry under the Inquiries Act 2005 | 316 |
| |     Inquiry proceedings – evidence and procedure | 317 |
| |     Public access to inquiry proceedings and information | 318 |

|  |  |  |
|---|---|---|
| | Restrictions on public access in a public inquiry | 318 |
| | Powers of chairperson to require the production of evidence | 320 |
| | Privileged information | 320 |
| | Public interest immunity | 322 |
| | Offences | 322 |
| | Enforcement by High Court or Court of Session | 323 |
| | Immunity from suit | 323 |
| | Time limit for applying for judicial review | 323 |
| | Expenses of witnesses and participants | 324 |
| **15** | **Civil Claims** | **325** |
| | Civil claims | 326 |
| | Judge hearing a civil case | 327 |
| | Judgment | 328 |
| | Costs | 328 |
| | Court of Appeal – Civil Division | 328 |
| | High Court – Queen's Bench Division | 328 |
| | Limitation period | 329 |
| | Personal injury and fatal accidents | 329 |
| | Enterprise and Regulatory Reform Act 2013 (ERRA 2013) | 329 |
| | *Stark v Post Office* | 330 |
| | Dismissal of a fraudulent claim | 331 |
| | Pre-Action Protocol for Personal Injury Claims | 331 |
| | Alternative dispute resolution (ADR) | 333 |
| | Fatal accident claims | 333 |
| | Dependant | 333 |
| | Assessment of dependency | 334 |
| | Causation | 335 |
| | How the claim is calculated | 335 |
| | Date for assessing the dependency | 336 |
| | Benefits resulting from death | 336 |
| | Settlement | 336 |
| | Provisional damages | 336 |
| | Appeal | 336 |
| | Enforcement | 337 |
| | Procedural defences | 337 |
| | Insurance | 337 |
| | Property damage | 338 |
| | Measure of damages | 338 |
| | Awarding damages | 338 |
| | Fire | 339 |
| | No strict liability for accidental fire damage | 340 |
| | Environmental claims | 340 |
| | Statutory duty | 340 |
| | Claims in negligence | 342 |
| | Private nuisance | 342 |
| | The current standing of public nuisance | 344 |

| | | |
|---|---|---|
| **16** | **Insurance** | **347** |
| | Business insurance | 347 |
| | Public liability insurance | 348 |
| | Employers' liability insurance | 348 |
| | Environmental liability insurance | 349 |
| | Product liability insurance | 350 |
| | Professional indemnity insurance | 350 |
| |     The claims-made nature of professional indemnity insurance | 351 |
| | Directors and officers liability insurance | 352 |
| | Business interruption insurance | 353 |
| | Insurance Act 2015 | 353 |
| |     Insurance contract law | 354 |
| |     The duty of fair presentation | 354 |
| |     Knowledge and fair presentation generally | 357 |
| |     Warranties and representations | 358 |
| |     Fraudulent claims and remedies | 359 |
| |     Remedies for breach | 360 |
| |     Contracting out: non-consumer insurance contracts | 360 |
| |     Amendments to the Third Parties (Rights against Insurers) Act 2010 | 361 |
| |     Consumer Insurance (Disclosure and Representations) Act 2012 | 361 |
| | Choice of solicitor | 362 |
| |     *Sneller v DAS Nederlandse Rechtsbijstand Verzekeringsmaatschappij* | 362 |
| |     The UK position | 363 |
| |     Cases decided after *Sneller* | 364 |
| |     Insurance Conduct of Business Sourcebook (ICOBS) | 365 |
| **Appendix** | | |
| | Cases | 367 |
| *Index* | | *455* |

# Table of Statutes

| | |
|---|---|
| Anti-Social Behaviour, Crime and Policing Act 2014 | 6.31 |
| Banking Act 1987 | |
| s 96(1) | 4.37 |
| Clean Air Act 1993 | 9.33 |
| Clean Neighbourhoods and Environment Act 2005 | 6.11 |
| Coal Mines Act 1911 | 4.30 |
| Companies Act 2006 | 1.13; 4.22 |
| s 172 | 1.9 |
| Company Directors Disqualification Act 1986 | 13.20 |
| ss 2, 6 | 13.20 |
| Consumer Act 2015 | 16.21 |
| Consumer Insurance (Disclosure and Representations) Act 2012 | 16.10, 16.18, 16.21 |
| ss 2–11 | 16.21 |
| Sch 1 | 16.21 |
| Sch 2 | 16.21 |
| Contempt of Court Act 1981 | |
| s 9 | 14.45 |
| Control of Pollution (Amendment) Act 1989 | |
| s 1 | 13.63 |
| Coroners and Justice Act 2009 | 13.2; 14.2, 14.4, 14.13, 14.24, 14.28 |
| s 1(7) | 14.6 |
| 7 | 14.19 |
| 8 | 14.20 |
| 16 | 14.23 |
| 47 | 14.13 |
| 125(1) | 13.2 |
| Sch 1 | 14.21 |
| paras 8, 9 | 14.23 |
| Sch 5 | 14.29 |
| paras 1, 2 | 14.10 |
| Corporate Manslaughter and Corporate Homicide Act 2007 | 4.1, 4.3, 4.7, 4.10, 4.11, 4.12, 4.13, 4.19, 4.20, 4.22, 4.27; 13.24, 13.37 |
| Corporate Manslaughter and Corporate Homicide Act 2007 – *contd* | |
| s 1 | 4.2 |
| (2) | 4.4 |
| (4)(c) | 4.16 |
| 2 | 4.13 |
| 8 | 4.14 |
| ss 9, 10 | 13.31 |
| Sch 1 | 4.4 |
| Criminal Justice Act 1925 | |
| s 33(6) | 12.13 |
| Criminal Justice Act 1967 | |
| s 9 | 11.31, 11.32; 12.8, 12.22, 12.30 |
| 10 | 12.31 |
| Criminal Justice Act 2003 | 5.13; 12.22; 13.4; 14.50 |
| s 98 | 12.23 |
| 101 | 12.23 |
| 113 | 12.23 |
| ss 116, 117 | 12.22 |
| s 118 | 12.22 |
| (1), (6) | 12.12 |
| 119 | 12.22 |
| ss 120, 127 | 12.22 |
| s 142 | 13.1 |
| 143(1) | 13.2 |
| 144 | 13.81, 13.97 |
| (1) | 13.105 |
| 162 | 13.16 |
| 164 | 13.3, 13.7, 13.17, 13.27, 13.68, 13.90 |
| 174 | 13.33, 13.84, 13.100 |
| 281(5) | 14.50 |
| Criminal Justice and Courts Act 2015 | |
| s 57 | 15.10 |
| Criminal Justice and Public Order Act 1994 | 11.25 |
| s 34 | 11.25; 12.36 |

*Table of Statutes*

Criminal Procedure and Investigations Act 1996 ......... 11.27; 12.15, 12.16, 12.21
  ss 6A, 6C ................................. 12.19
  s 7A ........................................... 12.17
  8 ................................................. 12.18
Criminal Procedure (Attendance of Witnesses) Act 1965 ........ 12.20
Crime and Disorder Act 1998
  s 51 ............................................ 12.24
  Sch 3
    para 2(2) ............................... 12.24
Employers' Liability (Compulsory Insurance) Act 1969 ......... 2.7; 9.10; 16.3

Employment Act 2002
  Explanatory Note
    para 2 (Pt 2, para 57) ............. 5.5
Enterprise and Regulatory Reform Act 2013 ......................... 15.8, 15.9
  s 69 ............................................ 15.8
Environment Act 1995 ................ 11.37
  s 108 ................................. 11.2, 11.32
    (4) ............................................ 11.37
      (a), (c), (d), (e),
      (f), (g), (h) ..................... 11.37
      (j) ................................... 11.32
      (k) .................................. 11.37
    (13) ........................................ 11.33
  Sch 18 ...................................... 11.37
Environment and Safety Information Act 1988 ........................ 8.27
Environment (Wales) Act 2016 ... 9.30
Environmental Protection Act 1990 ................... 6.9, 6.11; 7.5, 7.11; 15.40
  s 33 ................................... 6.6; 13.63
    33A ........................................ 6.13
    33C ........................................ 13.82
    34 ............................ 6.4, 6.5; 13.63
      (1) ...................................... 15.40
        (c) ................................... 15.40
    73(6) .................................... 15.40
    79 .......................................... 6.29
      (1) ...................................... 6.36
    80 ......................................... 13.63
    157 ........................................ 6.9
Fatal Accidents Act 1976 ... 15.19, 15.20, 15.23, 15.32
  s 3(2) ....................................... 15.29
Finance Act 1966 ........................ 4.38
  s 305(3) ................................... 4.22

Fire Precautions Act 1971 ........... 8.1, 8.7
  s 23 .......................................... 4.36
Fire (Scotland) Act 2005 ............ 2.8; 8.2, 8.5, 8.8, 8.16
  s 53(2)(a) ................................. 8.5
Fires Prevention (Metropolis) Act 1774
  s 86 .......................................... 15.37
Freedom of Information Act 2000 ............................ 11.38; 14.45
  s 30 .......................................... 11.38
  41 ............................................. 11.38
Health and Safety at Work etc Act 1974 ....................... 2.3, 2.4; 4.1, 4.8, 4.13, 4.15, 4.19, 4.27, 4.28; 5.1, 5.4; 8.23, 8.34; 9.1, 9.10; 11.24, 11.36, 11.37; 13.31, 13.60; 14.23; 15.8
  ss 2–6 ...................................... 4.27
  s 2 ............................ 4.27, 4.28, 4.29, 4.30, 4.31; 12.27; 13.4, 13.14, 13.34, 13.36, 13.39, 13.40, 13.41, 13.42, 13.43, 13.44, 13.45, 13.46, 13.47, 13.58
    (1) ........................... 4.27; 13.53
    (2) ........................................ 4.27
  3 ............................ 4.15, 4.27, 4.28, 4.29, 4.30, 4.31, 4.32; 12.27; 13.1, 13.3, 13.4, 13.14, 13.34, 13.35, 13.37, 13.38, 13.42, 13.43, 13.45, 13.46, 13.47
    (1) ................... 4.27; 13.51, 13.52, 13.54
  4 ................................. 4.27, 4.30; 13.4
  6 ..................................... 4.27; 13.4
  7 ...................................... 4.1, 4.40, 4.41; 11.33; 13.14
    (a) .......................... 4.40; 13.50
  8 ................................................ 4.41
  15 ..................................... 4.27; 15.8
  20 ....................... 11.2, 11.32, 11.36, 11.37; 13.54
    (2) ........................................ 11.37

Health and Safety at Work etc Act 1974 – *contd*
s 20(2)(a), (d), (e), (f),
    (g), (h), (i)........................ 11.36
    (j) .................................. 11.32
    (k) .................................. 11.36
  (4)........................................ 11.36
  (8)........................................ 11.33
21 ............................................ 5.2; 8.24
22 ............................................ 5.3; 8.24
24 ............................................ 5.4
25 ............................................ 5.3
30(1)(c).................................... 4.27
33 ............................................ 10.23
  (1)(a) ................................. 4.27
37 ............................................ 4.1, 4.22, 4.35,
                  4.36, 4.37, 4.39,
                  4.40; 6.9; 13.2,
                  13.14, 13.37, 13.41,
                  13.44, 13.53
  (1)........................................ 4.34
38 ............................................ 4.19
40 ............................................ 4.28, 4.32, 4.35
42(1), (4) ................................. 13.11
47(1)........................................ 4.27
53 ............................................ 4.27
  (1)........................................ 11.36
Health and Safety (Offences) Act 2008 ...................................... 13.14
Human Rights Act 1998 ............ 15.39
Sch 1
  Pt I, art 7 ............................. 15.43
Inquiries Act 2005............. 14.21, 14.33, 14.36, 14.43, 14.45
s 1............................................ 14.43
19 ............................................ 14.45
35(3)........................................ 14.50
Explanatory Note
  para 2 (s 22, para 54) ........... 14.48
Insurance Act 2015 ............ 16.10, 16.11, 16.12, 16.13, 16.14, 16.16, 16.17, 16.18, 16.19
Pt 1 (s 1) ................................. 16.10
s 4 ............................................ 16.13, 16.14
  (6)........................................ 16.13
s 6 ............................................ 16.15
10(1)........................................ 16.16
21(4), (5) ................................. 16.10
Interpretation Act 1978
ss 5, 11.................................... 4.27

Legal Aid, Sentencing and Punishment of Offenders Act 2012
  Sch 7 ...................................... 12.43
Licensing Act 2003..................... 8.7
Marine Insurance Act 1906......... 16.11
Police and Criminal Evidence Act 1984 .............. 11.2, 11.24
s 8 ............................................ 11.35, 11.37
10 ............................................ 11.33
ss 15, 16, 17, 18, 19................. 11.35
  20, 21, 22............................ 11.35
s 24 .......................................... 11.22
  (5).......................................... 11.22
24A .......................................... 11.22
78(1)........................................ 11.35, 11.37
Powers of Criminal Courts (Sentencing) Act 2000
s 143 ........................................ 18.81
Proceeds of Crime Act 2002 ... 6.13; 7.12, 7.13; 12.42
ss 6, 13.................................... 13.65
Prosecution of Offences Act 1985
s 10.......................................... 11.4
16 ............................................ 12.43
18 ............................................ 12.44
19 ............................................ 12.43
Protection of Badgers Act 1992 ... 6.39
Regulatory Enforcement and Sanctions Act 2008 .......... 7.1, 7.22, 7.42
Pt 3 (ss 36–71) ........................ 7.42
Serious Organised Crime and Police Act 2005
ss 73, 74.............. 13.9, 13.18, 13.80, 13.96
Pt 3 (ss 110–124) .................... 11.22
Third Parties (Rights against Insurers) Act 1930 ............... 16.20
Third Parties (Rights against Insurers) Act 2010 ............... 16.20
Tribunals of Inquiry (Evidence) Act 1921 ............................. 14.45
Water Industry Act 1991
s 111 ................................. 6.37; 13.63
209 .......................................... 15.42
Water Resources Act 1991 ......... 7.5
s 161A ...................................... 6.26
Wild Mammals (Protection) Act 1996 ................................. 6.39
Wildlife and Countryside Act 1981 ................................. 6.39
Sch 5 ........................................ 6.39

# Table of Statutory Instruments

Batteries and Accumulators (Placing on the Market) Regulations 2008, SI 2008/2164 ..... 6.20
Chemicals (Hazard Information and Packaging for Supply) Regulations 2009, SI 2009/716 ................. 2.8
Conservation of Habitats and Species Regulations 2010, SI 2010/490 ............... 6.39, 6.40
Construction (Design and Management) Regulations 2007, SI 2007/32 ..................... 13.35
Construction (Design and Management) Regulations 2015, SI 2015/51 ............ 2.8; 4.27; 12.20
Control of Major Accident Hazards Regulations 2015, SI 2015/483 ........................ 2.8
Control of Noise at Work Regulations 2005, SI 2005/1643 .... 2.7, 2.9
Control of Substances Hazardous to Health Regulations 2002, SI 2002/2677 ...................... 2.7
Control of Waste (Dealing with Seized Property) (England and Wales) Regulations 2015, SI 2015/426 ............... 7.21
Coroners (Inquests) Rules 2013, SI 2013/1616 ............... 14.2, 14.24
  r 8 ............................................ 14.9
  Pt 3 (rr 12–16) ........................ 14.12
  Pt 4 (rr 17–27)
    r 22 ............................... 14.18, 14.23
    26 ......................................... 14.23
Coroners (Investigations) Regulations 2013, SI 2013/1629 ..... 14.2
  reg 28 ..................................... 14.29
    (3), (4) ............................. 14.29
Costs in Criminal Cases (General) Regulations 1986, SI 1986/1335
  reg 3 ....................................... 12.43

Criminal Procedure Rules 2005, SI 2015/1490 ...... 12.1, 12.12, 12.21
  Pt 1 (rr 1.1–1.3) ....................... 12.1
  r 1.2 ......................................... 12.1
  Pt 2 (rr 2.1–2.3) ....................... 12.1
  Pt 3 (rr 3.1–3.12) ..................... 12.1
  Pt 8 (rr 8.1–8.4) ....................... 12.8
  Pt 15 (rr 15.1–15.9) ................ 12.15
  Pt 19 (rr 19.1–19.10) .............. 12.21
  Pt 20 (rr 20.1–20.5) ................ 12.22
  Pt 21 (rr 21.1–21.6) ................ 12.23
Criminal Procedure (Amendment) Rules 2018, SI 2018/132 ...... 12.1
Dangerous Substances and Explosive Atmospheres Regulations 2002, SI 2002/2776 ........... 2.8; 8.34
Electricity at Work Regulations 1989, SI 1989/635 ............... 2.7
Employment Tribunals (Constitution and Rules of Procedure) Regulations 2013, SI 2013/1237
  Sch 1 ........................................ 5.4
Environmental Civil Sanctions (England) Order 2010, SI 2010/1157 ....................... 7.1
  art 10 ...................................... 7.49
  Sch 1
    para 8 ................................ 7.45
  Sch 2
    para 8 ............................... 7.46, 7.48
  Sch 3
    para 3 ................................ 7.47
Environmental Civil Sanctions (Miscellaneous Amendments) (England) Regulations 2010, SI 2010/1159 ....................... 7.1
Environmental Civil Sanctions (Wales) Order 2010, SI 2010/1821 ................................... 7.1
  art 10 ...................................... 7.49
  Sch 1
    para 8 ................................ 7.45

*Table of Statutory Instruments*

Environmental Civil Sanctions (Wales) Order 2010 – *contd*
Sch 2
  para 8 .............................. 7.46, 7.48
Sch 3
  para 3 .............................. 7.47
Environmental Permitting (England and Wales) Regulations 2010, SI 2010/675 ...... 6.26; 7.2, 7.5
Environmental Permitting (England and Wales) Regulations 2016, SI 2016/1154
  reg 12.................... 6.25; 13.63
  38........................ 6.25
  (1), (2), (3) ............ 13.63, 13.82
  44....................... 13.82, 13.98
Explosives Regulations 2014, SI 2014/1638
  regs 6, 7 ................................. 10.18
Fire and Rescue Services (Northern Ireland) Order 2006, SI 2006/1254 .......... 8.2, 8.44
  art 25(2)(a) .............................. 8.6
  26(2)(a) .............................. 8.6
Fire Precautions (Workplace) Regulations 1997, SI 1997/1840 ...................... 8.1
Fire Precautions (Workplace) (Amendment) Regulations 1999, SI 1999/1877 ........ 8.1
Fire Safety Regulations (Northern Ireland) 2010, SI 2010/325 .. 8.2
Fire Safety (Scotland) Regulations 2006, SI 2006/456 .............. 8.2, 8.5
  reg 13(2)(h)............................... 8.13
Gas Safety (Installation and Use) Regulations 1998, SI 1998/2451 ...................... 2.8
Health and Safety and Nuclear (Fees) Regulations 2016, SI 2016/253 ...................... 5.7
Health and Safety (Display Screen Equipment) Regulations 1992, SI 1992/2792 .............. 2.7
Health and Safety (Fees) Regulations 2012, SI 2012/1652..... 5.7
Health and Safety (First-Aid) Regulations 1981, SI 1982/917 ...................... 2.7
Health and Safety Information for Employees Regulations 1989, SI 1989/682 ............... 2.7

Inquiry Rules 2006, SI 2006/1838 .................. 14.33
Insurance Companies (Legal Expenses Insurance) Regulations 1990, SI 1990/1159..... 16.24
  reg 2........................ 16.24
  6.................. 11.9; 16.24
Magistrates' Courts (Witnesses Addresses) Rules 1990, SI 1990/336 .................. 11.38
Management of Health and Safety at Work Regulations 1999, SI 1999/3242 ..................... 2.5; 4.27
  reg 3.................................. 13.4, 13.5, 13.35, 13.40
  (1)...................................... 2.11
  regs 16, 18 ............................... 2.17
Manual Handling Operations Regulations 1992, SI 1992/2793 ...................... 2.7
  reg 4.................................. 13.40
Notification of Accidents and Dangerous Occurrences Regulations 1980, SI 1980/804 ....... 10.1
Packaging (Essential Requirements) Regulations 2015, SI 2015/1640 ...................... 6.14
Personal Protective Equipment at Work Regulations 1992, SI 1992/2966 ..................... 2.7
  reg 4(1) .............................. 2.11
Personal Protective Equipment (Enforcement) Regulations 2018, SI 2018/390 ............... 2.7
Petroleum (Consolidation) Regulations 2014, SI 2014/1637... 8.34
Pressure Systems Safety Regulations 2000, SI 2000/128....... 10.18
Producer Responsibility Obligations (Packaging Waste) Regulations 2017, SI 2017/871 ...................... 6.14
Provision and Use of Work Equipment Regulations 1998, SI 1998/2306 ................. 2.7; 4.27; 15.9
  reg 5(1) .................................. 15.8
  11........................................ 13.36
Rail Vehicle Accessibility (Non-Interoperable Rail System) Regulations 2010, SI 2010/432 ....................................... 9.12

xxx

| | |
|---|---|
| Railway and Other Guided Transport (Safety) Regulations 2006, SI 2006/559 | 9.12 |
| Railways (Interoperability) Regulations 2011, SI 2011/3066 | 9.12 |
| Regulatory Reform (Fire Safety) Order 2005, SI 2005/1541 | 2.8; 8.2, 8.3, 8.8, 8.16, 8.19, 8.22, 8.24, 8.27, 8.32, 8.38; 13.2, 13.60 |
| art 3 | 8.3, 8.8 |
| 8(1) | 8.4 |
| 9 | 8.31 |
| 1 | 8.31 |
| 13 | 8.33 |
| 14 | 8.31, 8.33 |
| (2)(h) | 8.13 |
| 20 | 8.31 |
| 21 | 8.31 |
| 26 | 8.45 |
| 29 | 8.29 |
| 30 | 8.30 |
| 31 | 8.32, 8.33 |
| 36 | 8.46 |
| 37 | 8.35 |
| Reporting of Injuries, Diseases and Dangerous Occurrences Regulations 2013, SI 2013/1471 | 2.7; 10.1, 10.2, 10.6, 10.7, 10.10, 10.11, 10.12, 10.21, 10.22, 10.24, 10.26, 10.30, 10.33, 10.37; 11.19 |
| reg 3 | 10.23 |
| Social Security (Claims and Payments) Regulations 1979, SI 1979/628 | 10.16 |
| Statutory Nuisance (Appeals) Regulations 1995, SI 1995/2644 | 6.36 |
| Train Driving Licences and Certificates Regulations 2010, SI 2010/724 | 9.12 |
| Transfrontier Shipment of Waste Regulations 2007, SI 2007/1711 | 13.63 |
| Unauthorised Deposit of Waste (Fixed Penalties) Regulations 2016, SI 2016/334 | 6.13 |
| Waste Batteries and Accumulators Regulations 2009, SI 2009/890 | 6.20 |
| Waste Electrical and Electronic Equipment Regulations 2013, SI 2013/3113 | 6.23 |
| Water Abstraction and Impoundment (Licensing) Regulations (Northern Ireland) 2006, SI 2006/482 | 6.27 |
| Water Environment (Controlled Activities) (Scotland) Regulations 2011, SI 2011/209 | 6.27 |
| Water (Northern Ireland) Order 1999, SI 1999/662 | 6.27 |
| Workplace (Health, Safety and Welfare) Regulations 1992, SI 1992/3004 | 2.6 |

# Table of EC/EU Material

| | |
|---|---|
| Batteries Directive (2006/66/EC) | 6.20 |
| Controls on Animal By-Products Regulation (EC) 1069/2009 | 6.1 |
| Environmental Liability Directive (2004/35/CE) | 16.4 |
| European Convention on Human Rights | |
| Art 8 | 14.45 |
| Habitats Directive (92/43/EEC) | |
| Annexes II, IV | 6.39 |
| Industrial Emissions Directive (2010/75/EU) | 6.1 |
| Landfill Directive (1999/31/EC) | 6.1 |
| Legal Expenses Insurance Directive (87/344/EEC) | 16.23 |
| Art 4 | 16.23, 16.25 |
| (1) | 16.23 |
| (a) | 16.23 |
| Packaging and Packaging Waste Directive (94/62/EC) | 6.1 |
| Waste Electrical and Electronic Equipment (WEEE) Directive (2012/19/EU) | 6.1 |
| Waste Framework Directive (2008/98/EC) | 6.1 |

# Table of Cases

**A**

Amec Developments Ltd v Jury's Hotel Management (UK) Ltd [2000] EWHC Ch 454, [2002] TCLR 13, (2001) 82 P & CR 22.................. 15.35, 15.36
Amos v Worcester City Council (unreported, 1996)......................... 4.40
Argyll (Duchess of) v Beuselinck [1972] 2 Lloyd's Rep 172............ 4.33; 11.1; Appendix
Attorney General v PYA Quarries Ltd [1957] 2 QB 169, [1957] 2 WLR 770, [1957] 1 All ER 894.................................................. 15.43
Attorney General's Reference (No 1 of 1995) [1996] 1 WLR 970, [1996] 4 All ER 21, [1996] 5 Bank LR 173, [1996] 2 Cr App R 320, [1996] Crim LR 575.................................................................................. 4.37
Attorney General's Reference (No 2 of 1999) [2000] QB 796, [2000] 3 WLR 195, [2000] 3 All ER 182, [2001] BCC 210, [2000] 2 BCLC 257, [2000] 2 Cr App R 207, [2000] Crim LR 475.......................... 4.22

**B**

Baker v Quantum Clothing Group Ltd [2011] UKSC 17, [2011] 1 WLR 1003, [2011] 4 All ER 223.................................................. 4.29, 4.30; Appendix
Brown-Quinn v Equity Syndicate Management Ltd [2012] EWCA Civ 1633, [2013] 1 WLR 1740, [2013] 3 All ER 505, [2013] CP Rep 13, [2013] 1 Costs LR 1, [2013] 2 CMLR 20, [2013] Lloyd's Rep IR 371...... 16.24; Appendix
BT Fleet Ltd v McKenna [2005] EWHC 387 (Admin.................... 5.2; Appendix
Buyuktipi v Achmea Schadeverzekeringen NV (Case C-5/15) [2016] Lloyd's Rep IR 586 .......................................................... 16.25; Appendix

**C**

Cambridge Water Co v Eastern Counties Leather Plc [1994] 2 AC 264, [1994] 2 WLR 53, [1994] 1 All ER 53, [1994] 1 Lloyd's Rep 261, [1994] Env LR 105 ............................................................................ 15.42; Appendix
Caparo Industries Plc v Dickman [1990] 2 AC 605, [1990] 2 WLR 358, [1990] 1 All ER 568, [1990] BCC 164, [1990] BCLC 273 ............. 4.21, 4.39; Appendix
City Equitable Fire Insurance Co Ltd, Re [1925] Ch 407.................. 4.22
Colour Quest Ltd v Total Downstream UK Plc [2009] EWHC 540 (Comm), [2009] 2 Lloyd's Rep 1, [2009] 1 CLC 186.......................... 15.41; Appendix
Corby Group Litigation v Corby Borough Council [2008] EWCA Civ 463, [2009] QB 335, [2009] 2 WLR 609, [2009] 4 All ER 44, [2008] CP Rep 32, [2009] Env LR 2, [2008] PIQR P16, [2009] JPL 64.................. 15.42, 15.43
Corby Group Litigation v Corby District Council [2009] EWHC 1944 (TCC), [2010] Env LR D2 ............................................................. 15.40; Appendix
Corr v IBC Vehicles Ltd [2008] UKHL 13, [2008] 2 WLR 499, [2008] 2 All ER 943, [2008] ICR 372........................................................... 15.24
Cundall v Leeds City Council (unreported, 24 January 2017)............ 2.10

*Table of Cases*

## D

Davies v Taylor [1974] AC 207............................................................................ 15.21
Derry v Peek (1889) 14 App Cas 337, (1889) 5 TLR 625 ................. 16.17; Appendix
Dodds v Dodds [1978] QB 543.......................................................................... 15.24
DPP v Ara [2001] EWHC Admin 493, [2002] 1 WLR 815, [2001] 4 All ER
  559, [2002] 1 Cr App R 16..................................................................... 5.13; Appendix

## E

Edwards v National Coal Board [1949] 1 KB 704, [1949] 1 All ER 743, 65 TLR
  430 ................................................................................................................ 2.4; 4.30;
                                                                                                                Appendix
El-Aljou v Dollar Land Holdings Plc [1994] 2 All ER 685, [1994] BCC 143,
  [1994] 1 BCLC 464 .................................................................................. 4.16; Appendix

## F

Field v Leeds City Council [1999] EWCA Civ 3013, (2000) 32 HLR 618.......... 12.21;
                                                                                                                Appendix

## G

Goldscheider v Royal Opera House Covent Garden Foundation [2018] EWHC
  687 (QB)................................................................................................... 2.9; Appendix
Gore v Stannard (t/a Wyvern Tyres) [2012] EWCA Civ 1248, [2014] QB 1,
  [2013] 3 WLR 623, [2013] 1 All ER 694, [2013] Env LR 10..................... 15.38

## H

H v R [2014] EWCA Crim 1555, [2014] Crim LR 905....................... 12.21; Appendix
Hart v Lancashire & Yorkshire Railway Co (1869) 21 LT 261 ............ 4.33; Appendix
Hertfordshire Oil Storage Ltd v TAV Engineering Ltd *see* West London Pipeline
  & Storage Ltd v Total UK Ltd
HM Inspector of Health and Safety v Chevron North Sea Ltd [2018] UKSC 7,
  [2018] 1 WLR 964, [2018] 2 All ER 295, 2018 SC (UKSC) 132, 2018 SLT
  751, [2018] ICR 490................................................................... 5.4, 5.10; Appendix
Huckerby v Elliott [1970] 1 All ER 189 ................................................. 4.22, 4.38; 6.9;
                                                                                                                Appendix
Hughes, Re [1943] Ch 296, [1943] 2 All ER 269................................... 6.9; Appendix
Hui Chi-Ming v R [1992] 1 AC 34, [1991] 3 WLR 495, [1991] 3 All ER 897,
  (1992) 94 Cr App R 236, [1992] Crim LR 446........................... 12.25; Appendix
Hunter v Canary Wharf Ltd [1997] AC 655, [1997] 2 WLR 684, [1997] 2 All
  ER 426, [1997] CLC 1045, [1997] Env LR 488, [1997] 2 FLR 342, (1998)
  30 HLR 409, [1997] Fam Law 601................................ 15.42, 15.43, Appendix

## J

Jameson v Central Electricity Generating Board [1998] UKHL 51, [2000] 1 AC
  455, [1999] 2 WLR 141, [1999] 1 All ER 193............................................ 15.32

## K

Kennedy v Cordia (Services) LLP [2016] UKSC 6, [2016] 1 WLR 597, 2016 SC
  (UKSC) 59, 2016 SLT 209, 2016 SCLR 203 .................................. 2.11; Appendix

## L

London Borough of Wandsworth v Covent Garden Market Authority [2011]
  EWHC 1245 (QB), [2012] ICR D15 ................................................. 5.4; Appendix

*Table of Cases*

## M

Malcolm v DPP [2007] EWHC 363 (Admin), [2007] 1 WLR 1230, [2007] 3 All ER 578, [2007] 2 Cr App R 1, [2007] Crim LR 894 ..................... 12.1; Appendix
Manifest Shipping Co Ltd v Uni-Polaris Shipping Co Ltd [2001] UKHL 1, [2003] 1 AC 469, [2001] 2 WLR 170, [2001] 1 All ER 743, [2001] 1 All ER (Comm) 193, [2001] 1 Lloyd's Rep 389, [2001] CLC 608, [2001] Lloyd's Rep IR 247 ..................................................................................... 16.15
Manley v New Forest District Council [2007] EWHC 3188 (Admin), [2008] Env LR 26 .................................................................................... 6.36; Appendix
Massar v DAS Nederlandse Rechtsbijstand Verzekeringsmaatschappij NV (Case C-460/14) [2016] Lloyd's Rep IR 463 .............................. 16.25; Appendix
Mouatt v DPP [2001] EWHC Admin 130, [2001] 1 WLR 1293, [2001] 1 All ER 831, [2001] 2 Cr App R 23, [2001] Crim LR 741 ................................ 12.25
Mulholland v McCrea [1961] NI 135 ................................................................. 15.24

## N

New Look Retailers Ltd v London Fire and Emergency Planning Authority [2010] EWCA Crim 1268, [2011] 1 Cr App R (S) 57, [2010] CTLC 101 ..... 8.38; Appendix

## O

O'Brien v Chief Constable of South Wales Police [2005] UKHL 26, [2005] 2 AC 534, [2005] 2 WLR 1038, [2005] 2 All ER 931 ......................... 12.23; Appendix
Owen v Martin [1992] PIQR P151 ................................................................. 15.21

## P

Pan Atlantic Insurance Co Ltd v Pine Top Insurance Co Ltd [1995] 1 AC 501, [1994] 3 WLR 677, [1994] 3 All ER 581, [1994] 2 Lloyd's Rep 427, [1994] CLC 868 ................................................................................ 16.18; Appendix
Practice Direction (Costs in Criminal Proceedings) [2015] EWCA Crim 1568 .... 12.44

## R

R v Adaway [2004] EWCA Crim 2831, (2004) 168 JP 645, [2005] LLR 142, (2004) 168 JPN 956 ................................................................. 12.25; Appendix
R v Adomako [1995] 1 AC 171, [1994] 3 WLR 288, [1994] 3 All ER 79, (1994) 99 Cr App R 362 ............................................................ 4.20, 4.21, 4.26; Appendix
R v Argent [1996] EWCA Crim 1728, [1997] 2 Cr App R 27, [1997] Crim LR 346 ............................................................................. 11.25, 11.27; Appendix
R v Associated Octel Co Ltd [1996] 1 WLR 1543, [1996] 4 All ER 846, [1996] ICR 972, [1997] Crim LR 355 ..................................... 4.31; 12.44; Appendix
R v Balfour Beatty Rail Infrastructure Services Ltd [2006] EWCA Crim 1586, [2007] Bus LR 77, [2007] 1 Cr App R (S) 65 ...................... 13.1, 13.3; Appendix
R v Beckford [1996] 1 Cr App R 94, [1995] Crim LR 712 ................ 12.25; Appendix
R v Beckles [2004] EWCA Crim 2766, [2005] 1 WLR 2829, [2005] 1 All ER 705, [2005] 1 Cr App R 23, [2005] Crim LR 560 ...................... 11.27; Appendix
R v Beedie [1998] QB 356, [1997] 3 WLR 758, [1997] 2 Cr App R 167, [1997] Crim LR 747 ............................................................................ 12.25; Appendix
R v Boal [1992] QB 591, [1992] 2 WLR 890, [1992] 3 All ER 177, [1992] BCLC 872, (1992) 95 Cr App R 272, [1992] ICR 495 ................. 4.36; Appendix
R v Caley [2012] EWCA Crim 2821, [2013] 2 Cr App R (S) 47, (2013) 177 JP 111, [2013] Crim LR 342 ........................................................................ 13.105

*Table of Cases*

R v CAV Aerospace Ltd (unreported, 31 July 2015) .......................................... 4.6
R v Chaaban [2003] EWCA Crim 1012, [2003] Crim LR 658 ............ 12.1; Appendix
R v Chandler [2015] EWCA Crim 1825, [2016] BCC 212, [2016] 1 Cr App R
 (S) 37 ................................................................................................ 13.20; Appendix
R v Chargot Ltd [2008] UKHL 73, [2009] 1 WLR 1, [2009] 2 All ER 645 ....... 4.28,
 4.29, 4.37, 4.38, 4.39;
 11.33; Appendix
R v Cheshire [1991] 1 WLR 844, [1991] 3 All ER 670, (1991) 93 Cr App R
 251, [1991] Crim LR 709 .................................................... 4.12, 4.25; Appendix
R v Cornish [2016] EWHC 779 (QB), [2016] Crim LR 560 ............... 12.43; Appendix
R v DPP, ex p Manning [2000] EWHC Admin 342, [2001] QB 330, [2000] 3
 WLR 463 ............................................................................................ 11.3; Appendix
R v Ensor [2009] EWCA Crim 2519, [2010] 1 Cr App R 18, [2010] Crim LR
 731 ................................................................................................... 12.21; Appendix
R v F Howe & Son (Engineers) Ltd [1999] 2 All ER 249, [1999] 2 Cr App R (S)
 37, (1999) 163 JP 359, [1999] IRLR 434, [1999] Crim LR 238 .......... 4.12; 13.3;
 Appendix
R v Friskies Petcare (UK) Ltd [2000] EWCA Crim 95, [2000] 2 Cr App R (S)
 401 ............................................................................................. 12.8; 13.2; Appendix
R v Galbraith [1981] 1 WLR 1039, [1981] 2 All ER 1060, (1981) 73 Cr App R
 124, [1981] Crim LR 648 ............................................... 12.24, 12.35; Appendix
R v Gateway Foodmarkets Ltd [1997] 3 All ER 78, [1997] 2 Cr App R 40,
 [1997] ICR 382, [1997] Crim LR 512 ......................................... 4.31; Appendix
R v Goldstein [2003] EWCA Crim 3450, [2004] 1 WLR 2878, [2004] 2 All ER
 589, [2004] 1 Cr App R 27, [2004] UKHRR 296, [2004] Crim LR 303
 (CA); [2005] UKHL 63, [2006] 1 AC 459, [2005] 3 WLR 982, [2006] 2 All
 ER 257, [2006] 1 Cr App R 17, [2006] HRLR 3, [2006] UKHRR 1, [2006]
 Crim LR 153, [2006] Env LR D3 (HL) ........................... 15.42, 15.43; Appendix
R v Goodman [1993] 2 All ER 789, [1992] BCC 625, [1994] 1 BCLC 349,
 (1993) 97 Cr App R 210, (1993) 14 Cr App R (S) 147, [1992] Crim LR
 676 .................................................................................................. 13.20; Appendix
R v Harrison and Great Western Trains (unreported, 1999) ............................... 4.22
R v HM Coroner for Greater London (Southern District), ex p Ridley [1985] 1
 WLR 1347, [1986] 1 All ER 37, (1985) 149 JP 657 ................... 14.30; Appendix
R v HM Coroner for North Humberside and Scunthorpe, ex p Jamieson [1995]
 QB 1, [1994] 3 WLR 82, [1994] 3 All ER 972, (1994) 158 JP 1011 .......... 14.24
R v HTM Ltd [2006] EWCA Crim 1156, [2007] 2 All ER 665, [2006] ICR
 1383 ................................................................................... 4.15, 4.30, 4.32;
 Appendix
R v Ineos Chlorvinyls Ltd [2016] EWCA Crim 607, [2017] Env LR 7 .............. 13.6;
 Appendix
R v Jisl [2004] EWCA Crim 696 .................................................................... 12.1
R v Lion Steel Equipment Ltd (unreported, 2012) ............................................. 4.22
R v Maidstone and Tunbridge Wells NHS Trust (unreported, 27 January
 2016) ................................................................................................................ 4.5
R v Mirza [2012] EWCA Crim 3074 ................................................... 8.40; Appendix
R v Nelson Group Services (Maintenance) Ltd [1999] 1 WLR 1526, [1998] 4
 All ER 331, [1999] ICR 1004 ........................................................ 4.32; Appendix
R v Network Rail Infrastructure Ltd [2014] EWCA Crim 49, [2014] Env LR
 19 ........................................................................................................ 13.3; Appendix
R v New Look Ltd *see* New Look Retailers Ltd v London Fire and Emergency
 Planning Authority

R v Newell [2012] EWCA Crim 650, [2012] 1 WLR 3142, [2012] 2 Cr App R
   10, [2012] Crim LR 711 ...................................................................... 12.12; Appendix
R v Newton (1983) 77 Cr App R 13, (1982) 4 Cr App R (S) 388, [1983] Crim
   LR 198................................................................................................... 12.41; Appendix
R v Northallerton Magistrates' Court, ex p Dove [1999] EWHC Admin 499,
   [2000] 1 Cr App R (S) 136, [1999] Crim LR 760 ........................ 12.44; Appendix
R v P Ltd and G [2007] EWCA Crim 1937, [2008] ICR 96 ................   4.39; Appendix
R v Pabon [2018] EWCA Crim 420, [2018] Lloyd's Rep FC 258, [2018] Crim
   LR 662................................................................................................... 12.21; Appendix
R v Pearce (1979) 69 Cr App R 365, [1979] Crim LR 658 ................. 11.29; Appendix
R v R & S Recycling Ltd [2014] EWCA Crim 2302............................. 13.7; Appendix
R v Rimmington [2003] EWCA Crim 3450, [2004] 1 WLR 2878, [2004] 2 All
   ER 589, [2004] 1 Cr App R 27, [2004] UKHRR 296, [2004] Crim LR 303
   (CA); [2005] UKHL 63, [2006] 1 AC 459, [2005] 3 WLR 982, [2006] 2 All
   ER 257, [2006] 1 Cr App R 17, [2006] HRLR 3, [2006] UKHRR 1, [2006]
   Crim LR 153, [2006] Env LR D3 (HL) .............................. 15.42, 15.43; Appendix
R v Rose [2017] EWCA Crim 1168, [2018] QB 328, [2017] 3 WLR 1461,
   [2018] 2 All ER 430, [2017] 2 Cr App R 28, [2018] Crim LR 76 ........ 4.20, 4.21,
                                                                                                4.24, 4.26; 13.55;
                                                                                                              Appendix
R v Sandhu [2017] EWCA Crim 908, [2017] 4 WLR 160 ................... 13.2; Appendix
R v Sellafield Ltd [2014] EWCA Crim 49, [2014] Env LR 19 ............. 13.3; Appendix
R v Stubbs [2006] EWCA Crim 2312 ................................................ 12.21; Appendix
R v Takhar [2014] EWCA Crim 1619................................................. 8.40; Appendix
R v Tangerine Confectionary Ltd [2011] EWCA Crim 2015 ....... 4.29, 4.30; Appendix
R v Tata Steel UK Ltd [2017] EWCA Crim 704, [2017] 2 Cr App R (S) 29 ......   13.5;
                                                                                                              Appendix
R v Thames Water Utilities Ltd [2015] EWCA Crim 960, [2015] 1 WLR 4411,
   [2016] 3 All ER 919, [2015] 2 Cr App R (S) 63, [2015] Env LR 36, [2015]
   Crim LR 739.................................................................. 13.3, 13.4, 13.24; Appendix
R v Thelwall [2016] EWCA Crim 1755, [2016] CTLC 180 [2017] Crim LR
   240 ........................................................................... 12.8; 13.2, 13.16; Appendix
R v Underwood [2004] EWCA Crim 2256, [2005] 1 Cr App R 13, [2005] 1 Cr
   App R (S) 90......................................................................................... 12.41; Appendix
R v Whirlpool UK Appliances Ltd [2017] EWCA Crim 2186, [2018] 1 WLR
   1811, [2018] 1 Cr App R (S) 44, [2018] ICR 1010...................... 13.3; Appendix
R (on the application of Dennis) v DPP [2006] EWHC 3211 (Admin).............   11.3;
                                                                                                              Appendix
R (on the application of DPP) v Chorley Magistrates Court [2006] EWHC 1795
   (Admin) .................................................................................................. 12.1; Appendix
R (on the application of Ebrahim) v Feltham Magistrates Court [2001] EWHC
   Admin 130, [2001] 1 WLR 1293, [2001] 1 All ER 831, [2001] 2 Cr App R
   23, [2001] Crim LR 741 ...................................................................... 12.25; Appendix
R (on the application of Firth) v Epping Magistrates' Court [2011] EWHC 388
   (Admin), [2011] 1 WLR 1818, [2011] 4 All ER 326, [2011] 1 Cr App R
   32, [2011] Crim LR 717 ...................................................................... 12.12
R (on the application of Haigh) v City Westminster Magistrates' Court [2017]
   EWHC 232 (Admin), [2017] 1 Costs LR 175, (2017) 181 JP 325, [2017]
   Lloyd's Rep FC 193, [2017] ACD 47 .................................................. 12.43
R (on the application of Health and Safety Executive) v ATE Truck & Trailer
   Sales Ltd [2018] EWCA Crim 752, [2018] 4 WLR 142, [2018] 2 Cr App R
   (S) 29 ...................................................................................................... 13.5; Appendix

*Table of Cases*

R (on the application of IR Comrs) v Kingston Crown Court [2001] EWHC Admin 581, [2001] 4 All ER 721, [2001] STC 1615, [2001] BTC 322, [2001] STI 1240...................................................................................... 12.24; Appendix
R (for and on behalf of the Health and Safety Executive) v Jukes [2018] EWCA Crim 176, [2018] 2 Cr App R 9, [2018] Lloyd's Rep FC 157, [2018] Crim LR 658.................................................................................................... 11.33; Appendix
Reader v Molesworths Bright Clegg Solicitors [2007] EMCA Civ 169.............. 15.32
Ready Mixed Concrete (South East) Ltd v Minister of Pensions and National Insurance [1968] 2 QB 497, [1968] 2 WLR 775, [1968] 1 All ER 433...... 4.27; Appendix
Registrar of Restrictive Trading Agreements v WH Smith & Son Ltd [1969] 1 WLR 1460, [1969] 3 All ER 1065 ................................................. 4.36; Appendix
Rylands v Fletcher [1868] UKHL 1, (1868) LR 3 HL 330................... 15.42; Appendix

**S**

Scottish Power Generation Ltd v HM Advocate [2016] HCJAC 99, 2017 JC 85, 2016 SLT 1296, 2017 SCL 88, 2016 SCCR 569 ........................... 13.2; Appendix
Serious Fraud Office v Eurasian Natural Resources Corp Ltd [2018] EWCA Civ 2006, [2019] 1 WLR 791, [2019] 1 All ER 1026, [2018] Lloyd's Rep FC 635, [2019] Crim LR 44 ............................................................ 11.33; Appendix
Sneller v DAS Nederlandse Rechtsbijstand Verzekeringsmaatschappij (Case C-442/12) [2014] Bus LR 180, [2014] Lloyd's Rep IR 238 ........ 16.23; Appendix
Stark v Post Office [2000] ICR 1013, [2000] PIQR P105..................... 15.9; Appendix
Swift v Secretary of State for Justice [2012] EWHC 2000 (QB)......................... 15.23

**T**

Thompson v Arnold [2007] EWHC 1875 (QB)................................................. 15.32
Three Rivers District Council v Bank of England (No 5) [2003] EWCA Civ 474, [2003] QB 1556, [2003] 3 WLR 667......................................... 11.33; Appendix
Three Rivers District Council v Bank of England (No 6) [2004] EWCA Civ 218, [2004] QB 916, [2004] 2 WLR 1065, [2004] 3 All ER 168........ 11.33; Appendix
Transco Plc v Stockport Metropolitan Borough Council [2003] UKHL 61, [2004] 2 AC 1, [2003] 3 WLR 1467, [2004] 1 All ER 589, [2004] Env LR 24, [2004] 1 P & CR DG12............................................. 15.42, 15.43; Appendix

**W**

West London Pipeline & Storage Ltd v Total UK Ltd [2008] EWHC 1296 (Comm), [2008] CP Rep 35, [2008] 1 CLC 935, [2008] Lloyd's Rep IR 688 ............................................................................................. 15.41; Appendix
William v Summerfield [1972] 2 QB 512, [1972] 3 WLR 131, [1972] 2 All ER 1334, (1972) 56 Cr App R 597, [1972] Crim LR 424................................ 11.35
Wotherspoon v HM Advocate 1978 JC 74................................ 4.34, 4.39; Appendix
Wrotham Park Estate Co Ltd v Parkside Homes Ltd [1974] 1 WLR 798, [1974] 2 All ER 321, (1974) 27 P & CR 296........................................................ 15.35

# Part 1
# Managing Risk

# Chapter 1

# Corporate Governance, Directors' Duties

Introduction 1.1
History of corporate governance 1.2
UK Corporate Governance Code 1.3
    Board leadership and company purpose 1.4
    Division of responsibilities 1.5
    Composition, succession and evaluation 1.6
    Audit, risk and internal control 1.7
    Remuneration 1.8
Application of the latest Corporate Governance Report 1.9
Key highlights of the Corporate Governance Code 2018 1.10
    Guidance on the effectiveness of boards 1.11
    G20/OECD Principle of Corporate Governance 1.12
        Directors' duties – Companies Act 2006 1.13
        'Leading Health and Safety at Work' Guidance 1.14

## INTRODUCTION

**1.1** The principle that management is essential for the promotion of health and safety is not new. Lord Robens[1] said:

> 'Promotion of health and safety at work is an essential function of good management ... Good intentions at the board level are useless if managers further down the chain and closer to what happens on the shop floor remain preoccupied exclusively with production problems.'

The principles of good corporate governance flow through to good management of health and safety. The principles discussed in this chapter show how corporate governance has evolved in the UK, to the latest publications. It also discusses the same principles as ratified by the G20, through to directors duties in the Companies Act 2006 and the HSE's document 'Leading Health and Safety at Work'[2].

Corporate governance is increasingly in the media because of the investigation of high profile companies such as BHS and Sports Direct. In the summer of

---

1 Robens Report (Safety and Health at Work, Report of the Committee 1970–1972, Vol 1 London HMSO 1972), Ch 2.
2 HSE, 'Leading Health and Safety at Work', see http://www.hse.gov.uk/pubns/indg417.pdf.

**1.1** *Corporate Governance, Directors' Duties*

2016 there were inquiries into the failure of BHS and the employment practices at Sports Direct – which Parliament judged to be serious failings in corporate governance of these two major businesses[3]. It was found that in both cases there appeared to have been decisions taken in the board room which neglected the interest of the workers who worked hard to generate profits for the owners. There has also been growing dissatisfaction with the levels of executive pay where it is not reflected in the company's performance.

The sale and then collapse of BHS and the revelations about its pension fund focused attention on corporate governance. The purpose of corporate governance[4] is to facilitate effective entrepreneurial and prudent management that can deliver the long-term success of the company. Corporate governance is there to support effective decision making by companies for their own long-term success and provides a framework of law, rules and practices by which company boards balance the interests of shareholders with other stakeholders. That includes employees, customers, suppliers, creditors, pensioners and the local community.

Since the reports of July 2016, a new Prime Minster came to office, and her election campaign spoke of a 'need to get tough on irresponsible behaviour in big business'[5]. The Prime Minister has since described the scrutiny provided by those responsible for holding big business to account as 'not good enough' and she then spoke of the damage to the social contract between business and society caused when 'a small minority of business and business figures appear to game the system and work to a different set of rules'[6].

Following this the government published its Green Paper on corporate governance[7] in November 2016, which focused on three aspects:

- executive pay;
- private companies; and
- workers on boards.

The government then launched its own inquiry, which is complementary to its Green Paper, on industrial strategy[8] and proposed a new framework for informing long-term decision making for businesses and government[9]. This inquiry took oral evidence from 170 organisations and individuals who had

---

3   BHS First Report of the Work and Pensions Committee and Fourth Report of the Business, Innovation and Skills Committee Session 2016–17 HC54; Business Innovation and Skills Committee, Third Report of Session 2016–17, Employment Practices at Sports Direct, HC219.
4   ICAEW, 'What is Corporate Governance', see https://www.icaew.com/technical/corporate-governance/uk-corporate-governance/does-corporate-governance-matter.
5   Rt Hon Theresa May MP, Prime Minister, Speech on 11 July 2016.
6   Rt Hon Theresa May MP, Prime Minister, Speech at CBI, 21 November 2016.
7   Department for Business, Energy and Industrial Strategy, Corporate Governance Reform Green Paper, 29 November 2016.
8   HM Government Building our Industrial Strategy Green Paper 2017.
9   House of Commons, Business Energy and Industrial Strategy Committee, Industrial Strategy: First Review, Second Report of Session 2016–17, see https://publications.parliament.uk/pa/cm201617/cmselect/cmbeis/616/616.pdf.

submitted written evidence, plus discussions with a range of chairmen and chief executives of major companies at the Confederation of British Industry (CBI), the visiting professor of economics at the London School of Economics, Professor Paul Kay, and a range of businesses and trade unions during a visit to Sweden.

It is 25 years since the 'Cadbury Report' on the financial aspects of corporate governance and the government report found that the environment which businesses operate in has changed, with technological developments and new business models. Also business ownerships have changed and the global economy has created pressure to deliver short-term financial gains for shareholders rather than invest in long-term benefits. On this basis the government has proposed a series of reforms which are designed to require directors to take more seriously their duties to comply with the law and code relating to corporate governance.

This includes:

- more specific and accurate reporting;
- better engagement between boards and shareholders; and
- more accountable non-executive directors.

They have also recommended an expansion to the role and powers of the Financial Reporting Council so that it can call out poor practice and engage with the code.

# HISTORY OF CORPORATE GOVERNANCE

**1.2** 1992 – In the light of the *BCCI*[10] and *Maxwell* cases there was growing concern about standards of financial reporting and accountability. A committee was set up in 1991 to look at this and was chaired by Sir Adrian Cadbury and subsequently became known as the Cadbury Report[11]. It made three recommendations:

- the roles of chief executive officer and chairman of companies should be separated;
- boards should have at least three non-executive directors – two of whom should have no financial or personal ties to the executives;
- each board should have an audit committee composed of non-executive directors.

1995 – The Greenbury Committee was established by the CBI in response to a growing concern over the levels of salaries and bonuses paid to directors. It found that there should be remuneration committees made up of non-executive directors who determine the levels of executive directors'

---

10 Bingham LJ, *Inquiry into the Supervision of the Bank of Credit and Commerce International* see https://www.gov.uk/government/publications/inquiry-into-the-supervision-of-the-bank-of-credit-and-commerce-international.
11 'The Financial Aspects of Corporate Governance', see http://www.ecgi.org/codes/documents/cadbury.pdf.

**1.2** *Corporate Governance, Directors' Duties*

compensation packages and that there should be full disclosure of each executive's pay package and shareholders should be required to approve them. This was contained in the Greenbury Report[12].

1998 – The Hampel Committee was established to review the extent to which the objectives of the Cadbury and Greenbury reports were being achieved. The Hampel Report[13] was published in 1998 and produced the Combined Code on Corporate Governance ('the Combined Code') which applied to listed companies and said that:

- the chairman of the board should be the 'leader' of non-executive directors;
- institutional investors should consider voting on salaries at meetings;
- all kinds of remuneration, including pensions, should be disclosed.

1999 – The Turnbull Committee was established to provide direction on the internal control requirements of the Combined Code, including how to carry out risk management. The resulting Turnbull Report[14] helps boards meet the Code's requirements that they should maintain a sound system of internal control, conduct a review of the effectiveness of that system at least annually and report to shareholders that they have done so.

2003 – Sir Derek Higgs was commissioned by the UK government to review the roles of independent directors and of audit committees.

The resulting report[15] proposed that:

- at least half of a board (excluding the chairperson) be comprised of non-executive directors;
- that the non-executives should meet at least once a year in isolation to discuss company performance;
- that a senior independent director be nominated and made available for shareholders to express any concerns; and
- that potential non-executive directors should satisfy themselves that they possess the knowledge, experience, skills and time to carry out their duties with due diligence.

2005 – The Turnbull Guidance[16] was fully reviewed in 2004–05 and updated guidance was published in October 2005. Although there were no significant changes to the scope and content of the guidance, it was amended to encourage more informative disclosure, including by requiring boards

---

12 *Directors Remuneration – Report of a Study Group chaired by Sir Richard Greenbury*, see http://www.ecgi.org/codes/documents/greenbury.pdf.
13 *The Combined Code: Principles of Good Governance and Code of Best Practice* (May 2000), see https://www.frc.org.uk/getattachment/53db5ec9-810b-4e22-9ca2-99b116c3bc49/Combined-Code-1998.pdf.
14 Institute of Chartered Accountants, *Internal Control – Guidance for Directors on the Combined Code* http://www.ecgi.org/codes/documents/turnbul.pdf.
15 Derek Higgs, *Review of the Role and Effectiveness of Non-executive Directors* (January 2003), see http://www.ecgi.org/codes/documents/higgsreport.pdf.
16 FRC, *Internal Control – Reviewed Guidance for Directors on the Combined Code* (October 2005), see https://www.frc.org.uk/getattachment/fe1ba51a-578d-4467-a00c-f287825aced9/Revised-Turnbull-Guidance-October-2005.pdf.

*Corporate Governance, Directors' Duties* **1.2**

to confirm that necessary action has been or is being taken to remedy any significant failings or weaknesses identified from the annual review.

2006 – A revised version of the Combined Code on Corporate Governance[17] was published in June 2006 and applied to financial years beginning on or after 1 November 2006.

2008 – A revised version of the Combined Code on Corporate Governance[18] was published in June 2008 and applied to financial years beginning on or after 29 June 2008. Changes reflected new EU requirements relating to audit committees and corporate governance statements.

2010 – A revised UK Corporate Governance Code[19] was published in June 2010 and applied to financial years commencing on or after 29 June 2010. Changes included a revised format to give clearer advice on board composition; that all FTSE 350 directors be put forward for re-election every year; and improved risk management reporting provisions.

2011 – In March 2011 the FRC launched an enquiry led by Lord Sharman to identify lessons for companies and auditors addressing going concern and liquidity risk[20].

2012 – A revised UK Corporate Governance Code[21] was published in September 2012 and applied to financial years commencing on or after 1 October 2012. The changes included better reporting by audit committees; confirmation by boards that the annual report and accounts taken as whole are fair, balanced and understandable; and that companies explain and report on progress with their policies on boardroom diversity.

2014 – A revised UK Corporate Governance Code[22] was published in September 2014 and applied to financial years commencing on or after 1 October 2014. The Code was revised to enhance the quality of information received by investors about the long-term health and strategy of listed companies. It also updated the remuneration section to ensure executive remuneration is designed to promote the long-term success of the company and to demonstrate how this is being achieved more clearly to shareholders.

---

17 FRC, *The Combined Code on Corporate Governance* (June 2006), see https://www.frc.org.uk/getattachment/8238c251-5cfe-43b7-abc0-4318ccbdc0fd/Combined-Code-2006-(Oct-version).
18 FRC, *The Combined Code on Corporate Governance* (June 2008), see https://www.frc.org.uk/getattachment/56920102-feeb-4da7-84f7-1061840af9f0/Combined-Code-Web-Optimized-June-2008.pdf.
19 FRC, *The UK Corporate Governance Code* (June 2010), see https://www.frc.org.uk/getattachment/31631a7a-bc5c-4e7b-bc3a-972b7f17d5e2/UK-Corp-Gov-Code-June-2010.pdf.
20 The Sharman Inquiry, *Going Concern and Liquidity Risks: Lessons for Companies and Auditors* (June 2012), see https://www.frc.org.uk/getattachment/4a7f9880-0158-4cf0-b41e-b9e1bf006bd7/Sharman-Inquiry-final-report-FINAL.pdf.
21 FRC, *The UK Corporate Governance Code* (September 2012), see https://www.frc.org.uk/getattachment/e322c20a-1181-4ac8-a3d3-1fcfbcea7914/UK-Corporate-Governance-Code-(September-2012).pdf.
22 FRC, *The UK Corporate Governance Code* (September 2014), see https://www.frc.org.uk/getattachment/59a5171d-4163-4fb2-9e9d-daefcd7153b5/UK-Corporate-Governance-Code-2014.pdf.

*1.2 Corporate Governance, Directors' Duties*

2016 – A UK Corporate Governance Code[23] was published April 2016, following a consultation on changes needed to implement the EU Audit Regulation[24] and Directive[25]. It applies to financial years commencing on or after 17 June 2016.

2018 – The current UK Corporate Governance Code[26] was published in July 2018, focussing on the application of Principles. It applies to all accounting periods beginning on or after January 2019.

# UK CORPORATE GOVERNANCE CODE

**1.3** Since the first version of the UK Corporate Governance Code in 1992, corporate governance has been defined as[27]:

> 'The system by which companies are directed and controlled. Boards of directors are responsible for the governance of their companies. The shareholders' role in governance is to appoint the directors and the auditors and to satisfy themselves that an appropriate governance structure is in place.'

The 2018 UK Corporate Governance Code ('2018 Code')[28] focuses on the application of principles. The Listing Rules require companies to make a statement of how they have applied the principles in a manner that would enable shareholders to evaluate how the principles have been applied.

## Board leadership and company purpose

**1.4** The principles are:

- A successful company is led by an effective and entrepreneurial board, whose role is to promote the long-term sustainable success of the company, generating value for shareholders and contributing to wider society.

---

23 FRC, *The UK Corporate Governance Code* (April 2016), see https://www.frc.org.uk/getattachment/ca7e94c4-b9a9-49e2-a824-ad76a322873c/UK-Corporate-Governance-Code-April-2016.pdf.
24 Regulation (EU) No 537/2014 of the European Parliament and of the Council of 16 April 2014 on specific requirements regarding statutory audit of public-interest entities.
25 Directive 2014/56/EU of the European Parliament and of the Council of 16 April 2014 amending Directive 2006/43/EC on statutory audits of annual accounts and consolidated accounts Text with EEA relevance.
26 FRC, *The UK Corporate Governance Code* (July 2018) see https://www.frc.org.uk/getattachment/88bd8c45-50ea-4841-95b0-d2f4f48069a2/2018-UK-Corporate-Governance-Code-FINAL.PDF
27 'The Financial Aspects of Corporate Governance', see para 2.5 on Corporate Governance, http://www.ecgi.org/codes/documents/cadbury.pdf.
28 FRC, *The UK Corporate Governance Code* (July 2018), see https://www.frc.org.uk/getattachment/88bd8c45-50ea-4841-95b0-d2f4f48069a2/2018-UK-Corporate-Governance-Code-FINAL.pdf.

- The board should establish the company's purpose, values and strategy, and satisfy itself that these and its culture are aligned. All directors must act with integrity, lead by example and promote the desired culture.
- The board should ensure that the necessary resources are in place for the company to meet its objectives and measure performance against them. The board should also establish a framework of prudent and effective controls, which enable risk to be assessed and managed.
- In order for the company to meet its responsibilities to shareholders and stakeholders, the board should ensure effective engagement with, and encourage participation from, these parties.
- The board should ensure that workforce policies and practices are consistent with the company's values and support its long-term sustainable success. The workforce should be able to raise any matters of concern.

## Division of responsibilities

1.5     The principles are:

- The chairperson leads the board and is responsible for its overall effectiveness in directing the company. They should demonstrate objective judgement throughout their tenure and promote a culture of openness and debate. In addition, the chair facilitates constructive board relations and the effective contribution of all non-executive directors, and ensures that directors receive accurate, timely and clear information.
- The board should include an appropriate combination of executive and non-executive (and, in particular, independent non-executive) directors, such that no one individual or small group of individuals dominates the board's decision-making. There should be a clear division of responsibilities between the leadership of the board and the executive leadership of the company's business.
- Non-executive directors should have sufficient time to meet their board responsibilities. They should provide constructive challenge, strategic guidance, specialist advice and hold management to account.
- The board, supported by the company secretary, should ensure that it has the policies, processes, information, time and resources it needs in order to function effectively and efficiently.

## Composition, succession and evaluation

1.6     The principles are:

- Appointments to the board should be subject to a formal, rigorous and transparent procedure, and an effective succession plan should be maintained for board and senior management. Both appointments and succession plans should be based on merit and objective criteria and, within this context, should promote diversity of gender, social and ethnic backgrounds, cognitive and personal strengths.

1.6   *Corporate Governance, Directors' Duties*

- The board and its committees should have a combination of skills, experience and knowledge. Consideration should be given to the length of service of the board as a whole and membership should be regularly refreshed.
- Annual evaluation of the board should consider its composition and diversity and how effectively members work together to achieve objectives. Individual evaluation should demonstrate whether each director continues to contribute effectively.

## Audit, risk and internal control

1.7   The principles are:

- The board should establish formal and transparent policies and procedures to ensure the independence and effectiveness of internal and external audit functions and satisfy itself on the integrity of financial and narrative statements.
- The board should present a fair, balanced and understandable assessment of the company's position and prospects.
- The board should establish procedures to manage risk, oversee the internal control framework, and determine the nature and extent of the principal risks the company is willing to take in order to achieve its long-term strategic objectives.

## Remuneration

1.8   The principles are:

- Remuneration policies and practices should be designed to support strategy and promote long-term sustainable success. Executive remuneration should be aligned to company purpose and values, and be clearly linked to the successful delivery of the company's long-term strategy.
- A formal and transparent procedure for developing policy on executive remuneration and determining director and senior management remuneration should be established. No director should be involved in deciding their own remuneration outcome.
- Directors should exercise independent judgement and discretion when authorising remuneration outcomes, taking account of company and individual performance, and wider circumstances.

# APPLICATION OF THE LATEST CORPORATE GOVERNANCE REPORT

1.9   The 2018 Code is applicable to all companies with a Premium Listing. A Premium Listing is only available to equity shares issued by trading companies

*Corporate Governance, Directors' Duties* **1.9**

and close and open-ended investment entities. Issuers with Premium Listing are required to meet the UK's super-equivalent rules which are higher than the EU minimum requirements. A Premium Listing means the company is expected to meet the UK's highest standards of regulation and corporate governance – and as a consequence may enjoy a lower cost of capital through greater transparency and through building investor confidence[29]. The 2018 Code will apply to accounting periods beginning on or after 1 January 2019.

For parent companies with a Premium Listing, the board should ensure that there is adequate co-operation within the group to enable it to discharge its governance responsibilities under the 2018 Code effectively. This includes the communication of the parent company's purpose, values and strategy.

Externally managed investment companies (which typically have a different board and company structure that may affect the relevance of particular principles) may wish to use the Association of Investment Companies' Corporate Governance Code to meet their obligations under the 2018 Code. In addition, the Association of Financial Mutuals produces an annotated version of the 2018 Code for mutual insurers to use.

The principles are:

- A successful company is led by an effective and entrepreneurial board, whose role is to promote the long-term sustainable success of the company, generating value for shareholders and contributing to wider society.
- The board should establish the company's purpose, values and strategy, and satisfy itself that these and its culture are aligned. All directors must act with integrity, lead by example and promote the desired culture.
- The board should ensure that the necessary resources are in place for the company to meet its objectives and measure performance against them. The board should also establish a framework of prudent and effective controls, which enable risk to be assessed and managed.
- In order for the company to meet its responsibilities to shareholders and stakeholders, the board should ensure effective engagement with, and encourage participation from, these parties.
- The board should ensure that workforce policies and practices are consistent with the company's values and support its long-term sustainable success. The workforce should be able to raise any matters of concern.

The main changes are to:

- **Workforce and stakeholders** – there is a new provision to enable greater board engagement with the workforce to understand their views. The 2018 Code asks boards to describe how they have considered the interests of stakeholders when performing their duty under the Companies Act 2006, s 172.

---

29 See London Stock Exchange at https://www.londonstockexchange.com/companies-and-advisors/main-market/companies/primary-and-secondary-listing/listing-categories.htm.

**1.9** *Corporate Governance, Directors' Duties*

- **Culture** – boards are asked to create a culture which aligns company values with strategy and to assess how they preserve value over the long term.
- **Succession and diversity** – to ensure that the boards have the right mix of skills and experience, constructive challenge and to promote diversity, the 2018 Code emphasises the need to refresh boards and undertake succession planning. Boards should consider the length of term that chairs remain in post beyond nine years. The 2018 Code strengthens the role of the nomination committee on succession planning and establishing a diverse board. It identifies the importance of external board evaluation for all companies. Nomination committee reports should include details of the contact the external board evaluator has had with the board and individual directors.
- **Remuneration** – to address public concern over executive remuneration, the 2018 Code emphasises that remuneration committees should take into account workforce remuneration and related policies when setting director remuneration. Importantly formulaic calculations of performance-related pay should be rejected. Remuneration committees should apply discretion when the resulting outcome is not justified.

# KEY HIGHLIGHTS OF THE CORPORATE GOVERNANCE CODE 2018

**1.10** The 2018 Code[30] broadens the definition of governance and emphasises the importance of:

- 'Positive relationships between companies, shareholders and stakeholders.
- A clear purpose and strategy aligned with healthy corporate culture.
- High quality board composition and a focus on diversity.
- Remuneration which is proportionate and supports long-term success.

*Designed to:*

- Set higher standards of corporate governance to promote transparency and integrity in business.
- Attract investment in the UK for the long term, benefitting the economy and wider society. …

*Stakeholders*

- Emphasis on improving the quality of the board and company's relationships with a wider range of stakeholders.
- Taking effective action when receiving significant shareholder votes against resolutions and reporting back more promptly.
- Board responsibility for workforce policies and practices which reinforce a healthy culture.

---

30 FRC, 'Revised UK Corporate Governance Code 2018 Highlights', see https://www.frc.org.uk/getattachment/524d4f4b-62df-4c76-926a-66e223ca0893/2018-UK-Corporate-Governance-Code-highlights.pdf.

*Corporate Governance, Directors' Duties* **1.10**

- Engaging with the workforce through one, or a combination, of a director appointed from the workforce, a formal workforce advisory panel and a designated non-executive director, or other arrangements which meet the circumstances of the company and the workforce.
- The ability for directors and the workforce to be able to raise concerns and for effective enquiry of these concerns.

*The boardroom*

- Emphasis on importance of independence and constructive challenge of the boardroom.
- Strengthening consideration of "overboarding".
- A focus on diversity, the length of service of the board as a whole, and effective board refreshment.
- "Comply or explain" provision for a maximum nine-year length of service, allowing flexibility to extend "to facilitate effective succession planning and the development of a diverse board ... particularly in those cases where the chair was an existing non-executive director on appointment".
- Nomination committee responsibility for more effective succession planning that develops a more diverse pipeline. Reporting on the gender balance of senior management and their direct reports.
- Higher quality external board evaluations, emphasising the importance of the evaluator's direct contact with the board and individual directors.

*Remuneration*

- More demanding criteria for remuneration policies and practices.
- Clearer reporting on remuneration, how it delivers company strategy, long-term success and its alignment with workforce remuneration.
- Directors exercising independent judgement and discretion on remuneration outcomes, taking account of wider circumstances.
- Remuneration committee chair should have served on a remuneration committee for at least 12 months.

**Code structure and reporting**

The Code does not set out a rigid set of rules; instead it offers flexibility through the application of principles and through "comply or explain" Provisions and supporting guidance. It is the responsibility of boards to use this flexibility wisely and of investors and their advisors to assess differing company approaches thoughtfully. The 2018 Code:

- is shorter and sharper;
- "Supporting Principles" have been removed; and
- it has fewer Provisions.

*Renewed focus on the Principles*

- By reporting on the application of the Principles in a manner that can be evaluated, companies should demonstrate how the governance of the company contributes to its long-term sustainable success and achieves wider objectives
- The statement should cover the application of the Principles in the context of the particular circumstances of the company, how the board has set the company's purpose and strategy, met objectives and achieved outcomes through its decisions

**1.10** *Corporate Governance, Directors' Duties*

- High-quality reporting will include signposting and cross-referencing to other relevant parts of the annual report.

*The effective application of the Principles should be supported by high-quality reporting on the Provisions*

- The Provisions establish good practice on a "comply or explain" basis.
- Companies should avoid a "tick-box approach". An alternative to complying with a Provision may be justified in particular circumstances based on a range of factors, including the size, complexity, history and ownership structure of a company.
- Explanations should set out the background, provide a clear rationale for the action the company is taking, and explain the impact that the action has had.
- Where a departure from a Provision is intended to be limited in time, the explanation should indicate when the company expects to conform to the Provision.
- Explanations are a positive opportunity to communicate, not an onerous obligation.

*The role of investors and their advisors is very important*

- Investors should engage constructively and discuss with the company any departures from recommended practice.
- When considering explanations, investors and proxy advisors should pay due regard to a company's individual circumstances.
- Proxy advisors have every right to challenge explanations if they are unconvincing, but explanations must not be evaluated in a mechanistic way.
- Investors and proxy advisors should also give companies sufficient time to respond to enquiries about corporate governance reporting.'

## Guidance on the effectiveness of boards

**1.11** The Financial Reporting Council has produced a guide[31] which is aimed at making boards think about how effective they are and to continually focus on improving their effectiveness. The guide focuses on:

- board leadership and purpose;
- division of responsibility;
- composition, succession and evaluation;
- audit, risk and internal control; and
- remuneration

## G20/OECD Principle of Corporate Governance

**1.12** The updated principles of corporate governance[32] were launched at a meeting of G20 Finance Ministers and the Central Bank Governors in Ankara

---

31 FRC, 'Guidance on Board Effectiveness' (July 2018), see https://www.frc.org.uk/getattachment/61232f60-a338-471b-ba5a-bfed25219147/2018-Guidance-on-Board-Effectiveness-FINAL.PDF.
32 G20/OECD, 'Principles of Corporate Governance', see https://www.oecd.org/daf/ca/Corporate-Governance-Principles-ENG.pdf.

on 4–5 September 2015 and were subsequently endorsed at the G20 leaders' Summit in Antalya on 15–16 November 2015.

The principles say that good corporate governance is not an end in itself but a means to support economic efficiency, sustainable growth and financial stability. They also facilitate companies' access to capital for long-term investment and help ensure that shareholders who contribute to the success of the corporation are treated fairly.

The principles provide guidance on:

- ensuring the basis for effective corporate governance framework;
- the rights and equitable treatment of shareholders and key ownership functions;
- institutional investors, stock markets and other intermediaries;
- the role of stakeholders in corporate governance;
- disclosure and transparency; and
- the responsibilities of the board.

## Directors' duties – Companies Act 2006

**1.13** Directors have historically been subject to duties under English company law. The vast majority of duties were not set out in legislation but have evolved through common law. These duties included:

- a duty to act in good faith in the best interests of the company;
- a duty to exercise skill and care;
- a duty to avoid conflicting interests and duties; and
- a duty not to make a secret profit.

The Companies Act 2006 was intended to codify these duties; that is to translate them into legislation largely unchanged. The Act has however changed the scope of director's duties and now includes an 'overriding duty' to act in good faith.

## 'Leading Health and Safety at Work' Guidance

**1.14** The HSE worked together with the IOD (Institute of Directors) to produce guidance called 'Leading Health and Safety at Work'[33]. This lays down a number of guidelines and starts with essential principles[34].

> '• Strong and active leadership from the top:
>   – visible, active commitment from the board;

---

[33] IOD and HSE, 'Leading Health and Safety at Work' (INDG 417 (rev1) 06/13), see http://www.hse.gov.uk/pubns/indg417.pdf.
[34] Institute of Directors and the Health and Safety Executive, 'Leading Health and Safety at Work' (INDG 417 (rev1) 06/13), see http://www.hse.gov.uk/pubns/indg417.pdf, at p 1.

**1.14** *Corporate Governance, Directors' Duties*

- establishing effective "downward" communication systems and management structures;
- integration of good health and safety management with business decisions.
- Worker involvement:
  - engaging the workforce in the promotion and achievement of safe and healthy conditions;
  - effective "upward" communication;
  - providing high-quality training.
- Assessment and review:
  - identifying and managing health and safety risks;
  - accessing (and following) competent advice;
  - monitoring, reporting and reviewing performance.'

The HSE published HSG65[35] in 2013. The guidance explains the 'Plan, Do, Check, Act' approach which is used to help companies achieve a balance between systems and behavioural aspects of management. 'Leading Health and Safety at Work' has made a number of significant changes to this guidance as illustrated in the following table:

| HSG65 | Leading Health and Safety at Work |
| --- | --- |
| Systems and process orientated | Emphasis on behavioural aspects |
| Health and safety positioned as a separate business function | Health and safety management an integral part of good management generally |
| Contained in a manual | An HSE microsite providing links to further details |
| Provides detailed coverage of the key elements of a health and safety management system using POPIMAR: Policies-Organising-Planning-Implementing-Measurement-Audit-Review | Advocates a revised approach to putting health and safety arrangements in place or for overseeing them: Plan-Do-Check-Act |

---

35 HSE, 'Managing for Health and Safety' (HSG65), see http://www.hse.gov.uk/pubns/priced/hsg65.pdf.

# Chapter 2

# Risk Management

Introduction   2.1
Controlling risks in the workplace   2.2
Legislation   2.3
    Health and Safety at Work etc Act 1974   2.3
        ALARP – As low as is reasonably practicable   2.4
    Management of Health and Safety at Work Regulations 1999   2.5
    Workplace (Health, Safety and Welfare) Regulations 1992   2.6
    Other legislation   2.7
    Legislation with specific requirements   2.8
Prosecutions for a lack of a risk management system   2.9
    *Goldscheider v Royal Opera House Covent Garden Foundation*   2.9
    *Cundall v Leeds City Council*   2.10
    *Kennedy v Cordia (Services) LLP*   2.11
Risk assessment   2.12
    Definition of a hazard   2.13
    Definition of a risk   2.14
Five steps to risk assessment   2.15
    Step 1: Identify the hazards   2.16
    Step 2: Decide who might be harmed and how   2.17
    Step 3: Evaluate the risks   2.18
        Risk matrix   2.19
        Likelihood (probability)   2.20
        Consequences (impact)   2.21
        Risk = Likelihood × Consequence   2.22
        Reducing the likelihood   2.23
        Reducing the consequence by introducing risk controls which make the event less severe   2.24
        Reducing both the likelihood and the consequence   2.25
    Step 4: Record the significant findings   2.33
    Step 5: Review the risk assessment and update if necessary   2.34
Safety auditing   2.35
    Internal v external audits   2.36
        Internal   2.36
        External   2.37
Certification audits   2.38
    External certification   2.39
    ISO 45001 Occupational Health and Safety   2.40
        How does ISO 45001 relate to other standards?   2.41
        Stages of certification   2.42

2.1 *Risk Management*

# INTRODUCTION

**2.1** There are many types of risk management for a business to consider such as: strategic risk; compliance risk; operational risk; financial risk; and reputational risk.

All of these could be covered by the term 'business risk management' – a strategic process which supports the decision making at both strategic and operational levels. The Turnbull Committee's[1] guidance required businesses that are listed on the UK stock market to identify, record, and manage their significant risks. It is good practice for businesses and organisations, whether or not they are listed, to consider the significant risk to their businesses.

Health and safety hazards and controls will be included where they represent a significant operational and compliance risk. The principal of assessing the risks are common to both health and safety and other operational processes.

# CONTROLLING RISKS IN THE WORKPLACE

**2.2** To control risks in the workplace needs consideration of what might cause harm to people and decide whether the organisation is taking reasonable steps to prevent that harm. This is known as a risk assessment and it is something that is required by law to be carried out but if there are fewer than five employees, there is no requirement to write anything down – however it is good practice to have a record of the assessments that have been made – in case reference needs to be made to them in the event that something has happened.

A risk assessment is not about creating a lot of paperwork, but about identifying measures to control the risks in the workplace. There may already be systems in place to protect employees, the risk assessment will help a business decide whether all the measures that need to be taken are in place.

# LEGISLATION
## Health and Safety at Work etc Act 1974

**2.3** The Health and Safety at Work etc Act 1974 (HSWA 1974) sets down the general duties that employers have towards their employees, and that members of the public and employees have towards themselves and to each other.

---

1   Guidance on Risk Management, Internal Control and Related Financial and Business Reporting (Sept 2015) https://www.frc.org.uk/getattachment/d672c107-b1fb-4051-84b0-f5b83a1b93f6/Guidance-on-Risk-Management-Internal-Control-and-Related-Reporting.pdf.

## ALARP – As low as is reasonably practicable

**2.4** The duties under the HSWA 1974 are qualified by the principle of 'so far as is reasonably practicable' which means that the employer does not have to take measures to avoid a risk if the time, trouble or cost of the measures would make it grossly disproportionate from the risk. So, ALARP describes the level at which workplace risks are expected to be controlled.

'Reasonably practicable' was defined in the Court of Appeal decision *Edwards v National Coal Board*[2] where it was said[3]:

> '"Reasonably practicable" is a narrower term than "physically possible" and seems to me to imply that a computation must be made by the owner, in which the quantum of risk is placed on one scale and the sacrifice involved in the measures necessary for averting the risk (whether in money, time or trouble) is placed in the other; and that if it be shown that there is a gross disproportion between them – the risk being insignificant in relation to the sacrifice – the defendants discharge the onus on them.'

This means making sure a risk is reduced to ALARP whilst weighing the risk against the sacrifice needed to further reduce it. The decision is weighted in favour of health and safety as the presumption is that the duty-holder should implement the risk reduction measure. To avoid having to make this sacrifice, the duty-holder must be able to show that it would be grossly disproportionate to the benefits of risk reduction that would be achieved. Thus, the process is not one of balancing the costs and benefits of measures but, rather, of adopting measures except where they are ruled out because they involve grossly disproportionate sacrifices.

## Management of Health and Safety at Work Regulations 1999

**2.5** The Management of Health and Safety at Work Regulations 1999[4] is more explicit about what employers are required to do to manage health and safety under the HSWA 1974 and, like the Act, the regulations apply to every work activity. The regulations require the carrying out of risk assessments, the implementation of measures to control the risks, the appointment of competent people, and arranging for appropriate information and training to be given.

## Workplace (Health, Safety and Welfare) Regulations 1992

**2.6** The Workplace (Health, Safety and Welfare) Regulations 1992[5] cover basic health requirements and issues such as heating, lighting, ventilation, work stations, seating and welfare facilities.

---

2   [1949] 1 All ER 743.
3   [1949] 1 All ER 743 at [712].
4   SI 1999/3242.
5   SI 1992/3004.

2.7  *Risk Management*

## Other legislation

2.7    Other legislation that should be considered is as follows:

- Health and Safety (Display Screen Equipment) Regulations 1992[6] – set out requirements for working with visual display units (VDUs);
- Personal Protective Equipment at Work Regulations 1992[7] – require employers to provide appropriate protective clothing and equipment for their employees;
- Provision and Use of Work Equipment Regulations 1998[8] – require that equipment provided for use at work, including machinery, is safe;
- Personal Protective Equipment (Enforcement) Regulations 2018[9] apply to the whole supply chain rather than just manufacturers. These regulations also slightly modify the risk categorisation of products – life jackets and hearing protection are moved from category II (intermediate personal protective equipment (PPE)) to category III (complex PPE) – which means they are now subject to a stricter conformity assessment procedure and ongoing surveillance;
- Manual Handling Operations Regulations 1992[10] – cover the moving of objects by hand or bodily force;
- Health and Safety (First-Aid) Regulations 1981[11] – cover the requirements for first aid and require employers to provide adequate and appropriate equipment, facilities and personnel to ensure that their employees receive immediate attention if they are injured or taken ill at work;
- Health and Safety Information for Employees Regulations 1989[12] (as amended) – require employers to display a poster telling employees what they need to know about health and safety;
- Employers' Liability (Compulsory Insurance) Act 1969 – requires employers to take out insurance against accidents and ill-health suffered by their employees;
- Reporting of Injuries, Diseases and Dangerous Occurrences Regulations 2013[13] (RIDDOR) – require employers to notify certain occupational injuries, diseases and dangerous events to the appropriate authorities;
- Control of Noise at Work Regulations 2005[14] – require employers to take action to protect employees from hearing damage;
- Electricity at Work Regulations 1989[15] – require people in control of electrical systems to ensure they are safe to use and maintained in a safe condition;

6   SI 1992/2792.
7   SI 1992/2966.
8   SI 1998/2306.
9   SI 2018/390.
10  SI 1992/2793.
11  SI 1981/917.
12  SI 1989/682.
13  SI 2013/1471.
14  SI 2005/1643.
15  SI 1989/635.

- Control of Substances Hazardous to Health Regulations 2002[16] (as amended) (COSHH) – require employers to assess the risks from hazardous substances and prevent or reduce workers' exposure to these substances.

## Legislation with specific requirements

**2.8**

- Regulatory Reform (Fire Safety) Order 2005[17] – requires that the person who has some level of control in a premises must take reasonable steps to reduce the risk from fire and make sure that people can escape if there is a fire (see also the Fire (Scotland) Act 2005);
- Chemicals (Hazard Information and Packaging for Supply) Regulations 2009[18] – require suppliers to classify, label and package dangerous chemicals and provide safety data sheets for them;
- Construction (Design and Management) Regulations 2015[19] – cover safe systems of work on construction sites.
- Gas Safety (Installation and Use) Regulations 1998[20] (as amended) – cover the safe installation, maintenance and use of gas systems and appliances in domestic and commercial premises;
- Control of Major Accident Hazards Regulations 2015[21] (as amended) – require those who manufacture, store or transport dangerous chemicals or explosives in certain quantities to notify the relevant authority;
- Dangerous Substances and Explosive Atmospheres Regulations 2002[22] – require employers and the self-employed to carry out a risk assessment of work activities involving dangerous substances where dangerous substances can put peoples' safety at risk from fire, explosion and corrosion of metal.

# PROSECUTIONS FOR A LACK OF A RISK MANAGEMENT SYSTEM

## *Goldscheider v Royal Opera House Covent Garden Foundation*[23]

**2.9** The Opera House was liable to a viola player in its orchestra after he suffered acoustic shock due to noise levels during a rehearsal. The Opera House had breached its duties under the Control of Noise at Work Regulations

---

16 SI 2002/2677.
17 SI 2005/1541.
18 SI 2009/716.
19 SI 2015/51.
20 SI 1998/2451.
21 SI 2015/483.
22 SI 2002/2776.
23 [2018] EWHC 687 (QB).

*2.9 Risk Management*

2005[24]: it had failed to carry out an adequate risk assessment; failed to do everything reasonably practicable to eliminate the risk of noise exposure; failed to designate its orchestra pit as a mandatory hearing protection zone; and failed to train orchestra members about the risks. It could not compromise its standard of care for artistic considerations.

### *Cundall v Leeds City Council*[25]

**2.10** A local authority failed in its duty of care to a teaching assistant at a special needs school who was assaulted by a pupil. The pupil had been violent on several occasions in the previous two months but the local authority failed to assess the risk to which the teaching assistant was exposed, focusing exclusively on what it thought were the pupil's best interests.

### *Kennedy v Cordia (Services) LLP*[26]

**2.11** An employer was liable for injuries sustained by a home carer when she slipped and fell on an icy path during the course of her employment, as the failure to carry out a suitable risk assessment and provide personal protective equipment had breached the Management of Health and Safety at Work Regulations 1999[27], reg 3(1) and the Personal Protective Equipment at Work Regulations 1992[28], reg 4(1). The court gave guidance on the use of expert evidence in civil cases, the admissibility of such evidence, the responsibility of a party's legal team to make sure that the expert performed his role, the court's role in policing the performance of the expert's duties, and the consideration of economy in litigation.

## RISK ASSESSMENT

**2.12** Risk assessment is the systematic process of looking at the work people do and how this could cause them harm and decide whether there are reasonable steps taken to prevent the harm occurring. It is not about creating large amounts of paperwork but about identifying sensible measures to control the risks. For some risks there are regulations that require specific control measures.

---

24 SI 2005/1643.
25 Unreported.
26 [2016] UKSC 6.
27 SI 1999/3242.
28 SI 1992/2966.

## Definition of a hazard

**2.13** A 'hazard' is something (a property, substance or object or activity) that can cause an adverse effect. For example:
- liquid spilt on a staircase;
- excessive noise;
- asbestos dust in the air.

## Definition of a risk

**2.14** The 'risk' is the likelihood that the hazard will actually cause harm.

# FIVE STEPS TO RISK ASSESSMENT

**2.15** There are generally considered to be five steps to carrying out a risk assessment.

## Step 1: Identify the hazards

**2.16** The risk assessment should identify the potential hazards in the workplace – which is anything that could cause harm. Hazards can be classified into:
- physical – eg lifting, slips and trips, dust, machinery, noise, computer equipment;
- mental – eg working long hours, large workload, bullying, intense working – these hazards affect the mental health of people and affect their working relationships;
- chemical – eg cleaning fluids, aerosols, asbestos;
- biological – eg infectious diseases such as Weill's disease.

Walking round the workplace will help identify potential hazards – the following are issues to bear in mind:
- check manufacturers' instructions or data sheets for chemicals and equipment and ensure that they are being followed;
- review accident and ill-health records;
- review any non-routine work that is being carried out such as maintenance, cleaning operations or a change in production;
- consider long-term health hazards such as high levels of noise, exposure to harmful substance, and dust;
- there are some hazards with a recognised risk of harm, for example working at height, working with chemicals, machinery, and asbestos. Depending on the type of work being carried out, there may be other hazards that would be relevant to a business.

*2.17 Risk Management*

## Step 2: Decide who might be harmed and how

**2.17** This covers the organisation's full- and part-time employees and also agency staff, visitors, clients and members of the public who may come on to the premises. It is also important to review workers at all the different locations and situations, including people who work from home. There are also specific duties for people who are disabled, night workers, shift workers, or pregnant[29].

## Step 3: Evaluate the risks

**2.18** Having identified the hazards, then a decision about how likely it is that harm will occur will give an employer the level of risk, and then a further decision can be made about how acceptable that risk is. This can take the form of a simple list of hazards, and the steps that are being taken to control the risks from these hazards, with a date this will be carried out by and the person responsible for carrying it out.

*Risk matrix*

**2.19** A risk matrix can be used to define the level of the risk by looking at the level of the likelihood against that of the severity of the consequence. The commonest form is a 5 by 5 matrix.

*Likelihood (probability)*

**2.20**

| Score | Likelihood | Description |
|---|---|---|
| 5 | Almost certain | Will happen and possibly recur |
| 4 | Likely | Will happen – but not a persisting issue |
| 3 | Possible | Might happen or recur occasionally |
| 2 | Unlikely | Do not expect it to happen |
| 1 | Rare | Will probably never happen |

---

29 Pregnant workers – see the Management of Health and Safety at Work Regulations 1999 (SI 1999/3242), regs 16 and 18.

## Consequences (impact)

**2.21**

| Score | Consequence |
|---|---|
| 5 | Catastrophic |
| 4 | Major |
| 3 | Moderate |
| 2 | Minor |
| 1 | Negligible |

## Risk = Likelihood × Consequence

**2.22**

|  | Consequence ||||| 
|---|---|---|---|---|---|
| **Likelihood** | Negligible (1) | Minor (2) | Moderate (3) | Major (4) | Catastrophic (5) |
| Almost certain (5) | 5 | 10 | 15 | 20 | 25 |
| Likely (4) | 4 | 8 | 12 | 16 | 20 |
| Possible (3) | 3 | 6 | 9 | 12 | 15 |
| Unlikely (2) | 2 | 4 | 6 | 8 | 10 |
| Rare (1) | 1 | 2 | 3 | 4 | 5 |

If the level of risk is acceptable, then no further action needs to be taken. The level of risk is calculated by Risk = Likelihood × Consequence

Reducing the risk can be achieved by either lowering the likelihood, or the consequence, or both.

## Reducing the likelihood

**2.23** Examples of this are:
- guarding machinery;
- wearing a face visor when handling dangerous chemicals.

2.24  *Risk Management*

## Reducing the consequence by introducing risk controls which make the event less severe

2.24  Examples of this are:

- wearing a fall arrest harness when working from height;
- substitute a corrosive chemical with one which is less hazardous to handle and use;
- install handrails either side of a walkway.

## Reducing both the likelihood and the consequence

**Residual risk**

2.25  Whatever options are used to control the risk there will almost always be a residual risk. If the risk has been reduced to as low as is reasonably practicable then the residual risk should be acceptable.

**Deciding on the risk control**

2.26  The hierarchy of control is the system used in industry to minimise or eliminate exposure to hazards. This process has the acronym ERICPD and starts by trying to eliminate the risk altogether and then moves through to personal protective equipment (PPE) and discipline about how the procedures and methods of working are enforced. Note PPE is the last form of controlling the risk and not the first.

*Eliminate*

2.27  This is the option which is most effective and gets rid of the hazard. This can be done by changing the work activity or by automating the process.

For example:

- using material handling equipment rather than have workers lift, lower or carry materials manually;
- cleaning windows using a telescopic pole rather than from a ladder eliminates working from height.

*Reduce*

2.28  If the hazard cannot be eliminated, then it may be possible to reduce the hazard at source. For example:

- splitting large loads in to smaller ones;
- using less noisy processes;
- using a MEWP (mobile elevated working platform) instead of a ladder to work at height;
- using a liquid chemical rather than a powder.

*Isolate*

**2.29** This means preventing people from coming into contact with the hazard. For example:

- placing the hazard in an inaccessible location eg power lines on high pylons;
- locking chemicals in a hazardous chemical store;
- enclosing the hazard behind a barrier.

*Control*

**2.30** Safe systems of work rely upon people following the rules every time. For example:

- a set of procedures and rules which govern how the work is carried out;
- a permit to work system.

*PPE*

**2.31** This is the last resort and may also only be a temporary measure until an alternative process can be implemented. For example:

- Hi Vis vest, safety boots and hard hats;
- head shield to protect the face of a welder.

*Discipline*

**2.32** This consists of enforcing a safe system of work on site and a positive safety culture. For example:

- communication of clear safety rules;
- use of safety signs to remind people of the site rules;
- training and performance assessment.

Whatever controls are used need to be monitored and enforced. If the risk option relies on a particular behaviour then it is a less reliable risk control method than an option which does not.

## Step 4: Record the significant findings

**2.33** Even though a recorded risk assessment is not required for organisations with fewer than five people, it is good practice to record any significant findings: the hazards, how people might be harmed, and what there is in place to control the risks. Any record produced should be simple and focused on controls. The recorded findings can be reviewed at a later date, for example if something changes in the workplace.

## Step 5: Review the risk assessment and update if necessary

**2.34** Very few workplaces remain the same and so a risk assessment should be reviewed on a regular basis and when the nature of the work changes. This allows an employer to assess whether the control measures are working and if further or different controls are necessary.

# SAFETY AUDITING

**2.35** A safety audit – whether this is internally done or carried out by an external body – can provide an organisation with a review of the complete safety management system.

The Institute of Occupational Safety and Health (IOSH)[30] state that a component of a safety management system is measuring performance and that formal audits should evaluate the overall performance of the system. HSE[31] state that larger public and private sector organisations should have formal procedures for auditing and reporting health and safety performance.

The board should ensure that any audit is perceived as a positive management and boardroom tool. It should have unrestricted access to both external and internal auditors, keeping their cost-effectiveness, independence and objectivity under review.

ISO 45001[32], para 3.32 defines 'audit' as 'systematic, independent and documented process for obtaining audit evidence and evaluating it objectively to determine the extent to which the audit criteria are fulfilled'. An effective safety audit not only demonstrates compliance with legislation and how people are following company processes, but can also provide the opportunity to set standards for continuous improvement.

## Internal v external audits

### Internal

**2.36** People within the organisation can be trained to audit the safety management system. There are advantages in doing this such as:

- it is cost effective as the people are already employed and will know the business;

---

30 Institute of Occupational Safety and Health, *Systems in Focus – Guidance on occupational safety and health management systems* available at www.iosh.co.uk/freeguides. POL3742/110716/PDF.
31 HSE Auditing and Reporting see http://www.hse.gov.uk/leadership/auditing.htm.
32 International Organisation for Standardisation, ISO 45001:2018, *Occupational health and safety management systems — Requirements with guidance for use.*

*Risk Management* **2.38**

- it provides flexibility in how the audit is carried out – targeting specific areas of the business;
- it can be carried out with minimal disruption.

The disadvantages are:

- the audit may be seen as biased by people within the organisation;
- the internal audits may not be accepted by other people – eg companies that they bid for work from;
- priority may not be given to conducting the audit;
- the internal auditor is not allowed sufficient time from their normal role to audit.

## *External*

**2.37** External audit options are available – a number of companies run an audit system and provide certification whether to a standard such as ISO 45001 or to their own. The advantages of this are:

- the ability to benchmark the organisation against other similar industries using the same audit system;
- it is unbiased.

The disadvantages are:

- the organisation needs to allocate sufficient time for the audit and provide the auditor with access to areas which they want to visit;
- it can be expensive and time-consuming.

Whether an internal or external process is used, it is important to audit the safety management system to ascertain how it is operating in practice, and then make improvements. It is also a valuable record to show how the organisation is being run should anything happen.

# CERTIFICATION AUDITS

**2.38** A regular safety audit may be required of an organisation by someone they supply, or certification to a specified standard is required as part of the tendering process for work. Either way it makes sense to have a process for reviewing the company safety management system via an audit. It allows a company to:

- see that health and safety procedures are working;
- show that processes are in compliance with company policy and with regulations;
- discover and identify potential hazards;
- evaluate the effectiveness of existing controls;
- check the safety of the workplace and also of the equipment;
- evaluate the effectiveness of employee training.

## External certification

**2.39** There are a number of ways to have an external accreditation or certification of a safety management system. There are those run by organisations which provide certification of a specific standard, and there are those providing accreditation to an international standard. Using an external process provides an independent review of the safety management system.

## ISO 45001 Occupational Health and Safety

**2.40** ISO 45001:2018 is the replacement of OHSAS 18001 and was published on 12 March 2018.

ISO 45001 is an international standard that specifies requirements for occupational health and safety (OH&S) management systems to enable organisations to proactively improve their OH&S performance. It applies to any organisation irrespective of the organisation's size, nature or type. It also allows the integration of other aspects of worker health such as wellness/wellbeing.

As long as the organisation has people working on its behalf, or who may be affected by its activities, then using a systematic approach to managing health and safety will bring benefits to it. The standard can be applied to small low-risk operations as well as to high-risk and large complex organisations. Whilst the standard requires that OH&S risks are addressed and controlled, it also takes a risk-based approach to the OH&S management system itself, to ensure that it is effective and being improved to meet any changes the organisation may undergo. This risk-based approach is consistent with that used by organisations to manage their other 'business' risks and encourages the integration of the standard's requirements into the organisation's overall management processes.

### How does ISO 45001 relate to other standards?

**2.41** ISO 45001 follows the high-level structure approach that is being applied to other ISO management system standards, such as ISO 9001 (quality) and ISO 14001 (environment). When the standard was being developed consideration was given to the content of other international standards (such as OHSAS 18001 or the International Labour Organisation's 'ILO-OSH Guidelines') and national standards, as well as to the ILO's International labour standards and conventions (ILSs).

This allows for a relatively easy migration from using an existing OH&S management system standard to using ISO 45001, and will also allow for the alignment and integration with the requirements of other ISO management system standards into the organisation's overall management processes.

## Stages of certification

**2.42**

| Stage 1 | Initial assessment which determines if the mandatory requirements of the standard are being met and if the management system can move to stage 2. |
|---|---|
| Stage 2 | The second stage of assessment determines the effectiveness of the systems and tries to confirm if the management system is implemented and operational. |
| Recommendation for certification | This is where a review occurs of the corrective actions taken to address findings raised at stages 1 and 2; certification may be recommended. |
| Certification review and decision | The organisation's files are reviewed by an independent and impartial panel and the certification decision is made. |
| Certification achieved | Once ISO 45001 is released certification will last for three years and is subject to mandatory audits every year to ensure that the business is compliant. At the end of the three years, a business will be requested to complete a reassessment audit in order to become recertified to the standard. |

# Chapter 3

# Business Continuity

Introduction   3.1
    Business continuity plan   3.2
Business continuity management   3.3
Business impact analysis   3.4
    Step 1 – identify key products and services   3.5
    Step 2 – maximum time the organisation can manage   3.6
    Step 3 – recovery time   3.7
    Step 4 – critical activities   3.8
    Step 5 – quantify the resources   3.9
Creating a business continuity plan   3.10
    Assessment of the current situation   3.10
    Security   3.11
    Fire   3.12
    Services   3.13
    Insurance   3.14
    Salvage   3.15
    Planning   3.16
        Response to an incident – not the cause of the incident   3.17
        Integrate emergency plans into the organisation   3.18
        Integrate different departments and their response   3.19
        Co-ordinate arrangements with neighbours   3.20
        Elements of the plan   3.21
        Senior management involvement   3.22
        Implementing the plan   3.23
        Call out list   3.24
        Minimising damage   3.25
        Evacuation of the premises   3.26
        Relocation/alternative IT   3.27
Communications   3.28
    Relations with the public   3.29
    Liaison with emergency services   3.30
    Other issues to consider   3.31
        Data protection   3.31
        Personnel   3.32
        Security issues   3.33
        After the incident   3.34
Revision of plans after the event   3.35

3.1 *Business Continuity*

# INTRODUCTION

**3.1** A disruption can occur to a business at any time, whether a cyber-attack, an issue with the supply chain, floods or losing a key employee. Business continuity is about having a plan to deal with difficult situations, so that the organisation can continue to function with as little disruption as possible. Whether the organisation is a business, a public sector organisation, or a charity, it is important to understand how to carry on.

Examples of major disruption over the last few years include:

- in 2017, a global cyber-attack crippled NHS computers, and was found in 150 countries having infected more than 300,000 computers;
- in 2018, a supply chain failure closed more than half of the UK's KFC fast food outlets;
- the Holborn fire in April 2015, which was caused by an underground electrical fault and burned for 26 hours, caused 3,000 properties to be left without power and 5,000 evacuated from central London; in addition eight theatres had to cancel performances and many restaurants closed;
- the Forth Road Bridge closed in December 2015 because of a crack which left the crossing unusable for a month, causing chaos for commuters and having a significant impact on Christmas deliveries;
- a three-hour power cut in Terminal 5 at Heathrow Airport in August 2015, which affected the baggage system and impacted 50 BA flights, leaving thousands of people without their bags;
- between 19–21 December 2018 hundreds of flights at Gatwick Airport were cancelled following drone sightings close to the runway. The disruption affected approximately 140,000 passengers and 1,000 flights.

These are just some of the events that have had an impact on people and business beyond the original incident, and illustrate why it is important to have a plan in place.

# BUSINESS CONTINUITY PLAN

**3.2** An effective business continuity plan will:

- reduce the likelihood of disruption to a business;
- minimise the impact of disruption to a business;
- reduce the financial losses a business incurs;
- prevent loss of business to competitors;
- ensure a business brand and reputation are maintained;
- build customer confidence;
- build staff confidence; and
- ensure a business meets any relevant legislative and regulatory requirements.

Business continuity should become part of the way business is performed and should be considered by all organisations regardless of their size. The size and nature of an organisation will influence how comprehensive the business continuity plan is, and any plan should be clear and tailored to the specific needs of the business.

A business continuity plan should consider how business could be maintained under circumstances such as:

- loss of premises or loss of access to premises;
- loss of staff;
- loss of key suppliers;
- loss of, or interruption to, utility supplies;
- loss of, or interruption to, IT and telecommunications systems;
- loss of specialist equipment; or
- disruption to transport.

This plan should therefore be able to respond to:

> 'Any unwanted significant incident that threatens personnel, buildings and/or the operational effectiveness of an organisation, which requires special measures to be taken to restore the business back to normal.[1]'

For the programme to be effective, the ongoing management and governance process should be supported by senior management and resourced sufficiently to ensure that the necessary steps are taken to identify the impact of potential losses, maintain viable recovery strategies and plans, and ensure continuity of products/services through thorough training, testing and exercising.

# BUSINESS CONTINUITY MANAGEMENT

**3.3** Business continuity management is about identifying those essential parts of an organisation that it could not operate without (these could include information, stock, premises and staff) and then having a plan for how these could be maintained if such an incident was to occur. Whether an incident is natural, accidental or deliberate, and whether it is small or large, it can cause major disruption. If an organisation plans when things are going well, this plan will be ready if such events should happen and will help an organisation get back into business as quickly as possible. Delaying could mean business being lost to competitors, and customers losing confidence.

Consider:

- What are the organisation's key products and services?
- What are the critical activities and resources required to deliver these?
- What are the risks to these critical activities?
- How will these critical activities be maintained in the event of an incident (loss of access to premises, loss of utilities etc)?

---

1  Cabinet Office, *How Resilient is your Business to Disaster* (2006), Ch 2.

3.3 *Business Continuity*

There is no universal solution to business continuity, but that same basic process can be followed by each organisation when assessing their risks and making their plans.

Best practice in business continuity is built on the stages of the BCM (Business Continuity Management) Lifecycle[2].

This process guides organisations in identifying threats, designing responses, implementing a plan and measuring effectiveness. It is an ongoing process to continually build and improve organisational resilience, whereby businesses:

- identify and manage current and future threats to business;
- take a proactive approach to minimising the impact of incidents;
- keep critical functions up and running during a time of crisis;
- minimise downtime during incidents and improve recovery time; and
- demonstrate resilience to customers, suppliers and for tender requests.

# BUSINESS IMPACT ANALYSIS

3.4   A business impact analysis (BIA) will help identify the key documents and services that an organisation needs to function, and the impact their loss might have on the organisation.

## Step 1 – identify key products and services

3.5   An organisation should list the key products and services it organisation provides, which, if disrupted for any reason, would have the greatest impact. For each one identified, the organisation should consider what the impact of a disruption would be both in terms of the organisation's ability to meet its aims and objectives, and the impact on its stakeholders.

An organisation should document what the impact would be for:

- the first 24 hours;
- 24–48 hours;
- up to one week; and
- up to two weeks.

## Step 2 – maximum time the organisation can manage

3.6   An organisation should identify the maximum length of time that it can manage a disruption for each of the key products and services without it threatening the organisation's viability, either financially or through a loss of reputation.

---

2   Business Continuity Institute, *Introduction to Business Continuity*.

## Step 3 – recovery time

**3.7** An organisation should set the point at which each of the key products and services would need to be resumed in the event of a disruption, taking into account a margin for unforeseen difficulties with recovery.

## Step 4 – critical activities

**3.8** An organisation should document critical activities which are needed to deliver products and services.

## Step 5 – quantify the resources

**3.9** An organisation should quantify the resources required over time to maintain the critical activities at an acceptable level. These may include:
- people;
- premises;
- technology;
- information; and
- supplies and partners.

# CREATING A BUSINESS CONTINUITY PLAN
## Assessment of the current situation

**3.10** Reviewing existing loss prevention measures and risk assessments before making a plan will show any problems and issues that are present within the organisation. By correcting these it will automatically reduce the impact of the incident. Some insurers already insist that organisations have a plan in place as part of the condition of insurance cover.

It is important to look at the following prevention measures.

## Security

**3.11**
- Physical security of the site that the organisation occupies.
- Locks, intruder alarms and CCTV.
- Security arrangements for valuable items such as electronic equipment, merchandise and anything which is vital to the operation of the business.
- Security of personnel's belongings.
- Be aware of any pressure groups and protesters against the organisation's aims.

*3.12   Business Continuity*

# Fire

**3.12**

- Provision of fire extinguishing equipment, portable and fixed systems.
- Identification of escape routes.
- Fire resistant doors.
- Identification of all of the most significant hazards.
- Fire alarms and smoke detectors.
- Means of containing fire-fighting water so that it does not cause a pollution incident – companies have had large fines where water used during fire-fighting has caused pollution.

An aerospace and industrial surface treatments provider was sentenced at Birmingham Crown Court on a charge of failing to take measures to prevent major accidents and limit its consequences to the environment. They were ordered to pay £133,000 fines and £33,000 in costs for polluting the river which ran alongside their site following a fire. The fire brigade used pollution control equipment supplied by the Environment Agency to try and prevent the water used for fire-fighting from entering the river. However, despite their best efforts the water was contaminated[3].

# Services

**3.13**

- Maintenance of power supplies.
- If there is a back-up generator it is important to ensure that it is serviced and tested on a regular basis.
- Telephones and internal communications.
- The protection of valuable stock protected and vital documents.
- IT back-up systems – and alternative systems and equipment.

# Insurance

**3.14**   An organisation should understand the extent of insurance policies, covering such areas as maximum indemnity period, extent of cover, exclusions, limits of liability, business interruption, consequential loss, and legal liability to staff and public. Carrying out a site survey with photographs of particular items and areas will be useful when dealing with insurers and loss adjusters, and will greatly assist with repair and reinstatement. Ensure that one up-to-date set is kept off-site.

---

3   Unreported.

## Salvage

**3.15**

- Identification of all items of importance, including business records, with arrangements to protect them in a secure area after recovery.
- Identification of means to minimise damage to stock and artefacts by smoke or fire-fighting water.

## Planning

**3.16** The definition of a 'disaster' which can be understood by all within the organisation

A good business continuity plan recognises potential threats to the organisation and analyses what impact they might have on day-to-day operations. It also provides a way to mitigate these threats, allowing an organisation to put in place a framework which allows key functions of the business to continue even if the worst happens.

### Response to an incident, not the cause of the incident

**3.17** The principle is to respond to the incident, not the cause of the incident. The causes of incidents can be considered when carrying out a risk assessment, see Chapter 3 on Risk Management. There is no point in considering the cause of the incident – that will not help when looking at how to respond. Any plan must be flexible – being able, for example, to manage bank holidays and adverse weather conditions. It should be written clearly and be easy to understand.

### Integrate emergency plans into the organisation

**3.18** Any emergency plan should be built into the existing management structure of the organisation, and those involved in any incident should be part of that planning process. This will ensure that the emergency plan is not seen as a separate document; otherwise the plan might not form part of a regular review process nor part of an induction or training process.

### Integrate different departments and their response

**3.19** Different departments within the organisation will be able to contribute to the overall response and therefore it is vital to include them so that their contribution can be integrated into the plan. Failure to do this could lead to an unclear response to an incident.

**3.20** *Business Continuity*

## Co-ordinate arrangements with neighbours

**3.20** It is important that an organisation communicates with its neighbours and also with the police and Fire and Rescue Services. Also, if based in a multi-occupancy building, the organisation will need to ensure that it co-ordinates any potential response with the other tenants.

## Elements of the plan

**3.21** The plan should have a clear purpose and should allocate a time frame for the recovery of critical functions, rather than relying on a general statement of intent. In addition, it should contain:
- a clear statement showing that the plan has the support of senior management;
- a description of the premises, facilities and operations covered by the plan and an outline of activities or processes carried out in these premises;
- details of the main hazards faced by the organisation and the effect these hazards could have on the business;
- the team structure of those that are responsible for managing the recovery. There should be nominated team leaders and administrative support. In a larger organisation there may also be deputy team leaders.

## Senior management involvement

**3.22** Any plan needs to have the support of the most senior level of management and there needs to be a clear statement of this in the plan. This ensures that there is leadership in formulating the plan and also in its implementation.

## Implementing the plan

**3.23** When any plan is to be implemented it must be clear who has authority to implement it. Sometimes the decision to implement a plan may have to be taken outside normal working hours, so careful thought needs to be given as to who can implement the plan. Any plan must be clear about the circumstances when it should be implemented, including:
- exactly when and how to implement the plan;
- persons responsible for initiating the plan's implementation;
- delegation of authority for specific functions eg removal of specified items to a pre-planned place of safety;
- specialist support or authority to spend up to an increased financial limit;

- call out lists of key personnel (kept up to date); and
- designation of either an on-site office or an off-site facility.

Most important is ensuring that people know there is a plan and how and who will be responsible for putting the plan into action.

## Call out list

**3.24** These lists provide the names and position of people in the organisation and their contact numbers. The list needs to be updated regularly and should recognise the availability of staff at weekends and at night. People who have a key role to play should have a list of the actions they need to perform, including whom they should contact and update.

## Minimising damage

**3.25** The plan should contain instructions as to how to minimise and limit damage to equipment and premises. An organisation should consider whether it needs specialist expertise such as:

- the salvage of documents and computer data;
- smoke residue removal experts;
- plant hire contractors for pumps, generators or heating equipment;
- experts in decontamination (if appropriate);
- contact for all the utilities (gas, electricity, telephones, water) and local authority;
- contact for any national authorities which might be involved;
- contact for agencies such as the Environment Agency;
- transport and removal companies;
- building contractors, architects and structural engineers;
- computer equipment supplies;
- suppliers of office furniture and equipment; or
- contact for insurers.

## Evacuation of the premises

**3.26** When a fire alarm sounds, people exit the building through the designated fire-escape routes. However, this may not be the most appropriate exit during some emergencies, for example a ruptured gas main, or flood. It may also be necessary to keep people within the building. Therefore, consideration should be given to using a public address system or different alarms to ensure that people take the appropriate actions according to the type of incident. It is important that the plan identifies who is enabled to initiate an evacuation and call the emergency services.

### Relocation/alternative IT

**3.27** The plan should also include the arrangements for when the organisation will need to be relocated to other premises. It should include any pre-planning undertaken in acquiring an alternative location as well as details of sources of assistance which may be needed. This can include:

- alternative premises that have already been contracted for such an incident; and
- arrangements for alternative IT processes.

A business impact analysis (BIA) should be undertaken as part of the planning process detailing:

- an organisation's key products and services, critical activities and supporting resources;
- the maximum length of time an organisation can manage a disruption to each key product/service; and
- the resources required to resume the key products and services.

# COMMUNICATIONS

**3.28** The plan should include details of communication methods with:

- employees (who will need to be told what is happening and what they should do);
- people and organisations located nearby (so that they are kept informed about what is happening and any actions that they need to take);
- local authorities and enforcement bodies;
- customers/clients;
- suppliers;
- shareholders, bankers and the stock market; and
- media (social media, radio, television and newspapers).

The plan will have to cover not only emergency communications for immediately after the event (radios and mobile phones), but also longer-term measures, such as diverting telephone calls to other locations, possibly run by a specialist contractor. Also, mail will need to be redirected to pre-designated premises.

Key points to include in the plan are:

- internal and external communications;
- locations of existing facilities;
- sources of supply for additional telephones;
- diary/log keepers to ensure proper records of messages and decisions are kept;
- information to all staff if the disaster occurs outside normal working hours; and
- handling of calls from relatives and the public.

## Relations with the public

**3.29** The incident may attract the attention of the media. It is important that only people who are media-trained give interviews. The public relations part of the plan needs to cover a wide range of activities, especially if the incident is related to an act or omission of the organisation. Handling the media badly could lead to the end of the organisation.

The plan could include details of:

- the official media trained spokesperson;
- co-ordination of media management with the emergency services and other affected businesses nearby. This should also include the organisation's customers;
- lists of journalists and radio/television contacts; and
- pre-prepared facts on the organisation, what it does and its past safety record.

## Liaison with emergency services

**3.30** It is important to talk to the emergency services before they are needed. This way the organisation will know how they will react to an incident and the emergency services will be aware of any particular issue on-site such as cylinders of flammable gas or chemicals which may mean they need to take special precautions. The emergency services will already have emergency plans to deal with it.

## Other issues to consider

### Data protection

**3.31** There need to be good processes for:

- back-up and off-site storage – whether data can be accessed for home or other computers;
- sources of replacement equipment and software; and
- details and data relating to customers and suppliers – keeping in mind customer data security is very important.

### Personnel

**3.32** An organisation must consider:

- key staff – those who are vital to the running of the organisation;
- sources of external assistance and mutual aid (other organisations which can provide staff and facilities); and
- assistance with loss of personal effects such as house and car keys (changing home locks if keys have been lost), credit cards and money.

**3.33** *Business Continuity*

## Security issues

**3.33** An organisation must consider:

- site protection – CCTV, security personnel, barriers and passes, escort of visitors;
- availability of keys/passes for access to controlled areas or services;
- reception of emergency services, the HSE and the Environment Agency – whether staff know what to do when they arrive – where they should be directed to, what access they can have;
- management of the media and other visitors – is there a person dedicated to dealing with the media?

## After the incident

**3.34** Following the incident, access to the site may be restricted because of problems relating to the safety of the building, or for the investigation of the cause of the incident. If the incident is suspected to be the result of a crime, the police will require the scene to be preserved whilst evidence is gathered. The HSE and/or the Environment Agency may also be present. (See Chapter 11 on Responding to a Criminal Investigation.)

# REVISION OF PLANS AFTER THE EVENT

**3.35** When the organisation has returned to normal following the event it is important to review the performance of the contingency plan. This should highlight what was handled well and what could be improved upon. The review is to ensure that the lessons of a disaster are absorbed by the business, and any necessary improvements to the plan are made.

# Part 2
# The Law

# Chapter 4

# Manslaughter and Health and Safety Offences

Corporate manslaughter   4.1
    Introduction   4.1
    The offence   4.2
        Elements of the offence   4.3
    The organisation   4.4
        Corporations   4.5
        Parent companies   4.6
        Departments   4.7
        Police forces and constabularies   4.8
        Partnerships   4.9
        Foreign companies and subsidiaries   4.10
        Sub-contractors and charities   4.11
    Causation   4.12
    Relevant duty of care   4.13
    The gross breach   4.14
    Foreseeability   4.15
    Senior management   4.16
    Jurisdiction   4.17
    Exclusions   4.18
    Investigation   4.19
Gross negligence manslaughter   4.20
    The offence   4.20
    Duty of care   4.21
      In general   4.21
      Directors   4.22
      Breach of duty of care   4.23
      Foreseeability   4.24
      Causation   4.25
    Grossness of the breach   4.26
Health and Safety at Work etc Act 1974 offences   4.27
    Employers   4.27
      Prosecution for breaches of the HSWA 1974, ss 2 and 3   4.28
      Exposure to material risk   4.29
      'Reasonably practicable'   4.30
      Health and safety duties cannot be delegated   4.31
      Failures of frontline employees   4.32
      Post-accident changes to safe systems of work   4.33
      Directors and senior managers   4.34

*4.1 Manslaughter and Health and Safety Offences*

    Employees   4.40
       HSWA 1974, s 7   4.40
       HSWA 1974, s 8   4.41

# CORPORATE MANSLAUGHTER
## Introduction

**4.1** Before April 2008, it was possible for a corporate entity such as a company to be prosecuted for a number of criminal offences, including the offence of gross negligence manslaughter. However, for a company to be guilty of such an offence, it was also necessary for a senior individual who could be said to be the 'controlling mind' (alternatively referred to as the 'directing mind') of the organisation to be guilty of the offence. Although cases were brought, it proved to be difficult to find a 'single mind' who had been grossly negligent. There have been a number of high-profile cases – the Herald of Free Enterprise ferry which capsized in Zeebrugge harbour, the Kings Cross fire, the Southall train crash and the Hatfield train derailment – all of which failed to convict a corporation of corporate manslaughter. Of the successful prosecutions for corporate manslaughter these were usually of a small company where it was possible to identify the individual responsible for health and safety obligations. In larger organisations it was much more difficult since directors are not normally closely involved with the day-to-day running of the business.

Reform came in the form of the Corporate Manslaughter and Corporate Homicide Act 2007 (CMCHA 2007), which created a specific offence of 'corporate manslaughter'. The Corporate Manslaughter and Homicide Bill was put before Parliament in July 2006 and the 2007 Act came into force throughout the UK on 6 April 2008. In England, Wales and Northern Ireland the offence is called 'corporate manslaughter' and in Scotland it is called 'corporate homicide'. The offence was created to provide a means of accountability for serious management failings.

A corporation, whether a company, government department or Crown body, will be liable for prosecution where a gross failing by its senior managers to take reasonable care for the safety of their workers or other individuals causes a death.

An organisation charged with this offence will be tried in the Crown Court. On conviction a judge may impose an unlimited fine. The Act also provides for courts to impose a publicity order, requiring the organisation to publicise details of its conviction and fine, and may require an organisation to take steps to address the failures behind the death (a remedial order).

There is no individual liability under the Act, so an individual cannot be indicted for corporate manslaughter or for aiding, abetting, counselling or procuring the commission of this offence. However, an individual may still be prosecuted for common law gross negligence manslaughter and/or under the Health and Safety at Work etc Act 1974 (HSWA 1974), ss 7 or 37 (see paras **4.34** ff).

An individual cannot bring a private prosecution for this offence in England and Wales without the consent of the Director of Public Prosecutions, or in Northern Ireland without the consent of the Director of Public Prosecutions for Northern Ireland, unlike the position of allegations of gross negligence manslaughter against individuals where no such consent is required.

In advance of the Act coming into force the Ministry of Justice published *Understanding the Corporate Manslaughter and Corporate Homicide Act 2007*[1] which stated:

> 'The Government expects that cases of corporate manslaughter/homicide following a death at work will be rare as the new offence is intended to cover only the worst instances of failure across an organisation to manage health and safety properly.'

While there have been more prosecutions, the numbers remain small and the size of organisation prosecuted for the most part is still small (usually with only a few directors). Although the intention was that the offence should be reserved for the 'worst instances of failure', from the cases prosecuted to date it can be difficult to identify which features distinguish them from comparable prosecutions under the HSWA 1974.

# The offence

**4.2** The offence is set out in the CMCHA 2007, s 1. An organisation to which the Act applies is guilty of an offence if the way in which its activities are managed or organised:

- causes a person's death; and
- amounts to a gross breach of a relevant duty of care owed by the organisation to the deceased; and
- if the way in which its activities are managed or organised by its senior management is a substantial element of the organisation's breach of its duty of care.

Each of the elements of the offence must be proved by the prosecution to the criminal standard ie so that the jury is sure of the defendant's guilt.

## Elements of the offence

**4.3** For an organisation to be found guilty the following needs to be proved:

- the defendant is a qualifying *organisation*;
- the organisation *causes* a person's death;

---

1 See http://www.gkstill.com/Support/Links/Documents/2007-justice-1.pdf.

4.3 *Manslaughter and Health and Safety Offences*

- there was a *relevant duty of care* owed by the organisation to the deceased;
- there was a *gross breach* of that duty;
- a substantial element of that breach was in the way those activities were managed or organised *by senior management*; and
- the way in which its activities are managed or organised by its *senior management* is a *substantial element* of the organisation's breach of its duty of care.

Further, the defendant must not fall within one of the *exemptions* for prosecution under the CMCHA 2007.

## The organisation

**4.4** The CMCHA 2007, s 1(2) states that the offence applies to the following bodies:

- a corporation;
- a department or other body listed in the CMCHA 2007, Sch 1;
- a police force; and
- a partnership, or trade union or employer's association that is an employer.

### Corporations

**4.5** This means a body which is incorporated, usually a company limited by shares or guarantee. It usually has a suffix such as 'ltd' or 'plc' and can also include other organisations such as a local authority or an NHS Trust which has been incorporated (for an example of the latter see the failed prosecution against *R v Maidstone and Tunbridge Wells NHS Trust*[2] in 2016 which arose out of the tragic death of an obstetric patient who failed to recover fully from a general anaesthetic).

### Parent companies

**4.6** Usually the legal entity directly involved in the incident will be prosecuted. However, in 2015 CAV Aerospace[3] was convicted of corporate manslaughter in relation to an incident that occurred at its subsidiary CAV Cambridge. The prosecution concerned the death of a worker crushed by a dangerously high stack of Airbus parts. The prosecution's case was that there had been a series of management failures by the parent company that were causative of the death. No individual senior managers were specifically identified. This case demonstrates that prosecutors may, where possible, consider a prosecution against a more substantial parent company.

2  (unreported, 27 January 2016).
3  *R v CAV Aerospace Ltd* (unreported, 31 July 2015) (Central Crim Ct).

## Departments

**4.7** Crown immunity used to mean that Crown bodies (such as government departments) could not be prosecuted. However, they can now be prosecuted under the CMCHA 2007.

## Police forces and constabularies

**4.8** Subject to certain exemptions, the police can be prosecuted for the new offence. If a police force is prosecuted for corporate manslaughter it is the force itself which is indicted; however, if there is a prosecution under the HSWA 1974, it is the chief constable as a corporation sole who is the defendant.

## Partnerships

**4.9** A partnership can be prosecuted for corporate manslaughter, but only if it is an employer. The prosecutions must be against the partnership as a body, not its individual members, and the liability to pay the fine falls from the funds of the partnership only, not the personal assets of the individuals.

## Foreign companies and subsidiaries

**4.10** The offence applies to companies and other corporate bodies operating in the UK, whether they are incorporated in the UK or abroad. Companies that operate using a group structure are all separate legal entities for the purpose of the CMCHA 2007. If the subsidiaries are also incorporated they are individually subject to the offence. Where a company is registered abroad and is operating through an incorporated UK based subsidiary, if the subsidiary commits the offence it is the subsidiary which is the organisation for the purpose of prosecution.

## Sub-contractors and charities

**4.11** The offence applies to all companies and employing partnerships, including those in a contracting chain. Whether a particular contractor might be liable for the offence will depend on whether they owed a relevant duty of care to the victim. The CMCHA 2007 does not impose new duties of care but the offence will apply in respect of existing obligations on the main contractor and sub-contractors for the safety of worksites, employees and other workers whom they supervise.

## Causation

**4.12** Causation is not defined within the CMCHA 2007 but it was the intention to follow aspects of the law on gross negligence manslaughter. For causation of death to be proved (as with all homicide offences), the actions or omissions of the defendant must cause death but need not be the sole or main cause provided that the breach of duty contributed significantly to it, that is to say were more than minimal (see *R v Cheshire*[4]). The Court of Appeal observed in the health and safety case of *R v Howe & Son*[5] that 'it is often a matter of chance whether death or serious injury results from even a serious breach'.

## Relevant duty of care

**4.13** The CMCHA 2007, s 2 defines 'relevant duty of care'. The duty of care arises from certain specific functions or activities performed by an organisation, which means that its work activities should not harm either its employees or anyone else. The Act does not impose any new duty of care on an organisation (ie it does not go beyond the general duty of care imposed by the HSWA 1974). The offence only applies where an organisation owes a duty of care:

- *to its employees or to other persons working for the organisation*. This includes an employer's duty to provide a safe system of work for its employees. The organisation may also owe duties of care to those whose work it is able to control or direct, even though they are not formally employed by it. For example, contractors or volunteers. The offence does not impose any new duties of care where they are not currently owed, but where a duty is owed, a breach can trigger the offence;
- *as occupier* of premises (which also includes land). An organisation should ensure, for example, that buildings it occupies are kept in a safe condition;
- *when the organisation is supplying goods or services*. This includes duties owed by organisations to their customers, for example, duties owed by transport providers to their passengers and by retailers for the safety of their products. It also covers the supply of services by the public sector, for example, NHS bodies providing medical treatment;
- *when constructing or maintaining buildings, infrastructure or vehicles etc or when using plant or vehicles etc*. Duties of care are owed, for example, to ensure that adequate safety precautions are taken when repairing a road or in maintaining the safety of vehicles – these will be duties owed by an organisation in relation to the supply of a service or because it is operating commercially;
- *when carrying out other activities on a commercial basis*. This ensures that activities that are not the supply of goods and services but which are still performed by companies and others commercially, such as farming or mining, are covered by the offence; and

4  [1991] 1 WLR 844.
5  [1999] 2 Cr App R(S) 37.

- *because a person is being held in detention or custody.* This includes forms of custody or detention covered such as being detained in a prison or a similar establishment, in a custody area at a court or police station or in immigration detention facilities as well as being transported under immigration or prison escort arrangements. This part of the CMCHA 2007 came into force in 2012.

It will be for the trial judge to determine whether the organisation owed the deceased a duty of care, but for the jury to determine if there was a breach, the seriousness of it, and 'how much of a risk of death it posed'. This is a reflection of the legal nature of the tests relating to the existence of a duty of care in the law of negligence.

It is the company which owes the duty of care and it is not a necessary inference that the director, because of their role as director, owes a similar duty to others who may be affected by the actions/omissions of the company. For directors' duties see para **4.22**.

## The gross breach

**4.14** Once a relevant duty of care has been established, any breach must fall far below what could reasonably be expected of the organisation in the circumstances (see the CMCHA 2007, s 8).

The factors that the jury *must* consider in determining whether health and safety legislation was breached are:

- How serious was the breach?
- How much of a risk of death did it pose?

The breach which causes the death must be directly attributable to the senior management failure.

Other non-causative breaches might also be considered. The jury may also consider:

- the attitudes, policies, systems or accepted practices that were likely to have encouraged the breach or made people tolerant of it; and
- any health and safety guidance issued by the relevant enforcement authority that may relate to the breach.

## Foreseeability

**4.15** The foreseeability of risk is not in the definition of the offence because a corporation does not have the capacity to foresee risk as it is inanimate; however, the Law Commission did suggest that this would not prevent the jury considering whether the risk was or should have been obvious to senior managers.

*4.15 Manslaughter and Health and Safety Offences*

This approach has been used in the HSWA 1974, s 3[6] where foreseeability (or the lack of it) was permitted for the defence. The different tests may be a problem where both an individual and an organisation are prosecuted for manslaughter and also if either are charged with HSWA 1974 offences. Note also the approach to foreseeability in gross negligence manslaughter (see para **4.24**).

## Senior management

**4.16** The term 'senior management' is defined to mean those persons who play *a significant role in the management* of the whole, or *a substantial part* of the, organisation's activities (see the CMCHA 2007, s 1(4)(c)). Neither the term 'significant' nor the term 'substantial' are defined, but 'significant' is likely to be limited to those whose involvement is influential and will not include those who simply carry out the activity.

The test of senior management is wider than the previous 'controlling mind' test and can consider the failures of a number of senior individuals when determining whether there has been a management failure. Consideration will need to be given to the number of higher tiers of management, the diversity of the organisation's activities and the job descriptions of those identified in the senior management failure. Following the line of reasoning in *El-Ajou v Dollar Land Holdings*[7] (concerning the definition of a 'controlling mind') it is possible a person may be deemed to be in a senior management role for only part of their job function.

## Jurisdiction

**4.17** The CMCHA 2007 sets out specific rules for the jurisdiction of the new offence; ie to determine whether a death in a particular place will fall under the new offence.

A British company cannot be prosecuted for deaths abroad unless the harm occurs in the UK.

## Exclusions

**4.18** Corporate manslaughter will not apply to certain public and government functions where there exist wider questions of public policy, especially where there are already other forms of accountability. The exemptions fall into two broad types: comprehensive exemptions and partial exemptions.

---

6   *R v HTM Ltd* [2006] EWCA Crim 1156, [2006] ICR 1383.
7   [1994] 2 All ER 685.

## Investigation[8]

**4.19** The police will lead an investigation if a criminal offence (other than under health and safety law) is suspected and will work in partnership with the Health and Safety Executive (HSE), a local authority or other regulatory authority. A Protocol entitled *Work-Related Deaths: A Protocol for Liaison* has been agreed between the HSE, the Association of Chief Police Officers (ACPO), the British Transport Police, the Local Government Association, the Welsh Local Government Association, the Office of Rail Regulation, Maritime and Coastguard Agency, the Chief Fire Officers' Association and the Crown Prosecution Service (CPS)[9]. This sets out the principles for effective liaison and describes the initial action to be taken by investigators following a work-related death, how the investigation should be managed, the decision-making process, issues such as disclosure, when the coroner is involved, and the mechanisms by which the signatory agencies should co-operate.

Any proceedings for the offence will be the responsibility of the CPS in England and Wales. When the police investigate they must consider the possibility of a prosecution for corporate manslaughter under the CMCHA 2007 as well as looking at the actions of individuals for possible prosecution for gross negligence manslaughter. However, consideration may also be given to health and safety offences. A prosecution for health and safety offences in conjunction with an offence under the 2007 Act or gross negligence manslaughter can only proceed if the necessary consent has been obtained under the HSWA 1974, s 38.

If the decision taken is not to prosecute for corporate (or individual) manslaughter, the file is the handed to the HSE who will decide whether it will bring charges against the company and/or individuals under the HSWA 1974 and/or the relevant regulations.

Where a death has resulted from a road traffic accident caused by a defective vehicle, or where a driver has been allowed to work significantly long hours, consideration will be given as to whether the company is responsible under corporate manslaughter for any lack of maintenance of the vehicle concerned or for the driver's carelessness if that can be attributed to tiredness. Investigation will also take place as to whether the driver was using a phone and if this was on company business.

# GROSS NEGLIGENCE MANSLAUGHTER
## The offence

**4.20** When prosecuting an individual for manslaughter in relation to a workplace death, the form of common law manslaughter that will be relied

---

8   See also, more generally, Chapter 12 on Responding to a Criminal Investigation.
9   See http://www.hse.gov.uk/pubns/wrdp1.pdf.

**4.20** *Manslaughter and Health and Safety Offences*

upon is gross negligence manslaughter. This is where a death is the result of a grossly negligent act or omission on the part of the defendant. Common law means that the offence is derived from decided case law ie it is not a statutory offence like the offence pursuant to the CMCHA 2007.

This is an indictable offence so can be tried only in the Crown Court.

The leading modern authority on gross negligence manslaughter is the House of Lords decision in *R v Adomako*[10]. The case concerned the conduct of an anaesthetist during an eye operation, where the patient died on the operating table. The prosecution alleged that Adomako failed to notice, or respond appropriately, to the disconnection of an endotracheal tube inserted to enable the patient to breathe. His conviction was upheld on appeal.

Lord MacKay LC set out in his judgment[11] the essential elements of the offence:

> '[In] my opinion the ordinary principles of the law of negligence apply to ascertain whether or not the defendant has been in breach of a duty of care towards the victim who has died. If such breach of duty is established the next question is whether that breach of duty caused the death of the victim. If so, the jury must go on to consider whether that breach of duty should be characterised as gross negligence and therefore as a crime. This will depend on the seriousness of the breach of duty committed by the defendant in all the circumstances in which the defendant was placed when it occurred. The jury will have to consider whether the extent to which the defendant's conduct departed from the proper standard of care incumbent upon him, involving as it must have done a risk of death to the patient, was such that it should be judged criminal …
>
> The essence of the matter which is supremely a jury question is whether having regard to the risk of death involved, the conduct of the defendant was so bad in all the circumstances as to amount in their judgment to a criminal act or omission.'

This decision and subsequent case law concerning appeals against convictions of gross negligence manslaughter were reviewed by the Court of Appeal in *R v Honey Rose*[12]. Giving judgment, Sir Brian Leveson P stated there are five elements which the prosecution must prove in order for a defendant to be convicted of gross negligence manslaughter:

(i) the defendant owed an existing duty of care to the victim;
(ii) the defendant negligently breached that duty of care;
(iii) it was reasonably foreseeable that the breach of that duty gave rise to a serious and obvious risk of death;
(iv) the breach of that duty caused the death of the victim;
(v) the circumstances of the breach were 'truly exceptionally bad and so reprehensible as to justify the conclusion that it amounted to gross negligence and required criminal sanction'.

---

10 [1995] 1 AC 171.
11 *R v Adomako* [1994] 3 WLR 288, at [187].
12 [2017] EWCA Crim 1168, [2017] 3 WLR 1461, CA.

Each of the elements of the offence must be proved to the criminal standard of proof ie so that the jury is sure of the defendant's guilt. If the jury is not sure in respect of all the elements it must acquit.

Leveson said a further point emerged from the analysis of the legal authorities:

'... none of the authorities suggests that, in assessing either the foreseeability of risk or the grossness of the conduct in question, the court is entitled to take into account information which would, could or should have been available to the defendant following the breach of duty in question. The test is objective and prospective.'

The *Honey Rose* case concerned an optometrist who, during a routine eye examination of a seven-year-old boy, failed to identify that the child had swollen optic discs, an abnormality which is a symptom of hydrocephalus (fluid on the brain). Five months later he was taken ill at school and died later that day.

The optometrist's conviction was quashed; however, Leveson P observed at [95]:

'[This] decision does not, in any sense, condone the negligence that the jury must have found to have been established at a high level in relation to the way that Ms Rose examined [the deceased] and failed to identify the defect which ultimately led to his death. That serious breach of duty is a matter for her regulator; in the context of this case, however, it does not constitute the crime of gross negligence manslaughter.'

# Duty of care

## In general

**4.21** In many cases the existence of a duty of care will not be in issue (as with the medical practitioners in *Adomako* and *Honey Rose* above). However, in other cases (for example, the role of a senior manager), the scope of duty and whether any breach was causative of the death may not be straightforward.

The approach to determining the scope of a duty of care was considered by the coroner (Sir Michael Wright sitting as the Assistant Deputy Coroner for Inner South London) at the Inquest in 2008 into the death of Jean Charles de Menezes, when ruling on the verdicts to be left to the jury. Mr de Menezes was shot by police officers after he was incorrectly identified as a suspect involved in the previous day's failed bombing attempts in the wake of the 7/7 bombings in London.

When considering whether unlawful killing should be left to the jury, part of his determination required an assessment of the role (and scope of that role) of senior officers who bore responsibility for the police operation as a whole in the context of gross negligence manslaughter.

The coroner stated that it was helpful to begin with the general principles articulated in the House of Lords in *Caparo Industries Plc v Dickman*[13] by

---

13 [1990] 2 AC 605.

**4.21** *Manslaughter and Health and Safety Offences*

Lord Bridge, who, reviewing a number of authorities concerning the criteria for establishing a duty of care in negligence, stated:

> 'What emerges is that, in addition to the foreseeability of damage, necessary ingredients in any situation giving rise to a duty of care are that there should exist between the party owing the duty and the party to whom it is owed a relationship characterised by the law as one of "proximity" or "neighbourhood" and that the situation should be one in which the court considers it fair, just and reasonable that the law should impose a duty of a given scope upon the party for the benefit of the other. But it is implicit in the passages referred to that the concepts of proximity and fairness embodied in these additional ingredients are not susceptible of any such precise definition as would be necessary to give them utility as practical tests, but amount in effect to little more than convenient labels to attach to the features of different specific situations which, on detailed examination of all the circumstances, the law recognises pragmatically as giving rise to a duty of care of a given scope.'

Therefore, to establish a duty of care and scope there must be:

- foreseeability of damage (which, following the *Honey Rose* judgment, is of serious and obvious risk of death);
- a proximity of relationship between the defendant and the deceased;
- agreement that it is fair, just and reasonable to impose a duty of care.

## Directors

**4.22** The Companies Act 2006 imposes a number of general duties on directors of companies, including the duty to promote the success of the company, and the duty to exercise reasonable care, skill and diligence. However, there is no statutory duty upon a director under this legislation or any other legislation to manage health and safety.

In *Huckerby v Elliott*[14] a director was charged with an offence contrary to the Finance Act 1966, s 305(3) in that the offence was attributable to her neglect. Parker LCJ stated:

> '... I know of no authority for the proposition that it is the duty of a director to, as it were, supervise his co-directors or to acquaint himself with all the details of the running of the company. Indeed it has been said by Romer J in *Re City Equitable Fire Insurance Co Ltd* [1925] Ch 497 at 428–430 that amongst other things it is perfectly proper for a director to leave matters to another director or to an official of the company and that he is under no obligation to test the accuracy of anything that he is told by such a person, or even to make certain that he is complying with the law.'

The trial judge in *R v Harrison and Great Western Trains*[15], Scott Baker J (as he was then), dismissed corporate manslaughter proceedings against Great Western Trains brought under the common law. His ruling was considered in *Attorney*

---

14 [1970] 1 All ER 189 (DC).
15 (unreported, 1999).

*General's Reference (No 2 of 1999)*[16]. The case concerned the prosecution of the train driver involved in the Southall train crash of 1997, and his employer. During the course of his judgment Scott Baker J considered the duty of a director in relation to the issue of the 'controlling mind' of the company. He stated:

> 'The law is careful as to the circumstances in which a director acting in his capacity as such is personally liable. It would ordinarily require that he had procured, directed or authorised a commission of the tort in question'.

In *R v Lion Steel Equipment Ltd*[17] a company was prosecuted pursuant to the CMCHA 2007. Three of the company's directors (including the finance director) were prosecuted for gross negligence manslaughter and a breach of the HSWA 1974, s 37. The prosecution arose from the death of the company's maintenance man employed at its Hyde factory. He died when he fell 13m through a skylight in a roof, having gone onto the roof to repair a leak which he had discovered.

The trial judge ruled that the directors should be tried separately from the company. Their trial was heard first. At the conclusion of the prosecution's case submissions were made on behalf of the directors of no case to answer. These were partially successful. The prosecution then agreed to discontinue the charges that remained against two directors on the basis the company entered a plea to the corporate manslaughter charge.

During the course of the submissions of no case to answer the prosecution argued that the directors personally owed every employee a duty to keep them safe and that the obligation existed simply by being a director. This was rejected by the judge. He said that the position of director does not in itself create a duty of care to every employee, adding that it was a question of the 'measure and control and responsibility' of the director.

## Breach of duty of care

**4.23** Those who have a duty of care must act as a reasonable person would do in their position. A failure to do so is a breach of the duty of care. If the person has acted within a range of what would generally be accepted as being a standard practice it would be unlikely the failure would be described as falling below the standard of a reasonable person in their position.

## Foreseeability

**4.24** In the *Honey Rose* case[18] the deceased child had not experienced any of the more obvious symptoms of his condition such as headaches or nausea.

---

16 [2000] 3 WLR 195.
17 (unreported, 2012).
18 [2017] EWCA Crim 1168, [2017] 3 WLR 1461, CA.

**4.24** *Manslaughter and Health and Safety Offences*

The Court of Appeal said that in these circumstances the optometrist's failure to identify the swollen discs could not be said to have created a situation where it was reasonably foreseeable that an obvious and serious risk of death would arise.

Therefore, the question to be determined is whether a defendant's negligence led to a situation where it was reasonably foreseeable that, in consequence of that failure, there was an obvious and serious risk of death, as opposed to risk of injury or even very serious injury.

In many workplace incidents the defendant's negligence will lead to a situation where it is reasonably foreseeable that there is an obvious and serious risk of death, for example if the defendant's negligence gives rise to a risk of a fall from height.

## Causation

**4.25** As with corporate manslaughter, the breach of duty does not have to be the only cause of death, but can be one of a number of causes providing it was a significant cause (see *R v Cheshire*[19]).

## Grossness of the breach

**4.26** To be a gross breach, as stated in the *Honey Rose* case[20], the negligence has to be 'truly exceptionally bad' and warrant a criminal conviction. While this is, in the words of Lord Mckay in *Adomako*[21], 'supremely a jury question' there must be sufficient evidence, taken at its highest, that would allow a jury to safely conclude that the negligence was gross.

# HEALTH AND SAFETY AT WORK ETC ACT 1974 OFFENCES

## Employers

**4.27** The HSWA 1974, ss 2–6 set out general duties placed upon employers, the self-employed, manufacturers and suppliers to safeguard the health and safety of employees and others.

The HSWA 1974, s 2(1) sets out the general duty of an employer in respect of his employees. It states:

---

19  [1991] 1 WLR 844.
20  [2017] EWCA Crim 1168, [2017] 3 WLR 1461, CA.
21  [1995] 1 AC 171.

'It shall be the duty of every employer to ensure, so far as is reasonably practicable, the health, safety and welfare at work of all his employees.'

The HSWA 1974, s 2(2) states that this provision extends to:

'(a) the provision and maintenance of plant and systems of work that are, so far as is reasonably practicable, safe and without risks to health;
(b) arrangements for ensuring, so far as is reasonably practicable, safety and absence of risks to health in connection with the use, handling, storage and transport of articles and substances;
(c) the provision of such information, instruction, training and supervision as is necessary to ensure, so far as is reasonably practicable, the health and safety at work of his employees;
(d) so far as is reasonably practicable as regards any place of work under the employer's control, the maintenance of it in a condition that is safe and without risks to health and the provision and maintenance of means of access to and egress from it that are safe and without such risks;
(e) the provision and maintenance of a working environment for his employees that is, so far as is reasonably practicable, safe, without risks to health, and adequate as regards facilities and arrangements for their welfare at work.'

The term 'employee' is defined by the HSWA 1974, s 53 as someone under a contract of employment. This is different to an independent contractor working under a contract of service. However, whether someone is an employee or not is determined not only by the contract but also by the nature of the relationship between the parties ie whether, in reality, and despite the terms of the contract, there is an employer/employee relationship. Key questions to consider include:

- the degree of control exercised over the worker;
- whether the worker can properly be regarded as part of the employer's organisation;
- whether the 'employer' has the power to dismiss or suspend the worker; and
- whether the 'worker' receives holiday and sick pay.

There are a number of employment law cases where this issue has been considered, for example *Ready Mixed Concrete (South East) Ltd v Minister of Pensions and National Insurance*[22].

The HSWA 1974, s 3(1) imposes a similar duty in relation to anyone who may be affected by the health and safety risks from the employer's undertaking, in other words their business activity. So, for example, this can cover contractors or members if the public.

The section states:

'It shall be the duty of every employer to conduct his undertaking in such a way as to ensure, so far as is reasonably practicable, that persons not in his employment who may be affected thereby are not thereby exposed to risks to their health or safety.'

---

22 [1968] 2 QB 497.

**4.27** *Manslaughter and Health and Safety Offences*

The duty under the HSWA 1974, s 4 is owed by all those who have a degree of control over relevant premises (not domestic premises) which are made available for persons not employed by them 'as a place of work or as a place where they may use plant or substances provided for their use there'. Essentially the duty is to ensure those premises are safe, so far as is reasonably practicable.

The HSWA 1974, s 6 contains a series of interrelated complex provisions. It places duties on designers, importers, manufacturers and suppliers in respect of safety relating to articles and substances used for the purpose of work.

Breaches of the above duties do not give rise to civil liability (see the HSWA 1974, s 47(1)) but can give rise to criminal liability by virtue of the HSWA 1974, s 33(1)(a). This section refers to it being an offence for 'a person' to fail to discharge the duty. The word 'person' is not defined in the HSWA 1974, but is defined in the Interpretation Act 1978, ss 5 and 11, which define a person to include 'a body of person corporate or incorporate. Therefore, companies and the self-employed can be prosecuted for breach of these general duties. For unincorporated bodies, such as partnerships and trusts (not incorporated by statute), a prosecution will be against the partners or trustees individually.

There is no Crown exemption from the HSWA 1974 and the relevant statutory provisions. However, the Crown cannot be prosecuted for breaches of the law, including any failure to comply with improvement and prohibition notices but there are administrative arrangements in place by which Crown bodies maybe censured in respect of offences which would have led to prosecution.

The jurisdictional extent of the CMCHA 2007 is limited to UK territory and territorial waters, along with UK registered ships and aircrafts and offshore installations.

Most health and safety prosecutions are for breaches of the HSWA 1974, ss 2 or 3. However, an employer can also be prosecuted for breaches of health and safety regulations made pursuant to the HSWA 1974, s 15. The more commonly prosecuted regulations include the Management of Health and Safety at Work Regulations 1999[23] (in particular the failure to carry out a suitable and sufficient risk assessment), the Provision and Use of Work Equipment Regulations 1998[24] and the Construction (Design and Management) Regulations 2015[25] (CDM). A breach of health and safety regulations is an offence pursuant to the HSWA 1974, s 33(1)(c).

## Prosecution for breaches of the HSWA 1974, ss 2 and 3

**4.28** As observed in the Definitive Guideline for the sentencing of health and safety offences (*Health and Safety Offences, Corporate Manslaughter and Food*

---

23 SI 1999/3242.
24 SI 1998/2306.
25 SI 2015/51.

*Safety and Hygiene Offences*), health and safety offences concern 'failures to manage risks to health and safety' and that the offence is in 'creating a risk of harm'.

In order to establish a case against the employer for breaches of the HSWA 1974, ss 2 or 3, the prosecution does not have to prove that anyone was injured or killed or that there was any negligence on the part of the employer, only that the employees (HSWA 1974, s 2) or non-employees (HSWA 1974, s 3) were exposed to a 'material risk' to their health and safety. This must be proved to the criminal standard of proof (ie so that the court is sure). Once an exposure to material risk has been proved then it is for the employer, pursuant to the HSWA 1974, s 40, to prove to the civil standard of proof (ie on balance) that it took all reasonably practicable steps to control the risk which is the subject of the prosecution (often referred to as the 'reverse burden of proof')[26]. The HSWA 1974, s 40 states:

> 'In any proceedings for an offence under any of the relevant statutory provisions consisting of a failure to comply with a duty or requirement to do something so far as is practicable or so far as is reasonably practicable, or to use the best practicable means to do something, it shall be for the accused to prove (as the case may be) that it was not practicable or not reasonably practicable to do more than was in fact done to satisfy the duty or requirement, or that there was no better practicable means than was in fact used to satisfy the duty or requirement.'

Offences under the HSWA 1974 are 'either way' offences. This means that they can be tried either in the magistrates' court or the Crown Court. If an organisation is convicted of a health and safety offence then the court has power to impose an unlimited fine. Pursuant to the HSWA 1974, s 2 the court has the power to order the cause of the offence to be remedied; however, this power is rarely used.

## Exposure to material risk

**4.29** The prosecution must prove the exposure to risk was an exposure to a 'material risk'. In *Chargot*, Lord Hope held[27]:

> 'The first point to be made is that when the legislation refers to risks it is not contemplating risks that are trivial or fanciful. It is not its purpose to impose burdens on employers that are wholly unreasonable. Its aim is to spell out the basic duty of the employer to create a safe working environment. ... *The law does not aim to create an environment which is entirely risk free. It concerns itself with risks that are material.* That, in effect, is what the word 'risk' which the statute uses means. It is directed at situations where there is a material risk to health and safety, which any reasonable person would appreciate and take steps to guard against.' (Emphasis added).

---

26 See *R v Chargot Ltd* [2008] UKHL 73 in general in relation to these issues.
27 *R v Chargot Ltd* [2008] UKHL 73, at [27].

**4.29** *Manslaughter and Health and Safety Offences*

The concept of 'safety' and 'risk' was considered in detail by the Supreme Court in *Baker v Quantum Clothing Group Ltd*[28]. Lord Mance stated:

> 'Whether a place is safe involves a judgment, one which is objectively assessed of course, but by reference to the knowledge and standards of the time. There is no such thing as an unchanging concept of safety. ... Further, the fact that a single person has suffered injury due to some feature of the workplace is not, without more, proof that the workplace was unsafe.'

Also the majority of the Supreme Court in *Baker* held that foreseeability of risk is relevant to the assessment of risk, or lack of safety. Lord Mance concluded: 'If safety is a relative concept, then foreseeability must play a part in determining whether a place is or was safe.' Lord Dyson stated: 'Like Lord Mance, I prefer the approach of the judge, with the qualification that what is "safe" is an objective question in the sense that safety must be judged by reference to what might reasonably be foreseen by a reasonable and prudent employer.' Lord Saville agreed with the reasons of both Lord Mance and Lord Dyson.

The *Baker* case concerned personal injury claims for noise-induced deafness. However in *R v Tangerine Confectionary Ltd*[29] the Court of Appeal confirmed that the case applies to prosecutions under the HSWA 1974, ss 2 and 3 and that foreseeability of risk is relevant to the question of whether a risk to safety exists.

In a prosecution the relevant risk to which it is alleged that there has been an exposure must be identified. The exposure may be on a particular date (if related for example to an incident) or may be over a specified period.

The fact that there has been an accident or incident will usually be sufficient evidence to prove that there has been an exposure to risk by the employer. But this will not always be the case – there may be issues as to whether the particular risk identified was causative of the accident, or whether the risk arose from the employer's undertaking (see *Chargot* and *Tangerine*).

## 'Reasonably practicable'

**4.30** The Health and Safety Executive (HSE) relies upon the definition of what is 'reasonably practicable' given in the case of *Edwards v the National Coal Board*[30]. This case was a personal injury claim and concerned the Coal Mines Act 1911. The case revolved around whether it was reasonably practicable to prevent even the smallest possibility of a rock fall in a coal mine.

The Court of Appeal stated that a computation must be made in which the quantum of risk is placed on one side of the scale and on the other side the 'sacrifice', whether in money, time or trouble, involved in the measures necessary

---

28 [2011] UKSC 17, SC.
29 [2011] EWCA Crim 2015.
30 [1949] 1 All ER 743.

to avert the risk. Only if it is shown that there is a 'gross disproportion' between the risk and the sacrifice does the employer not have to take the measures to avert the risk. In *Reducing risks, protecting people* published by the HSE, it states that the HSE believes employers' duties qualified by 'so far as is reasonably practicable' (ie HSWA 1974, ss 2, 3) 'have not been complied with if the regime introduced by duty-holders to control risks fails the ... "gross disproportion" test'.

In relation to the gross disproportion test, Lord Mance said in *Baker*[31] that it represented an 'unjustified gloss on statutory wording which requires the employer simply to show that he did all that was reasonably practicable'. He stated further[32]:

> 'But this can only mean that some degree of risk may be acceptable, and what degree can only depend on current standards. The criteria relevant to reasonable practicability must on any view very largely reflect the criteria relevant to satisfaction of the common law duty to take care. Both require consideration of the nature, gravity and imminence of the risk and its consequences, as well as of the nature and proportionality of the steps by which it might be addressed, and a balancing of one against the other. Respectable general practice is no more than a factor, having more or less weight according to the circumstances, which may, on any view at common law, guide the court when performing this balancing exercise'.

Foreseeability is not only a factor in determining whether there has been an exposure to a material risk, but also whether the employer has taken all reasonably practicable steps to manage the risk. In *R v HTM*[33] the Court of Appeal stated:

> 'Foreseeability is merely a tool with which to assess the likelihood of a risk eventuating. ... it seems to us that a defendant to a charge under section 2 or indeed section 3 or 4, in asking the jury to consider whether it has established that it has done all that is reasonably practicable, cannot be prevented from adducing evidence as to the likelihood of the incidence of the relevant risk eventuating in support of its case that it had taken all reasonable means to eliminate it.'

In *Tangerine*[34] it was said:

> 'Whether a material risk exists or does not is, in these cases, a jury question and the foreseeability (or lack of it) of some danger or injury is part of the enquiry ... If a danger is not foreseeable it is difficult to see how it can be practicable, let alone reasonably practicable, for the defendant to take steps to avoid it ... What is reasonably practicable no doubt depends upon all the circumstances of the case, including principally the degree of foreseeable risk of injury, the gravity of injury if it occurs, and then implications of suggested methods of avoiding it.'

---

31 *Baker v Quantum Clothing Group Ltd* [2011] UKSC 17, SC.
32 [2011] UKSC 17, at [82].
33 [2006] EWCA Crim 1156, [2006] ICR 1383 at 21.
34 *R v Tangerine Confectionary Ltd* [2011] EWCA Crim 2015 at [36].

**4.31** *Manslaughter and Health and Safety Offences*

## Health and safety duties cannot be delegated

**4.31** Employers cannot delegate their health and safety duties or contract them out. When a certain activity has given rise to an exposure to health and safety risk, the issue is whether the exposure came within the employer's undertaking (ie work activities) and if so whether the employer has taken all reasonably practicable steps to manage the risk.

In the House of Lords case of *R v Associated Octel Co Ltd*[35], concerning a prosecution for a breach of the HSWA 1974, s 3, a specialist contractor was engaged by the defendant company to repair the lining of a tank on the defendant's chlorine plant. While carrying out this work one of the contractor's employees was badly burnt when a bucket of highly inflammable acetone used for cleaning ignited.

The House of Lords said it was a matter of fact whether an activity came within the defendant's undertaking. On the facts of this case the court found that a reasonable jury could conclude this: the contractors were engaged on a permanent basis, the defendant authorised the work being carried out, which enabled them to impose conditions upon the way the work was carried out, and the defendant provided the contractor's employees with the safety equipment.

*R v Gateway Foodmarkets Ltd*[36] concerned a prosecution for a breach of the HSWA 1974, s 2. Reputable contractors were engaged to provide regular maintenance and call out services for the defendant company' lifts at its supermarkets. At one of the sites one of the contractor's engineers left a trapdoor open. An employee of the defendant company fell through this and was killed. The Court of Appeal followed *Associated Octel* stating the duty under the HSWA 1974, s 2 could not be delegated.

## Failures of frontline employees

**4.32** In *R v Nelson Group Services (Maintenance) Ltd*[37] the defendant company installed, serviced and maintained gas appliances. One of its fitters removed a defective and dangerous gas fire in a private dwelling. The trial judge directed the jury that if it found the fitter had been negligent by not capping the gas pipe, the company was guilty of a breach of the HSWA 1974, s 3. The company was convicted.

The Court of Appeal, quashing the conviction, said an employer was not precluded from relying upon the HSWA 1974, s 40 merely because an employee carrying out the work was careless or omitted to take a precaution. The employer could show that it had done all that was reasonably practicable by proving appropriate instruction and training had been given and that there

---

35 [1996] 4 All ER 846.
36 [1997] 3 All ER 78.
37 [1998] 4 All ER 331.

were safety systems of work in place. It was held in *R v HTM*[38] that this case still remains good law.

## Post-accident changes to safe systems of work

**4.33** Changes that are made following an accident do not necessarily prove that an employer failed to take all reasonably practicable steps.

The coroner in the inquest into the 7/7 bombings in London, Hallett LJ, relied upon the 'wise words' of Megarry J in *Argyll v Beuselinck*[39]:

> 'In this world there are few things that could not have been done better if done with hindsight. The advantages of hindsight include the benefit of having a sufficient indication of which of the many factors present are important and which are unimportant. But hindsight is no touchstone of negligence.'

The same issue was dealt with by Baron Bramwell in *Hart v Lancashire & Yorkshire Railway Co*[40]:

> 'People do not furnish evidence against themselves simply by adopting a new plan in order to prevent the recurrence of an accident. I think that a proposition to the contrary would be barbarous. It would be ... to hold that, because the world gets wiser as it gets older, therefore it was foolish before.'

## Directors and senior managers

### HSWA 1974, s 37

**4.34** The HSWA 1974, s 37(1) provides:

> 'Where an offence under any of the relevant statutory provisions committed by a body corporate is proved to have been committed with the consent or connivance of, or to have been attributable to any neglect on the part of, any director, manager, secretary or other similar officer of the body corporate or a person who was purporting to act in any such capacity, he as well as the body corporate shall be guilty of that offence and shall be liable to be proceeded against and punished accordingly.'

This is known as a secondary liability offence, where a director or senior manager can also be guilty of an offence where their company has committed a health and safety offence with their consent or connivance or it was attributable to their neglect. To prove the case the prosecution must prove to the criminal standard (ie so that the court is sure) the following elements:

- that a health and safety offence has been committed under a relevant statutory provision by the body corporate; and

---

38 *R v HTM* [2006] EWCA Crim 1156, [2006] ICR 1383 and see para **4.30**.
39 [1972] 2 Lloyds Rep at 172.
40 (1869) 21 LT 261.

**4.34** *Manslaughter and Health and Safety Offences*

- that the defendant is a director, manager, secretary or other similar officer of the body corporate; and
- that the body corporate's offence was committed with the consent or connivance of the defendant or was attributable to the defendant's neglect.

In *Wotherspoon v HM Advocate*[41] (a Scottish case) it was held that the offence:

> '... is concerned primarily to provide a penal sanction against those persons charged with functions of management who can be shown to have been responsible for the commission of the offence by a body corporate, and that the functions of the office which he holds will be a highly relevant consideration.'

The offence is an either way offence (ie it can be tried in the magistrates' court or the Crown Court). If convicted in the Crown Court, the court has the power to imprison the defendant for a period of up to two years. The court can also impose an unlimited fine. Under the Company Directors Disqualification Act 1986 the court has the power to disqualify a defendant from being a director for up to five years (if convicted in the magistrates' court) and up to 15 years if convicted in the Crown Court.

### Offence by the body corporate

**4.35** It is not necessary for the company to be prosecuted and convicted in order to convict a defendant who is an officer or manager of that company pursuant to the HSWA 1974, s 37. It is possible to prosecute a defendant under this section without prosecuting the company. However the prosecution must prove that the company is guilty of committing a health and safety offence. The HSWA 1974, s 40 does not apply to proving this element of the offence ie the reverse burden of proof does not apply to the defendant.

### Persons liable under s 37

**4.36** While it is clear that directors and company secretaries of companies come within the HSWA 1974, s 37, as the HSE acknowledges in its enforcement guidance under the heading 'Proceedings against director, manager, secretary or other similar officer', '... that the liability does not fix on any person because of the name that attaches to his/her role in the company, but because of the authority and responsibility that s/he has within it'[42].

The meaning of 'manager' was considered in the case of *R v Boal*[43]. This concerned a prosecution pursuant to the Fire Precautions Act 1971, s 23 of which is analogous to the HSWA 1974, s 37. Boal was a manager of a bookshop. His conviction was set aside on appeal because he was responsible only for the day-to-day running of the premises. Simon Brown J ruled[44]:

---

41  1978 JC 74.
42  See *HSE Enforcement Guide* 'Where the section 37 duty rests' at http://www.hse.gov.uk/enforce/enforcementguide/investigation/identifying-directors.htm.
43  [1992] 3 All ER 177.
44  [1992] 3 All ER 177 at para 598.

'The intended scope of s 23 is, we accept, to fix with criminal liability only those who are in a position of real authority, the decision-makers within the company who have both the power and responsibility to decide corporate policy and strategy. It is to catch those responsible for putting proper procedures in place; it is not meant to strike at underlings.'

The court cited the judgment of Lord Denning in the *Registrar of Restrictive Trading Agreements v WH Smith & Son Ltd*[45] where he said:

'The word "manager" means a person who is managing the affairs of the company as a whole. The word "officer" has a similar connotation ... the only relevant "officer" here is an officer who is a "manager". In this context it means a person who is managing in a governing role the affairs of the company itself.'

Therefore, the critical criterion is the ability to affect the policies and strategies of the body corporate.

## Consent

**4.37** In *Att-Gen's Ref (No 1 of 1995)*[46] the Court of Appeal considered the Banking Act 1987, s 96(1), which is analogous to the HSWA 1974, s 37. Lord Taylor stated that for consent a defendant has to be proved to know of the material facts which constitute the offence by the body corporate and to have agreed to its conduct of the business on the basis of those facts. This was cited with approval by Lord Hope in *Chargot*[47] but added that consent can also be established by inference as well as by proof of an express agreement.

## Connivance

**4.38** In *Huckerby v Elliot*[48], which concerned a prosecution under the Finance Act 1966 in relation to a failure to hold the requisite gaming licence, connivance was described as a state of mind in which a director 'is well aware of what is going on but his agreement is tacit, not actively encouraging what happens but letting it continue and saying nothing about it'. Lord Hope in *Chargot*[49] observed that connivance can be established by inference.

## Neglect

**4.39** In *Wotherspoon*[50] the court stated in respect of 'neglect':

'... in considering in a given case whether there has been neglect within the meaning of section 37(1) on the part of a particular director or other particular officer charged, the search must be to discover whether the accused has failed to take some steps to prevent the commission of an offence by the corporation to

---

45 [1969] 3 All ER 1065 at para 1468.
46 [1996] 1 WLR 970.
47 *R v Chargot Ltd* [2008] UKHL 73, HL.
48 [1970] 1 All ER 189 (DC).
49 *R v Chargot Ltd* [2008] UKHL 73, HL.
50 *Wotherspoon v HM Advocate* 1978 JC 74 at 78.

**4.39** *Manslaughter and Health and Safety Offences*

which he belongs if the taking of those steps either expressly falls or should be held to fall within the scope of the functions of the office which he holds.'

This passage was cited with approval in *R v P Ltd and G*[51]. The Court of Appeal also said that 'neglect' does not necessarily require knowledge on the defendant's part of the material facts giving rise to the health and safety breach by the company and can include the situation where the defendant ought to have been aware of those circumstances. In *Chargot*[52] Lord Hope said it will be a relatively short step for the inference that there was neglect on the part of the defendant if the risk in question was under his direction or control adding the 'more remote his area of responsibility is from those circumstances, the harder it will be to draw that inference'.

The scope of the defendant's role within the company will be relevant and so it will be necessary to consider the general principles articulated by the House of Lords in *Caparo Industries Plc v Dickman*[53] (see duty of care in respect of gross negligence manslaughter at para **4.21**).

During the course of argument Latham LJ stated in *R v P Ltd and G* (which concerned the prosecution of a managing director pursuant to the HSWA 1974, s 37):

'If there is a proper system set up for health and safety that will usually be sufficient for [a director] to say "I have done my duty. I have set up that system", in the absence of material to make it plain to him that something was actually wrong with it.'

In terms of the meaning of the word 'attributable' in *Wotherspoon* the court said that it should be given its 'natural' meaning and that the offence must be proved to have been attributable in some way or to some extent and need not be wholly attributable to the defendant's neglect.

Therefore, for a case brought upon the basis of neglect the prosecution must prove:

- the extent of the defendant's responsibility;
- that the failure to discharge that responsibility amounted to neglect; and
- that the body corporate's offence was attributable to the defendant's neglect.

## Employees

*HSWA 1974, s 7*

**4.40** The HSWA 1974, s 7 states:

'It shall be the duty of every employee while at work—

---

51 [2007] EWCA Crim 1937, [2008] ICR 96, CA.
52 *R v Chargot Ltd* [2008] UKHL 73, HL.
53 [1990] 2 AC 605.

(a) to take reasonable care for the health and safety of himself and of other persons who may be affected by his acts or omissions at work; and
(b) as regards any duty or requirement imposed on his employer or any other person by or under any of the relevant statutory provisions, to co-operate with him so far as is necessary to enable that duty or requirement to be performed or complied with.'

Most prosecutions are pursuant to the HSWA 1974, s 7(a). This is an either way offence. The burden of proving the offence is upon the prosecution to the criminal standard (ie so that the court is sure). If convicted in the Crown Court the court has the power to impose a custodial sentence up to two years. The court can also impose an unlimited fine.

The offence is applicable to frontline workers up to senior managers who do not come within the terms of the HSWA 1974, s 37.

In terms of taking care of 'other persons' this does not just include fellow employees. In *Amos v Worcester City Council*[54] it was held that a store manager's duty extended to customers as well as other employees, including those inside the store and those entering or leaving the store.

The scope and nature of the defendant's duty of care will be relevant (see duty of care in respect of gross negligence manslaughter at para **4.21**).

In HSE's enforcement guide under the section entitled 'Prosecuting individuals' it states[55]:

'In general we are most likely to prosecute employees under section 7 where they have shown a reckless disregard for health and safety, and such a regard has resulted in serious risk'.

## HSWA 1974, s 8

**4.41** The HSWA 1974, s 8 states that no person shall intentionally or recklessly interfere with or misuse anything provided in the interests of health, safety or welfare. As with the HSWA 1974, s 7 it is for the prosecution to prove the offence to the criminal standard and the courts have the same powers of sentence. This provision is rarely prosecuted.

---

54 (unreported, 1996), QBD.
55 See HSE, *Prosecuting individuals* OC 130/8 ver 2 at http://www.hse.gov.uk/foi/internalops/ocs/100-199/130_8.htm.

# Chapter 5

# Health and Safety Enforcement Notices, Fee for Intervention (FFI) and Cautions

Health and safety enforcement notices   5.1
Improvement notices   5.2
Prohibition notices   5.3
Appeals   5.4
    The process   5.4
    Costs   5.5
    Why appeal?   5.6
Fee for intervention (FFI)   5.7
    What is FFI?   5.7
    Challenging an FFI invoice   5.8
        Query   5.9
        Dispute   5.10
        Repayment of money paid by the duty-holder under FFI   5.11
    Why raise a query/dispute?   5.12
Cautions   5.13

**Note** that in this chapter in respect of enforcement notices and cautions when the term 'inspector' is used this means an HM Inspector of Health and Safety or any other officer that enforces the Health and Safety at Work etc Act 1974 such as an environmental health officer at a local authority.

## HEALTH AND SAFETY ENFORCEMENT NOTICES

**5.1** Under the Health and Safety at Work etc Act 1974 (HSWA 1974), inspectors may issue enforcement notices against a business or person that, in the opinion of the inspector, is in breach of their legal duties. There are two kinds of notice:

- an Improvement Notice; and
- a Prohibition Notice.

Failure to comply with an enforcement notice is a criminal offence. If the duty-holder disagrees with the notice he can appeal to the employment tribunal. The notice will be cancelled, varied or affirmed.

5.2 *Health and Safety Enforcement Notices, Fee for Intervention (FFI) and Cautions*

# IMPROVEMENT NOTICES

5.2    An inspector may serve an improvement notice pursuant to the HSWA 1974, s 21 if, in his or her opinion, the person or business is contravening health and safety legislation or has contravened health and safety legislation in circumstances that make it likely that the contravention will continue or be repeated. An improvement notice requires positive action to be taken by a certain date. The notice must specify the date by when such action must be taken, the statutory provision(s) allegedly being breached, and the reasons for the inspector's opinion. In the notice, although not a requirement, the inspector may set out what needs to be done to put matters in order. An inspector can extend the time for complying with the notice, if appropriate. A request for an extension should be made before the date set for compliance. Once the remedial action has been taken the notice ceases to have effect.

In *BT Fleet Ltd v McKenna*[1] it was held that an improvement notice should enable the recipient to know what is wrong and why it is wrong, and should be clear and easily understood. It was also held that, in relation to directions to specify how compliance should be effected, these directions are part of the notice and, if they are confusing, they might render the notice invalid.

An inspector can withdraw a notice any time before the date set for compliance. If the improvement notice is appealed it is automatically suspended.

# PROHIBITION NOTICES

5.3    Pursuant to the HSWA 1974, s 22 an inspector may serve a prohibition notice if they are of the opinion that the activities under the control of a duty-holder involve, or will involve, a risk of serious personal injury.

The notice prohibits the carrying on of the work activity that, in the inspector's opinion, is creating the risk of injury. If there is an immediate risk of danger, the notice takes immediate effect and the work activity should be stopped at once. If not, the notice can be deferred.

The prohibition notice can be issued for any activity to which the relevant statutory provisions apply. However, there does not have to be an actual breach but if the inspector is of the opinion the law is being broken, the notice must state this and detail the alleged breaches. The notice must also state the matters which, in the inspector's view, are creating the risk of serious personal injury, and may include directions on what steps should be taken to rectify matters.

Note also, where there is an article or substance that the inspector is of the opinion creates an imminent risk of serious personal injury, under the HSWA 1974, s 25 the inspector can seize the article or substance or cause it to be rendered harmless.

1    [2005] EWHC 387 (Admin).

If a prohibition notice is appealed, unlike an improvement notice, it is not suspended, but the duty-holder can apply to the employment tribunal for a direction suspending the operation of the notice until the appeal is finally determined. An inspector cannot withdraw an immediate prohibition. There has to be an order of the court.

# APPEALS

## The process

**5.4** The HWSA 1974, s 24 provides that a duty-holder may appeal against a notice.

It states:

> '... the tribunal may either cancel or affirm the notice and, if it affirms it, may do so either in its original form or with such modifications as the tribunal may in the circumstances think fit.'

Appeals against notices are submitted to the employment tribunal on form ET1 (or ET1A if more than one notice is being appealed). This can be done online (see https://www.gov.uk/employment-tribunals/make-a-claim).

An appeal must be submitted within 21 days of the service of the notice (ie by the twentieth day after service). In the case of *London Borough of Wandsworth v Covent Garden Market Authority*[2] it was held the time limit can only be extended by the tribunal if it was not reasonably feasible to file the appeal in time. Therefore, the time limit will be strictly applied. An inspector cannot extend the time for submitting an appeal.

The principal rules applicable to these appeals are set out in the Employment Tribunals (Constitution and Rules of Procedure) Regulations 2013 (SI 2013/1237), Sch 1.

There will usually be a case management hearing where the tribunal will give directions such as:

- disclosure of documents;
- exchange of witness statements and experts' reports;
- the preparation of files of statements and documents for use at the hearing; and/or
- the preparation of case summaries and/or skeleton arguments on the law.

The hearing will usually be before a chairman who is legally qualified and two other members (one representing employers, the other, employees).

The approach to be taken by the tribunal has now been settled in the Supreme Court decision of *HM Inspector of Health and Safety v Chevron North Sea*

---

2 [2011] EWHC 1245 (QB).

5.4 *Health and Safety Enforcement Notices, Fee for Intervention (FFI) and Cautions*

*Ltd*[3]. Before the judgment a different approach was taken in England and Wales to that taken in Scotland. The issue in the appeal was whether a tribunal is confined to the material which was known, or could reasonably have been known, to the inspector at the time the notice was served (the approach in England or Wales) or whether it can take account of additional evidence which has since become available (the approach in Scotland). The appeal concerned a prohibition notice but is applicable to both appeals against prohibition and improvement notices.

The Supreme Court found in favour of the Scottish approach.

Lady Black concluded[4]:

> 'In my view, on an appeal under section 24, the tribunal is not limited to considering the matter on the basis of the material which was or should have been available to the inspector. It is entitled to take into account all the available evidence relevant to the state of affairs at the time of the service of the prohibition notice, including information coming to light after it was served.'

The court said that it was vital for an inspector to be able to take prompt and effective action to ensure compliance with the HSWA 1974 and that a prohibition notice is a powerful tool for an inspector. However, the court acknowledged that the service of a prohibition notice on a business has the potential to do financial and reputational damage.

The court said that an appeal against an inspector's notice is not against the inspector's opinion but against the notice itself. It is no criticism of the inspector when new material leads to a different conclusion about risk from the one reached. The decision to serve a notice is often taken as a matter of urgency when comprehensive information may not be available. The court observed[5]:

> ' ... a forum is required in which to determine the continuing dispute between the inspector and the employer or, putting it more constructively and in the spirit of the health and safety legislation, to determine whether the circumstances that concerned the inspector did in fact give rise to a relevant risk. The appeal process provides that necessary forum.'

## Costs

5.5 For the tribunal to make a costs order, a party (or that party's representative) has to have acted 'vexatiously, abusively, disruptively or otherwise unreasonably in the bringing of the proceedings (or part) or in the way the proceedings (or part) have been conducted or if any claim or response had no reasonable prospect of success'[6]. In practice, it is the latter ground that is most likely to be relevant.

---

3 [2018] UKSC 7.
4 [2018] UKSC 7 at [24].
5 [2018] UKSC 7 at [23].
6 Explanatory Notes to the Employment Act 2002, Ch 22, Pt 2, para 57.

If costs are ordered, the tribunal has power to order an amount up to £20,000. Where a tribunal is of the view that costs greater than £20,000 are appropriate, these will need to be assessed or referred to the civil courts for resolution.

## Why appeal?

**5.6** On its website the HSE has a public register of enforcement notices that it has served (that have not been appealed). Notices will appear on this database for a period of five years. After five years, notices served on organisations are removed from this database and placed in the HSE's notice history database[7].

It is not uncommon for the HSE, when prosecuting an organisation, to seek to rely on previous notices as part of its case. This can be by introducing the notices as evidence of 'bad character' and a propensity to commit health and safety breaches.

Having an enforcement notice issued might impact upon the approval of a business under a contractor approval scheme or impact upon its chances of success when tendering for work, especially from public authorities and government bodies.

# FEE FOR INTERVENTION (FFI)
## What is FFI?

**5.7** In 2011 the government published its proposals for the reform of health and safety, entitled *Good Health and Safety, Good for Everyone*. This stated:

> ' ... it is reasonable that businesses that are found to be in serious breach of health and safety law – rather than the taxpayer – should bear the related costs incurred by the regulator in helping them put things right.'

In October 2012 FFI was introduced under the Health and Safety (Fees) Regulations 2012[8]. It is now currently set out in the Health and Safety and Nuclear (Fees) Regulations 2016[9].

FFI does not apply to health and safety investigations carried out by anyone other than the HSE, for example local authority environmental health officers.

Under the scheme, if an inspector is of the opinion a duty-holder is in 'material breach' of health and safety legislation, the inspector will serve a 'Notification of Contravention' (NoC) setting out the material breach with reasons for his/her opinion and often what steps are required to remedy the breach. This then

---

7 See http://www.hse.gov.uk/noticeshistory/.
8 SI 2012/1652.
9 SI 2016/253.

### 5.7 Health and Safety Enforcement Notices, Fee for Intervention (FFI) and Cautions

triggers recovery of the cost of the inspector's time, currently charged at £154 per hour.

Recoverable time includes:
- carrying out visits;
- writing reports;
- taking statements; and
- obtaining specialist advice/evidence, where required.

Invoices are raised every two months (duty-holders can receive more than one) and are payable within 30 days. While the average FFI invoice is in the region of £700 there have been some significantly larger ones. The HSE's Small Business Trade Association Forum's Hot Topics Fact Sheet Number 11, dated 15 March 2016, details invoices of £201,150.14, £93,558.00, £86,200.16 and £76,929.60.

On occasions a letter is sent by the inspector to the duty-holder advising that a notification of contravention may be served at a future date if the investigation reveals a material breach by the duty-holder.

If a prohibition notice or improvement notice is served a notification of contravention will usually be served with the notice or subsequently.

In prosecutions brought by the HSE, if there is a conviction, the claim for costs by the HSE against the defendant organisation will include solely the claim for the cost of bringing the prosecution, and not investigation costs, as these will have already been claimed by the HSE under the FFI scheme.

If the duty-holder disagrees that there has been a material breach and/or wishes to challenge the amount charged, then the duty-holder can raise a 'query'. If the duty-holder wishes to challenge the outcome of the query this can be done by raising a dispute (see para **5.10**).

In 2013 the Department for Work and Pensions appointed Martin Temple, at the time Chair of the Engineering Employers' Federation (EEF), the Manufacturers' Organisation, and since May 2016 the Chair of the HSE, to undertake a review of the HSE. His report was published on 9 January 2014. A section of the report addressed FFI.

He stated that while the principle behind FFI is valid, its introduction has primarily been driven by the HSE's need to raise income. Mr Temple noted concerns expressed by stakeholders that FFI was understood to be a penalty and that:

> 'At its worst stakeholders told me that it is against the principle of justice for HSE to act as police, prosecutor, judge and jury.'

The concern was that the dispute process was not sufficiently independent since a dispute was determined by a dispute panel comprising two senior HSE managers and an independent person from an HSE panel. Following a judicial review brought by OCS Group (UK) Ltd, the HSE introduced a new dispute process on 1 September 2017. One of the key changes was that the dispute panel should

*Health and Safety Enforcement Notices, Fee for Intervention (FFI) and Cautions* **5.10**

comprise a lawyer chosen from the Attorney General's Civil Panel and two independent people with practical experience of health and safety management.

## Challenging an FFI invoice

**5.8** The HSE has published *Fee for intervention – query and dispute process* which can be downloaded at http://www.hse.gov.uk/fee-for-intervention/assets/docs/ffi-queries-dispute-process.pdf.

### Query

**5.9** The first stage is to raise a query in writing setting out why the finding of material breach is challenged and/or the amount charged is challenged. This should be sent to the FFI Team either by email – feeforintervention@hse.gov.uk – which the HSE prefers, or by letter to:

Fee for Intervention Team
Health and Safety Executive
6.4 Redgrave Court
Merton Road, Bootle L20 7HS

The query must be raised no later than 21 days after the invoice date. It should detail the invoice number, the date of the invoice and the amount queried.

The query will be determined usually by the principal inspector for the inspector (ie his/her line manager) who served the notification of contravention. There is provision for the principal inspector to speak to both the inspector and the duty-holder in order to better understand or clarify any aspect of the query. On completing their review, the principal inspector will make a decision to uphold, partially uphold or not uphold the query.

If the query is upheld the invoice will be cancelled. If the query is upheld in part, then the timescales for payment may be varied. If the invoice remains unchanged, payment will be required. However, if the duty-holder is not satisfied with the response, they can raise a dispute.

There is no charge for the principal inspector considering the query, even if query is not upheld.

### Dispute

**5.10** A dispute must be raised in writing (either by email or letter) to the FFI Team no later than 21 days after the date of the HSE's response setting out the determination of the query. The dispute should include the following:

- invoice number and date;
- customer reference;

**5.10**  *Health and Safety Enforcement Notices, Fee for Intervention (FFI) and Cautions*

- name of the organisation to which the invoice was sent;
- name of the individual disputing the invoice;
- specific reason(s) for disputing the invoice; and
- confirmation of whether the dispute relates to the entire invoice or only part, specifying the appropriate entries.

The dispute will be considered by a 'Disputes Panel' which, as explained above, comprises a lawyer as chair, together with two other independent members. Details of the panel members along with their experience are provided to the duty-holder before the panel meeting.

The HSE will provide to the duty-holder, within 21 days of the dispute being received, all the relevant information that was available to the inspector on which their decision was based, and why a contravention was considered to be a material breach.

Depending on the nature of the dispute, it will include:

- what provisions have been contravened;
- why the HSE is of that opinion;
- evidence upon which the opinion is based (additional information that was not available or known to the inspector at the time the notice of contravention was served or enforcement notice was issued will not be provided or submitted to the panel);
- why contraventions are considered to be material breaches;
- an explanation of the decision in the context of the Enforcement Management Model;
- what functions have been performed as a result of the contravention;
- how the performance of those functions can be attributed to the duty-holder;
- the HSE's opinion as to how and why the costs have been reasonably incurred;
- the HSE's response to any issue raised by the duty-holder as a query or in requesting the dispute; and
- any information in the HSE's possession which could reasonably be considered to indicate that the fees were not payable.

On receipt of this information, the duty-holder can provide further representations or information to the HSE for the panel to consider within 21 days.

The submissions and information provided by the HSE and the duty-holder will be considered on the papers when the panel meets to consider the dispute. The panel may request, if necessary, additional written information either from the HSE or the duty-holder. The panel has discretion in exceptional cases to convene a meeting with the duty-holder and the HSE but only if both agree.

In light of the *Chevron*[10] decision (see para **5.4**), it must follow that the panel is entitled to take into account all the available evidence relevant to the state of

---

10   *HM Inspector of Health and Safety v Chevron North Sea Ltd* [2018] UKSC 7.

*Health and Safety Enforcement Notices, Fee for Intervention (FFI) and Cautions* **5.12**

affairs when the notification of contravention was served including information that comes to light afterwards.

Where the investigation is ongoing or there is an appeal against an enforcement notice in the employment tribunal, the dispute process will be suspended until the outcome of the appeal or enforcement action is known.

As with a query, if the dispute is upheld the invoice will be cancelled. If the dispute is upheld in part, then the timescales for payment may be varied. If the invoice remains unchanged, payment will be required. Unlike a query there is a cost associated with raising a dispute. If the dispute is unsuccessful there will be an added cost of the panel considering the dispute but not any in relation to the time spent by the HSE preparing for or providing information to the panel.

The decision of the panel does not bind the duty-holder or the HSE (although the HSE will normally accept the decision of the panel). It is possible even if a dispute is upheld for the HSE to institute debt recovery proceedings in the civil court, albeit unlikely.

## *Repayment of money paid by the duty-holder under FFI*

**5.11** If a duty-holder successfully defends a criminal prosecution or is successful in their appeal against an enforcement notice, then any money paid under FFI must be repaid to the duty-holder.

## Why raise a query/dispute?

**5.12** In an interview with Ben Rich of 2 Hare Court[11], Peter McNaught, Chief Legal Advisor to the HSE, did not rule out that a notification of contravention that had not been challenged could be used in future criminal proceedings. It is not uncommon for the HSE to refer the court in the sentencing hearing to previous relevant notifications of contravention that have been served on the defendant.

It can also have an impact upon a defendant company commercially, particularly when tendering for work. It is now becoming more common for prospective clients to ask in pre-qualification questionnaires not only whether the defendant has had any prosecutions or enforcement notices, in say the last three years, but also whether the company has been served with any notifications of contravention.

It is not possible to dispute the hourly rate that is applied. However, it can be worth examining the time the inspector has spent engaged in the investigation and whether that time is reasonable in all the circumstances.

---

11 Published in March 2013 and at http://2harecourt.newsweaver.com/regulatorycrimenewsletter/3j4wo3ho19k.

*5.13  Health and Safety Enforcement Notices, Fee for Intervention (FFI) and Cautions*

# CAUTIONS

**5.13**  A 'simple' caution can be given by an inspector to an organisation or individual in respect of a health and safety offence rather than instituting court proceedings. It should not be confused with the caution given at the start of an interview under caution.

A caution is a statement by an inspector, accepted in writing by the organisation or individual, that an offence has been committed for which there is a realistic prospect of conviction. These are only used in exceptional circumstances where the public interest firmly weighs against prosecution. The existence of a previous caution might influence the decision to prosecute if there is re-offending, and in the event of a conviction, that caution might be brought to the attention of the court when sentencing. If an offender refuses to accept the caution, a prosecution will usually follow. The offender is entitled to disclosure of evidence before agreeing to accept a simple caution (see *DPP v Ara*[12]).

A 'simple' caution is different from a 'conditional' caution, which was introduced under the Criminal Justice Act 2003. Inspectors are not authorised to give a conditional caution.

---

12  [2001] EWHC Admin 493.

# Chapter 6

# Environmental Offences

Environmental offences   6.1
    Strict liability   6.2
Waste   6.3
    What is waste?   6.3
    Waste offences   6.4
    Penalties   6.5
    Unlawful deposit of controlled waste   6.6
    Waste carriers brokers registration   6.7
    Examples of penalties   6.8
EPA 1990, s 157 – Offences by bodies corporate   6.9
Fly-tipping   6.10
    Penalties   6.11
    Examples of prosecutions   6.12
    Fixed penalty notices   6.13
Packaging waste   6.14
    Definition of packaging   6.15
    Obligated packing producer   6.16
    Definition of handling   6.17
    Activity list: definition/description   6.18
    Registration   6.19
Batteries   6.20
    Penalties   6.21
    Example of a prosecution   6.22
WEEE Regulations   6.23
Water offences   6.24
    In England and Wales   6.25
    Anti-pollution works notice under the Water Resources Act 1991   6.26
    In Scotland and Northern Ireland   6.27
    Examples of penalties   6.28
Noise nuisance   6.29
    Penalties for not complying with a noise abatement notice   6.30
    Criminal behaviour orders for noise pollution   6.31
Statutory nuisance   6.32
    An abatement notice   6.33
    Penalties for not complying with an abatement notice   6.34
    Appeals   6.35
    Examples of abatement notices and appeal   6.36
    Restrictions on use of public sewers   6.37

*6.1 Environmental Offences*

Wildlife crime   6.38
    Examples of wildlife crime   6.39
    Examples of prosecutions   6.40

# ENVIRONMENTAL OFFENCES

**6.1** There are relatively few offences related to harming the environment which are crimes in themselves. The criminal law has been used to address unacceptable behaviour and enforce the system of environmental regulation. Environmental crime itself includes offences created either by statute or developed under common law that relate to such issues as littering and abandoned vehicles.

The majority of the UK's environmental law is based upon EU directives and UK laws relating to waste, chemicals, nature conservation, environmental protection, climate change, producer responsibility and industrial emissions. These come from the EU's development of environmental law over the last 25 years.

Some environmental law within the UK is there to ensure that EU targets are met. For example, the requirement to reduce landfill to 50% by 2020. This requirement led to the introduction of a landfill tax, which both provides money for the Treasury and also makes recycling the more economic option.

Other examples include:

- *Packaging and Packaging Waste Directive (94/62/EC)* – sets escalating targets for reducing packaging waste and for promoting recycling, reuse and other forms of waste recovery;
- *Landfill Directive (1999/31/EC)* – outlines the rules for landfilling and sets targets to reduce the amount of municipal waste going to landfill;
- *Waste Framework Directive (2008/98/EC)* – the overarching EU policy on waste covering recycling targets, a definition of waste and national waste management plans as well as creating the 'Waste Hierarchy';
- *Controls on Animal By-Products Regulation (EC) 1069/2009* – sets rules for the disposal of animal carcasses and other animal parts;
- *Impact in food waste collection and treatment* – the disposal of food waste is a devolved issue. In Scotland, Northern Ireland and Wales regulations require that food waste is collected separately for anaerobic digestion rather than landfill. In England food waste still mainly goes to landfill;
- *Industrial Emissions Directive (2010/75/EU)* – introduces a holistic approach to environmental permitting in industrial activity;
- Waste management of industrial sites and environmental management of waste operators;
- *Waste Electrical and Electronic Equipment (WEEE) Directive (2012/19/EU)* – sets targets for electronic waste recycling and lays out rules for recycling electronic waste;
- *Producers finance* – cost of collection, treatment and recovery.

## Strict liability

6.2    In law, strict liability makes a person or organisation legally responsible for damage and loss caused by their acts and omissions regardless of fault. Where strict liability exists there is no requirement to prove fault, negligence or intention. Whether or not the damage was intended is not relevant.

The reasons for strict liability for environmental crimes are:

- it is in the public interest;
- it acts as a deterrent so that those who have to comply with the law do not take risks; and
- it is easier for the regulators to enforce and prosecute environmental offences.

Where an environmental crime is committed by an employee, the company that employs him/her is liable to be prosecuted. It is also possible to prosecute senior managers within a company in their capacity as managers if the environmental offence is committed either with their consent or connivance, or is attributable to their neglect.

# WASTE

## What is waste?

6.3    The legal definition of waste in the UK is derived from the EU Waste Framework Directive and covers anything that is required, or will need to be, thrown away. This includes situations where the article is given to someone else to be reused or recycled; it is still largely considered to be waste if it is no longer required by the person who produced it.

## Waste offences

6.4    The Environmental Protection Act 1990 (EPA 1990), s 34 relates to a duty of care in respect to waste. This requires that anyone who:

- produces;
- imports;
- keeps;
- stores;
- transports;
- treats; or
- disposes

of waste must take reasonable steps to ensure that the waste is managed properly. This duty of care also applies to anyone who acts as broker and has control of waste.

6.4 *Environmental Offences*

If somebody has waste they must:
- ensure that any person who takes control of the waste is licensed;
- take steps to prevent it escaping from their control;
- store it safely and securely;
- prevent it from causing environmental pollution or harm to anyone; and
- describe the waste in writing and prepare a waste transfer note if they intend to pass the waste on to someone else.

Someone who collects waste from others must:
- be authorised under the law to collect and receive waste;
- obtain a description of the collected waste in writing; and
- complete and retain a transfer note.

## Penalties

6.5  Charges under the EPA 1990, s 34 can be tried either in the Crown Court or the magistrates' court.

Both courts can apply an unlimited fine.

## Unlawful deposit of controlled waste

6.6  Under the EPA 1990, s 33 it is an offence to:
- deposit or knowingly cause or knowingly permit to be deposited (controlled) waste in or on land unless in accordance with the terms of a waste management licence;
- treat, keep or dispose of controlled waste in land or by means of any mobile plant unless in accordance with the terms of a waste management licence; or
- treat, keep or dispose of controlled waste that could cause environmental pollution or harm human health (applies when a waste management licence is not required).

## Waste carriers brokers registration

6.7  A person or organisation must be registered if they:
- transport waste;
- buy, sell or dispose of waste; or
- arrange for someone else to buy, sell or dispose of waste.

Once the business is registered then the organisation details will appear on a public register of waste carriers[1].

---

1  See the public register of waste carriers at https://environment.data.gov.uk/public-register/view/index.

## Examples of penalties

**6.8** A Nottingham man was fined £880 plus £1,989 costs and £88 victim surcharge after a driver was found transporting waste without a licence[2]. Following a multi-agency operation in May 2017 a Ford Transit van driven by the man was found to be fully laden with waste including plastic, furniture, toys, a fridge and soiled mattress. In the vehicle a number of waste transfer notes and weighbridge tickets were found which suggested that he had previously taken scrap metal to two separate sites. A search of the public register confirmed that he did not have a waste carrier's licence.

# EPA 1990, S 157 – OFFENCES BY BODIES CORPORATE

**6.9** Where an offence committed by a body corporate under any provision of the EPA 1990 is proved to have been committed with the consent or connivance of, or to have been attributable to any neglect on the part of, any director, manager, secretary or other similar officer of the body corporate, or a person who was purporting to act in any such capacity, he as well as the body corporate shall be guilty of that offence and shall be liable to be proceeded against and punished accordingly.

In addition to being committed by a relevant employee of the company, the offence has to have been committed with consent, through the connivance or due to neglect of the individual concerned:

- *consent* – *Huckerby v Elliott*[3] held that a company director must be aware of the breach or offence and actively encourage and approve it. So consent covers a situation where a company director deliberately commits the offence and this is the reason that the Environment Agency may well consider personal prosecutions;
- *connivance* – in the case of *Huckerby v Elliott* the situation was one where the director was equally aware of what was going on but his agreement was tacit – not actively encouraging what was happening but letting it continue without saying anything;
- *neglect* – neglect was defined in the case of *Re Hughes*[4] as a 'failure to perform a duty which the person knows or ought to know'. It is then not necessary for the prosecution to show that the director knew of the offence, only that they should have known.

The terms of this type of prosecution are very similar to those of the HSWA 1974, s 37.

---

2  See https://www.gov.uk/government/news/nottingham-man-fined-for-carrying-waste-without-a-licence.
3  [1970] 1 All ER 189.
4  [1943] 2 All ER 269.

6.10  *Environmental Offences*

# FLY-TIPPING

**6.10**  Fly-tipping is the illegal dumping of waste instead of using an authorised method such as an authorised rubbish dump or a kerbside collector. It is illegal to deposit any waste onto land, and this includes waste dumped or tipped on a site with no licence to accept waste.

There were 1,602 prosecutions for fly-tipping in England in 2016/17 and 98% of prosecutions resulted in conviction. In the same period councils handed out 56,000 penalty notices with a maximum fine of £400.

## Penalties

**6.11**  The penalties for fly-tipping are set out in the EPA 1990 and were increased through the Clean Neighbourhoods and Environment Act 2005. It is a criminal offence punishable by a fine of up to £50,000 or 12 months' imprisonment if convicted at a magistrates' court and an unlimited fine and up to five years' imprisonment if convicted at a Crown Court. The Sentencing Guidelines 2015 have increased the maximum penalties.

## Examples of prosecutions

**6.12**  Three men from Plymouth[5] were banned from the waste trade for fly-tipping in Cornish beauty spots. They were given community orders requiring 100 hours of work after admitting depositing household, industrial and commercial waste and not being waste carriers.

A Devon haulage company[6] and site clearance company was given a bill for more than £100,000 for dumping thousands of tonnes of soil and stone on farmland. The family owned and ran a company based at a farm in Crediton. Farmers are allowed to accept up to 1,000 tonnes of non-hazardous waste including soil and stone under a permission known as an 'exemption' that is commonly used on farms to construct hard-standings, bases for buildings and tracks, and hence an environmental permit is not required.

Inquiries by the Environment Agency revealed that the haulage company had deposited 7,820 tonnes of waste at the farm. Excessive quantities of waste, much of it from building and construction sites, had also been tipped at three other Devon farms. The offences came to light after the Environment Agency examined waste transfer notes that showed the haulage company was the source of the excessive amounts of waste material. The company benefited

---

5   See https://www.gov.uk/government/news/plymouth-trio-banned-from-waste-trade-for-fly-tipping-around-cornwall.
6   See https://www.gov.uk/government/news/cc-haulage-sons-ltd-to-pay-109000-for-dumping-on-devon-farms.

*Environmental Offences* **6.14**

financially by paying the farmers less to accept the waste than it was charging its clients to take the material away.

There are also a range of other possible penalties which will be discussed in the following paragraphs.

## Fixed penalty notices

**6.13** Since 9 May 2016, local authorities in England have been able to issue fixed penalty notices for between £150 to £400 for small-scale fly-tipping offences pursuant to the Unauthorised Deposit of Waste (Fixed Penalties) Regulations 2016[7]. These may be served as a criminal penalty in lieu of prosecution for a criminal offence. They are not a civil penalty (see further below).

In Scotland, fixed penalty notices can be used for any fly-tipping incidents under the EPA 1990, s 33A (as amended).

Some organisations have claimed that the penalties handed down are too low to discourage fly-tipping. A government consultation on proposals to enhance measures to tackle waste crime ran between 26 February 2015 and 6 May 2015. The consultation sought views on enhancing enforcement powers and other measures to tackle waste crime in England and Wales. It included a call for evidence on adopting fixed penalties for small-scale fly-tipping.

In its *Report on Litter and Fly-tipping in England* (published when the waste crime consultation was still open in March 2015) the Communities and Local Government Select Committee recommended that the government introduce a national fixed penalty notice for small amounts of fly-tipping.

Under the Proceeds of Crime Act 2002 offenders can also have assets frozen.

# PACKAGING WASTE

**6.14** This is covered by the Packaging (Essential Requirements) Regulations 2015[8] and the Producer Responsibility Obligations (Packaging Waste) Regulations 2017[9].

If a business or organisation produces or uses packaging or sells packaged goods, they may be classed as a packaging producer. Packaging producers must:

- reduce the amount of packaging produced in the first place;
- reduce how much packaging waste goes to landfill; and
- increase the amount of packaging waste that is recycled and recovered.

---

7   SI 2016/334.
8   SI 2015/1640.
9   SI 2017/871.

## Definition of packaging

**6.15** 'Packaging' is any material used to hold, protect, handle, deliver and present goods.

This includes packaging for raw materials, right through to packaging finished goods to be sold, or being sold. For example: bags; boxes; tape for wrapping; rolls; tubes; and clothes hangers sold as part of the clothing item.

## Obligated packing producer

**6.16** An 'obligated' packing producer is one who handles or is part of a group of companies that handle, more than 50 tonnes of packaging materials or packaging in the previous calendar year, and has a turnover of more than £2 million (based on the last financial year).

## Definition of handling

**6.17** 'Handling' is defined as:

- carrying out one or more of the activities in the activity list (see para **6.18**) or having these activities carried out by another party on behalf of the first party;
- owning the packaging on which the activities are carried out; or
- supplying packaging or packaging materials at any stage in the chain or to the final user of the packaging.

A person is not 'handling' packaging or packaging materials if they are being used internally within the business.

## Activity list: definition/description

**6.18** Activities included in the activity list are as follows:

- *raw material manufacture* – producing raw materials for packaging manufacture;
- *packaging conversion* – converting raw materials into packaging;
- *packing/filling* – putting goods into packaging or put packaging around goods;
- *selling* – supplying packaged goods to the end user;
- *importing* – importing packaged goods or packaging materials from outside the UK; this includes raw materials that will become packaging, for example, plastic pellets used to make bottles;
- *service provider* – a business that supplies packaging by hiring it out or lending it.

## Registration

**6.19** Packaging producers must be registered, either to a compliance scheme or to the National Packaging Waste Database. Wine and sherry producer Gonzalez Byass UK Limited failed to register with a scheme and take steps to recycle packaging. It paid a contribution of £120,000 to the Woodland Trust and has since registered with Biffpack.

Biscuit producer Bahlsen Management Limited, fruit and vegetable supplier Cobell Limited, and Hameln Pharmaceuticals Limited were similarly all also found not to have registered, and agreed to contribute £39,800, £33,723, and £35,000 respectively to charity.

Apart from the Woodland Trust, other charities that benefit from the enforcement undertakings include the New Forest Trust, the Marine Conservation Society, the Bedfordshire, Cambridgeshire, Northamptonshire, Dorset, Sussex and Kent Wildlife Trusts, Friends of Westonbirt Arboretum, the British Beekeepers Association, Carrymoor Environmental Trust, Howhill Trust, and Freshwater Habitats Trust.

These enforcement undertaking are published by the Environment Agency[10].

# BATTERIES

**6.20** Enforcement provisions and offences arise from breaches of the Batteries and Accumulators (Placing on the Market) Regulations 2008[11], and the Waste Batteries and Accumulators Regulations 2009[12]. These regulations implement the Batteries Directive 2006/66/EC.

Anyone who puts batteries in their own appliances and vehicles has producer obligations. Anyone supplying end users with batteries, excluding battery products, has distributor obligations.

The law affects those who:

- make one tonne or more of portable batteries, on their own or in appliances or vehicles, on the UK market for the first time *(producer activity)*;
- make less than one tonne of portable batteries, on their own or in appliance or vehicles, on the UK market for the first time *(small producer activity)*;
- provide 32 kg per annum of portable batteries (on their own, not in appliances) to end users on a professional basis *(distributor activity)*;
- provide less than 32 kg per annum of portable batteries (on their own, not in appliances) to end users on a professional basis *(small distributor activity)*;

---

10 See https://www.gov.uk/government/publications/enforcement-undertakings-accepted-by-the-environment-agency.
11 SI 2008/2164.
12 SI 2009/890.

6.20  *Environmental Offences*

- place industrial batteries, on their own or in appliances or vehicles, on the UK market for the first time *(industrial producer activity)*;
- place automotive batteries, on their own or in appliances or vehicles, on the UK market for the first time *(automotive producer activity)*.

## Penalties

6.21  A number of criminal offences are possible, including:
- failing to meet finance obligations;
- failing to join a compliance scheme if required to do so;
- failing to provide accurate information to a compliance scheme;
- failing to report on industrial or automotive batteries placed on the market;
- failing to report on waste industrial or automotive batteries taken back;
- failing to provide a registration number to customers;
- failing to keep adequate and correct records;
- failing to provide documents or information when required to do so;
- providing false or misleading information;
- failing to provide free take-back if required to do so.

Penalties are currently up to £5,000 per offence with the possibility of unlimited fines and imprisonment for directors/statutory officers in some cases. Battery offences are subject to criminal prosecution as they do not currently fall under the civil sanctions regime.

## Example of a prosecution

6.22  In an unreported case, Babz Media was fined £45,000 and £8,724.98 in costs for non-compliance with environmental legislation for packaging, waste, and electrical equipment.

# WEEE REGULATIONS

6.23  The Waste Electric and Electronic Equipment (WEEE) Regulations 2013[13] (WEEE Regulations) require all manufactures to fund the collection and recycling of their products when they come to their end of life.

Most light bulbs and lamps are covered by the WEEE Regulations. The following are all lighting equipment covered by the regulations:

- compact fluorescent lamps – otherwise known as energy-saving light bulbs;
- fluorescent tubes;
- metal halide lamps;

---

13  SI 2013/3113.

- mercury and blended lamps;
- sodium lamps;
- LEDs.

Filament lamps are excluded by the regulations, but ordinary household light bulbs are fine to be recycled.

Larger items covered by the WEEE rules are split into categories:

- large household appliances – white goods;
- small household appliances – irons, kettles, toasters etc;
- IT and telecommunications equipment;
- entertainment devices – radios, cd players;
- lighting equipment;
- electric tools;
- toys and sports equipment;
- medical devices – dialysis machines, ventilators etc;
- monitoring and control instruments – for example smoke detectors;
- automatic dispensers – vending machines;
- display equipment – televisions;
- cooling equipment – fridges and freezers;
- gas discharge lamps.

# WATER OFFENCES

6.24 Water discharge and ground water activities offences are regulated by the Environmental Permitting (England and Wales) Regulations 2016 (EPR 2016)[14], reg 12, which deals with the elements of the offence of breaching environmental permit conditions and penalties for committing the offences. This note also covers the offence of a person making a false or misleading statement under the EPR 2016, reg 38.

## In England and Wales

6.25 Water offences in England and Wales are covered by the Environmental Permitting (England and Wales) Regulations 2010 (as amended)[15]:

- 'a person must not, except under and to the extent authorised by an environmental permit, (a) operate a regulated facility; or (b) cause or knowingly permit a water discharge activity or groundwater activity'.

    Water discharge activities include:

    – discharging poisonous, polluting or noxious matter or solid waste into inland freshwater, coastal waters or relevant territorial waters;

---

14 SI 2016/1154.
15 SI 2010/675.

*6.25 Environmental Offences*

- – discharging any trade or sewage effluent into inland freshwater coastal waters and relevant territorial waters;
 - – cutting or uprooting substantial amounts of vegetation of any inland fresh waters;
- penalties:
 - – magistrates' court – a fine not exceeding £50,000 or imprisonment for a term not exceeding 12 months, or both;
 - – Crown Court – unlimited fine or imprisonment not exceeding a term of five years, or both.

## Anti-pollution works notice under the Water Resources Act 1991

**6.26** This Act requires that if a person or their business causes pollution or a risk of pollution to any water course then the Environment Agency can serve a works notice under s 161A of the Water Resources Act 1991 which requires preventative works to be carried out to minimise the risk and future risk and any failure to do so may lead to a prosecution.

An example of this can be seen in the unreported case of the owner of a leisure park in South Devon who held a consent to discharge sewage effluent into the nearby stream provided that the effluent was first treated and met the standards set out in the consent. Shortly after the company took over operations at the site in 2008, Environment Agency officers informed them that their on-site sewage treatment plant was not functioning properly. This resulted in sewage being discharged into the stream without being properly treated first, thereby causing serious pollution.

During 2009 and 2010, the Environment Agency took samples from the stream to test the levels of sewage effluent being discharged and on each occasion the levels were well above the permitted levels under the consent.

A site visit in October 2009 revealed evidence of poor site maintenance and a general disregard by the company for the pollution issues. In particular, the area immediately surrounding the pipe used to discharge the sewage waste was covered in thick brown sludge. Further investigations of the sewage treatment plant indicated that this was in a state of disrepair meaning that the effluent was still not being properly treated prior to discharge. As a result, the Environment Agency served the company with an anti-pollution works notice requiring it to take remedial steps.

## In Scotland and Northern Ireland

**6.27** The following legislation covers water offences in Scotland and Northern Ireland:

- Water Environment (Controlled Activities) (Scotland) Regulations 2011 (as amended) – more commonly known as CAR:

  These regulations apply regulatory controls over activities which may affect Scotland's water environment. The regulations cover:
  - discharges;
  - diffuse pollution;
  - abstractions;
  - engineering works in inland waterways;
  - groundwater.

  The Scottish Environmental Protection Agency (SEPA) implement the regulations, charging schemes, and compliance with the regulations.

- Water (NI) Order 1999 and Water Abstraction and Impoundment (Licensing) Regulations (Northern Ireland) 2006:

  Monitoring of water pollution in Northern Ireland is divided into nine areas and each is staffed by an Environmental Health (Rivers) Officer or a Senior Water Quality Inspector and a number of water quality inspectors who act as field agents on behalf of the Department of Agriculture, Environment and Rural Affairs.

## Examples of penalties

6.28 Thames Water[16] was prosecuted for six separate cases where repeated discharges of sewage into the River Thames and its tributaries resulted in major environmental damage. It was fined over £20 million in fines and costs.

# NOISE NUISANCE

6.29 Noise nuisance offences can be committed under the EPA 1990, s 79. For a noise to count as a statutory nuisance it must be unreasonable and substantially interfere with the use or enjoyment of a home or other premises, or injure health or be likely to injure health.

Duties are conferred on local authorities to investigate any complaint about excessive noise. Councils are responsible for looking into complaints about noise from:

- premises – including land like gardens and certain vessels (for example loud barking dogs), vehicles, machinery;
- equipment on the streets (for example music from car stereos).

---

16 See https://www.gov.uk/government/news/thames-water-ordered-to-pay-record-20-million-for-river-pollution.

6.29  *Environmental Offences*

Statutory noise nuisance laws do not apply to:

- noise from traffic or planes (but do apply to model planes);
- political demonstrations and demonstrations about a cause;
- premises occupied by the armed forces or visiting forces.

Complaints fall into different categories and each has a number of notices and penalties for non-compliance. These categories are:

- noise at night – warning notices;
- noise from intruder alarms;
- noise from construction works;
- loudspeakers on the street;
- model aircraft noise;
- noise from industrial, trade or business premises – special rules.

Councils also have powers to deal with anti-social noise and consider noise in planning decisions, entertainment licences and decisions about building control.

The Environment Agency controls some potential noise nuisances, with environmental permits, as part of pollution control.

## Penalties for not complying with a noise abatement notice

6.30  Councils can:

- give a fixed penalty notice (FPN) giving the offender the chance to pay a fine (up to £110 for dwellings and £500 for licensed premises) within 14 days, instead of being prosecuted;
- prosecute the offender if the council does not issue a FPN or if the person responsible does not pay the fine on time (conviction can result in a fine of up to £1,000 for dwellings and an unlimited amount for licensed premises);
- remove noise-making equipment like loudspeakers.

## Criminal behaviour orders for noise pollution

6.31  Failure to comply with a noise abatement notice can lead to a criminal behaviour order. An example of this can be seen in the case of a man in Poulton[17] who pleaded guilty to failing to comply with a noise abatement notice served to stop the continuous barking of a dog in his ownership. The criminal behaviour order prohibited him from keeping the dog in question at his address or from kennelling any other dog outdoors at the address. He was fined £70 and ordered to pay £1,000 costs. This comes under the Anti-Social Behaviour, Crime and Policing Act 2014.

17  See http://www.wyre.gov.uk/news/article/1573/resident_issued_with_wyre_s_first_criminal_behaviour_order_over_nuisance_dog.

# STATUTORY NUISANCE

6.32    A statutory nuisance may include:

- noise from premises or from vehicle, equipment or machinery in the street;
- smoke from premises;
- smells from industry, trade or business premises (for example sewage treatment works, factories or restaurants);
- artificial light from premises;
- insect infestations from industrial, trade or business premises;
- accumulation or deposits on premises (ie piles of rotting rubbish).

For one of the above to be a statutory nuisance it must:

- unreasonably and substantially interfere with the use or enjoyment of a home or other premises; or
- injure health or be likely to injure health.


## An abatement notice

6.33    Councils must serve an abatement notice on people responsible for statutory nuisance, or a premises owner or occupier if this is not possible.

The abatement notice may require the person responsible for the activity to stop or limit the times that the activity is carried out, and may include actions to reduce the problem.


## Penalties for not complying with an abatement notice

6.34    Non-compliance is triable at the magistrates' court only. Penalties vary according to the following circumstances:

- where the offence is committed on industrial, trade, business premises the fine is unlimited;
- where the offence is committed on non-industrial premises the fine is unlimited with a further fine of an amount equal to one-tenth of that level for each day on which the offence continues after the conviction.

Fines may be a lump sum, and further fines may also be decided by the court for each day that there is a failure to comply (also set by the court).

The council may also take action to stop or restrict the nuisance by:

- carrying out works and making the person given the notice pay for them (this can include seizure and confiscation of equipment); or
- applying to the High Court for an injunction (if the prosecution is not adequate).

**6.35** *Environmental Offences*

## Appeals

6.35 Anyone served with an abatement notice can appeal to the magistrates' court within 21 days of receiving the notice.

The grounds for appeal are:
- legal tests have not been met to show that the issue is a statutory nuisance;
- the notice was served to the wrong person;
- the notice was defective;
- the authority has unreasonably refused to accept compliance with alternative requirements, where the requirements of the notices are unreasonable in character or extent or are unnecessary;
- the time limit for compliance with any of the requirements of the notice is insufficient for the purpose.

In certain cases, where the best practicable means were used to prevent or to counteract the effects of the nuisance, this will be the foundation of both a successful appeal against the service of an abatement notice and a prosecution for breach of such a notice.

## Examples of abatement notices and appeal

6.36 In the case of *Manley v New Forest DC*[18], a couple owned a house and operated dog kennels containing 24 Siberian Huskies. The local authority had served an abatement notice and suggested that the Manley's could line the kennels or build new kennels where the huskies could be kept during the night. The Manley's appealed against the abatement notice to the district judge and then to the Crown Court. The Crown Court agreed that these were business premises but that the Manley's had not demonstrated that the best practicable means had been used to counteract the noise and therefore the notice was justified. The noise from the dogs fell within the descriptions of statutory nuisances in the EPA 1990, s 79(1). If the Manley's sought to resist the service of an abatement notice pursuant to the Statutory Nuisance (Appeals) Regulations 1995[19], then the burden was upon the Manley's to demonstrate that at the time of the abatement notice the best practicable means were in use to prevent the noise. It was for the Manley's to demonstrate that they were doing something and that those were the best practicable means. If they had done nothing, the only way they could succeed in having the abatement notice set aside was to show that nothing could be done. In this case that would be an almost impossible task. There was plenty of evidence to demonstrate that the question of boxing in or lining of the kennels was properly canvassed before the court and that the Manley's had a fair opportunity to deal with it. The judgment of the Crown Court had made it clear that after considering veterinary evidence,

18 [2007] EWHC 3188 (Admin).
19 SI 1995/2644.

either lining or new buildings were practicable methods for abating the noise, neither of which the Manley's had adopted. In those circumstances there was no possibility of the Manley's demonstrating that the best practicable means had been used.

## Restrictions on the use of public sewers

6.37    The Water Industry Act 1991, s 111 provides for restrictions on the use of public sewers.

Offences under this section are triable in either the magistrates' or the Crown Court. Penalties are as follows:

- when tried at the Crown Court, imprisonment of up to two years or a fine or both;
- when tried at the magistrates' court, a fine not exceeding the statutory maximum and a further fine not exceeding £50 for each day on which the offence continues after conviction.

# WILDLIFE CRIME

6.38    Wildlife crime can take many forms and ranges from organised crime, such as the trade in endangered species, to the shooting of birds.

## Examples of wildlife crime

6.39

- Badger persecution – the Protection of Badgers Act 1992.
- Bat persecution – Conservation of Habitats and Species Regulations 2010[20] and the Wildlife and Countryside Act 1981.
- Illegal trades in endangered species – Convention on International Trade in Endangered Species (CITES).
- Fresh water mussels – endangered species in rivers in England and Scotland.
- Poaching/coursing.
- Raptor persecution.
- Theft or disturbance of wild birds, their eggs and/or nests – Wildlife and Countryside Act 1981.
- Theft or disturbance of wild animals, plants or habitat – the Wildlife and Countryside Act 1981, Sch 5.
- Animal cruelty – the Wild Mammals (Protection) Act 1996.
- Invasive species – Wildlife and Countryside Act 1981.

20   SI 2010/490.

*6.39   Environmental Offences*

- European protected species – the European Habitats Directive Annexes II and IV and protected by law throughout the EU. Member States of the EU are required to protect these species.

## Examples of prosecutions

**6.40** In 2017 a real estate company based in London pleaded guilty at the magistrates' court to three offences relating to the destruction of a bat roost, contrary to the Conservation of Habitats and Species Regulations 2010[21]. The case has been adjourned for a proceeds of crime hearing.

A man was jailed for attempting to sell rhino and elephant tusks. He was sentenced to 14 months' imprisonment.

---

21   SI 2010/490.

# Chapter 7

# Environmental Notices and Sanctions

Environmental notices and sanctions   7.1
Injunctions   7.2
Warnings   7.3
Formal caution   7.4
Enforcement notice   7.5
Criminal sanctions   7.6
    Fixed penalty notices (FPNs)   7.6
    Formal caution   7.7
    Prosecution   7.8
Orders imposed by the court ancillary to prosecution   7.9
    Disqualification of directors   7.10
      Example   7.11
    Confiscation of assets – Proceeds of Crime Act 2002   7.12
      Example   7.13
    Criminal behaviour orders   7.14
      Example   7.15
    Forfeiture of equipment used to commit the offence   7.16
      Example   7.17
    Compensation   7.18
      Example   7.19
    Vehicle seizure   7.20
      Example   7.21
Regulatory Enforcement and Sanctions Act 2008   7.22
    Fixed monetary penalties (FMPs)   7.23
    Variable monetary penalties (VMPs)   7.24
    Compliance notices   7.25
    Restoration notices   7.26
    Stop notices   7.27
    Suspension notice   7.28
      Challenge to a suspension notice   7.29
    Enforcement undertakings (EUs)   7.30
Non-compliance penalties   7.31
    VMP, FMP or other monetary penalty   7.32
    Enforcement undertakings   7.33
    Restoration notice or compliance notice imposed without VMP   7.35
    Non-compliance penalty notice (NCP)   7.36
    Restoration notice or compliance notice imposed with a VMP or
        a third party undertaking accepted by the regulator   7.37
    Stop notices   7.38

*7.1* *Environmental Notices and Sanctions*

Other options   7.39
    Enforcement cost recovery notices   7.39
    Application of NCPs   7.40
Climate change regimes   7.41
Appeals   7.42
    Environment tribunal   7.42
    Who sits on the tribunal?   7.43
    What can be appealed against?   7.44
    Grounds of appeal   7.45
      Fixed monetary penalty (FMP)   7.45
      Variable monetary penalty (VMP)   7.46
      Stop notice   7.47
      Compliance/restoration notice   7.48
    Tribunals powers   7.49

# ENVIRONMENTAL NOTICES AND SANCTIONS

**7.1** Civil sanctions for criminal offences were introduced by the Regulatory Enforcement and Sanctions Act 2008 (RESA 2008), which aims to make the enforcement of environmental compliance quicker and more effective. The introduction of the Environmental Civil Sanctions (England) Order 2010[1] (for mainly water-related offences), the Environmental Civil Sanctions (Miscellaneous Amendments) (England) Regulations 2010[2] (for mainly waste-related offences), and the Environmental Civil Sanctions (Wales) Order 2010[3] granted to both the Environment Agency (EA) and Natural England the power to use these sanctions to better regulate environmental compliance. This gave the authorities the ability to use these powers to deal with an offence, and to secure a clean-up far quicker than using a lengthy and expensive criminal prosecution.

Offences that are committed deliberately or recklessly or with gross negligence are more likely to result in prosecution.

Where an offence has been committed and the delivery of advice and guidance does not achieve the required outcome, the regulator will consider issuing some form of sanction as well as taking any other preventive or remedial action necessary to protect the environment and people.

# INJUNCTIONS

**7.2** An injunction is an order of a court directing an individual (or company) to either:

1    SI 2010/1157.
2    SI 2010/1159.
3    SI 2010/1821.

- stop a particular activity (a prohibitory injunction); or
- carry out a particular activity (a mandatory injunction).

Failure to comply with an injunction is treated as a contempt of court and is punishable by an unlimited fine and/or up to two years' imprisonment.

A court order under the Environmental Permitting (England and Wales) Regulations 2010 (SI 2010/675) is similar to an injunction.

# WARNINGS

7.3   A warning is a written notification when it is believed an offence has been committed. The notification can be either:

- a warning letter; or
- a site warning that is normally issued on-site or otherwise as a result of a compliance visit to a permitted site or activity.

The warning is recorded and may, in the event of further non-compliance, influence subsequent choice of sanction.

# FORMAL CAUTION

7.4   A formal caution is the written acceptance by an offender that they have committed an offence, and can only be used where a prosecution could have been brought. This differs from the warning at para 7.3 which is simply a record and warning about an offence that has been or may be committed. A formal caution is a criminal sanction which will be produced in court if there is further offending. It is different from a civil sanction as the circumstances which led to the offence are considered to be appropriate for a prosecution and a repetition of similar offending would likely lead to prosecution.

Formal cautions are intended to be a deterrent and are suitable where other factors mitigate against prosecution. Where a formal caution is not accepted, this will normally lead to a prosecution.

# ENFORCEMENT NOTICE

7.5   This requires that the recipient of the enforcement notice ceases offending, restore or remediate the affected environment, or comply with regulatory requirements. There are already existing provisions for this, namely under the Environmental Permitting (England and Wales) Regulations 2010[4]. Enforcement notices are made by court order and enforced by the High Court.

---

4   SI 2010/675.

7.5  *Environmental Notices and Sanctions*

There are various remediation powers which aim to prevent or remedy pollution and recover costs, and allow for disposal of radioactive orphan sources.

*Enforcement notices:*

- variation notice;
- suspension notice;
- revocation notice;
- groundwater prohibition notice.

*Court order:*

- enforcement by the High Court.

*Remediation powers:*

- power to prevent or remedy pollution and recover costs;
- power to dispose of radioactive orphan sources.

*Environmental Protection Act 1990:*

- notice to remove waste.

*Water Resources Act 1991:*

- anti-pollution works notice.

# CRIMINAL SANCTIONS

## Fixed penalty notices (FPNs)

7.6  A fixed penalty notice (FPN) is a financial penalty for an offence, imposed by the regulator, which, if unpaid, can be dealt with by way of prosecution in the criminal courts. FPNs are available for a limited number of offences.

Where an FPN is served, payment of the penalty discharges the liability. Where this happens, a record of the payment of the FPN will be kept and treated in the same way as a record arising from a warning.

Where an FPN is imposed but not paid, the recipient will normally be prosecuted for the original offence.

## Formal caution

7.7  A formal caution is the written acceptance by an offender that they have committed an offence. This may only be used where a prosecution could also have been brought. It differs from a warning, which is simply a record and warning about an offence that has been or may be committed. The formal caution is a formal recorded criminal sanction which will be produced in court if there is further offending. It differs from the imposition of a civil sanction as the circumstances which led to the offence have been considered to be appropriate for a prosecution and a repetition of similar offending would be likely to lead to such a prosecution.

Formal cautions are intended to be a specific deterrent to an offender and are suitable for cases where, although a prosecution could be taken, other factors mitigate against this.

Before bringing a prosecution the regulator will consider the test under the Code for Crown Prosecutors, that is whether there is sufficient evidence, and also the public interest factors involved.

Where a formal caution is not accepted the original offence will normally be prosecuted by the regulator.

## Prosecution

7.8 The legislation gives the courts considerable scope to punish offenders and to deter others. In some cases, imprisonment and unlimited fines may be imposed (see **Chapter 13** on Sentencing).

Where it is decided that a criminal sanction is appropriate, the case will be looked at in accordance with the requirements of the Code for Crown Prosecutors before the regulator commences a prosecution.

Prosecutions are serious and are only taken after full consideration of the implications and consequences. Where it is decided that a prosecution is the most appropriate choice of sanction, the test set out in the Code for Crown Prosecutors[5], to determine whether there is sufficient evidence, and whether the prosecution is in the public interest, must be satisfied. The decision must then be taken as to whether prosecution is an appropriate response or whether an alternative to prosecution may be more appropriate.

# ORDERS IMPOSED BY THE COURT ANCILLARY TO PROSECUTION

7.9 The Code for Crown Prosecutors requires the consideration of compensation and ancillary orders ie confiscation orders and criminal behaviour orders.

## Disqualification of directors

7.10 A person can be banned from being a company director if they do not meet their legal responsibilities. Disqualification can be for up to 15 years and means that the person cannot be:

5   See https://www.cps.gov.uk/publication/code-crown-prosecutors.

**7.10** *Environmental Notices and Sanctions*

- a director of any company registered in the UK or an overseas company that has connections with the UK;
- be involved in forming, marketing or running a company.

## *Example*

**7.11** Following an insolvency investigation, the county court disqualified directors for failing to ensure that the company complied with its statutory obligation under the Environmental Protection Act 1990 resulting in a risk of serious pollution. Between May 2015 and June 2015 three fires broke out at the trading site. This ultimately led to an enforcement notice from the Environment Agency prohibiting the company from receiving certain types of waste and requiring the company to take steps to remove the risk of serious pollution with immediate effect. Soon after the enforcement notice was served the company entered liquidation. The directors were disqualified for a period of seven and nine years[6].

## Confiscation of assets – Proceeds of Crime Act 2002

**7.12** 'Proceeds of crime' is the term given to money or assets gained by criminals from a criminal activity. The Proceeds of Crime Act 2002 gave the court powers to seek to confiscate assets to ensure that no profit is made from the criminal activity.

## *Example*

**7.13** A man who ran an illegal waste site for 15 months has been forced to sell his home to pay towards the clean-up of land off the A38 at Eggington near Burton-on–Trent. The Environment Agency took confiscation proceedings under the Proceeds of Crime Act 2002 against Robert Murphy, 49, of Carver Road, Burton-on-Trent. This followed a hearing in May 2015 at Stafford Crown Court when he was sentenced to seven months' imprisonment for operating a site he did not own or have an environmental permit for. As part of his sentence, a confiscation order was made, requiring him to pay compensation of £20,793 to the landowner. The Environment Agency was also awarded prosecution costs of £10,000. Murphy failed to make any payments and has since served an additional 12-month default sentence for his failure to comply with the confiscation order[7].

---

6   See https://www.gov.uk/government/news/ban-for-waste-management-directors-who-failed-to-comply-with-environmental-laws.
7   See https://www.gov.uk/government/news/waste-criminal-pays-up-after-proceeds-of-crime-confiscation-order.

## Criminal behaviour orders

**7.14** Criminal behaviour orders (CBOs) (formerly anti-social behaviour orders (ASBOs)) are civil orders designed to protect the public from behaviour that causes or is likely to cause harassment, alarm or distress. The order contains conditions preventing an individual from carrying out specific anti-social acts[8].

### Example

**7.15** The Environment Agency has secured its first CBO, against a self-employed builder who dumped illegal waste in a field in Somerset on numerous occasions. The builder, of Shepton Beauchamp, admitted at Taunton Crown Court to transporting, depositing and transferring waste to Wall Ditch Lane, Merriot, Somerset. Under the terms of the five-year CBO the builder must not collect, carry, transport or deposit any waste in the course of his or any other business. Also he must not use any vehicle to collect, carry, transport or deposit waste as a business. The last term of the CBO states that he must not enter on foot or in a vehicle Wall Ditch Lane or the field where the waste was dumped. If the order is breached, he will risk a prison sentence of up to five years[9].

## Forfeiture of equipment used to commit the offence

**7.16** This is the removal of the property that the offender used for the purpose of committing or facilitating the commission of the offence.

### Example

**7.17** In February 2016, Preston City Council and the Environment Agency had identified an illegal waste transfer site being operated in Preston. Enforcement officers found that a large amount of mixed waste (approximately 30 tonnes in weight) was being stored on the site in an unsafe manner. The officers also confirmed reports that there had been regular burning of waste in close proximity to local housing. This operation was linked to a skip hire business operated by the three defendants. Following the intervention of enforcement officers from Preston City Council and the Environment Agency, the waste transfer site was closed down.

---

8 The Anti-Social Behaviour Crime and Policing Act 2014 has now consolidated ASBOs and they are now called criminal behaviour orders. See the Home Office guidance – 'Anti-social Behaviour, Crime and Policing Act 2014 Statutory guidance for frontline professionals' – https://assets.publishing.service.gov.uk/government/uploads/system/uploads/attachment_data/file/679712/2017-12-13_ASB_Revised_Statutory_Guidance_V2.1_Final.pdf.
9 Unreported.

*7.17 Environmental Notices and Sanctions*

The skip hire business was then found to be linked to other fly-tipping offences, including the abandonment of skips loaded with waste. In April 2016, Preston City Council seized the skip lorry together with several of the skips used by the business. All three defendants declined to register a claim of owning the lorry and it was subsequently sold at auction.

The three defendants appeared before the Preston Magistrates' Court on 22 September 2017 where they were sentenced in respect of their respective levels of involvement in the offences committed during the operation of the skip hire business[10].

## Compensation

7.18 Compensation can be required to put right damage that has been done.

### Example

7.19 A Sunderland-based firm was ordered to pay over £14,700 for breaking environmental laws, which contributed to the illegal dumping of 585 tonnes of waste. The company ran a waste transfer station at The Parade in Hendon and was handed the fine in 2017 after pleading guilty to charges brought by the Environment Agency for failing to comply with duty of care legislation. The legislation requires businesses to ensure their waste is transferred and disposed of legally.

An investigation showed that between September 2015 and January 2016, the company paid a local man below market rates to remove waste from their site without fulfilling their legal requirement to check it was being taken to a permitted destination. The paperwork completed failed to include required details such as the origin of the waste or an accurate description. The court ruled that the company had acted recklessly. Thompson Waste Ltd was fined £3,335 and ordered to pay compensation of £5,394 and costs of £6,000[11].

## Vehicle seizure

7.20 A vehicle can be seized and impounded if it is suspected that:
- waste is being carried without a valid waste carriers licence;
- the vehicle has been or is about to be used in an alleged waste crime offence; or
- the waste duty of care is being or has been breached.

---

10 Unreported.
11 See https://www.gov.uk/government/news/sunderland-firm-fined-for-waste-offences.

## Example

**7.21** A council received evidence that a white van was used in fly-tipping incidents. A neighbourhood officer spotted the van and found it was packed with waste. The vehicle was seized, an action supported by the police in accordance with the Control of Waste (Dealing with Seized Property) (England and Wales) Regulations 2015 (SI 2015/426).

# REGULATORY ENFORCEMENT AND SANCTIONS ACT 2008

**7.22** In some cases the best outcome can be obtained by using civil sanctions made under the Regulatory Enforcement and Sanctions Act 2008 (RESA 2008). Civil sanctions are not available for all offences.

## Fixed monetary penalties (FMPs)

**7.23** In order to issue a fixed monetary penalty (FMP) the regulator must be satisfied beyond reasonable doubt that an offence has been committed. FMPs should be used for offences with minor or no direct environmental impact, such as paperwork or administrative errors.

The regulator must serve a notice of intent before payment is demanded. The person receiving the notice has the opportunity to make representations on the notice or to receive 50% off the penalty if they pay within 28 days. If payment is not made within 28 days, the regulator can serve a final notice demanding payment. If payment is not received in the period then allowed, the amount of the penalty increases by 50%. For rights of appeal see para **7.42**. The regulator cannot serve an FMP if it has already issued a variable monetary penalty (VMP), compliance notice, stop notice or restoration notice for the same incident. EA cannot start a criminal prosecution in relation to the same offence that is the subject of the FMP.

FMPs are set at:

- £300 for businesses;
- £100 for individuals.

## Variable monetary penalties (VMPs)

**7.24** A VMP is a penalty where the sum is dictated by the severity of the offence. The maximum amount that can be imposed must be lower than the

*7.24 Environmental Notices and Sanctions*

maximum which a court could impose for the same offence. The highest possible amount for a VMP is £250,000.

A VMP is only available for certain environmental offences. The regulator must be satisfied beyond reasonable doubt that an offence has been committed. It is used for more serious environmental offences, particularly where the offender has made some profit or saving by committing the offence. A VMP cannot be served if an FMP has already been issued or payment following a notice of intent has been made in respect of the same incident.

The Environment Agency (EA) must serve a notice of intent before payment is demanded. The person receiving the notice has 28 days in which to make representations or objections on the notice and/or the suggested amount of the penalty. If representations are not made within 28 days, the regulator can serve a final notice demanding payment. For rights of appeal see para 7.42. A VMP cannot be imposed on a person on more than one occasion in relation to the same act or omission. The regulator can only start a criminal prosecution in relation to the same offence that is the subject of the VMP if the offender fails to comply with the VMP. The offender can make a formal undertaking to the regulator to take certain steps or make certain payments to those affected by the offender's actions. These are known as 'third party undertakings' and the regulator can choose whether to accept such undertakings or not.

A VMP is not a criminal conviction and may save the recipient the need to pay for representation, and enable the recipient to offer a third party undertaking to make restitution to adversely affected third parties, including local communities, for example in cases where there has been more significant environmental damage but other factors indicate that imposing a VMP may be appropriate. VMPs will also be used, where appropriate, to remove an identifiable financial gain or saving resulting from the non-compliance.

## Compliance notices

7.25   These require the offender to come back into compliance. They may be used in a case where the offender has previously been in compliance with a requirement, such as regularly submitting returns, but is currently not fulfilling their obligations. The notice should ensure that the offender takes action to stop the non-compliance, addresses the underlying causes and comes back into compliance. They may be used where previous advice or guidance to encourage compliance has not been followed and a formal notice has become necessary to ensure compliance. They can be combined with a VMP and a restoration notice.

A compliance notice can only be served if the regulator is satisfied beyond reasonable doubt that an offence has been committed. This will be used when previous advice or guidance to encourage compliance has not been followed and a formal notice has become necessary. A compliance notice cannot be served if an FMP has already been issued or payment following a notice of intent has been made in respect of the same incident.

*Environmental Notices and Sanctions* **7.27**

A compliance notice may not be imposed on a person on more than one occasion in relation to the same act or omission. The regulator must first serve a notice of intent advising the offender of its intention to serve the notice and their reasons for doing so. The person receiving the notice then has 28 days in which to make representations or objections on the notice. If representations are not made within 28 days, the regulator can serve a final notice demanding the action to be taken. For rights of appeal see para **7.42**. The regulator can only start a criminal prosecution in relation to the same offence that is the subject of the compliance notice if the offender fails to comply with it. The offender can make a formal undertaking to the regulator to take certain steps or make certain payments to those affected by the offender's actions. The regulator can choose whether to accept such third party undertakings or not.

## Restoration notices

**7.26** These require the offender to take steps to put right any damage caused as a result of the non-compliance with a requirement and address any harm within a specified time frame. These notices can be used where damage has been caused to the environment and the action and work needed to address the damage can be identified and carried out by the offender.

This notice can only be served if the regulator is satisfied beyond reasonable doubt that an offence has been committed. Such notices should be expected when restoration has not been undertaken voluntarily and no other suitable enforcement notice is available. They may also be used when previous advice or guidance to encourage restoration has not been followed. A restoration notice cannot be served if an FMP has already been issued or payment following a notice of intent has been made in respect of the same incident. They can be combined with a VMP and a compliance notice.

A restoration notice may not be imposed on a person on more than one occasion in relation to the same act or omission. The regulator must first serve a notice of intent advising the offender of its intention to serve the notice and their reasons for doing so. The receiver of the notice then has 28 days in which to make representations or objections on the notice. If representations are not made within 28 days, the regulator can serve a final notice demanding the action to be taken. For rights of appeal see para **7.42**. The regulator can only start a criminal prosecution in relation to the same offence that is the subject of the restoration notice if the offender fails to comply with it. It is open for an offender to make a formal undertaking to the EA to take certain steps or make certain payments to those affected by the offender's actions. The regulator can choose whether to accept such third party undertakings or not.

## Stop notices

**7.27** A stop notice prohibits a person from carrying on a specified activity or prevents a specified activity until set steps have been taken by the offender.

7.27   *Environmental Notices and Sanctions*

A stop notice is only available for certain environmental offences. Stop Notices will be used where the regulator reasonably believes that an activity is causing, or presents a significant risk of causing, serious harm to either human health or the environment. These notices can also be served where the regulator reasonably believes that an activity involves or is likely to involve the commission of an applicable offence. A stop notice cannot be served if an FMP has already been issued or payment following a notice of intent has been made in respect of the same incident.

As a lower standard of proof is required for a stop notice to be served, it gives regulators the flexibility to use stop notices as preventative rather than reactionary measures. The stop notice must contain the reason for issue as well as other prescribed information. For rights of appeal see para **7.42**. If the notice is compiled with, the regulator must serve a compliance notice to confirm this. Failure to comply with a stop notice is a criminal offence. If the stop notice is successfully challenged or is withdrawn, the regulator could be liable to pay the recipient compensation for any losses they have incurred as a result.

A stop notice can be used in two sets of circumstances to immediately stop an activity that is causing, or presents a significant risk of:

- causing serious harm to human health or the environment and where a specified offence is being, or is likely to be, committed; or
- to immediately stop an activity that is likely to be carried on that will cause, or will present a significant risk of causing, serious harm to human health or the environment, and the activity likely to be carried on involves or will be likely to involve a specified offence being committed.

## Suspension notice

7.28   If the operation of a regulated facility involves the risk of serious pollution the regulator can serve a 'suspension notice'. This applies whether or not the operator has breached a permit condition. A suspension notice can also be served by a local authority regulator for non-payment of a charge.

The suspension notice must describe the nature of the risk of pollution and the actions necessary to remove the risk. The notice must also specify the deadline for the action. When a suspension notice is issued then the permit ceases to authorise the operation of the entire facility or specified activities depending upon what is specified in the notice. A suspension notice should allow activities to continue unless they need to cease to address the risk of pollution. When a suspension notice is in force then additional steps may need to be taken in relation to any activities that are allowed to continue. However, if this is the case then the notice must set this out. When the remedial steps have been taken that are described within the notice then the regulator must withdraw the notice.

## Challenge to a suspension notice

**7.29** In an unreported a case, a judge sitting in the High Court Queen's Bench Division (Manchester) overturned a suspension notice served in February 2012 to the international giant metal reclamation outfit EMR regarding scrap yard in Stoke on Trent. The notice in question related to levels of noise which had prompted 1,103 complaints within 12 months.

This suspension notice can only be utilised when there is a 'risk of serious pollution'. It suspends the operation of an environmental permit to the extent specified in the notice.

## Enforcement undertakings (EUs)

**7.30** An EU is a legally binding written agreement between offender and the regulator whereby the offender takes agreed steps within an agreed time limit either to stop offending or prevent further offences or to make right any harm caused by its offending. This can also be accompanied by a promise to compensate anyone who has suffered loss as a result of the offender's actions.

An EU is only available for certain environmental offences. The regulator will only accept an Enforcement Undertaking where it has reasonable grounds to suspect the person has committed a relevant offence. The regulator also needs to be confident that the terms of the EU will be delivered.

EUs are seen as an acceptance of responsibility and a willingness to make amends. Once the regulator is satisfied that the undertaking has been complied with, they can serve a compliance certificate. There is a right of appeal against any decision of the regulator not to serve a compliance certificate. Once a regulator has accepted an EU, the offender cannot be served with an FMP, VMP, compliance notice or restoration notice in respect of that act or omission unless the undertaking is not satisfied. Neither can the offender be prosecuted for the same offence, unless that person fails to comply with the undertaking. For rights of appeal see para **7.42**.

The terms of the EU may also contain an element of restoration as well as steps to ensure future compliance such as long-term investment in environmental management systems.

# NON-COMPLIANCE PENALTIES

**7.31** The process of enforcement differs between the different sanctions.

## FMP, VMP or other monetary penalty

**7.32** Where an FMP or VMP has been imposed and the person has failed to pay it, no prosecution can be brought for the original offence and unpaid

*7.32 Environmental Notices and Sanctions*

penalties will be enforced through the civil courts. Orders allow regulators to recover unpaid sums in the same way as going to a county court or High Court. The regulator will also be able to recover unpaid enforcement cost recovery notices and non-compliance penalties in the same way.

## Enforcement undertakings

7.33 Should there be a failure to comply with an EU or only a partial compliance, the regulator has the choice as to whether it:

- extends the period of the enforcement undertaking;
- imposes a different civil sanction; or
- pursues a criminal prosecution for the original offence.

7.34 If there has been partial compliance, this will be taken into account in deciding whether to prosecute. If the person involved provides misleading or inaccurate information, they will have been deemed to have not complied with the undertaking, and the regulator can then decide whether to impose a civil sanction or pursue a prosecution.

## Restoration notice or compliance notice imposed without VMP

7.35 Failing to comply with either of these notices would normally result in a prosecution unless there are strong mitigating factors. Where there are mitigating factors, a non-compliance penalty notice (NCP) can be served.

## Non-compliance penalty notice (NCP)

7.36 This is a written notice issued by the regulator which is imposing the monetary penalty. The original restoration notice, compliance notice or third party undertaking remain outstanding and should it be a continued non-compliance the regulator will be able to prosecute for the original offence, whether or not the NCP is paid.

## Restoration notice or compliance notice imposed with a VMP or a third party undertaking accepted by the regulator

7.37 When a restoration notice imposed with a VMP is not complied with, no prosecution is allowed as the VMP provides immunity. The regulator can, however, impose an NCP notice (NCP). An NCP would also be needed if the person has failed to fulfil a third party undertaking it has made. The restoration notice, compliance notice or third party undertaking would remain in force.

## Stop notices

7.38  As a stop notice is issued for a serious situation, non-compliance would normally result in a criminal prosecution.

# OTHER OPTIONS
## Enforcement cost recovery notices

7.39  These unpaid notices are pursued through the civil courts.

## Application of NCPs

7.40  The regulator determines the amount of the NCP by looking at the original notice or third party undertaking and calculating a percentage of the costs of the outstanding requirements. This percentage can be up to 100% dependent on the circumstances of the case. The monies gained from the NCP are not retained by the regulator but paid into the consolidated fund. A consolidated fund is the main bank account of the government.

There is no notice of intent as the consequences of non-compliance with the original civil sanction would have been set out when the final restoration or compliance notice was served, or third party undertaking accepted. There are 28 days to pay the NCP unless the regulator stipulates a longer period. Should the compliance notice, restoration notice or third party undertaking be complied with during the NCP payment period, the penalty does not have to be paid. There are no late payment charges. The regulator has the power to withdraw or vary the notice if it finds grounds to do so.

When serving an NCP, the notice must contain the following information:

- the grounds for imposing the notice;
- the amount to be paid;
- the period within which the amount must be paid;
- if appropriate, the circumstances, such as partial completion of the necessary work, that may lead the regulator to reduce the NCP, or withdraw and extend the period of the NCP;
- how payment should be made;
- rights of appeal;
- the consequences of failing to comply with the notice; and
- a revised time period in which the original notice must be complied with.

As with unpaid monetary penalties, if a person fails to pay an NCP for non-compliance with a compliance notice, restoration notice or third party undertaking combined with a VMP, then regulators may enforce through the civil courts.

7.41   *Environmental Notices and Sanctions*

# CLIMATE CHANGE REGIMES

7.41   The climate change regimes (CRC Energy Efficiency Scheme, the EU Emissions Trading System, the Climate Change Agreements Scheme and the Energy Savings Opportunity Scheme) have a different civil sanctions framework. In relation to the Landfill Allowance scheme, the legislation requires suspected non-compliance to be reported to the Secretary of State.

# APPEALS

## Environment tribunal

7.42   The Hampton and Macrory reviews brought about the introduction of a civil sanction in the Regulatory Enforcement and Sanctions Act 2008 (RESA 2008), Pt 3. This enactment resulted in the First Tier Tribunal (Environment) (General Regulatory Chamber) (established in 2010 and known as the 'Environmental Tribunal') which hears appeals against the imposition of civil sanctions as required by the RESA 2008. The tribunal only deals with appeals against civil sanctions and not criminal offences.

## Who sits on the tribunal?

7.43   The Environmental Tribunal has six legally qualified judges and ten non-legal members. Panels consist of the tribunal judge and two other members. A list of members can be found on the Department of Justice's website[12].

## What can be appealed against?

7.44   A fine or a notice for an environment offence imposed by:

- Environment Agency;
- Natural England;
- Department for Environment, Food and Rural Affairs;
- National Measurement Office;
- local flood authorities;
- Department of Energy and Climate Change;
- Department of Enterprise, Trade and Investment;
- Welsh ministers;
- local authorities in England and Wales;
- Marine Management Organisation.

---

12   See https://www.gov.uk/guidance/environmental-fines-or-notices-appeal-against-a-regulator.

# Grounds for appeal

## Fixed monetary penalty (FMP)

**7.45** Grounds for appeal[13]:

- decision to impose a FMP was based on an error of fact;
- the decision was wrong in law;
- the decision was unreasonable;
- for any other reason.

## Variable monetary penalty (VMP)

**7.46** Grounds for appeal[14]:

- the decision to impose a VMP was based on an error of fact;
- the decision was wrong in law;
- the amount of the penalty is unreasonable; and
- the decision was unreasonable;
- for any other reason.

## Stop notice

**7.47** Grounds for appeal[15]:

- the decision to impose a stop notice was based on an error of fact;
- the decision was wrong in law;
- the decision was unreasonable;
- any step specified in the stop notice is unreasonable;
- the person has not committed the relevant offence and would not have committed it had the stop notice not been served; and
- that the person would not, by reason of any defence, have been liable to be convicted of the relevant offence had the stop notice not been served;
- for any other reason.

## Compliance/restoration notice

**7.48** Grounds for appeal[16]:

---

13 VMP grounds for appeal – see the Environmental Civil Sanctions (England) Order 2010 (SI 2010/1157), Sch 1, para 8; Environmental Civil Sanctions (Wales) Order 2010 (SI 2010/1821), Sch 1, para 8.
14 VMP grounds for appeal – see SI 2010/1157, Sch 2, para 8; SI 2010/1821, Sch 2, para 8.
15 Stop notice grounds for appeal – see SI 2010/1157, Sch 3, para 3; SI 2010/1821, Sch 3, para 3.
16 VMP grounds for appeal – see SI 2010/1157, Sch 2, para 8; SI 2010/1821, Sch 2, para 8.

*7.48 Environmental Notices and Sanctions*

- the decision to impose a compliance/restoration notice was based on an error of fact;
- the decision was wrong in law;
- the nature of the requirement is unreasonable and the decision was unreasonable for any other reason;
- for any other reason.

## Tribunal powers

7.49 The Environmental Tribunal may[17]:

- withdraw the requirement or notice;
- confirm the requirement or notice;
- vary the requirement or notice;
- take such steps as the regulator could take in relation to the act or omission giving rise to the requirement or notice;
- remit the decision whether to confirm the requirement or notice, or any matter relating to that decision, to the regulator.

17 See SI 2010/1157, Pt 4, art 10 (appeals); SI 2010/1821, Pt 4, art 10 (appeals).

# Chapter 8

# Fire Safety Offences and Notices

Introduction   8.1
Legislation   8.2
    England and Wales   8.3
        Responsible person requirements   8.4
    Scotland   8.5
    Northern Ireland   8.6
    Fire certificates   8.7
Requirements of the Regulatory Reform (Fire Safety) Order 2005   8.8
    Fire risk assessment   8.9
    Fire extinguishers   8.10
    Fire safety signs   8.11
    Fire alarm systems   8.12
    Emergency lighting   8.13
    Fire safety training   8.14
Enforcement   8.15
    Fire and Rescue Service   8.16
        England and Wales Fire and Rescue Services and the Primary Authority Scheme   8.17
    Local authority   8.20
    Health and Safety Executive   8.21
    Crown Fire Inspectors   8.22
Fire inspections   8.23
Public register of notices   8.24
    Public register   8.25
        Viewing the public register of notices   8.26
Enforcement options for England, Wales and Scotland   8.27
    Notices   8.28
        Alteration notice   8.29
        Enforcement notice   8.30
        Prohibition notice   8.32
        Notices under the RRO, art 37 (fire fighters' switches for luminous tube signs)   8.35
    Prosecution   8.36
    Factors which affect choice of enforcement action   8.37
Examples of prosecutions   8.38
    Companies   8.38
    Individual fire safety prosecutions   8.39
    Responsible person prosecution   8.40
Appeals   8.41

**8.1** *Fire Safety Offences and Notices*

      England and Wales  8.41
      Scotland  8.42
      Northern Ireland  8.43
        Action plan  8.44
Determinations  8.45
      England and Wales  8.45
        Example  8.46
        Applying for a determination  8.47
      Scotland  8.48
        When a determination can be made  8.49
        Making an application  8.50

# INTRODUCTION

**8.1** There has generally been a significant increase in the level of fines imposed for fire safety breaches and a growing trend to impose prison sentences on individuals with the responsibility for ensuring compliance with fire safety law.

In England during 2015/16[1] there were 63,000 fire safety audits carried out, which is 7% more than the previous year but 25% lower than five years before. Many prosecutions have been imposed due to the poor quality of fire risk assessments carried out by some fire risk assessors. Previously the UK was covered by many pieces of fire safety legislation, the main legislation being the Fire Precautions Act 1971; the Fire Precautions (Workplace) Regulations 1997[2]; and the Fire Precautions (Workplace) (Amendment) Regulations 1999[3]. In 2001 it was decided that the legislation needed to be simplified and therefore new legislation was introduced.

# LEGISLATION

**8.2** Significant changes were made to fire legislation in 2005 and 2006 with the introduction of the Regulatory Reform (Fire Safety) Order 2005 (RRO)[4] which covers England and Wales, and the Fire (Scotland) Act 2005 supported by the Fire Safety (Scotland) Regulations 2006[5].

---

1    Fire and Rescue Authorities: operational statistics bulletin for England 2015 to 2016. https://www.gov.uk/government/uploads/system/uploads/attachment_data/file/563118/fire-rescue-operational-statistics-201516-hosb1216.pdf.
2    SI 1997/1840.
3    SI 1999/1877.
4    SI 2005/1541.
5    SI 2005/1541.

The Fire and Rescue Services (Northern Ireland) Order 2006[6] and the Fire Safety Regulations (Northern Ireland) 2010[7] cover fire safety in Northern Ireland.

There are some differences between the legislation.

## England and Wales

8.3    In England and Wales, the RRO requires that the responsible person, on which the order imposes requirements, must make a suitable and sufficient assessment of the risks to which the relevant persons are exposed for the purpose of identifying the general fire precautions that need to be taken to comply with the requirements and prohibitions imposed on them by or under this regime.

A 'responsible person'[8] means:

- in relation to a workplace, the employer, if the workplace is under their control;
- if the premises are not a workplace, the person who has control of the premises (as occupier or otherwise) in connection with the carrying on by them of a trade, business or other undertaking (for profit or not); or
- where the person in control of the premises does not have control in this way, the 'responsible person' is deemed to be the owner.

### Responsible person requirements

8.4    The RRO[9] requires that the responsible person takes 'general fire precautions'. This includes: measures to reduce the risk of fire on the premises, including safe escape routes and emergency escape lighting; measures in relation to fire fighting; and measures in relation to the detection of fire and the ability to warn of fire. Therefore, 'general fire precautions' are not simply restricted to fire precautions identified under other articles in the legislation. Some of the duties and responsibilities of the 'responsible person' are as follows:

- to make suitable and sufficient risk assessments of the risks that people may be exposed to. This assessment is to identify the general fire precautions that are needed to comply with the requirements and prohibition imposed on them under the order;
- ensure that the premises are, to the extent that it is appropriate, fitted with fire detectors and alarms;
- to evacuate the building in the event of danger, (ie fire) as quickly and safely as possible;

---

6    SI 2006/1254.
7    SI 2006/456.
8    Regulatory Reform (Fire Safety) Order 2005, art 3.
9    Regulatory Reform (Fire Safety) Order 2005, art 8(1).

8.4 *Fire Safety Offences and Notices*

- to ensure emergency doors are not locked or fastened so that they cannot be easily and immediately opened by someone escaping a fire;
- where necessary, provide emergency escape lighting within fire escape routes so that in the event of a fire and the failure of normal lighting, the escape routes can be illuminated;
- where necessary ensure that the facilities and any equipment and devices provided at the premises are subject to a suitable system of maintenance and are maintained in an efficient state, working order and in good repair.

## Scotland

8.5 In Scotland the duty to carry out a fire risk assessment is imposed on every employer by the Fire (Scotland) Act 2005, s 53(2)(a). The Act requires that the risk assessment identifies any risks to the safety of the employers and employees in respect of harm caused by fire in the workplace. The Act also imposes a duty, on any person who has control to any extent of the relevant premises, to carry out a fire risk assessment, and this risk assessment must identify any risks to any relevant persons in respect of harm that could be caused by fire in the relevant premises. 'Relevant persons' are defined in much the same manner as in the RRO in England and Wales. In Scotland, further requirements in respect of the assessments required by the Fire (Scotland) Act 2005 are imposed by the Fire Safety (Scotland) Regulations 2006. Guidance on the requirements of this legislation and the required fire risk assessment is published by the Scottish government.

## Northern Ireland

8.6 In Northern Ireland, the responsibility for fire safety in the workplace rests with the employer and those with any degree of control of premises (deemed the 'appropriate person').

The appropriate person must take steps to:

- reduce the risk from fire;
- ensure people are able to escape safely if there is a fire.

In Northern Ireland the requirements for the assessments are identical to those in Scotland, but are imposed by the Fire and Rescue Services (Northern Ireland) Order 2006, arts 25(2)(a) and 26(2)(a). Guidance is available from the Department of Health, Social Services, and Public Safety (in Northern Ireland).

## Fire certificates

8.7 Under the later legislation any fire certificate issued under the Fire Precautions Act 1971 ceases to have any effect. However, a fire risk assessment must be carried out for all premises and be kept up to date. Premises may also be subject to the provisions of a licence or registration (eg under the Licensing Act 2003). In that case the fire authority may wish to review the risk assessment as part of the requirements under the Licensing Act 2003.

# REQUIREMENTS OF THE REGULATORY REFORM (FIRE SAFETY) ORDER 2005

**8.8** The legislation under the RRO[10] will apply in relation to a workplace which is to any extent under the control of the employer and if it is in relation to a premises the person who has control over the premises. Under the Fire (Scotland) Act 2005 similar duties for employers apply.

Domestic premises do not generally fall within the scope of the RRO or that of the Fire (Scotland) Act 2005, but there are exceptions which include those requiring a licence under the houses in multiple occupation mandatory licensing scheme, and care home premises.

A person having a degree of control over premises covered by the fire safety regime is likely to have some responsibility for fire safety but this responsibility will be in direct proportion to their level of control ie the more control, the greater the responsibility.

Additionally, an employer will always retain responsibility for the safety of his or her employees.

It is important to note that more than one person can have fire safety responsibilities for the premises. For example, an employer, owner, landlord, tenant or a contractor carrying out repair work may each have fire safety responsibilities for the premises and will be required to co-operate with each other and co-ordinate their fire safety measures.

The overriding duty is to ensure, so far as is reasonably practicable, safety in respect of harm that could be caused by fire in the workplace. The overriding duty is supplemented by a number of prescriptive duties:

- to carry out a fire safety risk assessment of the premises. If there are five or more employees the risk assessment must be recorded in writing;
- to identify the fire safety measures necessary as a result of the fire safety risk assessment;
- to implement these fire safety measures using risk reduction principles – avoiding the risk so far as possible; combating the risk at source; adapting technical processes; developing a coherent overall fire prevention policy which covers technology and the organisation of work;
- to inform employees of the fire safety risks and provide fire safety training;

---

10 Regulatory Reform (Fire Safety) Order 2005, Pt 1, art 3.

8.8   *Fire Safety Offences and Notices*

- to co-ordinate and co-operate with other duty-holders in the same premises in relation to fire safety;
- to review the risk assessment if there is a significant change to the premises or the work, or if there is any other reason to suspect that the risk assessment is no longer valid.

## Fire risk assessment

8.9   All businesses must have carried out a fire risk assessment. This is the basis of fire protection in the business and, along with the fire safety log book, is one of the first things that a fire inspector will ask to see.

The fire risk assessment does not have to be written down unless there are five or more employees, however it is useful to have it documented for easy reference.

The fire risk assessment must:

- be reviewed regularly;
- be documented if:
    - there are five or more employees in the business; or
    - the premises require a licence; or
    - the fire brigade has issued an alterations notice stating that it must be documented. The fire risk assessment document must record main findings and any action to be taken.

It is not necessary to use a professional to carry out the fire risk assessment, however if that person is not a professional, the person who carries out a fire risk assessment must be able to:

- correctly identify the potential causes of fire in the business;
- identify the people at risk;
- assess the suitability of fire safety measures in place, such as fire alarm systems and escape routes;
- assess the ongoing management of fire safety in the business, such as fire drills and staff training;
- develop a fire safety action plan if changes are needed;
- record all the significant findings;
- implement the action plan if one is needed;
- keep the fire risk assessment updated on an ongoing basis.

## Fire extinguishers

8.10   UK fire safety legislation states that a business must provide 'appropriate fire-fighting equipment'. This usually means portable fire extinguishers, but some businesses may also have sprinklers. Fire extinguishers must:

- be the right type for the business and location;
- be maintained in good working order;
- undergo an annual maintenance test;
- be maintained by a 'competent' person; and
- may need to be certified to industry standards.

## Fire safety signs

**8.11** Most businesses will need at least two signs (a fire action notice, and an extinguisher ID sign). Other signage includes:

- fire action notice – explains what to do in case of fire and is mandatory for all premises;
- fire extinguisher ID sign – explains and locates each type of extinguisher and is mandatory for all premises;
- fire exit signs – show how to exit the premises in case of fire. These are needed for all but the smallest and simplest of properties;
- fire alarm call point signs – identify where to activate the fire alarm. These are mandatory if there is an alarm on the premises;
- other fire equipment signs – for example signposting the presence and location of a hose reel or a dry riser;
- warning and prohibition signs – used to highlight danger.

## Fire alarm systems

**8.12** A fire alarm system may not be needed if a business is operating out of small premises, such as a shop, where it would be possible to see a fire developing, and a shout of 'FIRE' would be heard throughout the premises.

However, for some higher-risk businesses, such as restaurants, it is recommended to install alarms as an extra safeguard.

According to UK fire safety legislation, all other businesses must have an appropriate fire detection system. This means:

- either a manual or an automatic system;
- an automatic system if it is likely that a fire could go undetected;
- everyone in the building must be able to hear the alarm clearly – if people have a disability which would make this difficult then other provisions must be made;
- there must be an alarm call point by every exit on every floor.

Also:

- the fire detection system must be maintained in good working order;
- there must be a weekly fire alarm test;
- the fire alarm must be serviced at least every six months;

**8.12** *Fire Safety Offences and Notices*

- the person who carries out the testing and maintenance must be competent.

## Emergency lighting

**8.13** The RRO[11] specifies the requirements for emergency lighting in emergency routes and exits which require illumination with an adequate intensity in the case of failure of normal lighting. The Fire Safety (Scotland) Regulations 2006 similarly require emergency lighting[12]. In the UK the lighting must conform to the British Standard. There are three main purposes of emergency lighting:

- escape route lighting – illuminates exit routes and helps occupants find fire-fighting equipment in a fire;
- open area lighting – also called 'panic lighting'. Keeps communal areas lit in a fire to reduce panic;
- high-risk task area lighting – provides light to shut down potentially dangerous processes in the event of a fire.

The latest British Standard recommends a three-hour emergency lighting test once a year, during which the main light circuit should be switched off and the emergency lights left on for a three-hour period, to test if any fail to work for the full duration. The three-hour time window is to allow the fire brigade time to work in the event of a fire once all of the building's occupants have been safely evacuated.

## Fire safety training

**8.14** Everyone on the premises should know what to do in the event of fire and new employees must be shown what to do when joining a business. Also:

- refresher training should be delivered regularly – typically this is annually;
- fire safety training updates are needed if there are any changes such as building alterations;
- fire drills should be carried out; and
- fire marshals or wardens should be appointed to do the following in case of an alarm:
    - use fire extinguishers where appropriate;
    - make contact with the emergency services;
    - assist with the evacuation.

---

11  Regulatory Reform (Fire Safety) Order 2005, Pt 2, art 14(2)(h).
12  Fire Safety (Scotland) Regulations 2006, SI 2006/456, Pt III, reg 13(2)(h).

# ENFORCEMENT

**8.15** For the majority of premises, the local fire and rescue authorities are responsible for enforcing the fire safety legislation. The Health and Safety Executive (HSE) has enforcement responsibility for construction sites, nuclear premises and on ships under construction or undergoing repair.

Premises covered by the fire safety regime may be inspected or audited by an enforcement officer to ensure compliance with the law. An enforcement officer has the power to enter and inspect premises at any reasonable time and they may also look at facilities, information, documents and records. The enforcing officer must be given any assistance required with regard to facilities, information, documents, records, or any other assistance needed.

If the enforcing officer is dissatisfied with the outcome of the fire safety risk assessment or the action taken, they may:

- serve a notice specifying the actions to be taken to comply with the law within a prescribed period (at least 28 days); or
- if they consider there to be a serious fire risk, issue a prohibition notice that restricts the use of all or part of the premises until improvements are made; or
- serve a notice requiring the premises to be physically altered.

These enforcement notices can be appealed, but any appeal must be made within 21 days of the notice being served.

## Fire and Rescue Service

**8.16** The Fire and Rescue Service (FRS), operating through the local fire authority, is the primary enforcer of the RRO. Similarly, under the Fire (Scotland) Act 2005, the Scottish Fire and Rescue Service (SFRS) have similar responsibilities. They can undertake audits and issue enforcement orders to any premises within the area of the authority.

### England and Wales Fire and Rescue Services and the Primary Authority Scheme

**8.17** From 6 April 2014 FRSs in England and Wales have been able to enter into partnerships with businesses, charities or other organisations which operate across more than one local authority fire enforcement area – becoming their single point of contact for fire safety regulation advice.

The aim of the Primary Authority Scheme is for FRSs to develop effective partnerships with businesses in order to achieve a national consistency in delivering fire safety enforcement advice. The scheme will also allow fire authorities to recover costs from its partner organisations.

8.18 *Fire Safety Offences and Notices*

**Elements of Primary Authority Schemes**

8.18 The main elements of Primary Authority Schemes are as follows:
- to provide reliable and consistent regulatory advice that a business requires in relation to fire safety;
- when a FRS has concerns about how a business, which has a Primary Authority partnership with a different FRS, is complying with fire safety regulations, it will at an early stage discuss the issue with the Primary Authority;
- if a FRS believes that there is a statutory requirement for taking enforcement action it will notify the Primary Authority of the action it proposes to take. In some cases there will be a need for enforcement action to start immediately, for example, where action is needed urgently to ensure the safety of employees or members of the public;
- where actions of a business may be subject to an enforcement action by a FRS, the business's Primary Authority will advise the FRS on whether it has given the relevant fire safety advice to the business and whether the enforcement action would be consistent with that advice.

**Who can enter into a Primary Authority Scheme?**

8.19 The Primary Authority Scheme can include any business, charity or other organisation that is regulated by two or more FRSs under the RRO. A Primary Authority Scheme will benefit businesses with premises in a number of local authority areas. It is possible for a business to choose which FRS will be the Primary Authority Scheme and this does not have to be the one nearest to the head office or in the county where the business has the greatest number of outlets.

# Local authority

8.20 Domestic buildings which include housing association accommodation and blocks of flats are the responsibility of the Environmental Health Office for the enforcement of fire safety. This also applies to sports grounds and any premises which require a fire safety certificate issued by the local authority. The principles of enforcement are the same as for the FRS.

# Health and Safety Executive

8.21 The Health and Safety Executive (HSE) is responsible for enforcing fire safety precautions on all off-shore installations, nuclear sites, ships under construction and underground mines. The HSE is also the enforcing authority for fire safety on construction sites.

## Crown Fire Inspectors

**8.22** The Crown Fire Inspectors are responsible for enforcing the RRO in Crown premises.

# FIRE INSPECTIONS

**8.23** Fire and Rescue Services (FRSs) conduct regular inspections on high-risk non-domestic premises to ensure that they comply with the fire regulations. There are a number of reasons why the authority may be prompted to make an inspection:

- following a fire;
- following a complaint relating to fire safety on the premises;
- following an unwanted signal from 'problem premises';
- information received from other enforcing authorities;
- because it was requested;
- as part of a risk-based re-inspection programme.

The fire inspector will check the workplace, the activities that are undertaken and the management of fire safety. They will also audit the fire risk assessment to ensure that it is complying with the fire safety law.

The inspection programme is based on risk assessed principles and high-risk premises are mainly those premises that have sleeping accommodation such as hotels, hostels, and residential homes. Other premises may come to their attention if they are involved in fire or brought to their attention by other people.

During an inspection visit, a check is made of the arrangements that are in place for consulting and informing employees or their representatives, for example safety representatives, about fire safety matters.

During the inspection employees and their representative may be spoken to, unless this is clearly inappropriate because of the purpose of the visit. When they meet, employees or their representatives should always be given the opportunity to speak privately to the enforcement officer if they so wish.

In Scotland the enforcing officer may also report any breaches to the Procurator Fiscal for prosecution. Failure to comply with a notice issued by the enforcing authority, or placing persons at risk by failing to carry out any duty imposed by fire safety law, is an offence punishable by up to two years' imprisonment or an unlimited fine.

The fire safety regime has adopted an approach similar to the health and safety regime under the Health and Safety at Work etc Act 1974 (HSWA 1974). Health and safety is enforced with thousands of enforcement notices served and prosecutions brought every year.

8.24 *Fire Safety Offences and Notices*

# PUBLIC REGISTER OF NOTICES

8.24   The national enforcement registers are where an FRS[13] can publicly display the details of enforcement action taken in line with its statutory responsibilities:

- the enforcement register – this register details enforcement, prohibition and alteration notices that have been served on business premises under the Regulatory Reform (Fire Safety) Order 2005;
- the prosecution register – this register details prosecutions taken in relation to breaches of the RRO.

The registers provide interested parties with the ability to access details of enforcement actions taken by a FRS.

Notices included on the register are as follows:

Under the RRO:

- alterations notices;
- enforcement notices;
- prohibition/restriction notices.

Under the HSWA 1974:

- section 21 improvement notices;
- section 22 prohibition notices.

## Public register

8.25   Notices appear in the enforcement register database for a period of five years. Notices served on individuals under the age of 18 will be removed earlier. Notices which are subject to appeal are not included.

### *Viewing the public register of notices*

8.26   The register can be found on the Chief Fire Officers Association website:

**England and Wales:**

Enforcement Register – see http://www.cfoa.org.uk/11823

Prosecution Register – see http://www.cfoa.org.uk/15251

**Northern Ireland:**

See https://www.nifrs.org/firesafe/register.php

---

13   Fire and Rescue Services duty under the Environment and Safety Information Act 1988.

# ENFORCEMENT OPTIONS FOR ENGLAND, WALES AND SCOTLAND

8.27  Under the RRO there are four kinds of notice which a fire authority may serve.

A notification of fire safety deficiencies identifies provisions and or procedures, which the regulatory authority considers as either lacking or not suitable and sufficient in regards to the premises.

This notice carries no statutory force but may result in formal action being considered if agreed improvements do not take place to bring the premises up to minimal standards. The notice should indicate that failure to comply with any requirement of the legislation is an offence and the person responsible is liable to prosecution.

The enforcement agency can verify the required standards of any required improvements and can ensure that full discussion takes place and that all options are considered, and agreed, by all involved parties before any proposals are formulated.

Although the notice and attached schedule will be issued without prejudice to any legal action which may subsequently be taken regarding the perceived failures to comply with the RRO legislation, the FRS routinely 'copy in' relevant third party organisations including governing bodies, licensing authorities, ruling councils, an association, institution and/or commission. This in itself could bring about further action.

The four 'relevant notices' are as follows:

- alteration notice;
- enforcement notice;
- prohibition notice;
- fire fighters' cut-off switch notice.

A 'relevant notice' is any notice issued by any enforcing authority which is required by the Environment and Safety Information Act 1988 to be entered into the public register of notices.

## Notices

8.28  All notices contain some basic details:

- address to which the notice applies;
- borough or area that the premises are situated in;
- property type;
- date of the notice;
- notice type;

8.28 *Fire Safety Offences and Notices*

- name and address on whom the notice has been served;
- responsibility of the person on whom the notice was served;
- applicable legislation;
- date of expiry of the notice;
- date remedial works completed.

## Alteration notice[14]

8.29 There are two purposes of an alteration notice:

- it is intended to assist the enforcing authorities in maintaining a risk-based inspection programme as it highlights the premises where there is a potentially high risk to life and where the levels of risk may change depending on the result of the fire risk assessment;
- it informs the responsible person (and anyone else with a duty in regard to the premises) that the enforcing authority considers the premises to be a high or potentially high-risk premises.

An alterations notice may be issued if the premises have high safety risks or will have high safety risks if the use of the premises changes. An alterations notice requires the responsible person to notify the enforcing authority of any proposed changes (alterations) to the premises to which the notice applies. They are issued when the inspector:

- considers that the premises constitute a serious risk to a relevant person (either due to the features of the premises, their use, any hazard present or any other circumstances) or may constitute a risk if changes are made.

An alterations notice does not mean that the responsible person has failed to comply with the RRO.

## Enforcement notice[15]

8.30 An enforcement notice can only be issued when the enforcing authority believes that the responsible person has failed to comply with any provision of the RRO (or any regulation made under it). They may be issued if the fire and rescue authority finds a serious risk that is not being managed. It will state what improvements are needed and specify a time period for compliance. This is a document sent to the responsible person by a FRS stating that the enforcing authority (fire service) is of the opinion that the responsible person or any other person as applicable has failed to comply with the provision of the RRO or any of the regulations under it.

---

14   Alterations notice under the Regulatory Reform (Fire Safety) Order 2005, art 29.
15   Enforcement notice under the Regulatory Reform (Fire Safety) Order 2005, art 30.

Example of an enforcement notice

**8.31** Regulatory Reform (Fire Safety) Order 2005, art 20
Schedule

| Article | Details of failure to comply with order | Necessary steps to comply with order |
|---|---|---|
| Article 9 | Failure to review the fire risk assessment. | Implement regular programme to review fire risk assessment. |
| Article 11 | Failure in the effective management of the preventive and protective measures. | Implement arrangement for the effective planning, organisation, control, monitoring and review of the preventive and protective measures. |
| Article 14 | Failure to provide and/or maintain adequate and clearly indicated emergency routes and exits that lead to a place of safety. | Ensure that adequate escape routes and exits leading to a place of safety are provided and that these are maintained clear and available for use at all times that the premises is occupied. |
| Article 21 | Failure to ensure employees receive adequate safety training. | Implement/review training programme to ensure employees receive adequate safety training. |

## Prohibition notice[16]

**8.32** These take effect immediately if the FRS considers that the fire risk is so great that access to the premises needs to be prohibited or restricted. A prohibition notice is issued where the use of the premises may constitute an imminent risk of death or serious injury to the persons using them. This may be a restriction of use, for example imposing a maximum number of persons allowed in the premises, or a prohibition of a specific use of all or part of the premises, for example prohibiting the use of specific floors or rooms for sleeping accommodation.

The issue of a prohibition notice under the Regulatory Reform (Fire Safety) Order 2005 is the most serious enforcement option available to the FRS other than prosecution and can only be authorised by identified senior officers.

---

16 Prohibition notice under the Regulatory Reform (Fire Safety) Order 2005, art 31.

## 8.33 Fire Safety Offences and Notices

Example of a prohibition notice

**8.33 Applicable legislation: Regulatory Reform (Fire Safety) Order 2005, art 31**

| Article | Details of failure to comply with order | Necessary steps to comply with order |
| --- | --- | --- |
| Article 13 | Failure to provide a suitable method of giving warning in case of fire. | Provide a suitable method of giving warning in case of fire. |
| Article 14 | Failure to provide and/or maintain adequate and clearly indicated emergency routes and exits that lead to a place of safety. | Ensure that adequate escape routes and exits leading to a place of safety are provided and that these are maintained clear and available for use at all times that the premises is occupied. |

**Improvement and prohibition notices under the Health and Safety at Work etc Act 1974**

8.34 The Petroleum Enforcing Authority (PEA) is the enforcing authority within its area. For example the London Fire Brigade (LFB) is the enforcing authority for London and is responsible for ensuring those that keep and dispense petrol do not cause a risk to the public or the environment and are compliant with the Dangerous Substances and Explosive Atmospheres Regulations 2002[17]. The Petroleum (Consolidation) Regulations 2014[18] (P(C)R) are in force and replaced the petroleum licensing system with the Petroleum Storage Certificate (PSC). If a petroleum licensee fails to comply with the licence conditions an improvement notice may be served detailing corrective measures that they are legally obliged to complete within a set timescale.

If an inspector discovers premises being used as a petrol filling station that may constitute an imminent risk of death or serious injury to persons, a prohibition notice may be issued prohibiting activities or the use of equipment associated with the storage of petrol.

## Notices under the RRO, art 37 (fire fighters' switches for luminous tube signs)

8.35 This applies to luminous tube signs designed to work at a voltage normally exceeding the prescribed voltage, or other equipment so designed,

---

17 SI 2002/2776.
18 SI 2014/1637.

and references to a cut-off switch apply where a transformer is provided to raise the voltage to operate the apparatus.

Under the RRO, art 37(1), the 'prescribed voltage' means:

'(a) 1000 volts AC or 1500 volts DC if measured between any two conductors, or
(b) 600 volts AC or 900 volts DC if measured between a conductor and earth.'

It is an offence if:

- any failure by the 'responsible person' to provide notification to the FRS regarding existing or proposed installation;
- there is any failure by the 'responsible person' to comply with the requirements of a notice issued by the FRS in the time specified as above.

Any person guilty of an offence under the above is liable on summary conviction to a fine not exceeding level 3 on the standard scale.

## Prosecution

**8.36** Prosecution is considered where, for example, there is failure to comply with the fire safety duties imposed by the RRO and that 'failure has put one or more RRO relevant persons at risk of death or serious injury in case of fire'. In addition, if there has been a failure to comply with any requirement or restriction imposed by a notice issued under the RRO, then consideration will be given to prosecution. If the recommendation is to pursue a prosecution, then the enforcing authority will prepare the legal bundle ready for court.

## Factors which affect choice of enforcement action

**8.37** Each FRS has an enforcement policy statement which includes a number of factors which enforcement officers will consider when deciding which course of action to take:

- the seriousness of the alleged offence;
- the previous history of the party concerned;
- the likelihood of the defendant being able to establish a satisfactory defence, such as 'due diligence' and all reasonable precautions;
- the willingness of the party to prevent a recurrence of the problem;
- whether there is satisfactory evidence;
- any relevant explanation offered by the affected party;
- the probable public benefit of the action and the importance of the case, such as whether a prosecution might establish legal precedent in other companies or nationally.

8.38 *Fire Safety Offences and Notices*

# EXAMPLES OF PROSECUTIONS
## Companies

8.38

**New Look**

New Look received the maximum possible fine of £400,000 following a fire that gutted the Oxford Street store in 2007. It required 35 fire engines and 135 fire fighters to tackle the blaze and the crews remained on the scene for three days. New Look pleaded guilty to two breaches of the RRO following prosecution by the London Fire Brigade, namely:

- insufficient staff training;
- storage blocking escape routes.

**Shell International**

Shell was fined over significant failings in fire safety at the Shell centre in central London. Shell pleaded guilty to three breaches of the RRO. Fire officers found extensive breaches including:

- blocked fire escapes;
- blocked fire exits;
- defective fire doors;
- excessive fire loading.

**The Co-operative Group**

The Co-operative Group was in court in Southampton for six breaches under the RRO. It was fined £210,000 for:

- failing to maintain the rear emergency exit doors;
- a fitted lock requiring a security code on the emergency door;
- fire alarm call point obstruction;
- failing to ensure that the store manager was provided with suitable and sufficient fire safety training;
- failing to ensure that the fire alarm system was being regularly tested;
- failing to ensure a means of early detection of fire.

## Individual fire safety prosecutions

8.39 The law also enables the prosecution of private fire risk assessors who fail to provide adequate fire risk assessment reports. For example, the unreported case of Mr Craig Stonelake, who pleaded guilty in March 2015 for failure to provide an adequate fire risk assessment report for a large restaurant in Newton Abbot. He was fined £7,000 for failing in his duty to undertake this work to an appropriate standard, which placed people using the premises at the risk of death or serious injury in the event of a fire occurring.

Another serious offence can be seen in the unreported case of Lui and O'Rourke in 2011. One was an external fire risk assessor and the other a hotel operator who were both jailed for eight months after admitting multiple breaches of the RRO. In addition, fines issued across the pair amounted to £20,000.

## Responsible person prosecution

8.40    In *R v Mirza (Zulfiqar Baig)*[19] the person owned a small business selling furniture, household electrical goods and flooring. The business premises were inspected and routes to exits were found to be obstructed, a fire door was obstructed and deadlocked, there was inadequate signage and no emergency lighting. There had been an enforcement notice issued and the person had failed to fully comply with it despite the fact that two extensions of time had been granted. The original sentence was one of three months' custody, suspended. He was also ordered to carry out 200 hours of unpaid work and pay prosecution costs of £2,000. On appeal a suspended custodial sentence was held not to be wrong in principle given the offender's history of failing to comply with previous assessments and enforcement notices, but the 200 hours of community work was excessive and was reduced to 100 hours.

In *R v Takhar*[20] the appellant had managed a hotel and following a complaint fire officers inspected the hotel and found a series of fire safety breaches. A later follow-up inspection occurred and the person had remedied some of the existing breaches but further breaches were found. The 61-year-old, who was in ill-health at the time of sentencing, had pleaded guilty and was of previous good character. He was sentenced to concurrent sentences of six months which were found on appeal to be appropriate.

# APPEALS[21]
## England and Wales

8.41    It may be possible to arrange an informal review from the FRS if there is disagreement with the decision to issue a fire safety notice.

An appeal can be made to the local magistrates' court within 21 days of receiving a notice and, in certain circumstances, the appellant and the FRS can ask for a 'determination' from the Secretary of State for Housing Communities and Local Government to resolve a dispute.

---

19   [2012] EWCA Crim 3074.
20   [2014] EWCA Crim 1619.
21   Fire Safety in the Workplace, see https://www.gov.uk/workplace-fire-safety-your-responsibilities/enforcement-appeals-and-penalties.

8.41 *Fire Safety Offences and Notices*

A person will be told in writing about the right of appeal when an enforcement, improvement or prohibition notice is served. They will be told how to appeal, where and within what period an appeal may be brought.

If the enforcing authority and the responsible person cannot agree on the measures which are necessary to remedy the failure they may agree to have the question as to what measures are necessary to remedy the failure referred to the Minister of State for Policing and the Fire Service for his determination.

There are three grounds for appeal:

- the enforcement notice was based upon an error of fact(s);
- the enforcement notice was wrong in law;
- the fire authority erred in the exercise of its discretion in serving the enforcement notice.

## Scotland

8.42   There is a provision for an appeal to the sheriff against the operation of a prohibition, enforcement or alteration notice.

Where an appeal is made it allows the sheriff to make an order revoking, varying or confirming the notice. The appeal can be made by the person on whom the notice is served or, where it is a prohibition notice, in respect of the premises to which the prohibition notice relates. Appeals should be made to the sheriff within 21 days from the day that the notice is served.

Where there is an appeal against an alterations notice or an enforcement notice then this has the effect of suspending the operation of the notice until the order is made by the sheriff or until the appeal is abandoned. An appeal against the prohibition notice does not have the effect of suspending the operation of the prohibition notice.

## Northern Ireland

8.43   Where the Northern Ireland Fire and Rescue Service (NIFRS) is of the opinion that there is a failure to comply with the requirements imposed by the fire regulations but the breach does not warrant the service of an enforcement notice then the 'Notification of Fire Safety Deficiencies Form' will be used. This is served by the inspector. This notification will identify the matters that need to be addressed and the steps that are considered necessary to remedy the issues.

The Fire Safety Deficiencies Form is not an enforcement notice but identifies deficiencies which are required to be addressed to meet the obligations under the fire regulations and is issued by the NIFRS before any formal enforcement action is taken.

*Action plan*

**8.44** Where the NIFRS is of the opinion that there is a failure to comply with a series of requirements imposed by the Fire and Rescue Services (Northern Ireland) Order 2006[22] but the breaches are considered not to warrant service of an enforcement notice then an Action plan may be used. This identifies deficiencies, sets out a programme of remedies, and prioritises the order for completion. This is not an enforcement notice, but identifies the deficiencies, sets an agreed programme of remedies, and prioritises the order of their completion.

# DETERMINATIONS
## England and Wales

**8.45** Where both parties (the enforcing authority and the responsible person) agree that there is a need for improvement to the fire precautions but disagree on the technical solution to be used, they may agree to refer to the Minister of State for Policing and the Fire Service for independent determination[23].

*Example*

**8.46** An occupier has begun to use a new mezzanine floor in a warehouse. Both the enforcing authority and the responsible person agree that the distance to a place of safety is excessive. The enforcing authority feels that it is necessary to provide an alternative escape route from the mezzanine floor. The responsible person believes that a smoke detection system in the whole building will reduce the time for escape to an acceptable level with the existing escape route. Both agree to approach the Minister of State to seek a determination under art 36 of the RRO.

Consideration should be given at the earliest suitable opportunity and if possible before a formal enforcement notice has been issued. If the enforcing authority considers the breach is so serious that it has served an enforcement notice, a determination may not be appropriate.

Either party can refuse to agree to the determination – for example if the enforcing authority considers that any delay brought about by the process would put people's safety at an unacceptable risk – then the expected enforcement action would be taken without a referral for a determination.

A determination can only be made with respect to a technical disagreement – it is not possible for the Minister of State to determine the law itself.

---

22   SI 2006/1254.
23   Regulatory Reform (Fire Safety) Order 2005, art 26.

**8.46** *Fire Safety Offences and Notices*

The Minister of State can seek technical advice from parties other than those seeking the determination. When the Minister of State has made a determination, the enforcing authority may not take the enforcement action that would conflict with the determination. Following the determination, the Minister of State has no further jurisdiction in the case and any matters that follow should be referred back to the enforcing authority.

## Applying for a determination

8.47 The application should contain three paper copies of the following:
- names and addresses of the enforcing authority and the responsible person;
- full postal address of the premises;
- statement from both parties requesting the Minister of State to determine the question;
- whether any formal enforcement action has been taken and, if so, full details of the action, with copies of any enforcement notice etc;
- the most recent risk assessment for the premises;
- statement setting out the provision of the order at issue and the measures proposed by both parties to meet the provision;
- any relevant correspondence involved;
- any enforcement notice;
- any other documentation, supporting the case for compliance, including any calculations, plans etc.

# Scotland

8.48 For non-domestic premises in Scotland[24], then the Scottish Fire and Rescue Service (SFRS) is the enforcing authority. If a person disagrees with what they have been asked to do by the SFRS they can apply for a dispute resolution. This dispute resolution service allows fire safety disputes to be resolved without the need for appeal to the court. Dispute determinations are made by the Chief Inspector of the Scottish Fire and Rescue Service which is independent of the SFRS.

## When a determination can be made

8.49 A determination can be made where the SFRS considers that the duty-holder has failed to comply with the fire safety duties and the SFRS and the duty-holder fail to agree on what action should be taken. Where the legislation

---

24 Applying for a determination if you have a fire safety dispute – see http://www.gov.scot/Resource/0048/00481729.pdf.

allows the duty holder to dispute the case then the case will only be considered if it is reasonable and appropriate.

If the duty-holder disagrees with the view of the local enforcement officer, then they can challenge the view but this is then through the SFRS's own internal review system and not through the dispute determination procedure.

The dispute determination procedure is only relevant to action required to satisfy technical fire safety matters and cannot be established to determine law. The process does not cover disputes that relate to procedural, conduct or administrative aspects of the SFRS enforcement – these are dealt with through the SFRS internal processes.

## Making an application

8.50   There should first be an informal discussion about the appropriateness of using this procedure.

Confirmation will need to be made that:

- notification of non-compliance from the SFRS has been received;
- full negotiation and discussion with the SFRS has taken place;
- there is a failure to agree on technical matters; and
- the case may involve disproportionate or inappropriate fire safety measures.

If the determination process is not the correct one, then reasons will be given. If it is the correct process, then the following will need to be submitted:

- name and contact details;
- name and contact details of any agent acting in the case;
- the address and use of the relevant premises to which the dispute applies;
- a statement explaining the matter(s) under dispute and specifically identifying what the determination expected to look at;
- argument or reasoning in support of the argument;
- a copy of any document or evidence in support the application.

The SFRS will make its own submission.

# Part 3

# Enforcement and Sentencing

# Chapter 9

# Enforcement Agencies and Enforcement Policies

Health and safety enforcement   9.1
    How the HSE and LAs work together   9.2
    HELA (Health and Safety Executive/Local Authorities
        Enforcement Liaison Committee)   9.3
    Health and Safety Executive (HSE)   9.4
        Enforcement policy statement   9.5
    Local Authority (LA)   9.6
        Local authority enforcement   9.7
        National local authority enforcement code   9.8
        LA intervention and enforcement activity   9.9
    Office of the Rail Regulator (ORR)   9.10
        Enforcement policy   9.11
        Powers   9.12
        Compliance and enforcement   9.13
        Formal enforcement tools   9.14
        Prosecution   9.15
    Office of Nuclear Regulations (ONR)   9.16
        Enforcement policy   9.17
    Health and Safety Executive Northern Ireland (HSENI)   9.18
        Five key mission objectives of the HSENI   9.19
        HSENI and local councils   9.20
    Other enforcing authorities   9.23
Environmental enforcement   9.24
    Environment Agency   9.24
        England   9.25
        Enforcement policy   9.26
    Scottish Environment Protection Agency (SEPA)   9.27
        Enforcement policy   9.28
    Natural Resources Wales (NRW)   9.29
        Enforcement policy   9.30
    Northern Ireland Environment Agency (NIEA)   9.31
        Enforcement policy   9.32
    Local authorities   9.33

*9.1   Enforcement Agencies and Enforcement Policies*

# HEALTH AND SAFETY ENFORCEMENT

**9.1**   Health and safety is regulated by both the local authority (LA) and the Health and Safety Executive (HSE). The HSE owns some primary and secondary legislation. Primary legislation consists of Acts of Parliament which include the Health and Safety at Work Act etc 1974 (HSWA 1974). Secondary legislation is made up of statutory instruments (SIs), referred to as regulations.

The statistics for 2016/17 show that the HSE issued 9495 enforcement notices and the LA issued 2418. The 2016/17 data shows a large annual increase in the total amount of fines raising from £38.8 million in 2015/16 to 69.9 million in 2016/17. 2016/17 is the first full year when the new sentencing guidelines have been in place.

## How the HSE and LAs work together

**9.2**   The HSE takes the national lead for health and safety policy, with HSE and LA enforcement officers ensuring that duty-holders manage their work place with regard to health and safety. Both the HSE and the LAs provide advice and support and will take enforcement action where appropriate[1].

## HELA (Health and Safety Executive/Local Authorities Enforcement Liaison Committee)

**9.3**   The HELA provides a strategic oversight of the co-regulatory relationship that is between the HSE and local authorities and aims to maximise effectiveness, improve health and safety outcomes, and ensure the delivery of HSE strategy. The HELA meets twice a year and is chaired jointly by a senior representative of the HSE and the chair of the Local Authority Health and Safety Practitioner Forum. The membership is made up of senior HSE officials concerned with policy development and operations, and senior LA officers which represent:

- Local Government Association (LGA) in England;
- Convention of Scottish Authorities (COSLA) in Scotland;
- Welsh LGA (WLGA) in Wales;
- Royal Environmental Health Institute of Scotland (REHIS);
- Chartered Institute of Environmental Health (CIEH).

## Health and Safety Executive (HSE)

**9.4**   The HSE is the enforcing authority for the following types of premises:

---

1   See Statement of Commitment between HSE and local authority representative bodies at http://www.hse.gov.uk/lau/statement.htm.

*Enforcement Agencies and Enforcement Policies* 9.7

- factories;
- farms;
- building sites;
- mines;
- schools and colleges;
- fairgrounds;
- gas, electricity and water systems;
- hospitals or nursing homes;
- central and local government premises;
- offshore installations.

## *Enforcement policy statement*[2]

**9.5** The policy statement is issued by the HSE, but LA inspectors are also obliged to follow this policy when looking at the workplaces that are allocated to them. In Scotland decisions to prosecute are made by the Crown Office and Procurator Fiscal Service (COPFS) and recommendation are made by the COPFS in line with this policy.

Other regulators enforcing health and safety legislation include: the Office of Road and Rail; the Office of Nuclear Regulations; and the Petroleum Enforcement Authorities (PEAs). Each has its own enforcement policy statements[3].

## Local Authority (LA)

**9.6** In the following premises health and safety law is enforced by the LA:

- offices (except government offices);
- shops;
- hotels;
- restaurants;
- leisure premises;
- nurseries and playgroups;
- pubs and clubs;
- museums (privately owned);
- places of worship;
- sheltered accommodation and care homes.

## *Local authority enforcement*

**9.7** The LA is the enforcing authority for retail, wholesale distribution and warehousing, hotel and catering premises, offices and consumer leisure

---

2   Enforcement Policy Statement HSE – 2015 – http://www.hse.gov.uk/pubns/hse41.pdf.
3   Office of Rail and Road – Policies and Statements, see http://orr.gov.uk/rail/publications/policies-and-statements; Office of Nuclear Regulations – Enforcement Policy Statement, see http://www.onr.org.uk/documents/enforcement-policy-statement.pdf.

## 9.7 Enforcement Agencies and Enforcement Policies

industries. Each LA must make adequate provision for enforcement and the LA National Enforcement Code introduced in May 2013 sets out the principles that each LA should follow to ensure a consistent, proportionate and targeted approach to regulation based on risk.

There are a number of intervention approaches available to the LA including:

- provision of advice and guidance to individual businesses and groups;
- proactive interventions including inspection;
- reactive interventions eg investigating an incident or complaint.

LA inspectors can also use enforcement powers, including formal enforcement notices, and take prosecution action.

### National local authority enforcement code

**9.8** The national local authority enforcement code[4] sets out the risk-based approach to targeting health and safety interventions which should be followed by the LA regulators. The code is a framework which concentrates on four objectives:

- clarifying the roles and responsibilities of business, regulator and professional bodies;
- outlining the risk-based approach to regulation that LAs should adopt;
- setting out the need for training and competence of LA health and safety regulators;
- explaining the arrangements for collection/publication of LA data and peer review to give assurance on meeting the requirements of the code.

### LA intervention and enforcement activity

**9.9** Local authorities provide data on their health and safety intervention, enforcement and prosecution activity on an annual basis. The latest annual return data was presented to the HELA at their meeting in October 2017 and the HSE published the data to allow the LAs to benchmark and peer review their work with other LAs[5].

Occupational injuries, ill-health and enforcement action for Scotland, Wales and English regions can be found on the HSE website: http://www.hse.gov.uk/statistics/regions/index.htm.

---

4   National Local Authority Enforcement Code Health and Safety at Work England, Scotland and Wales. see http://www.hse.gov.uk/lau/national-la-code.pdf.
5   LAE1 Annual Return data 1 April 2016 to 31 March 2017, see http://www.hse.gov.uk/lau/lae1-return-2016-17.xlsx.

## Office of the Rail Regulator (ORR)

**9.10** The Office of Rail and Road (ORR) is an independent safety and economic regulator for Britain's railways. It is responsible for ensuring that railway operators comply with health and safety law. It regulates Network Rail's activities and funding requirements; regulates access to the network; licenses the operators of railway assets; and publishes rail statistics. The ORR is also the competition authority for the railways and enforces consumer protection.

### Enforcement policy[6]

**9.11** The purpose of an enforcement policy is to ensure that the network operates safely, reliably and provides value for taxpayers and customers. The ORR regulator is the enforcing authority for mainline railway, High Speed 1, light rail, heritage railways, tram networks and metro systems. Its vision is for: 'Zero workforce and industry-caused passenger facilities, with an ever-decreasing overall safety risk'.

### Powers

**9.12** The ORR's powers come from a number of sources:

- the HSWA 1974 and regulations made under the Act;
- specified powers allocated to the ORR inspectors not associated with the HSWA 1974, for example REACH (European Regulation on the Registration, Evaluation, Authorisation and restriction of Chemicals), Employers Liability (Compulsory Insurance) Act 1969;
- railway industry specific legislation, for example the Railway and Other Guided Transport (Safety) Regulations 2006[7] (ROGS);
- 'relevant non-health and safety legislation' for which the ORR is the enforcing authority which stems from European legislative requirements;
- the Railways (Interoperability) Regulations 2011[8];
- the Rail Vehicle Accessibility (Non-Interoperable Rail System) Regulations 2010[9];
- the Train Driving Licences and Certificates Regulations 2010[10].

### Compliance and enforcement

**9.13** The ORR has a selection of compliance and enforcement strategies which range from information, advice, persuasion, cooperation, inspection,

---

6   ORR's health and safety compliance and enforcement policy statement 2016.
7   SI 2006/559.
8   SI 2011/3066.
9   SI 2010/432.
10  SI 2010/724.

**9.13** *Enforcement Agencies and Enforcement Policies*

audit, permissioning, verification and compulsion through to the deterrence activities of formal enforcement.

## Formal enforcement tools

**9.14** The following enforcement tools can be used by the ORR[11]:

- 'where we find an article or substance that we believe may be a cause of imminent danger, we can require it to be made harmless;
- seize plant equipment and substances;
- an improvement notice requiring compliance by a certain date;
- a prohibition notice that prohibits a practice or use of plant, equipment or a substance until it can be undertaken or used safely;
- revocation of a safety certificate or safety authorisation issued under ROGS. A transport undertaking cannot operate without the necessary certificate or authorisation;
- issue of a simple caution (out of court disposal) in England and Wales;
- prosecution in the courts in England and Wales; and
- report to the Crown Office and Procurator Fiscal Service in Scotland.'

When deciding whether or not take formal enforcement activity the ORR uses an Enforcement Management Model (EMM) and supplementary ORR specific guidance.

## Prosecution

**9.15** The decision to prosecute is made by a senior inspector of principal level or above, who is independent from the investigation and who has no prior dealings with the prospective defendant in respect of the matter. In Scotland the decision to prosecute is made by the Procurator Fiscal on the basis of a report and recommendation made by the ORR health and safety inspectors.

# Office of Nuclear Regulations (ONR)[12]

**9.16** The ONR provides efficient and effective regulation of the nuclear industry, holding it to account on behalf of the public. It must take enforcement action when licensees are found to be failing to meet the safety and security standards required by law. To do this the ONR has been provided with a range of enforcement powers which range from providing advice to instigating court proceedings.

---

11 ORR's Health and Safety Compliance and Enforcement Policy Statement 2016, see http://orr.gov.uk/__data/assets/pdf_file/0016/5650/health-and-safety-compliance-and-enforcement-policy-statement-2016.pdf at 22.
12 Nuclear Installations – Office for Nuclear Regulation – see http://www.onr.org.uk.

## Enforcement policy[13]

**9.17** Enforcement can range from advice by inspectors, to warnings, letters, notices, use of powers under the licence conditions, and the other nuclear safety and security legislation or prosecutions.

## Health and Safety Executive Northern Ireland (HSENI)

**9.18** The HSENI is an executive non-departmental public body sponsored by the Department for the Economy (DfE). The HSENI is the lead body responsible for the promotion and enforcement of health and safety at work standards in Northern Ireland.

## Five key mission objectives of the HSENI

**9.19** HSENI's mission objectives are as follows[14]:

- 'To provide the highest standards of service delivery at a regional level.
- To promote key workplace health and safety messages and themes to targeted sectors and groups.
- To communicate appropriate, timely and practical workplace health and safety information and advice.
- To improve compliance with health and safety standards through inspection and investigation activities.
- To ensure that an effective and up-to-date health and safety at work regulatory framework is maintained.'

## HSENI and local councils

**9.20** HSENI is the lead body for health and safety promotion and enforcement but this responsibility is shared with 11 local councils.

The responsibility for the enforcement of health and safety depends on the type of workplace concerned.

### HSENI's enforcement responsibilities

**9.21**

- Factories.
- Building sites.
- Farms.

---

13 Office for Nuclear Regulations – Enforcement Policy Statement, see http://www.onr.org.uk/documents/2014/enforcement-policy-statement.pdf.
14 See https://www.hseni.gov.uk/content/about-hseni.

9.21   *Enforcement Agencies and Enforcement Policies*

- Motor vehicle repairs.
- Mines and quarries.
- Chemical plants.
- Schools and universities.
- Leisure and entertainment facilities (owned by local councils).
- Fairgrounds.
- Hospitals and nursing homes.
- Fire and police.
- Government departments.
- Railways.
- Any other workplaces not listed under local councils.

**Local councils' enforcement responsibilities**

9.22

- Offices.
- Retail and wholesale shops.
- Tyre and exhaust fitters.
- Restaurants, take away food shops, mobile snack bars and catering services.
- Hotels, guest houses and residential homes.
- Whole sale and retail warehouses.
- Leisure and entertainment facilities (privately owned).
- Exhibitions.
- Religious activities.
- Undertakers.
- The practice or presentation of the arts, sports, games, entertainment or other cultural or recreational activities.
- Therapeutic and beauty services.
- Animal care.

# Other enforcing authorities

9.23

- Poor food hygiene – Environmental Health Department (Local Authority) – https://www.gov.uk/find-local-council.
- Pollution including nuisance noise – Environmental Health (Local Government) – https://www.gov.uk/find-local-council.
- Problems with purchased goods and services – Trading Standards (Local Authority) – https://www.gov.uk/find-local-council.
- Roads Highways and Pavements – Highways Department (Local Authority) – https://www.gov.uk/find-local-council.
- Unstable/dangerous buildings – Building Control (Local Authority) – https://www.gov.uk/find-local-council.
- Road traffic issues – Police – https://www.police.uk.

*Enforcement Agencies and Enforcement Policies* **9.25**

- Road worthiness of vehicles – Driver and Vehicle Standards Agency – https://www.gov.uk/government/organisations/driver-and-vehicle-standards-agency.
- Railway Health and Safety – Office of Road and Rail – http://orr.gov.uk/rail/health-and-safety.
- Waste disposal, contaminated ground, some air pollution issues – Environment Agency – https://www.gov.uk/government/organisations/environment-agency.
- Care of patients in health services Scotland – Health Improvement Scotland – http://www.healthcareimprovementscotland.org.
- Care of patients in health services Wales – Healthcare Inspectorate Wales – http://hiw.org.uk/splash?orig=/.
- Care of users of social care services in Scotland – Social Care and Social Improvement Scotland – http://www.careinspectorate.com.
- Care of social health services users Wales – Social Care and Social Services Inspectorate Wales – http://careinspectorate.wales/?lang=en.
- Repairs to council owned property – Ombudsman – https://www.lgo.org.uk.
- Conditions for and treatment of those in prison – Her Majesty's Inspectorate of Prisons – https://www.justiceinspectorates.gov.uk/hmiprisons/contact-us/.
- Concerns about patient safety – Doctors – General Medical Council – https://www.gmc-uk.org/guidance/ethical_guidance/decision_tool.asp.
- Concerns about patient safety Nurses and Midwives – Nursing and Midwifery Council – https://www.nmc.org.uk.
- Welfare facilities in schools – Department of Education – https://form.education.gov.uk/en/AchieveForms/?form_uri=sandbox-publish://AF-Process-f1453496-7d8a-463f-9f33-1da2ac47ed76/AF-Stage-1e64d4cc-25fb-499a-a8d7-74e98203ac00/definition.json&redirectlink=%2Fen&cancelRedirectLink=%2Fen.
- Occupational health and safety of flight crew and cabin crew in aircraft and health of passengers on aircraft – Civil Aviation Authority – http://www.caa.co.uk/home/.
- Concerns about marine safety including certification, pollution, and health, safety and welfare of seafarers – Maritime and Coastguard Agency – https://www.gov.uk/government/organisations/maritime-and-coastguard-agency/about/access-and-opening.

# ENVIRONMENTAL ENFORCEMENT

## Environment Agency

**9.24** The Environment Agency was established in 1996 to protect and improve the environment.

### England

**9.25** Within England the Environment Agency is responsible for:

**9.25** *Enforcement Agencies and Enforcement Policies*

- regulating major industry and waste;
- treatment of contaminated land;
- water quality and resources;
- fisheries;
- island river, estuary and harbour navigations;
- conservation and ecology;
- managing the risk of flooding from main rivers, reservoirs, estuaries and the sea;
- taking action against businesses who do not take responsible environmental action;
- protection of wildlife and habitats;
- helping to improve the quality of inner city areas and parks by restoring rivers and lakes;
- influencing and working with government, industry and local authorities to make the environment a priority.

## Enforcement policy

**9.26** The Environment Agency's aim is to improve the environment through education, advice and by regulating activities. The general approach is to engage with businesses to educate and enable compliance. When individuals or organisations are not complying then it may use formal enforcement powers and sanctions. It publishes information about enforcement action taken and issues press releases to raise awareness. The Environment Agency always seeks to recover the costs of investigations and enforcement proceedings, for instance, if costs have been incurred because the Environment Agency has carried out remedial works, it will seek to recover all the costs from those responsible in accordance with the 'polluter pays' principle.

Enforcement and sanctions should:

- aim to change the behaviour of the offender;
- aim to eliminate any financial gain or benefit from non-compliance;
- be responsive and consider what is appropriate for the particular offender and regulatory issue, which can include punishment and the public stigma that should be associated with a criminal conviction;
- be proportionate to the nature of the offence and the harm caused;
- aim to restore the harm caused by regulatory non-compliance, where appropriate; and
- aim to deter future non-compliance.

The Environment Agency takes account of the provisions in the Regulator's Code[15] when devising and implementing regulatory policies. This requires that if immediate enforcement action is required then it is taken to respond to a serious breach.

---

15 Regulators' Code – see https://www.gov.uk/government/publications/regulators-code.

Regulation and enforcement follow the principles of:

- proportionality in the application of law in securing compliance;
- consistency of approach;
- transparency about how the Environment Agency operates and what those that regulate expect from it;
- targeting of enforcement action accountability for the enforcement action that has been taken.

## Scottish Environment Protection Agency (SEPA)

9.27   SEPA was established in 1996 and is responsible for the protection of the natural environment in Scotland.

The purpose is to protect the environment (including managing natural resources in a sustainable way) and enforcement action will only be carried out as part of a broader, evidence-based approach to regulation.

Responsibilities are similar to the Environment Agency's, with some differences:

- all pollution prevention and control (PPC) requirements are regulated (there are no local authority powers under PPC in Scotland);
- flood defence is limited to issuing flood warnings;
- there is no fisheries involvement;
- water resources (abstraction licensing) responsibilities were acquired in 2005 under the Water Framework Directive.

### Enforcement policy

9.28   The intent behind the enforcement action is to:

- secure compliance and change behaviour;
- stop or reduce the risk of harm arising from non-compliance to an acceptable level;
- ensure restoration and remediation of the environment.

## Natural Resources Wales (NRW)

9.29   Natural Resources Wales is a Welsh government sponsored body formed in 2013 which largely took over the functions of the Countryside Council for Wales, Forestry Commission Wales and the Environment Agency in Wales, as well as some Welsh government functions. According to the NRW website, it has the following roles and responsibilities[16]:

---

16   See https://naturalresources.wales/about-us/what-we-do/our-roles-and-responsibilities/?lang=en.

9.29   *Enforcement Agencies and Enforcement Policies*

'• **Adviser:** principal adviser to Welsh Government, and adviser to industry and the wider public and voluntary sector, and communicator about issues relating to the environment and its natural resources.
- **Regulator:** protecting people and the environment including marine, forest and waste industries, and prosecuting those who breach the regulations that we are responsible for.
- **Designator:** for Sites of Special Scientific Interest – areas of particular value for their wildlife or geology, Areas of Outstanding Natural Beauty (AONBs), and National Parks, as well as declaring National Nature Reserves.
- **Responder:** to some 9,000 reported environmental incidents a year as a Category 1 emergency responder.
- **Statutory consultee:** to some 9,000 planning applications a year.
- **Manager/Operator:** managing seven per cent of Wales' land area including woodlands, National Nature Reserves, water and flood defences, and operating our visitor centres, recreation facilities, hatcheries and a laboratory.
- **Partner, Educator and Enabler:** key collaborator with the public, private and voluntary sectors, providing grant aid, and helping a wide range of people use the environment as a learning resource; acting as a catalyst for others' work.
- **Evidence gatherer:** monitoring our environment, commissioning and undertaking research, developing our knowledge, and being a public records body.'

## Enforcement policy

9.30   This means acting in a manner which seeks to ensure that the needs of the present are met without compromising the ability of future generations to meet their own needs.

Reinforcing, and complementing this, is the Environment (Wales) Act 2016, which states that it must:

- pursue sustainable management of natural resources in relation to Wales; and
- apply the principles of sustainable management of natural resources, in the exercise of its functions, so far as consistent with their proper exercise.

In response to this, Natural Resources Wales has produced '*Our regulatory approach to deliver sustainable management of natural resources – Our Regulatory Principles*'[17]. This outlines its principles as follows:

'These principles are:
- Deliver outcomes
- Be intelligent
- Prepared to challenge
- Use the full range of tools available

17   Natural resources Wales – Our Regulatory Principles, see https://naturalresources.wales/about-us/what-we-do/how-we-regulate-you/regulatory-principles/?lang=en.

- Be flexible
- Bring the right skills/expertise together
- Be efficient and effective
- Be clear on what we do and why

In order to deliver the aspirations of the sustainable management of natural resources, we believe that:

- Regulation is more than the application of the law;
- Formal regulation (underpinned by the law) can contribute to delivery of sustainable management of natural resources and well-being, but the pressures on our natural environment show this is not the whole solution;
- The solution is about doing something – intervening and regulating actions and behaviours, and means doing things and looking at problems differently;
- We need to understand the impact of our behaviours, as well as understanding the behaviours of others; and
- We need to recognise our limitations and constraints, and value the benefit of collaboration to deliver the wider objectives for Wales – it's not just about looking at what we, NRW, can do – it is what we, Wales, can do

We use our Regulatory Principles to guide our regulatory approach to the sustainable management of natural resources and deliver well-being outcomes. Regulation is about doing something, a clear "intervention" that makes a difference. In the delivery of this, we remain committed to the applications of the principles of good regulation, and to our commitments under the Regulators' Code.'

## Northern Ireland Environment Agency (NIEA)

9.31   The NIEA is an executive agency within the Department of Agriculture, Environment and Rural Affairs. It aims to:

- deliver effective compliance and implementation of legislation and international obligations;
- improve understanding and appreciation of the environment;
- support a sustainable economy;
- deliver reformed and effective planning.

### Enforcement policy

9.32   The NIEA enforces environment legislation to ensure that people take environmental protection seriously; that they realise the cost of environmental crime; and where damage is done intentionally, that the cost plus restoration is borne by the person or company which has caused the damage, ie the 'polluter pays' principle. It also publicises enforcement and raises awareness of the significance of environmental crime so that people can recognise that the costs of ignoring or wilfully contravening environmental legislation is far greater than the costs of complying.

9.33 *Enforcement Agencies and Enforcement Policies*

## Local authorities

**9.33** Local authorities have a range of environmental regulation responsibilities delivered through their environmental health, trading standards and planning functions (and across district, county and unitary authorities). These include:

- land use planning;
- local air quality strategies (to reflect the national Air Quality Strategy);
- Local Authority Air Pollution Control (LAAPC) including PPC Part B;
- installations in England and Wales;
- Clean Air Act 1993;
- noise and statutory nuisance (eg dust and odour);
- environmental health;
- contaminated land;
- tree preservation orders.

# Chapter 10

# RIDDOR and Internal Investigations

RIDDOR (Reporting Injuries, Diseases and Dangerous Occurrences
    Regulations) and Incident Investigation   10.1
    Purpose of a RIDDOR report   10.1
    Who makes the report?   10.2
        Employer   10.3
        Control of premises   10.4
        Self-employed   10.5
        Members of the public, employees, injured persons and their
            representatives   10.6
        Employment agency   10.7
        Gas supplier   10.8
        Gas engineer   10.9
        Why reports must be made   10.10
    What must be reported?   10.11
        The death of any person   10.12
        Specified injuries to workers   10.13
        Over-seven-day incapacitation of a worker   10.14
        Over-three-day incapacitation of a worker   10.15
        Non-fatal accidents to non-workers (eg members of the
            public)   10.16
        Occupational diseases   10.17
        Dangerous occurrences   10.18
        Gas incidents   10.20
    How to make a RIDDOR report   10.21
    Insurance   10.22
    Failure to report   10.23
    Over reporting   10.24
    Records that need to be kept   10.25
    HSE investigation   10.26
    Mandatory investigations   10.27
        Fatalities (work-related deaths)   10.28
        'Specified injuries' (work-related)   10.29
        Cases of occupational disease   10.30
        Incidents that indicate a likelihood of a serious breach of
            health and safety law   10.31
        Major hazard precursor events   10.32
        Discretionary investigation   10.33
    Records that need to be kept   10.34
    When does an incident need to be reported?   10.35

**10.1** *RIDDOR and Internal Investigations*

    Exemptions   10.36
    How long must RIDDOR records be kept?   10.37
Carrying out internal investigations   10.38
    Incident   10.39
    Reasons to investigate a workplace incident   10.40
    What to investigate and who investigates   10.41
    Should the immediate supervisor be on the team?   10.42
    The decision to investigate   10.43
    The investigation   10.44
        Root cause   10.45
    Gathering information   10.46
    Information analysis   10.47
    Recommendations   10.48

# RIDDOR (REPORTING INJURIES, DISEASES AND DANGEROUS OCCURRENCES REGULATIONS) AND INCIDENT INVESTIGATION

## Purpose of a RIDDOR report

**10.1** In 1980 the Notification of Accidents and Dangerous Occurrences Regulations (NADOR)[1] were introduced and they required employers and the self-employed to keep a record of any accidents or certain types of dangerous occurrences and report them to the Health and Safety Executive (HSE). The Regulations included lists of types of dangerous occurrences that are reportable including those that occur in any situation and those that relate specifically to mines, quarries and railways. Now, the Reporting of Injuries, Diseases and Dangerous Occurrences Regulations 2013 (RIDDOR)[2] have replaced NADOR.

RIDDOR requires employers, or in certain circumstances others who control or manage premises, to report to the relevant enforcing authority and to keep records of:

- work-related deaths;
- work-related accidents which cause certain specific serious injuries to workers, or which result in a worker being incapacitated for more than seven consecutive days (this was changed from three days to seven in the 2013 revision);
- occurrences of the industrial diseases listed in RIDDOR;
- certain 'dangerous occurrences' (near miss accidents);
- injuries to a person who is not at work, such as a member of the public, which are caused by an accident at work, and which results in the person being taken to hospital from the site for treatment.

1    SI 1980/804.
2    SI 2013/1471.

## Who makes the report?

**10.2** Only 'responsible persons' including employers, the self-employed, and people in control of work premises should submit a report under RIDDOR.

### Employer

**10.3** An *employer* must report work-related deaths and certain work-related injuries, cases of disease and near misses involving their employees wherever they are working.

### Control of premises

**10.4** If a person is in *control of premises* they must report any work-related deaths, certain injuries to members of the public and self-employed people on their premises and dangerous occurrences (some near misses) that occur on their premises.

### Self-employed

**10.5** If a person is self-employed and working on someone else's premises, and suffers either a specified injury or an over seven-day injury, then it is the responsibility of the *person in control of the premises* for reporting that injury. The self-employed person should ensure they are familiar with this.

If there is a reportable incident whilst the self-employed person is working on their own premises, or a doctor informs that person of the presence of a work-related disease or condition, then the self-employed person can decide to report it.

### Members of the public, employees, injured persons and their representatives

**10.6** The RIDDOR reporting system is only for those that have duties under the regulations so it is not appropriate for members of the public, employees, injured persons and their representatives to use the reporting system.

### Employment agency

**10.7** Where the employment agency is the legal employer then they are under the same obligations as an employer and therefore have a duty to report ill-health and accidents. Agencies should ensure that the responsibility for

## 10.7 RIDDOR and Internal Investigations

reporting under RIDDOR is clearly assigned to the appropriate person based on the details of the employment relationship.

### Gas supplier

**10.8** If someone who is a conveyor, filler, importer or supplier of flammable gas finds that someone has died, been taken to hospital, or has been found unconscious in connection with the gas that has been distributed, filled, imported or supplied, they must report such instances. This also includes exposure to carbon monoxide or fire/explosion incidents.

### Gas engineer

**10.9** Gas engineers who are registered with the Gas Safe Register must, either themselves or through their employers, provide details of gas fittings (which includes appliances and flues or ventilation used with the appliances) that are considered dangerous to such an extent that people could die, be rendered unconscious or need to go to hospital. This is because the design, construction, installation, modifications or incorrect servicing of such fittings could result in:

- an accidental leakage of gas;
- incomplete combustion of gas; or
- inadequate removal of products of the combustion of gas.

## Why reports must be made

**10.10** It is a legal requirement to report certain incidents. These reports inform the enforcing authorities (HSE, local authorities and the Office of the Rail Regulator (ORR)) about the deaths, injuries, occupational diseases and dangerous occurrences. This allows them to identify where and how risks arise and whether the enforcing authority needs to investigate. This means that advice can be targeted to help companies avoid deaths and injuries.

RIDDOR reports are only required when:

- the accident is work-related; and
- it results in an injury of the type that is reportable.

A RIDDOR event must be reported as failure to do so is a criminal offence which could result in prosecution. Reporting an incident is NOT an admission of liability!

## What must be reported?

**10.11** The law requires the responsible person to report to the HSE under RIDDOR the following events that 'arise out of or in connection with work'.

## The death of any person

**10.12** All deaths to workers and non-workers, with the exception of suicides, must be reported if they arise from a work-related accident, including an act of physical violence to a worker.

## Specified injuries to workers

**10.13** The following specified injuries to workers must be reported:
- fractures, other than to fingers, thumbs and toes;
- amputations;
- any injury likely to lead to permanent loss of sight or reduction in sight;
- any crush injury to the head or torso causing damage to the brain or internal organs;
- serious burns (including scalding) which:
  - cover more than 10% of the body;
  - cause significant damage to the eyes, respiratory system or other vital organs;
- any scalping requiring hospital treatment;
- any loss of consciousness caused by head injury or asphyxia;
- any other injury arising from working in an enclosed space which:
  - leads to hypothermia or heat-induced illness;
  - requires resuscitation or admittance to hospital for more than 24 hours.

## Over-seven-day incapacitation of a worker

**10.14** Accidents must be reported where they result in an employee or self-employed person being away from work, or unable to perform their normal work duties, for more than seven consecutive days as the result of their injury. This seven-day period does not include the day of the accident, but does include weekends and rest days. The report must be made within 15 days of the accident.

## Over-three-day incapacitation of a worker

**10.15** Accidents must be recorded, *but not reported*, where they result in a worker being incapacitated for more than three consecutive days. If the employer is one that keeps an accident book under the Social Security (Claims and Payments) Regulations 1979[3], that record will be enough.

---

3   SI 1979/628.

**10.16** *RIDDOR and Internal Investigations*

## Non-fatal accidents to non-workers (eg members of the public)

**10.16** Accidents to members of the public or others who are not at work must be reported if they result in an injury and the person is taken directly from the scene of the accident to hospital for treatment to that injury. Examinations and diagnostic tests do not constitute 'treatment' in such circumstances.

There is no need to report incidents where people are taken to hospital purely as a precaution when no injury is apparent.

## Occupational diseases

**10.17** Employers and self-employed people must report diagnoses of certain occupational diseases where these are likely to have been caused or made worse by their work.

## Dangerous occurrences

**10.18** Dangerous occurrences are certain, specified near miss events. Not all such events require reporting. There are 27 categories of dangerous occurrences that are relevant to most workplaces.

**Lifting equipment** – the collapse, overturning or failure of any load-bearing part of any lifting equipment, other than an accessory for lifting.

**Pressure systems** – the failure of any closed vessel or of any associated pipework (other than a pipeline) forming part of a pressure system as defined by the Pressure Systems Safety Regulations 2000[4], where that failure could cause the death of any person.

**Overhead electric lines** – any plant or equipment unintentionally coming into:

- contact with an uninsulated overhead electric line in which the voltage exceeds 200 volts; or
- close proximity with such an electric line, such that it causes an electrical discharge.

**Electrical incidents causing explosion or fire** – any explosion or fire caused by an electrical short circuit or overload (including those resulting from accidental damage to the electrical plant) which either:

- results in the stoppage of the plant involved for more than 24 hours; or
- causes a significant risk of death.

---

4  SI 2000/128.

**Explosives** – any unintentional:

- fire, explosion or ignition at a site where the manufacture or storage of explosives requires a licence or registration, as the case may be, under regs 6 or 7 of the Explosives Regulations 2014[5]; or
- explosion or ignition of explosives (unless caused by the unintentional discharge of a weapon, where, apart from that unintentional discharge, the weapon and explosives functioned as they were designed to),

except where a fail-safe device or safe system of work prevented any person being endangered as a result of the fire, explosion or ignition.

The misfire of explosives (other than at a mine or quarry, inside a well or involving a weapon) except where a fail-safe device or safe system of work prevented any person being endangered as a result of the misfire.

Any explosion, discharge or intentional fire or ignition which causes any injury to a person requiring first-aid or medical treatment, other than at a mine or quarry.

The projection of material beyond the boundary of the site on which the explosives are being used, or beyond the danger zone of the site, which caused or might have caused injury, except at a quarry ('danger zone' means the area from which persons have been excluded or forbidden to enter to avoid being endangered by any explosion or ignition of explosives).

The failure of shots to cause the intended extent of collapse or direction of fall of a structure in any demolition operation.

**Biological agents** – any accident or incident which results or could have resulted in the release or escape of a biological agent likely to cause severe human infection or illness.

**Radiation generators and radiography** – the malfunction of:

- a radiation generator or its ancillary equipment used in fixed or mobile industrial radiography, the irradiation of food or the processing of products by irradiation, which causes it to fail to de-energise at the end of the intended exposure period; or
- equipment used in fixed or mobile industrial radiography or gamma irradiation, which causes a radioactive source to fail to return to its safe position by the normal means at the end of the intended exposure period.

'Radiation generator' means any electrical equipment emitting ionising radiation and containing components operating at a potential difference of more than 5kV.

**Breathing apparatus** – the malfunction of breathing apparatus:

- where the malfunction causes a significant risk of personal injury to the user; or

---

5   SI 2014/1638.

**10.18** *RIDDOR and Internal Investigations*

- during testing immediately prior to use, where the malfunction would have caused a significant risk to the health and safety of the user had it occurred during use other than at a mine.

**Diving operations** – the failure, damaging or endangering of:

- any life support equipment, including control panels, hoses and breathing apparatus; or
- the dive platform, or any failure of the dive platform to remain on station, which causes a significant risk of personal injury to a diver.
- the failure or endangering of any lifting equipment associated with a diving operation;
- the trapping of a diver;
- any explosion in the vicinity of a diver;
- any uncontrolled ascent or any omitted decompression which causes a significant risk of personal injury to a diver.

**Collapse of scaffolding** – the complete or partial collapse (including falling, buckling or overturning) of:

- a substantial part of any scaffold more than 5m in height;
- any supporting part of any slung or suspended scaffold which causes a working platform to fall (whether or not in use); or
- any part of any scaffold in circumstances such that there would be a significant risk of death to a person falling from the scaffold.

**Train collisions** – the collision of a train with any other train or vehicle, other than a collision reportable under Part 5 of RIDDOR, Sch 2, which could have caused the death, or specified injury, of any person.

**Wells** – in relation to a well (other than a well sunk for the purpose of the abstraction of water):

- a blow-out (which includes any uncontrolled flow of well-fluids from a well);
- the coming into operation of a blow-out prevention or diversion system to control flow of well-fluids where normal control procedures fail;
- the detection of hydrogen sulphide at a well or in samples of well-fluids where the responsible person did not anticipate its presence in the reservoir drawn on by the well;
- the taking of precautionary measures additional to any contained in the original drilling programme where a planned minimum separation distance between adjacent wells was not maintained; or
- the mechanical failure of any part of a well whose purpose is to prevent or limit the effect of the unintentional release of fluids from a well or a reservoir being drawn on by a well, or whose failure would cause or contribute to such a release.

**Pipelines or pipeline works** – in relation to a pipeline or pipeline works:

- any damage to, accidental or uncontrolled release from or inrush of anything into a pipeline;

- the failure of any pipeline isolation device, associated equipment or system; or
- the failure of equipment involved with pipeline works,

which could cause personal injury to any person, or which results in the pipeline being shut down for more than 24 hours.

The unintentional change in position of a pipeline, or in the subsoil or seabed in the vicinity, which requires immediate attention to safeguard the pipeline's integrity or safety.

**Reportable incidents except in relation to an offshore workplace**

**10.19** The following incidents do not need a RIDDOR report if they occur at an offshore workplace.

**Structural collapse** – the unintentional collapse or partial collapse of:

- any structure, which involves a fall of more than five tonnes of material; or
- any floor or wall of any place of work

arising from, or in connection with, ongoing construction work (including demolition, refurbishment and maintenance), whether above or below ground.

The unintentional collapse or partial collapse of any falsework.

**Explosion or fire** – any unintentional explosion or fire in any plant or premises which results in the stoppage of that plant, or the suspension of normal work in those premises, for more than 24 hours.

**Release of flammable liquids and gases** – the sudden, unintentional and uncontrolled release:

- inside a building:
  - of 100 kilograms or more of a flammable liquid;
  - of 10 kilograms or more of a flammable liquid at a temperature above its normal boiling point;
  - of 10 kilograms or more of a flammable gas; or
- in the open air, of 500 kilograms or more of a flammable liquid or gas.

**Hazardous escapes of substances** – the unintentional release or escape of any substance which could cause personal injury to any person other than through the combustion of flammable liquids or gases.

## Gas incidents

**10.20** Distributors, fillers, importers and suppliers of flammable gas must report incidents where someone has died, lost consciousness, or been taken to hospital for treatment to an injury arising in connection with that gas.

10.20 *RIDDOR and Internal Investigations*

Registered gas engineers (under the Gas Safe Register) must provide details of any gas appliances or fittings that they consider to be dangerous, to such an extent that people could die, lose consciousness or require hospital treatment. The danger could be due to the design, construction, installation, modification or servicing of that appliance or fitting, which could cause:

- an accidental leakage of gas;
- incomplete combustion of gas; or
- inadequate removal of products of the combustion of gas.

## How to make a RIDDOR report

**10.21** RIDDOR reporting is mainly done by the completion of an online form[6]. For fatal accidents or accidents resulting in specified injuries to workers only the incident can be reported by phone[7].

In relation to out of hours reporting for serious incidents such as a work-related death, serious incidents involving multiple casualties or serious incidents causing major disruption eg evacuation, road closures, large numbers of people going to hospital, a call can be made to the HSE's Duty Officer[8].

## Insurance

**10.22** Information supplied to the HSE on a RIDDOR form is not passed to the insurer. If the insurer needs to be informed then it is the responsibility of the insured to inform them.

An employer that fails to follow the RIDDOR reporting requirements is taking a big risk. The HSE and local authorities, both of whom enforce RIDDOR, regularly trawl through the local papers looking for accidents which should have been reported to them. They may also receive direct complaints from the injured parties and information from hospitals.

It is worth noting that if a personal injury claim is made against an employer, the lawyers involved will ask for a copy of the RIDDOR report. Failure to produce one will cause difficulty and may lead to the injured party tipping off the authorities many years after the event.

Inspectors will take a view as to whether the incident needs to be followed up. This will depend on a number of factors, such as the seriousness of the accident and whether there is habitual evidence of late reporting.

---

6   Online forms are being updated on the HSE website, see http://www.hse.gov.uk/riddor/report.htm.
7   On 0345 300 9923.
8   On 0151 922 9235.

Whilst it is clearly best practice to ensure that delay is avoided, the authorities are used to receiving late reports, and therefore a late report is not necessarily a problem. Unless it is a very bad accident or there is an appalling record, it is unlikely that there will be an investigation.

The person making the late report should explain why the report is being made late and show the actions they intend to take to prevent a recurrence of the incident and how late reports will be prevented in the future.

Reporting an incident late is better than not at all. Whether the report is followed up will depend on the nature of the accident, whether there is a poor accident record and how late the report is being made.

## Failure to report

**10.23** Failing to report 'reportable' accidents is a criminal offence under the Health and Safety at Work etc Act 1974[9], and the responsible person can be sentenced in the magistrates' court with a fine up to £20,000, or in the Crown Court with an unlimited fine. Individuals deemed responsible for non-reporting can also face a period of imprisonment for up to two years.

Tesco failed to report two employee accidents at a store in Warfield and another in the Meadows Sandhurst. The company did not train its operational and management staff properly to load and unload vehicles and had no safe system of work in place. For the failure to ensure a safe system of work, Tesco was fined £14,000 and a further £34,000 after pleading guilty to three breaches of RIDDOR, reg 3. Tesco also had to pay prosecution costs of £25,000.

## Over reporting

**10.24** It is important that if an accident occurs which is 'reportable' that it is reported and recorded in accordance with RIDDOR's requirements. However, businesses should be certain that an accident is 'reportable' before reporting; *making an unnecessary report may bring unwanted scrutiny and investigation by the HSE.*

## Records that need to be kept

**10.25** A record must be kept of any reportable injury, over-three-day injury, disease or dangerous occurrence. Records must be kept in an accident book under social security law and this can be used for the records of injuries, although a separate method will be needed for that of diseases. The accident book does not have to be a physical book but can be an electronic recording system.

---

9   HSWA 1974, Pt 1, s 33(1) (provision of offences).

10.26 *RIDDOR and Internal Investigations*

## HSE investigation

**10.26** The RIDDOR report received by the HSE may trigger an investigation. Not all accidents which are reported are then investigated. Regulators only have a limited amount of resources, so will prioritise which incidents are investigated. The HSE will determine this using its incident selection criteria and the enforcement policy. Local authorities select incidents for investigation under their duty in the National Local Authority Enforcement Code[10].

The HSE decides which incidents to investigate and the level of resource to be allocated by considering the following:

- severity and scale of potential or actual harm;
- seriousness of any potential breach of the law;
- duty-holder's known past health and safety performance;
- enforcement priorities;
- practicality of achieving results;
- wider relevance of the event, including serious public concern; and
- national guidance on targeting interventions (see LAC 67/2[11]).

## Mandatory investigations

**10.27** There are a number of incidents which will always be investigated. These are as follows.

### *Fatalities (work-related deaths)*

**10.28**
- All work-related accidents which result in a fatality including non-workers – this excludes suicides.
- Other deaths arising from preventable work-related causes and where there is a likelihood that there has been a serious breach of safety law and where is it appropriate for the authorities to investigate.

### *'Specified injuries' (work-related)*

**10.29** All work-related accidents resulting in a 'specified injury' to any person including non-workers that meet any of the following conditions:

- serious multiple fractures (more than one bone, not including wrist or ankle);

---

10 HSE, *National Local Authority Enforcement Code: Health and Safety at Work: England, Scotland & Wales*, see http://www.hse.gov.uk/lau/national-la-code.pdf.
11 LAC 67/2 'Setting Local Authority Priorities and Targeting Interventions'.

*RIDDOR and Internal Investigations* **10.33**

- all amputations other than amputation of digit(s) above the first joint (eg fingertip);
- permanent blinding in one or both eyes;
- crush injuries leading to internal organ damage, eg ruptured spleen;
- any burn injury (including scalding) which covers more than 10% of the surface area of the body or causes significant damage to the eyes, respiratory system or vital organs;
- any degree of scalping requiring hospital treatment;
- loss of consciousness caused by head injury or asphyxia;
- any injury arising from working in an enclosed space which leads to hypothermia or heat induced illness, or requires resuscitation or hospital admittance for more than 24 hours.

## Cases of occupational disease

**10.30** All reports of occupational disease that are reported under RIDDOR, specifically:

- carpal tunnel syndrome;
- cramp in the arm or leg;
- occupational dermatitis;
- hand arm vibration syndrome (HAVS);
- occupational asthma;
- tendonitis or tenosynovitis in the arm or forearm;
- any cancer attributed to an occupational exposure to a known human carcinogen or mutagen;
- any disease attributed to an occupational exposure to a biological agent.

## Incidents that indicate a likelihood of a serious breach of health and safety law

**10.31** This will include an incident which may give rise to a serious public concern and that may give rise to a notice or prosecution.

## Major hazard precursor events

**10.32** This is a precursor identified within the HSE business plan and work plans of relevant HSE operational directorates.

## Discretionary investigation

**10.33** These are incidents which do not fall into any of the other categories but can be investigated by a local authority according to the following factors:

10.33   *RIDDOR and Internal Investigations*

- the incident may not have caused a RIDDOR defined major injury but may be in line with the HSE's national guidance to local authorities on targeting interventions or one which arises from a specific health and safety initiative that may be contained within the Local Authorities Service Plan;
- poor health and safety track record of the duty-holder and whether or not there has been a history of similar events;
- the incident has the potential for high public profile\media attention or has received considerable media attention leading to reputational risk through inaction\perceived inaction;
- the incident may give rise to complaint(s). Depending on the circumstances, this should be dealt with as a normal complaint procedure and not necessarily require a full incident investigation unless found to be appropriate, or any incident that has been identified as being useful for:
  - enhancing sector good practice\technical knowledge; or
  - training and developing staff as recognised from any Regulators' Development Needs Analysis (RDNA) discussions.

The result of the investigation is covered in **Chapter 9** on Enforcement and Sentencing.

## Records that need to be kept

10.34   Records must be kept of the following:

- any reportable injury;
- over-three-day injury;
- disease or dangerous occurrence.

Online forms are available which can be saved and printed, or the form can be emailed. Note that if the online form is not used the following information should be included: the date and method of reporting; the date, time and place of the event; personal details of those involved; and a brief description of the nature of the event or disease.

## When does an incident need to be reported?

10.35   The responsible person must notify the enforcing authority of an incident without delay, and a report must be received within ten days of the incident. For accidents resulting in the over-seven-day incapacitation of a worker, the enforcing authority should be notified within 15 days of the incident.

## Exemptions

10.36   Deaths and injuries do not require reports if they result from:

- medical or dental treatment, or an examination carried out by, or under the supervision of a doctor or registered dentist;

- duties carried out by the armed forces while on duty; or
- road traffic accidents unless the accident involved:
  - the loading or unloading of a vehicle;
  - work alongside the road, eg construction or maintenance work;
  - the escape of a substance being conveyed by a vehicle; or
  - a train.

## How long must RIDDOR records be kept?

**10.37**  RIDDOR records must be kept for a minimum of three years after the date of the last incident. However good practice recommends keeping them for at least six years (five in Scotland) in order to allow time for any civil litigation to be made.

# CARRYING OUT INTERNAL INVESTIGATIONS

**10.38**  The most important reason for investigating incidents and near misses is so that similar events can be prevented in the future and there are financial reasons for reducing accidents and ill-health. Carrying out an investigation will also provide a deeper understanding about the level of risk of the tasks carried out. Learning lessons from incidents is important to help improve safety.

There are many difference methods of incident investigation available. Wherever one of these methods is used or whether an organisation develops its own method, it is important that any investigation is methodical, and has a structured approach to information gathering, collation and analysis. Any investigation finding will form the basis for a series of actions to prevent the incident recurring and may make wider recommendations which effect more than just that one type of incident, for instance training or a change in the way employees communicate.

## Incident

**10.39**  The term 'incident' can be defined as an occurrence, condition, or situation arising in the course of work that resulted in, or could have resulted in, injuries, illnesses, damage to health, or fatalities. Using the term 'accident' implies that there was no fault or cause. It is now much more common to call all unwanted events 'incidents'.

## Reasons to investigate a workplace incident

**10.40**  There are several reasons to investigate incidents in the workplace:

- to find the root cause of incidents and to prevent similar incidents in the future;
- to fulfil any legal requirements;
- to determine the cost of an incident;
- to determine compliance with applicable regulations (eg occupational health and safety, criminal, etc).

The same principles apply to an investigation of a minor incident or near miss and to the more formal investigation of a serious event.

## What to investigate and who investigates

**10.41** Ideally, an investigation would be conducted by a person or a group of people who are experienced in incident investigation and who are:
- knowledgeable of any legal or organisational requirements;
- knowledgeable in the work processes, procedures, persons, and industrial relations environment for that particular situation;
- able to use interview effectively;
- knowledgeable of requirements for documents, records, and data collection; and
- able to analyse the data gathered to determine findings and reach recommendations.

Members of the team can include:
- employees with a knowledge of the work;
- supervisor of the area or work;
- safety manager/advisor;
- health and safety committee;
- union representative;
- employees with experience in investigations;
- 'outside' experts.

## Should the immediate supervisor be on the team?

**10.42** The advantage is that this person is likely to know most about the work and persons involved and the current conditions. Any issues of conflicts of interest should not arise if the incident is investigated by a team of people, and if the worker representative(s) and the investigation team members review all incident investigation findings and recommendations thoroughly.

An investigator or team who believes that incidents are caused by unsafe conditions is likely to try to uncover conditions as causes. On the other hand, an investigator who believes the incidents are caused by unsafe acts will attempt to find the human errors that are causes. Therefore, it is necessary to examine all underlying factors in a chain of events that ends in an incident.

## The decision to investigate

**10.43** The level of investigation time and effort should be related to the incident that occurred or the seriousness of the near miss. There are many different investigation techniques available – but the key issue is to have a process that people understand and one that looks for the root cause.

## The investigation

**10.44** An investigation will involve an analysis of all the information available, ie physical (the scene of the incident), verbal (the accounts of witnesses) and written (risk assessments, procedures, instructions, job guides etc), to identify what went wrong and determine what steps must be taken to prevent the adverse event from happening again.

It is important to be open, honest and objective throughout the investigation process. Pre-conceived ideas about the process, the equipment, or the people involved in an adverse event may result in the real cause being missed. An investigator should question everything and be wary of blaming individuals.

### Root cause

**10.45** A root cause is the initiating cause of either a condition or a chain of events that led to the incident. It is important not to find an immediate reason and stop at that point. For instance, if a piece of machinery fails then that failure in itself is not a root cause. In order to ascertain the root cause, inquiries will need to be made of the management processes around the maintenance of the equipment and establish if those were followed. Similarly, human error is not a root cause. People make mistakes for many reasons, lack of training, lack of procedure, or lack of control over the way the work was carried out.

Any investigation should be carried out with the aim of preventing further incidents – not to find out who to blame. That, if necessary, should be a separate process.

## Gathering information

**10.46** This should be a structured process, which looks at any records, including those of training. It should be carried out in a timely manner and look at all reasonable lines of enquiry.

## Information analysis

**10.47** This should be objective and unbiased and create a time line of events to look at the conditions which led up to the incident. It should identify the

*10.47 RIDDOR and Internal Investigations*

immediate and root causes. The analysis should also look at any organisational issues, training and communication issues.

## Recommendations

**10.48** Recommendations to prevent similar incidents are often of different types. Measures can be recommended which would prevent the same incident happening again. Other recommendations will take longer to implement, such as a training programme, or some physical alteration to the building.

Recommendations should be assigned to a person responsible for delivering them and also should be subject to a timescale. Actions should be SMART:

- Specific;
- Measureable;
- Agreed;
- Realistic;
- Timescale,

with a formal report being completed later. These notes should be kept at least until the investigation is complete.

The analysis should be conducted with employee or trade union health and safety representatives and other experts or specialists, as appropriate. This team approach can often be highly productive in enabling all the relevant causal factors to emerge.

# Chapter 11

# Responding to a Criminal Investigation

When an incident occurs   11.1
Investigators' powers   11.2
Fatal incidents: Work-related Deaths – A Protocol for Liaison   11.3
Code for Crown Prosecutors   11.4
    The evidential test   11.5
    The public interest test   11.6
Protocol – co-ordinating the response   11.7
    1    Inform insurers of the incident   11.8
    2    Do not delay in obtaining legal advice   11.9
    3    Appoint one person as contact with the investigating authority   11.10
    4    Do not assume the organisation only is being investigated   11.11
    5    Ensure individuals understand their legal rights in respect to interviews   11.12
    6    Nominate someone to speak on behalf of the organisation   11.13
    7    Identify early on an internal advisory team to assist in the criminal/civil defence   11.14
    8    Do not allow investigating authorities to exceed their authority   11.15
    9    Make a record of potential witnesses/collect evidence of the scene   11.16
    10    Do not rush to provide an internal investigation report   11.17
    11    Do not ignore other associated legal proceedings   11.18
    12    RIDDOR (health and safety incidents)   11.19
    13    Experts   11.20
    14    Do not ignore the media   11.21
Power of arrest   11.22
Conflicts of interest – interviews   11.23
Interviews under caution   11.24
    When do interviews under caution take place?   11.24
    Adverse inference   11.25
    Option for interviews under caution   11.26
    'No comment' interviews   11.27
    Full interview   11.28
    Prepared statement   11.29
    Interviews under caution of organisations   11.30
Voluntary witness statements   11.31
Compelled interviews of witnesses   11.32
Legal professional privilege   11.33

**11.1** *Responding to a Criminal Investigation*

Internal accident/incident investigation report   11.34
Obtaining documentary and other evidence – the powers' of the
    investigators   11.35
    Powers of the police   11.35
    Health and safety investigations   11.36
    Environment investigations   11.37
Freedom of Information Act 2000   11.38

# WHEN AN INCIDENT OCCURS

**11.1** While a criminal investigation can result from a routine inspection or a complaint alleging non-compliance, it is much more likely to follow from an incident. In these situations the central enquiry will be about whether there is evidence to support a prosecution of the organisations involved and possibly individuals working for those organisations.

Professor James Reason in his book *Managing the Risks of Organizational Accidents*[1] writes that it is natural for people to believe that bad events are due to 'monstrous blunders'. He observes that the best people can make the worst mistakes and that terrible incidents can happen to conscientious and well-run organisations.

When a criminal investigation is instigated it should not be assumed that those investigating have the necessary experience or expertise to appreciate the mechanics and causes of the incident. It can be difficult to explain to the investigating authority the circumstances as a whole and why the incident may have occurred. There can be a tendency for the investigators to concentrate, to the exclusion of other factors, upon what they believe the individuals or organisations have done wrong, focusing on the proximal and more obvious causes.

It is not uncommon for criminal investigations to be swayed by the consequences of a failure or series of failures, rather than to put the incident into context. Investigations can become influenced by hindsight.

The courts have warned of the dangers of applying hindsight. Mr Justice Hidden (as he was then) in his report following the public inquiry into the Clapham Rail Disaster of 1988 wrote[2]:

> 'In my review I have attempted at all times to remind myself of the dangers of using the powerful beam of hindsight to illuminate the situations revealed in the evidence. The power of that beam has its disadvantages. Hindsight also possesses a lens which can distort and can therefore present a misleading picture: it has to be avoided if fairness and accuracy of judgement is to be sought.'

---

1   James Reason, *Managing the Risks of Organizational Accidents* (Ashgate 1997).
2   See http://www.weathercharts.org/railway/Clapham_Junction_Collision_1988.pdf.

## Responding to a Criminal Investigation  11.1

The Rt Hon Lady Justice Hallett DBE in her report following the inquests into the deaths resulting from the London Bombings on 7 July 2005[3] reminded herself of the 'wise words' of Megarry J in the case of *Duchess of Argyll v Beuselinck*[4] in which he said:

> 'In this world there are few things that could not have been better done if done with hindsight. The advantages of hindsight include the benefit of having a sufficient indication of which of the many factors present are important and which are unimportant. But hindsight is no touchstone of negligence'.

Often directors and senior managers within an organisation being investigated believe if they simply explain what has happened to the investigating authority that will be an end to the matter. Unfortunately this may not be the case.

The early stages of a criminal investigation are crucial. Tactical decisions taken in the days and weeks following the incident can have a significant bearing on whether enforcement action is taken, the nature of that enforcement action, and the eventual outcome.

It should also be borne in mind that if prosecution does follow then cases will be determined in England and Wales more quickly than in the past. This is due to: (i) more cases being determined in the magistrates' court because the court now has the power to impose unlimited fines; (ii) CrimPR, Transforming Summary Justice[5] in the magistrates' court and Better Case Management[6] with their respective case management forms resulting in fewer hearings and limited scope for adjournment along with the requirement upon defendants to set out at an early stage the 'real issues in dispute' (see **Chapter 12** on Prosecution – the Court Process); (iii) pressure on defendants to indicate at an early stage if they intend to plead guilty or otherwise lose credit for a guilty plea (see **Chapter 13** on Sentencing); and (iv) in terms of cases involving a fatality, accelerated timescales for inquests (see **Chapter 14** on Coroners' Inquests and Public Inquiry).

All too often the first time an organisation considers how to respond to a criminal investigation is when an incident has occurred. It is therefore prudent for an organisation to have in place a protocol for the management of and response to a criminal investigation (see para **11.7**).

This chapter considers issues that may arise during a criminal investigation. It is written from the point of view of the procedure and the law as it applies to England and Wales. However many of the topics covered will be relevant to other jurisdictions.

---

3   See http://7julyinquests.independent.gov.uk/docs/orders/rule43-report.pdf.
4   [1972] 2 Lloyd's Rep 172 at 185.
5   See https://www.justiceinspectorates.gov.uk/hmcpsi/inspections/transforming-summary-justice/.
6   See https://www.judiciary.uk/wp-content/uploads/2015/09/better-case-management-information-pack-1.pdf.

**11.2** *Responding to a Criminal Investigation*

## INVESTIGATORS' POWERS

**11.2** Investigating bodies do not have identical powers. Criminal investigations can involve more than one body. For example a work-related death would involve the police and relevant regulatory body eg the Health and Safety Executive (HSE). Some incidents where environmental and health and safety issues arise might involve an investigation by the Environment Agency and the HSE (eg the Buncefield explosion in 2005). It is therefore important to be familiar the powers of the respective investigating bodies.

The powers of police officers are contained in the Police and Criminal Evidence Act 1984 (PACE) and the accompanying Codes of Practice. The powers of HSE inspectors (or other officers enforcing health and safety legislation) are set out in the Health and Safety at Work etc Act 1974, s 20 (HSWA 1974) and the powers of the Environment Agency officers (or other officers that enforce environmental legislation) are set out in the Environment Act 1995, s 108.

## FATAL INCIDENTS: WORK-RELATED DEATHS – A PROTOCOL FOR LIAISON

**11.3** *Work-related Deaths – A Protocol for Liaison*[7] and the accompanying *Work-related Deaths – Practical Guide*[8] is an agreement that sets out the working practices for the investigation of workplace deaths. A work-related death is defined as a fatality resulting from an incident arising out of, or in connection with, work. There are a number of signatories to the Protocol including:

- the police through the Association of Chief Police Officers;
- Crown Prosecution Service (CPS);
- HSE;
- Local Government Association and the Welsh Local Government Association;
- fire and rescue services through the Chief Fire Officers Association.

The police will investigate the incident jointly with the support of the appropriate regulatory body, for example, in relation to a construction site that appropriate body will be the HSE. The police will investigate corporate manslaughter and gross negligence manslaughter (in respect of individuals). If there is a prosecution, this will be prosecuted by the CPS.

If there is insufficient evidence to bring a corporate manslaughter/gross negligence manslaughter prosecution, the case will be passed to the regulatory authority who will investigate whether there is evidence to support a prosecution for the respective regulatory offences. If during the investigation,

---

7   See http://www.hse.gov.uk/pubns/wrdp1.pdf.
8   See http://www.hse.gov.uk/pubns/wrdp2.pdf.

evidence emerges which indicates the manslaughter investigation should be reopened, the matter will be passed back to the police to reconsider.

Regulatory bodies such as the HSE do not usually take their final decision on prosecution until after the Coroner's inquest has taken place. If the inquest jury reach a conclusion of unlawful killing this will also lead to the police being asked to reconsider the matter. In *R v DPP, ex p Manning*[9] it was stated that:

> 'where an inquest following a proper direction to the jury culminates in a [conclusion] of unlawful killing … the ordinary expectation would naturally be that a prosecution would follow.'

Where no prosecution follows, the court said that 'solid grounds' should exist to explain why this decision has been taken. In *R (on the application of Dennis) v DPP*[10] it was further said 'where an inquest jury has found unlawful killing the reasons why a prosecution should not follow need to be clearly expressed'.

# CODE FOR CROWN PROSECUTORS

**11.4** The Code for Crown Prosecutors is issued by the Director of Public Prosecutions (DPP) under the Prosecution of Offences Act 1985, s 10[11].

This Code gives guidance to all prosecutors on the general principles to be applied when making decisions about prosecutions. Although issued primarily for prosecutors in the CPS it is also applies to decisions to prosecute health and safety and environmental cases in conjunction with the respective enforcement policy of the enforcing body.

The decision to prosecute must be kept under review, even after proceedings have begun.

The Code sets out two fundamental steps in deciding whether to prosecute: (i) the evidential test; and (ii) the public interest test. In approaching tactics and preparation during a criminal investigation it is worth keeping in mind what the prosecutor will need to consider when applying the Code.

## The evidential test

**11.5** Prosecutors must be satisfied that there is sufficient evidence to provide a 'realistic prospect of conviction' against the defendant on each charge. They must consider what the defence may be and how that is likely to affect the prosecution case.

---

9   [2000] EWHC 342 (Admin), para 33.
10  [2006] EWHC 3211 (Admin), para 30.
11  It can be downloaded at: https://www.cps.gov.uk/sites/default/files/documents/publications/code_2013_accessible_english.pdf.

**11.5** *Responding to a Criminal Investigation*

Deciding whether there is a realistic prospect of conviction is an objective test. It means that the magistrates/district judge (in a magistrates' court) or jury (in a Crown Court) properly directed in accordance with the law is more likely than not to convict the defendant on each alleged offence.

## The public interest test

**11.6** Where prosecutors conclude there is sufficient evidence to justify a prosecution, they must then go on to consider whether a prosecution is required in the public interest ie to balance factors for and against prosecution.

In 1951 Lord Shawcross, when he was Attorney General, said:

> 'It has never been the rule in this country – I hope it never will be – that suspected criminal offences must automatically be the subject of prosecution.'[12]

The Code sets out a number of factors to be considered including:

- seriousness of the offence – the more serious the more likely a prosecution;
- the level of culpability of the suspect – the more culpable the more likely the prosecution;
- whether prosecution is a proportionate response.

In terms of the HSE's *Enforcement Policy Statement*[13] the factors that point towards prosecution in a health and safety case include:

- death was a result of a breach of the legislation;
- the gravity of an alleged offence, taken together with the seriousness of any actual or potential harm, or the general record and approach of the offender warrants it;
- there has been reckless disregard of health and safety requirements;
- there have been repeated breaches which give rise to significant risk, or persistent and significant poor compliance;
- there has been a failure to comply with an improvement or prohibition notice;

or there has been a repetition of a breach that was subject to a simple caution.

In terms of environmental cases, the factors where the Environment Agency is more likely to prosecute include where[14]:

- the offence was committed deliberately, recklessly or because of serious negligence;
- the circumstances leading to an offence could reasonably have been foreseen and no action to avoid or prevent it was taken;
- the environmental effect was serious;
- the offending was motivated by financial gain.

12  483 HC Official Report, 29 January 1951, col 681.
13  See http://www.hse.gov.uk/pubns/hse41.pdf.
14  See https://www.gov.uk/government/publications/environment-agency-enforcement-and-sanctions-policy/environment-agency-enforcement-and-sanctions-policy.

# PROTOCOL – CO-ORDINATING THE RESPONSE

**11.7** It is important for an organisation to have in place a protocol for responding to an incident and possible criminal investigation. The early stages of an investigation are crucial and can have a significant bearing on the eventual outcome. Arguably the most important part of any protocol is ensuring that the managers of the organisation are familiar with the protocol and that the appropriate people within the organisation are informed of the incident so that steps can be taken to control the response.

The following paragraphs list the issues that may be considered in a protocol. The protocol should be written taking into account the nature of the organisation's operations and the regulators that regulate the business. This list should not be viewed as an exhaustive one.

## 1   Inform insurers of the incident

**11.8**   As soon as possible after an incident the organisation's insurer and/or broker should be informed. It is important that the insurers are placed on notice. Insurance issues are covered in **Chapter 16**.

## 2   Do not delay in obtaining legal advice

**11.9**   In many cases it is prudent to have access to legal advice from the start to advise on the investigation and requests from the police/regulator. Defending a prosecution in relation to a work-related incident requires a combination of legal skills comprising knowledge and understanding of the regulatory framework and experience of representing defendants in criminal cases. Depending on the terms of the policy insurers may authorise or provide legal representation. Insurers may insist on a firm from its panel being instructed. Note that pursuant to the Insurance Companies (Legal Expenses Insurance) Regulations 1990[15], reg 6 an insured is entitled to instruct a solicitor of its choice.

## 3   Appoint one person as contact with the investigating authority

**11.10**   Ensure that requests for interviews and documents are made through one person and a record is kept of all requests and copies kept of all evidence handed over and attendances logged. It is usually prudent to draw up a schedule of documents handed over and to ask the inspector to sign a copy to acknowledge receipt.

---

15   SI 1990/1159.

**11.10** *Responding to a Criminal Investigation*

To avoid misunderstanding and to minimise disruption it is important to open a direct line of communication between the appointed person and the investigator. This may assist in an early understanding of the direction of the investigation and establish who the investigating officers/inspectors wish to interview (and if necessary make appropriate representations).

Sometimes a request will be made for the appointed person to provide a statement exhibiting the documents. If a statement is required then this should be given by someone else in the company as otherwise the appointed person may become a prosecution witnesses which could cause difficulties for the person to assist the legal team in event of a prosecution.

## 4 Do not assume the organisation only is being investigated

**11.11** The investigating authority may be considering prosecuting not only the organisation but also individual directors/managers and/or employees. Beware of conflicts of interest arising between individuals requiring separate legal representation (see para **11.23** on conflicts of interest).

## 5 Ensure individuals understand their legal rights in respect to interviews

**11.12** As will be explained below there are three types of interviews: (i) interviews under caution; (ii) voluntary statements; and (iii) compelled interviews. It is permissible for the lawyer instructed to explain the nature of the different interviews but not to provide advice to employees (see para **11.23** on conflicts of interest.

## 6 Nominate someone to speak on behalf of the organisation

**11.13** Anyone who speaks on behalf of the organisation at any time should have authority to do so. Senior persons within an organisation should exercise caution since what they say to an investigator may be deemed to be an admission on behalf of the organisation.

If a person is attending an interview on behalf of the company as its representative they should not be a suspect in their own right nor should they be a potential prosecution witness. When attending the interview they should provide a written authority to speak on behalf of the organisation (eg for a company a letter of authority from one of the directors).

## 7 Identify early on an internal advisory team to assist in the criminal/civil defence

**11.14** The legal team will benefit from assistance from people within the organisation with relevant expertise/technical knowledge. Ideally these people should not provide witness statements to the investigating authorities as this will hinder the legal team's ability to be able to rely upon their assistance.

## 8  Do not allow investigating authorities to exceed their authority

**11.15**  Be familiar with the powers of investigators to search and require disclosure of documents (see para **11.35**).

## 9  Make a record of potential witnesses/collect evidence of the scene

**11.16**  Ensure that the addresses and telephone numbers are obtained of potential witnesses whether employees or others. It is easy to lose track of witnesses over the lengthy course of the investigation process. Photographs/videos of the scene of the incident can be valuable evidence. If there is relevant CCTV evidence this should be downloaded.

## 10  Do not rush to provide an internal investigation report

**11.17**  Those investigating may be entitled to a copy of an internal investigation report. Any report produced shortly after the incident should ideally be written as an interim report. A report only has the potential to attract legal professional privilege if the investigation was instigated on the instructions of lawyers acting for the organisation and its dominant purpose is for litigation (see para **11.23**).

## 11  Do not ignore other associated legal proceedings

**11.18**  The criminal investigation is unlikely to be the only litigation that may result from the incident. For example there may be civil claims for compensation, an inquest if there is a work-related death or an appeal against an enforcement notice if one is served.

## 12  RIDDOR (health and safety incidents)

**11.19**  The Reporting of Injuries, Diseases and Dangerous Occurrences Regulations 2013[16] place a legal duty upon the 'responsible person to notify and report certain work related accidents to the HSE (see **Chapter 10** on

---

16  SI 2013/1471.

**11.19** *Responding to a Criminal Investigation*

RIDDOR and Internal Investigations). The responsible person is usually the employer or the company having control of the work activity[17].

Accidents that have to be reported include deaths, major injuries and where the employee is absent for over seven days.

Care should be taken when completing a RIDDOR form. This can determine whether there is a visit by the HSE following an incident. The information should be kept succinct and supposition avoided.

## 13 Experts

**11.20** Experts can often be crucial to defending proceedings. Because of the timetable of a case if a prosecution is instigated it is often prudent to begin the search for appropriate experts while the matter is being investigated and to retain them. The rules governing expert evidence are covered in **Chapter 12**.

## 14 Do not ignore the media

**11.21** The way the incident is reported can impact upon an organisation's reputation. There needs to be close co-ordination between those dealing with media issues and the legal team. Consideration will also need to be given to communications with staff, management, its investors, stakeholders and financial analysts. Consideration will also need to be given to social media: it can be advisable to monitor and record any social media posts to allow later cross-checking of witness statements.

# POWER OF ARREST

**11.22** For an arrest of an individual to be lawful it must comply with s 24 of PACE (as amended by the Serious Organised Crime and Police Act 2005, Pt 3). Police officers are able to arrest a person for any offence provided that:

- the officer, on the information known at the time, actually believes that the arrest is necessary for one of the reasons set out in PACE, s 24(5); and
- the belief is objectively reasonable.

Reasons under PACE, s 24(5) include:

- the need for prompt and effective investigation of the offence or conduct of the person; and
- to prevent any prosecution of the offence from being hindered by the disappearance of the person in question.

---

17 HSE has published guidance which can be found at http://www.hse.gov.uk/pubns/indg453.pdf.

The power of arrest is governed by Code G of the Code of Practice to PACE.

If arrested by a police officer a suspect will usually be detained in a police station. Detention when arrested is governed by Code C of PACE. The custody officer at the police station must explain to the suspect their rights which include to:

- consult privately with a solicitor and that free independent legal advice is available;
- have someone informed of their arrest;
- consult the PACE Codes of Practice.

The suspect will be searched and their possessions will be kept by the police custody officer while they are at the police station. The police also have the right to take photographs of the suspect and take fingerprints and a DNA sample.

The powers of arrest of those who are not police officers, which includes HSE inspectors and Environment Agency officers, are set out in PACE, s 24A. The powers of such persons are restricted to indictable offences ie offences that are not summary so therefore the power of arrest includes most health and safety and environmental offences which are either way offences ie can be heard in both the magistrates' court and Crown Court (see **Chapter 12** on Prosecution – the Court Process). The powers will be exercisable only if the person making the arrest has reasonable grounds for believing that any of the grounds set out below make it necessary *and* it appears to the person making the arrest that it is not practicable for a police officer to make the arrest instead. The grounds are to prevent the person:

- causing injury to him/herself or any other person;
- suffering physical injury;
- causing loss of damage to property;
- making off before a police officer can assume responsibility for the person.

The restrictions on this power of arrest make it very unlikely that an HSE inspector or Environment Agency officer would use it.

Obviously it is only possible to arrest a person. It is not possible to arrest an organisation. Therefore while directors, managers and employees may be arrested in relation to offences that they are suspected of having committed, they cannot be arrested in relation to offences suspected to have been committed by an organisation that they are employed by.

# CONFLICTS OF INTEREST – INTERVIEWS

**11.23** The Solicitors Regulation Authority (SRA) has issued specific guidance entitled *Employer's solicitors attending HSE interviews with employees*[18]. The

---

18 Which can be downloaded at https://www.sra.org.uk/solicitors/code-of-conduct/guidance/Employer-s-solicitors-attending-HSE-interviews-with-employees.page.

**11.23** *Responding to a Criminal Investigation*

guidance states that investigations by other authorities may give rise to similar considerations. Therefore it is applicable to police interviews in relation to work-related fatalities and investigation by the Environment Agency. The guidance states it is not mandatory but that the SRA may take it into account when exercising its regulatory functions.

A conflict of interest is where the solicitor owes separate duties to act in the best interests of two or more clients in relation to the same or related matters, and those duties conflict, or there is a significant risk that those duties may conflict. The guidance considers a number of scenarios.

The first is the solicitor acting for both the employer and employee. It states that very careful consideration should be given by the solicitor before accepting instructions to act for both due to the risk of a conflict of interests. In assessing the risk the solicitor needs to consider the duty to disclose and the duty of confidentiality. The guidance says that the duty to tell the employer client about information provided by the employee to the HSE inspector may conflict with the duty of confidentiality owed to the employee client.

The guidance then considers a solicitor acting for employees and not the employer but where the employer is funding the representation. The guidance says that this is permissible providing the solicitor acts solely for the employee. The solicitor may provide information to the employer about the interview only if the employee consents to this. The solicitor may act for more than one employee, providing there is no conflict of interest between the employees.

Section 5 of the guidance concerns solicitors acting for the employer. It says that the solicitor in this circumstance may provide the employee with information about the process and must make sure that the employee understands that the solicitor is not acting for them and cannot advise them. The employee should be advised before the interview with the HSE to obtain their own legal advice. The guidance goes on to say:

> '5.2 But even if these precautions are taken, it is difficult to justify the employer's solicitor accompanying the employee to the interview. The employer's solicitor's conduct obligation is to pass on to the employer all information which is material to the client's business, regardless of the source of that information (Outcome 4.2). This means that the solicitor will be obliged to pass material information to the employer, whether or not to do so is detrimental to the interests of the employee. The solicitor would be present at the interview at the employee's behest, in the knowledge that this situation might arise. The solicitor would be exposing himself to the possibility of obtaining information detrimental to the employee which he/she would be duty bound to pass on to the employer. The solicitor could even be perceived as taking unfair advantage of the employee, in that the employee's right to be accompanied would have been exercised in favour of a solicitor whose duty was owed to the employer and not to the employee (Outcome 11.1).
> 
> 5.3 There are other more general public interest issues to be considered. Would the presence of the employer's solicitor inhibit the employee from making a full and proper disclosure of facts relevant to the enquiry? An employee may understandably be reluctant to say anything which may have an adverse effect on their continuing employment or prospects of promotion, in the

presence of an employer's solicitor, whose presence may have the effect of constraining the employee in what they will say (Principle 1).
5.4 There should be no pressure on the employee to accede to having the employer's solicitor attend the interview. Otherwise employees might feel that merely by refusing the offer of attendance by the employer's solicitor they might be alienating their employer.
5.5 For these reasons it is generally inappropriate for the employer's solicitor to attend such interviews as the employee's nominee, or to seek to obtain the employee's consent to being present at the interview.'

# INTERVIEWS UNDER CAUTION
## When do interviews under caution take place?

**11.24** A person suspected of a criminal offence will usually be interviewed under caution (or be invited to an interview under caution) as part of the investigation. However there is no express legal requirement for this to take place before the decision on prosecution is taken.

The interview may provide:

- important evidence against the suspect that might not otherwise be possible to obtain;
- information leading to further lines of inquiry;
- an opportunity for the suspect to answer the allegations against him which may lead to lines of inquiry leading away from the suspect;
- evidence relevant to the prosecution decision.

The caution, which must be given at the start of the interview, is as follows:

'You do not have to say anything. But, it may harm your defence if you do not mention when questioned something which you later rely on in court. Anything you do say may be given in evidence.'

A caution must be given to a person suspected of committing a criminal offence where that person is to be questioned about that offence. This is to ensure that the answers (or silence) will be admissible in court proceedings as evidence against that person. However any evidence given in the interview under caution that incriminates others cannot be relied upon as evidence against those other persons. The evidence is only admissible against the person being interviewed.

Once a suspect has been charged with the offence under investigation, they should not be questioned further in relation to that offence (there are though exceptions to this rule but these are unlikely to arise in health and safety/environmental cases).

The police can compel an individual to be interviewed under caution because they have the power of arrest. The police may ask a suspect to attend a police station on a voluntary basis and not be arrested prior to interview. The suspect will be informed they are free to leave the police station at any time. However

**11.24** *Responding to a Criminal Investigation*

if the suspect refused to attend the interview under caution then the likelihood is that the police would use their power of arrest to compel the interview.

Because of the limited power of arrest for those agencies investigating health and safety offences and environmental offences they in practice will not be able to compel an individual to be interviewed under caution. Therefore if a request is made to an individual to attend an interview under caution, then consideration will need to be given as to whether it is in the interests of the individual to attend.

Where there is a joint investigation by the police and regulatory authority the police may seek to have the officer of the regulatory authority present in the interview. The question to consider is whether it is in the interests of the suspect to have the officer of the regulatory authority excluded from the interview under caution. The conflict is that if the officer of the regulatory authority is allowed into the interview they will be able to ask questions relating to the offences they are investigating which they would otherwise not be able to compel the individual to answer. An example of this situation is a workplace fatality where the police would be investigating manslaughter allegations and the HSE inspector alleged breaches of the HSWA 1974: but for the manslaughter investigation the HSE inspector would not be able to compel the suspect to answer questions in relation an alleged HSWA 1974 offence.

Interviews under caution are often referred to as 'PACE interviews'. All interviews under caution, whether by the police or those investigating health and safety offences or environmental offences, are governed by Code C of the Codes of Practice to PACE. Interviews under caution will usually be audio recorded, the requirements of which are governed by Code E.

## Adverse inference

**11.25** Prior to the Criminal Justice and Public Order Act 1994 coming into force a suspect had the right to remain silent when interviewed under caution. However, s 34 of the Act changed this. It states that a court, in determining whether or not a defendant is guilty, may draw such inferences as appears proper from the evidence of silence either when the defendant was interviewed under caution or when charged, the defendant failed to mention any fact that they later rely on in court in their defence which in the circumstances existing at the time they could reasonably be expected to have mentioned. A defendant cannot be convicted upon an inference from silence alone.

The key objectives of s 34 are:

- to discourage defendants from running 'ambush' defences (although note the requirement for defence statements – see **Chapter 12** on Prosecution – the Court Process);
- to encourage defendants to make early disclosure of any defence or fact that is consistent with their innocence.

In the case of *R v Argent*[19] the Court of Appeal gave six conditions which must be met before an adverse inference can be drawn:

(1) there must be proceedings against the defendant for an offence;
(2) the failure to mention a relevant fact must have occurred prior to charge or on charge;
(3) the failure must have occurred when the defendant was interviewed under caution;
(4) the questioning had to be directed to trying to discover whether or by whom the alleged offence was committed;
(5) the failure by the defendant has to relate to a fact relied on in their defence;
(6) the failure was one that, in the circumstances existing at the time of the interview, the defendant could reasonably be expected to mention when questioned.

Where an individual cannot be compelled to give an interview under caution (for example if the request was made by an HSE inspector) and does not attend the interview, then no adverse inference can be drawn by refusing to attend an interview to answer questions. An adverse inference can only be drawn if the individual attends the interview under caution and then fails to answer questions in interview.

## Option for interviews under caution

**11.26** There are three options for dealing with the interview under caution:

(1) give a 'no comment' interview;
(2) give a full interview where the suspect answers all the questions;
(3) hand in a prepared statement and then make 'no comment' to the questions asked at the interview.

## 'No comment' interviews

**11.27** The danger of failing to answer questions in the interview is that an adverse inference may be drawn at court from the silence. However this danger must be balanced with competing factors.

Under the Criminal Procedure and Investigations Act 1996 there is no obligation on the investigator to make disclosure to the suspect or his legal advisor prior to the interview. However the Court of Appeal has held in a number of cases, including *R v Argent*[20], that where little or no disclosure of the case is given so that the legal adviser is unable to properly advise their client, then giving a no comment interview may be justified.

---

19 [1996] EWCA Crim 1728.
20 [1996] EWCA Crim 1728.

**11.27** *Responding to a Criminal Investigation*

Remaining silent may also be justified where the material disclosed is so complex or relates to matters that occurred a long time ago that an immediate response is not appropriate. If the suspect is given appropriate time to consider the documentation and the allegation, then remaining silent may not be justifiable.

There may be rare occasions where the legal adviser believes their client is vulnerable and it would be in the client's interest to remain silent. An example would be if the police wanted to interview a train driver under caution soon after they have been involved in a train crash which is being investigated by the police supported by the Office of Rail and Road, in relation to potential criminal offences.

If the accused later at trial seeks to argue that the reason they remained silent was upon legal advice, then there is a two-stage test set out in the case of *R v Beckles*[21], whether an adverse inference can be drawn:

(1) Did the accused genuinely rely on the advice and believe that he was entitled to follow it?
(2) Was it reasonable in all the circumstances for the accused to rely on that advice?

If the accused gives evidence at trial that they followed legal advice to remain silence then this may amount to a waiver of privilege (legal professional privilege is explained below) and result in the legal adviser being called to give evidence. For this reason it is important for the legal adviser to make a full note as to why this advice was given.

When there is a 'no comment' interview' it is likely the officer/inspector will still put all the questions that they would have asked to the accused as if there was a full flowing interview. It is important that the accused replies 'no comment' to each question. If they answer some questions but refuse to answer others then an adverse inference is likely to be drawn.

## Full interview

**11.28** Where those investigating have made clear the allegations against the suspect and have given appropriate disclosure the suspect may decide to give a full interview answering all the questions put by the investigator. If the suspect is able to give an account that is consistent with their innocence and stands up to robust examination then this may cause the investigator to consider whether there is sufficient evidence to charge or at least cause the investigator to make further enquiries.

However, the challenge where the interview is in relation to a health and safety matter or environmental incident is being able to explain to the investigator, who may be unfamiliar with the context in which the alleged offence has occurred, the context and the nature of the industry. The suspect may feel they

---

21 [2004] EWCA Crim 2766.

are being asked questions about matters before being able to give the relevant background and explanation. Therefore care needs to be taken before deciding to give a full interview.

There may be occasions where the suspect wishes to make a full and frank admission to the allegations where the suspect accepts they are guilty which then forms the basis of a plea in mitigation if prosecuted.

## Prepared statement

**11.29** It is not uncommon, in health and safety and environmental investigations, for the suspect (or their lawyers) to read out a prepared statement rather than give a full interview. The advantage of this approach is that the suspect has control over the way in which their explanation is presented and allows them to set out the necessary context and background information. The suspect can then decide whether to then answer the investigator's questions (if so all the questions must be answered), or to respond 'no comment' once the statement has been read out, in which circumstance the fact that no comment has been made means no adverse inference can be drawn. It should be borne in mind that a prepared statement will most likely be ruled as self-serving and inadmissible as part of the defence case[22].

An adverse inference can be drawn if at trial the suspect contradicts the prepared statement or mentions a fact which they could reasonably have been expected to mention when interviewed under caution. In those circumstances the prepared statement can be put to the suspect in cross-examination.

## Interviews under caution of organisations

**11.30** If an organisation is requested to attend an interview under caution, then the organisation will be asked to nominate a representative to speak on its behalf. This person will need a letter of authority to represent the company (eg a letter from the director of a company).

It can happen that the organisation nominates a representative to attend an interview under caution who is suspected of committing an offence in their own right and may be interviewed under caution as an individual. In those circumstances the organisation should nominate someone else to attend as the nominated representative. Where the organisation is so small it is not possible for someone else to be nominated (eg a company where there is only one director) then there should be two interviews – one for the organisation and one for the individual.

Care should also be taken to ensure that the nominated person is not a potential prosecution witness (ie has not given a witness statement to the investigators).

---

22  See *R v Pearce* (1979) 69 Cr App R 365, CA.

**11.30** *Responding to a Criminal Investigation*

The investigator rather than inviting the organisation to an interview under caution may invite the organisation to send submissions. In those circumstances the investigator, in addition to setting out the allegations against the organisation, may also ask specific questions for the organisation to respond to.

## VOLUNTARY WITNESS STATEMENTS

**11.31** Voluntary witness statements taken by the police or inspector for the HSE of officer for the Environment Agency will be in 'section 9' form. This refers to the Criminal Justice Act 1967, s 9.

The start of a section 9 statement has the following declaration:

> 'This statement, consisting of [x] pages, each signed by me, is true to the best of my knowledge and belief and I make it knowing that, if it is tendered in evidence, I shall be liable to prosecution if I have wilfully stated in it anything which I know to be false or do not believe to be true.'

The witness is required to sign this declaration and then the foot of each page of his statement. There is no requirement under s 9 for the witness' signature to be witnessed, although this is the practice of the police.

A s 9 statement is admissible as evidence in a future prosecution without the need for the witness to attend court to give evidence orally, providing the defendant does not object to this.

Because it is voluntary, the witness does not have to give a statement at all if they do not wish to. Further, if the witness does decide to make a statement, they are under no obligation to answer all the questions that may be asked of them.

The statement should be in the witness' own words and before signing the witness should check carefully that it is correct and reflects the evidence he has given. Witnesses should 'stick to the facts' and avoid speculating.

If at any point the police officer/HSE inspector/Environment Agency officer believes the witness is incriminating themselves then the interview must be terminated and the witness cautioned and advised of his legal rights.

The witness can ask to have a person (nominated by that witness) to be present at the interview. This can be a colleague, union representative or legal representative (this legal representative should be independent ie not the employer's lawyer). This may be refused. Investigating authorities are usually reluctant to provide a copy of the statement to the witness (for example in a work-related accident where the witness is an employee the HSE inspector may be concerned that the witness may show the statement to their employer).

Where the statement is being taken by the police in a manslaughter investigation and the witness is viewed as a 'significant witness' there is a growing trend for these statements to be recorded.

## COMPELLED INTERVIEWS OF WITNESSES

**11.32** Those enforcing health and safety legislation can compel a witness to be interviewed pursuant to their powers under the HSWA 1974, s 20(2)(j) (often referred to as a 'section 20 interview'). An inspector can require any person who they have reasonable cause to believe is able to give information relevant to an investigation to answer questions asked by the inspector that they reasonably believe are required as part of the investigation. A person interviewed under this provision will be required to sign a declaration of truth. Those investigating environmental offences have an equivalent power under the Environment Act 1995, s 108(4)(j).

When the power under the HSWA 1974, s 20/the Environment Act 1995, s 108 is used it is an offence for the witness not to answer the questions. However any answers given in interview cannot be used against the witness to prosecute them. Unlike a section 9 statement, the witness cannot refuse to answer any of the questions.

If a person is concerned that there is a possibility they might incriminate themselves then it is appropriate for that person to refuse to give a section 9 statement, and require that they be interviewed under the s 20/s 108 power.

The witness being interviewed may ask to have a person nominated by them to be present at the interview.

The police do not have an equivalent power to compel a witness to be interviewed.

## LEGAL PROFESSIONAL PRIVILEGE

**11.33** Section 10 of PACE gives a definition of legally privileged material. It states:

'(1) Subject to subsection (2) below, in this Act "items subject to legal privilege" means—
 (a) communications between a professional legal adviser and his client or any person representing his client made in connection with the giving of legal advice to the client;
 (b) communications between a professional legal adviser and his client or any person representing his client or between such an adviser or his client or any such representative and any other person made in connection with or in contemplation of legal proceedings and for the purposes of such proceedings; and
 (c) items enclosed with or referred to in such communications and made—
  (i) in connection with the giving of legal advice; or
  (ii) in connection with or in contemplation of legal proceedings and for the purposes of such proceedings, when they are in the possession of a person who is entitled to possession of them.
(2) Items held with the intention of furthering a criminal purpose are not items subject to legal privilege.'

**11.33**  *Responding to a Criminal Investigation*

Under the police powers of search and seizure and obtaining a warrant the police are not entitled to documentation that is covered by legal professional privilege.

Similarly those investigating health and safety offences and environmental offences cannot require the production of documentation that is legally privileged. In relation to health and safety criminal investigations, the HSWA 1974, s 20(8) states:

> 'Nothing in this section shall be taken to compel the production by any person of a document of which he would on grounds of legal professional privilege be entitled to withhold production on an order for discovery in an action in the High Court or, as the case may be, on an order for the production of documents in an action in the Court of Session.'

The same wording is used in the Environment Act 1995, s 108(13) in relation to environmental criminal investigations.

There are two types of legal professional privilege (as set out in the PACE definition):

(1) **Advice privilege** – this extends to all confidential communications between a lawyer and client that are made for the purposes of giving or obtaining legal advice. It also covers lawyer's working papers. As the law stands legal advice privilege does not apply to communications between a client or a client's lawyers and third parties (ie anyone who is not the client). The term 'client' was been narrowly defined in *Three Rivers District Council v Governor and Company of the Bank of England (No 5)*[23]. This stated that most employees of an organisation are not the client for the purposes of legal advice. Therefore in the context of a large company advice privilege usually covers a defined group as the 'client' covering for example the directors and the chief executive officer.

(2) **Litigation privilege** – this is wider than legal advice privilege and can cover communications with third parties or documents created by third parties (eg investigation reports) providing the following test, set out in *Three Rivers District Council v Governor and Company of the Bank of England (No 6)*[24] is met: (i) litigation is in process or in reasonable contemplation (eg criminal prosecution or civil litigation); (ii) the communication was made for the sole or dominant purpose of conducting that litigation; and (iii) the litigation is adversarial and not investigative or inquisitorial.

The nature and extent of legal professional privilege in criminal investigations has in recent times been the subject of a number of cases brought by the Serious Fraud Office (SFO), the most significant of which is *Serious Fraud Office v Eurasian Natural Resources Corporation*[25].

---

23   [2003] EWCA Civ 474.
24   [2004] EWCA Civ 218.
25   [2018] EWCA Civ 2006.

In this case Eurasian Natural Resources Corporation (ENRC) received notification from a whistleblower about alleged bribery. ENRC did not know whether there was any evidence to support the allegation and so instructed lawyers to carry out a fact finding investigation. The SFO sought disclosure of various documents from ENRC, the most important of which were notes of interviews between ENRC's lawyers and employees, and materials and reports generated by forensic accountants appointed to undertake a 'books and records' review. ENRC refused to supply these documents to the SFO on the basis that they were covered by legal profession privilege. The SFO applied to the High Court for disclosure.

The SFO sought to argue a significant curtailment to legal professional privilege, in particular litigation privilege. Geraldine Andrews J at first instance accepted the SFO's arguments.

In relation to advice privilege, following *Three Rivers (No 5)*, which was binding on her, discussions with the company's employees to ascertain the facts about a particular work matter were not protected. She also found that these were not protected either by the wider litigation privilege. The judge found that litigation was not reasonably contemplated when the interviews were conducted and the forensic review undertaken. She said that the SFO had commenced an investigation, but that was not the same as a criminal prosecution. In her judgment a criminal prosecution was only in reasonable contemplation once the potential defendant had sufficient knowledge of the facts to be able to conclude there was sufficient evidence for there to be a prosecution. She said that avoiding litigation is not a good reason for invoking litigation privilege.

The Court of Appeal was critical of Andrews J approach to litigation privilege and upheld ENRC's position that the interview notes and the forensic review were covered by litigation privilege. On the facts the Court of Appeal found that litigation (ie potential prosecution) was in contemplation and that the documents had been created for the dominant purpose of litigation. It was relevant that before the creation of these documents, ENRC was aware of the whistleblowing allegations, was told that a SFO investigation was to be expected and had appointed external lawyers and forensic accountants to investigate.

The Court of Appeal said that there should be no distinction between contemplation of civil or criminal proceedings when considering litigation privilege. The fact that the underlying facts may be unclear initially does not in itself prevent litigation from being reasonably contemplated and that heading off, avoiding or settling proceedings comes within the scope of litigation privilege. The Court of Appeal held that it was in the public interest that companies should not lose the benefit of legal professional privilege when investigating alleged wrongdoing within the company.

The Court of Appeal did not consider the issue of advice privilege, but made it clear that it did not agree with the decision in *Three Rivers (No 5)*. It stated that this was an issue to be decided by the Supreme Court. Following the

**11.33** *Responding to a Criminal Investigation*

decision the SFO announced that it was not appealing the Court of Appeal's ruling.

Another relevant case concerning litigation privilege is *R (for and on behalf of the Health and Safety Executive) v Paul Jukes*[26]. Jukes was the transport and operation manager at a waste and recycling plant. In 2010 an employee of the company at which Jukes was employed was killed in a work-related incident. A few weeks after the incident Jukes gave a statement to his employer's solicitors, who were investigating the accident, which he signed. He said in that statement that he had responsibility for health and safety on site. The police and the HSE interviewed Jukes 16 months later under caution when he denied his responsibility for health and safety. Jukes was prosecuted for a breach of the HSWA 1974, s 7. At trial the prosecution relied upon Jukes's statement to his employer's solicitors that he was responsible for health and safety. Jukes was convicted and sentenced to nine months' imprisonment.

The case came before the Court of Appeal after the first instance decision in *SFO v ENRC*[27] but before the Court of Appeal judgment. The Court of Appeal followed the analysis of Andrews J in *SFO v ENRC* and determined that litigation could not reasonably have been in contemplation at the time Jukes gave his statement. It was therefore not covered by litigation privilege and his appeal against conviction was dismissed.

In a health and safety case, following *R v Chargot*[28] in which the House of Lords found that an accident is usually sufficient proof that there has been an exposure to a material risk to health and safety, then given the reverse burden of proof it is arguable that from the start, in terms of an employer, it is reasonable to conclude there may be a prosecution, particularly following the approach of the Court of Appeal in *SFO v ENRC*.

While Jukes claimed his employer's solicitors were also his lawyers, this was denied by the solicitors. Therefore the legal professional privilege was his employers not his. Therefore his employers could always waive that privilege. The Jukes case identifies the potential for conflict of interest between their corporate client and their client's employees when taking statements in the course of an investigation.

# INTERNAL ACCIDENT/INCIDENT INVESTIGATION REPORT

**11.34** Those investigating potential criminal charges are likely to request a copy of the internal investigation report of the organisation being investigated. Any report produced shortly after the incident should ideally be written as an

---

26 [2018] EWCA Crim 176.
27 *Serious Fraud Office v Eurasian Natural Resources Corporation* [2018] EWCA Civ 2006.
28 [2008] UKHL 73.

interim report (setting out the further information that is required before a final report can be prepared). A report only has the potential to attract litigation privilege if the investigation was the instruction of the organisation's lawyers and its dominant purpose is for litigation (as explained above). Therefore there needs to be instructions from the lawyer to those carrying out the investigation setting out that litigation is contemplated and that the purpose of the report is so that the lawyer may advise the company upon that potential litigation. It is also important that to maintain legal privilege the report should be restricted to a defined group within the organisation and its legal advisors.

Internal investigations are covered in **Chapter 10**. However, below is a suggest list of matters to consider in terms of presentation when there is the potential for there to be a criminal prosecution:

- Make clear the terms of reference of the report. Sometimes reports stray into issues that are outside the investigation into the incident. In those cases separate reports may be required.
- Keep the report succinct. It is often better to put detailed information in the appendix.
- The report may one day go before a jury. Therefore think of the potential end user. Try to avoid jargon and make sure processes etc are explained.
- Use diagrams, plans and photographs where appropriate.
- Make sure the mechanics of the incident are clearly explained.
- Ensure the person investigating the incident understands the operation.
- Evidence referred to in the report (ie statements and documents) should ideally be in appendices.
- It is often useful to have a discussion section in the report of the issues followed by a conclusion (which may be structured to set out the immediate, underlying and root causes).
- Often a report with many recommendations is an indication that the incident is not fully understood. Recommendations should ideally be discussed with those with operational responsibility and where appropriate review the recommendations to assess their effectiveness. There can be occasions when the 'do nothing option' is the most appropriate.

# OBTAINING DOCUMENTARY AND OTHER EVIDENCE – THE POWERS OF THE INVESTIGATORS

## Powers of the police

**11.35** The police have the power to search without a warrant. PACE, s 17 gives a police officer the power to enter premises in order to make an arrest provided certain conditions are met. PACE, s 18 gives a police officer the power to search premises occupied or controlled by the arrested person, again provided that certain conditions are met – essentially that the police officer has

**11.35** *Responding to a Criminal Investigation*

reasonable grounds for suspecting there is evidence at the premises, other than legally privileged items, that relates to a suspected offence. Section 18 is not relevant to an organisation since it is not possible to arrest an organisation the provision is only relevant to individuals.

There is power to obtain a search warrant pursuant to PACE, s 8. In those circumstances a justice of the peace at a magistrates' court must be satisfied that there are 'reasonable grounds for believing' there is material on the premises which is likely to be of substantial value to the investigation of the offence.

In the case of *William v Summerfield*[29] it was said:

> 'The issue of a search warrant is a serious interference with the liberty of the subject, and a step which should only be taken after most serious consideration of all the facts of the case'.

PACE, s 15 sets out safeguards for the granting of warrants and s 16 deals with the execution of warrants.

PACE, s 19 provides the police with a general power in relation to seizure. It states that a police officer who is lawfully on any premises has the following powers:

'(3) The constable may seize anything which is on the premises if he has reasonable grounds for believing—

　(a) that it is evidence in relation to an offence which he is investigating or any other offence; and
　(b) that it is necessary to seize it in order to prevent the evidence being concealed, lost, altered or destroyed.

(4) The constable may require any information which is stored in any electronic form and is accessible from the premises to be produced in a form in which it can be taken away and in which it is visible and legible or from which it can readily be produced in a visible and legible form if he has reasonable grounds for believing—

　(a) that—
　　(i) it is evidence in relation to an offence which he is investigating or any other offence; or
　　(ii) it has been obtained in consequence of the commission of an offence; and
　(b) that it is necessary to do so in order to prevent it being concealed, lost, tampered with or destroyed.'

PACE, s 20 extends the power of seizure to computer records. Section 21 sets out the police's powers regarding access and copying of items seized. PACE, s 22 sets out the powers of the police to retain anything seized pursuant to ss 19 and 20. These can be retained 'so long as is necessary in all the circumstances'.

---

29 [1972] 2 All ER 1334.

Code B of the Codes of Practice to PACE deals with police powers to search premises and to seize and retain property found on premises and persons.

It is an offence, by the Police Act 1996 to wilfully obstruct a police officer in the execution of his duty. However, if a police officer obtains evidence improperly a court may exclude the evidence in any subsequent prosecution pursuant to PACE, s 78(1) which provides:

> 'In any proceedings the court may refuse to allow evidence on which the prosecution proposes to rely to be given if it appears to the court that, having regard to all the circumstances, including the circumstances in which the evidence was obtained, the admission of the evidence would have such an adverse effect on the fairness of the proceedings that the court ought not to admit it.'

## Health and safety investigations

**11.36** Under the HSWA 1974, s 20(2)(a) an inspector can at any reasonable time (or in a situation which the inspector believes is or may be dangerous, at any time) enter premises which he has reason to believe is necessary for him to enter to exercise his powers under the HSWA 1974, s 20. The word 'premises' has a wide meaning and can include any installation or vehicle. Unlike a police officer, the power is not related to either arrest or obtaining a warrant. The inspector does not have the power to search premises or to enter the premises in order to carry out a search: their powers of entry are covered by the *Powers of entry: code of practice*[30]. The code provides guidance and sets out considerations that apply to the exercise of powers of entry including, where appropriate, the need to minimise disruption to business. As part of this code, inspectors may be required to give 48 hours' notice before entering the premises.

The HSWA 1974, s 20(2)(d) confers a power on the inspector to make such examination and investigation as may in the circumstances be necessary for the purposes of exercising their powers. 'Examination' and 'investigation' are not defined in the HSWA 1974.

Under s 20(2)(e) the inspector can direct that the entered premises or part of the premises be left 'undisturbed' for so long as is necessary to carry out the examination and investigation.

Section 20(2)(f) allows the inspector to be able to take measurements and photographs and make such recordings as he thinks necessary for the purpose of any examination or investigation.

Section 20(2)(g) gives an inspector power to take samples of any article or substance found in any premises and on the premises and of the atmosphere in or in the vicinity of the premises. The word 'article' is not defined but the term

---

30 This can be downloaded at https://assets.publishing.service.gov.uk/government/uploads/system/uploads/attachment_data/file/383079/Code_of_Practice_-_Powers_of_Entry__web_.pdf.

**11.36** *Responding to a Criminal Investigation*

'article for use at work' is defined by the HSWA 1974, s 53(1) as plant used or operated by a person at work and any article used as a component in such plant. 'Substance' is also defined in s 53(1) and includes any natural or artificial substance irrespective of its form.

Under the HSWA 1974, s 20(2)(h) if the article or substance appears to caused or to be likely to cause danger to health and safety, the inspector can require it to be dismantled or subjected to any process or test. Section 20(4) requires testing to be carried out in front of a person responsible for the premises if they request this (unless there is a danger to safety).

Section 20(2)(i) states that in the case of an article or substance to which s 20(2)(h) applies, the inspector has the power to take possession of it and detain it for as long as necessary for all or any of the following purposes:

- to examine it and do to it anything which the inspector has power to do under that paragraph;
- to ensure that it is not tampered with before the examination of it is completed;
- to ensure that it is available for use as evidence in any proceedings for an offence under any of the relevant statutory provisions or any proceedings relating to an improvement or prohibition notice.

Section 20(2)(k) gives an inspector the power to require the production of, inspect and take copies of (the inspector cannot take the originals into his possession) any entry in:

- any books or documents which by virtue of any of the relevant statutory provisions are required to be kept; and
- any other books or documents which it is necessary for the inspector to see for the purposes of any examination or investigation under s 20(2)(d).

Pursuant to the HSWA 1974, s 33(1)(h) it is an offence to obstruct an inspector in the exercise of any of these powers. Guidance in relation to a similar provision concerning the exercise of powers by Environment Agency officers has recently been given by the Divisional Court (see below). Note that if an inspector obtains evidence improperly by exceeding any of these powers a court may exclude the evidence in any subsequent prosecution pursuant to PACE, s 78(1) (see para **11.35**).

## Environment investigations

**11.37** Environment Agency officers under the EA 1995, s 108(4) have powers that almost mirror those of an HSE inspector under the HSWA 1974, s 20(2).

Under the EA 1995, s 108(4)(a) an Environmental Agency officer can enter at any reasonable time (or in an emergency, at any time and, if need be, by force) any premises to exercise his/her powers. Unlike an HSE inspector, the officer can apply to a justice of the peace at a magistrates' court for an entry warrant pursuant to the EA 1995, Sch 18 to be granted. The justice of the peace must have reasonable grounds for granting the entry warrant and one or more of the following conditions must apply:

- that the exercise of the power in relation to the premises has been refused;
- that such a refusal is reasonably apprehended;
- that the premises are unoccupied;
- that the occupier is temporarily absent from the premises and the case is one of urgency; or
- that an application for admission to the premises would defeat the object of the proposed entry.

An officer does not have the power to search premises or to enter the premises in order to carry out a search. The warrant under Sch 18 is an entry warrant, and not a search warrant like a PACE, section 8 warrant and so an officer is not permitted search if entry has been obtained by an entry warrant. Like HSE inspectors Environment Agency officers' power of entry are covered by the *Powers of entry: code of practice* (see para **11.36**).

Under the EA 1995, s 108(4)(c) the officer can make such examination and investigation as may in the circumstances be necessary for carrying out the purposes of exercising their powers. As with the HSWA 1974, the EA 1995 does not define 'examination' or 'investigation'.

Pursuant to s 108(4)(d) an officer can direct that the premises or part of the premises be left 'undisturbed' for as long as is necessary to carry out the examination and investigation.

Section 108(4)(e) allows the officer to be able to take measurements and photographs and make such recordings as thought necessary for the purpose of any examination or investigation.

The EA 1995, s 108(4)(f) provides that an officer can take samples, or cause samples to be taken, of any article in or on the premises and of the air, water or land in, or in the vicinity of the premises. Under s 108(4)(g) the officer can require any article or substance to be dismantled or subjected to any test or process if it appears to have caused or to be likely to cause pollution of the environment or harm human health. Section 108(4)(h) allows the officer to take into their possession the article or substance and detain it for any of the following reasons:

- to examine it, or cause it to be examined, and to do, or cause to be done, to it anything which he has power to do under that paragraph;
- to ensure that it is not tampered with before examination of it is completed;
- to ensure that it is available for use as evidence in any proceedings for an offence under the pollution control enactments in the case of the enforcing authority under whose authorisation the officer acts or in any other proceedings relating to a variation notice, enforcement notice or prohibition notice under those enactments.

Section 108(4)(k) gives an officer the power to require the production of, or where the information is recorded in computerised for, the extracts from any records and to take copies of them:

**11.37** *Responding to a Criminal Investigation*

- which are required to be kept under the pollution control enactments for the enforcing authority under whose authorisation the officer acts; or
- which it is necessary for the officer to see for the purposes of an examination or investigation under s 108(4)(c).

As with the powers under the HSWA 1974, s 20, it is an offence for a person to obstruct an officer in the excise of the above powers, pursuant to the EA 1995, s 110(1). In *Millmore v Environment Agency*[31] the convictions of five employees for obstruction were considered by the Divisional Court by way of case stated. Two of the convictions were quashed. The court found that it is not necessary to prove a positive action for a prosecution to succeed and that mere omission can amount to obstruction.

The prosecutions arose out of an investigation in 2016 by the Environment Agency into Southern Water Services Ltd. As part of the investigation, officers visited a number of waste water treatment works, during which various documents were requested.

In relation to the two employees whose convictions were quashed, one was a management scientist who was instructed by the company's legal team to prevent officers from removing documents. She communicated the company's position but did not physically obstruct the officers. The other, again on the instruction of the company's lawyers, requested the officers leave site. With respect to the convictions upheld, two related to employees (one said to be on the instruction of the company's lawyers) who removed a number of site diaries and locked them in a van and then refused to answer questions, and one in respect of a process operator who picked up a number of site diaries which had been given to the officers and then locked them in a cupboard. Southern Water Services Ltd was also prosecuted for obstruction but the Environment Agency was unable to prove that the company was criminally liable for the relevant actions of their employees.

Note that if an officer obtains evidence improperly by exceeding any of the powers conferred under the EA 1996, s 108(4) a court may exclude the evidence in any subsequent prosecution pursuant to PACE, s 78(1) (see para **11.35**).

# FREEDOM OF INFORMATION ACT 2000

**11.38** The Freedom of Information Act 2000 (FIA 2000) places an obligation upon 'public authorities' to give access to certain information that they hold or control. Enforcing authorities such as the HSE and the Environment Agency are 'public authorities' for the purpose of the Act. An application is made by writing a letter or email to the public authority in question.

The question arises as to what happens to the statements and documents obtained as part of its investigation and are requested under the Act by a third

---

31 [2019] EWHC 443 (Admin).

party, for example a request to the HSE by the lawyers for a personal injury claimant injured at work where the incident has led to a criminal investigation.

There are a number of exemptions to providing the information, including:

- **FIA 2000, s 30** – *investigations and proceedings:* under s 30(1) information will be exempt if it has at any time been held by a public authority for the purposes of:
  - any investigation which the public authority has a duty to conduct to ascertain whether a person should be charged with, or is guilty of, an offence;
  - any investigation conducted by a public authority that may lead to a decision to institute criminal proceedings that the authority has power to conduct; or
  - any criminal proceedings which the authority has power to conduct.

  The exemption is not absolute. The information will not be disclosed if the public interest not to disclose outweighs the public interest to disclose.

- **FIA 2000, s 41** – *confidential information:* the Act gives some protection if the information was provided in confidence to the public authority by a private body. However, protection is limited. It only applies if it would be an actionable breach of confidence for the information to be disclosed.

Note in relation to witness statements, the witness would have given the statement on the understanding that it would only be used for potential criminal proceedings. Also under the Magistrates' Courts (Witnesses Addresses) Rules 1990[32] most witnesses will have provided statements on the understanding that their addresses will not be disclosed without their consent. Therefore if a request is made for witness statements, the public authority will not usually disclose them to a third party without first obtaining the consent of the witness.

It is perhaps prudent for the person co-ordinating the response to the criminal investigation to discuss with the investigator what processes are in place if a request is made under the Act and that the organisation will be given the opportunity to make representations to the enforcing authority.

---

32   SI 1990/336.

# Chapter 12

# Prosecution – the Court Process

Criminal Procedure Rules   12.1
Magistrates' court   12.2
Crown Court   12.3
Types of offences and where they are heard   12.4
    Summary offences   12.5
    Either way offences   12.6
    Indictable offences   12.7
The start of proceedings   12.8
Case management   12.9
    Transforming summary justice/better case management   12.9
    Preparation for trial form – magistrates' court   12.10
    Plea and trial preparation hearing (PTPH) and form – the Crown
        Court   12.11
    Statements made in case management forms   12.12
    Entering a plea – corporate body   12.13
    Bail   12.14
Disclosure and defence statement   12.15
    Unused material   12.15
    Duty of the investigator and disclosure officer   12.16
    Disclosure test   12.17
    The stages of disclosure   12.18
Defence statement   12.19
    Third party disclosure   12.20
Expert evidence   12.21
Hearsay evidence   12.22
Bad character   12.23
Dismissal   12.24
Abuse of process   12.25
Trial   12.26
    Burden of proof   12.27
    Trial file/jury bundle   12.28
    Witnesses giving evidence   12.29
    Reading witness statements   12.30
    Admissions   12.31
    Points of law   12.32
    Start of the trial   12.33
    Prosecution case   12.34
    No case to answer   12.35
    Defence case   12.36

**12.1** *Prosecution – the Court Process*

    Closing addresses   12.37
    Judge's summing up   12.38
    Verdict   12.39
Sentencing   12.40
    Sentencing hearing   12.40
    Newton hearing   12.41
    Confiscation (environmental prosecutions)   12.42
Costs   12.43
    Defendant's costs order   12.43
    Order that the defendant pay the prosecution costs   12.44
Appeals   12.45
    Appeals from the magistrates' court   12.46
    Appeals from the Crown Court   12.47

The aim of this chapter is to give an overview of the court process as it relates to health and safety and environmental cases for those readers unfamiliar with criminal proceedings.

# CRIMINAL PROCEDURE RULES

**12.1** The Criminal Procedure Rules[1] (CrimPR) first came into force in 2005. These, along with the associated Criminal Practice Directions (CPD), govern the practice and procedure to be followed in the criminal courts in England and Wales. The CrimPR are arranged to reflect the main stages of a criminal case. The CPD contain the case progression forms and all other prescribed forms which the rules require should be used.

The first three parts of the CrimPR are particularly important: Pt 1 – the overriding objective; Pt 2 – understanding and applying the rules; and Pt 3 – case management.

Part 1 of the CrimPR sets out the overriding objective of the rules which is to deal with cases justly. In *R (DPP) v Chorley Justices*[2] the Court of Appeal said that the CrimPR had brought about a 'sea change' in the way criminal cases are dealt with stating[3]:

> 'The rules make clear that the overriding objective is that criminal cases be dealt with justly; that includes acquitting the innocent and convicting the guilty, dealing with the prosecution and the defence fairly, respecting the interests of witnesses, dealing with the case efficiently and expeditiously, and also, of great importance, dealing with the case in a way that takes into account the gravity of the offence, the complexity of what is in issue, the severity of the consequences to

---

1   SI 2005/1490.
2   [2006] EWHC 1795 (Admin).
3   [2006] EWHC 1795 (Admin) at [24].

the defendant and others affected and the needs of other cases. Rule 1.2 imposes upon the duty of participants in a criminal case to prepare and conduct the case in accordance with the overriding objective, to comply with the rules and, importantly, to inform the court and all parties of any significant failure, whether or not the participant is responsible for that failure, to take any procedural step required by the rules.'

The Court of Appeal also added:

'The days of ambushing and taking last-minute technical points are gone. They are not consistent with the overriding objective of deciding cases justly, acquitting the innocent and convicting the guilty.'

Part 3 requires the courts to manage the progression of cases. In the cases of *Chaaban*[4] and *Jisl*[5], the Court of Appeal held that courts have a duty to manage criminal cases effectively. Moreover, Part 3 states that all courts must further the overriding objective by active case management which includes:

- early identification of the issues in the case (there is a duty on the defence to identify early on the 'real issues' in the case, see *Malcolm v DPP*[6]);
- early identification of witness requirements;
- setting a timetable for the progression of the case;
- monitoring the progress of the case and compliance with directions given by the court; and
- ensuring that evidence, whether disputed or not, is presented in the shortest and clearest way.

If a party fails to comply with a rule or court direction the court can make a cost order or impose 'other sanctions' as appropriate.

The CrimPR and the CPD can be viewed at http://www.justice.gov.uk/courts/procedure-rules/criminal/rulesmenu-2015. The rules are usually amended twice a year in April and October. The most recent changes to the CrimPRs were made by the Criminal Procedure (Amendment) Rules 2018[7].

# MAGISTRATES' COURT

**12.2** In the magistrates' court cases are heard either by three lay magistrates or one district judge. The lay magistrates (also known as justices of the peace) are local people who volunteer their services. They do not have formal legal qualifications, but are given legal and procedural advice by a qualified justices' legal adviser (clerk to the court). District judges are legally qualified, paid and full-time professionals. An authorised district judge must deal with all hearings, including trial, where:

---

4   [2003] EWCA Crim 1012.
5   [2004] EWCA Crim 696.
6   [2007] EWHC 363 (Admin).
7   SI 2018/132.

**12.2** *Prosecution – the Court Process*

- the case involves (or there was a high risk of) death or a significant life changing injury;
- the case involves substantial environmental damage or polluting material of a dangerous nature;
- the case resulted in major adverse effect on human health or quality of life, animal health or flora;
- major costs through clean up, site restoration or animal rehabilitation have been incurred;
- the case involves a defendant corporation that has a turnover in excess of £10 million but does not exceed £250 million, and the defendant has acted in a deliberate, reckless or negligent manner;
- the case involves a defendant corporation with a turnover in excess of £250 million;
- the case requires the court to analyse complex company accounts;
- the case is high profile or of an exceptionally sensitive nature.

# CROWN COURT

**12.3** The Crown Court sentences defendants committed from the magistrates' court, tries cases with a judge and jury, and sentences defendants that have either pleaded guilty in the Crown Court or have been convicted following a jury trial. The Crown Court also hears appeals from the magistrates' court.

The judge deals with all pre-trial hearings and sentences. Trials are before a judge sitting with a jury of 12 people. The judge decides issues of law and directs the jury. It is the jury who decides issues of fact and whether the defendant is guilty or not.

The jury is required to return a unanimous verdict. If it is unable to do so the judge may decide that a verdict can be returned if a majority of the jury can reach an agreement on whether they are sure of the defendant's guilt or innocence, referred to as 'majority verdict'. This means that the judge will be content with a verdict if ten or more of the jurors are in agreement. If agreement cannot be reached (known as a 'hung jury') the jury will be dismissed and the prosecution will consider whether to seek a re-trial.

Judges at the Crown Court are usually either a circuit judge or a recorder (a barrister or solicitor who sits as part-time judge). Very serious criminal cases may be heard by a High Court judge.

# TYPES OF OFFENCES AND WHERE THEY ARE HEARD

**12.4** There are three types of offences: summary offences; offences triable either way; and indictable offences. Summary offences can only be tried in the magistrates' court. Either way offences can be tried in the magistrates' court or the Crown Court. Indictable offences can only be tried in the Crown Court.

A few health and safety offences and environmental offences are summary only. The vast majority however are either way offences. There are no indictable only offences. However, gross negligence manslaughter and corporate manslaughter are indictable offences.

## Summary offences

**12.5** Prosecutions for summary offences must be commenced within the specified time period, generally no more than six months after the date of the offence, or otherwise the prosecution will be time barred.

At that first hearing in the magistrates' court the defendant is likely to be asked to enter a plea. If the defendant pleads guilty, the court may proceed immediately to sentence. If the defendant pleads not guilty (or does not enter a plea), then the court will likely want to fix a date for trial and complete the 'preparation for trial' form (see para **12.10**). If not, the case will be adjourned to another date for this to take place.

## Either way offences

**12.6** For an either way offence the magistrates' court will determine (usually at the first hearing) whether the case should be heard in the magistrates' court or the Crown Court.

The justices' legal adviser will first ask the defendant to confirm that he has received the 'initial details of the prosecution case' (see para **12.10**). If not then the hearing may be adjourned if the defendant requests this. The defendant will then be asked to indicate his plea (known as 'plea before venue').

If the defendant pleads guilty then the magistrates' court can proceed to sentencing immediately if it considers it has sufficient sentencing powers. If not, the case will be committed to the Crown Court for sentencing by a judge at a later date. For offences committed after 12 March 2015 the magistrates' court has the power to impose unlimited fines. For custodial sentences for individuals, the maximum sentence the magistrates' court can impose is six months.

If the defendant indicates a not guilty plea (or does not indicate a plea) the court goes on to consider the venue (known as the 'mode of trial' hearing). The prosecution and defence make representations as to whether the case is suitable for summary trial. The *Allocation Definitive Guideline*[8] gives guidance as to whether cases should be dealt with by a magistrates' court or Crown Court. It states that in general either way offences should be tried summarily, unless:

---

8   See https://www.sentencingcouncil.org.uk/wp-content/uploads/Allocation_Guideline_2015.pdf.

### 12.6 *Prosecution – the Court Process*

- the outcome would clearly be a sentence in excess of the court's powers for the offence(s) concerned after taking into account personal mitigation and any potential reduction for a guilty plea; or
- for reasons of unusual legal, procedural or factual complexity, the case should be tried in the Crown Court. This exception may apply in cases where a very substantial fine is the likely sentence. Other circumstances where this exception will apply are likely to be rare and case specific; the court will rely on the submissions of the parties to identify relevant cases.

The guideline continues:

> 'In cases with no factual or legal complications the court should bear in mind its power to commit for sentence [to the Crown Court] after a trial and may retain jurisdiction notwithstanding that the likely sentence might exceed its powers.'

Given that most health and safety and environmental prosecutions are of organisations rather than individuals and given that the magistrates' court has the power to impose unlimited fines, many will be considered suitable for summary trial, with a significant number being allocated to a district judge.

If the court accepts jurisdiction the defendant is then asked whether he wishes to be tried in the magistrates' court or the Crown Court. If he wishes to be tried in the magistrates' court then the court will usually at the first hearing fix a date for trial and complete the 'preparation for trial'.

If the defendant elects trial in the Crown Court the case will be sent to the court. A date will be set for a plea and trial preparation hearing (PTPH) in the Crown Court (see para **12.11**) usually 28 days from the date of the magistrates' court hearing. A short form has to be completed by the court and parties setting out the offences and pleas, concisely the 'real issues' in the case.

There are a number of factors to consider when deciding whether to elect trial at the Crown Court. These include the following.

- There is a view amongst some lawyers that district judges and magistrates become 'case hardened' over time and so are more likely to convict. The conviction rate in the magistrates' court is certainly significantly higher than in the Crown Court, although the figures need to be treated with care as they can include guilty pleas as well as those convicted after trial. Some feel that a jury is more likely to give a defendant the benefit of the doubt.
- Health and safety and environmental prosecutions often concern industries with which the general public will have little if any knowledge of how they operate. In a jury trial the judge will often allow time for the evidence to be given to assist the jury's understanding. As a consequence there can be more time for the evidence to be examined.
- Where an application is made during trial for evidence to be excluded, in the magistrates' court this will be decided by the magistrates/district judge. Even if they agreed to exclude the evidence they will still have heard it and it might be difficult to remove that information from their minds when deliberating upon their verdict. In the Crown Court the issue is determined by the judge in the absence of the jury.

- Some lawyers are of the view that if there are complex legal issues in the case then these are best determined by a judge at a jury trial.
- Cases progress through the magistrates' court far more quickly than in the Crown Court.
- If the defendant is convicted, particularly if a company, then the defendant may be ordered to pay the prosecution's costs. The costs in the Crown Court are likely to be much higher. Note that if the prosecution is by the Health and Safety Executive (HSE), investigation costs will be recovered under the fee for intervention scheme (FFI).
- There is the perception that defendants sentenced in the Crown Court are given tougher sentences. So in terms of a company the concern will be a higher fine. However, the Crown Court and the magistrates' court apply the same sentencing guidelines but the reality is that a Crown Court judge is more used to imposing greater sentences.
- A defendant may consider appealing against conviction and/or sentence. Appeals from the magistrates' court are to the Crown Court and the procedure is relatively straightforward. The appeal is a rehearing of the case before a judge and two magistrates (who have not previously been involved in the case). If the appeal is dismissed then the Crown Court could increase the sentence imposed. Unlike in the magistrates' court, to appeal from the Crown Court the defendant will first have to obtain permission (from a High Court judge). If permission is granted, the appeal is heard in the Court of Appeal by three appeal judges. It is not a rehearing of the case. To appeal conviction the defendant must satisfy the court that something went wrong at the trial that makes the conviction unsafe eg the judge misdirected the jury. An appeal against sentence is usually on the grounds that it was 'manifestly excessive'.

## Indictable offences

**12.7** Where the charge is an indictable offence, if the first hearing is in the magistrates' court the matter will automatically be sent to the Crown Court 'forthwith'. The first hearing in the Crown Court will usually be 28 days from the date of the hearing in the magistrates' court for a PTPH, see para **12.11**. If it is a guilty plea the aim is to sentence the defendant at this hearing (unless, in relation to an individual, a pre-sentencing report is required in which case the hearing will be adjourned). If it is a not guilty plea (or no plea is entered) the judge will aim to fix a trial date and make appropriate orders to progress the case in a way that minimises the need for further hearings and ensures an effective trial.

# THE START OF PROCEEDINGS

**12.8** Health and safety and environmental prosecutions against individual and corporate defendants start by the service of a summons. For a charge of

**12.8** *Prosecution – the Court Process*

corporate manslaughter against a corporate defendant, this also starts by the service of a summons. Where an individual is prosecuted for gross negligence manslaughter then the proceedings start when the defendant is charged with the offence at the police station.

To issue a summons the regulator must lay an 'information' at the magistrates' court. This is the application to issue the summons. An information is a statement that tells the court what offence the defendant has allegedly committed. The information should:

- identify the defendant by giving the defendant's name and address;
- describe the offence;
- give sufficient detail of the alleged offence, which will include the date of the alleged offence or the period over which it is said to have been committed and usually the location at which it is said the alleged offence occurred; and
- refer to the statutory provision which creates the offence.

Once the information has been laid, the court can issue a summons. The summons must specify each offence against the defendant and contain a notice of when and where the defendant has to attend court.

The summons will usually be served by the regulator by sending, in terms of an individual, to an address whether the regulator believes the individual will receive it eg home address, or in the case of an organisation to its principal office, or (if no identifiable office) to its place of business. Summonses can also be served by electronic means or by handing the summons to the defendant if an individual, or if an organisation, a person holding a senior position in the organisation.

In either way cases, the covering letter with the summons will refer to the mode of trial and the right to 'initial details' of the prosecution case. Part 8 of the CrimPR requires that initial details should include:

- a summary of the circumstances of the offence;
- any account given by the defendant (or if an organisation the representative) in an interview under caution;
- any witness statements or exhibits that the prosecution has available and considers material to plea, allocation of the case for trial, or to sentence;
- the defendant's previous convictions, if any;
- any available victim impact statements.

In practice the regulator will usually serve the witness statements upon which the prosecution intend to rely (which will be in s 9 of the Criminal Justice Act 1967 form – see **Chapter 10** on RIDDOR and Internal Investigations), documentary evidence, photographs, expert reports and record of the defendant's interview under caution along with a case summary/outline of the case (the level of detail given will depend on the nature of the case).

Many prosecutors still serve a 'Friskies Schedule' detailing what it alleges are the aggravating and mitigating features of the case relevant to sentencing (named after the case *R v Friskies Petcare (UK) Ltd*[9]). However the Court of Appeal in *R v Thelwall*[10] said these were no longer of 'any materiality'. It is now more usual for prosecutors in the case summary to include a section that sets out the regulator's position on the application of the relevant sentencing guideline in the event of conviction[11].

# CASE MANAGEMENT
## Transforming summary justice/better case management

**12.9** In recent years there has been an emphasis on trying to make the criminal justice system more efficient and effective. This began with 'Transforming Summary Justice' (TSJ) in the magistrates' court setting out a number of principles (including early provision to the defendant of the initial details of the prosecution case, streamlined disclosure and a clear expectation of effectiveness), followed by 'Better Case Management' (BCM) in relation to Crown Court cases. There is a *Better Case Management Handbook* which sets out how cases are to be progressed in the Crown Court[12].

In January 2015 the Rt Hon Sir Brian Leveson, President of the Queen's Bench Division, published his report entitled 'Review in Efficiency in Criminal Proceedings'[13]. At para 22 he states:

> 'It is ... necessary to ensure that the scarce resources are not wasted or used inefficiently. Demands on public funds must be kept to a minimum while, at the same time, ensuring that the delivery of justice is effective and meets the highest standards that any democratic society is entitled to expect.'

The report emphasises the importance of the CrimPR and the role of judges in effectively managing the work of the court.

The aim of TSJ and BCM is to encourage cases to be dealt with more quickly meaning that every hearing should count towards reducing or eliminating wasted hearings and wasted time. Since many cases do not go to trial, there is an emphasis on guilty pleas being entered sooner rather than later. Consequently, the defendant is expected to indicate their plea at an early stage and to say what they believe are the real issues in the case.

Central to the case management of contested cases is the completion of the preparation for trial form for summary trials, normally completed at the first hearing in the magistrates' court, and for jury trials the PTPH form usually

---

9  [2000] EWCA Crim 95.
10 [2016] EWCA Crim 1755.
11 Sentencing Council, *Health and Safety Offences, Corporate Manslaughter and Food Safety and Hygiene Offences – Definitive Guideline* (February 2016).
12 See https://www.judiciary.gov.uk/wp-content/uploads/2018/02/bcm-guide-for-practitioners-20180207.pdf.
13 See https://www.judiciary.gov.uk/wp-content/uploads/2015/01/review-of-efficiency-in-criminal-proceedings-20151.pdf.

**12.9**  *Prosecution – the Court Process*

completed at the first hearing in the Crown Court. These forms are described below. If there is more than one defendant then the form has to be completed by each defendant. A number of the issues referred to in the forms, for example disclosure and hearsay evidence, are explained later in this chapter.

## Preparation for trial form – magistrates' court

**12.10**   Where the defendant pleads not guilty and the case is to be tried in the magistrates' court, the preparation for trial form must be completed by the parties and the court. This form can be viewed at https://www.justice.gov.uk/courts/procedure-rules/criminal/docs/2014/crimpr-part3-magistrates-courts-trial-preparation-form.pdf. This is a general form and so not all elements of the form are relevant to health and safety and environmental cases.

Part 1 of the form is for the prosecutor to complete and includes their contact details, whether more evidence is to be served, whether the prosecution relies on expert, hearsay and or bad character evidence, and whether the prosecutor wants to vary the standard court directions.

Part 2 of the form is for the defendant's legal representative to complete and includes the defendant's and their legal representative's contact details, whether the defendant has been advised that they will receive credit for a guilty plea (ie a discount on sentence), what facts can be recorded as written admissions, what are the disputed issues of fact or law for trial, whether the defendant will give a defence statement (not compulsory in the magistrates' court) and whether the defendant wants to vary the standard court directions.

Part 3 is to be completed by both parties and concerns witness evidence. The prosecution witnesses are listed and the prosecution indicates which witnesses they intend calling. The defence must state which prosecution witnesses' statements can be read (ie are not disputed), which prosecution witnesses they require to attend and identifying to which disputed issue in the case the evidence is relevant. In terms of defence witnesses it must state if the defendant is likely to give evidence (if a company, a company representative) and how many witnesses the defence intends to call (the defence must give details separately of intended defence witnesses).

After Part 3 the prosecution and the defendant's legal representative are required to sign the form.

Part 4 is the court's directions for trial. This section starts with dates being given for the prosecution to serve any further evidence and to complete initial disclosure. There are then standard directions annexed to this section with time limits (which are required to be completed in six weeks or nine weeks where expert evidence is to be called) however these can be varied which will usually be the case in health and safety and environmental cases. The ones that may be relevant to health and safety and environmental cases are: written admissions; defence statement; defence witnesses; application for disclosure; expert evidence; hearsay evidence; bad character evidence, and the service of skeleton arguments in relation to the law. There is provision for other directions that may be required that are not included in the standard directions. In health and safety and environmental cases it is common to request the prosecution to serve in advance of the trial an opening note setting out how the prosecutor intends to open the case and to serve a draft file of the documents the prosecution intends to rely on at trial. A date for trial is entered on the form with a time estimate for the length of trial. The parties are required to certify readiness for trial at least 14 days before trial and confirm which witnesses will give evidence and what the time estimate for trial is.

## Plea and trial preparation hearing (PTPH) and form – the Crown Court

**12.11** Where the defendant pleads not guilty and the case is to be tried in the Crown Court, the PTPH form must be completed by the parties and the court. This form can be viewed at https://www.justice.gov.uk/courts/procedure-rules/criminal/docs/october-2015/cm008.pdf. As with the magistrates' court form, this is a general form and so not all elements of the form are relevant.

The hearing will usually be held 28 days after sending from the magistrates' court. There is a discretion to vary this timescale up to a maximum of 35 days. One reason for doing so is to enable the trial advocate to attend the PTPH.

Crown Courts have a digital case system where documents are 'served' once they are uploaded to the system and notification sent by email to the defendant. However this only applies to cases prosecuted by the Crown Prosecution Service (CPS) (and so applies to gross negligence manslaughter and corporate manslaughter cases). However, the HSE and local authorities who prosecute health and safety offences and the Environment Agency that prosecutes environmental cases (along with other regulators) are not at present part of this scheme. Therefore in these cases documents still have to be served and hard copies provided to the court and the defendant.

The prosecution is required to complete its sections of the form and send to the defendant in no less than seven days. The defendant is then required to complete his sections and return to the prosecution and the court in advance of the hearing. The court will provide copies of the completed form to the parties after the hearing.

The defendant will usually be arraigned at the PTPH (ie enter his plea) unless there is good reason not to do so eg there is going to be an abuse of process argument or a dismissal application is likely. If the defendant cannot be arraigned the court will usually give full PTPH directions towards a trial but make provision for a further case management hearing (FCMH).

Where the defendant pleads 'not guilty' or does not enter a plea, the court will:

- set the trial date;
- identify, so far as can be determined, the issues for trial;

**12.11** *Prosecution – the Court Process*

- consider with the parties the witness requirements that can be determined;
- provide a timetable for the necessary pre-trial preparation and give appropriate directions for an effective trial;
- make provision for any FCMH.

Unless otherwise ordered the prosecution and the defendant must file a certificate of readiness no less than 28 days before the start of the trial.

Part 1 of the PTPH form – the parties and their advocates have to enter their details and appoint a 'case progression officer'. The defence is required to set out as far as it is known the 'real issues' in the case. There is then a 'state of preparation' section which for the prosecution relates to such matters as what evidence has been served and whether a draft indictment (which sets out the offence and particulars of offence) has been served. For the defence, the issues include whether it is an abuse of process issue or a dismissal application is anticipated, whether the defendant can be arraigned and if a defence statement is available. There is then a section where the prosecution witnesses are listed, and where the parties indicate which witnesses they require to attend court stating the relevant issue in dispute for each witness and which witnesses' evidence can be read.

Part 2 of the form is completed by the court and is where it sets out its directions.

The court records the pleas entered if there was arraignment, and if not, the reasons why arraignment did not take place. The judge must record that the defendant has been informed that, if pleading guilty, credit for the plea will be given, and that if the defendant fails to provide a sufficiently detailed defence statement this may count against them. For health and safety and environmental prosecutions the court will usually fix a date for trial with a time estimate (these cases are unsuitable for the 'warned list' where cases are listed for trial on any day within a defined window).

The directions are in four stages:

- **Stage 1** – is to be completed usually by 70 days from the date of sending for corporate defendants and individuals on bail. This stage is for the prosecution to serve the bulk of its evidence, make initial disclosure (if not already done), serve any bad character notice or hearsay application and, if applicable, deal with third party disclosure;
- **Stage 2** – is for the service of the defence response including the defence statement, details of defence witnesses and the service of expert evidence. This date will ordinarily be 28 days after Stage 1 reflecting the time provided for the service of a defence statement;
- **Stage 3** – is for the prosecution response to the defence statement and other defence items. This date will ordinarily be 14 or 28 days after Stage 2 depending on the date of trial;
- **Stage 4** – for the defence to provide final materials including any defence expert evidence not served at Stage 2 or make applications that arise out of prosecution disclosure. This date will ordinarily be 14 or 28 days after Stage 2 depending on the date of trial.

In health and safety and environmental cases the court will usually order that the experts meet in advance of trial and provide a statement of what issues are agreed and what issues are in dispute. The judge is likely to make an order for the prosecution to serve an opening note in advance of trial and a draft file of documents to be put before the jury (often referred to as the 'jury bundle'). Because the PTPH may not be before the judge who will hear the case, a pre-trial review may be listed, often 28 days before the trial date to ensure that the case is ready for trial.

## Statements made in case management forms

**12.12** In *R v Newell*[14] the appellant was charged with possession of cocaine with intent to supply. He had made no comment when interviewed under caution and did not serve a defence statement. In the equivalent of the PTPH form that was in use at the Crown Court at the time in response to the question 'what are the real issues' his barrister had written 'No Possession'. He later changed solicitors and a new barrister was instructed. A defence statement was served on the first day of trial which accepted possession but denied intent to supply the cocaine.

At trial the judge allowed the prosecution to put to the appellant in cross examination the answer given in the form.

The Court of Appeal held that statements made in case management forms are admissible as evidence under the Criminal Justice Act 2003 (CJA 2003), s 118(1) but they would rarely be admitted at trial where the case has been conducted within the letter and the spirit of CrimPR. The court however made clear that in certain circumstances there might be exceptions to this general rule where the spirit of the CrimPR had not been followed.

The court distinguished the case of *Firth v Epping Magistrates Court*[15] which was a judicial review. Here the defendant was charged with assault in the magistrates' court and had pleaded not guilty. She indicated in the 'trial issues' part of the form that her defence was self defence. The prosecutor then indicated that the charge was to be upgraded to actual bodily harm and was allowed to rely upon the response in the form as an admission of involvement. The judicial review failed.

In *Newell* the Court of Appeal acknowledged that the trial preparation form in the magistrates' court is different to the case management form in the Crown Court in that the form provides for the making of admissions or the acknowledgment that matters are not in issue.

14 [2012] EWCA Crim 650.
15 [2011] EWHC 388 (Admin).

### Entering a plea – corporate body

**12.13** The usual practice for a corporate body to enter a plea is for the lawyer representing the corporate body at the hearing to have a written statement from an officer of the corporate body (eg the managing director or other person having the management of the corporation's affairs) appointing the lawyer to act in the matter (see the Criminal Justice Act 1925, s 33(6)). This written authority will be handed to the court. The lawyer will then enter the plea to the charge on behalf of the corporate body. The lawyer may be asked to hand to the court the plea in writing.

### Bail

**12.14** In relation to individuals bail will need to be considered. The vast majority of defendants prosecuted in relation to a work-related accident or environmental incident do not have a criminal record and are not likely to commit other offences while on bail. Therefore the court is very likely to grant unconditional bail.

# DISCLOSURE AND DEFENCE STATEMENT
### Unused material

**12.15** Unused material includes statements or documents obtained during the course of the investigation that is not being relied upon by the prosecution. It may also be draft witness statements of the prosecution witnesses being called, or records of their interview under caution if originally a suspect in the investigation. Further potentially disclosable as unused material are the investigator's notebooks and instruction to, and draft reports of, the prosecution's experts.

Disclosure is covered by the Criminal Procedure and Investigations Act 1996 (CPIA 1996) which has a Code of Practice[16]. There is also the *Attorney General's Guidelines on Disclosure for Investigators, Prosecutors and Defence Practitioners*[17] and Part 15 of the CrimPR.

### Duty of the investigator and disclosure officer

**12.16** All investigators have a responsibility to carry out their investigation in accordance with the CPIA 1996 and its code including recording information

---

16 See https://assets.publishing.service.gov.uk/government/uploads/system/uploads/attachment_data/file/447967/code-of-practice-approved.pdf.
17 See https://assets.publishing.service.gov.uk/government/uploads/system/uploads/attachment_data/file/262994/AG_Disclosure_Guidelines_-_December_2013.pdf.

and retaining records of information and other material. The investigator must pursue all reasonable lines of enquiry, whether these point towards or away from a suspect. What is reasonable will depend on the circumstances of the case.

The investigator in charge of the investigation is responsible for directing the investigation and ensuring that there are proper procedures in place for recording information and retaining records of information and other material.

The investigation will have a disclosure officer (in larger cases there may be more than one). The duties of the disclosure officer include:

- examining material retained during the investigation;
- drawing to the attention of the prosecutor material that may be disclosable;
- at the request of the prosecutor disclosing unused material to the defence.

The disclosure officer prepares a schedule of relevant unused material from the investigation and identifies the material that meets the disclosure test (which will be disclosed to the defence or made available for inspection) and that material which does not meet the test.

The disclosure officer must prepare the unused material when:

- the accused is charged with an indictable offence; or
- the accused is charged with an either way offence which is likely to be tried at the Crown Court or the accused is likely to plead not guilty at a summary trial; or
- the accused is charged with a summary offence and is likely to plead not guilty.

## Disclosure test

**12.17** Material must be disclosed if it 'might reasonably be considered capable of undermining the case for the prosecution or of assisting the case for the accused'[18]. Material should not be viewed in isolation. It may be that certain items of material together meet the disclosure test.

The CPIA 1996, s 7A requires the disclosure officer and prosecutor a requirement to keep disclosure under continual review throughout the investigation and prosecution. The position on disclosure must be reviewed on receipt of a defence statement and when details of the issues in dispute are identified on the case management form.

## The stages of disclosure

**12.18** There are three stages to disclosure:

---

18 CPS, *Disclosure Manual* (February 2018), Ch 10.

**12.18** *Prosecution – the Court Process*

- **Stage 1** – the prosecution provides 'initial disclosure' by serving the unused schedule along with copies of any material that it considers meets the disclosure test;
- **Stage 2** – often referred to as 'defence disclosure' which is when the defendant serves a 'defence statement' (see para **12.19**) which is mandatory in the court but voluntary in the magistrates' court (although in health and safety and environmental cases it is likely to be beneficial to serve a defence statement so the court is aware of the issues that are disputed);
- **Stage 3** – the prosecution then review the position in respect of disclosure in light of the defence statement.

If the defence reasonably believes there are documents in possession of the prosecution that should be disclosed but the prosecution has objected to disclosing, the defence can make an application to the court for disclosure using a form under the CPIA 1996, s 8.

# DEFENCE STATEMENT

**12.19** A defence statement should (see CPIA 1996, s 6A):

- include the nature of the defence, including any particular defences on which the defendant intends to rely;
- indicate the matters of fact on which the defendant takes issue with the prosecutor, and in respect of each why;
- include particulars of the matters of fact on which the defendant relies upon for the purposes of the defence;
- include any point of law that the defendant wishes to take, including any point about the admissibility of evidence or about abuse of process, and identify any legal authority relied on.

Defence statements are required to be clear and sufficiently detailed. In the Crown Court judges will say if they are of the view the defence statement is inadequate and give appropriate warnings.

The period for the service of the defence statement is taken from the day on which the prosecutor complies or purports to comply with its duty to provide initial disclosure. In the Crown Court this is 28 days and in the magistrates' court 14 days. An application to extend the period for service of the defence statement must be made within the relevant period (ie 14 or 28 days), and specify the reason for the extension and the number of days' extension required. If still within the time period when the case management form is being considered by the court the date for service will be addressed then.

The defence statement must be signed by the defendant or his legal representative. In the case of a corporate defendant anyone signing the statement should have written authorisation from the company to sign on its behalf.

Note the time period for the service of the defence statement is also the time period for the defence to inform the prosecution and court of the details of the defence witnesses likely to be called (CPIA 1996, s 6C), which once again is voluntary in the magistrates' court.

### Third party disclosure

**12.20** The requirement for the prosecution to keep disclosure under review extends to unused material held by third parties which may become relevant.

This is not an uncommon issue in health and safety and environment cases where there may be a number of duty-holders, some of whom are not being prosecuted (eg in a work-related accident on a construction site where under the Construction (Design and Management) Regulations 2015[19] there could be the client, the principal contractor, sub-contractors, designers and principal designer). If the prosecutor does not pursue this line of enquiry then the only option is to apply for a witness summons against the third party under the Criminal Procedure (Attendance of Witnesses) Act 1965. To be able to obtain the summons the defendant must be able to establish:

- the person on whom the summons is served is likely to be able to give evidence likely to be material evidence or produce any document likely to be material; and
- it is in the interests of justice to issue the summons to secure the attendance of that person to give evidence or produce the document/item.

## EXPERT EVIDENCE

**12.21** Health and safety and environmental prosecutions often involve expert evidence. Expert assistance may be useful in two ways:

- for the investigation, helping the investigators understand technical issues and assisting with lines of enquiry. For the defence, helping the defence lawyer to understand the technical issues and analyse the prosecution's evidence to determine lines of enquiry and cross-examination;
- to give opinion evidence at court.

The rules governing evidence given at court in criminal cases (whether at trial or at sentencing hearings) are set out in Pt 19 of the CrimPR. For an expert's opinion to be admissible as evidence:

- it must be relevant to an issue in the proceedings;
- it is required to provide the court with information likely to be outside the court's own knowledge and experience; and
- the expert witness must be competent to give that opinion.

---

19  SI 2015/51.

**12.21**  *Prosecution – the Court Process*

An expert's duty is to the court and not to the party that instructs them. Their role is to assist the court by giving objective and unbiased opinion on matters within their area of expertise. An expert witness may give opinion evidence to assist in resolving issues concerning matters of knowledge which can only be acquired by special training or experience in order to enable the court to adequately consider those issues in the case. The facts on which the expert's opinions are based must be either admitted or proved by admissible evidence. Usually those facts are established by witnesses of fact in the case but they may also include facts observed by the expert themselves.

*H (Stephen) v R*[20] was an historic sexual abuse prosecution where the defence sought to call an expert on 'false memory syndrome'. It was the defence case that the victim's allegations were untrue and the likely product of mental illness. The trial judge accepted that this was a matter appropriate for expert evidence but that the report of the defence expert was inadmissible as evidence as it was 'littered with wholly inappropriate, adverse comments on the credibility and reliability' of the victim and 'had assumed the role of the advocate arguing the case for the defence'.

The Court of Appeal upheld this ruling and observed that the CrimPR, which had recently been amended in respect of expert evidence, now requires a 'more rigorous approach on the part of advocates and the courts to the handling of expert evidence' and that expert 'comment based only on analysis of the evidence which effectively usurps the task of the jury is to be avoided: the task of the expert is only to provide assistance'[21] to the court.

The CrimPR sets out a number of factors which the court may take into account when determining the reliability of expert opinion. These include:

- the extent and quality of the data on which the expert's opinion is based;
- if the expert's opinion relies on the results of the use of any method, whether the opinion takes account of matters such as the degree of precision or margin or uncertainty;
- the extent to which the expert's opinion is based on material falling outside the expert's own field of expertise;
- the completeness of the information, which was available to the expert, and whether the expert took account of all relevant information;
- if there is a range of expert opinion on the matter in question, whether the expert's preference has been properly explained.

The fact that an expert may be employed by the investigator or by the defendant company does not prevent that person from being an expert. In *Field v Leeds City Council*[22] (a civil case concerning disputed repairs to a tenanted property) the Court of Appeal stated[23]:

---

20  [2014] EWCA Crim 1555.
21  [2014] EWCA Crim 1555 at [909].
22  [1999] EWCA Civ 3013.
23  [1999] EWCA Civ 3013 at [27].

'The question whether someone should be able to give expert evidence should depend on whether, (i) it can be demonstrated whether that person has relevant expertise in an area in issue in the case; and (ii) that it can be demonstrated that he or she is aware of their primary duty to the court if they give expert evidence.'

In *R v Stubbs*[24] a bank employee was convicted of conspiracy to defraud. The Court of Appeal held that the trial judge had been correct to allow the prosecution to call another employee of the same bank to give expert evidence on the online banking system that was in use when the passwords of account-holders were reset without their authority. The witness's limitations had been clearly put to the jury, and the fact that he was an employee of the bank affected only the weight and not the admissibility of his evidence.

When parties intend to call expert evidence they should alert the court and the other side at the earliest practicable moment. Permission can be refused where service is so late as to constitute a 'grave breach' of the rules (see *R v Ensor*[25]).

The statement and declaration required for an expert's report is given in the CPD. It should be in the same terms or terms substantially the same. The statement and declaration is reproduced below:

'I (Insert Full Name) DECLARE THAT:

1. I understand that my duty is to help the court to achieve the overriding objective by giving independent assistance by way of objective, unbiased opinion on matters within my expertise, both in preparing reports and giving oral evidence. I understand that this duty overrides any obligation to the party by whom I am engaged or the person who has paid or is liable to pay me. I confirm that I have complied with and will continue to comply with that duty.
2. I confirm that I have not entered into any arrangement where the amount or payment of my fees is in any way dependent on the outcome of the case.
3. I know of no conflict of interest of any kind, other than any which I have disclosed in my report.
4. I do not consider that any interest which I have disclosed affects my suitability as an expert witness on any issues on which I have given evidence.
5. I will advise the party by whom I am instructed if, between the date of my report and the trial, there is any change in circumstances which affect my answers to points 3 and 4 above.
6. I have shown the sources of all information I have used.
7. I have exercised reasonable care and skill in order to be accurate and complete in preparing this report.
8. I have endeavoured to include in my report those matters, of which I have knowledge or of which I have been made aware, that might adversely affect the validity of my opinion. I have clearly stated any qualifications to my opinion.
9. I have not, without forming an independent view, included or excluded anything which has been suggested to me by others including my instructing lawyers.
10. I will notify those instructing me immediately and confirm in writing if for any reason my existing report requires any correction or qualification.

---

24 [2006] EWCA Crim 2312.
25 [2009] EWCA Crim 2519.

## 12.21 Prosecution – the Court Process

11. I understand that:
    a. my report will form the evidence to be given under oath or affirmation;
    b. the court may at any stage direct a discussion to take place between experts;
    c. the court may direct that, following a discussion between the experts, a statement should be prepared showing those issues which are agreed and those issues which are not agreed, together with the reasons;
    d. I may be required to attend court to be cross-examined on my report by a cross-examiner assisted by an expert.
    e. I am likely to be the subject of public adverse criticism by the judge if the Court concludes that I have not taken reasonable care in trying to meet the standards set out above.

I have read Part 19 of the Criminal Procedure rules and I have complied with its requirements.

I confirm that I have acted in accordance with the code of practice or conduct for experts of my discipline, namely [identify the code].

[For Experts instructed by the Prosecution only] I confirm that I have read guidance contained in a booklet known as *Disclosure: Experts' Evidence and Unused Material* which details my role and documents my responsibilities, in relation to disclosure as an expert witness. I have followed the guidance and recognise the continuing nature of my responsibilities of revelation. In accordance with my duties of disclosure, as documented in the guidance booklet, I confirm that:

I have complied with my duties to record, retain and reveal material in accordance with the Criminal Procedure and Investigations Act 1996, as amended;

  a. I have compiled an Index of all material. I will ensure that the Index is updated in the event I am provided with or generate additional material;
  b. in the event my opinion changes on any material issue, I will inform the investigating officer, as soon as reasonably practicable and give reasons.

STATEMENT OF TRUTH

I confirm that the contents of this report are true to the best of my knowledge and belief and that I make this report knowing that, if it is tendered in evidence, I would be liable to prosecution if I have wilfully stated anything which I know to be false or that I do not believe to be true.'

The CrimPR requires the parties to consider with their experts whether it would assist the court if the experts were to hold a meeting between the experts in order to try to agree and narrow the issues and in particular to identify:

- the extent of the agreement between them;
- the points of and short reasons for any disagreement;
- actions, if any, which may be taken to resolve any outstanding points of disagreement; and
- any further material issues not raised and the extent to which these issues are agreed.

A meeting between the parties is not compulsory under the CrimPR but may be directed by the court. This direction is included in the magistrates' court trial preparation form and the Crown Court's PTPH form.

It is important that any expert who is being considered to give evidence is properly instructed and understands their duty to the court. If the expert has given evidence in civil claims but not criminal prosecutions it is important that they appreciate the difference between the two types of proceedings. It is also important that the expert understands the nature of the charges against the defendant and the elements of the offence.

It is essential that the expert keeps to their area of expertise. It might be that the expert comes to a conclusion that there are other areas which they believe may be relevant to the case but that they do not have the relevant expertise to be able to give an opinion. In those circumstances it may be necessary to instruct another expert to address these issues.

The need to ensure the expert has appropriate expertise and understands their duty as an expert was emphasised by the Court of Appeal in *R v Pabon*[26]. This was a prosecution brought by the Serious Fraud Office (SFO). The case was that Pabon along with his co-defendants faced a charge of conspiracy to defraud, alleging that they dishonestly rigged LIBOR which is shorthand for the 'London Inter-Bank Offered Rate': a global benchmark interest rate for many types of financial transactions (in other words the interest rate at which banks can borrow money from each other on a particular day). The defendants fell into two categories: traders; and LIBOR submitters.

The sole focus of the appeal against conviction concerned the conduct of an expert witness, Saul Haydon Rowe, called by the prosecution. The central issue for the jury was dishonesty. Rowe was called by the SFO to assist the court on the complexities of LIBOR and the banking system. Although the conviction was upheld the Court of Appeal was very critical of the SFO's expert and found he was only a suitable expert in relation to basic banking and financial matters (which were not in dispute). Key issues addressed in the judgment were:

- experts must be aware of their duties and obligations to the court. Rowe had signed the declaration to his report without reading without reading Pt 19 of the CrimPR and associated material. The Court of Appeal noted that Rowe had 'signally failed to comply with his basic duties as an expert';
- the evidence must be within the expert's expertise. The court found that Rowe had strayed beyond his areas of expertise;
- experts should not pass off the work of others as their own. The court was very critical of the fact that parts of Rowe's report had been drafted by someone else. Rowe had been in discussions with a number of others in respect of areas outside his purported areas of expertise;
- experts must not discuss their evidence with anyone while giving evidence. Rowe gave evidence over two days. At the end of the first day the judge gave the usual warning to him not to discuss his evidence whilst in the witness box, but after leaving court Rowe called a number of people in an attempt to bolster his understanding of matters on which he was being questioned.

---

26 [2018] EWCA Crim 420.

# HEARSAY EVIDENCE

**12.22** Hearsay is evidence of fact which is not given in oral evidence by someone with direct knowledge of that fact. The general rule is that hearsay evidence is not admissible in a criminal trial. However, there are limited circumstances in which hearsay evidence is admissible:

- where all parties (eg the prosecution, the defence and the judge) agree to the hearsay evidence being admitted;
- where admitting the hearsay evidence is in the best interests of justice;
- where there is a statutory provision under the CJA 2003 or a common law exception making the hearsay statement admissible.

The rules on hearsay evidence are set out in Pt 20 of the CrimPR.

There are many exceptions to the rule against hearsay, allowing hearsay evidence to be admitted at trial. Some of the exceptions that occur in health and safety and environmental cases include:

- a statement taken in section 9 (Criminal Justice Act 1967) form where the witness is no longer available to give evidence (see the CJA 2003, s 116). This could be because the witnesses is dead or cannot be found (despite reasonably practicable steps having been taken to find them) or is outside of the UK and it is not reasonably practicable to secure their attendance (although this is less likely these days as evidence can be given via video link);
- the CJA 2003, s 117 allows business records to be admitted into evidence, however the information has to be reliable. The document must have been created or received by a person in the course of a trade, business, profession or other occupation or as the holder of an office;
- the CJA 2003, s 118 reserves certain common law exceptions such as public records, admissions by an agent eg company director, and experts' reference to the works of others within their field;
- where a person gives evidence in person and admits having made a statement previously which is not the same as what they have said in the witness box, the previous statement can be used and can be accepted as good evidence by the court. See the CJA 2003, s 119;
- where a witness has been cross-examined on a previous statement, the statement itself can be admissible in certain circumstances. See the CJA 2003, s 120;
- the CJA 2003, s 127 relates to the admissibility of preparatory work for expert evidence.

# BAD CHARACTER

**12.23** The rules on bad-character evidence are contained in the CJA 2003, ss 98 to 113 and the CrimPR, Pt 21.

The CJA 2003 defines[27] 'bad character' as where there is evidence of, or a disposition towards, misconduct by the defendant, other than the evidence concerning the charge the defendant is currently facing. 'Misconduct', means the commission of an offence, or other 'reprehensible behaviour'. Bad character is therefore all about the personal characteristics of the defendant.

The CJA 2003 lays down[28] a number of circumstances in which this type of evidence is 'admissible' (ie can be relied upon) at trial. These are known as 'gateways' and are as follows:

- **Gateway 1** – all parties to the proceedings agree to the evidence being admissible;
- **Gateway 2** – the evidence is adduced by the defendant himself, or is given in answer to a question asked by him in cross-examination and he intended to elicit it;
- **Gateway 3** – it is important explanatory evidence;
- **Gateway 4** – it is relevant to an important matter in issue between the defendant and the prosecution;
- **Gateway 5** – it is evidence to correct a false impression given by the defendant; or
- **Gateway 6** – the defendant has made an attack on another person's character.

To be admissible, the evidence must be 'relevant' and 'important'. The prosecution has no absolute right to have the evidence admitted, and the defendant can apply to the court to have the evidence excluded on the grounds it would make the proceedings unfair. In the case of *O'Brien v Chief Constable of South Wales Police*[29] the House of Lords said that, to be admissible, the evidence must have an 'enhanced probative value'.

The likely gateways to be relied on in a health and safety or environmental prosecution are 3 and 4 above. Gateway 3 concerns evidence without which the jury would find it impossible, or difficult, to understand properly other evidence in the case, and the value of this evidence substantially helps the understanding of the case as a whole.

In relation to gateway 4, the issue is likely to be whether the defendant has a 'propensity to commit the offence'. This will usually be the route relied upon by a prosecutor for admitting as evidence the fact that the defendant has previous convictions or there has been other enforcement action, but this has to be relevant to the nature of the prosecution being faced.

# DISMISSAL

**12.24** Where an either way case is sent to the Crown Court or the offence is indictable only, the defendant may apply for the charge(s) to be dismissed.

---

27 CJA 2003, Pt 11, s 98.
28 CJA 2003, Pt 11, s 101.
29 [2005] UKHL 26.

**12.24** *Prosecution – the Court Process*

The application has to be made in writing within 14 days of receipt of the prosecution evidence and must be heard before the defendant is arraigned. The Crime and Disorder Act 1998, s 51 and Sch 3, para 2(2) provide:

> 'The judge shall dismiss a charge (and accordingly quash any count relating to it in any indictment preferred against the applicant) which is the subject of any such application if it appears to him that the evidence against the applicant would not be sufficient for him to be properly convicted'.

In *R (Inland Revenue Commissioners) v Kingston Crown Court*[30], it was said that when an application is considered the court reviews whether there is evidence to go to a jury and whether that evidence is sufficient for a jury properly to convict. The relevant test is *R v Galbraith*[31] (see para **12.35** in respect of 'no case to answer').

As to whether a dismissal application is a tactical decision is a question that needs careful consideration. The danger of making an application and failing is that the prosecution will have insight into how the defence intends to defend the case; and the prosecution has advanced warning of any weaknesses in its own case which it may try to address before trial.

# ABUSE OF PROCESS

**12.25** An abuse of process has been defined as 'something so unfair and wrong that the court should not allow a prosecutor to proceed with what is, in all other respects, a regular proceeding'[32]. If the court finds that there has been an abuse of process the proceedings are stayed ie halted.

In *R v Crawley*[33] the Court of Appeal set out the scope of the two broad categories that the abuse process can be brought under: (i) cases where the defendant cannot receive a fair trial; and (ii) cases where it would be unfair for the defendant to be tried[34]. In the magistrates' court the power to stay proceedings is limited to cases where the defendant cannot obtain a fair trial.

Examples of abuse of process are as follows:

- **Delay** – Where there has been substantial delay in bringing a prosecution and the defendant will suffer such serious prejudice that a fair trial cannot be held. Health and safety and environmental prosecutions are often subject to delay. However a stay on the basis of delay will only be granted in exceptional circumstances.
- **Loss of evidence/failure to disclose unused material** – Where the prosecution fails to take action to obtain relevant evidence or evidence is lost or destroyed this may be a ground for abuse of process. There may also

---

30 [2001] EWHC Admin 581.
31 (1981) 73 Cr App R 124.
32 *Hui Chi-Ming v R* [1992] 1 AC 34 (PC).
33 *R v Crawley* [2014] EWCA Crim 1028.
34 See *R v Beckford* [1996] 1 Cr App R 94, 101.

be an abuse of process if the prosecution fails to comply with disclosure obligations in respect of unused material. To order a stay of proceedings (see *R (Ebrahim) v Feltham Magistrates Court: Mouatt v DPP*[35] the court needs to consider: (i) the extent of the duty, if any, on the investigating authority and/or prosecutor to obtain and/or retain the evidence; (ii) if there was a breach, then proceedings will only be halted if the defence prove on the balance of probabilities that there would be serious prejudice so that no fair trial can be held; and (iii) if the behaviour of the prosecution was so bad that it would not be fair for the defendant to be tried – the defence will need to show bad faith or serious fault on the part of the investigators and/or the prosecution.

- **Double jeopardy** – It is likely to be an abuse to prosecute a defendant for an offence which arises out of the same set of facts for which the defendant has already been prosecuted. This is what happened in the case of *R v Beedie*[36] and is an example of where proceedings were stayed. The CPS prosecuted Beedie for manslaughter after he had already been prosecuted by the HSE for health and safety offences in relation to a defective gas installation that caused a fatality. This case led to the *Work-related Deaths: A protocol for liaison*[37]. If the circumstances meant that prosecutions could be brought by both the HSE and the Environment Agency then it is likely this would be a joint prosecution (eg the prosecution that followed the Buncefield explosion in 2008).

- **Breach of promise** – It can occur that a regulator makes representations to the duty-holder that there will be no prosecution but later that decision is reversed and a prosecution started. Reneging on such a promise may amount to an abuse of process. The longer a defendant is given to thinking that he will not be prosecuted, the more likely it is that a prosecution will amount to an abuse of process.

- **Decision to prosecute is contrary to the regulator's policy** – It may be possible to argue that a prosecution is contrary to a regulator's enforcement policy and is oppressive. An example of this is the case of *R v Adaway*[38]. This was a trading standards case prosecuted by a local authority that had a policy of only prosecuting where there was fraud or persistent and repeated offences. As a result of the evidence called the trial judge formed the view that the decision was not on this basis but solely on the insistence of the aggrieved party. The Court of Appeal said[39]: 'Trading standards officers must exercise discretion when deciding whether or not a particular case warrants the intervention of the criminal law ... The Trade Descriptions Act is essentially concerned with consumer protection. It does not seem ... that this case falls within the type of mischief which the Act is directed'.

---

35 [2001] EWHC Admin 130.
36 [1997] 2 Cr App R 167, CA.
37 National Liaison Committee for Work-related Deaths Protocol, *Work-related Deaths: A protocol for liaison (England and Wales)* (England and Wales WRDP2 Rev 02/16).
38 [2004] EWCA Crim 2831.
39 [2004] EWCA Crim 2831 at [13].

# TRIAL

**12.26** The format of a trial in the magistrates' court and in the Crown Court is very similar. However, because there is a jury in the Crown Court this alters some of the procedures.

## Burden of proof

**12.27** It is for the prosecution to prove the case against a defendant to the 'criminal standard' of proof ie the prosecution must prove its case beyond reasonable doubt, often referred to as making the magistrates/district judge in the magistrates' court or the jury in a Crown Court trial 'satisfied so that they are sure' of the defendant's guilt.

However there are some regulatory offences where there is a reverse burden of proof upon the defendant. For example in a health and safety prosecution pursuant to ss 2 or 3 of the Health and Safety at Work etc Act 1974 the prosecution must prove to the criminal standard that there has been an exposure to a material risk. Once this is proved it is for the defendant to prove to the 'civil standard' which is on the balance of probabilities, ie more likely than not, that the defendant took all reasonably practicable steps to manage the risk.

## Trial file/jury bundle

**12.28** In health and safety and environmental cases there are usually a large number of documents along with photographs, diagrams and plans that are served by the prosecution in support of its case. Some of these documents the prosecution (and defence) may wish the court to examine during the trial with witnesses giving evidence. It is usual for these to be placed in a file (or files) with copies for the parties, the witness box, and the magistrates/district judge in the magistrates' court or the judge and jury in the Crown Court (often referred to as the 'jury bundle'). It may be appropriate for the defence to add documents to this file as the trial progresses or to have a separate defence file.

## Witnesses giving evidence

**12.29** A witness gives evidence from the witness box. When a defendant gives evidence this is from the witness box not the dock. A witness is required to swear an oath (the Bible if Christian or another holy book if of another faith) to tell the truth. Alternatively the witness can affirm.

With the exception of the defendant, the officer in the case for the prosecution and experts (who give opinion evidence), a witness who has not given evidence cannot sit in the court during the proceedings until they have given evidence. In terms of experts it is usually advisable to have them sitting in court from the start of the evidence: if there is a change in evidence from the written statement of a witness that is being called this might alter their opinion.

When a witness is called to give evidence he is first asked questions by the party's advocate. This is known as 'evidence in chief'. The object is to elicit from the witness all the facts supporting that party's case that are within the personal knowledge of that witness. The advocate should not ask in general 'leading questions'. These are questions which invite a witness to give a particular response. There are some limited exceptions such as questions on introductory matters or facts that are not in dispute.

After a witness has given evidence in chief, he may be cross-examined on behalf of the other parties in the trial (including co-defendants asking questions of another defendant's witness). The advocate is permitted to ask leading questions in cross-examination.

After a witness has been cross-examined he may be questioned again by the party's advocate that called the witness. This is known as 're-examination'. Once again the advocate cannot ask leading questions and can only ask questions in respect of matters that have arisen during cross-examination ie it is not a second bite of the cherry for the advocate to ask questions that were forgotten during the examination in chief.

The magistrates/district judge can ask questions of the witnesses. In the Crown Court the judge may ask questions if it is believed an issue needs exploring or clarification. If a member of the jury wishes to ask a question they will have to send a note of that question to the judge. If the judge believes the question is relevant, the judge will ask the question.

## Reading witness statements

**12.30** Where witness evidence is not controversial and the parties agree, a written witness statement can be read out in court and accepted as evidence. For this to occur, the statement must be in s 9 of the Criminal Justice Act 1967 form. It may be that in order to agree the evidence the statement will be edited and only the agreed content read out.

## Admissions

**12.31** The prosecution and defence are able to make formal admissions to the court which means that the prosecution does not have to call evidence to prove those facts. These are made pursuant to the Criminal Justice Act 1967, s 10. An example in a health and safety case would be that the deceased died as a result of a workplace accident. These are usually referred to by the prosecution when the case is opened at the start of the trial. However in health and safety and environmental prosecutions it is not uncommon for these admissions not to be finalised until the end of the prosecution's case.

## Points of law

**12.32** During the case, points of law or procedural issues may arise. In a Crown Court trial the jury will be sent out of the court while the parties' advocates address the judge. In the magistrates' court these matters are determined by the magistrates/district judge.

## Start of the trial

**12.33** In the magistrates' court the defendant is asked to confirm their not guilty plea. If there are any legal issues these are then addressed. In more complex cases these are sometimes determined at a pre-trial hearing ordered specifically for that purpose.

The trial then starts with the prosecution opening its case to the magistrates/district judge setting out what the allegation is with a summary of what the evidence against the defendant is and any relevant matters of law. After the prosecution opening speech, the magistrates/district judge sometimes invite the defence advocate to address them briefly on what the defence is and to clearly identify what the issues in the case are.

In the Crown Court, arraignment will have taken place at an earlier hearing. Before the prosecution opens the case to the jury the judge will deal with any preliminary legal issues that need to be resolved (that have not been resolved at previous hearings). Once this has been addressed a jury of 12 will be chosen at random from a jury panel. Where the case is due to last for more than four weeks the court can start a case with two extra jurors who can take the place of any juror unable to continue. Once the jury is chosen the jury are sworn in.

The judge will tell the jury that the evidence upon which they will decide the case is the evidence that will be presented to them in court and that they should only discuss the case among themselves. The judge will warn them not to be influenced by any media reporting of the case and not to carry out research of their own eg on the internet. The jury will be told that they decide matters of fact and return a verdict and that matters of law are for the judge who will direct them on the law.

The trial then starts with the prosecution opening its case to the jury when the prosecuting advocate will explain what the case is all about by telling them what the charges are against defendant and what the case is against them. In health and safety cases and environmental cases the advocate will usually explain briefly what needs to be proved but tell the jury that the judge will direct them upon this at the end of the trial. The judge may then invite the defence advocate to give a short address to the jury on what the issues are.

The purpose of this is to help the jury understand the case and focus on those matters which are in dispute.

## Prosecution case

**12.34** The prosecution then calls its witnesses who will be cross-examined by the defence advocate. During the course of the evidence the prosecution will read out agreed witness statements. The prosecution will also read out any admissions agreed between the parties. The prosecution will call any expert evidence it relies upon. At some trials the court will require the prosecution and expert evidence to give evidence 'back to back' during the prosecution case. The case will conclude with the inspector/officer in the case adducing the defendant's (or in the case of a company defendant, the company representative's) record of interview under caution if the defendant attended an interview under caution.

## No case to answer

**12.35** At the close of the prosecution's case the defence can submit to the judge or magistrates/district judge that there is no case for the defendant to answer. If the court agrees, the case is dismissed, and the defendant acquitted. If the court does not accept the submission the case proceeds.

The relevant test is set out in *R v Galbraith*[40] where Lord Lane CJ said[41]:

> '(1) If there is no evidence that the crime alleged has been committed by the defendant, there is no difficulty. The judge will of course stop the case.
> (2) The difficulty arises where there is some evidence but it is of a tenuous character, for example because of inherent weakness or vagueness or because it is inconsistent with other evidence.
>
>> (a) Where the judge comes to the conclusion that the prosecution evidence, taken at its highest, is such that a jury properly directed could not properly convict upon it, it is his duty, upon a submission being made, to stop the case.
>> (b) Where however the prosecution evidence is such that its strength or weakness depends on the view to be taken of a witness's reliability or other matters which are generally speaking within the province of the jury and where on one possible view of the facts there is evidence upon which a jury could properly come to the conclusion that the defendant is guilty, then the judge should allow the matter to be tried by the jury.
>> ...
>
> There will of course, as always in this branch of the law, be borderline cases. They can safely be left to the discretion of the judge.'

---

40 (1981) 73 Cr App R 124.
41 (1981) 73 Cr App R 124 at 127.

**12.35** *Prosecution – the Court Process*

In a trial in the Crown Court, a submission of no case to answer is heard in the absence of the jury.

A submission of no case to answer may also be made at the close of the defence case as well as at the end of the prosecution case.

## Defence case

**12.36** The defence will then call their evidence including any expert evidence.

The defendant does not have to give evidence. If the defendant decides not to do so they will be warned that the court may draw such inferences as appear proper from the failure to give evidence (see the Criminal Justice and Public Order Act 1994, s 34). Similarly if the defendant does give evidence but then refuses to answer some questions, then an adverse inference can be drawn. A defendant cannot be convicted alone upon adverse inferences. Arguably the adverse inference provision does not apply to a company defendant.

## Closing addresses

**12.37** When all the evidence has been given, the prosecution and then defence advocates make their closing speeches. In a jury trial they will address the jury as they argue their respective cases. In the magistrates' court after the closing addresses the magistrates/district judge will consider their verdict. In a jury trial after the closing addresses the judge will give his summing up.

## Judge's summing up

**12.38** In a jury trial the judge will explain the law to the jury and what has to be proved. Sometimes in health and safety and environmental cases a judge in discussion with the advocates will draft a document known as a 'route to verdict' to assist the jury. The judge will then sum up the evidence for the jury stressing that evidence may have been included that the jury do not think is relevant and that they may have noted evidence which they think is relevant which the judge has not referred to in summing up. The judge will then give directions about the duties of the jury and then the jury will retire to consider their verdict.

## Verdict

**12.39** If the defendant is convicted the court will then proceed to sentence (see para **12.40**). If acquitted, the defendant will be released from court.

Where a company has been prosecuted and the case has attracted media interest it is prudent to have a press release prepared in advance covering both eventualities.

# SENTENCING

## Sentencing hearing

**12.40** Sentencing will take place either after the defendant has been convicted following a trial or the defendant has pleaded guilty. Sentencing procedure is similar in the magistrates' court and Crown Court.

Where a defendant pleads guilty, it is not uncommon in health and safety and environmental cases, for the defendant to submit a 'basis of plea', a document that sets out the basis on which the plea is entered, identifying what part of the prosecution case is accepted and what part is not. If this is not accepted by the prosecution and the judge believes this will impact upon the level of sentence then there may be a Newton hearing (see para **12.41**).

Sentence is determined by the magistrates/district judge in the magistrates' court and the judge in the Crown Court.

Where the defendant has pleaded guilty the prosecution will open the case. This will not be necessary if the defendant is convicted after a trial. It is not for the prosecution to tell the court what sentence to impose. However the prosecution will provide their submissions on the application of the relevant sentencing guideline. It may well be that certain elements of the sentencing guideline can be agreed in advance eg the level of culpability. It is not uncommon where there is dispute regarding the application of the sentencing guideline for the defence to submit a note on the issue in addition to the basis of plea.

The prosecution will draw the court's attention to any victim personal statement. The prosecution will also inform the court of any previous convictions or other enforcement action (and in health and safety cases prosecuted by the HSE may draw to the court's attention notifications of contravention served under the fee for intervention scheme). In terms of corporate defendants the prosecution may also address the court on the company accounts. Where an application for costs is being made, and these have not been agreed with the defence, the prosecution will address the court on their schedule of costs.

When the prosecutor has finished, the defence makes a plea in mitigation. In the mitigation the defence will tell the court about the defendant and explain the circumstances of the offence and will address the court on any aggravating features (eg previous convictions) and mitigating features (no relevant/recent convictions, steps taken to remedy the problem that led to the offence, co-operation with the investigator) – see the list of aggravating and mitigating features set out in the relevant sentencing guidelines[42]. The defence may submit (or sometimes call) evidence to support the plea in mitigation.

In terms of corporate defendants the defence will want to make submissions on the company accounts. It should be appreciated that the magistrates/district

---

42 Sentencing Guidelines Council, see https://www.sentencingcouncil.org.uk/about-sentencing/about-guidelines/.

**12.40** *Prosecution – the Court Process*

judge/judge may not be familiar with company accounts. It is becoming more common for the defence to rely on expert evidence from a forensic accountant as part of its submission in order, for example, to explain the profitability of the company.

If the prosecution has made an application for costs and these are not agreed the defence will then make submissions on the costs claimed.

After the plea in mitigation the magistrates/district judge/judge will either retire to consider sentence or proceed directly to sentence. When sentencing they will set out their reasons for the sentence imposed (sentencing remarks). The court will also make any order for costs.

In terms of a convicted individual if an immediate custodial sentence has been imposed the defendant will be taken from the dock into the court cells as soon as the sentence is passed. Where a fine and costs are imposed upon a company (or an individual) the court will order by when the fine and costs are to be paid. This might be by instalments in appropriate cases.

## Newton hearings

**12.41** A 'Newton hearing' occurs where the defendant admits their guilt but does not accept the facts (or interpretation of those) as a basis of his guilt and the court concludes that the differences between the prosecution and defence cases would make a material difference to the sentence. The purpose of a Newton hearing is for the court to resolve the dispute and determine the basis for sentence. The name of the hearing comes from the case *R v Newton*[43].

Evidence is called at the hearing to determine the issues. The same rules of evidence and procedure apply as at a trial. Where the issues are in respect of the interpretation of facts then there may be a quasi-Newton hearing where the parties may make submissions on the evidence. In the Crown Court a Newton hearing is before the judge sitting without a jury. In the circumstances where the court rejects the defendant's version then the reduction in sentence that the defendant would have been entitled to for a guilty plea will be reduced (see *Reduction in Sentence for a Guilty plea – Definitive Guideline*[44]).

In *R v Underwood*[45] the Court of Appeal set out a summary of the limitations of a Newton hearing where it stated:

- at the end of a Newton hearing the court cannot make findings of fact and sentence on a basis which is inconsistent with the pleas of guilty which have already been accepted by the prosecution and approved by the court. Particular care is needed in relation to where one defendant faces a number of charges or a case involving a number of defendants, and to

---

43 [1982] 4 Cr App R (S) 388.
44 See **Chapter 13** on Sentencing.
45 [2004] EWCA Crim 2256.

circumstances in which the prosecution accepts, and the court approves, a guilty plea to a reduced charge;
- matters of mitigation are not normally dealt with by way of a Newton hearing. It is always open to the court to allow the defendant to call evidence in support of their mitigation;
- where the impact of the dispute on the eventual sentencing decision is minimal, a Newton hearing is unnecessary.

## Confiscation (environmental prosecutions)

**12.42** At step 2 of the *Environmental Offences: Definitive Guideline*[46] (whether the court is sentencing an organisation or an individual), the court is required to consider confiscation. The purpose of confiscation is to deprive offenders of the proceeds of their criminal conduct. The legislation covering confiscation is the Proceeds of Crime Act 2002 (often referred to as POCA). Committal to the Crown Court for sentence is mandatory if confiscation is being considered. Confiscation must be dealt with before any other fine or financial order.

For a POCA confiscation the defendant must first have been convicted and then the prosecutor has to request confiscation proceedings. The defendant is required subsequently to disclose details of assets. The prosecutor then provides a statement of information to which the defendant is required to respond. The prosecution and defendant will then agree the value order of the amount to be recovered or the case is set down for hearing and the value of order determined by the court.

# COSTS

## Defendant's costs order

**12.43** Section 16 of the Prosecution of Offences Act 1985 provides for costs orders from central funds to be made in favour of acquitted defendants. However, this entitlement has been substantially reduced by the Legal Aid, Sentencing and Punishment of Offenders Act 2012, Sch 7. Acquitted organisations can no longer recover their legal costs under this provision nor can acquitted individuals not in receipt of legal aid unless they have applied for legal aid and been refused (in which case their costs will be limited to legal aid rates).

Following this change there were attempts to recover costs following an unsuccessful prosecution, some of which were successful, under the Prosecution

---

[46] Environmental Offences: Definitive Guideline Sentencing Council, see https://www.sentencingcouncil.org.uk/wp-content/uploads/Final_Environmental_Offences_Definitive_Guideline_web1.pdf.

**12.43** *Prosecution – the Court Process*

of Offences Act 1985, s 19 (orders against a party to pay costs thrown away) and the Costs in Criminal Cases (General) Regulations 1986[47], reg 3 as a result of a party's 'unnecessary or improper act or omission'. Guidelines have now been set down in *R v Cornish*[48] (which arose from a failed corporate manslaughter prosecution of a hospital and gross negligence manslaughter prosecution of one of its consultants) that mean it will be very difficult to recover costs under this provision:

- simply because a prosecution fails, even if the defendant is found to have no case to answer, does not of itself overcome the threshold criteria for s 19;
- improper conduct means an act or omission that would not have occurred if the party concerned had conducted his case properly;
- the test is one of impropriety, not merely unreasonableness;
- where the case fails as a matter of law, the prosecutor may be more open to a claim that the decision to charge was improper – however, even then, that does not necessarily follow because 'no one has a monopoly of legal wisdom, and many legal points are properly arguable';
- it is important that s 19 applications are not used to attack decisions to prosecute by way of a collateral challenge, and the courts must be ever vigilant to avoid any temptation to impose too high a burden or standard on a public prosecuting authority in respect of prosecution decisions;
- the granting of a s 19 application will be 'very rare' and will be 'restricted to those exceptional cases where the prosecution has made a clear and stark error as a result of which a defendant has incurred costs for which it is appropriate to compensate him'[49].

## Order that the defendant pay the prosecution costs

**12.44** The Prosecution of Offences Act 1985, s 18 concerns orders against convicted defendants to pay prosecution costs. Paragraph 3.4 of the *Practice Direction (Costs in Criminal Proceedings)*[50] states that an order should be made for the defendant to pay the prosecution costs where the court is satisfied the defendant has the ability and the means to pay. Costs are assessed by the court when the defendant is sentenced.

In *R v Associated Octel Co Ltd*[51], which concerned a prosecution by the HSE, it was said that the costs order can include not only the costs of prosecution but also the costs of investigation (but note since October 2012 investigation costs incurred by the HSE have been recovered under the fee for intervention scheme).

---

47 SI 1986/1335.
48 [2016] EWHC 779 (QB).
49 *R (Haigh) v City of Westminster Magistrates' Court* [2017] EWHC 232 (Admin) at 32.
50 [2015] EWCA Crim 1568.
51 [1996] CACD 15 Nov 1996.

*Prosecution – the Court Process* **12.46**

In the same case it was observed that:

- the prosecution should serve on the defence in advance full details of its costs so that these may be considered;
- the defence should then respond to the prosecution stating which items of costs it accepts and which it objects to, giving reasons for those objections.

The Division Court gave guidance for the imposition of costs in *R v Northallerton Magistrates' Court, ex p Dove*[52]:

(1) an order to pay costs to the prosecutor should never exceed the amount the defendant is able to pay having regard to the defendant's means and any other financial order imposed upon him;
(2) the amount awarded should never exceed the amount the prosecutor has actually and reasonably incurred;
(3) the purpose of costs order is to compensate the prosecutor and not to punish the defendant. The defendant should not be punished for exercising a constitutional right to defend oneself;
(4) the costs ordered should not be grossly disproportionate to the fine. If the fine and the costs together exceed the amount which the defendant is able to pay, the costs order should be reduced rather than the fine;
(5) it is for the convicted defendant to provide to the court the relevant information setting out their financial position so that the court can assess what the defendant can reasonably afford. Failure to provide this information could lead to the court drawing reasonable inferences regarding the defendant's means;
(6) it is incumbent on the court to give the defendant a fair opportunity to provide the relevant financial information and make submissions prior to determination.

The definitive sentencing guidelines for health and safety offences and environment offences expect convicted organisations to provide comprehensive financial information.

# APPEALS

**12.45** A convicted defendant can appeal against conviction and/or sentence.

## Appeals from the magistrates' court

**12.46** An appeal from the magistrates' court against conviction and/or sentence is usually to the Crown Court. The matter will be heard by a judge and two magistrates who have not been involved in the case previously. In relation to an appeal against conviction, the appeal is a trial of the case again.

---

52 [1999] EWHC Admin 499.

**12.46** *Prosecution – the Court Process*

Both the prosecution and defence present their evidence and they are entitled to call witnesses. A notice of appeal must be completed and served on the magistrates' court and the prosecution within 21 days of the date of sentence.

There is another route of appeal by way of case stated to the Divisional Court of the Queen's Bench Division of the High Court. These appeals are for cases based upon legal arguments where there is no factual dispute.

## Appeals from the Crown Court

**12.47** An appeal against conviction and/or sentence in the Crown Court is to the Criminal Division of the Court of Appeal. To appeal the defendant will have to get permission, usually from a single judge on the papers. This will only be granted if the defendant has grounds which are considered to be properly arguable. If permission is granted then the appeal will be before three judges in the Court of Appeal.

In appeals against conviction there are numerous grounds upon which appeals against conviction are based. These include errors of law where it is suggested that the judge has wrongly directed the jury on a legal issue, the judge was biased in his summing or a 'material irregularity' occurred during trial. An appeal against conviction from the Crown Court is not a rehearing of the trial.

Generally appeals against sentence are on the basis the sentence was 'manifestly excessive'. The sentencing guidelines will be referred to during an appeal with the argument being that the Crown Court judge failed to apply the guidelines correctly.

An application for permission to appeal against conviction and grounds of appeal must be served within 28 days of conviction on the Crown Court where the defendant was convicted. If sentence is due to take place more than 28 days after conviction the application for permission to appeal against conviction must be served before sentencing takes place. For appeals against sentence the time period is 28 days from sentence.

# Chapter 13

# Sentencing

Introduction   13.1
    The purposes of sentencing   13.1
    Sentencing guidelines   13.2
    Setting a fine   13.3
Health and Safety Offences, Corporate Manslaughter and Food Safety
    and Hygiene Offences – Definitive Guideline   13.4
    Health and safety offences – organisations   13.4
        Step one – determining the offence category   13.5
        Step two – starting point and category range   13.6
        Step three – check whether the proposed fine based on
            turnover is proportionate to the overall means of the
            offender   13.7
        Step four – consider other factors that may warrant
            adjustment of the proposed fine   13.8
        Step five – consider any other factors which indicate a
            reduction, such as assistance to the prosecution   13.9
        Step six – reduction for guilty plea   13.10
        Step seven – compensation and ancillary orders   13.11
        Step eight – totality principle   13.12
        Step nine – reasons   13.13
    Health and safety offences – individuals   13.14
        Step one – determining the offence category   13.15
        Step two – starting point and category range   13.16
        Step three – review any financial element of the sentence   13.17
        Step four – consider the factors which indicate a reduction,
            such as assistance to the prosecution   13.18
        Step five – reduction for guilty plea   13.19
        Step six – compensation and ancillary orders   13.20
        Step seven – totality principle   13.21
        Step eight – reasons   13.22
        Step nine – consideration for time spent on bail   13.23
    Corporate manslaughter   13.24
        Step one – determining the seriousness of the offence   13.25
        Step two – starting point and category range   13.26
        Step three – check whether the proposed fine based on
            turnover is proportionate to the overall means of the
            offender   13.27
        Step four – consider other factors that may warrant
            adjustment of the proposed fine   13.28

**13.1** *Sentencing*

>    Step five – consider any factors which indicate a reduction, such as assistance to the prosecution   13.29
>    Step six – reduction for guilty plea   13.30
>    Step seven – compensation and ancillary orders   13.31
>    Step eight – totality principle   13.32
>    Step nine – reasons   13.33
>  Examples of sentences   13.34
> Manslaughter – Definitive Guideline   13.55
>  Gross negligence manslaughter   13.55
>    Examples of pre-guideline sentencing   13.56
> Fire safety   13.60
> Environmental Offences – Definitive Guideline   13.61
>  Structure ranges and starting points   13.62
>  Guidelines for offenders that are organisations   13.63
>    Step one – compensation   13.64
>    Step two – confiscation (Crown Court only)   13.65
>    Step three – determining the offence category   13.66
>    Step four – starting point and category range   13.67
>    General principles to follow when setting a fine   13.68
>    Steps five to twelve   13.76
>  Guidelines for offenders that are individuals   13.85
>    Step one – compensation   13.86
>    Step two – confiscation (Crown Court only)   13.87
>    Step three – determining the offence category   13.88
>    Step four – starting point and category range   13.89
>    General principles to follow in setting a fine   13.90
>    Steps five to twelve   13.93
>  Other environmental offences   13.102
>  Fine bands and community orders   13.103
> Reduction in Sentence for Guilty Plea – Definitive Guideline   13.105
> Offences Taken into Consideration and Totality – Definitive Guideline   13.106

# INTRODUCTION

## The purposes of sentencing

**13.1** The purposes of sentencing are set out in s 142 of the Criminal Justice Act 2003 (CJA 2003). This states that a court when sentencing an offender in respect of his/her offence must have regard to the following:

>  '(a) the punishment of offenders;
>  (b) the reduction of crime (including its reduction by deterrence);
>  (c) the reform and rehabilitation of offenders;
>  (d) the protection of the public; and
>  (e) the making of reparation by offenders to persons affected by their offences.'

The Court of Appeal in *R v Balfour Beatty Rail Infrastructure Services Ltd*[1] when sentencing the defendant for a breach of s 3 of the Health and Safety at Work etc Act 1974 (HSWA 1974) observed that most of these can be applied in the case of a company, although there are 'obvious difficulties' in applying subsection (c).

## Sentencing guidelines

**13.2** The Sentencing Council for England and Wales, which replaced the Sentencing Guidelines Council, was created by the Coroners and Justice Act 2009 (CJA 2009). The council is responsible for developing sentencing guidelines, monitoring the use of guidelines and reviewing decisions relating to sentencing.

Section 125(1) of the CJA 2009 requires that Crown Courts and magistrates' courts in England and Wales when sentencing *must* follow any relevant sentencing guidelines, unless it is contrary to the interests of justice to do so. There are two types of guidelines:

- those in relation to specific offences; and
- those giving guidance on general sentencing issues and principles.

The aim of the sentencing guidelines is to help ensure that courts across England and Wales are consistent in their approach to sentencing.

Where no guideline exists, courts are required to refer to relevant Court of Appeal judgments in similar cases to examine how sentences have been determined in the past.

The relevant sentencing guidelines for corporate manslaughter, health and safety offences, gross negligence manslaughter and environmental offences are:

- *Health and Safety Offences, Corporate Manslaughter and Food Safety and Hygiene Offences – Definitive Guideline*[2]*–* which came into force on 1 February 2016;
- *Manslaughter: Definitive Guideline*[3] – which came into force on 1 November 2018 – it covers all manslaughter offences including gross negligence manslaughter;
- *Environmental Offences – Definitive Guideline*[4] – which came into force on 1 July 2014;

---

1 [2006] EWCA Crim 1586, [2007] Bus LR 77.
2 See https://www.sentencingcouncil.org.uk/wp-content/uploads/HS-offences-definitive-guideline-FINAL-web.pdf.
3 See https://www.sentencingcouncil.org.uk/wp-content/uploads/Manslaughter_Definitive-Guideline_WEB.pdf.
4 See https://www.sentencingcouncil.org.uk/wp-content/uploads/Final_Environmental_Offences_Definitive_Guideline_web1.pdf.

**13.2** *Sentencing*

- *Reduction in Sentence for Guilty Plea – Definitive Guideline*[5] – which came into force on 1 June 2017;
- *Offences Taken into Consideration and Totality – Definitive Guideline*[6] – which came into force on 6 March 2012.

Surprisingly there is no sentencing guideline for offences pursuant to the Regulatory Reform (Fire Safety) Order 2005[7].

The sentencing guidelines follow the same approach. In brief this is as follows:

(1) The offence category is determined by considering the seriousness of the offence. This means assessing culpability and harm. This is required by s 143(1) of the CJA 2003 which states:

> 'In considering the seriousness of any offence, the court must consider the offender's culpability in committing the offence and any harm which the offence caused, was intended to cause or might foreseeably have caused.'

(2) Once the category of offence has been determined the guidelines give a category range with a starting point for sentence. The sentence will move up or down the category range depending on aggravating factors (which increase the sentence) and mitigating factors (which decrease the sentence).
(3) The court is then required to take a 'step back' to ensure the sentence meets the objectives of sentencing. The court may adjust the sentence upwards or downwards, including moving outside the range.
(4) Once the sentence has been determined the court will consider a reduction for a guilty plea if one has been entered and if there is more than one offence the 'totality principle' is applied to consider whether the total sentence is 'just and proportionate'.

The Court of Appeal has made it clear that courts should only consider the relevant guidelines for the purposes of sentencing. In the case of *R v Thelwall*[8], concerning the prosecution of a sole director of a company who was sentenced 12 months' imprisonment for a breach s 37 of the HSWA 1974), the Court of Appeal stated:

> 'The court would like to add three observations in relation to this kind of case. As the court has made clear in other cases where the offence is the subject of a Sentencing Council Guideline …, guidelines are guidelines. The citation of decisions of the Court of Appeal Criminal Division in the application and interpretation of guidelines is generally of no assistance. There may be cases where the court is asked to say something about a guideline where, in wholly exceptional circumstances – and we wish to emphasise that these are rare – the guideline may be unclear. In such circumstances the court will make observations

---

5 See https://www.sentencingcouncil.org.uk/wp-content/uploads/Reduction-in-Sentence-for-Guilty-plea-Definitive-Guide_FINAL_WEB.pdf.
6 See https://www.sentencingcouncil.org.uk/wp-content/uploads/Definitive_guideline_TICs__totality_Final_web.pdf.
7 SI 2005/1541.
8 [2016] EWCA Crim 1755.

which may be cited to the court in the future. However, in those circumstances it is highly likely that the Council will revise the guideline and the authority will cease to be of any application.'

There has been a practice in health and safety and environmental cases of providing the court with reports of sentences for similar breaches from databases on the regulator's website and newspaper articles. The court made it clear in *Thelwall* that this practice was 'impermissible'. This point was repeated by the Court of Appeal in the appeal against sentence for breaches of the Regulatory Reform (Fire Safety) Order 2005 in *R v Sandhu*[9].

It has been usual practice in health and safety and environmental cases for the prosecution to serve what is known as a 'Friskies Schedule' (from the case *R v Friskies Petcare (UK) Ltd*[10]) setting out what in its view are the aggravating and mitigating factors. However the Court of Appeal in *Thelwall* said these were no longer of 'any materiality'. However, many prosecutors still follow the practice.

The Sentencing Council's guidelines only apply to England and Wales; however they may have relevance for health and safety and environmental cases sentenced in Scotland. In *Scottish Power Generation Ltd v HMA*[11], which concerned a breach of health and safety regulations following an accident at a power station in which one of its employees was severely injured, the High Court of Justiciary stated[12]:

> '[G]uidelines from the Sentencing Council will often provide a useful cross check, especially where the offences are regulated by a UK statute'.

And:

> '… it is important to look at existing Scottish precedent to discover what levels of penalty are appropriate, albeit that this task may involve a cross check with relevant guidelines.'

## Setting a fine

**13.3** Where the sentence involves imposing a fine the CJA 2003, s 164 requires:

> '(1) Before fixing the amount of any fine to be imposed on an offender who is an individual, a court must inquire into his financial circumstances.
> (2) The amount of any fine fixed by a court must be such as, in the opinion of the court, reflects the seriousness of the offence.
> (3) In fixing the amount of any fine to be imposed on an offender (whether an individual or other person), a court must take into account the circumstances of the case including, among other things, the financial circumstances of the offender so far as they are known, or appear, to the court.

---

9 [2017] EWCA Crim 908.
10 [2000] EWCA Crim 95, [2000] Cr App R (S) 401.
11 [2016] HCJAC 99.
12 [2016] HCJAC 99, at para 59.

## 13.3 Sentencing

(4) Subsection (3) applies whether taking into account the financial circumstances of the offender has the effect of increasing or reducing the amount of the fine.'

In relation to corporate manslaughter, health and safety and environmental offences the only (or main) sentence upon an organisation will be a fine. The sentencing range for a fine of an organisation in the respective guidelines is by reference to its turnover. The categories are:

| Large: | Turnover or equivalent of £50 million and over |
|---|---|
| Medium: | Turnover or equivalent of between £10 million and £50 million |
| Small: | Turnover or equivalent of between £2 million and £10 million |
| Micro: | Turnover or equivalent of not more than £2 million |

The sentencing ranges and starting point for the fine for each category is given with reference to culpability and harm.

The guidelines require a convicted organisation to provide comprehensive accounts for the last three years to enable the court to make an assessment of its financial status.

Courts will scrutinise the accounts which will also include how directors have been remunerated. In the joint unsuccessful appeals against sentence of *R v Sellafield Ltd; R v Network Rail Infrastructure Ltd*[13] (the former an environmental case, the latter a health and safety case) the Court of Appeal noted in the *Network Rail* case that directors were paid between £577,000 and £348,000 plus performance-related bonuses. While acknowledging bonuses had been slightly reduced, the court said there should have been 'very significant reductions'. It commented that the prospect of a significant reduction of a bonus will incentivise directors to pay the highest attention to health and safety.

Since the introduction of the guidelines an issue has arisen as to how an organisation with a turnover far exceeding £500 million should be dealt with. In *R v Whirlpool UK Appliances Ltd*[14] the defendant company had a turnover of £700,000. The fine was reduced on appeal from £700,000 to £300,000 with the Court of Appeal stating it was unusual in that the breach of s 3 of the HSWA 1974 flowed from an offence of low culpability and low likelihood. It concerned the death of a contractor on the defendant company's premises involved in maintenance work.

The Court of Appeal observed that the sentencing guideline did not refer to an upper limit of turnover for a large organisation. It said that most organisations with a turnover which 'very greatly exceeds £50 million' would be treated as very large organisations and in those circumstances it was permissible to move outside the appropriate range in order to achieve a proportionate sentence. However, the court stressed, following the environmental case of *R v Thames*

---

13 [2014] EWCA Crim 49.
14 [2017] EWCA Crim 2186.

*Water Utilities Ltd*[15], that that there should be 'no mechanistic extrapolation' to determine the levels for very large organisations.

Concern that the levels of fines imposed upon companies were not high enough for health and safety offences (and environmental offences) have been expressed for many years. In *R v F Howe & Son*[16], until the publication of the sentencing guidelines the leading authority upon the sentencing of health and safety and environmental cases, the Court of Appeal, observed:

> 'Disquiet has been expressed in several quarters that the level of fine for health and safety offences is too low. We think there is force in this and the figure with which we have been supplied supports the concern'.

Since the introduction of the sentencing guidelines fines have significantly increased.

In March 2017 the record fine for environmental offences of £20.3 million was imposed at Aylesbury Crown Court on Thames Water Utilities Ltd for a series of significant pollution incidents on the River Thames between 2012 and 2014.

The largest fines imposed in health and safety cases predate the introduction of the sentencing guidelines. In 2005 Transco in the High Court of Scotland was fined £15 million for a breach of s 3 of the HSWA 1974 for failing to maintain a leaking gas main that resulted in an explosion killing a family of four in their home. In the same year Balfour Beatty Rail Infrastructure Services Limited was fined £10 million, which was later reduced on appeal to £7.5 million (*R v Balfour Beatty Rail Infrastructure Services Ltd*[17]) also for a breach of s 3 of the HSWA 1974 relating to the Hatfield train derailment caused by gauge corner cracking. Both of these cases concerned very large companies and followed unsuccessful prosecutions for corporate homicide (Transco) and corporate manslaughter (Balfour Beatty Rail Infrastructure Services Ltd) prior to the introduction of the Corporate Manslaughter and Corporate Homicide Act 2007.

However, whereas £1 million plus fines were rare and reserved for cases where fatalities had occurred, following the introduction of the sentencing guidelines fines above £1 million are commonplace with a number of cases not involving any fatality. This is because, as the guidelines observe, a health and safety breach is 'in creating the risk of harm'. In other words the sentencing process is concerned with the harm that could have resulted from the breach not necessarily the harm that did result. According to figures published by IOSH (the Institution of Occupational Health and Safety) in its publication *Health and safety sentencing guidelines one year on* (2017) in 2014 there were no fines over £1 million, in 2015 there were three but in 2016 there were 19 fines.

The largest fine imposed so far has been £5 million for a non-fatal accident against Merlin Attraction Operations Limited in September 2016 which

---

15 [2015] EWCA Crim 960, [2015] 1 WLR 4411.
16 [1999] 2 All ER 249.
17 [2006] EWCA Crim 1586, [2007] Bus LR 77.

operates the Alton Towers Amusement Park. This followed the incident involving the Smiler Ride in 2015 where 16 people were injured, five of them seriously.

Although the *Whirlpool* case resulted in the fine being reduced the Court of Appeal made clear that very large fines are here to stay[18]:

> 'Large commercial entities in many areas of business are vulnerable to very substantial financial penalties for regulatory failings. The same is true for breaches of health and safety or environmental law in appropriate cases.'

In the environmental case *R v Thames Water Utilities Ltd*[19] where the defendant's turnover was £1.9 billion the Court of Appeal warned[20]:

> 'In the worst cases ... [t]his may well result in a fine equal to a substantial percentage, up to 100% of the company's pre-tax net profit for the year ... even if this results in fines in excess of £100m'.

# HEALTH AND SAFETY OFFENCES, CORPORATE MANSLAUGHTER AND FOOD SAFETY AND HYGIENE OFFENCES – DEFINITIVE GUIDELINE

## Health and safety offences – organisations

**13.4** Health and safety offences are triable either way ie either tried in the magistrates' court or the Crown Court. For offences committed after 12 March 2015 magistrates have had the power to impose unlimited fines (previously there had been a limit of £20,000 per offence). However, cases where there is an unusual legal, procedural or factual complexity will be heard in the Crown Court along with those where a very substantial fine is likely to be imposed.

Most prosecutions are for breaches of ss 2 or 3 of the HSWA 1974 ie for failing to ensure the health and safety of employees (s 2), or non-employees affected by the organisation's undertaking (s 3) so far as is reasonably practicable. The guideline also covers prosecutions for breaches of specific health and safety legislation eg the Management of Health and Safety at Work Regulations 1999[21], reg 3, for failing to undertake a suitable and sufficient risk assessment. However, the guideline does not cover prosecutions for breaches of ss 4 (general duties of persons concerned with premises to persons other than their employees) and 6 (general duties of manufacturers etc as regards articles and substances for use at work) of the HSWA 1974, although it is likely these will be considered when applying the general principles under CJA 2003 when sentencing for these offences.

---

18 [2017] EWCA Crim 2186, at para 43.
19 [2015] EWCA Crim 960.
20 [2015] EWCA Crim 960, at para 40.
21 SI 999/3242.

The offence range is: £50 fine to £10 million fine. Although *R v Thames Water Utilities Ltd*[22] makes clear the court may go beyond the £10 million fine in appropriate cases.

The sentencing process has nine steps.

## Step one – determining the offence category

**13.5** In this step the court first determines the level of *culpability*. There are four levels: very high; high; medium; or low. The conduct described in the guideline ranges from 'deliberate breach of or flagrant disregard of the law' at the top end, down to 'offender did not fall far short of the appropriate standard' at the bottom end.

The court is then required to consider the potential *harm* that could have resulted from the breach. To do this the court must determine both the seriousness of the harm risked and the likelihood of that harm occurring in order to arrive at a 'harm category', which has four levels ranging from 1, the lowest, to 4, the highest. This is done by reference to the table below[23].

|  | Seriousness of harm risked | | |
|---|---|---|---|
|  | **Level A**<br>• Death<br>• Physical or mental impairment resulting in lifelong dependency on third party care for basic needs<br>• Significantly reduced life expectancy | **Level B**<br>• Physical or mental impairment, not amounting to Level A, which has a substanctial and long-term effect on the sufferer's ability to carry out normal day-to-day activities or on their ability to return to work<br>• A progressive, permanent or irreversible condition | **Level C**<br>• All other cases not falling within Level A or Level B |
| **High likelihood of harm** | Harm category 1 | Harm category 2 | Harm category 3 |
| **Medium likelihood of harm** | Harm category 2 | Harm category 3 | Harm category 4 |
| **Low likelihood of harm** | Harm category 3 | Harm category 4 | Harm category 4 (start towards bottom of range) |

Having identified the harm category the guideline requires the court to consider two further factors: (i) whether the offence exposed a number of workers or members of the public to risk; and (ii) whether the offence was a significant cause of actual harm. The guide continues:

> 'If one or both of these factors apply the court must consider either moving up a harm category or substantially moving up within the category range at step two … The court should not move up a harm category if actual harm was caused but to a lesser degree than the harm that was risked, as identified in the scale of seriousness …'

---

22 [2015] EWCA Crim 960.
23 Sentencing Council, *Health and Safety Offences, Corporate Manslaughter and Food Safety and Hygiene Offences – Definitive Guideline* (February 2016), p 5.

## 13.5 Sentencing

But note in *R v Whirlpool UK Appliances Ltd*[24], which concerned a fatality, the Court of Appeal stated[25]:

> '... the systemic failings were a significant cause of harm, indeed the most serious harm imaginable, namely death. That would justify an upward movement within the appropriate category range or a move into the next harm category'.

The guide also states that the actions of victims are unlikely to be considered contributory events for the purposes of sentences. It makes the point that organisations are:

> 'required to protect workers or others who may be neglectful of their own safety in a way that is reasonably foreseeable'.

There can be a danger that when actual harm has occurred this may influence the categorisation of the likelihood of harm. In *R v Tata Steel UK Ltd*[26] there were two offences, which occurred within six months of each other in 2016, relating to inadequate guarding. Both related to incidents which had resulted in partial finger amputation. The Court of Appeal found that the categorisation of the likelihood of harm for offence 2 should have been medium, not high, and consequently reduced the fine to £1.315 million for offence 2 from £1.8 million. The court noted the previous incident, the estimated use of the equipment without incident of 150,000 man hours and that the second incident occurred during training rather than normal operations. It stated at para 44:

> 'None of this detracts from the admitted high culpability for the incident – which could have been prevented by simple precautions – but it does tell against the high likelihood characterisation. ... We conclude accordingly that offence 2 was to be characterised as one of medium likelihood.'

In the case of *R v Squibb Group Ltd*[27] the fine was reduced from £400,000 to £190,000. The defendant, a demolition contractor, was prosecuted for breaches of the HSWA 1974, ss 2(1) and 3(1) following exposure of employees and others to asbestos during a construction project. In respect to the likelihood of harm, the sentencing judge was provided with a report from an independent expert which gave an estimate of the risk to employees and others of contracting an asbestos-related disease as a result of their likely exposure. This was based on statistical data derived from published studies. The expert estimated that if 100,000 people were exposed to a similar extent to the defendant's employees, about 90 deaths would occur. While acknowledging the limitation of such evidence and that the estimates were necessarily 'very rough', the Court of Appeal found that the judge was wrong to have assessed the likelihood of harm as medium concluding the appropriate assessment was low. Given the impact on sentence of this element of the sentencing process, the reliance upon expert statistical evidence may become more common in the future.

---

24 [2017] EWCA Crim 2186.
25 At [30].
26 [2017] EWCA Crim 704.
27 [2019] EWCA Crim 227.

The Court of Appeal has encouraged judges to take into account agreement reached between the prosecution and defence in respect of step 1, although ultimately it is a matter for the sentencing judge. In *R (Health and Safety Executive) v ATE Truck and Trailer Sales Ltd*[28] the Court of Appeal said at para 51:

> 'There is much to be said in an area such as this – with a specialist prosecution agency – for sensible agreement between the parties, not least saving resources and court time and permitting a focus on remedial measures. Such sensible agreement is to be encouraged and it is to be expected will be weighed carefully by any Court before departing from it. However and ultimately, no such agreement can bind the Court.'

In this case the parties had reached agreement which the judge significantly departed from when sentencing; in particular finding high culpability when the parties had agreed low culpability. ATE, a truck sale and leasing company, had pleaded guilty to a breach of the Management of Health and Safety at Work Regulations 1999, reg 3 for failing to have a written risk assessment in place covering trailer dismantling which it accepted contributed to the death of a contractor. The Court of Appeal reduced the fine from £475,000 to £200,000.

## Step two – starting point and category range

**13.6** An organisation is expected to provide comprehensive accounts for the last three years (from the date of sentence not offence). If the organisation does not provide any financial information or if the information is insufficient then the court will be entitled to draw reasonable inferences of the financial position.

The guideline sets out the information the court requires for different types of organisation:

- **For companies:** annual accounts. The court will pay particular attention to turnover; profit before tax; directors' remuneration, loan accounts and pension provision; and assets as disclosed by the balance sheet. Most companies are required to file audited accounts at Companies House. It is not uncommon for the prosecution to obtain these and place them before the court if the organisation does not. In order to obtain an up to date position of the company the court may also be interested in seeing the company's management accounts.
- **For partnerships:** annual accounts. Particular attention will be paid to turnover; profit before tax; partners' drawings, loan accounts and pension provision; assets as above.
- **For local authorities, fire authorities and similar public bodies:** the annual revenue budget ('ARB') is the equivalent of turnover and the guideline

---

28 [2018] EWCA Crim 752.

## 13.6 *Sentencing*

says this is the best indication of the size of the organisation. The court will not usually analyse relevant specific expenditure or reserves 'unless inappropriate expenditure is suggested'.
- **For health trusts – the independent regulator of NHS foundation trusts:** The quarterly reports of Monitor[29] will be considered. The court is unlikely to require detailed analysis of expenditure or reserves.
- **For charities:** annual audited accounts. Detailed analysis of expenditure or reserves is unlikely to be called for unless there is a suggestion of unusual or unnecessary expenditure.

From the financial information it will then be determined whether the organisation is large, medium, small or micro depending on turnover or the equivalent (see para **13.3**). The harm category and culpability level is then applied to the appropriate table for the size of the organisation to determine the starting point for the fine and the category range. Below is the table for large companies[30].

| **Large** Turnover or equivalent: £50 million and over | Starting point | Category range |
|---|---|---|
| **Very high culpability** | | |
| Harm category 1 | £4,000,000 | £2,600,000 – £10,000,000 |
| Harm category 2 | £2,000,000 | £1,000,000 – £5,250,000 |
| Harm category 3 | £1,000,000 | £500,000 – £2,700,000 |
| Harm category 4 | £500,000 | £240,000 – £1,300,000 |
| **High culpability** | | |
| Harm category 1 | £2,400,000 | £1,500,000 – £6,000,000 |
| Harm category 2 | £1,100,000 | £550,000 – £2,900,000 |
| Harm category 3 | £540,000 | £250,000 – £1,450,000 |
| Harm category 4 | £240,000 | £120,000 – £700,000 |
| **Medium culpability** | | |
| Harm category 1 | £1,300,000 | £800,000 – £3,250,000 |
| Harm category 2 | £600,000 | £300,000 – £1,500,000 |
| Harm category 3 | £300,000 | £130,000 – £750,000 |
| Harm category 4 | £130,000 | £50,000 – £350,000 |
| **Low culpability** | | |
| Harm category 1 | £300,000 | £180,000 – £700,000 |
| Harm category 2 | £100,000 | £35,000 – £250,000 |
| Harm category 3 | £35,000 | £10,000 – £140,000 |
| Harm category 4 | £10,000 | £3,000 – £60,000 |

By way of example, using the above table for a large company with harm category 1 and high culpability the starting point for the fine will be £2.4 million, with a category range of fine between £1.5 million and £6 million.

Normally only the financial position of the organisation being sentenced will be considered. However the guideline states: 'unless exceptionally it is

---

29 See www.monitor-nhsft.gov.uk.
30 Sentencing Council, *Health and Safety Offences, Corporate Manslaughter and Food Safety and Hygiene Offences – Definitive Guideline*, p 7.

*Sentencing* **13.6**

demonstrated to the court that the resources of a linked organisation are available and can properly be taken into account'[31].

In *R v Ineos Chlorvinyls Ltd*[32] where the turnover of the defendant company was £904 million but there was a loss of £37 million the Court of Appeal said the court was entitled to consider the available resources of the parent company. In the *Tata Steel*[33] case, where the defendant was also making a loss, the support of the parent company was taken into account. However, it is not enough for the prosecution to simply show that the defendant is part of a wider group: the court should only be looking at the wider group if the accounts of the defendant do not reflect the true position. In *R v NPS London*[34] the Court of Appeal made clear that it is the offending organisation's turnover, not that of a linked organisation, which should be used in step 2 to identify an organisation's size. However, such resources can be taken into account in step 3 (see below) when examining the financial circumstances of the organisation in the round.

There is now greater scrutiny of an organisation's accounts than used to occur in the past. That said, the criminal courts in general are not familiar with considering the accounts of organisations, particularly large ones. Therefore consideration will need to be given to obtaining evidence to explain the accounts, say from the organisation's accountants, or to instruct a forensic account expert (for the role of an expert in criminal proceedings see para **12.21**). The circumstances when a forensic account might be considered include: where there are large or unexplained financial movements; unusual expenditure; or turnover is not a fair indicator of the size of the company.

Once the starting point for the fine has been determined, aggravating factors, which increase the fine in the range, and mitigating factors, which decrease the fine in the range are considered. A non- exhaustive list of factors are set out in the guideline that include:

- *aggravating factors* – relevant previous convictions (which are likely to result in a significant increase from the starting point), cost cutting at the expense of safety and a poor health and safety record; and
- *mitigating factors* – no relevant previous convictions, a good safety record, steps taken voluntarily to remedy the problem and a high level of co-operation with the investigation but the guideline makes clear this must be 'beyond that which will always be expected'.

---

31 Sentencing Council, *Health and Safety Offences, Corporate Manslaughter and Food Safety and Hygiene Offences – Definitive Guideline Obtaining financial information*, p 6.
32 [2016] EWCA Crim 607.
33 *R v Tata Steel UK Ltd* [2017] EWCA Crim 704.
34 [2019] EWCA Crim 228.

13.7 *Sentencing*

## Step three – check whether the proposed fine based on turnover is proportionate to the overall means of the offender

**13.7** In steps three and four the court is required to take a 'step back' to ensure the fine fulfils the objectives of sentencing required by the CJA 2003, s 164. This can result in the fine being adjusted upwards or downwards including going outside of the category range.

At step three the guideline emphasises that the fine must be: 'Sufficiently substantial to have a real economic impact which will bring home to both management and shareholders the need to comply with health and safety legislation'.

In order to meet this aim it is now becoming more common, rather than to reduce the fine, to give the organisation time to pay the fine in instalments, which as the guideline advises can be over a number of years. In the case of *R v R and S Recycling Ltd*[35], a case predating the guideline, the company had experienced difficult trading conditions and in some years made losses. On appeal the fine of £80,000 was reduced to £65,000 but the costs order was unaltered making the total amount to be paid by the defendant company £122,927. The Court of Appeal agreed with the sentencing judge that the fine and costs should be paid by instalments but reduced this from £25,000 per year to £15,000 (making the period of payment just over eight years).

The court is required to examine the financial circumstances of the organisation 'in the round' to assess the economic realities. The guideline states that in finalising the sentence the court should have regard to:

- **Profitability** – if profit margins are small relative to turnover, downward adjustment may be needed, but if these are large profit margins an upward adjustment might be appropriate. No mention is made in respect of the position where the organisation is making a loss. As mentioned in the *Ineos* and *Tata Steel* cases the offenders were loss making and in those circumstances the support of the respective parent companies were taken into account and no adjustments were made.
- **Any quantifiable economic benefit derived for the offence** – eg through avoided costs or operating savings.
- **Whether the fine will put the organisation out of business** – the guideline says that in some bad cases this may be an acceptable outcome.

## Step four – consider other factors that may warrant adjustment of the proposed fine

**13.8** The guideline says that any wider impact should be considered in respect of within the organisation or on innocent third parties. Examples given are:

---

35 [2014] EWCA Crim 2302.

*Sentencing* **13.12**

- the fine impacts the offender's ability to make restitution to victims;
- the impact of the fine upon the offender's ability to improve conditions in respect of health and safety;
- the impact of the fine on employment of staff, service users, customers and local economy 'but not shareholders or directors'.

In the case of public bodies and charities the guidelines says that the fine should normally be substantially reduced if it can be demonstrated the fine 'would have a significant impact on the provision of its services'.

## *Step five – consider any other factors which indicate a reduction, such as assistance to the prosecution*

**13.9** Reference is made to the Serious Organised Crime and Police Act 2005, ss 73 and 74. It is suggested in health and safety cases there is unlikely to be any reduction of sentence – the aspect of assistance to the prosecution is more likely to be considered at step two in considering mitigation.

## *Step six – reduction for guilty plea*

**13.10** The reduction for guilty plea is dependent upon when the plea was entered in the proceedings. See *Reduction in Sentence for Guilty Plea – Definitive Guideline* (see para **13.105**).

## *Step seven – compensation and ancillary orders*

**13.11** These include:

- remediation under the HSWA 1974, s 42(1). This provision is rarely used. The reality is that given the time it takes for these cases to come to court, the remedial action required will have already been taken and will form part of the organisation's mitigation;
- forfeiture of an explosive article or substance pursuant to the HSWA 1974, s 42(4);
- compensation – where damage or injury has been caused. This rarely occurs as such matters will be met through insurance and if there is any issue as to the level of compensation, this will be determined through civil proceedings. Because of the time that prosecutions can take to come to court it is often the case that claims for personal injury have been settled or are in the process of settlement.

## *Step eight – totality principle*

**13.12** This is where there is more than one offence being sentenced at the same time. See *Offences Taken into Consideration and Totality – Definitive Guideline* (see para **13.106**).

## Step nine – reasons

**13.13** The sentencing court has a duty to give reasons for the sentence and to explain the effect. Given the nature of the sentencing process the 'sentencing remarks' now tend to be more detailed than in the past.

## Health and safety offences – individuals

**13.14** This covers individuals convicted of health and safety offences. This can be individuals prosecuted for breaching the HSWA 1974, ss 2 or 3 (eg if they are operating as a sole trader), for employees for breaching the HSWA 1974, s 7 or directors/senior managers prosecuted pursuant to the HSWA 1974, s 37 where it is alleged that their company is in breach of health and safety law and that this breach was due to their consent or connivance, or attributable to their neglect.

Since the Health and Safety (Offences) Act 2008 came into force the magistrates' court have had the power to impose custodial sentences of up to six months for individuals convicted of health and safety offences and the Crown Court up to two years. Prior to the introduction of the guideline custodial sentences were imposed. This has now changed. The impact of the guideline is that the threshold for custody has been lowered making imprisonment a real possibility particularly where the prosecution results from a fatal incident.

The sentencing steps mirror those for sentencing an organisation.

## Step one – determining the offence category

**13.15** In this step the court first determines the level of *culpability*. There are four levels: very high; high; medium; or low. The conduct described in the guideline ranges from 'intentionally, or flagrantly disregarded, the law' down to '[o]ffence committed with little fault'.

Using the same table as used in step one for sentencing an organisation (see para **13.5**), the court is then required to consider *harm* and determine the harm category to be applied ranging from category 1, the lowest, to category 4, the highest. As with sentencing an organisation the court then must consider whether the harm category should be raised or move up the starting point in the category range in step two if the offence exposed a number of workers or members of the public to risk of harm or if actual harm was caused.

## Step two – starting point and category range

**13.16** The harm category and level of culpability is then applied to the table below[36].

---

36 Sentencing Council, *Health and Safety Offences, Corporate Manslaughter and Food Safety and Hygiene Offences Definitive Guideline*, p 17.

*Sentencing* **13.17**

|  | Starting point | Category range |
|---|---|---|
| **Very high culpability** | | |
| Harm category 1 | 18 months' custody | 1 – 2 years' custody |
| Harm category 2 | 1 year's custody | 26 weeks' – 18 months' custody |
| Harm category 3 | 26 weeks' custody | Band F fine or high level community order – 1 year's custody |
| Harm category 4 | Band F fine | Band E fine – 26 weeks' custody |
| **High culpability** | | |
| Harm category 1 | 1 year's custody | 26 weeks' – 18 months' custody |
| Harm category 2 | 26 weeks' custody | Band F fine or high level community order – 1 year's custody |
| Harm category 3 | Band F fine | Band E fine or medium level community order – 26 weeks' custody |
| Harm category 4 | Band E fine | Band D fine – Band E fine |
| **Medium culpability** | | |
| Harm category 1 | 26 weeks' custody | Band F fine or high level community order – 1 year's custody |
| Harm category 2 | Band F fine | Band E fine or medium level community order – 26 weeks' custody |
| Harm category 3 | Band E fine | Band D fine or low level community order – Band E fine |
| Harm category 4 | Band D fine | Band C fine – Band D fine |
| **Low culpability** | | |
| Harm category 1 | Band F fine | Band E fine or medium level community order – 26 weeks' custody |
| Harm category 2 | Band D fine | Band C fine – Band D fine |
| Harm category 3 | Band C fine | Band B fine – Band C fine |
| Harm category 4 | Band A fine | Conditional discharge – Band A fine |

Once the starting point for the fine has been determined, aggravating factors, which increase the fine in the range, and mitigating factors, which decrease the fine in the range are considered. A non-exhaustive list of factors are set out in the guideline that include:

- *aggravating factors* – relevant previous convictions (which are likely to result in a significant increase from the starting point – see for example the Court of Appeal's comments in the case of *R v Thelwall* in relation to a previous conviction), cost cutting at the expense of safety and a poor health and safety record; and
- *mitigating factors* – no relevant previous convictions, a good safety record and good character and/or exemplary conduct.

For high levels of culpability and serious injury risked, only custody is considered, which in appropriate cases could be suspended. As can be seen even where the culpability is only medium but with a harm category of 1, the starting point is 26 weeks' custody. For lower levels of culpability and harm risked the sentence will be a fine or in some cases a community order. Fines and community service is covered in the appendix to the guideline. The fine bands are bands based on percentages of weekly income: band 'A', the lowest, ranging from 25% to 75% of income to the highest band 'F', 500% to 700%. Defendants will be expected to provide financial information and if they do not the court can compel the disclosure of the offender's financial circumstances pursuant to the CJA 2003, s 162.

## Step three – review any financial element of the sentence

**13.17** Where the court proposes to impose a fine as the sentence or part of the sentence it should 'step back' to ensure it complies with the principles set

**13.17** *Sentencing*

out in the CJA 2003, s 164. The court can also consider the wider impact of a fine ie the offender's ability to comply with the law or impact on employment of staff etc. The 'step back' provision is unlikely to be as relevant as in the sentencing of an organisation, particularly given the range of sentences that can result in imprisonment.

## Step four – consider the factors which indicate a reduction, such as assistance to the prosecution

**13.18** As with sentencing an organisation, reference is made to the Serious Organised Crime and Police Act 2005, ss 73 and 74 which is unlikely to be relevant in the vast majority of cases.

## Step five – reduction for guilty plea

**13.19** The relevant guideline is the *Reduction in Sentence for Guilty Plea – Definitive Guideline* (see para **13.104**).

## Step six – compensation and ancillary orders

**13.20** As with the sentencing of organisations, compensation, particularly in regard to personal injury claims, is likely to be dealt with by insurance.

Perhaps the most significant ancillary order is the disqualification of acting as a director of a company. The court may also disqualify a defendant from being a director for up to five years if sentenced in the magistrates' court and up to 15 years if sentenced in the Crown Court under the Company Directors Disqualification Act 1986.

In order for the court to be able to disqualify the offender from being a director the offence must be in connection with the promotion, formation or management of a company (s 2 of the 1986 Act). The test of whether an offence is in connection with the management of a company is whether it has 'some relevant factual connection with the management of the company' (see *R v Goodman*[37]).

In *R v Chandler*[38] the defendant's company purchased two cars at auction. The vehicles were later advertised for sale on eBay with significantly reduced mileage. The defendant, the managing director of the company, pleaded guilty to three regulatory offences. In his basis of plea, he stated that he did not know an employee had altered the odometers on the cars. At appeal the disqualification order made by the sentencing judge was quashed because the judge had not identified the conduct which was said to have made the defendant unfit to be a company director for the purposes of s 6 of the 1986 Act.

37 [1993] 2 All ER 789.
38 [2015] EWCA Crim 1825.

## Step seven – totality principle

**13.21** The relevant guideline is the *Offences Taken into Consideration and Totality – Definitive Guideline* (see para **13.106**).

## Step eight – reasons

**13.22** The court is required to set out its reasons for the sentence imposed.

## Step nine – consideration for time spent on bail

**13.23** The court must consider whether to give credit for any time spent on bail. However, this is unlikely to arise in a health and safety case as individuals are usually granted unconditional bail.

# Corporate manslaughter

**13.24** This is a conviction of an organisation pursuant to the Corporate Manslaughter and Corporate Homicide Act 2007. Corporate manslaughter cases can only be heard in the Crown Court. The court has the power to impose an unlimited fine.

The offence range is: £180,000 fine to £20 million fine. Although *R v Thames Water Utilities Ltd*[39] makes clear the court may go beyond the £20 million fine in appropriate cases.

There have not been the large fines for corporate manslaughter convictions that have been seen in health and safety sentencing. This is because the companies that have been convicted to date have been small/micro organisations.

The sentencing steps take a similar approach to the sentencing of organisations for health and safety offences. However, as the guideline points out, by definition the harm and culpability involved will be very serious as every case will involve death and corporate failure at a high level.

## Step one – determining the seriousness of the offence

**13.25** The court is required to assess the following factors affecting seriousness:

(1) How foreseeable was serious injury?
(2) How far short of the appropriate standard did the organisation fall?

---

39 [2015] EWCA Crim 960.

**13.25** *Sentencing*

(3) How common is this kind of breach in the organisation?
(4) Was there more than one death, or a high risk of further deaths, or serious personal injury in addition to death?

Where the answers to questions (1) to (4) indicate a high level of harm or culpability within the context of the offence, the offence will be category 'A'. If the answers indicate lower culpability the offence will be category 'B'.

## Step two – starting point and category range

**13.26** The starting point is determined by the size of the company ie large, medium, small or micro (see para **13.3**) and the offence category of A or B and then applied to the table below[40].

| Large organisation<br>Turnover more than £50 million | | |
|---|---|---|
| Offence category | Starting point | Category range |
| A | £7,500,000 | £4,800,000 – £20,000,000 |
| B | £5,000,000 | £3,000,000 – £12,500,000 |

| Medium organisation<br>Turnover £10 million to £50 million | | |
|---|---|---|
| Offence category | Starting point | Category range |
| A | £3,000,000 | £1,800,000 – £7,500,000 |
| B | £2,000,000 | £1,200,000 – £5,000,000 |

| Small organisation<br>Turnover £2 million to £10 million | | |
|---|---|---|
| Offence category | Starting point | Category range |
| A | £800,000 | £540,000 – £2,800,000 |
| B | £540,000 | £350,000 – £5,000,000 |

| Micro organisation<br>Turnover up to $2 million | | |
|---|---|---|
| Offence category | Starting point | Category range |
| A | £450,000 | £270,000 – £800,000 |
| B | £300,000 | £180,000 – £540,000 |

By way of example, a micro company with an offence category of A would have a sentencing starting point of £450,000 with a category range of £270,000 to £800,000.

---

40 Sentencing Council, *Health and Safety Offences, Corporate Manslaughter and Food Safety and Hygiene Offences Definitive Guideline*, p 24.

The type of financial information required is the same as set out in step two for sentencing an organisation for a health and safety offence (see para **13.6**).

Once the starting point has been determined, aggravating and mitigating factors are applied to move the fine upwards or downwards within the category range. This section makes the point made in sentencing for health and safety offences that organisations are required to protect workers or others who are neglectful of their own safety in a way which is reasonably foreseeable.

## Step three – check whether the proposed fine based on turnover is proportionate to the overall means of the offender

**13.27**   As with sentencing an organisation for health and safety offences, steps three and four require the court to take a 'step back' to ensure the fine fulfils the objectives of sentencing required by the CJA 2003, s 164.

The guideline acknowledges that fines cannot attempt to value human life in money. The fine 'must be sufficiently substantial to have a real economic impact which will bring home to management and shareholders the need to achieve a safe environment for workers and members of the public affected by their activities'[41].

As with health and safety fines, the court should consider the organisation's financial circumstances in the round and adjust if necessary upwards or downwards or even go outside the category range. Consideration should also be given to profitability, any quantifiable economic benefit derived from the offence and whether the fine will put the organisation out of business. There is also power to order that the amount be paid in instalments.

## Step four – consider other factors that may warrant adjustment of the proposed fine

**13.28**   The court can consider the wider impact such as the:

- impact of the fine on the offender's ability to improve conditions;
- impact of the fine on the employment of staff, service users, customers and local economy (but not shareholders or directors).

As with health and safety fines, if the offender is a public body or charity, the fine should normally be substantially reduced if the organisation is able to demonstrate the proposed fine would have a significant impact on the provision of their services.

---

41   Sentencing Council, *Health and Safety Offences, Corporate Manslaughter and Food Safety and Hygiene Offences – Definitive Guideline*, p 25.

**13.29** *Sentencing*

## Step five – consider any factors which indicate a reduction, such as assistance to the prosecution

**13.29** As with health and safety offences, this is unlikely to be applicable in the vast majority of cases.

## Step six – reduction for guilty plea

**13.30** As with health and safety offences, *Reduction in Sentence for Guilty Plea – Definitive Guideline* is to be applied (see para **13.105**).

## Step seven – compensation and ancillary orders

**13.31** The Corporate Manslaughter and Corporate Homicide Act 2007 makes provision for other ancillary orders. The guidelines state that a *Publicity Order* (s 10) should ordinarily be imposed. It may require publication in a specified manner of:

- the fact of conviction;
- specified particulars of the offence;
- the amount of any fine;
- the terms of any remedial order.

The reality is that as corporate manslaughter convictions are still a relative rarity, there will automatically be publicity.

Under s 9 of the Act the court can make a remediation order but as commented above the remediation provision under the HSWA 1974 is rarely used. Similarly, there is unlikely to be any order for compensation as this will be covered by insurance.

## Step eight – totality principle

**13.32** As with health and safety offences, the *Offences Taken into Consideration and Totality – Definitive Guideline* is to be applied (see para **13.106**).

## Step nine – reasons

**13.33** The sentencing court has a duty to give reasons for the sentence and to explain the effect[42].

---

42  Criminal Justice Act 2003, Pt 12, Ch 1, s 174 – duty to explain sentence.

*Examples of sentences*

**Travis Perkins Trading Company Limited (unreported, April 2016)**

**13.34** Travis Perkins was fined £2 million for breaches of the HSWA 1974, ss 2 and 3 in relation to an incident at one of its sites when a customer was fatally run over by a lorry in one of its yards. The company's turnover was £2,198 million.

The customer was loading planks of wood onto the roof rack of his Land Rover when he fell backwards onto the yard surface. He was then run over by a company vehicle operating in the yard. There was no banksman contrary to company policy.

The judge found the company's culpability as medium, the harm as level A with likelihood of harm as high giving harm category 1. An aggravating factor was the company's previous conviction in 2006. The judge took into account the defence's mitigation and used the range for large organisations, which is between £800,000 and £3.25 million. He set the fine near the top of the range, but discounted it to £2 million in recognition of Travis Perkins' guilty plea.

**Balfour Beatty Utility Solutions Limited (unreported, May 2016)**

**13.35** The company was fined £2.6 million for admitted breaches of the HSWA 1974, s 3, the Construction (Design and Management) Regulations 2007[43], and the Management of Health and Safety at Work Regulations 1999[44], reg 3 (risk assessment).

Balfour Beatty was the appointed principal contractor for a construction project that was laying ducting for new cable for an offshore windfarm that was being built off the coast by Heysham, Lancashire. On 14 April 2010 an employee of a sub-contractor died when a trench he was working in collapsed on him. The investigation found there was inadequate shoring for the trench.

The reason for the delay in the case coming to court is because there was a lengthy police investigation which determined there was no corporate manslaughter case. The company fell to be sentenced under the guidelines as it had taken effect by the time of sentence.

The company at the time of sentence was dormant but the turnover of the group of which it was part was £8,235 million.

**McCain Foods (GB) Limited (unreported, May 2016)**

**13.36** McCain Foods (GB) Limited pleaded guilty to breaching the Provision and Use of Work Equipment Regulations 1998[45], reg 11 and the HSWA 1974,

---

43 SI 2007/320.
44 SI 1999/3242.
45 SI 1998/2306.

**13.36** *Sentencing*

s 2 following an incident when one of its employees was examining a conveyor belt and his arm become caught in the machine. The investigation found that the conveyor belt did not have the correct guards.

Sentencing the company, the judge categorised the seriousness of harm risked as category A and the likelihood of harm as high, giving a harm category of 1. He also found the level of culpability to be high. McCain is a large company for the purposes of sentencing.

The judge reduced the fine to £1.2 million (below the sentencing range) for factors such as the prompt action to fix guarding across the site and McCain's full co-operation with the HSE. The fine was reduced by a third to £800,000 to reflect the guilty plea.

### Monovan Construction Limited (unreported, July 2016)

**13.37** Monavon Construction Ltd pleaded guilty to two counts of corporate manslaughter pursuant to the Corporate Manslaughter and Corporate Homicide Act 2007 and a breach of the HSWA1974, s 3. The company was prosecuted after two men fell into a 3.7m light well that only had perimeter edge protection, rather than metal railings, fixed around it. The pleas were entered after the prosecution of one of the directors for a breach of the HSWA 1974, s 37 was dropped.

The company was fined £250,000 for each corporate manslaughter offence and £50,000 for the health and safety offence making a total fine of £550,000. The level of the fine was based on the fact that Monavon was a micro organisation with a turnover of much less than £2 million.

### Merlin Attractions Operations Limited (unreported, September 2016)

**13.38** Merlin Attractions was fined £5 million for a breach of s 3 of the HSWA 1974 (a full third discount was given for the guilty plea).

The prosecution related to a rollercoaster crash on 2 June 2015 involving the Smiler ride at Alton Towers amusement park when five passengers suffered life-changing injuries and others were seriously hurt. The judge in his sentencing remarks said the incident was the result of the company's catastrophic failure to assess risk and have a structured system of work.

The judge concluded that culpability was high and that the harm risked was death or serious injury. The judge found that there was a high risk and that the harm category was 1. Because injury occurred and a number of people were exposed to risk the judge said it was appropriate to move up the category range for the starting point. Despite the company's turnover of £421 million, the judge concluded that a proportionate sentence could be achieved within the category range for large companies with a harm category 1: £1.5 million to £6 million.

## Kentucky Fried Chicken (Great Britain) Limited (unreported, January 2017)

**13.39** Kentucky Fried Chicken was fined £950,000 for a breach of the HSWA 1974, s 2. The prosecution related to an incident in which a 16-year-old employee at the business's Teesside Park restaurant suffered serious burns to his hands and arms after he was asked to remove hot gravy from a microwave while he was not wearing protective gloves. There was a further incident four months later when an employee at the chain's Wellington Square branch in Stockton removed a tub of hot gravy from a microwave and it spilled, also causing serious burns to her body.

## Wilko (unreported, January 2017)

**13.40** Retailer Wilko was fined £2.2 million after a part-time worker and student was paralysed when a container of paint tins fell on her. The court heard that the floor of the goods lift being used was not level with the shop floor and that the roll cage which fell on her was incorrectly loaded.

Wilko pleaded guilty to breaching the HSWA 1974, s 2, the Manual Handling Operations Regulations 1992[46], reg 4, and the Management of Health and Safety at Work Regulations 1999[47], reg 3 (risk assessment).

The judge found that culpability was high, the seriousness of harm risked was level A and the likelihood of harm was medium. Multiple employees were exposed to risk. He determined harm category 2. He further found that a previous conviction justified an upward adjustment to the fine.

The turnover of Wilko was £1.4 billion. The judge said he would move outside the range of £550,000 to £2.9 million to achieve a proportionate sentence. The fine of £2.2 million was determined taking into account mitigation and applying a discount of a third for the guilty pleas.

## Thorn Warehouse Ltd and Kenneth Thelwall (unreported, October 2016 – Appeal)

**13.41** An employee of Thorn Warehousing died when a remote controlled Mobile Elevated Working Platform (MEWP) he was loading on to a truck fell from the ramps and crushed him. The HSE's investigation found he had not been adequately trained and that there was no risk assessment and no safe system of work.

The company pleaded guilty to a breach of the HSWA 1974, s 2 and was fined £166,000. At the time of sentence the company was in administration. Kenneth Thelwall, the company director was sentenced to 12 months' imprisonment (based on a third reduction from 18 months in view of his guilty plea) for a

---

46  SI 1992/2793.
47  SI 1999/3242.

**13.41** *Sentencing*

breach of the HSWA 1974, s 37. He was also disqualified from being a director for seven years.

Thelwall appealed his sentence which was dismissed. The Court of Appeal upheld the judge's ruling that culpability was high on the cusp of very high, based on a finding that Thelwall's attitude to health and safety was 'cavalier'. It also upheld its view that the risk of harm was high giving category harm 1.

### Nottinghamshire County Council (unreported, April 2017)

**13.42** Nottinghamshire County Council of County Hall, Nottingham, pleaded guilty to breaching ss 2 and 3 of the HSWA 1974, in relation to an incident at a country park when one of its workers at the wheel of a tractor collided with a disabled member of the public. The man suffered serious bruising and injuries to arms legs and head. Workers were transporting branches to be burned, using a grab attachment mounted on the tractor.

The prosecution's case was that the council had not properly planned and supervised the work and that the tractor was not suitable for transporting materials long distances.

The council was fined £1 million.

### Aldi (unreported, July 2017)

**13.43** The prosecution arose from an accident at one of Aldi stores when an agency worker sustained severe crush injuries to his foot when he was manoeuvring an electric-powered pallet truck into a tight space which ran over his foot. The prosecution's case was that he had received inadequate training.

Aldi pleaded guilty to breaching ss 2 and 3 of the HSWA 1974 and were fined £1 million. Culpability was determined as medium, the harm risked level B with the likelihood of harm giving harm category 2. With turnover of £7.7 billion the company was very large but the judge stayed within the large business category due to a low profit margin of 2.2%. A full discount of a third was given for the guilty plea.

### Martinisation (London) Limited and Martin Gutaj (unreported, July 2017)

**13.44** The prosecution related to the deaths of two employees who were working on the renovation of a Victorian apartment in London and fell from a balcony as they tried to haul a 115 kg sofa up to a first floor.

The company was found guilty of two counts of corporate manslaughter pursuant to the Corporate Manslaughter and Corporate Homicide etc Act 2007 and a breach of the HSWA 1974, s 2. At the time of sentence, the company had gone into liquidation although had had a turnover of £9.7 million. The judge treated the company as 'small' for the purposes of the sentence. He fined the company £1.2 million on each corporate manslaughter charge and £650,000 on the health and safety charge to run concurrently (ie the total sentence was £1.2 million).

Martin Gutaj, who was one of two directors of the company was convicted of a breach of the HSWA 1974, s 37 and was sentenced to 14 months' imprisonment.

### Iceland Foods (unreported, September 2017)

**13.45** Iceland Foods was found guilty of breaching ss 2 and 3 of the HSWA 1974 in relation to a fatal accident when a contractor fell 3m through a ceiling while replacing filters in an air handling unit. While the company had a turnover of over £2.5 billion it was sentenced within the range for large companies. Culpability was deemed to be medium with level A harm risked with a likelihood of harm as high giving harm category 1. The company was fined £2.5 million on each offence making a total of £2.5 million.

### Sembcorp Utilities (UK) Ltd, Central Industrial Services (Northern) and R&A Kay Inspection Services Ltd (unreported, October 2017)

**13.46** The prosecution arose from an accident during pressure testing of a boiler at Sembcorp's biomass power station. A valve on a pressure test rig was pressurised above the safe working limit and failed, causing the hose and metal fitting assembly to whip round, striking an employee of R&A Kay on his right leg which was later amputated. Sembcorp carried out the test with the assistance of Central Industrial Services. R&A Kay's role was to monitor the test.

Sembcorp and Central Industrial Services both pleaded guilty to breaching the HSWA 1974, ss 2 and 3 and were fined £1.35 million and £125,000 respectively. Sembcorp's turnover was £149.9 million with a profit of £14.2 million. R&A Kay pleaded guilty to a breach of the HSWA 1974, s 2 and was fined £37,500.

### London and South Eastern Railway and Wetton Cleaning Services Ltd (unreported, November 2017)

**13.47** London and South Eastern Railway (trading as Southeastern) and its cleaning company Wetton Cleaning Services Ltd were prosecuted by the Office of Rail and Road (ORR) for breaching ss 2 and 3 of the HSWA 1974. Both were convicted following a contested trial.

The prosecution arose out of the death of an employee of the cleaning company who fell onto a live 750-volt rail while cleaning the exterior of a train at a depot near Hastings, East Sussex. ORR's case was that there was a 'culture of cost cutting' which exposed workers to serious risk. Southeastern was fined £2.6 million and Wetton £1.1 million.

### Poundstretcher (unreported, January 2018)

**13.48** Poundstretcher pleaded guilty to 24 safety offences brought against it by three local authorities in relation to three of its 400 hundred stores. All counts related to the overstocking of goods and a failure to train staff. The company was fined a total of £1 million.

### Martin-Baker Aircraft Ltd (unreported, February 2018)

**13.49** The ejection seat manufacturer was fined £1.1 million and agreed to pay HSE's costs of £550,000 following its plea of guilty to breaching the HSWA 1974, s 3(1). The prosecution followed the death of Red Arrows pilot Flt Lt Sean Cunningham who was ejected from his jet while conducting pre-flight safety checks in November 2011.

The ejection seat inadvertently fired shooting the pilot into the air. The parachute on the seat then failed to open and he fell to the ground. The pilot died later in hospital from multiple injuries.

The parachute failed to deploy because two shackles jammed together. An investigation found that this had occurred because during an earlier routine inspection an engineer had overtightened the locknut on one of the shackles. The company had been aware since the early 1990s that this could occur if the locknut was overtightened. While the company had advised a number of customers of this issue it had failed to warn the RAF.

Mrs Justice Carr when sentencing the company said it was 'an entirely preventable tragedy' and that 'A significant number of pilots, and also potential passengers, were exposed to the risk of harm over a lengthy period.'

Applying the sentencing guidelines the judge stated that the culpability level was medium, the seriousness of harm risked was level A, commenting 'Here the risk of harm was of the highest level – death' and that the likelihood of harm occurring was low (at an earlier hearing the court was told an assessment by the Ministry of Defence (MoD) was that such an incident would happen only once in more than 100 years). The resultant harm category of 3 was increased to 2 because of the number of people exposed to the risk over a lengthy period.

The company's turnover was in excess of £200 million a year making it a large company (turnover in excess of £50 million). The starting point for the fine was £600,000 but the judge increased this to £1.45 million to reflect the fact that the company's turnover was significantly larger than £50 million. Following consideration of mitigating factors and applying a discount for a guilty plea the fine was reduced to £1.1 million.

### Terrence Murray (unreported, February 2018)

**13.50** Terrence Murray pleaded guilty to breaching the HSWA 1974, s 7(a). In June 2017 he was photographed by a retired health and safety inspector erecting scaffolding at a height of approximate 18m without building a safety rail or taking any other precautions to prevent him falling. Although he was wearing a harness it was not clipped to either the building or the scaffold.

HSE's investigation found that Murray's employers had taken reasonable steps to avoid working at height unsafely and that Murray had the appropriate training and was experienced. The correct safety equipment had been made available to him.

Murray was given a 26-week custodial sentence suspended for 12 months.

### Bupa Care Homes (unreported, June 2018)

**13.51** Bupa Care Homes, part of Bupa Care Services, pleaded guilty to breaching the HSWA 1974, s 3(1) following the death of an elderly resident from Legionnaires' disease at its Hutton Village care home in Brentwood, Essex. It was fined £3 million and was ordered to pay costs of just over £150,000.

The HSE investigation found that for over a year the company had failed to implement the required monitoring and measuring measures to manage the hot and cold water systems in the home during which major refurbishment was taking place. Samples taken from the deceased resident's bathroom contained a concentration of legionella bacteria in the water.

### Willmott Partnership Homes (unreported, September 2018)

**13.52** Willmott Partnership Homes, a subsidiary of the Willmott Dixon construction group, pleaded guilty to breaching the HSWA 1974, s 3(1). The company was fined £1.25 million and ordered to pay costs of just under £24,000. The prosecution followed a failure to isolate live boilers in Hamilton House in Wolverton, Buckinghamshire, when it carried out remedial works in 2014, exposing residents to a carbon monoxide poisoning risk (however the HSE investigation found that there was only one flat where there was a proven high likelihood of risk to the occupant).

### Gaskell's (North West) Ltd and Jonathan Gaskell (unreported, October 2018)

**13.53** Waste and recycling company Gaskell's (North West) Ltd pleaded guilty to breaching the HSWA 1974, s 2(1) and its director Jonathan Gaskell pleaded guilty to a breach of the HSWA, s 37. The company was fined £700,000 and ordered to pay costs of just under £100,000. Gaskell was sentenced to a custodial sentence of eight months.

In December 2010 one of its employees entered the bailing chamber of a machine used to compress recyclable and waste materials into small bales in order to clear a blockage. The safety interlock system on the machine had been defeated by the company. The machine automatically activated causing severe injuries to the employee which he later died of.

**13.53** *Sentencing*

In July 2015 HSE made a site visit having been informed that the company was still using the machine, with the safety systems defeated, five years after the employee's death.

### DB Cargo (UK) Ltd (unreported, March 2019)

**13.54** DB Cargo was prosecuted by the Office of Rail and Road for a breach of the HSWA 1974, s 3(1). Following a contested trial it was fined £2.7 million and ordered to pay costs of £188,873.89. The prosecution arose from an incident in which a 13-year-old boy suffered life-changing injuries after receiving an electric shock from 25,000 volt overhead line equipment at Tyne Yard in Gateshead. He along with another boy of the same age climbed onto the top of a wagon and came into contact with the overhead line equipment. The investigation found that trespassers often visited the disused signal box in the yard.

At the conclusion of the trial, the company also pleaded guilty to an offence of failing to provide documentation requested by the investigating inspector pursuant to the powers under the HSWA 1974, s 20. For this offence DB Cargo was fined £33,500.

# MANSLAUGHTER – DEFINITIVE GUIDELINE
## Gross negligence manslaughter

**13.55** The Manslaughter Definitive Guideline covers four types of manslaughter: unlawful act; gross negligence; by reason of loss of control; and by reason of diminished responsibility. The guideline came into force on 1 November 2018.

Gross negligence manslaughter can occur in a number of different types of ways. It is where the offender is in breach of a duty of care towards the victim which causes the death of the victim and amounts to a criminal act or omission. The types of circumstances of these cases vary greatly. In a domestic setting it could include parents or carers who fail to protect the victim from an obvious danger. In a work setting, it could cover an individual who is an employer who disregards the safety of employees. It could also arise in a medical setting when a practitioner falls far below the required standard in the treatment of a patient.

It is clear that the aim of the guideline as a whole is to increase the custodial sentences for manslaughter generally.

For gross negligence manslaughter step one is to determine the culpability category of which there are four:

A   very high culpability;
B   high culpability;

C   medium culpability;
D   lower culpability.

Step two is to apply these to the table below, which gives the starting point and the category range, and then apply the aggravating and mitigating factors which will move the sentence upwards or downwards in the category range.

| Culpability ||||
| --- | --- | --- | --- |
| A | B | C | D |
| Starting Point | Starting Point | Starting Point | Starting Point |
| 12 years' custody | 8 years' custody | 4 years' custody | 2 years' custody |
| Category Range | Category Range | Category Range | Category Range |
| 10–18 years' custody | 6–12 years' custody | 2–7 years' custody | 1–4 years' custody |

Arguably the culpability categories do not sit easily with the analysis of the law of gross negligence manslaughter as set out in the judgment of the Court of Appeal in *R v Honey Rose*[48] in which it is stated for negligence to be gross it must be:

> 'truly exceptionally bad and so reprehensible as to justify the conclusion that it amounted to gross negligence and required criminal sanction'.

## Examples of pre-guideline sentencing

### Matthew Gordon and Peter Wood (unreported, January 2017)

**13.56** Matthew Gordon, the owner and director of a haulage company, and his mechanic, Peter Wood, were found guilty of gross negligence manslaughter following an incident in which the company's tipper truck drove down a 'rat run' in Bath with a one in five gradient and collided with pedestrians killing four people including a four-year-old child. The 19-year-old driver of the truck was cleared of gross negligence manslaughter and causing death by dangerous driving.

The case against Gordon and Wood was that they failed to properly maintain the vehicle's braking system: when tested after the incident the brakes were found to have an overall efficiency of only 28%.

Following a contested trial Gordon was given a custodial sentence of seven-and-a-half years and Wood five years three months. Gordon was also disqualified from being a director for 12 years.

---

48   [2017] EWCA Crim 1168, at [45].

**13.57** *Sentencing*

### Kelvin Adsett (unreported, May 2017)

**13.57** Kelvin Adsett, a construction supervisor of a company that was fitting window frames at a site on London's Hanover Square when three of them (weighing 655 kg that had been propped against a wall) fell killing a passer-by, was jailed for a year for gross negligence manslaughter. The judge when sentencing Adsett said he had shown 'reckless disregard' for the life-threatening situation.

### Andrew Winterton (unreported, June 2017)

**13.58** Andrew Winterton, site manager and director of a housing development company – Conquest Homes – was found guilty of gross negligence manslaughter when a trench collapsed on a building site killing a worker. The sides of the trench had not been properly or adequately secured. Conquest Homes was also convicted of breaching the HSWA 1974, s 2. Winterton was sentenced to four years' imprisonment.

### William and Shelby Thurston (unreported, June 2018)

**13.59** Husband and wife William and Shelby Thurston were two fairground workers. They were convicted of gross negligence manslaughter after a bouncy castle blew away with a young girl inside it. They were both sentenced to three years' imprisonment. The prosecution's case was that the defendants failed to ensure the bouncy castle was adequately anchored to the ground and that they had failed to monitor weather conditions to ensure it was safe to use. A yellow Met Office weather warning was in place on the day of the incident.

# FIRE SAFETY

**13.60** Although the sentencing guidelines on health and safety are clear and are often used for sentencing health and safety cases, they do not apply to breaches of the fire regulations. Respondents to the consultation on the sentencing guidelines did suggest that fire safety offences could be included. However, the council felt that the application of the guidelines in such cases could result in a distortion of the sentencing levels.

This has led to some discrepancies in sentencing for fire safety breaches. In December 2017, Poundstretcher was fined £1 million for health and safety breaches at three of its stores – Swindon, Newhaven and Newbury. Environmental officers found on inspection that emergency exits were blocked, stock stored in a dangerous way and there was inadequate safety training. Poundstretcher pleaded guilty to 24 counts of breaching the HSWA 1974.

This case can be contrasted to that of JD Sports who earlier in 2017 were convicted of six breaches of the Regulatory Reform (Fire Safety) Order 2005 and were fined £60,000. Although Poundstretcher had previously been prosecuted for similar offences, there still seems to be a large difference in fines for a similar offence, which has been prosecuted under a different Act.

# ENVIRONMENTAL OFFENCES – DEFINITIVE GUIDELINE

**13.61** These definitive guidelines apply to individual offenders aged over 18 and organisations that are sentenced after 1 July 2014 – regardless of the date of the offence.

## Structure ranges and starting points

**13.62** The guidelines specify offence ranges – the range of sentences that are appropriate for each type of offence and there are a number of categories which reflect the various degrees of seriousness; the guidelines also identify a starting point within each range. These starting points define the position within the category range from which to start calculating a provisional sentence.

## Guidelines for offenders that are organisations

**13.63** Offences include:
- illegal discharges to air, land and water;
- unauthorised or harmful deposit, treatment or disposal etc of waste;
- offences which are under:
  - Environmental Protection Act 1990 (s 33);
  - Environmental Permitting (England and Wales) Regulations 2016 (regs 12 and 38(1), (2) and (3));
- other environmental offences – when sentencing other offences the court should refer to the sentencing approach in steps one to three and five to seven of the guidelines making adjustments to the starting points and ranges bearing in mind the statutory maxima for those offences.

The following table provides an indicative list of these other environmental offences[49]:

---

49 Sentencing Council, *Environmental Offences – Definitive Guideline*, p 23.

**13.63** *Sentencing*

| Offence | Mode of trial | Statutory maxima |
|---|---|---|
| Section 1 Control of Pollution (Amendment) Act 1989 – transporting controlled waste without registering | Triable summarily only | • level 5 fine |
| Section 34 Environment Protection Act 1990 – breach of duty of care | Triable either way | • when tried on indictment: unlimited fine<br>• when tried summarily: level 5 fine |
| Section 80 Evvironmental Protection Act 1990 – breach of an abatement notice | Triable summarily only | • where the offence is committed on industrial, trade or business premises: £20,000 fine<br>• where the offence is committed on non-industrial etc premises: level 5 fine with a further fine of an amount equal to one-tenth of that level for each day on which the offence continues after the conviction |
| Section 111 Water Industry Act 1991 – restrictions on use of public sewers | Triable either way | • when tried on indictment: imprisonment of a term not exceeding two years or a fine or both<br>• when tried summarily: a fine not exceeding the statutory maximum and a further fine not exceeding £50 for each day on which the offence continues after conviction |
| Offences under the Transfrontier Shipment of Waste Regulations 2007 | Triable either way | • when tried on indictment: a fine or two years imprisonment or both<br>• when tried summarily: a fine not exceeding the statutory maximum or three months' imprisonment or both |

These offences are triable either way.

Maximum sentence: when tried on indictment – unlimited fine; when tried summarily – £50,000 fine.

The offence range is: between £100 fine and £3 million fine.

## Step one – compensation

**13.64** The court must consider making a compensation order requiring the offender to pay for any personal injury, loss or damage resulting from the offence an amount that the court considers appropriate. If the offender has limited means then the priority is given to the payment of compensation over the payment of any other financial penalty.

Reason must be given if no compensation order is made.

## Step two – confiscation (Crown Court only)

**13.65** Confiscation must be considered if either the Crown asks for it or the court thinks it may be appropriate. Confiscation must be dealt with before any other fine or financial order (except compensation) (Proceeds of Crime Act 2002, ss 6 and 13).

## Step three – determining the offence category

**13.66**  The court should use only the culpability and harm categories when determining the offence category. The culpability and offence categories are on a sliding scale and where an offence does not fall into a specific category then individual factors may require a degree of weighting before making an overall assessment to determine the appropriate offence category.

The issue of dealing with the risk of harm involves the consideration of both the likelihood of harm occurring and the extent of the harm if it does. Risk of harm is less serious than the same actual harm. Where the offence has caused a risk of harm but no (or less) actual harm the normal approach is to move down a category of harm (see table below[50]).

| Culpability | Harm | |
|---|---|---|
| **Deliberate** Intentional breach of or flagrant disregard for the law by person(s) whose position of responsibility in the organisation is such that their acts/omissions can properly be attributed to the organisation; **OR** deliberate failure by organisation to put in place and to enforce such systems as could reasonably be expected in all the circumstances to avoid commission of the offence. | Category 1 | • Polluting material of a dangerous nature, for example, hazardous chemicals or sharp objects<br>• Major adverse effect or damage to air or water quality, amenity value, or property<br>• Polluting material was noxious, widespread or pervasive with long-lasting effects on human health or quality of life, animal health or flora<br>• Major costs incurred through clean-up, site restoration or animal rehabilitation<br>• Major interference with, prevention or undermining of other lawful activities or regulatory regime due to offence |
| **Reckless** Actual foresight of, or wilful blindness to, risk of offending but risk nevertheless taken by person(s) whose position of responsibility in the organisation is such that their acts/omissions can properly be attributed to the organisation; **OR** reckless failure by organisation to put in place and to enforce such systems as could reasonably be expected in all the circumstances to avoid commission of the offence. | Category 2 | • Significant adverse effect or damage to air or water quality, amenity value, or property<br>• Significant adverse effect on human health or quality of life, animal health or flora<br>• Significant costs incurred through clean-up, site restoration or animal rehabilitation<br>• Significant interference with or undermining of other lawful activities or regulatory regime due to offence<br>• Risk of category 1 harm |
| **Negligent** Failure by the organisation as a whole to take reasonable care to put in place and enforce proper systems for avoiding commission of the offence. | Category 3 | • Minor, localised adverse effect or damage to air or water quality, amenity value, or property<br>• Minor adverse effect on human health or quality of life, animal health or flora<br>• Low costs incurred through clean-up, site restoration or animal rehabilitation<br>• Limited interference with or undermining of other lawful activities or regulatory regime due to offence<br>• Risk of category 2 harm |
| **Low or no culpability** Offence committed with little or no fault on the part of the organisation as a whole, for example by accident or the act of a rogue employee and despite the presence and due enforcement of all reasonably required preventive measures, or where such proper preventive measures were unforeseeably overcome by exceptional events. | Category 4 | • Risk of category 3 harm |

---

50  Sentencing Council, *Environmental Offences – Definitive Guideline*, p 5.

**13.67** *Sentencing*

## Step four – starting point and category range

**13.67** Having determined the category then the court will refer to the tables. There are four tables of starting points and ranges:

- one for large organisations;
- one for medium organisations;
- one for small organisations;
- one for micro organisations.

The court will then use the corresponding starting point to reach a sentence within each category range and further adjustment can be made for aggravating and mitigating features.

## General principles to follow when setting a fine

**13.68** Under the CJA 2003, s 164, the appropriate level of fine should be set to take into account the financial circumstances of the offender and the level of fine should reflect the extent to which the offender fell below the required standard. The fine should meet in a fair and proportionate way the objectives of the punishment deterrence and the removal of any gain made during the commission of the offence. It should not be cheaper to offend than to take the appropriate precautions.

### Obtaining financial information

**13.69** An offender which is a company partnership, or a body which delivers public or charitable services, is expected to provide comprehensive accounts for the last three years to enable a court to make an accurate assessment of their financial status. The court can draw inference form the circumstances of the case if the court thinks it has not been given accurate or reliable information. It is normal that only the information about the organisation that is before the court is relevant, unless the resources of linked organisations can be properly taken into account.

### For companies

**13.70** In the case of a company, annual accounts consideration will be given to:

- turnover;
- profit before tax;
- directors' remuneration;
- loan accounts;
- pension provision;
- assets as disclosed by the balance sheet.

Most companies are required to have filed audited accounts at Companies House.

*Sentencing* **13.75**

Failure to produce the relevant recent accounts on request may properly lead to the conclusion that the company can pay any appropriate fine.

*For partnerships*

**13.71** In the case of a partnership, annual accounts consideration will be given to:

- turnover;
- profit before tax;
- partners drawings;
- loan accounts;
- pension provision;
- assets as above.

Limited liability partnerships (LLP) may be required to file audited accounts with Companies House. Failure to produce the relevant recent accounts on request may properly lead to the conclusion that the company can pay any appropriate fine.

*For local authorities, fire authorities and similar public bodies*

**13.72** The annual revenue budget (ARB) is the equivalent of turnover and the best indication of the size of the defendant organisation. It is unlikely to be necessary to analyse specific expenditure or reserves unless appropriate expenditure is suggested.

*For health trusts*

**13.73** The independent regulator of NHS foundation trusts is Monitor. It publishes quarterly reports and annual figures for the financial strength and stability of trusts from which the annual expenditure income can be seen.

*For charities*

**13.74** In the case of charities it will be appropriate to inspect the annual audited accounts. At this step the court will look at the organisation's annual turnover or equivalent to reach a starting point.

**Very large organisation**

**13.75** Where the defendant company's turnover or equivalent greatly exceeds the threshold for large companies, it may be necessary to move outside the suggested range to achieve a proportionate sentence.

There is a table (see below[51]) which contains a non-exhaustive list of factual elements providing the context of the offence and factors relating to the

---

51 Sentencing Council, *Environmental Offences – Definitive Guideline*, p 11.

13.75 *Sentencing*

offender, identity of any combination of these, or relevant factors which could result in a downward or upward adjustment from the starting point.

| Factors increasing seriousness | Factors reducing seriousness or reflecting mitigation |
|---|---|
| *Statutory aggravating factors:* | No previous convictions **or** no relevant/recent convictions |
| Previous convictions, having regard to a) the nature of the offence to which the conviction relates and its relevance to the current offence; and b) the time that has elapsed since the conviction | Evidence of steps taken to remedy problem |
| | Remorse |
| | Compensation paid voluntarily to remedy harm caused |
| *Other aggravating factors include:* | One-off event not commercially motivated |
| History of non-compliance with warnings by regulator | Little or no financial gain |
| Location of the offence, for example, near housing, schools, livestock or environmentally sensitive sites | Effective compliance and ethics programme |
| Repeated incidents of offending or offending over an extended period of time, where not charged separately | Self-reporting, co-operation and acceptance of responsibility |
| Deliberate concealment of illegal nature of activity | Good character and/or exemplary conduct |
| Ignoring risks identified by employees or others | |
| Established evidence of wider/community impact | |
| Breach of any order | |
| Offence committed for financial gain | |
| Obstruction of justice | |

## Steps five to twelve

**13.76** The court next reviews whether the sentence as a whole meets, in a fair way, the objectives of punishment, deterrence and removal of gain derived through the commission of the offence.

**Step five – ensure that the combination of financial orders (compensation, confiscation if appropriate, and fine) removes any economic benefit derived from the offending**

**13.77** The court will remove any economic benefit the offender has derived through the commission of the offence including:

- avoided costs;
- operating savings;
- any gain made as a direct result of the offence.

When a fine is levied then the amount of economic benefit should normally be added to the fine arrived at in step four. If a confiscation order is made, then when considering the economic benefit, the court should avoid double recovery.

**Step six – check whether the proposed fine based on turnover is proportionate to the means of the offender**

**13.78** The combination of financial orders should be substantial enough to have a real economic impact to make both shareholders and management understand that regulatory compliance is important. When the court considers the ability of the offender to pay it has the power to allow time for payment by instalments.

### Step seven – consider the factors that may warrant adjustment of the proposed fine

**13.79** Where a fine is on a public charity or public body then it can be substantially reduced if the offending organisation is able to demonstrate that the proposed fine would have a significant impact on the provision of services.

Some of the factors that a court should consider are:

- whether the fine impairs the offender's ability to make restitution to victims;
- the impact on the offender's ability to improve conditions in the organisation and comply with the law;
- the impact of the fine on the employment of staff, service users, customers and the local economy.

### Step eight – consider any factors which indicate a reduction, such as assistance to the prosecution

**13.80** The court needs to take into account the Serious Organised Crime and Police Act 2005, ss 73 (assistance by the defendant: reduction in sentence) and 74 (assistance by the defendant: review of sentence) and any other rule of law by which a defendant may receive a discounted sentence as a consequence of providing (or offering) assistance to the prosecutor or investigator.

### Step nine – reduction for guilty plea

**13.81** The court should take account of any potential reduction for a guilty plea in accordance with the CJA 2003, s 144 and the Sentencing Council's *Reduction in Sentence for a Guilty Plea – Definitive Guideline*[52].

Section 144 of the CJA 2003 states:

> '(1) In determining what sentence to pass on an offender who has pleaded guilty to an offence in proceedings before that or another court, a court must take into account—
>
> (a) the stage in the proceedings for the offence at which the offender indicated his intention to plead guilty, and
> (b) the circumstances in which this indication was given.'

---

52 Sentencing Council, *Reduction in Sentence for a Guilty Plea – Definitive Guideline*: https://www.sentencingcouncil.org.uk/wp-content/uploads/Reduction-in-Sentence-for-Guilty-plea-Definitive-Guide_FINAL_WEB.pdf.

**13.81** *Sentencing*

There are five stages to the approach:
- Stage 1 – determine the appropriate sentence for the offence(s) in accordance with any offence specific sentencing guideline;
- Stage 2 – determine the level of reduction for a guilty plea in accordance with this guideline;
- Stage 3 – state the amount of that reduction;
- Stage 4 – apply the reduction to the appropriate sentence;
- Stage 5 – follow any further steps in the offence specific guideline to determine the final sentence.

### Step ten – ancillary orders

**13.82** Ancillary orders may include:
- **forfeiture of a vehicle** – if the vehicle is used in or for the purposes for the commission of the offence (Environmental Protection Act 1990, s 33C);
- **deprivation of property** – where the Environmental Protection Act 1990, s 33C does not apply, the court may order the offender to be deprived of property used to commit crime or intended for that purpose in accordance with the Powers of Criminal Courts (Sentencing) Act 2000, s 143. The court must have regard to the value of the property and the likely effects on the offender of making the order taken together with any other order the court makes;
- **remediation** – where the offender is convicted of an offence under the Environmental Permitting (England and Wales) Regulations 2016[53], reg 38(1), (2) or (3) a court may order the offender to take steps to remedy the cause of the offence within a specified period in accordance with the Environmental Permitting (England and Wales) Regulations 2016, reg 44.

### Step eleven – totality principle

**13.83** If sentencing the offender for more than one offence, or where the offender is already serving a sentence, then consideration will be given to whether the total sentence is just and proportionate to the offending behaviour.

### Step twelve – reasons

**13.84** Section 174 of the CJA 2003 imposes a duty to give reasons for, and explain the effect of the sentence.

---

53  SI 2010/675.

# Guidelines for offenders that are individuals

**13.85** Offences are triable either way and on indictment subject to an unlimited fine and/or five years' custody; and when tried summarily then subject to a £50 thousand maximum fine and/or six months' custody.

The offence range is: conditional discharge – three years' custody.

## Step one – compensation

**13.86** The court must consider making a compensation order requiring an offender to pay compensation for personal injury, loss or damage resulting from the offence in such an amount that the court considers appropriate having regards to the means of the offender.

## Step two – confiscation (Crown Court only)

**13.87** Confiscation must be considered if either the Crown asks for it or the court thinks that it may be appropriate. Confiscation must be dealt with before any fine or financial order (except compensation).

## Step three – determining the offence category

**13.88** The court will determine the offence category using the culpability and harm factors which are on a sliding scale (see table below[54]). Dealing with the risk of harm involves consideration of both the likelihood of the harm occurring and the extent of it if it does.

---

54 Sentencing Council, *Environmental Offences – Definitive Guideline*, p 17.

**13.88** *Sentencing*

| Culpability | Harm | |
|---|---|---|
| **Deliberate** Where the offender intentionally breached, or flagrantly disregarded, the law | Category 1 | • Polluting material of a dangerous nature, for example, hazardous chemicals or sharp objects
• Major adverse effect or damage to air or water quality, amenity value, or property
• Polluting material was noxious, widespread or pervasive with long-lasting effects on human health or quality of life, animal health, or flora
• Major costs incurred through clean-up, site restoration or animal rehabilitation
• Major interference with, prevention or undermining of other lawful activities or regulatory regime due to offence |
| **Reckless** Actual foresight of, or wilful blindness to, risk of offending but risk nevertheless taken | | |
| **Negligent** Offence committed through act or omission which a person exercising reasonable care would not commit | | |
| **Low or no culpability** Offence committed with little or no fault, for example by genuine accident despite the presence of proper preventive measures, or where such proper preventive measures were unforeseeably overcome by exceptional events | | |
| | Category 2 | • Significant adverse effect or damage to air or water quality, amenity value, or property
• Significant adverse effect on human health or quality of life, animal health or flora
• Significant costs incurred through clean-up, site restoration or animal rehabilitation
• Significant interference with or undermining of other lawful activities or regulatory regime due to offence
• Risk of category 1 harm |
| | Category 3 | • Minor, localised adverse effect or damage to air or water quality, amenity value, or property
• Minor adverse effect on human health or quality of life, animal health or flora
• Low costs incurred through clean-up, site restoration or animal rehabilitation
• Limited interference with or undermining of other lawful activities or regulatory regime due to offence
• Risk of category 2 harm |
| | Category 4 | • Risk of category 3 harm |

## Step four – starting point and category range

**13.89** Having determined the category, the court will refer to the starting points and reach a sentence within the category range, with any further adjustment for aggravating and mitigating features.

## General principles to follow in setting a fine

**13.90** The level of fine will be considered in accordance with the CJA 2003, s 164 which means it must reflect the seriousness of the offence and the financial circumstances of the offender.

### Obtaining financial information

**13.91** It is for the offender to disclose to the court such financial data as is relevant so the court can see what they can afford to pay. If necessary, the court

*Sentencing* **13.92**

may compel the disclosure of an individual offender's financial circumstances. On the absence of such disclosure or where the court is not satisfied that it has been given sufficient reliable information, the court will be entitled to draw reasonable inferences as to the offender's means from the evidence it has heard and from all the circumstances of the case.

### Starting points and ranges

**13.92** Where the range includes a potential custodial sentence the court should consider the custody threshold as follows:

- Has the custody threshold been passed?
- If so, is it avoidable that a custodial sentence could be imposed?
- If so, can that sentence be suspended?

Where the range includes a potential sentence of a community order, the court should consider the community order threshold as follows:

- Has the community order threshold been passed?

The guidelines indicate that even when the community order threshold has been passed then a fine would normally be the most appropriate disposal[55].

The guidelines also contain a list of factors which increase or reduce the seriousness of the offence[56].

| Factors increasing seriousness | Factors reducing seriousness or reflecting personal mitigation |
|---|---|
| *Statutory aggravating factors:* | No previous convictions **or** no relevant/recent convictions |
| Previous convictions, having regard to a) the nature of the offence to which the conviction relates and its relevance to the current offence; and b) the time that has elapsed since the conviction | Remorse |
| | Compensation paid voluntarily to remedy harm caused |
| Offence committed whilst on bail | Evidence of steps taken to remedy problem |
| *Other aggravating factors include:* | One-off event not commercially motivated |
| History of non-compliance with warnings by regulator | Little or no financial gain |
| Location of the offence, for example, near housing, schools, livestock or environmentally sensitive sites | Self-reporting, co-operation and acceptance of responsibility |
| Repeated incidents of offending or offending over an extended period of time, where not charged separately | Good character and/or exemplary conduct |
| Deliberate concealment of illegal nature of activity | Mental disorder or learning disability, where linked to the commission of the offence |
| Ignoring risks identified by employees or others | Serious medical conditions requiring urgent, intensive or long-term treatment |
| Established evidence of wider/community impact | Age and/or lack of maturity where it affects the responsibility of the offender |
| Breach of any order | |
| Offence committed for financial gain | Sole or primary carer for dependent relatives |
| Obstruction of justice | |
| Offence committed whilst on licence | |

---

55 Sentencing Council, *Environmental Offences – Definitive Guideline*, p 17.
56 Sentencing Council, *Environmental Offences – Definitive Guideline*, p 20.

## Steps five to twelve

**13.93** Where the sentence is or includes a fine the court should 'step back' and review whether the sentence as a whole meets the objective of punishment, deterrent and removal of gain derived through the commission of the offence.

**Step five – ensure that the financial orders (compensation, confiscation if appropriate and fine) removes any economic benefit derived from the offending**

**13.94** Any economic benefit includes:
- avoided costs;
- operating savings;
- any gain made as a direct result of the offence.

**Step six – consider the factors that warrant adjustment of the proposed fine**

**13.95** Some of the additional elements that a court could consider in deciding whether to increase a fine are:
- the fine impairs the offender's ability to make restitution of the victims;
- impact of the fine on the offender's ability to improve conditions to comply with the law;
- impact of the fine on the employment of staff, service users, customers and local economy.

**Step seven – consider factors which indicate a reduction, such as assistance to the prosecution**

**13.96** Consider any factors which indicate a reduction, such as assistance to the prosecution.

The court should take into account the Serious Organised Crime and Police Act 2005, ss 73 and 74 (assistance by defendants: reduction or review of sentence) and any other rule of law by virtue of which an offender may receive a discounted sentence in consequence of assistance given (or offered) to the prosecutor or investigator.

**Step eight – reduction for guilty plea**

**13.97** The court should take account of any potential reduction for a guilty plea in accordance with the CJA 2003, s 144 and the Sentencing Council's *Reduction in Sentence for a Guilty Plea – Definitive Guideline*.

**Step nine – ancillary orders**

**13.98** The following ancillary orders can be considered:

- **Disqualification of director** – the maximum period of disqualification is 15 years (Crown Court) or five years (magistrates' court)'.
- **Disqualification from driving** – the court may consider this where a vehicle has been used in connection with the commission of the offence. The court may also disqualify from driving on conviction of any offence either in addition to or instead of any other sentence.
- **Forfeiture of the vehicle** – if the vehicle has been used in the commission of the offence.
- **Deprivation of property** – the offender can be deprived of property used to commit the offence – but the court must consider the value of the property and the effects on the offender:
  The Environment Agency took confiscation proceedings under the proceeds of Crime Act 2002 against a man who ran an illegal waste site for 15 months. Following a hearing at the Crown Court he received a seven month sentence for operating a site he did not own or have an environmental permit for. He was forced to sell his home to pay towards the cost of the clean-up of land off the A38 at Eggington.
- **Remediation** – the court can order the offender to take steps to remedy the cause of the offence within a specified period in accordance with the Environmental Permitting (England and Wales) Regulations 2016[57], reg 44.

### Step ten – totality principle

**13.99** If sentencing an offender for more than one offence, or where the offender is already serving a sentence, consider whether the total sentence is just and proportionate to the offending behaviour.

### Step eleven – reasons

**13.100** Section 174 of the CJA 2003 imposes the duty to give reasons for and explain the effect of the sentence.

### Step twelve – consideration of time spent on bail

**13.101** The court must give credit for time spent on bail.

## Other environmental offences

**13.102** When sentencing other environmental offences, the court will have regard to steps two to three and five and six of the guideline – adjusting the starting points accordingly. See Table at para **13.63**.

---

[57] SI 2010/675.

**13.103** *Sentencing*

## Fine bands and community orders

**13.103** The appropriate fine bands and community orders are listed in at table in the Sentencing Council, *Environmental Offences – Definitive Guideline* (p 24). Band F is an alternative to a community order or custody[58].

| Fine Band | Starting point *(applicable to all offenders)* | Category range *(applicable to all offenders)* |
|---|---|---|
| Band A | 50% of relevant weekly income | 25–75% of relevant weekly income |
| Band B | 100% of relevant weekly income | 75–125% of relevant weekly income |
| Band C | 150% of relevant weekly income | 125–175% of relevant weekly income |
| Band D | 250% of relevant weekly income | 200–300% of relevant weekly income |
| Band E | 400% of relevant weekly income | 300–500% of relevant weekly income |
| Band F | 600% of relevant weekly income | 500–700% of relevant weekly income |

### Community orders

**13.104** These are expressed as being of three levels, low, medium and high[59].

| LOW | MEDIUM | HIGH |
|---|---|---|
| In general, only one requirement will be appropriate and the length may be curtailed if additional requirements are necessary | | More intensive sentences which combine two or more requirements may be appropriate |
| Suitable requirements might include one or more of:<br>• 40–80 hours unpaid work;<br>• prohibited activity requirement;<br>• curfew requirement within in the lowest range (for example, up to 12 hours per day of a few weeks). | Suitable requirements might include one or more of:<br>• greater number of hours of unpaid work (for example, 80–150 hours);<br>• prohibited activity requirement.<br>• an activity requirement in the middle range (20–30 days);<br>• curfew requirement within the middle range (for example, up to 12 hours for 2–3 months). | Suitable requirements might include one or more of:<br>• 150–300 hours unpaid work;<br>• activity requirement up to the maximum of 60 days;<br>• curfew requirement up to 12 hours per day for 4–6 months;<br>• exclusion order lasting in the region of 12 months. |

# REDUCTION IN SENTENCE FOR GUILTY PLEA – DEFINITIVE GUIDELINE

**13.105** Section 144(1) of the CJA 2003 states:

> 'In determining what sentence to pass on an offender who has pleaded guilty to an offence in proceedings before that or another court, a court must take into account—

---

58 Sentencing Council, *Environmental Offences – Definitive Guideline*, p 24.
59 Sentencing Council, *Environmental Offences – Definitive Guideline*, p 24.

(a) the stage in the proceedings for the offence at which the offender indicated his intention to plead guilty, and
(b) the circumstances in which this indication was given.'

The guideline[60] sets out the reduction in sentence to be applied which depends upon when the guilty plea was entered.

A discount in sentence of one third will be given if the plea of guilty is entered at the 'first stage' of the proceedings which will normally be the first hearing at which a plea or indication of plea is first sought by the court. Most health and safety and environmental offences are 'either way' offences. For either way offences the guilty plea must be given at the first appearance in the magistrates' court to obtain a one-third reduction (unless one of the exceptions applies).

Admissions at interview, co-operation with the investigation and remorse are not to be taken into account for the purposes of discount but in mitigation. In *Caley v The Queen*[61] (in respect of the previous guideline upon reduction for guilty pleas) the Court of Appeal said an admission in interview would be treated as mitigation not as an 'indication of guilty plea' for a percentage adjustment.

After the first stage there is a sliding scale of reduction ranging from a quarter to a maximum of one tenth if given on the first day of trial. There may be no reduction if the plea is entered during the trial.

There are a number of exceptions which include the following:

- **Further information, assistance or advice necessary before indicating plea:** if the sentencing court is satisfied that there were 'particular circumstances which significantly reduced the defendant's ability to understand what was alleged or otherwise made it unreasonable to expect the defendant to indicate a guilty plea sooner than was done' it should still make a reduction of one third. The guideline expressly distinguishes between circumstances where the defendant is engaging in delaying tactics and where 'it is necessary to receive advice and/or have sight or evidence in order to understand whether the defendant is in fact and law guilty of the offence charged'.
- **Newton hearings:** a Newton hearing is where the defendant admits guilt but challenges the level of guilt. The hearing, at which evidence may be called, is for the judge to determine the level of guilt. The guideline states that where a defendant's version of events is rejected at a Newton hearing the reduction which would have been available at the stage the guilty plea was indicated should normally be halved. Where witnesses are called during the hearing the reduction may be further reduced.
- **Offender convicted of a lesser or different offence:** if a defendant is convicted of a lesser or different offence to that originally charged and they have made an unequivocal indication of a guilty plea to that charge they should be given the level of reduction that is appropriate to the stage of proceedings at which the indication was given.

---

60 Sentencing Council, *Reduction in Sentence for Guilty Plea – Definitive Guideline* (June 2017).
61 [2012] EWCA Crim 2821.

13.105 *Sentencing*

The first exception appears appropriate for many health and safety and environmental cases where often there are multiple parties, complex factual and technical information, and many witnesses of fact and expert evidence. However, this exception should be regarded with care.

It is clear the guideline is intended to encourage cases to be dealt with more quickly. This must be seen in the context of the reforms known as *Transforming Summary Justice* in the magistrates' court and *Better Case Management* in the Crown Courts which aim to make every hearing count thus reducing or eliminating wasted hearings and wasted time. Consequently, the defendant is expected to indicate their plea at an early stage, and to say what they believe are the real issues in the case.

In health and safety and environmental prosecutions it is unlikely that there will be an immediate charging decision. A defendant organisation will usually have carried out an internal investigation and in health and safety cases will have some idea of the HSE's views from the notification of contravention served under the fee for intervention scheme. There will have usually been an invitation to an interview under caution or to provide submissions at which time the outline of the case will have been given. In health and safety cases involving a fatality there will usually have been an inquest before the organisation is prosecuted. Therefore, to rely on this exemption the court is going to need to be persuaded of the particular circumstances that merit its application.

# OFFENCES TAKEN INTO CONSIDERATION AND TOTALITY – DEFINITIVE GUIDELINE

**13.106** This guideline applies when sentencing an offender for multiple offences. In health and safety and environmental cases these often arise from a specific incident. The guideline states 'all courts, when sentencing for more than a single offence, should pass a total sentence which reflects *all* the offending behaviour before it and is just and proportionate'[62].

In terms of custodial sentences, concurrent (where the sentences run at the same time) as opposed to consecutive sentences, will usually be appropriate where the offences arise out of the same incident or facts.

In terms of fines, the court should determine the fine for each individual offence based on the seriousness of the offence, taking into account the circumstances of the case, including the financial circumstances of the defendant. The court should add up the fines for each offence and consider if they are just and proportionate. If the total fine is not just and proportionate the court should consider how to reach a just and proportionate fine.

---

62 Sentencing Council, *Offences Taken into Consideration and Totality – Definitive Guideline* (June 2012), p 5.

Two examples are given[63].

- **Example 1:** Where a defendant is to be fined for two or more offences that arose out of the same incident or where there are multiple offences of a repetitive kind, it will often be appropriate to impose a fine for the most serious offence which reflects the totality of the offending where this can be achieved within the maximum penalty for that offence. No separate penalty should be imposed for the other offences.
- **Example 2:** Where a defendant is to be fined for two or more offences that arose out of different incidents, it will often be appropriate to impose a separate fine for each of the offences. The court should add up the fines for each offence and consider if they are just and proportionate. If the total fine is not just and proportionate the court should consider whether all of the fines can be proportionately reduced. Separate fines should then be passed.

The guideline says that where separate fines are passed, the court must be careful to ensure that there is no double-counting.

---

63 Sentencing Council, *Offences Taken into Consideration and Totality – Definitive Guideline* (June 2012), p 12.

# Part 4

# Inquests and Claims

# Chapter 14

# Coroners' Inquests and Public Inquiry

Introduction   14.1
Coroners' inquests   14.2
    Coroner areas   14.3
        Eligibility and qualifications   14.4
        Coroners' officer   14.5
Calling an inquest   14.6
    A coroner's duty to investigate   14.7
    Duty to hold an inquest   14.8
    Timing of an inquest   14.9
Evidence   14.10
    Coroner's powers in relation to evidence   14.10
    Disclosure   14.11
    Disclosure by coroners to interested persons   14.12
    Interested persons   14.13
        Restrictions on disclosure   14.14
            Charge for disclosure   14.15
The inquest hearing   14.16
        Witness evidence   14.17
        Self-incrimination   14.18
When is a jury required?   14.19
        The jury   14.20
Duty to suspend or adjourn an inquest   14.21
Determinations and findings of an inquest   14.22
        Summing up   14.23
        Conclusions   14.24
            Short-form inquest conclusions   14.25
            Narrative conclusions   14.26
        Standard of proof   14.27
Investigations lasting more than a year   14.28
Reports to prevent further deaths   14.29
Post-mortem examinations   14.30
Conflicts of interest – insured and insurer at inquests   14.31
Conflicts of interest – insured and insurer – inquest disclosure   14.32
Public inquiry   14.33
    Scope of any public inquiry   14.34
    Power to establish a public inquiry   14.35
    There is to be no determination of liability   14.36
    Composition of the inquiry panel   14.37
    Setting-up date and terms of reference   14.38

**14.1** *Coroners' Inquests and Public Inquiry*

>Requirement of impartiality    14.39
>Assessors    14.40
>Power to suspend inquiry    14.41
>End of inquiry    14.42
>Power to convert another inquiry into inquiry under the Inquiries Act 2005    14.43
>Inquiry proceedings – evidence and procedure    14.44
>Public access to inquiry proceedings and information    14.45
>Restrictions on public access in a public inquiry    14.46
>Powers of chairperson to require the production of evidence    14.47
>Privileged information    14.48
>Public interest immunity    14.49
>Offences    14.50

Enforcement by High Court or Court of Session    14.51
Immunity from suit    14.52
Time limit for applying for judicial review    14.53
Expenses of witnesses and participants    14.54

# INTRODUCTION

**14.1**

>'Coroners perform an important service. They investigate the death with a view to explaining the unexplained and where appropriate they make a report to prevent future deaths. And it must be remembered that this is a public service, first and foremost for bereaved families who must be placed at the heart of the process and secondly for the wider public good, learning lessons for the health and welfare of others.'
>
>HH Judge Peter Thornton QC, the Chief Coroner for England and Wales, *Inquests A Practitioner's Guide* Legal Action Group (LAG).

Both public inquiries and coroners' inquests are independent of the government in their operation and findings and can allow the participation of families of victims by enabling their legal representatives to question witnesses. A statutory inquiry may have a remit which is wider than an inquest. This chapter explains the way in which each of these work and also what happens to a coroner's investigation if there is a public enquiry.

# CORONERS' INQUESTS

**14.2**    A coroners' inquest is a legal inquiry into a death when the cause of death is unknown. The coroner's inquest is held in public and the investigation into the person's death is to determine:

- who the deceased was;
- how, when and where the deceased came by his or her death; and
- the particulars required for registering death.

The way in which coroners are organised, and their powers, has undergone a significant overhaul in the last decade with the introduction of the Coroners and Justice Act 2009 (CJA 2009), Coroners (Inquests) Rules 2013[1] and the Coroners (Investigations) Regulations 2013[2]. These are significant changes and their effect should not be underestimated.

The CJA 2009[3] created the post of Chief Coroner. The first appointment was made in September 2002, HH Judge Peter Thornton QC. He retired on 30 September 2016 and Judge Mark Lucraft QC was appointed as Chief Coroner of England and Wales with effect from 1 October 2016. This appointment is made by the Lord Chief Justice in consultation with the Lord Chancellor. To be eligible the role holder is required to be a High Court or circuit judge. The Chief Coroner receives reports on all inquests and makes an annual report to the Lord Chief Justice.

## Coroner areas

**14.3** England and Wales is divided into coroner areas (previously known as coroner districts). A coroner area is a local authority area or a combination of more than one local authority area. If the coroner area consists of a single local authority area then it is that local authority which is the relevant authority. If the coroner area consists of two or more local authorities then the authorities jointly nominate which one is to be the relevant authority. Each relevant authority must appoint a coroner known as the senior coroner for that area. The Coroners' Society website provides an interactive map showing listing Coroner in each area[4].

There is one senior coroner per coroner area. Each area has a minimum of one assistant coroner. The funding is via the local authority which is obliged under the CJA 2009 to provide adequate facilities.

It is possible for a new coroner area to be created by combining two or more old coroner areas. There were three mergers in 2017–18: Central Lincolnshire and South Lincolnshire were merged to form the new Lincolnshire Area; Preston and West Lancashire, East Lancashire and Blackburn, Hyndburn and Ribble Valley were merged to form the Lancashire and Blackburn with Darwen Area; and most recently the Teeside and Hartlepool areas were merged to form a combined Teeside and Hartlepool Area[5].

1   SI 2013/1616.
2   SI 2013/1629.
3   See www.legislation.gov.uk/ukpga/2009/25/contents.
4   See https://www.coronersociety.org.uk/coroners/.
5   See https://www.gov.uk/government/publications/chief-coroners-annual-report-2017-to-2018 at para 26.

**14.3** *Coroners' Inquests and Public Inquiry*

The Lord Chancellor may, after consultation, make orders altering coroner areas by either combining or dividing coroner areas. The current thinking is that there is benefit from the reduction in the number of coroner areas across England and Wales. In the period since implementation of the Coroners and Justice Act 2009, in July 2013, the number of areas has reduced from 110 to 88. In the First Annual Report of the Chief Coroner it was stated that under the then current planning with the Ministry of Justice, the target of a reduction to about 80 coroner areas in total for England and Wales in the relatively short to medium term was realistic and that 75 was the longer-term objective. That remains to be the case.

## Eligibility and qualifications

**14.4** A coroner must have practised as a solicitor or barrister for at least five years. Existing medically trained coroners are able to continue although those without legal qualifications will not be able to apply for any new appointments. The senior coroner has overall responsibility for the coroner area.

The CJA 2009 has made significant changes to the way in which an inquest is conducted. The Act, its schedules and subsequent regulations identified new types of coroner and coroner investigations and inquests.

## Coroners' officer

**14.5** A coroners' officer acts as the representative of the coroner in the investigation and is the person who usually deals with the parties involved. They are quite often the first to be notified of a death and undertake many of the delegated and administrative duties of a coroner.

Their key duties are:
- record, assess and investigate all deaths reported to the coroner service and obtain all relevant information including social and medical history;
- attend and record scenes of death as directed by the coroner and ensure that all evidence for the coroner is safeguarded;
- gather evidence to assist the coroner in establishing the identity of the deceased;
- provide accurate and timely information and appropriate guidance to bereaved people for the duration of the coroner's inquiry;
- arrange for the transfer of the deceased to the designated mortuary;
- gather information for the coroner and pathologist and arrange and attend the post-mortem examination as the coroner directs;
- ensure adequate information is provided to the coroner to facilitate the release of the body to the person legally entitled;
- inform and provide guidance to other properly interested persons and other agencies/professionals as appropriate;

- collate and record evidence of witnesses including that obtained by other agencies, professionals as appropriate and produce a case file;
- co-ordinate and attend inquest hearings as appropriate;
- record, assess and investigate reports of potential treasure;
- undertake such other reasonable duties as specified by the coroner or employer that are commensurate with the grade and responsibilities of the post.

# CALLING AN INQUEST

**14.6** Under the CJA 2009, a coroner may make 'whatever enquiries seem necessary'[6] in order to ascertain whether there is a duty or power to investigate a particular death. There are particular situations which require coroners to hold an inquest and in relation to fatal accidents at work there must be an inquest with a jury.

### A coroner's duty to investigate

**14.7** A senior coroner who is made aware that a body of a deceased person is within their coroner area must, as soon as practicable, conduct an investigation into the person's death if the coroner has reason to suspect that the deceased died a violent or unnatural death, the cause of death is unknown, or the deceased died while in custody or other state detention.

### Duty to hold an inquest

**14.8** A senior coroner who conducts an investigation into a person's death must, as part of the investigation, hold an inquest into the death.

### Timing of an inquest

**14.9** Under the Coroners (Inquests) Rules 2013[7], r 8, the coroner must complete an inquest within six months of the date on which the coroner was made aware of the death or as soon as practicable after that date.

---

6  CJA 2009, s 1(7).
7  SI 2013/1616.

# EVIDENCE

## Coroner's powers in relation to evidence

**14.10** The CJA 2009, Sch 5, para 1 provides that the coroner has the power to summon witnesses and to compel the production of evidence for the purposes of the investigation or inquest. This power does not extend to requiring a person to produce anything that could be withheld from a civil court, for example, privileged legal correspondence, see Sch 5, para 2. Failing to give to the coroner documents which have been summonsed is punishable by way of contempt of court.

## Disclosure

**14.11** Under previous law the coroner had no powers to require the disclosure of documents, or insist on the provision of witness statements. Their powers were confined to issuing a summons for a witness to attend and give oral evidence. Coroners now have the powers to require evidence to be given or produced:

- at the inquest by giving evidence and producing any document that the person may have or have control of which relates to a matter relevant to the inquest;
- to provide a written statement during the investigation (previously such statements were a voluntary matter);
- any documents of anything else which is relevant to the investigation.

There is a caveat that applies to privileged material that would not be required to be disclosed in civil proceedings. There are also powers of entry, search and seizure.

## Disclosure by coroners to interested persons

**14.12** Part 3 of the Coroners (Inquests) Rules 2013 deals with disclosure of information by the coroner to interested persons. The onus is on the interested person to request disclosure even if they do not know what information the coroner holds, but a blanket request for information can be made. The coroner must disclose the documents which in their opinion are relevant as soon as is reasonably practical, for example, post-mortem examination reports.

## Interested persons

**14.13** The CJA 2009 sets out who is treated as an interested person for the purposes of an inquest. Under s 47 an interested person is:

- a spouse, civil partner, partner, parent, child, brother, sister, grandparent, grandchild, child of a brother or sister, stepfather, stepmother, half-brother or half-sister;
- a personal representative of the deceased;
- a medical examiner exercising functions in relation to the death of the deceased;
- a beneficiary under a policy of insurance issued on the life of the deceased;
- the insurer who issued such a policy of insurance;
- a person who may by any act or omission have caused or contributed to the death of the deceased, or whose employee or agent may have done so;
- in a case where the death may have been caused by an injury in the course of employment or a prescribed industrial disease, a representative of a trade union for which the deceased was a member at the time of death;
- a person by or a representative of an enforcing authority, for example, the Health and Safety Executive (HSE);
- any other person who the senior coroner thinks has sufficient interest.

## Restrictions on disclosure

**14.14** There are some restrictions on disclosure and a coroner may refuse where:

- there is legal or statutory prohibition to disclosure (which may cover legal privileged material shared only with the coroner);
- the consent of an author with copyright cannot reasonably be obtained for documents subject to copyright;
- the request is unreasonable;
- the document relates to criminal proceedings or where criminal proceedings are expected.

### Charge for disclosure

**14.15** A coroner may no longer charge a fee for disclosing documents to interested parties either before or during the inquest.

# THE INQUEST HEARING

**14.16** All inquest hearings are to be held in public. The next of kin and interested persons must be notified by the coroner within one week of the coroner setting a date for the inquest or inquest hearing. The notification must include the date, time and place of the inquest. The details must be made publicly available before the inquest hearing commences.

*14.17 Coroners' Inquests and Public Inquiry*

## Witness evidence

**14.17** Witnesses are questioned by the coroner either under oath or affirmation. The coroner must also allow properly interested persons to do the same although the coroner has the power to disallow any question put to a witness which the coroner considers to be irrelevant. It is a criminal offence to fail to comply with a coroner's notice requiring evidence to be given or produced. All pre-inquest review hearings and inquest hearings are recorded.

According to guidance issued by the Chief Coroner in July 2013 all recordings must be kept for at least 15 years. All recordings should be digital and stored with a back-up and the bereaved family should be told of their right to request a copy of the recording of that inquest. If a recording is used by an interested party or bereaved family for the purpose of producing a transcript the transcript must be shown to the coroner before being used for the purpose(s) of any further proceedings so as to give the coroner the opportunity should he or she wish to check any part of it including the quality of the transcript.

## Self-incrimination

**14.18** The Coroners (Inquests) Rules 2013, Pt 4, r 22 states:

> '22(1) No witness at an inquest is obliged to answer any question tending to incriminate him or her.
>
> (2) Where it appears to the coroner that a witness has been asked such a question, the coroner must inform the witness that he or she may refuse to answer it.'

Rule 22 does not enable a witness to refuse to give evidence at all. The rule only permits objection to a particular question that tends to incriminate the person in the sense of exposing them to a criminal prosecution.

Unlike criminal courts, witnesses may be present in court throughout the inquest.

At the inquest touching upon the death of Poppi Worthington[8], her father exercised his right under r 22 to refuse to answer 252 questions during the course of his evidence. The coroner David Roberts HM Senior Coroner for the County of Cumbria explained[9]:

> 'I must emphasise that the entitlement to refuse to answer questions at an inquest if there is a risk of self-incrimination is an important one. Mr Worthington was quite entitled to decline to answer the questions he did and I emphasise that I draw no adverse inference against him for his decision to do so. In consequence, however, the fact is that Paul Worthington's evidence to this inquest amounts to little more than the previous accounts and evidence he had already given elsewhere.'

---

8   See https://www.bbc.co.uk/news/uk-england-cumbria-42682796.
9   See http://www.cumbria.gov.uk/elibrary/Content/Internet/17318/43115155356.pdf – David Roberts HM Senior Coroner for the County of Cumbria in the Matter of Poppi Iris Worthington Deceased, *Review of Evidence, Findings and Conclusion* Inquest 27 November–14 December 2017 at Kendal (5 January 2018), p 20, para 25.

*Coroners' Inquests and Public Inquiry* **14.20**

The right against self-incrimination is a fundamental right in UK law and applies to both criminal proceedings and inquests. However, the making of any application will need to be made with sensitivity if distress to the families is to be avoided. At the pre-inquest review hearing for the Hillsborough inquest, when the Police Federation indicated that some police witnesses might also exercise that right under r 22, there were reports of the families shaking their heads and someone shouting 'outrageous'[10].

Inquests touching deaths, such as those of Poppi Worthington where there was other evidence as to the baby's injuries and likely cause of death, are difficult when r 22 is invoked; but what about the workplace accidents when the physical injuries are known but the question that remains unanswered is 'how' the deceased came by the injuries? The 'how' may only be capable of being answered by the one or two witnesses who, if r 22 is invoked, can hinder the coroner's ability to determine the cause of death and reach a conclusion and the families' right to utilise the process to establish the facts.

There is a balance to be made between ensuring the witnesses rights are properly protected and avoiding unnecessary and avoidable distress and upset for the deceased's family.

# WHEN IS A JURY REQUIRED?

**14.19** Under the CJA 2009, s 7 the circumstances in which a coroner is obliged to call a jury to hear evidence is more limited than prior to the Act. Only a senior coroner can make the decision that a jury is required. These circumstances can include:

- the deceased died while in custody or otherwise in state detention and the death was violent or an unnatural one or the cause of death is unknown;
- the death resulted from an act or omission of a police officer or member of a service police force in the execution of their duty;
- the death was caused by a notifiable accident, poisoning or disease (it should be reported to the HSE). Such notifiable incidents include deaths caused by an accident in the workplace or a death in a healthcare setting where the patient has committed suicide or been killed by another patient.

## The jury

**14.20** The jury at an inquest can consist of seven, eight, nine, ten or 11 people[11]. The jury will be summonsed to attend by the senior coroner at a time

---

10 See https://www.channel4.com/news/hillsborough-inquests-police-may-refuse-to-answer-questions.
11 CJA 2009, s 8.

and place stated in the summons. Once assembled, the members of the jury are sworn in by or before the coroner, to enquire into the death of the deceased and to give a true determination according to the evidence.

## DUTY TO SUSPEND OR ADJOURN AN INQUEST

**14.21** The CJA 2009, Sch 1 sets out when a coroner must suspend an investigation:

- if asked to do so by a prosecuting authority because someone may be charged with a homicide or related offence involving the death of the deceased;
- when criminal proceedings have been brought in connection with the death;
- where there is an inquiry under the Inquiries Act 2005.

If, during the course of the inquest, it appears to the coroner that the death of the deceased is likely to have been due to a homicide offence and that a person may be charged in relation to that offence, the coroner is under a duty to adjourn the inquest and notify the Director of Public Prosecutions (DPP). The subject may be raised by an interested person by way of application or by the coroner. The investigation and inquest cannot be resumed until the criminal proceedings which triggered the suspension have come to an end unless the prosecuting authority has confirmed that it has no objection to the coroner resuming their investigation and/or inquest. For example, in a work-related death situation, if a coroner hears evidence which appears to suggest that the death was caused by the witness having committed the offence of gross negligence manslaughter then the coroner is under a duty to adjourn and notify the DPP so that a decision can be made as to whether a prosecution should take place.

Where the investigation has been suspended because of an ongoing inquiry under the Inquiries Act 2005, the investigation and/or inquest can be resumed after 28 days from either the date of the Lord Chancellor notifying the coroner as to the date of the conclusion of the inquiry or, where the coroner has received no such notification, the date of publication of the findings of that inquiry.

## DETERMINATIONS AND FINDINGS OF AN INQUEST

**14.22** The coroner makes a 'finding of fact' at the end of an inquest. The corner cannot attribute blame to any individual and cannot imply a criminal or civil liability. The conclusion can be a 'short-form' or a narrative, or a combination of both.

## Summing up

**14.23** The coroner must direct the jury as to the law and provide the jury with a summary of the evidence. In doing so they must summarise the evidence fairly and direct the jury as to law and possible conclusions as to death, determination and findings before the jury retires to consider the evidence.

In relation to all other criminal proceedings except homicide, for example prosecutions under the Health and Safety at Work etc Act 1974, the coroner has no specific duty to suspend the inquest. That said, there is always the overriding power and duty under the CJA 2009, Sch 1, paras 8 and 9 which state that an inquest must be resumed if the coroner is of the opinion that there is sufficient cause to do so. It is a common experience to see attempts made by interested persons, who are subject to an ongoing health and safety investigation and possible prosecution, to submit arguments before the coroner which would result in suspension.

It could be argued that this makes a mockery of the system if inquests are suspended without very good reason for doing so. If interested persons and witnesses are concerned that they will expose themselves to prosecution by virtue of giving evidence in an inquest then they have the ability to rely on the Coroners (Inquests) Rules 2013, r 22.

It must be remembered at all times that the primary focus of an inquest is to establish who the deceased was; where the deceased came by his or her death; when the deceased came by his or her death; and how the deceased came by his or her death. It is a public service foremost for the bereaved families[12].

## Conclusions

**14.24** The Chief Coroner has provided guidance[13] to assist coroners in the use of short-form and narrative conclusions and with a view to achieving greater consistency across England and Wales. It provides a suggested approach, consistent with case law, to making public findings and conclusions clear, accessible and complete[14].

The outcome of an inquest is recorded in the Record of Inquest (Form 2) and this shows the medical cause of death and the conclusion, either short-form or narrative. There are five sections or boxes to be completed:

---

12 Note: memorandum of understanding: the memorandum of understanding between the Crown Prosecution Service, the Association of Chief Police Officers, the Chief Coroner and the Coroners' Society of England and Wales. As part of a coroner's decision-making process when deciding whether to suspend or adjourn an inquest they must consider the legislation which sets out the intent that the inquest should take place promptly and in any event as soon as practicable: CJA 2009, s 16 and Coroners (Inquests) Rules 2013, r 26.
13 Chief Coroners *Guidance No 17 Conclusions: Short-Form and Narrative.*
14 See https://www.judiciary.uk/wp-content/uploads/2013/09/guidance-no-17-conclusions.pdf.

**14.24** *Coroners' Inquests and Public Inquiry*

(1) name of the deceased;
(2) the medical cause of death;
(3) how, when and where the deceased came by his or her death;
(4) conclusion;
(5) the particulars required for death registration.

The record will be signed by the coroner and by the jury and ordinarily should be treated as a public document available for inspection by the public with minor redactions in relation to the signatures of jurors and the address of the deceased, where there is good reason for doing so.

The jury is required, having heard the evidence, and in addition to deciding the medical cause of death (box 2), to arrive at a conclusion by way of a staged process:

(a) to make findings of fact based upon the evidence;
(b) to distil from the findings of fact 'how' the deceased came by his or her death and to record that briefly in box 3.

Normally, the answer to 'how' will be a brief one sentence summary taken from the findings of fact in (a) above. 'How' means 'by what means' rather than in what broad circumstances[15].

There will usually be a description of the mechanism of death, for example:

- from trauma consistent with an un-witnessed fall from a roof a person was working on (the box 4 conclusion showing 'accident');
- by exposure to asbestos fibres during the course of the person's occupation as manufacturing operative (the box 4 conclusion showing 'industrial disease').

The words used must be brief, neutral and clear and they must not appear to determine any question of criminal liability on the part of a named person.

There are two alternative conclusions which are sanctioned by the CJA 2009 and the Coroners (Inquests) Rules 2013: (i) a short-form conclusion; and (ii) a narrative conclusion. It is permissible to combine the two types of conclusion.

In most complex work-related death inquests where interested persons are represented, the coroner will invite submissions on the type of conclusion, short-form or narrative; the short-form conclusions that the coroner is considering leaving to the jury; what written directions (if any) will be given to the jury; and what questions (if any) may be asked of them.

## Short-form inquest conclusions

**14.25** These are some of the most common short-form conclusions and their explanation.

---

15 See *R v HM Coroner for North Humberside and Scunthorpe, ex p Jamieson* [1995] QB 1.

- **Natural causes** – the death was caused by the normal development of a natural illness which was not significantly contributed to by human intervention.
- **Accidental death** – the cause of death was unnatural but not unlawful.
- **Misadventure** – this is nearly the same verdict as 'accidental death' but would imply that the deceased has taken a deliberate action that has then resulted in his or her death.
- **Suicide** – it is decided that the person has voluntarily acted to destroy his or her life in a conscious way.
- **Neglect** – there has been a gross failure to provide the deceased with his or her basic needs ie the provision of nourishment, liquid, warmth or medicine. There must be a clear causal link between this gross failure and the death of the dependent person. This is a rare conclusion and commonly associated with the failure to provide even basic medical attention. More commonly the coroner would consider neglect as a contributing factor rather than the sole cause of death.
- **Unlawful killing** – the death was caused by murder, manslaughter, infanticide or through a serious driving offence.
- **Open verdict** – there is simply not enough evidence to return a verdict. This is a rare verdict and really only used as a 'last resort'.

## Narrative conclusions

14.26 There is no obligation for a coroner to use a short-form conclusion they can use a narrative conclusion. This is where the coroner sets out the circumstances of the death in a detailed way based on the evidence that was heard.

In a non-art 2 case (which is the case for most work-related deaths) a narrative conclusion should be a brief, neutral, factual statement; it should not express any judgment or opinion. Words or phrases such as 'missed opportunities' or 'inadequate failures' should probably be avoided. The Chief Coroners Guidance[16] gives the following example:

> 'But rather than, for example, saying that "There was a missed opportunity when the registrar failed to seek advice from the consultant", the coroner could say just as effectively: "The evidence leads me to find that the registrar did not seek advice from the consultant who was nearby and available at the time and the registrar knew that. The registrar acted on his own."'

## Standard of proof

14.27 Most inquests are decided on 'the balance of probabilities'. This means that 'it is more likely than not' that the death of the person happened in

---

16 *Chief Coroners Guidance No 17, Conclusions: Short-Form and Narrative*, para 34.

this way. If the conclusion is for suicide or unlawful killing, then this must be decided on the basis of 'beyond reasonable doubt'.

# INVESTIGATIONS LASTING MORE THAN A YEAR

**14.28** One aim of the CJA 2009 was to reduce the time between a person's death and the inquest hearing concluding within a year. A senior coroner who is conducting an investigation into a person's death that has not been completed or is not discontinued within a year is under a duty to notify the Chief Coroner of that fact and the date on which the investigation is to be completed or discontinued. The Chief Coroner must in turn keep a register of all death notifications.

The Report of the Chief Coroner to the Lord Chancellor 2017–18 contains an Annex C table showing the numbers of cases over 12 months per area[17].

As can be seen from the table, following the introduction by the Chief Coroner in 2014 of a standard procedure for reporting on cases over 12 months, there has been a decrease in the numbers of cases outstanding. There has been a reduction from 2,673 cases first reported in 2014 to 2,161 cases reported in 2018. The number of cases over 12 months has increased slightly over the last two years due to the increase of more complex and lengthy inquests. Suspended cases have also contributed to the increase with ongoing external investigations in incidents such as the Shoreham Airshow disaster and MH17 plane crash abroad. Practice would indicate that in relation to industrial or work-related fatalities, completion of cases within the 12-month timescale is a long way from being achieved.

The Coroners (Inquests) Rules 2013, r 8 requires that a 'coroner must complete an inquest within six months of the date on which the coroner is made aware of the death, or as soon as reasonably practicable after that date.'

What amounts to 'reasonably practicable' depends on the particular facts and circumstances of each case. There are often good and clear reasons why some cases are outstanding. For example, if there are ongoing police enquiries, criminal investigations and prosecutions, investigations overseas, Health and Safety Executive (HSE) investigations, the coroner's inquest is put on 'hold' pending the outcome of those enquiries or investigations. In some cases, those other investigations are very lengthy. The net result can be that a coroner can only hold an inquest on a case after a period of two years or more. Homicide investigations by the police, manslaughter or health and safety investigations by the HSE and investigations by the PPO or IPOC will have a particular impact on the figures for cases over 12 months in those coroner areas covering the major cities of England and Wales where the majority of homicides take place or where the major prisons are located.

---

17  See https://assets.publishing.service.gov.uk/government/uploads/system/uploads/attachment_data/file/764720/report-of-the-chief-coroner-lord-chancellor-2017-18.pdf.

# REPORTS TO PREVENT FURTHER DEATHS

**14.29** A coroner has the power to make reports to prevent further deaths ('PFD Report'). A coroner's duty arises under the CJA 2009, Sch 5, para 7 and is exercised under the Coroners (Investigations) Regulations 2013[18], reg 28. This means that if in the opinion of the coroner the death could have been prevented if a different action had been taken by a particular person or organisation, then the coroner can make a recommendation for change. The coroner should make the report where a concern is identified. A coroner must compile a PFD Report if their investigation has led them to conclude that circumstances creating a risk of a future death exist or will occur and action should be taken to prevent the occurrence or continuation of such circumstances or to eliminate or reduce the risk of death created by such circumstances.

The reports should be intended to improve public health, welfare and safety. The coroner must send the report to the person the coroner believes may have the power to take the actions identified within the report. The person or organisation which received the coroner's recommendation (usually in the form of a report) must respond within 56 days or longer if the coroner grants an extension.

Between July 2017 and June 2018 there were 377 PFD Reports issued by coroners. All reports are published by the Chief Coroner on the judiciary website (although sometimes with redaction for data protection purposes).

Whilst all PFD Reports are different, because they deal with individual cases, the following themes could be identified by the Chief Coroner as appearing in several reports issued concerning deaths in prison in 2016 there were 354. These themes include:

- evidence of a lack of awareness amongst some staff about procedures (for example one PFD Report highlighted the lack of awareness amongst staff of the different procedures in day and night working);
- lack of clarity amongst staff about how to trigger an emergency medical response;
- the inconsistent application of procedures (this is a common observation in reports; for example, in one report it referred to the inconsistent or incorrect application of established procedures such as for cell observation checks);
- failure to pass on information between agencies and within institutions;
- issues around buildings and estate (such as exposed ligature points in cells);
- several reports also identified the need for extra or reinforced training for staff.

The Chief Coroner encourages all coroners to write and submit PFD Reports where appropriate. The Chief Coroner is keen to undertake additional work on PFD Reports.

---

18 SI 2013/1629.

**14.29** *Coroners' Inquests and Public Inquiry*

A report may not be made until the coroner has considered all the documents, evidence and information that in the opinion of the coroner are relevant to the investigation[19].

The coroner must send a copy of the report to the Chief Coroner and every interested person who in the coroner's opinion should receive it; to the appropriate Local Safeguarding Children Board where the coroner believes the deceased was under the age of 18; and may send a copy of the report to any other person who the coroner believes may find it useful or of interest[20].

The coroner's duty arises when something revealed by the investigation (including evidence at the inquest) which gives rise to a concern. Giving rise to a concern is a relatively low threshold[21]:

> 'The effect of the amendment to rule 43 in 2008 was significantly to enlarge its scope. Whereas previously the power could only be exercised with a view to preventing similar deaths to those under investigation at the inquest, a report can now be made relating to any risk of further deaths, whether or not similar to the deaths under investigation.'

The concern is that circumstances creating a risk of further deaths will occur, or will continue to exist, in the future. The coroner has a duty to report (ie 'must report') the matter to a person or organisation who the coroner believes may have power to take such action.

# POST-MORTEM EXAMINATIONS

**14.30** A senior coroner may request a suitable practitioner to undertake a post-mortem examination of the body if a post-mortem examination is necessary to enable the coroner to decide whether the death is one into which the coroner has a duty to conduct an investigation.

There is a duty on the practitioner to report to the coroner following a post-mortem as soon as practicable after the examination.

If the bereaved family of the deceased are dissatisfied with the post-mortem they may request the coroner permit them to arrange a second post-mortem. This will, however, be at their own expense. Similarly, a defendant charged with an offence in relation to the death may also request a second post-mortem. The coroner should grant such a request unless there are reasonable grounds for refusing it[22].

---

19 SI 2013/1629, reg 28(3).
20 SI 2013/1629, reg 28(4).
21 London Bombings of 7 July 2005, per Lady Justice Heather Hallett, Assistant Deputy Coroner for Inner West London, ruling 6 May 2011, transcript p15, see http://webarchive.nationalarchives.gov.uk/20120216072447/http://7julyinquests.independent.gov.uk/hearing_transcripts/06052011am.htm.
22 *R v South London Coroner, ex p Ridley* [1985] 1 WLR 1347.

With the advancement of technology, it is possible for post-mortem imaging to be undertaken by means of a computerised tomography (CT) scan as an alternative to more invasive post-mortem examination (autopsy). This area continues to develop, but slowly, and as the law currently stands, an autopsy ordered by a coroner is free of charge to the family and is paid for by the state. CT scanning is more expensive and there is no state funding for it at present. There are only a limited amount of post-mortem scanning facilities provided by the state although private companies have provided these services in some areas. Provision is geographically variable and in those parts of England and Wales where it is available, families may be asked to pay for it. The facilities are becoming available and importantly the Chief Coroner encourages the availability and use of imaging so a shift towards more imaging may be seen in the foreseeable future.

In 2017 there were a number of events that have resulted in mass fatalities. Westminster Bridge, the Manchester Arena, London Bridge and Borough Market were the subject of terrorist activity with the loss of many lives and numerous serious injuries. On 14 June fire broke out at Grenfell Tower. Each of these incidents led to the extensive involvement of the coroner service and of the local senior coroner. When a mass fatality incident occurs, depending on where and how it takes place, the senior coroner with responsibility for the area will be notified by the police and will be involved in the process of the identification of the victims.

# CONFLICTS OF INTEREST – INSURED AND INSURER AT INQUESTS

**14.31** Insurers funding defence costs may also cover the costs of attending an inquest where the coroner has decided the company is an 'interested person'. Depending on whether there is a co-existing civil claim, the interests of the insured and the insurer may or may not be aligned.

A typical clause may for example be in the following terms:

> 'We, the insurer, have the right, but not the obligation, to take control of and conduct in your name, the investigation, settlement or defence of any claim …'

In most civil claims interests are normally aligned, that is to say, the insurer pays the legal fees and the compensation awarded to the employee or third party and, save for reputational and publicity issues, the parties' aims of settling any valid claim at the most cost-effective point. Criminal and regulatory claims (such as health and safety investigations and prosecutions) is a different situation altogether. Given that for the most part the HSE is still waiting for the outcome and the evidence to be unveiled in an inquest before making any decision on prosecution, the interests of a party at an inquest are often closely aligned with those of a criminal defence rather than a civil claim.

**14.31** *Coroners' Inquests and Public Inquiry*

The insurer has no responsibility for paying any criminal fine that may be imposed and there is no financial incentive (save for commercial obligation) for it to deploy the expertise and resources needed to properly defend or mitigate any alleged breaches.

## CONFLICTS OF INTEREST – INSURED AND INSURER – INQUEST DISCLOSURE

**14.32** Policy obligations requiring disclosure differ from policy to policy, but the following would be typical obligation in most legal expenses insurance policy wording:

> 'What you and your representative must do for us [the insurer]:
>
> If we ask for this, we must be able to have access to your representative's files. This includes the truthful account of the facts of your case and any paperwork you have supplied to your representative.'

An obligation on insureds to make available to insurers all documents may lead to a conflict where documents have been provided to the interested person to the inquest by the coroner for the sole purpose of concluding the investigation. Documents may be provided under restrictions imposed by the coroner whereby it is not permissible for them to be used by any other party or for any other purpose.

Careful thought should be given to the basis on which documents are held and whether such disclosure is in the interests of the insured, before any disclosure is made.

## PUBLIC INQUIRY

**14.33** Public inquiries such as the Ladbroke Grove Rail Crash, the death of Victoria Climbié, Anthony Grainger Shooting, Alexander Litvinenki Poisoning, Grenfell Tower are not to be confused with large inquests such as the Hillsborough Disaster, Lakanall House Fire, 7th July London Bombings, Mark Duggan Shooting and London Bridge Terror Attack.

Public inquiries are set up by the government under the Inquiries Act 2005 and the Inquiry Rules 2006[23].

A minister may have an inquiry under the Inquiries Act 2005 where it appears to them that:

- particular events have caused, or are capable of causing, public concern; or
- there is public concern that particular events may have occurred.

---

23 SI 2006/1838.

Inquiries can be held by one person or a panel and they can take evidence in the form of documents and oral evidence about the events in questions. Often the inquiry will be chaired by a currently serving or retired judge.

## Scope of any public inquiry

**14.34** The scope of a public inquiry can be very broad and tends to focus on establishing what went wrong and making recommendations to prevent similar incidents occurring. A public inquiry makes no decision about liability. An inquiry panel is not to rule on, and has no power to determine, any person's civil or criminal liability and an inquiry panel is not to be inhibited in the discharge of its functions by any likelihood of liability being inferred from facts that it determines or recommendations that it makes.

Ministers are able to set up formal, independent inquiries relating to particular events which have caused or have potential to cause public concern, or where there is public concern that particular events may have occurred. Ministers also have the power to set the terms of reference, to appoint a chairperson to conduct the inquiry, and also additional panel members and assessors where appropriate.

## Power to establish a public inquiry

**14.35** A minister can cause an independent inquiry to be held. An inquiry could be called into a particular event, for example the Dunblane inquiry 1996, or a series of events; for example the BSE inquiry 1997. In the past most inquiries have been triggered by events, they have also been held where there is a concern that something has failed to happen or that particular systems have not operated properly, for example the Climbié inquiry 2001.

## There is to be no determination of liability

**14.36** Inquiries brought under the Inquiries Act 2005 have no power to determine civil or criminal liability and must not purport to do so. The aim of inquiries is to help to restore public confidence in systems or services by investigating the facts and making recommendations to prevent recurrence, not to establish liability or to punish anyone. Whilst there are often strong public feelings, particularly following high profile and controversial events, that an inquiry should determine who is to blame for what has occurred, inquiries are not courts and their findings cannot and do not have legal effect.

## Composition of the inquiry panel

**14.37** Ministers are provided with the flexibility to appoint an inquiry panel that is appropriate to the circumstances under investigation. The panel can be either a chairperson sitting alone, for example as Lord Cullen did as the chairman to the inquiry into the shootings at Dunblane Primary School 1996 and the inquiry into the Ladbroke Grove Rail Crash 1999; or they may sit with one or more panel members, for example the Royal Liverpool Children's Hospital inquiry 1999 into the removal and retention of organ and tissue following post-mortems on children was chaired by Michael Redfern QC as one of a three-person panel with Dr Jean Keeling Consultant Paediatric Pathologist and Mrs Elizabeth Powell Chief Officer Liverpool Community Health Council.

## Setting-up date and terms of reference

**14.38** The minister must consult with the chairperson when either setting or changing the terms of reference. The type of information contained in the terms of reference will vary from inquiry to inquiry and some will be more expansive than others. For example, the terms for the Royal Liverpool Children's Hospital inquiry were set out as six simple bullet points, whereas others are a page long.

The terms of reference means:
- the matters to which the inquiry relates;
- any particular matters as to which the inquiry panel is to determine the facts;
- whether the inquiry panel is to make recommendations;
- any other matters relating to the scope of the inquiry that the minister may specify.

The minister must specify whether the inquiry is asked to make recommendations when reporting however, the panel may make recommendations even if this was not a requirement in the terms set by the minister.

## Requirement of impartiality

**14.39** There is a requirement for the panel to be impartial. The minister must not appoint a person as a member of the inquiry panel if the person has a direct interest in the matters to which the inquiry relates, or a close association with an interested party, unless, despite the person's interest or association, their appointment could not reasonably be regarded as affecting the impartiality of the inquiry panel. A person might be said to have an 'interest' in the events where the matters raised impinge on issues which they are concerned about, either personally or professionally. A 'direct interest' would be present where the individual's concern with the events is particularly strong. A 'close association' focuses not so much on the interests of the individual, but on the links (whether personal or professional) that the individual has. For example, were an inquiry panel member to have ties with a witness, there might be concerns about the weight which that inquiry panel member would give to the evidence.

## Assessors

14.40 The role of assessors will vary from inquiry to inquiry, but in essence they are experts in their own particular field, whose knowledge can provide the panel with the expertise it needs in order to fulfil an inquiry's terms of reference. For example in the Victoria Climbié inquiry, four expert assessors joined the chairman, Lord Laming: Dr Nellie Adjaye, a Fellow of the Royal College of Paediatrics and Child Health and a consultant paediatrician with the Maidstone and Tunbridge Wells NHS Trust; John Fox, a detective superintendent and the head of the Specialist Investigations Department in the Hampshire Constabulary; Donna Kinnair, a nurse and health visitor and formerly the strategic commissioner for children's services for the Lambeth, Southwark and Lewisham Health Authority; Nigel Richardson, the Assistant Director of Children and Families for North Lincolnshire Council.

An assessor could be appointed for the duration of the inquiry, but it would also be possible to appoint an assessor only for part of the inquiry, to assist when evidence on a particular subject was being considered.

Assessors do not have any of the inquiry panel's powers and are not responsible for the inquiry report or findings, although it is of note that the assessors that Lord Laming chose for the Climbié inquiry are referred to in the Report as the 'Inquiry Panel' and sat with Lord Laming through the evidence.

## Power to suspend inquiry

14.41 An inquiry may be suspended to allow for the completion of any other investigation relating to any of the matters to which the inquiry relates, or for the determination of any civil or criminal proceedings (including proceedings before a disciplinary tribunal) arising out of any of those matters. Given the subject matter and importance of the underlying events that cause a public inquiry to be called, it is inevitable that it is only going to be one of a number of investigations running concurrently. It is important that an inquiry does not prejudice, for example, a criminal prosecution. If new investigations or proceedings come to light, or are commenced after the inquiry has started, it may be necessary to halt the inquiry temporarily.

## End of inquiry

14.42 In most cases an inquiry will end when the chairperson has submitted a report and has confirmed to the minister that the inquiry has fulfilled its terms of reference and has done any further work necessary to wind up the inquiry, such as a costs assessment. There might however, be situations before the submission of the report in which it is no longer necessary or possible for the inquiry to continue. Evidence may emerge that there is no further need for an inquiry or which demonstrates that the inquiry has the wrong focus,

**14.42** *Coroners' Inquests and Public Inquiry*

for example, if it emerged during an inquiry that the event being investigated was an act of sabotage rather than failings of a particular system, and ought to be dealt with by the police rather than an inquiry. Other events might occur which also need to be investigated, and it may be more appropriate to set up a single, wider-ranging, inquiry perhaps with a different panel. An event may occur, such as a fire or the death of a witness, which means that an inquiry will no longer have access to the evidence it needs to conduct an effective investigation, and it may no longer be in the public interest for it to continue.

Such scenarios are unlikely, but possible. In such cases, the minister, after consulting the chairperson, is able to bring the inquiry to a close. There may also be situations where there is in fact a need for a series of reports not just one. For example, Dame Janet Smith as chair of the Shipman inquiry produced six reports:

(1) how many patients Shipman killed, the means employed, and the period over which the killings took place;
(2) conduct of the police investigation that took place in March 1998 and failed to uncover Shipman's crimes;
(3) the present system for death and cremation certification and for the investigation of deaths by coroners, together with the conduct of those who had operated those systems in the aftermath of the deaths of Shipman's victims for which she has made recommendations for change based on her findings;
(4) the systems for the management and regulation of controlled drugs, together with the conduct of those who operated those systems;
(5) the handling of complaints against general practitioners (GPs), the raising of concerns about GPs, General Medical Council procedures and its proposal for revalidation of doctors;
(6) how many patients Shipman killed during his career as a junior doctor at Pontefract General Infirmary between 1970 and 1974.

She also considered a small number of cases from Shipman's time in Hyde, which the inquiry became aware of after the publication of the First Report. She also considered the claims by a former inmate at HMP Preston regarding alleged claims by Shipman about the number of patients he had killed.

## Power to convert another inquiry into inquiry under the Inquiries Act 2005

**14.43** The minister can convert an inquiry that is not being held under the Inquiries Act 2005 into an inquiry held under that Act. Examples of non-statutory inquiries include the Hutton Inquiry and the Bichard inquiry.

The Hutton inquiry was a 2003 judicial inquiry in the UK chaired by Lord Hutton, who was appointed by the Labour government to investigate the circumstances surrounding the death of David Kelly, a biological warfare expert and former UN weapons inspector in Iraq. Mr Kelly, an employee of the Ministry of Defence, was found dead after he had been named as the source of quotations used by BBC journalist Andrew Gilligan. These quotations had formed the basis of media reports claiming that the government had knowingly 'sexed up' the report into Iraq and weapons of mass destruction.

The Bichard inquiry was an independent inquiry set up by the Home Secretary to[24]:

> 'Urgently enquire into child protection procedures in Humberside Police and Cambridgeshire Constabulary in the light of the recent trial and conviction of Ian Huntley for the murder of Jessica Chapman and Holly Wells. In particular to assess the effectiveness of the relevant intelligence-based record keeping, the vetting practices in those forces since 1995 and information sharing with other agencies, and to report to the Home Secretary on matters of local and national relevance and make recommendations as appropriate.'

The purpose of this power is to convert a non-statutory inquiry – ie one requested by a minster but not under the Inquiries Act 2005, into one which has the powers under the Act. The inquiry panel has the ability to use formal powers, if they become necessary.

The minister may convert a non-statutory inquiry provided the matter that the original inquiry was investigating fell within the scope of the circumstances set out in s 1 of the Inquiries Act 2005. It is not intended that this power should be used to convert other types of inquiries, such as planning inquiries, but it is intended that the power would extend to Department of Health inquiries where the subject matter and issues to be covered dictate the need for statutory powers.

In 2001 the Secretary of State for Health announced the setting up of three separate, independent statutory inquiries, none of which was to be held in public. One of those inquiries was the independent investigation into how the NHS handled the allegations about the conduct of medical practitioner Clifford Ayling chaired by Dame Anna Pauffley; the second about Richard Neale, a consultant obstetrician and gynaecologist who worked in a number of hospitals in North Yorkshire; and the third about William Kerr and Michael Haslam, two consultant psychiatrists who practised in North Yorkshire.

## Inquiry proceedings – evidence and procedure

**14.44** The chairperson of the inquiry may direct evidence on oath, and for that purpose may administer oaths. The chairperson is required to act fairly throughout the inquiry and may consider, for example, if certain participants require some form of legal advice or representation.

---

24 The Bichard Inquiry Report: HC653 Introduction and Summary, at p 1, para 3, see http://dera.ioe.ac.uk/6394/1/report.pdf.

**14.45** *Coroners' Inquests and Public Inquiry*

## Public access to inquiry proceedings and information

**14.45** The chairperson has the powers under the Inquiries Act 2005, s 19 to impose restriction on public access to inquiry proceedings and information in some circumstances. However, the chairperson is required to do what is considered reasonable to ensure public access to evidence (including the media), such as permitting individuals:

- to attend the inquiry or to see and hear a simultaneous transmission of proceedings at the inquiry;
- to obtain or to view a record of evidence and documents given, produced or provided to the inquiry or inquiry panel.

Unless it is requested by the clairman or permission is given, no recording or broadcast of proceedings at an inquiry may be made.

The chairperson will have discretion on broadcasting: some have allowed broadcasting of particular stages, such as the opening statements. In deciding whether to allow broadcasting, the chairperson will need to consider whether it would interfere with witnesses' human rights and, in particular, with the right to respect for a private and family life[25]. Unlike inquiries under the Tribunals of Inquiry (Evidence) Act 1921, inquiries under the Inquiries Act 2005 will not be covered by s 9 of the Contempt of Court Act 1981, which places restrictions on sound recording.

An active inquiry held under the Inquiries Act 2005 is not a public authority for the purposes of the Freedom of Information Act 2000. However, once an inquiry is over, its records are generally held by a public authority, such as a government department or the National Archives.

## Restrictions on public access in a public inquiry

**14.46** Restrictions may be imposed on:

- attendance at an inquiry, or at any particular part of an inquiry;
- disclosure or publication of any evidence or documents given, produced or provided to an inquiry.

Restrictions are permissible if the chairperson considers them helpful to the inquiry in fulfilling its terms of reference, or to be necessary in the public interest.

Those matters are:

- the extent to which any restriction on attendance, disclosure or publication might inhibit the allaying of public concern;
- any risk of harm or damage that could be avoided or reduced by any such restriction;

---

25 Article 8 of the European Convention on Human Rights.

- any conditions as to confidentiality subject to which a person acquired information that he is to give, or has given, to the inquiry;
- the extent to which not imposing any particular restriction would be likely:
  - to cause delay or to impair the efficiency or effectiveness of the inquiry; or
  - otherwise to result in additional cost (whether to public funds or to witnesses or others).

Inquiry proceedings can be held in private and evidence can be withheld from the public if the circumstances require it. Over a third of the notable inquiries held in the past 15 years, such as the Penrose inquiry into the collapse of Equitable Life, and the inquiry into the government's handling of the outbreak of foot and mouth disease, to mainly public inquiries such as the Bloody Sunday inquiry and the Hutton inquiry, in which a small amount of highly sensitive material was withheld from the public, have had some sort of restriction on public access.

Restrictions can be imposed on attendance which might range from the exclusion of the press or general public, allowing those with an interest in the inquiry to attend, as was the case in Dame Pauffley's Clifford Ayling inquiry.

There might be situations in which restrictions could prevent a person from passing on information that they have learnt as a result of their attendance at, or involvement in, the inquiry. This could include insurers see paras **14.31** and **14.32** on conflicts of interest.

Restriction notices and orders continue indefinitely unless otherwise specified or unless they are revoked. Orders restricting attendance will only be relevant during the course of the inquiry, but some orders restricting disclosure or publication of evidence might need to continue beyond the end of the inquiry. For example, if an inquiry chairperson issued an order that the identity of a particular witness was to be kept confidential, because the witness could be at risk if their identity were disclosed, that order would remain in place and would need to continue to protect their identify.

Disclosure restrictions would not prevent a person not involved in the inquiry from disclosing or publishing information that had come into their possession through means unconnected with the inquiry, even if some of that information might be included in documents or hearings that were covered by a restriction order or notice. For example, if an inquiry were set up into the death of a hospital patient, a restriction notice could be issued to exclude the general public from the proceedings and to prevent the publication of transcripts of evidence, because it could be considered that an inquiry held partly in private would be more effective. The inquiry might consider information already in the public domain, such as papers from the inquest, or statements of hospital policy. The fact that a restriction notice was in place for the inquiry would not prevent a member of staff at the hospital from providing a patient with a copy of the hospital policy.

Another example is of a government department providing information to an inquiry held in private and, after the end of the inquiry, a request being made under the Freedom of Information Act 2000 for some of that information. The department could not refuse to provide the information purely because it happened to have been covered by the restriction notice, because the department would have held that information even if the inquiry had never happened. The purpose of a restriction notice is to restrict disclosure of information in the context of the inquiry or to restrict disclosure by those who have received the information only by virtue of it being present.

## Powers of chairperson to require the production of evidence

**14.47** The chairperson of an inquiry may require a person to attend at a time and place stated in the notice:

- to give evidence;
- to produce any documents in that person's custody or under their control that relate to a matter in question at the inquiry;
- to produce any other thing in that person's custody or under their control for inspection, examination or testing by or on behalf of the inquiry panel.

The notice must explain the possible consequences of non-compliance and indicate what the recipient should do if they are unable to comply with a notice under this section, or it is not reasonable in all the circumstances to require them to comply with such a notice.

The chairperson may revoke or vary the notice but must consider the public interest and the likely importance of the information.

Inquiries are provided with statutory powers to compel evidence. An inquiry panel will usually ask for information informally first, and experience from past inquiries has shown that the vast majority of informal requests, where they can be, will be complied with. There are three main scenarios in which powers of compulsion are likely to be used:

- a person is unwilling to comply with an informal request for information;
- a person is willing to comply with an informal request, but is worried about the possible consequences of disclosure, for example if disclosure were to break confidentiality agreements, and therefore asks the chairperson to issue a formal notice; or
- a person is unable to provide the information without a formal notice because there is a statutory bar on disclosure.

## Privileged information

**14.48** A person may not be required to give, produce or provide any evidence or document if:

- they could not be required to do so if the proceedings of the inquiry were civil proceedings in a court in the relevant part of the UK; or

*Coroners' Inquests and Public Inquiry* **14.48**

- the requirement would be incompatible with a European Community obligation.

The rules of law under which evidence or documents are permitted or required to be withheld on grounds of public interest immunity apply in relation to an inquiry as they apply in relation to civil proceedings in a court in the relevant part of the UK.

Witnesses at inquiries will have the same privileges, in relation to requests for information, as witnesses in civil proceedings. In particular, this means that a witness will be able to refuse to provide evidence if:

- it is covered by legal professional privilege;
- it might incriminate the witness or their spouse or civil partner; or
- it relates to what has taken place in Parliament.

In some recent inquiries, the Attorney General has given undertakings along the following lines[26]:

> 'To undertake in respect of any person who provides evidence to the inquiry that no evidence he or she may give before the inquiry, whether orally or by written statement, nor any written statement made preparatory to giving evidence nor any document produced by that person to the inquiry will be used in evidence against him or her in any criminal proceedings, except in proceedings where he or she is charged with having given false evidence in the course of this inquiry or having conspired with or procured others to do so.'

In the report of the Al-Sweady inquiry an undertaking was given in the following terms[27]:

> 'No evidence ... will be used in evidence against that person in any criminal proceedings or for the purpose of deciding whether to bring such proceedings against that person (including any proceedings for an offence against military law, whether by court martial or summary hearing before a commanding officer or appropriate senior authority) ...'

The Attorney General further undertook that[28]:

> '... in any criminal proceedings brought, or in any decision as to whether to bring such proceedings, against any person who provides such evidence [as defined] to the Inquiry, no reliance will be placed upon evidence which is obtained during an investigation as a result of the provision by that person of evidence to the Inquiry. This undertaking does not preclude the use of information and/or evidence identified independently of the evidence provided by that person to the Inquiry.'

The intention of this provision is to encourage all witnesses to give full and truthful accounts, free from any concern that might otherwise have caused witnesses to refuse to give evidence and/or to answer questions by invoking

---

26 Inquiries Act 2005, Explanatory Notes, Ch 12, s 22, para 54.
27 Sir Thane Forbes, *The Report of the Al Sweady Inquiry*, Vol 1 (Dec 2014), Ch 4: Procedural Issues, at 1.144.
28 Sir Thane Forbes, *The Report of the Al Sweady Inquiry*, Vol 1 (Dec 2014), Ch 4: Procedural Issues, at 1.146.

the privilege against self-incrimination. In this matter the Al-Sweady inquiry endeavoured to ensure that it would receive the unqualified assistance of all witnesses in carrying out its task of establishing the true facts relating to the matters it was required to investigate.

## Public interest immunity

**14.49** The right to withhold disclosure on the grounds of public interest immunity, as in civil proceedings, exists. Applications can be made on the grounds that disclosure of the information would be prejudicial to national security when it is believed that disclosure would cause real damage or harm to the public interest and that this outweighs the public interest in open justice. A claim will need to be supported by evidence and it is the responsibility of the inquiry panel, having viewed the documents or information, to balance the public interest in disclosure against the public interest in maintaining confidentiality. If the claim is upheld, it does not automatically follow that a document would be withheld. Where it is possible to redact documents so that the information giving rise to the issue of national security is removed, it is open to the inquiry chairperson to order that this is done.

## Offences

**14.50** A person is guilty of an offence if:
- they fail without reasonable excuse to do anything that they are required to do by a notice;
- if during the course of an inquiry that person does anything that is intended to have the effect of:
  - distorting or otherwise altering any evidence, document or other thing that is given, produced or provided to the inquiry panel; or
  - preventing any evidence, document or other thing from being given, produced or provided to the inquiry panel, or anything that they know or believe is likely to have that effect.

A person is guilty of an offence if during the course of an inquiry[29]:
- they intentionally suppress or conceal a document that is, and that they know or believe to be, a relevant document. A document is a 'relevant document' if it is likely that the inquiry panel would (if aware of its existence) wish to be provided with it; or
- they intentionally alter or destroy any such document. For the purposes of this subsection a document is a 'relevant document' if it is likely that the inquiry panel would (if aware of its existence) wish to be provided with it.

---

29 Inquiries Act 2005, s 35(3).

A person who is guilty of an offence is liable on conviction at the magistrates' court to a fine or to imprisonment for a term not exceeding the relevant maximum (currently 51 weeks in England and Wales under the Criminal Justice Act 2003, s 281(5)), or to both. Although the Criminal Justice Act 2003 wanted to raise the maximum sentencing powers of magistrates to a year, this is still currently at six months.

## ENFORCEMENT BY HIGH COURT OR COURT OF SESSION

**14.51**  The chairperson has the option of two sanctions for non-compliance with an inquiry, or for actions that are likely to hinder the inquiry.

In England and Wales and Northern Ireland, it is the chairperson that can institute a prosecution for non-compliance with a notice issued. This is because it is for the chairperson to decide whether to enforce notices issued under their powers of compulsion, and how best to do this.

Where a person fails to comply with, or acts in breach of, a notice or an order made by an inquiry, or threatens to do so, the chairperson of the inquiry – or after the end of the inquiry – the minister, may certify the matter to the appropriate court.

## IMMUNITY FROM SUIT

**14.52**  A member of an inquiry panel has immunity from law suits. No action lies against the panel, an assessor, counsel or solicitor to an inquiry, or a person who is engaged to provide assistance to an inquiry, in respect of any act done or omission made in the execution of their duty as such, or any act done or omission made in good faith in the execution of their duty as such.

## TIME LIMIT FOR APPLYING FOR JUDICIAL REVIEW

**14.53**  Any challenge made to a decision by a minister or inquiry panel by judicial review must be brought within 14 days of the day on which the applicant became aware of the decision, unless that time limit is extended by the court.

This is to reduce the time limit for judicial reviews of decisions that could delay an inquiry: the prospect of a challenge to a procedural decision can halt the inquiry until it has been resolved by a court. For example, in the case of Clifford Ayling, when the Secretary of State announced in July 2001 that there

**14.53** *Coroners' Inquests and Public Inquiry*

was to be an independent statutory inquiry but that it was not to be held in public, solicitors acting for a number of women, including some who had been indecently assaulted by Ayling, commenced judicial review proceedings of the decision of the Secretary of State not to hold an inquiry in public. The claims for judicial review were not heard until February 2002 and judgment was given in March 2002.

Unlike that in the Civil Procedure Rules, the time limit runs from the date on which an applicant became aware of the decision, not from the date on which the decision was made.

## EXPENSES OF WITNESSES AND PARTICIPANTS

**14.54** The chairperson may award reasonable expenses to a person by way of compensation for loss of time, or in respect of expenses properly incurred, or to be incurred in relation to, the inquiry and this includes where appropriate to award amounts in respect of legal representation.

A person may be eligible if it can be shown that they are:

- a person attending the inquiry to give evidence or to produce any document or other thing; or
- a person who, in the opinion of the chairperson, has such a particular interest in the proceedings or outcome of the inquiry as to justify such an award.

Legal costs of participants are often the most significant part of the total cost of an inquiry. The non-statutory position adopted in some inquiries has been for the minister to decide, in consultation with the chairperson, whether to fund those participating that require representation but who may be unable to pay for representation themselves.

The government would not normally meet the costs of large organisations and although the chairperson has the power to pay costs, the minister can place qualifications on that power. The minister will generally set out any broad conditions under which payment may be granted, and the chairperson will then take the individual decisions.

# Chapter 15

# Civil Claims

Civil claims   15.1
    Judge hearing a civil case   15.2
    Judgment   15.3
    Costs   15.4
    Court of Appeal – Civil Division   15.5
    High Court – Queen's Bench Division   15.6
    Limitation period   15.7
Personal injury and fatal accidents   15.8
    Enterprise and Regulatory Reform Act 2013 (ERRA 2013)   15.8
    *Stark v Post Office*   15.9
    Dismissal of a fraudulent claim   15.10
    Pre-Action Protocol for Personal Injury Claims   15.11
        Letter of notification   15.12
        Rehabilitation   15.13
        Letter of claim   15.14
        Claim and response   15.15
        Disclosure   15.16
        Experts   15.17
    Alternative dispute resolution (ADR)   15.18
Fatal accident claims   15.19
    Dependant   15.20
    Assessment of dependency   15.21
        Re-marriage   15.22
        Cohabitees   15.23
    Causation   15.24
    How the claim is calculated   15.25
        Dependency multiplicand   15.25
    Date for assessing the dependency   15.26
        Dependency should be assessed at the date of death   15.26
    Benefits resulting from death   15.27
    Settlement   15.28
    Provisional damages   15.29
    Appeal   15.30
    Enforcement   15.31
    Procedural defences   15.32
    Insurance   15.33
Property damage   15.34
    Measure of damages   15.35
    Awarding damages   15.36

**15.1** *Civil Claims*

Fire   15.37
    No strict liability for accidental fire damage   15.38
Environmental claims   15.39
    Statutory duty   15.40
    Claims in negligence   15.41
    Private nuisance   15.42
    The current standing of public nuisance   15.43

# CIVIL CLAIMS

**15.1** When an incident happens it is easy to concentrate on the criminal investigation side of any potential health and safety or environmental failure and potential prosecution. Knowledge of potential civil claims, how they can arise, who is entitled to bring a claim, under what circumstances and the damages (amount of money) that a party could be liable for is equally as important to a company board trying to understand all of its potential liabilities.

Civil claims are started by private individuals, companies or organisations for their own benefit. In the criminal court a convicted defendant may be forced to pay a fine as a punishment for their crime, and the legal costs of both the prosecution and defence. The victim of the crime will generally pursue their claim for compensation through a civil and not a criminal action. A victim of crime may also be awarded compensation by a judge in a criminal court.

Evidence used in a criminal trial may also be admissible as evidence in a civil action about the same matter. It is also possible that a civil case could be proved when a criminal case has failed. This is because the standard of proof in the criminal trial is 'beyond reasonable doubt' which is a higher burden of proof than in the civil trial which is 'on the balance of probabilities'.

If it is shown that a person is liable in a civil court, then damages (the amount of money) which should be paid to the claimant will be decided. However, this could also be a civil remedy such as restitution, transfer of property or an injunction to restrain or order certain actions.

Civil claims within England and Wales are mainly dealt with in the county courts and in the case of more substantial or complex cases, the High Court. A civil case involves a hearing in open court which the public may attend, a hearing in the judge's private room from which the public are excluded and the matters are decided by a judge in private on the basis of papers alone. Civil cases in Scotland are dealt with by the Sheriff Courts, and the Court of Sessions in Edinburgh deals with complex cases and appeals.

Often a civil claim can be resolved without determination by the court – for example through a process of mediation or an established complaints procedure. A judge in a civil case does not have the power to imprison a losing party.

## Judge hearing a civil case

**15.2** A judge will read the papers in a case before any hearing. Most civil cases do not have a jury (a libel or slander trial would be the exception), and the judge hears them on their own, deciding them by finding facts and applying the relevant law and giving a reasoned judgment.

Judges also play an active role in managing civil cases once they have started and help them to proceed as quickly as possible. This includes:

- encouraging parties to co-operate with each other in the conduct of the case;
- helping parties to settle the case;
- encouraging the parties to use an alternative dispute resolution procedure (ADR) as appropriate;
- controlling the progress of the case.

As part of the management process parties are required to complete and submit to the court directions, questionnaires and a draft order of directions setting out how they believe the case should be managed, what steps should be taken, and by what dates.

Guidance is provided in the *White Book*[1] and a proforma draft order is provided on the Justice website[2].

The main stages to be completed in each case before a trial can proceed are:

(1) **disclosure** – standard disclosure involves each party creating a list of documents they hold on which they rely; and the documents which: (a) adversely affect their own case; (b) adversely affect another party's case; or (c) support another party's case; and

(2) **witness statements of fact** – the general rule is that any fact which needs to be proved by the evidence of witnesses is to be proved: (a) at trial, by their oral evidence given in public; and (b) at any other hearing, by their evidence in writing. A witness statement is a written statement signed by a person which contains the evidence which that person would be allowed to give orally. The court may give directions: (a) identifying or limiting the issues to which factual evidence may be directed; (b) identifying the witnesses who may be called or whose evidence may be read; or (c) limiting the length or format of witness statements;

(3) **expert evidence** – no party may call an expert, or put in evidence an expert's report, without the court's permission. When parties apply for permission they must provide an estimate of the costs of the proposed expert evidence and identify: (a) the field in which expert evidence is required and the issues which the expert evidence will address; and (b) where practicable, the name of the proposed expert. Experts should be given written instructions so that they understand the nature and scope of their instruction under

---

1 *The White Book Service* (2019), Vols 1 and 2.
2 See https://www.justice-ni.gov.uk/publications/draft-order-template.

15.2 *Civil Claims*

Part 35 of the Civil Procedure Rules and importantly understand their duty is to the court and to help the court on matters within their expertise. This duty overrides any obligation to the person from whom experts have received instructions or by whom they are paid and is an important feature of expert witnesses.

## Judgment

**15.3** Once all the evidence has been heard and submissions put forward, the judgment is delivered. This can be immediately, or if the matter is complex, at a later date. If it is decided that damages should be paid to the claimant, the judge will decide on the amount. The judge may also decide any other appropriate remedy.

## Costs

**15.4** The costs are dealt with by the judge and those can include legal fees, court fees, any fees paid to expert witnesses, allowances to people who are represented themselves, loss of earnings, travel and subsistence. Usually the unsuccessful party will pay the successful party's costs – however the judge has discretion on this.

## Court of Appeal – Civil Division

**15.5** The Civil Division of the Court of Appeal hears appeals from all Divisions of the High Court, in some circumstances the county courts and certain tribunals. 'Permission' is needed to bring an appeal. This may be granted from a court below or more usually from the Court of Appeal itself. Applications for appeal are usually determined by a single Lord Justice, or for a full appeal by two or three judges.

## High Court – Queen's Bench Division

**15.6** This bench deals with common law business, for example actions relating to contract except those specifically allocated to the Chancery Division and civil wrongs. They most commonly handle cases involving personal injury, fatal accidents, negligence, breach of contract, breach of statutory duty, breach of the Human Rights Act 1988, libel, slander and other torts and the non-payment of debt and 'enforcement orders' which allow the court to ensure that a party complies with the judgment against them. They also hear more specialist matters such as applications for judicial review.

## Limitation period

**15.7** Limitation periods under civil law in England and Wales are fixed by the Limitation Act 1980. These indicate the fixed periods of time in which formal proceedings must be started and the limitation period varies depending on the type of civil claim involved.

The reason for limitation periods is that it is unfair and contrary to public policy for individuals or organisations to be perpetually exposed to litigation for wrongful acts or omissions. When a long time has passed then witnesses' recollection will fade and documentary evidence may be lost, which would make it difficult to properly adjudicate the case.

In theory, the time limit does not automatically apply, and a claim can still be made if it is outside the limitation period. If the defence is that the claim is time limited then this must be raised as a defence.

The Limitation Act 1980 sets out the limitation periods. There may also be other limitation periods set in other statutes. The main limitation periods are as follows:

- claims in relation to a contract – six years;
- claims in relation to awards in arbitration – six years;
- claims in relation to personal injury – three years;
- claims in relation to negligence – six years;
- claims in relation to recovery of land – 12 years;
- claims in relation to breach of trust – six years;
- claims in relation to defamation and malicious falsehood – one year.

The Limitation Act 1980 only applies to a civil claim. In the case of criminal acts there are no statutory limits on the prosecution of crimes in the UK except for 'summary' offences (those tried at a magistrates' court).

# PERSONAL INJURY AND FATAL ACCIDENTS
## Enterprise and Regulatory Reform Act 2013 (ERRA 2013)

**15.8** Claimants have been able to rely on health and safety legislation in order to establish civil liability and obtain an award for damages. This was changed by the Enterprise and Regulatory Reform Act 2013 (ERRA 2013). The aim of the Act was to '… remove the right of civil action against employers for breach of statutory duty in relation to certain health and safety legislation, other than where such a right is specifically provided for'.

This amendment to s 69 of the ERRA 2013, means that there is no automatic civil liability for:

- breaches of regulations made under s 15 of the Health and Safety at Work etc Act 1974 (HSWA 1974) (where most of health and safety legislation comes from);

**15.8** *Civil Claims*

- breaches of health and safety related statutes or regulations listed in the Health and Safety at Work Act 1974.

It is also possible that regulations can be made to determine the extent of civil liability for breaches of 'other than health and safety legislation'.

Before ERRA 2013, for an employee to have a successful action against their employer, negligence did not need to be proved. For example, if there was defective equipment then the employer had strict liability.

Regulation 5(1) of the Provision and Use of Work Equipment Regulations 1998[3] provides:

> 'Every employer shall ensure that work equipment is maintained in an efficient state, in efficient working order and good repair.'

An employee will know nothing of the maintenance regime and cannot investigate why the accident occurred. They also have no access to inspection regimes, the creation of risk assessments, and reports of any other failure that the equipment may have had.

After ERRA 2013, the burden is now on the employee to prove the negligence of the employer. Many regulations have a defence of 'reasonably practicable' and will also now require the person making the claim to prove that a failure to take steps required by the regulations resulted in the injury.

This will make it harder for workplace claims to be successful and the employee will now have to prove that the employer's standard fell below what would be expected of a reasonable and prudent employer.

## Stark v Post Office[4]

**15.9** Mr Stark was a postman, in 1994, and was injured when the brakes on his bicycle failed. He brought a claim against his employer, the Post Office. It was found that the failure of those brakes would not have been apparent on inspection of the bicycle and the claim would have failed in common law. However, Mr Stark succeeded in his claim (decided by the Court of Appeal in 2000) because he was able to show that the Post Office was in breach of its statutory duty. There was an obligation placed on the employer by the Provision and Use of Work Equipment Regulations 1998[5] that he should have been provided with safe equipment.

The consequences of post regulation reform, if Mr Stark was to have an accident on his bicycle now, his claim would arguably fail in the civil courts. He would be unable to establish the claim in common law. Now that the Regulatory Reform Act is in place he could not rely on a breach of the health

---

3 SI 1998/2306.
4 [2000] ICR 1013.
5 SI 1998/2306.

and safety regulations which established the liability in his original claim, and in this situation his claim would fail.

## Dismissal of a fraudulent claim

**15.10** Section 57 of the Criminal Justice and Courts Act 2015 requires a court to dismiss the entire claim for any personal injury where the claimant has been fundamentally dishonest, unless it would cause substantial injustice to the claimant to do so. Previous to this, the court's discretion to dismiss an entire claim was limited by case law to 'exceptional circumstance', with the result that the claimant was usually still awarded compensation in relation to the 'genuine' element of the claim. This measure means that dismissal of the claim where there is dishonesty will now be the norm.

## Pre-Action Protocol for Personal Injury Claims

**15.11** This protocol for personal injury claims sets standards which a party claiming for personal injury is expected to observe before court proceedings are issued. This protocol is to encourage parties to exchange information at an early stage and to consider using a form of ADR.

The protocol applies to all claims which include a claim for personal injury except for medical negligence, disease or illness claims and low value claims arising from road traffic accidents. Where a claim involves a personal injury type of claim, for example a claim from property damage, the entire claim will be covered by the protocol.

The protocol is not intended to apply to claims which proceed under:

- the Pre-Action Protocol for Low Value Personal Injury Claims in Road Accidents from July 2013;
- the Pre-Action Protocol for Low Value Personal Injury (Employers' Liability and Public Liability) Claims;
- the Pre-Action Protocol for the Resolution of Clinical Disputes;
- the Pre-Action Protocol for Disease and Illness Claims.

### Letter of notification

**15.12** The person making the claim or their legal representative, may wish to notify the defendant and/or insurer as soon as they know a claim is likely to be made, but before they can make a detailed letter of claim. This letter should provide the person or insurer with any relevant information to assist in determining the issues of liability/suitability of the claim for an interim payment and/or early rehabilitation. This letter, sent before the letter of claim, does not start the timetable for a letter of response but should be replied to within 14 days.

### Rehabilitation

**15.13** Parties should consider as early as possible whether the claimant has reasonable needs which need to be met by medical treatment or other rehabilitation.

### Letter of claim

**15.14** Before starting court proceedings, the claimant is expected to send a letter of claim which sets out a summary of the facts of the case together with an indication of the nature of the injuries suffered and of any financial loss that has been incurred.

The claimant is expected to send the defendant, as soon as practicable, a schedule of special damages with supporting documents. This may accompany the letter of claim.

Parties are required to inform other parties about any funding agreements they have entered into. If the claimant has entered into a funding arrangement, for example where they have entered into a conditional fee agreement, then this should be stated in the letter of claim.

The Protocol is intended to encourage parties to exchange information at an early stage.

The claimant should specify in the letter of claim when he expects the defendant to respond: normally within 21 days to acknowledge receipt; and three months to provide a full response. This is not always possible, for instance where it is close to the limit of an expiry period. Once the letter of claim has been sent, the claimant should not normally carry out any further investigation on liability until the defendant has responded indicating whether liability is in dispute.

### Claim and response

**15.15** The defendant should acknowledge receipt of the letter of claim within 21 calendar days of the date of posting of the letter and in their reply they should identify their insurer (if any) and, where appropriate, any significant omissions from the letter of claim.

Within the time set for responding to the letter of claim, the defendant, or their insurers, should respond to the letter of claim, stating whether liability is denied. If it is, then reasons should be given including any alternative version of events relied upon.

If the defendant admits liability, but says there is contributory negligence by the claimant, the defendant should give reasons and disclose any documents he may have which are material to the allegation of contributory negligence. If the defendant, or his insurers, fails to acknowledge the letter of claim, the claimant is entitled to commence court proceedings.

## Disclosure

**15.16** Disclosure of documents is to promote an early exchange of relevant information to help with clarifying or resolving issues in dispute. Pre-action disclosure will usually be limited to documents required to be enclosed with the letter of claim and the response. Where the liability is admitted in full, disclosure will be limited to the documents relevant to the amount under discussion.

## Experts

**15.17** The process encourages the joint selection of an expert. Before a party can instruct an expert they should give the other party the name of that expert.

### Alternative dispute resolution (ADR)

**15.18** There is no accepted definition of ADR but in the UK ADR is understood to describe the dispute resolution methods other than court proceedings and arbitration, or just non-adjudicative dispute resolution methods such as mediation.

# FATAL ACCIDENT CLAIMS

**15.19** Under the Fatal Accidents Act 1976 (FAA 1976), dependents of the deceased are entitled to file a claim for compensation if the accident was a result of somebody else's error or negligence.

### Dependant

**15.20** Under the FAA 1976, s 1(3) a dependant is defined as:

- the wife or husband, or former wife or husband, of the deceased;
- the civil partner, or former civil partner, of the deceased;
- any person who:
  - was living with the deceased in the same household immediately before the death; and
  - had been living with the deceased in the same household for a least two years before that date; and
  - was living during the whole of that period as the husband or wife or civil partner of the deceased;
- any parent or other ascendant of the deceased;

**15.20** *Civil Claims*

- any person who was treated by the deceased as his parent;
- any child or other descendant of the deceased;
- any person (not being a child of the deceased) who, in the case of any marriage to which the deceased was at any time a party, was treated by the deceased as a child of the family in relation to that marriage;
- any person (not being a child of the deceased) who, in the case of any civil partnership in which the deceased was at any time a civil partner, was treated by the deceased as a child of the family in relation to that civil partnership;
- any person who is, or is the issue of, a brother, sister, uncle or aunt of the deceased.

## Assessment of dependency

**15.21** Damages 'may be awarded as are proportioned to the injury resulting from the death to the defendants respectively'[6].

The test is not whether the claimant would have been a dependant but whether they had a substantial possibility of it. In the case of *Davies v Taylor*[7] the deceased had separated from the widow concerned and had commenced divorce proceedings for adultery and so had not established any loss. In the case of *Owen v Martin*[8] the marriage had been for a year when the claimant committed adultery and so the court reduced both the multiplier from 15 to 11 and the multiplicand (by reducing the dependency on the marriage).

### Re-marriage

**15.22** When assessing the dependant, the court needs to consider the remarriage of a widow or the prospects of remarriage.

### Cohabitees

**15.23** To claim under this FAA 1976, cohabitees will only be considered to be dependent if they are living with the deceased in the same household for two years immediately before the date of death, and during the whole of the two year period they must have lived as husband and wife.

This was challenged in the case of *Swift v Secretary of State for Justice*[9]. Ms Swift had been cohabiting with the deceased partner for six months when he was fatally injured at work and she subsequently gave birth to a child six

---

6 Fatal Accidents Act 1976, s 3(1).
7 [1974] AC 207.
8 [1992] PIQR P151.
9 [2012] EWCH 2000 (QB).

months later. She had a limited payment of compensation made by her partner's former employers. She challenged the award and brought a dependency claim under the FAA 1976. Her case was dismissed by the High Court in 2012 on the grounds that she had been living with the deceased for less than two years immediately before his death. The claimant subsequently appealed to the Court of Appeal.

## Causation

**15.24** A dependant may claim if 'death is caused by any wrongful act, neglect or default which is such as would (if death had not ensued) have entitled the person injured to maintain and action …' [10].

Injury is defined as including any disease and any impairment of a person's physical or mental condition.

The claimant must establish that the death occurred on the balance of probabilities as a result of the cause of action which gives rise to the claim. Suicide does not necessarily break the chain of causation; it is possible for a claim to made where the psychological injuries to a person lead them to commit suicide[11]. For example, in *Corr v IBC Vehicles Ltd*[12] the deceased became depressed as the result of an accident in a factory and committed suicide some six years after the incident the claim was not barred by principles of causation, remoteness and foreseeability.

Where the dependant is responsible for causing the death then their claim will be reduced proportionately[13]; and where a dependant is partly responsible for the death this does not affect the claims made by other dependants who can recover their claim without any reduction[14].

## How the claim is calculated

### Dependency multiplicand

**15.25** A dependency percentage is applied to the sum of both incomes and then the claimant's residual earning capacity is subtracted. The usual dependency percentage is 75% with a dependent spouse and one or more children; and is two thirds with no dependent children, although this can be changed where a more rigorous analysis is made of family finances. The proportion may also change where there is a significant difference in age, there are significant savings, and where dependent children were never reliant on what their mother could earn.

---

10 Fatal Accident Act 1976, s 1(1).
11 *Corr v IBC Vehicles Ltd* [2008] UKHL 131.
12 [2008] UKHL 131.
13 *Mulholland v McCrea* [1961] NI 135.
14 *Dodds v Dodds* [1978] QB 543.

## Date for assessing the dependency

*Dependency should be assessed at the date of death*

Dependency multipliers

**15.26** There are five considerations given to the multiplier:
- the likelihood of the provider of the support continuing to exist;
- the likelihood of the dependant being alive to benefit from that support;
- the possibility of the providing capacity of the provider being affected, and chances of life either in a positive or negative manner;
- the possibility of the needs of the dependant being altered by the changes and chances of life in a positive or negative way;
- the actuarial account to compensate:
    - for immediate receipt;
    - for the principle capital being exhausted before the end of the dependency.

## Benefits resulting from death

**15.27** In the case of *Jameson v Central Electricity Generating Board*[15] it was stated:

> 'In assessing damages in respect of a person's death in an action under this Act, benefits which have accrued or will or may accrue to any person from his estate or otherwise as a result of his death shall be disregarded.'

## Settlement

**15.28** For a settlement each dependent that wishes to and is party to the claim, has approved the agreement and the court has approved the settlement in respect of each protected party.

## Provisional damages

**15.29** An award made for provisional damages within the lifetime of the deceased does not itself prevent a subsequent claim under the FAA 1976, s 3(2), or the Damages Act 1996.

## Appeal

**15.30** An individual dependent may appeal an award for damages and the Court of Appeal can increase the original award without altering awards to other dependents.

---

15 *Jameson v Central Electricity Generating Board* [1998] UKHL 51.

## Enforcement

**15.31** Although the statutes create only one cause of action, each dependent is entitled for the loss to them personally.

## Procedural defences

**15.32** The FAA 1976 does not itself create a cause for action. It allows it to persist despite the death for the benefit of the dependants. A claim maybe barred by a previous claim.

In *Thompson v Christine Arnold*[16] the defendant wrongly diagnosed a cancerous lump as benign. Thompson issued proceedings, the schedule of loss and damage made no claim for the lost years. Thompson obtained a judgment in default of the defence and the claim was subsequently settled. Late proceedings were commenced for dependency. The purpose of the FAA 1976 was not to ensure that there was a benefit for the children of the deceased, rather the Act's focus was on ensuring that the person who caused this did not escape paying damages. If death brought the right of action, then this would give rise to the prospect of double recovery for the same wrongful act.

*Jameson v Central Electricity Generating Board*[17] established that a claim against one defendant will bar a claim against another defendant concurrently liable unless the settlement is clearly restricted to only part of the value of the claim.

The issue of proceeding without service during the deceased life does not stop a dependent's claim[18]. If a deceased person started proceedings which were subsequently discontinued after their death then a Court of Appeal hearing in *Reader v Molesworths Bright Clegg Solicitors*[19] held that the deceased wife had a separate action which could be brought despite the discontinuance of the deceased action.

## Insurance

**15.33** In cases of compensation claims for mesothelioma, employer's liability insurance policies covered employers for diseases contracted or injury sustained during the relevant insurance period, not merely when the disease or injury manifested itself. Additionally, exposure of an employee to asbestos in breach of a duty could have a sufficient causal link for an insurance policy to be invoked.

---

16 [2007] EWQB 1875.
17 [1999] 1 All ER 193.
18 *Cachia v Faluyi* [2001] EWCA Civ 998.
19 [2007] EWCA Civ 169.

# PROPERTY DAMAGE

**15.34** When one party breaches its obligations to another then there is an entitlement by the wronged party to claim for damages. The court has three methods for assessing what damages are payable:

(1) as compensation for losses resulting from the breach, but not from the loss of the obligation itself;
(2) a sum based on what reasonable people in the position of the parties would have negotiated to get rid of the obligation ('buy out damages');
(3) a sum based on any profit that the party who breached the obligation made from the breach ('account for profits damages').

## Measure of damages

**15.35** A case in 1973 is still a leading case in the measure and availability of damages. A property developer, Parkside Homes, built houses on its own land which was in breach of a freehold covenant agreement with Wrotham Park Estate[20]. Wrotham Park subsequently sued for breach of covenant.

The decision:

- damages are capped at the sum the injured party might reasonably have demanded in return for granting permission to build the houses;
- the application of the decision is only related to cases involving properties;
- the power to award damages is instead of an injunction. The court could have issued an injunction for this beach and made an order to demolish the houses.

There have been some more recent cases, for example, in 2000 Jury's Hotel Management[21] began to carry out works in breach of a covenant with AMEC Developments which prohibited the work. The judge decided that it was necessary to consider the sum that would have been reached in negotiations between the parties.

## Awarding damages

**15.36** The process of assessing damages on a buy out basis is becoming increasingly common. For damages to be awarded on an account for profits basis the wronged party should have a 'legitimate interest' in preventing the unlawful profit making activity or there should be a deliberate intention on the part of the offending party to profit from the breach.

---

20 *Wrotham Park Estate Co Ltd v Parkside Homes Ltd* [1974] 1 WLR 798.
21 *Amec Developments Ltd v Jury's Hotel Management (UK) Ltd* [2000] EWHC Ch 454.

In the case of *AMEC Developments Ltd v Jury's Hotel Management (UK) Ltd* the judge considered the effect of a 'negotiation' and made the following points:

- the party committing the breach was in a position of trust. This makes the breach more serious and the offender's accountability greater;
- the breach was a right/obligation between the offending parties;
- the breach was neither a matter of public interest nor a private matter;
- the offending party made a calculated attempt to profit from the breach with no thought for the innocent party payment;
- the seriousness of the breach and the covenant in the first place was highlighted.

The distinction was made between accounts for profits damages and buy out – ie buy out is what the parties would have hypothetically agreed for the covenant to be relaxed.

# FIRE

**15.37** In common law, a person is liable for damage caused by fire if the damage was caused:

- wilfully;
- by negligence; or
- by the escape, without negligence, of a fire which is brought into existence by some non-natural user of the land.

The defendant is liable if:

- they brought onto their land items likely to catch fire and kept them in such conditions that, if they did ignite, the fire would be likely to spread to the claimant's land;
- this was done in the course of some non-natural use;
- the item ignited and the fire spread.

Section 86 of the Fires Prevention (Metropolis) Act 1774 modified the common law above to say:

> 'And no action, suit or process whatever shall be had, maintained or prosecuted against any person in whose house, chamber, stable, barn or other building, or on whose estate any fire shall, accidentally begin, nor shall any recompense be made by such person for any damage suffered thereby, any law, usage or custom to the contrary notwithstanding; provided that no contract or agreement made between landlord and tenant shall be hereby defeated or made void.'

This statement means that no negligence is required on the part of the defendant and that liability is strict. 'Non-natural' has been interpreted by the courts to mean something that is an extraordinary use of the land.

## No strict liability for accidental fire damage

**15.38** In the case of *Gore v Stannard*[22] an appeal was considered on the basis of liability for damage arising from a fire started on one person's land and escaping to another. The issue was whether there was a strict liability for the escape.

In this case the Court of Appeal said that the items brought onto the land – ie tyres – were not exceptionally dangerous and the company had no reason to expect that escaping tyres would pose a risk to their neighbours. However, the court decided that it was the fire that escaped, and not the tyres, and that keeping the tyres for a tyre fitting business was not an unusual use of the land. The Court of Appeal said that the object (tyres) and the fire needed to escape in order for the rule to apply. Also the occupier of the offending property must have had reason to suspect that the 'item' that was brought onto the property posed a threat to the neighbours.

This ruling makes it difficult to see situations where the rule can be applied to property damage caused by the spread of a fire. One case may be where a chemical stored on the property catches fire and is either spread through the air to neighbouring areas or runs over boundaries of the neighbouring properties.

However, despite its limited use, the rule still exists, and landowners should be cautious that their activities and things stored on their land are not likely to do damage to neighbouring property. A note of caution from the Court of Appeal: 'Make sure you have insurance cover for losses occasioned by fire on your premises.'[23]

# ENVIRONMENTAL CLAIMS

**15.39** The legal basis for a claim for damages arising out of an environmental incident can be found in the following causes of action:

- breach of a statutory duty;
- negligence;
- public or private nuisance;
- claim under the Human Rights Act 1998.

## Statutory duty

**15.40** Whilst the law of negligence is based on common law (judge/case-made law), statute has clarified, changed and expanded on the common law

---

22 *Gore v Stannard (t/a Wyvern Tyres)* [2012] EWCA Civ 1248.
23 [2012] EWCA Civ 1248, at [50].

(judge-made law). Statutory duties have been created which are actionable by those for whom the particular statute was enacted to protect. Not all statutes confer a private right of action for a breach of a statutory duty but one such act that does and has been used for environmental claims is the Environmental Protection Act 1990.

The Act provides that a person shall not dispose of controlled waste in a manner likely to cause pollution of the environment or harm to human health. Section 34(1)(c) describes the duty of a person who disposes of controlled waste to take all measures applicable to him:

'34 Duty of care etc, as respects waste

(1) Subject to subsection (2) below, it shall be the duty of any person who imports, produces, carries, keeps, treats or disposes of controlled waste or, as a dealer or broker, has control of such waste, to take all such measures applicable to him in that capacity as are reasonable in the circumstances—

...

(c) on the transfer of the waste, to secure—

   (i) that the transfer is only to an authorised person or to a person for authorised transport purposes; and
   (ii) that there is transferred such a written description of the waste as will enable other persons to avoid a contravention of that section or regulation 12 of the Environmental Permitting Regulation, or a contravention of a condition of an environmental permit, and to comply with the duty under this subsection as respects the escape of waste.'

Section 73(6) provides for a breach to give rise to a civil claim for damages:

'73 Appeals and other provisions relating to legal proceedings and civil liability

(6) Where any damage is caused by waste which has been deposited in or on land, any person who deposited it, or knowingly caused or knowingly permitted it to be deposited, in either case so as to commit an offence under section 33(1) or 63(2) above, is liable for the damage except where the damage—

   (a) was due wholly to the fault of the person who suffered it; or
   (b) was suffered by a person who voluntarily accepted the risk of the damage being caused,

but without prejudice to any liability arising otherwise than under this subsection.

(7) The matters which may be proved by way of defence under section 33(7) above may be proved also by way of defence to an action brought under subsection (6) above.

(8) In subsection (6) above—

"damage" includes the death of, or injury to, any person (including any disease and any impairment of physical or mental condition); ...'

## Claims in negligence

**15.41** A claimant will need to prove that they were owed a duty of care by the proposed defendant, that the defendant breached that duty, that there was damage which was caused by that breach, and the losses/damage were foreseeable.

In December 2005 a number of large explosions and fires occurred at the Buncefield Oil Storage terminal in Hertfordshire. The incident was caused by the negligent overfilling of a fuel storage tank located on one of the three main sites that comprised the terminal. This led to the creation of a large hydrocarbon-rich vapour cloud which then ignited. The incident caused widespread damage to the land in and around the terminal, including fuel storage tanks, pipelines and associated equipment within the terminal and considerable damage to houses and property outside the site's perimeter fence. Substantial claims for compensation were brought by a number of claimants including Total Downstream UK plc, Total UK Limited and Hertfordshire Oil Storage Limited. Total in turn brought a claim against Chevron[24].

Summary judgment was entered for the claimants – negligence having been admitted.

The respective defendants' admissions were subject to issues regarding foreseeability of the resulting loss, recoverability of economic loss, the proof of title to sue and quantum aspects generally. This resulted in further litigation[25].

## Private nuisance

**15.42** This is primarily the right to enjoy one's own property. It historically has not extended to damages for personal injury. Private nuisance is based on the interference by one occupier of land with the right of enjoyment of land by another.

Three decisions of the House of Lords should be considered here: first is the case of *Cambridge Water Company v Eastern Counties Leather plc*[26], which looked at the pollution of an underground water supply by an industrial process and the spillage resulting in chemicals percolating into the plaintiff's borehole. It was decided that foreseeability is the prerequisite to the recovery of damages. It also cited the case of *Rylands v Fletcher*[27] which held that a person who, for his own purposes, brought on his land and collected and kept there anything likely to do mischief if it escaped, had to keep it at their

---

24 *West London Pipeline & Storage Ltd, United Kingdom Oil Pipelines Ltd v Total UK Ltd, Total Downstream UK plc, Hertfordshire Oil Storage Ltd v TAV Engineering Ltd, Motherwell Control Systems 2003 Ltd* [2008] EWHC 1296 (Comm), David Steel J.
25 *Colour Quest Ltd v Total Downstream UK plc* [2009] EWHC 540 (Comm).
26 [1994] 2 AC 264.
27 [1868] UKHL 1, (1868) LR 3 HL 330.

peril. The second decision is that of *Hunter v Canary Wharf Ltd*[28] where action was brought against the construction of Canary Wharf tower as the claimant's argued that it would interfere with their television reception. The case decided that a person's right to their land was not restricted because a building might interfere with the neighbours' enjoyment of the land, for example a nuisance action based on interference due to noise, dirt or smell might succeed but interference with a television signal would not. In the third case of *Transco plc v Stockport Metropolitan Borough Council*[29] a claim arose out of a water pipe to a block of flats which fractured. The result of this was that large quantities of water escaped underground and caused the collapse of an embankment which left the Transco gas main exposed and unsupported. The claimant carried out emergency repair work to its gas main and brought an action against the owner of the land for the cost of the remedial work. The claimant did not allege that the fracture of the pipe and consequent escape of the water was caused by any lack of care or negligence. Transco's main claim was that the council was liable without proof of negligence under the rule of *Rylands v Fletcher*.

The Water Industry Act 1991, s 209 states as follows:

'209 Civil liability of undertakers for escapes of water etc.

(1) Where an escape of water, however caused, from a pipe vested in a water undertaker causes loss or damage, the undertaker shall be liable, except as otherwise provided in this section, for the loss or damage.
(2) A water undertaker shall not incur any liability under subsection (1) above if the escape was due wholly to the fault of the person who sustained the loss or damage or of any servant, agent or contractor of his.
(3) A water undertaker shall not incur any liability under subsection (1) above in respect of any loss or damage for which the undertaker would not be liable apart from that subsection and which is sustained—

   (a) by the Environment Agency, a relevant undertaker or any statutory undertakers, within the meaning of section 336(1) of the Town and Country Planning Act 1990;
   (b) by any public gas supplier within the meaning of Part I of the Gas Act 1986 or the holder of a licence under section 6(1) of the Electricity Act 1989;
   (c) by any highway authority; or
   (d) by any person on whom a right to compensation is conferred by section 82 of the New Roads and Street Works Act 1991.'

The appellants in *Transco* contended: (i) that conduct formerly chargeable as the crime of public nuisance had now become the subject of express statutory provision; (ii) that where conduct was the subject of express statutory provision it should be charged under the appropriate statutory provision and not as public nuisance; and (iii) that accordingly the crime of public nuisance had ceased to have any practical application or legal existence.

---

28  [1997] AC 655.
29  [2003] UKHL 61, [2004] 2 AC 1, HL.

15.43 *Civil Claims*

## The current standing of public nuisance

**15.43** A more recent approach is summarised by the House of Lords in *R v Rimmington*[30] which stated that the offence of public nuisance was clear, precise, adequately defined, and based on a discernible rational principle and was not therefore contrary to common law principles or incompatible with the Human Rights Act 1998, Sch 1, Pt I, art 7.

The appellants in this case contended: (i) that conduct formerly chargeable as the crime of public nuisance had now become the subject of express statutory provision; (ii) that where conduct was the subject of express statutory provision it should be charged under the appropriate statutory provision and not as public nuisance; and (iii) that accordingly the crime of public nuisance had ceased to have any practical application or legal existence.

In *R v Rimmington Court of Appeal*[31] there were two appellants, Rimmington (R) and Goldstone (G). R had sent a large number of separate postal packages containing racist material to individual members of the public based on their perceived ethnicity and was charged with a single count of public nuisance contrary to common law. G was charged with the indictment of causing a public nuisance by posting a letter containing salt. G, the supplier of kosher foods in Manchester, owed money to one of its suppliers which was owned by a friend. He sent the cheque for the sum that he owed in an ordinary brown envelope and put a small quantity of salt in the envelope which he described as the size of about half a Smartie. When it arrived at the sorting office in Wembley in October 2001, some five weeks or so after the events of 11 September 2001 and at the height of the anthrax scare where two US postmen had died of anthrax poisoning whilst working in a sorting office, the package created a scare where the building had to be evacuated and a special unit created by the Metropolitan Police called to the incident. G claimed that the salt had been intended as a joke, but accepted that the escape of salt could have terrified a postal worker in light of the climate at the time.

On appeal both appellants said that the conduct formerly chargeable as the crime of public nuisance had now become the subject of a statutory provision and so the charge of public nuisance had therefore ceased to exist and that the crime of causing a public nuisance lacked the certainty and predictability necessary to meet the requirements of the common law itself.

The most typical cause of public nuisance is where there is statutory prohibition and there are definitions of the offences and possible defences and mode of trial and penalties. Where these cases exist then it is right to prosecute. However, the guiding principle of common law is that no one should be punished under it unless it was clear that they knew the conduct was forbidden before they did it and so the appeal in the case of *R v Rimmington* was allowed.

---

30 [2005] UKHL 63.
31 [2003] EWCA Crim 3450.

*Civil Claims* **15.43**

In the case of *Re Corby Group Litigation*[32], there were 18 claimants who were all born between 1986 and 1999 with deformities of their upper limbs. Between 1983 and 1989 Corby Borough Council acquired 180 acres of land in Corby, Northamptonshire from the British Steel Corporation with a view to reclamation and redevelopment. The land was heavily contaminated and the claimants alleged that their mothers, who lived close to the land, were exposed during the embryonic stage of their pregnancies to toxic materials in the course of the council's reclamation and decontamination programme and it was this exposure that caused the deformities. The claimants originally pleaded the case in negligence alone. The council admitted a duty of care but denied any breach and also denied that the deformities were caused by the exposure to toxic materials emanating from the land.

In April 2007 the claimants served additional points of claim to introduce allegations of a breach of statutory duty under ss 33(1)(c) and/or 34(1)(b) of the Environmental Protection Act 1990 and public nuisance. The council did not object to the introduction of a claim for breach of statutory duty but they did object to the introduction of a claim in public nuisance on the grounds that, as a matter of law, damages for personal injury could not be recovered in public nuisance. On application to the court to strike out the claim in nuisance Master Lesley said that this was a developing area of law and he was not satisfied that the claim in public nuisance had no real prospect of success. The public nuisance claim was pleaded in the following terms[33]:

> 'Further, the reclamation programme arose directly from the Defendant's use and/or control and/or occupation of the various sites which made up the former Steel Works complex. The Defendant allowed toxic material to escape from the Deene Quarry, Willowbrook North, and Soothills and Southbanks sites into the community and surrounding area and/or allowed the spread of contaminated liquids and toxic sludges on to and along the public highway by vehicles during the reclamation works above which thereby endangered the health of the public and caused personal injury to the Claimants and their mothers.
>
> In the premises, the Defendant is guilty of a public nuisance.'

The local authority argued that in light of the House of Lords' decisions in *Hunter v Canary Wharf Ltd*[34] and *Transco plc v Stockport MBC*[35] the assumption that damages for personal injury were recoverable in nuisance was wrong.

In *Hunter v Canary Wharf* an action in nuisance was brought as there was interference with a television signal following the construction of Canary Wharf Tower. The court of appeal had ruled that no action lay in private nuisance for interference with a television signal caused by the mere presence of a building.

In *Transco plc v Stockport MBC*, the claimant was the owner of a gas pipe which passed under the surface of an old railway. The council was responsible

---

32 *Re Corby Group Litigation* [2008] EWCA Civ 463.
33 *Re Corby Group Litigation* [2008] EWCA Civ 463, at [11] and [12].
34 [1997] AC 655.
35 [2003] UKHL 61, [2004] 2 AC 1.

**15.43** *Civil Claims*

for a water pipe which supplied water to a block of flats. A leak developed in the water pipe which was fixed but had not immediately been detected and the water saturated the embankment where the claimants pipe was and this then collapsed, leaving the gas pipe unsupported and in need of remedial work. The claimant argued that the council were liable. The court however, found that the council were not liable as this was natural use of the land and the supply of water was neither unnatural nor specifically dangerous behaviour.

Common law has long recognised the crime of causing a public nuisance[36]. The current definition of the offence in the 2003 edition of *Archbold* at para 31–40 is as follows:

> 'Public nuisance is an offence at common law. A person is guilty of a public nuisance (also known as a common nuisance) who (a) does an act not warranted by law, or (b) omits to discharge a legal duty, if the effect of the act or omission is to endanger the life, health, property, morals, or comfort of the public, or to obstruct the public in the exercise or enjoyment rights common to all Her Majesty's subjects.'

This definition is taken from Stephen's *Digest of the Criminal* Law[37] which defined the offence at p 184 in the following terms:

> 'A common nuisance is an act not warranted by law or an omission to discharge a legal duty, which act or omission obstructs or causes inconvenience or damage to the public in the exercise of rights common to all His Majesty's subjects.'

This latter definition is the one adopted in Smith and Hogan[38]. It was also relied upon by the Court of Appeal in *Attorney General v PYA Quarries*[39], which was a relator action for an injunction to restrain a public nuisance caused by dust and vibration in a quarry.

> 'I do not propose to attempt a more precise definition of a public nuisance than those which emerge in the text books and authorities to which I referred. It is, however, clear in my opinion, that any nuisance is "public" which materially affects the reasonable comfort and convenience of life of a class of Her Majesty's subjects. The sphere of the nuisance may be described generally as "the neighbourhood"; but the question whether the local community within that sphere comprises a sufficient number of persons to constitute a class of the public is a question of fact in every case. It is not necessary, in my judgment, to prove that every member of the class has been injuriously affected; it is sufficient to show that a representative cross-section of the class has so been affected for an injunction to issue.'

---

36 These have been set out in an article by JR Spencer JR Spencer 'Public nuisance – A critical Examination' Cambridge Law Journal (March 1989).
37 9th edn, 1900.
38 (10th edn), p 772.
39 [1957] 1 All ER 894.

# Chapter 16

# Insurance

Business insurance   16.1
Public liability insurance   16.2
Employers liability insurance   16.3
Environmental liability insurance   16.4
Product liability insurance   16.5
Professional indemnity insurance   16.6
    The claims-made nature of professional indemnity insurance   16.7
Directors and officers liability insurance   16.8
Business interruption insurance   16.9
Insurance Act 2015   16.10
    Insurance contract law   16.11
    The duty of fair presentation   16.12
      Knowledge of the insured   16.13
      Knowledge of the insurer   16.14
    Knowledge and fair presentation generally   16.15
    Warranties and representations   16.16
    Fraudulent claims and remedies   16.17
    Remedies for breach   16.18
    Contracting out: non-consumer insurance contracts   16.19
    Amendments to the Third Parties (Rights against Insurers) Act 2010   16.20
    Consumer Insurance (Disclosure and Representations) Act 2012   16.21
Choice of solicitor   16.22
    *Sneller v DAS Nederlandse Rechtsbijstand Verzekeringsmaatschappij*   16.23
    The UK position   16.24
    Cases decided after *Sneller*   16.25
    Insurance Conduct of Business Sourcebook (ICOBS)   16.26

## BUSINESS INSURANCE

**16.1** The millions of people who set up and lead businesses up and down the country are to be admired – running a business is risky and the investment of money, time, talent and energy is high. Ensuring directors understand what types of insurance are available to assist with the managing of those risks is essential.

**16.1** *Insurance*

Insurance can be an essential safety net. Floods, fires and employee and third-party accidents can hit hard. The consequences of not having the right cover in place can be devastating to a business and there are many examples of companies that have traded successfully for years being wiped out completely where they have not understood what insurance they had in place or the insurance has not responded as they thought it might when an incident happens.

The following chapter offers a practical explanation of the most common types of business insurance and, in broad terms, the cover they offer:

- public liability insurance;
- employers liability insurance;
- environmental liability insurance;
- professional indemnity insurance; and
- directors and officers insurance.

# PUBLIC LIABILITY INSURANCE

**16.2** Public liability insurance is an insurance which is designed to cover the cost of claims for compensation for personal injuries, loss of or damage to property and death, made by members of the public for incidents that occur in connection with the activities of the business.

Public liability insurance provides cover for members of the public and third parties the insured business interacts with. The following list, although not exhaustive, is provided by the Association of British Insurers (ABI):

- people visiting a business's sites and premises;
- customers;
- clients;
- people taking part in events or activities the business has organised;
- people watching events or activities the business has organised.

Public liability insurance does not cover employees, temporary staff, students or people on work placements (see employers liability insurance).

# EMPLOYERS' LIABILITY INSURANCE

**16.3** Employers' liability (EL) insurance was made compulsory under the Employers' Liability (Compulsory Insurance) Act 1969. It effectively means that employers need EL insurance in place in order to trade.

EL insurance is designed to cover the cost of compensating employees who are injured at, or who become ill through activities related to the work they do, at the business premises or off-site.

Employers are legally obliged to have EL cover of a least £5 million and can be fined up to £2,500 for every day it is not in place. It is normal for EL to cover the cost of compensation and any associated legal fees although the level of cover varies from insurer to insurer, so it is advisable to check exactly what the chosen policy does and does not include, and at what level.

Companies with no employees or those who employ only family members are exempt of the obligation to have EL and further guidance on this is provided by the Health and Safety Executive (HSE)[1].

An EL policy should respond to claims brought by all employees whether permanent, contract, casual, temporary, students and people on work placements or seasonal employees, volunteers, advisers, referees and marshals and also labour-only sub-contractors.

Insurers and brokers are required by the Financial Conduct Authority to collect additional information from their clients. This information will be used by employees to help trace their former employer's EL insurer should they need to make a claim for illness or injury at work.

EL polices are recorded on a central database and can be traced through The Employers' Liability Tracing Office (ELTO)[2]. The ELTO service was introduced by the insurance industry to make it easier to search for EL insurance policies using a central database containing all new and renewed EL insurance policies from April 2011. Policies from before April 2011 can be traced through its voluntary predecessor, the Employers' Liability Code of Practice (ELCOP) tracing service, which was in place from 1999.

The ELTO is an independent industry body comprising members who are EL insurers.

# ENVIRONMENTAL LIABILITY INSURANCE

**16.4** Environmental liability insurance (ELI) is designed to cover the cost of restoring damage caused by environmental accidents, such as pollution of land, water, air, and biodiversity damage.

Examples provided by the ABI of ways in which environmental damage could be caused are as follows:

- businesses' use of land or the historical use of the site;
- malfunction of holding tanks eg an oil tank;
- transportation issue eg when transporting pollutants such as pesticides;
- fire on a business's land;
- poorly operating drains causing run-off of oil into water supply eg in a car park;
- dust arising from construction work.

---

1  See http://www.hse.gov.uk/toolbox/managing/insurance.htm.
2  See http://www.elto.org.uk/.

**16.4** *Insurance*

UK and EU legislation has significantly increased the potential costs of the remedial works that will be required[3].

In particular, ELI policies will normally provide cover for:

- pollution – sudden and gradual;
- first-party (own property or site) clean-up costs imposed by regulatory authorities;
- third-party liability including impact on property value;
- nuisance claims;
- legal costs and expenses.

Some environmental liabilities may be covered under other liability policies but that cover will be limited in scope. For example, environmental liabilities arising from tort law such as negligence or nuisance may be covered by public liability insurance; the costs of defending a civil or criminal environmental claim may be covered under a directors and officers insurance; the cost of compensating an employee who has suffered injury or disease as a result of exposure to a dangerous substance may be covered by an EL insurance.

# PRODUCT LIABILITY INSURANCE

**16.5** Product liability (PL) insurance is designed to cover the cost of compensating anyone who is injured by a faulty product that the insured business designs, manufactures or supplies.

The cover under these policies normally includes the cost of compensation for personal injuries caused by the faulty product, loss of or damage to property caused by the faulty product, unforeseeable circumstances such as product faults that the insured's quality control system could not identify.

PL insurance is unlikely to cover faulty products resulting from bad workmanship and financial losses to a business or person caused by a faulty product.

# PROFESSIONAL INDEMNITY INSURANCE

**16.6** Professional indemnity insurance (PII) is designed to cover the cost of compensating clients for loss or damage resulting from negligent services or advice provided by a business or an individual. This has in the past been available to the traditional professions that are required to have insurance by their professional bodies or regulators such as solicitors, accountants, architects, chartered surveyors, and financial advisers.

---

3    Directive 2004/35/CE of the European Parliament and of the Council of 21 April 2004 on environmental liability with regard to the prevention and remedying of environmental damage.

There has over the past ten years been an emergence of professional indemnity insurance for other types of business that may choose to take out such cover for instance:

- consultancies;
- design agencies;
- contractors.

Although PII is designed to cover negligent advice and services some policies do offer legal advice and assistance which extends to health and safety or environmental prosecutions or investigations. It is important to note that many of the extensions currently available on the market limit the provision of that cover and the policy responds only where there is a 'prosecution' or where there is an 'investigation' rather than when an incident occurs and when advice and assistance is needed most. There is a void in availability of insurance funded legal advice between the incident and the time a prosecuting authority has made up its mind the policyholder is likely to have committed an offence and requires investigation.

## The claims-made nature of professional indemnity insurance

**16.7** Professional indemnity cover is offered on a claims-made basis. This means that cover will only be provided in respect of claims that are brought against the business during the term of the policy or policy year.

If a claim is made against the business after the policy has expired, and there has been no notification to the insurer that a circumstance which might give rise to a claim during the policy year, the claim is unlikely to be covered. For example, if an incident occurred in April 2016, the policy year ended in December 2016 and a claim was brought against the business in April 2017, that claim would ordinarily not be covered by the December 2015 to December 2016 policy but would fall to the next policy year when the claim was made, being December 2016 to December 2017. This contrasts with EL insurance which allows the claim to be made against the policy at the time of the incident even if the claim is made many years later.

It has become fashionable for companies as part of their procurement process to ask sub-contractors and consultants, including health and safety consultants, to prove they have PII in place. However, what many companies fail to appreciate is that the claims-made nature of the insurance means that not only does PII cover need to be in place during the course of the work undertaken, but also for the years following the work when a claim could be made. Under the Limitation Act 1980 the entire time a claim could be made for professional negligence is six years. This is a large undertaking for most small businesses.

When ceasing to trade, traditional professional practices purchase a 'run-off policy' which has the effect of extending the cover for any new claims that are brought against the company after their PII has expired.

**16.7** *Insurance*

Before changing insurer, it is sensible to speak to a broker or seek professional advice as to whether a run-off policy will protect a company against new claims for incidents that occurred during the period with the previous insurer. It is possible that the new insurer may agree to provide cover for claims relating to prior incidents but many will want to exclude anything that has been notified to the previous insurer.

Professional bodies and regulators often insist that their members are insured for a minimum amount – for solicitors, the minimum is £2 million for a partnership, and £3 million for a limited liability partnership.

# DIRECTORS AND OFFICERS LIABILITY INSURANCE

**16.8** 'D&O' is a form of liability insurance which is designed to provide protection for a company's senior executives from the financial implications of legal action, both criminal investigations and prosecutions and civil claims for compensation associated with alleged wrongful acts – in effect errors and omissions of an officer of the company.

Wrongful acts include:

- breach of trust;
- breach of duty;
- neglect;
- error;
- misleading statements;
- wrongful trading.

Employment practices liability insurance can often be bought as an extension of D&O liability insurance. It covers employee discrimination claims, eg for unfair dismissal, harassment, or failure to promote a person.

D&O sometimes covers defence costs arising from criminal and regulatory investigations into a company where no actual wrongful act has been alleged against a director but the precise wording will need to be checked and there are variations in the market as to the point in the investigation that the cover will become available. One questions whether cover which does not allow for advice from a specialist solicitor at the earliest opportunity fails to address the true needs of the insured.

D&O does not cover claims made against the business as a whole, only claims or investigations against individuals for alleged wrongful acts carried out in their capacity as directors or officers. The types of claims that could be covered will be dependent upon the nature of the company's business. Investigations and prosecutions of individual officers by the HSE, HM Revenue and Customs or the Financial Conduct Authority are the type of investigations normally covered. There seems to be an increased appetite for prosecutors to investigate officers for any individual failing following an incident which can now lead to imprisonment and directors' disqualification to prevent directors from being involved in, setting up or running a company for up to 15 years.

D&O liability insurance can be written to cover the directors and officers of for-profit businesses, private businesses, not-for-profit organisations, and educational institutions.

Defence costs often reduce the policy's limits unlike other liability insurance where the defence costs are covered in addition to policy limits. Other features of D&O policies which make the type of cover different is that they are written on a claims-made basis (see para **16.7** for a description of claims-made) and it often includes monetary damages but excludes bodily injury and property damage.

## BUSINESS INTERRUPTION INSURANCE

**16.9** Business interruption (BI) insurance is designed to cover loss of income during periods when the business cannot be carried out as usual due to an expected event and aims to put the business back in the same trading position as it was in before the event occurred which is likely to include (pre-tax) shortfall in profits and any increased costs of working ie running the business as a result of the event.

Although there are various policies on the market with differing levels of cover, many policies will cover business interruption as a result of:

- damage caused to business premises or equipment by fire, storm or flooding; and
- the breakdown of essential equipment.

Specialist policies, including cyber policies, are now available to insure business's computers against viruses, hackers and other cyber risks.

Pool Reinsurance Company Limited offer terrorism cover which is backed by Her Majesty's Treasury (HMT) and is specifically designed to cover terrorist acts designed to overthrow or influence the government. This has some limitations:

- it is only available in England, Wales and Scotland;
- the full value cover for all properties must be bought;
- there is no BI cover for property not damaged in an attack;
- there is no loss of attraction or event cancellation;
- threat and hoax are excluded;
- the terrorist attack must be by a terrorist group.

## INSURANCE ACT 2015

**16.10** The Insurance Act 2015 (IA 2015) applies to all non-consumer insurance contracts. There is no definition per se of non-consumer other than

16.10 *Insurance*

by reference to the consumer insurance contracts. A non-consumer insurance contract is defined in Part 1 of the IA 2015 as 'a contract of insurance which is not a consumer contract of insurance' and a 'consumer insurance contract has the same meaning as in the Consumer Insurance (Disclosure and Representations) Act 2012'[4]. In essence this means that the insured is not an individual and the contract is entered into mainly or wholly for business purposes and thereby falls outside the consumer insurance contract as defined in the Consumer Insurance (Disclosure and Representations) Act 2012 (CIDR 2012). It is a rather long-winded way to go about defining 'non-consumer' but one presumes the rationale is to avoid being too prescriptive and prevent certain types of insured falling between the two definitions.

The Act extends to the whole of the UK, apart from the consequential amendments in s 21(4) and (5). Section 21(4) of the Act extends only to England, Wales and Scotland and s 21(5) extends only to Northern Ireland.

## Insurance contract law

**16.11** The main provisions of the IA 2015 give effect to the recommendations set out in a joint Report published in July 2014 by the Law Commission and the Scottish Law Commission ('the Commissions'): *Insurance Contract Law: Business Disclosure; Warranties; Insurers' Remedies for Fraudulent Claims; and Late Payment*[5].

British insurance law developed during the eighteenth and nineteenth centuries, codified by the need for the 1906 Act arose from the need to protect insurance companies from exploitation by the insured. Although strictly the 1906 Act applies only to marine insurance, most of its principles have been applied to non-marine insurance on the basis that the 1906 Act embodies the common law.

Criticism had been made to the effect that the law (the 1906 Act and common law) was out of line with best practice in the modern insurance market and that the law had not kept pace with developments in other areas of commercial contract and consumer law.

The purpose of the IA 2015 was to update the statutory framework in these areas, in line with best practice in the modern UK insurance market, and overall the insurance market was largely supportive of its provisions.

## The duty of fair presentation

**16.12** The IA 2015 updates and replaces the existing duty on non-consumer policyholders to disclose risk information to insurers before entering into an insurance contract. It redefines its boundaries under the banner of the 'duty of

---

4   IA 2015, Pt 1, s 1.
5   Law Com No 353; Scot Law Com No 238.

fair presentation', effectively requiring policyholders to undertake a reasonable search of information available to them, and defining what a policyholder knows or ought to know.

Before a contract of insurance is entered into, the insured must make to the insurer a fair presentation of the risk. A fair presentation of the risk is one which makes the disclosure of every material circumstance which the insured knows or ought to know, or failing that, disclosure which gives the insurer sufficient information to put a prudent insurer on notice that it needs to make further enquiries for the purpose of revealing those material circumstances. A fair presentation requires the disclosure in a manner which would be reasonably clear and accessible and any material representations as to a matter of fact is substantially correct, and every material representation as to a matter of expectation or belief is made in good faith.

The IA 2015 also requires insurers to play a more active role, asking questions in some circumstances. Importantly, the Act introduced a new system of proportionate remedies where the duty has been breached. This replaces the existing single remedy of avoidance of the contract, except where the policyholder has breached the duty deliberately or recklessly. In particular, an insurer has a remedy against the insured for a breach of the duty of fair presentation only if the insurer shows that, but for the breach, the insurer would not have entered into the contract of insurance at all, or would have done so only on different terms.

There has been little case law on the duty of fair presentation since the IA 2015 although the Financial Ombudsman's decisions are available on its website[6].

The IA 2015 provides that the remedy of retrospective voidance should only be available to an insurer if, contrary to his duty of fair presentation, the insured fails to disclose material circumstances which he knows or ought to know; and if that qualifying breach of duty induces the insurer to insure, ie it would not have entered into the contract on the same terms or at all. Even then, voidance would only be available if the insurer can show that the breach was deliberate or reckless or, if neither, that it would still not have entered into that insurance contract (as opposed to merely offering different terms). The IA 2015 provides for lesser remedies where the duty-holder's failure is not deliberate.

An example of failing to comply with the duty of fair presentation would be the failure to answer clear and unambiguous questions posed by the insurer. The fact that an insurer has posed specific questions would tend to suggest that the insurer regards the questions and answers to be relevant to the risk it is considering to underwrite. If a proposer is asked clear and specific questions, they ought reasonably to realise that their answers are material from the insurer's point of view – accordingly, they need to disclose what they know or ought to know in order to comply with their duty of fair presentation.

6   See http://www.ombudsman-decisions.org.uk/.

**16.12** *Insurance*

The Financial Ombudsman has been satisfied that by signing a form with incorrect answers to clear questions, insureds have failed to disclose material circumstances contrary to what they knew or ought to have known, and that a breach of their duty of fair presentation occurred.

## Knowledge of the insured

**16.13** The IA 2015, s 4 defines what the insured 'knows' and 'ought to know' for the purposes of the duty of disclosure. It is based on the existing duty to disclose every material circumstance known to them, including everything which 'in the ordinary course of business, ought to be known' to them.

It also addresses the position of an insured who is an individual (such as a sole trader or practitioner) and what they will be taken to 'know'. This includes anything which is known by an individual who is 'responsible for the insured's insurance' and defines the individuals whose knowledge will be directly attributed to the insured where the insured is not an individual (such as a company) as the insured's senior management and the person or people responsible for the insured's insurance.

Senior management captures those individuals who play significant roles in the making of decisions about how the insured's activities are to be managed or organised. In a corporate context, this is likely to include members of the board of directors but may extend beyond this, depending on the structure and management arrangements of the insured whose knowledge is directly imputed to the insured for the purposes of the duty of fair presentation[7].

The IA 2015 also defines what an insured 'ought to know' by reference to information that could reasonably be expected to be revealed by a search of available information[8]. The insured should seek out information about their business by undertaking a reasonable search, which may include making enquiries of their staff and agents (including their insurance broker).

The IA 2015 does not define a reasonable search save for providing that:

- information includes any information held within the policyholder's organisation or by any other person, for example third parties;
- the search may take many forms either by enquiries or any other means.

What is reasonable will depend on the circumstances and requires the policyholder to determine what is necessary to meet their obligations of fair presentation. The reasonable search should also be proportionate to the type and size of the insurance and nature and complexity of the business.

---

7 Detailed explanation of the roles and duties is outside the scope of this book, but helpful guidance can be found in the explanatory notes to the IA 2015: see http://www.legislation.gov.uk/ukpga/2015/4/notes/contents.
8 IA 2015, s 4(6).

## Knowledge of the insurer

**16.14** There is also a definition in the IA 2015 of what the insurer 'knows', 'ought to know' and 'is presumed to know' for the purposes of duty of disclosure[9].

It sets out the individuals whose knowledge will be directly attributed to the insurer, being what the insurer 'knows'. This includes those making the particular underwriting decision. The relevant individuals also include employees of the insurer, or of the insurer's agent, and this is important to note when insurers are using underwriting agencies.

It also sets out two types of information which an insurer 'ought to know'. This includes information which an employee or agent of the insurer knows and ought reasonably to have passed on to the underwriter and is intended to include information held by claims teams, an expert's report for the purpose of assessing the risk but could include, depending on the circumstances, a loss adjuster's report and records.

The insurer is required to make a reasonable effort to search for such information as is available to them within the insurer's organisation, such as in the insurer's electronic records, and is 'presumed to know' which things are common knowledge, and which things an insurer offering insurance of the class in question to insureds in the field of activity in question would reasonably be expected to know in the ordinary course of business. Underwriters are only presumed to know about, or have insight into, the industry or type of insurance it writes.

## Knowledge and fair presentation generally

**16.15** References to an individual's knowledge include not only actual knowledge, but also matters which the individual suspected, and of which the individual would have had knowledge but for deliberately refraining from confirming them or enquiring about them, so-called 'blind eye' knowledge. The IA 2015, s 6 contains general provisions regarding knowledge: 'knowledge' includes not only actual knowledge, but also what has been termed 'blind eye' knowledge: things which the individual suspected but deliberately chose to ignore.

Blind eye knowledge may, for example, be held by a person who deliberately refrains from examining a ship in order not to gain direct knowledge of what they had reason to believe was the unseaworthy state of a ship. In *Manifest Shipping Co Ltd v Uni-Polaris Shipping Co Ltd*[10], the underwriters argued that the assured had 'blind eye knowledge' of the two particular respects in which the ship was unseaworthy.

---

9   IA 2015, s 4.
10  [2001] UKHL 1, [2001] 2 WLR 170.

**16.15** *Insurance*

'Blind eye knowledge in my judgment requires a conscious reason for blinding the eye. There must be at least a suspicion of a truth about which you do not want to know and which you refuse to investigate.'[11]

Blind eye knowledge requires a suspicion that the relevant facts do exist and a deliberate decision to avoid confirming that they exist. The deliberate decision must be a decision to avoid obtaining confirmation of facts in whose existence the individual has good reason to believe.

A 'fair presentation' confirms that a presentation can come in variety of forms and does not have to form a single document or oral presentation. The insurer may ask questions about the information that has been presented, before it is in a position to make the underwriting decision. All information which has been provided to the insurer by the time the contract is entered into will therefore form part of the presentation to be assessed.

The term 'circumstance' includes any communication made to, or information received by, the insured. A circumstance or representation is material if it would influence the judgment of a prudent insurer in determining whether to take the risk and, if so, on what terms. Examples of things which may be material circumstances are special or unusual facts relating to the risk, any particular concerns which led the insured to seek insurance cover for the risk, anything which those concerned with the class of insurance and field of activity in question would generally understand as being something that should be dealt with in a fair presentation of risks of the type in question. A material representation is substantially correct if a prudent insurer would not consider the difference between what is represented, and what is actually correct, to be material. A representation may be withdrawn or corrected before the contract of insurance is entered into.

## Warranties and representations

**16.16** Before the IA 2015 came into force, a breach of a warranty in an insurance contract discharged the insurer from liability completely from that point onwards, even if the breach was remedied.

The IA 2015 now provides that non-compliance with a warranty or other term relating to a particular type of loss should not allow the insurer to escape liability for a different type of loss, on which the non-compliance could have had no effect.

Previously, the rule had been that if an insured breaches a warranty in the policy, the insurer may avoid liability under the policy even though the breach is irrelevant to the circumstances of the claim. The IA assess this[12] by abolishing 'any rule of law that breach of a warranty (express or implied) in a contract of insurance results in the discharge of the insurer's liability under the contract'.

---

11  [1995] 1 Lloyd's Rep 651 at [644].
12  IA 2015, s 10(1).

The insurer's liability will now be suspended, rather than discharged, in the event of breach of warranty, so that the insurer is liable for valid claims which arise after a breach has been remedied.

An insurer has no liability under a contract of insurance in respect of any loss occurring, or attributable to something happening, after a warranty (express or implied) in the contract has been breached but before the breach has been remedied. This does not affect the liability of the insurer in respect of losses occurring, or attributable to something happening, before the breach of warranty, or after the breach can be remedied (providing it is capable of being remedied).

Basis of the contract clauses have been abolished. These clauses historically had the effect of converting pre-contractual information supplied to insurers into warranties.

## Fraudulent claims and remedies

**16.17** The IA 2015 provides the insurer with clear statutory remedies when a policyholder submits a fraudulent claim. The main remedy in the IA 2015 is the one already established by the courts: namely if a claim is tainted by fraud, the policyholder forfeits the whole claim.

If the insured makes a fraudulent claim under a contract of insurance the insurer is not liable to pay the claim, the insurer may recover from the insured any sums paid by the insurer to the insured in respect of the claim and, in addition, the insurer may by notice to the insured treat the contract as having been terminated with effect from the time of the fraudulent act.

If the insurer treats the contract as having been terminated, the rights and obligations of the parties to the contract with respect to events occurring before the time of the fraudulent act are not affected.

The IA 2015 does not define 'fraud' or 'fraudulent claim'. The remedies will apply once fraud has been determined in accordance with common law test for fraud in *Derry v Peek*[13].

The 'fraudulent claim' is to be distinguished from the 'fraudulent act'.

The fraudulent act is the behaviour that makes a claim fraudulent. The timing of the fraudulent act is relevant in determining when the liability of the insurer ceases. If an insured makes a claim that is genuine but adds in a fraudulent element later (for example, adding a claim for something known not to be lost or increasing the losses when it is known to be false), the fraudulent act takes place at this later time. The contract may be treated as having been terminated at that later point and the insurer's liability ceases.

Where the insured commits a fraud against the insurer, the insurer is not liable to pay the insurance claim to which the fraud relates. Where the insurer has

---

13 (1889) 14 App Cas 337.

already paid out insurance monies on the claim and later discovers the fraud, the insurer may recover those monies from the insured.

Many group schemes are set up by employers to provide protection for their employees. The policyholder is typically the employer, who arranges the scheme directly with the insurer. This means that the insurer has the same remedies against the employee or group member as it would have against a policyholder who makes a fraudulent claim. It may treat the employee or group member's insurance cover as having been terminated at the time of the fraudulent act, but the insurer may not treat its entire liability under the contract as terminated, only its liability to the fraudulent group member.

## Remedies for breach

**16.18** The insurer must show that it would have acted differently if the insured had not failed to make a fair presentation; that is, that the insurer would not have entered into the contract or variation at all, or would only have done so on different terms. This reflects the current law on inducement as developed following the decision in *Pan Atlantic Insurance Co Ltd v Pine Top Insurance Co Ltd*[14].

A breach for which the insurer has a remedy is a 'qualifying breach'.

Under the IA 2015, the insurer has different remedies depending on the situation. One distinction is whether or not the proposer's breach of the duty of fair presentation was deliberate or reckless.

An insured will have acted deliberately if it knew that it did not make a fair presentation. An insured will have acted recklessly if it 'did not care' whether or not it was in breach of the duty, but this is intended to indicate a greater degree of culpability than acting 'carelessly'. 'Deliberate or reckless' will include fraudulent behaviour.

The deliberate or reckless definition echoes that in CIDRA 2012. However, in CIDRA a 'qualifying breach' must be either deliberate, reckless, or careless, since the consumer's duty is to take reasonable care not to make a misrepresentation to the insurer. In the case of non-consumer insurance, breaches do not have to be careless or deliberate/reckless in order to be actionable. 'Innocent' breaches of the duty will also give an insurer a remedy if the insurer can show inducement.

## Contracting out: non-consumer insurance contracts

**16.19** Within consumer insurance contracts, an insurer will not be able to use a contractual term to put a consumer in a worse position than they would be in under the terms of the IA 2015. For non-consumer insurance,

---

14 [1995] 1 AC 501, [1994] 3 All ER 581.

the provisions of the Act are intended to provide default rules and parties are free to agree alternative regimes, provided that the insurer satisfies two transparency requirements.

- the insurer must take sufficient steps to draw the disadvantageous term to the insured's attention before the contract is entered into or the variation agreed;
- the disadvantageous term must be clear and unambiguous as to its effect.

## Amendments to the Third Parties (Rights against Insurers) Act 2010

**16.20** The intention behind the Third Parties (Rights against Insurers) Act 2010 (and the 1930's Act) is to enable payments of compensation by insurers directly to the third party (claimant/injured party) rather than any insurance claim payment forming part of the assets available to the general creditors of an insolvent insured. The aim is to allow a statutory transfer of the rights the policyholder has against the insurer to the third party. Unlike the 1930 Act, the 2010 Act does not require the claimant/injured party to first establish the liability of the policyholder, whether by legal proceedings or otherwise.

## Consumer Insurance (Disclosure and Representations) Act 2012

**16.21** CIDRA 2012 received Royal Assent on 8 March 2012. Sections 2–11 and Schs 1 and 2 came into force on 6 April 2013.

CIDRA 2012 applies only to consumers and deals only with the issue of what the consumer must tell the insurer before entering into or renewing an insurance contract. The Act creates a duty on consumers to take reasonable care not to make a misrepresentation during pre-contractual negotiations. The Consumer Act 2015 fails in this regard as the insurer will have a remedy and that remedy will depend on the nature of the breach. For example, a misrepresentation which was made in honest and reasonable belief would no longer afford an insurer the right to refuse to pay any claim.

If the consumer answers a question posed by an insurer in a careless manner, and if an insurer had had the correct information it would not have entered into the contract at all or would have done so on different terms, the insurer may have a remedy.

The remedy will depend on what the insurer would or would not have done had it received the information at the inception, ranging from returning the premium and refusing to pay all claims if it would not have entered the contract at all, through to refusing to pay that particular claim which it otherwise would have if a careful response had been provided. Being subject to a particular exclusion clause, or if the premium would have been higher, then the insurer may have the right to only pay a proportion of the claim which would be in

16.21 *Insurance*

line with the premium it actually received rather than should have received for the particular risk it had accepted.

A deliberate or reckless misrepresentation permits the insurer to avoid the policy altogether and treat the contract as if it had never existed, refusing all claims. There is a question mark over whether an insurer would have to return the premium in this scenario and it will no doubt be a matter of case law in years to come.

A deliberate or reckless misrepresentation is where, on the balance of probabilities, the consumer:

- knew that the statement was untrue or misleading, or did not care whether it was or not; and
- knew that the matter was relevant to the insurer, or did not care whether it was or not.

# CHOICE OF SOLICITOR

**16.22** Most insurance companies providing legal expense insurance (LEI) offer a panel of solicitors that are highly-qualified and experienced. However, many organisations are unaware that UK and EU legislation and case law provides that a person or company is free to choose their own solicitor, outside of the insurance company's panel. In the context of regulatory investigations, health and safety and environmental in particular, many of the insurers acknowledge the insured's choice for a specialist and will accommodate without too much negotiation.

## Sneller v DAS Nederlandse Rechtsbijstand Verzekeringsmaatschappij

**16.23** In 2013, the European Court of Justice (ECJ) in *Sneller v DAS Nederlandse Rechtsbijstand Verzekeringsmaatschappij*[15] provided guidance in accordance with Art 4 of Council Directive 87/344/EEC on the coordination of laws, regulations and administrative provisions relating to legal expenses insurance[16]:

'Article 4

1. Any contract of legal expenses insurance shall expressly recognize that:

(a) where recourse is had to a lawyer or other person appropriately qualified according to national law in order to defend, represent or serve the interests of the insured person in any inquiry or proceedings, that insured person shall be free to choose such lawyer or other person;

---

15 Case C-442/12, [2013] WLR (D) 426.
16 Council Directive 87/344/EEC of 22 June 1987 on the coordination of laws, regulations and administrative provisions relating to legal expenses insurance.

(b) the insured person shall be free to choose a lawyer or, if he so prefers and to the extent that national law so permits, any other appropriately qualified person, to serve his interests whenever a conflict of interests arises.'

The two questions before the court were effectively[17]:

- Whether Art 4(1) entitles an insurer, which defines in its policy that it has its own panel of solicitors, to indemnify the costs of external legal advisors freely chosen by the insured only in cases where that insurer takes the view that the case must be assigned to an external lawyer?
- Whether the answer to that question will differ, depending on whether or not legal assistance is compulsory in the inquiry or proceedings concerned?

In this case, Mr Sneller was bringing a claim against his former employer for unfair dismissal. Legal assistance is not compulsory for such claims in the Netherlands.

Mr Sneller wanted to appoint his own lawyer under his LEI cover with DAS (the insurer). However, the insurer was only prepared to allow him representation from one of its (non-qualified) employees. Following an adverse decision against Mr Sneller in the Dutch Court of Appeal, the issue was referred to the ECJ because of the wider social implications relating to the freedom of choice of legal representation.

The court ruled that Art 4(1)(a) cannot be interpreted in such a way as to allow any insurer who stipulates in its LEI policies that legal assistance will principally be provided by its own employees or insurance legal panel, to restrict indemnity for costs incurred by the insured if they use their own lawyer solely to those circumstances in which that insurer considers the handling of the case must be sub-contracted to an external lawyer.

Importantly, the court also confirmed that the insured's right to choose their own lawyer will not differ depending on whether or not legal assistance is compulsory under national law in the particular proceedings.

## The UK position

**16.24** The Insurance Companies (Legal Expenses Insurance) Regulations 1990 ('the 1990 Regulations')[18], reg 2 defines 'legal expenses insurance business' as the business of effecting or carrying out contracts of insurance (other than contracts of reinsurance) which insure against a risk arising from legal expense.

Thus, any insurance policy such as an EL policy or public liability policy that provides cover for legal expenses comes within the 1990 Regulations.

---

17 See *Sneller v DAS Nederlandse Rechtsbijstand Verzekeringsmaatschappij* Case C-442/12, para 17.
18 SI 1990/1159.

**16.24** *Insurance*

Regulation 6 states:

> 'Freedom to choose lawyer
> 
> (1) Where under a legal expenses insurance contract recourse is had to a lawyer (or other person having such qualifications as may be necessary) to defend, represent or serve the interests of the insured in any inquiry or proceedings, the insured shall be free to choose that lawyer (or other person).
> (2) The insured shall also be free to choose a lawyer (or other person having such qualifications as may be necessary) to serve his interests whenever a conflict of interests arises.
> (3) The above rights shall be expressly recognised in the policy.'

The UK Court of Appeal was called on to interpret how the EEC Directive related to LEI in the case of *Brown-Quinn v Equity Syndicate Management Ltd*[19].

This case concerned the question of whether an insurer's refusal to accept the insured's choice of solicitor where their fees exceeded the insurer's prescribed rates restricted the insured's choice of legal representative and was consequently in breach of reg 6.

The Court of Appeal held that the insurer was not entitled to deny the respondent the benefit of LEI. It is clear from that case that the policyholder is entitled to recover at least the non-panel fee rates under the policy, and if the insurer refused to pay any legal costs because the non-panel solicitor did not accept the fixed non-panel fee rate in its terms of appointment, that would be a breach of the 1990 Regulations. The case did not conclude that the amount offered by the insurer would always be acceptable but it is implied that an insurer has the right to restrict what it would pay to a non-panel solicitor, provided the remuneration is not so low as to render the policyholder's freedom of choice meaningless.

## Cases decided after *Sneller*

**16.25** There have been two subsequent decisions by the ECJ following on from *Sneller*.

In both *Massar v DAS Nederlandse Rechtsbijstand Verzekeringsmaatschappij NV*[20] and in *Buyuktipi v Achmea Schadeverzekeringen NV and Stichting Achmea Rechtsbijstand*[21] the court found in favour of the insured party. In both cases, the judges refused to interpret Art 4 narrowly and emphasised the 'obligatory nature' of an insured party's right to choose their own legal representative.

These cases are consistent with previous rulings which upheld the rights of an insured party to choose a legal firm from outside the insurer's panel.

---

19 [2012] EWCA Civ 1633, [2013] 3 All ER 505.
20 Case C-460/14.
21 Case C-5/15.

The Financial Ombudsman Service (FOS) set up by Parliament, is the UK's official consumer and micro-business service for sorting out and deciding upon problems with financial services including complaints against insurance companies. A micro-business is a EU term which describes a small business with an annual turnover of up to €2million *and* fewer than ten employees. On the subject of choosing a solicitor, the FOS gives a case study[22]:

> 'Mr A claimed for the cost of suing his former employer for age discrimination and unfair dismissal.
>
> As proceedings had been issued, the business accepted Mr A was free to choose his own solicitors – so long as they agreed to its standard terms of appointment. These said that the legal fees payable would be no more than the business would pay two of its panel solicitors (a fixed fee of £1,500 inclusive of VAT).
>
> Mr A's solicitor wasn't prepared to accept this. So the business refused to accept Mr A's claim saying that it was within its rights to set budgets for certain types of work.
>
> Mr A said that no other solicitor would take on the case for less than £10,000 plus VAT. He didn't accept that the panel solicitors were sufficiently qualified to represent him and brought his complaint to us.
>
> **Complaint upheld**
>
> Having considered the terms of the policy and the cover that it was supposed to provide, we decided it wasn't fair or reasonable for the business to restrict the legal fees it was prepared to pay Mr A's own solicitor. The choice of two panel solicitors wasn't sufficient to provide a *meaningful* choice to Mr A.
>
> We didn't think it was fair and reasonable for the business to restrict the level of indemnity to the fixed fee it proposed. The scope of this significant limitation in its standard terms of appointment hadn't been expressly drawn to Mr A's attention – either within the policy or some other document – until he wished to instruct his own solicitor.
>
> We decided the hourly rate charged was reasonable, and had been reasonably incurred by Mr A's solicitors. So we decided this should be the applicable level of hourly rate when the business indemnified him.'

## Insurance Conduct of Business Sourcebook (ICOBS)

**16.26** The overall aim of ICOBS[23] is to ensure that insured are treated fairly. Insurers are required to give insureds clear, fair information when insurance is sold. ICOBS outlines high-level standards that apply to general insurance and protection policies:

- **suitability** – insurance providers must ensure the advice is suitable for their customers/insureds;

---

22 See http://www.financial-ombudsman.org.uk/publications/technical_notes/legal-expenses.html.
23 For further information see FCA Handbook, ICOBS rules, at https://www.handbook.fca.org.uk/handbook/ICOBS/.

**16.26** *Insurance*

- **product disclosure** – insurance providers must take reasonable steps to ensure the customer/insured is given appropriate information about a policy in good time and in a comprehensible way so they can make an informed decision. This applies before and after they buy the product and it includes price. The information insurers give will depend on the customer/insured, the policy's terms and its complexity;
- **claims handling** – insurance providers or those acting for them must treat the customer/insured fairly when handling claims.

# Appendix

# Cases

## CONTENTS

| | |
|---|---|
| Baker v Quantum Clothing Group Ltd (Supreme Court) [2011] UKSC 17 | 370 |
| Brown-Quinn v Equity Syndicate Management Ltd Baxter v Equity Syndicate Management Ltd, Webster Dixon LLP v Equity Syndicate Management Ltd [2012] EWCA Civ 1633, [2013] 3 All ER 505 | 371 |
| BT Fleet Ltd v McKenna [2005] EWHC 387 (Admin) | 373 |
| Cambridge Water Company v Eastern Counties Leather plc [1994] 2 AC 264 | 373 |
| Caparo Industries Plc v Dickman [1990] 2 AC 605 | 374 |
| Colour Quest Ltd v Total Downsteam UK plc, Total UK Ltd, Hertfordshire Oil Storage Ltd [2009] EWHC 540 (Comm) | 374 |
| Corby Group Litigation v Corby DC [2009] EWHC 1944 (TCC) | 376 |
| Derry v Peek (1889) 14 App Cas 337 | 377 |
| DPP v Ara [2001] EWHC Admin 493 | 378 |
| Duchess of Argyll v Beuselinck [1972] 2 Lloyd's Rep 172 | 378 |
| Edwards v the National Coal Board [1949] 1 All ER 743 | 379 |
| El-Ajou v Dollar Holdings Plc (No 1) [1994] 2 All ER 685 | 379 |
| Field v Leeds City Council [1999] EWCA Civ 3013 | 380 |
| Goldscheider v Royal Opera House Covent Garden Foundation [2018] EWHC 687 (QB) | 380 |
| H (Stephen) v R [2014] EWCA Crim 1555 | 381 |
| Hart v Lancashire & Yorkshire Railway Co (1869) 21 LT 261 | 382 |
| Herald of Free Enterprise ferry | 383 |
| Hertfordshire Oil Storage Ltd v TAV Engineering Ltd, Motherwell Control Systems 2003 Ltd [2008] EWHC 1296 (Comm) | 383 |
| HM Inspector of Health and Safety v Chevron North Sea Ltd [2018] UKSC 7 | 384 |
| Huckerby v Elliot [1970] 1 All ER 189 (DC) | 385 |
| Hughes, Re [1943] 2 All ER 269 | 385 |
| Hui-Chi-Ming v R [1992] 1 AC 34 (PC) | 385 |
| Hunter v Canary Wharf Ltd [1997] AC 655 | 386 |
| Kennedy v Cordia (Services) LLP Supreme Court (Scotland) [2016] UKSC 6 | 387 |
| Kings Cross Fire | 387 |
| London Borough of Wandsworth v Covent Garden Market Authority [2011] EWHC 1245 (QB) | 388 |

## Cases

| | |
|---|---|
| Malcolm v DPP [2007] EWHC 363 (Admin) | 388 |
| Manley v New Forest DC [2007] EWCH 3188 (Admin) | 390 |
| Massar v DAS Nederlandse Rechtsbijstand Verzekeringsmaatschappij NV (Case C-460/14) [2016] Lloyd's Rep IR 463 and in Buyuktupi v Achmea Schadeverzekeringen NV and Stichting Achmea Rechtsbijstand (Case C-5/15) [2016] Lloyd's Rep IR 586 | 391 |
| O'Brien v Chief Constable of South Wales Police [2005] UKHL 26 | 392 |
| Pan Atlantic Insurance Co Ltd v Pine Top Insurance Co Ltd [1995] 1AC 501, [1994] 3 All ER 581 | 392 |
| R (DPP) v Chorley Justices [2006] EWHC 1795 (Admin), [2002] EWHC 2162 (Admin) | 393 |
| R (Ebrahim) v Feltham Magistrates Court: Mouatt v DPP [2001] EWHC Admin 130 | 393 |
| R (for and on behalf of the Health and Safety Executive) v Paul Jukes [2018] EWCA Crim 176 | 394 |
| R (Inland Revenue Commissioners) v Kingston Crown Court [2001] EWCH Admin 581 | 396 |
| R v (on application of Dennis) v DPP [2006] EWCH 3211 (Admin) | 396 |
| R v Adaway [2004] EWCA Crim 2831 | 397 |
| R v Adomako [1995] 1 AC 171 | 398 |
| R v Argent [1996] EWCA Crim 1728 | 398 |
| R v Associated Octel Co Ltd [1996] 4 All ER 846 | 399 |
| R v Balfour Beatty Rail Infrastructure Services Ltd [2006] EWCA Crim 1586, [2007] Bus LR 77 | 400 |
| R v Beckford [1996] 1 Cr App R 94 | 401 |
| R v Beckles [2004] EWCA Crim 2766 | 401 |
| R v Beedie [1997] 2 Cr App R 167, CA | 402 |
| R v Boal [1992]3 All ER 177 | 403 |
| R v Chaaban [2003] EWCA Crim 1012 | 403 |
| R v Chandler [2015] EWCA Crim 1825 | 404 |
| R v Chargot [2008] UKHL 73 | 405 |
| R v Cheshire [1991] 1 WLR 844 | 407 |
| R v Cornish [2016] EWHC 779 (QB) | 407 |
| R v DPP, ex p Manning [2000] EWHC Admin 342 | 409 |
| R v Ensor [2009] EWCA Crim 2519 | 410 |
| R v F Howe & Son [1999] 2 All ER 249 | 411 |
| R v Friskies Petcare (UK) Ltd [2000] EWCA Crim 95 | 411 |
| R v Galbraith (1981) 73 Cr App R 124 | 412 |
| R v Gateway Foodmarkets Ltd [1997] 3 All ER 78 | 413 |
| R v Goodman [1993] 2 All ER 789 | 413 |
| R (Health and Safety Executive) v ATE Truck and Trailer Sales Ltd [2018] EWCA Crim 752 | 414 |
| R v HM Coroner for Greater London, ex p Ridley [1985] 1 WLR 1347 | 415 |
| R v Honey Rose [2017] EWCA Crim 1168 | 416 |
| R v HT-M [2006] ICR 1383 Ltd [2006] EWCA Crim 1156 | 417 |
| R v Ineos Chlorvinyls Ltd [2016] EWCA Crim 607 | 418 |

| | |
|---|---|
| R v Mirza (Zulfiqar Baig) [2012] EWCA Crim 3074 | 419 |
| R v Nelson Group Services (Maintenance) Ltd [1998] 4 All ER 331 | 420 |
| R v New Look Ltd [2010] EWCA Crim 1268 | 421 |
| R v Newell [2012] EWCA Crim 650 | 422 |
| R v Newton (1982) 4 Cr App R(S) 388 | 423 |
| R v Northallerton Magistrates' Court, ex p Dove [1999] EWHC Admin 499 | 424 |
| R v P Ltd and G [2007] EWCA Crim 1937, [2008] ICR 96, CA | 424 |
| R v Pabon [2018] EWCA Crim 420 | 425 |
| R v Pearce (1979) 69 Cr App 365, CA | 427 |
| R v R and S Recycling Ltd [2014] EWCA Crim 2302 | 427 |
| R v Rimmington (Anthony); R v Goldstein (Harry Chaim) [2005] UKHL 63 | 429 |
| R v Sadhu [2017] EWCA Crim 908 | 430 |
| R v Sellafield Ltd and R v Network Rail Infrastructure Ltd [2014] EWCA Crim 49 | 431 |
| R v Squibb Group Ltd [2019] ECWA Crim 227 | 433 |
| R v Stubbs [2006] EWCA Crim 2312 | 434 |
| R v Takhar [2014] EWCA Crim 1619 | 435 |
| R v Tangerine Confectionery Ltd [2011] EWCA Crim 2015 | 436 |
| R v Tata Steel UK Ltd [2017] EWCA Crim 704 | 437 |
| R v Thames Water Utilities Ltd [2015] EWCA Crim 960, [2015] 1 WLR 4411 | 438 |
| R v Thelwall [2016] EWCA Crim 1755 | 440 |
| R v Underwood [2004] EWCA Crim 2256 | 441 |
| R v Whirlpool UK Appliances Ltd [2017] EWCA Crim 2186 | 441 |
| Ready Mixed Concrete (South East) Ltd v Minister of Pensions and National Insurance [1968] 2 QB 497 | 443 |
| Registrar of Restrictive Trading Agreements v WH Smith & Son Ltd [1969] 3 All ER 1065 | 444 |
| Rylands v Fletcher (1868)LR 3 HL 330 | 445 |
| Scottish Power Generation Ltd v HM Advocate [2016] HCJAC 99 | 445 |
| Serious Fraud Office v Eurasian Natural Resources Corp Ltd [2018] EWCA Civ 2006 | 447 |
| Sneller v DAS Nederlandse Rechtsbijstand Verzekeringsmaatschappij (Case C-442/12) [2014] Bus LR 180 | 449 |
| Southall Train Crash | 450 |
| Stark v Post Office [2000] ICR 1013 | 450 |
| Three Rivers District Council v Governor and Company of the Bank of England (No 5) [2003] EWCA Civ 474 | 451 |
| Three Rivers District Council v Governor and Company of the Bank of England (No 6) [2004] EWCA Civ 218 | 451 |
| Transco plc v Stockport Metropolitan Borough Council [2003] UKHL 61, [2004] 2 AC 1 | 452 |
| West London Pipeline & Storage Ltd v Total UK Ltd [2008] EWHC 1296 (Comm) | 453 |
| Wotherspoon (John Maxwell) v HM Advocate 1978 JC 74 | 454 |

*Cases*

## Baker v Quantum Clothing Group Ltd (Supreme Court) [2011] UKSC 17

Employers in the knitting industry were not liable at common law or under the Factories Act 1961, s 29 for hearing loss sustained by their employees before the Noise at Work Regulations 1989, SI 1989/1790 came into force.

The employers in the knitting industry Quantum Clothing and Meridian appealed against a decision that they were liable for hearing loss sustained by employees before the Noise at Work Regulations 1989 came into force. The person had been employed by Quantum and Meridian in the decades before the regulations came into force. Quantum were average-sized employers and Meridian were larger. The employees had allegedly been subjected to noise levels at work between 85 and 90dB(A)lepd (daily personal exposure level). The government issued a Code of Practice in 1972 stating that 90dB(A)lepd was not to be exceeded. In 1983 a Directive had been proposed which would require employers to provide hearing protection for workers exposed to noise levels above 85dB(A)lepd. The employees were given ear protection in the late 1980s. The employees alleged that the noise levels had induced noise-related hearing loss, but the judge rejected their claims on the grounds that the employers had been entitled to rely on the Code of Practice until the terms of the Directive had become generally known and that they had been entitled to two years from then to implement policies. The judge held that Meridian would have had a greater understanding of the risks by 1983 and so should have taken action from 1985, but found that their employees had not been exposed to levels above 85dB(A)lepd. The employees successfully appealed. The issues before the Supreme Court were whether the judge had been correct to treat Meridian differently to average employers and find that Quantum and Meridian had been entitled to rely on the code and had not breached their common law duty.

The appeal found that Quantum and Meridian had not breached their duty under the Factories Act 1961, s 29.

- The judge's assessment that Meridian had had an earlier understanding would not be changed, on the basis that they had greater resources and research and the discussion generated by the European proposals, larger employers had appreciated by 1983 that the 90dB(A)lepd limit was no longer acceptable. That appreciation was sufficient to find liability. There was no reason to change the judge's conclusion that the code had been official and clear guidance which set an appropriate standard upon which a reasonable and prudent employer could legitimately rely until the late 1980s.
- The underlying statistics did not undermine the code's appropriateness as a guide to acceptable practice. The judge had correctly formed a judgment on the whole of the expert, documentary and factual evidence before him. The date when the employers should have been aware that it was no longer acceptable simply to comply with the code was when the terms of the 1986 Directive became generally known. The judge had allowed two years from the end of the consultation process for the Directive in 1988, meaning

that Quantum had no potential common law liability before 1990, when the regulations required the provision of protection anyway. The Court of Appeal had not been justified in interfering with that conclusion. As Meridian were in a special position and should have taken steps from 1983, they were liable as from 1985.

- A workplace was unsafe under s 29 if operations constantly and regularly carried out in it made it so. The noise generated by the knitting machines was a permanent feature of the operations intrinsic to the workplace. That would make the place unsafe if s 29 related to noise. Although s 29 had been enacted without any appreciation that it could cover noise, whether it could cover noise was linked to whether safety was an absolute or relative concept. Although the judgement of whether a place was safe was objective, that was by reference to the knowledge and standards of the time, and the onus was on the employee to show that the workplace was unsafe. There was no such thing as an unchanging concept of safety.

As safety was a relative concept, foreseeability had to play a part in determining whether a place was safe. The judge had been entitled to find that the standard of safety was determined by the code and judged by that standard, the workplaces had been safe. Had reasonable foreseeability not been imported into the meaning of safety, it would have been imported into reasonable practicability that meant that some degree of risk was acceptable, and that degree had to depend on current standards.

## Brown-Quinn v Equity Syndicate Management Ltd Baxter v Equity Syndicate Management Ltd, Webster Dixon LLP v Equity Syndicate Management Ltd [2012] EWCA Civ 1633, [2013] 3 All ER 505

Certain conditions in a legal expenses insurance contract which restricted the insured's choice of legal representative were in breach of the Insurance Companies (Legal Expenses Insurance) Regulations 1990, SI 1990/1159, reg 6. Insurers could limit the costs for which they were liable to the insured to their non-panel rates provided that the freedom of choice guaranteed by Directive 2009/138 was not rendered meaningless.

Equity Syndicate appealed against a decision (*Brown-Quinn v Equity Syndicate Management Ltd* [2011] EWHC 2661 (Comm), [2012] 1 All ER 778) making declarations in relation to provisions in before the event insurance policies restricting the insureds' choice of solicitors and their remuneration.

The respondent firm of solicitors Webster Dixon acted for three claimant insureds, also respondents to this appeal, who had before the event insurance issued by Equity Syndicate and wished to pursue employment and discrimination claims. Equity Syndicate had retained a panel of solicitors to act for its insureds. Webster Dixon were not on the panel. Equity Syndicate would not agree to Webster Dixon acting for the claimants unless they agreed not to charge more than the fixed hourly rate (the non-panel rate) prescribed under

*Cases*

Equity Syndicate's terms. Webster Dixon and the claimants brought proceedings for a declaration that Equity Syndicate's position limited the right of the client to choose his solicitor in breach of the Insurance Companies (Legal Expenses Insurance) Regulations 1990, reg 6, implementing Directive 2009/138, Art 201. Equity Syndicate conceded at trial that the insureds were not restricted to recovering the non-panel rate. The judge declared that Equity Syndicate were not entitled to decline to accept the insureds' choice of solicitors on the basis that their rates of remuneration were higher than the non-panel rate, and that those solicitors' fees were to be assessed pursuant to the Criminal Procedure Rules 1998 (CPR) Pt 48 and were not to be restricted to the non-panel rate. On appeal Equity Syndicate sought to withdraw their concession that the insureds were not restricted to recovering the non-panel rate.

Equity Syndicate accepted that their pre-trial argument – that they were entitled to refuse to accept the appointment of Webster Dixon unless Webster Dixon and the insureds agreed to the non-panel rates – was wrong, but submitted that they were only bound to pay the rates set out in the standard terms of appointment.

The appeal was allowed in part.

- Equity Syndicate could withdraw the concession they had made before the judge. To the extent that Equity Syndicate had argued in pre-trial correspondence that they were entitled to refuse to accept the appointment of Webster Dixon unless Webster Dixon and the insureds agreed to the non-panel rates, that was wrong. They were right to concede on the appeal that that argument was inconsistent with the right of the insured to instruct a lawyer of their choice. A refusal to accept the appointment of an insured's lawyer of choice on the basis that he would only be accepted if they charged no more than the non-panel rates would be a serious inhibition of freedom of choice and thus contrary to the Insurance Companies (Legal Expenses Insurance) Regulations 1990. The judge's conclusion that the non-panel rate could be a comparator when assessing the lawyers' remuneration was understandable in light of Equity Syndicate's concession before him. Given the withdrawal of that concession, the question of whether the insured were restricted to recovering the non-panel rate had to be decided by the terms of the policy. In the terms, the insureds were entitled to recover the non-panel rate set out in the standard terms and conditions and no more. They were, however, entitled to recover at least at those rates. If that meant they would have to pay more to their chosen solicitors and arrange some other way to make such payment, that would then be their decision. Neither the Insurance Companies (Legal Expenses Insurance) Regulations 1990 nor the Directive made any reference to charging rates. The fact that some potential insureds might be unable to pay extra to secure the solicitor of their choice could hardly mean that all insureds could always choose any solicitor however expensive and expect the insurers to pay. Insurers could limit the costs for which they were liable to the insured provided that the freedom of choice guaranteed by the Directive was not rendered meaningless. A court determining whether the remuneration offered by an insurance policy was so insufficient as to render the insured's freedom of choice meaningless would have to have evidence of such insufficiency before it could avoid or strike down any provision in an insurance contract relating to the level of costs and expenses payable in respect of a solicitor's services. In the absence of such evidence in this case, it was not possible to say that Equity Syndicate could not rely on the term restricting the insured's indemnity to the non-panel rate. Therefore, Equity Syndicate were obliged to pay the appropriate non-panel rates to their insureds but no more.

- The condition in the insurance contract which provided that Equity Syndicate could choose not to accept the insured's choice of representative was in breach of the regulations. So too was the condition which provided that if the insured's appointed representative refused to continue to act, or if the insured dismissed an appointed representative, the cover would end at once unless Equity Syndicate agreed to appoint another representative. Those conditions had to be deleted or comprehensively redrafted.

## BT Fleet Ltd v McKenna [2005] EWHC 387 (Admin)

Recipients of improvement notices issued under the Health and Safety at Work etc Act 1974, s 21 were entitled to know what was wrong and why it was wrong, and the notice had to be clear and easy to understand. Where a statute provided an option to prescribe how a recipient could comply with a notice, any directions given as to compliance formed part of the notice and, if confusing, could operate to make the notice invalid.

## Cambridge Water Company v Eastern Counties Leather plc [1994] 2 AC 264

Foreseeability of harm by the defendant is required for the recovery of damages both in nuisance and under the rule in *Rylands* (see *Rylands v Fletcher* (1868) LR 3 HL 350). Eastern Counties Leather plc used and stored a chlorinated solvent at its tannery, situated just over a mile from the Cambridge Water Company's borehole where water was abstracted for domestic use. The water became unfit for human consumption, having been contaminated by the solvent which had seeped into the ground below Eastern Counties Leather plc's premises and conveyed in percolating water towards the borehole. The Cambridge Water Company claimed damages on three alternate grounds: negligence; nuisance; and the rule in *Rylands*. The actions in negligence and nuisance were dismissed by the trial judge on the grounds that Eastern Counties Leather plc could not reasonably have foreseen the damage that occurred, and the claim based on the rule in *Rylands* was dismissed on the ground that the storage and use of the solvent was, in the circumstances, a natural use of Eastern Counties Leather plc's land. On the Cambridge Water Company's appeal against the dismissal of the third cause of action, the Court of Appeal allowed the appeal, but declined to determine it on the basis of the rule in *Rylands*, deciding instead that there was a parallel rule of strict liability in nuisance. Eastern Counties Leather plc appealed.

The appeal was allowed in that:
- foreseeability of harm by the defendant was a prerequisite of the recovery of damages both in nuisance and under the rule in *Rylands*;
- notwithstanding that the storage of the solvent constituted a non-natural use of Eastern Counties Leather plc's land, since the Cambridge Water Company could not establish that the pollution which occurred was in the circumstances foreseeable, the action failed.

## Caparo Industries Plc v Dickman [1990] 2 AC 605

A firm of accountants, appealed against a decision of the Court of Appeal that they owed a duty of care to shareholders when preparing an auditor's report as required by statute. Caparo Industries had brought an action against Dickman and another, directors of a public company, about the report which had been prepared, alleging negligent misstatement. Caparo had purchased shares in the company as part of a takeover bid and placed reliance on the report, then bought further shares. The report was subsequently proved to have given a false picture of the company's profits and Caparo suffered a loss. The Court of Appeal had drawn a distinction between existing shareholders, to whom a duty was owed, and potential investors, in respect of whom no duty was owed.

The appeal was allowed as no duty was owed either to existing shareholders, or to potential investors, since for a duty to arise, three factors had to exist:
- a sufficient degree of proximity in the relationship between the parties;
- the knowledge that the report would be communicated to the shareholder or investor in connection with a particular transaction in the contemplation of the parties; and
- the shareholder or investor would place reliance on the report when deciding whether to enter into the relevant transaction.

Auditors of a public company routinely preparing accounts, in contrast to the preparation of a report for a specific purpose for an identified party, owed no duty to the public at large who might place reliance on company accounts when making investment decisions. Furthermore, it was necessary to impose some limit on liability for economic loss arising in the absence of a contractual relationship between the parties.

## Colour Quest Ltd v Total Downsteam UK plc, Total UK Ltd, Hertfordshire Oil Storage Ltd [2009] EWHC 540 (Comm)

Companies in the Total group had control of tank filling operations at the part of the Buncefield oil storage depot where an explosion occurred and were vicariously liable for the careless tank filling activities of their employees. One of the causes of the explosion was the failure to have an adequate system to prevent overfilling of a tank.

The cause of the explosions was the ignition of an enormous vapour cloud that had developed from the spillage of some 300 tons of petrol from a storage tank. The tank was part of the operations of the third defendant H, which was a joint venture company between two oil companies (T and C) which owned 60% and 40% respectively of the joint venture. There was a large fire which engulfed a further 20 fuel storage tanks. Apart from damage to a large proportion of the Buncefield site, significant damage was also caused to both commercial and residential properties outside the perimeter of the depot, in particular on the adjacent industrial estate. The claimants consisted of companies, many situated on the industrial estate, individuals resident in the vicinity of the depot and companies which owned the other storage facilities and a warehouse at the site. Summary judgment was given for the claimants in the light of admissions made by T and H that either one or the other was vicariously liable for various acts of negligence by the relevant supervisor on duty at Buncefield on the night of the explosions. The main preliminary issue was whether T or H was vicariously liable for the faults in the operation of the site which were causative of the explosion: the relevant employee (N) was employed by T and the issue was whether, having been seconded to H, he was to be regarded as the employee of H, thus rendering H liable in place of T.

T submitted that the effect of the relevant joint venture agreements was that, as between T and C, the site was to be operated by H, the relevant employees worked under the immediate direction of the board of H and H retained ultimate responsibility for directing and controlling the manner of tank filling operations. C submitted that H discharged its obligations by delegating its functions to T, such functions being performed by employees of T both on and off site.

Preliminary issues were determined:

- the identity of the person vicariously liable for the careless tank filling activities of N was a question of fact. As a matter of fact, T had control of tank filling operations. T failed to establish that H was responsible for the negligence of N. The activities of the on-site staff were under the control of T and not H;
- one of the causes of the explosion was the failure to promulgate an adequate system to prevent overfilling of a tank. That was a fault of T's head office staff;
- T was not entitled to a contractual indemnity as against C or H, because the relevant clauses were not intended to indemnify a party in respect of its own negligence;
- T was liable to claimants outside the site under *Rylands v Fletcher*. It could not avoid liability under *Rylands v Fletcher* and in nuisance to those within the site on the basis that they had consented to the oil storage. Where there was negligence there was no defence available because the consent was vitiated;

*Cases*

- the claimants, subject to proof of damage, had a claim in private nuisance. There could be liability in private nuisance for a single or isolated escape as opposed to a state of affairs where there was both unreasonable or negligent user of land and foreseeability of escape. The explosion endangered the health and comfort of the public at large. Subject to establishing loss, there was a claim in public nuisance. The causes of action in public and private nuisance were not mutually exclusive. A claimant could recover damages in public nuisance where access to or from the premises was obstructed so as to occasion a loss of trade. There was no requirement that those who suffered special damage in proximity to the explosion had to show a proprietary interest before they could recover;
- the claims of an oil company (S) arising out of its inability to use the pipelines from the site failed. S did not have the necessary legal ownership of the pipeline or right to possession. S's claim did not fall within any exception to the usual rule.

## Corby Group Litigation v Corby DC [2009] EWHC 1944 (TCC)

A local authority had been in breach of its duty to take reasonable care to prevent the dispersal of mud and dust containing a range of contaminants from land reclamation sites which it owned or operated. Pregnant women in the local area had thereby been exposed to teratogenic substances which had caused some children to be born with birth defects consisting of shortened or missing arms, legs and fingers. The local authority was also liable for public nuisance in causing, allowing or permitting the dispersal of dangerous or noxious contaminants and was in breach of its statutory duty under the Environmental Protection Act 1990, s 34.

Corby Group Litigation alleged negligence, breach of statutory duty and public nuisance on the part of the defendant local authority in connection with the reclamation of an extensive industrial site to the east of the town of Corby. The claim related to birth defects said to have been caused to a group of children born between 1986 and 1999. It was Corby Group Litigation's case that the birth defects had been caused as the result of their pregnant mothers' ingestion or inhalation of harmful substances generated by the reclamation works and spread in various ways through many parts of Corby. The court was required to consider and address specific issues which were generic and common to Corby Group Litigation and to determine the liability to any individual claimant.

The judgment was for the claimants:

- in the management and execution of land reclamation contracts which involved toxic waste management, the local authority had owed a duty of care to Corby Group Litigation to take reasonable care to prevent the airborne exposure of Corby Group Litigation's mothers to such toxic waste before or during the embryonic stage of pregnancy. In practice, that duty involved taking reasonable care to prevent the dispersal of mud and dust containing contaminants from the sites which it owned or operated;

- the local authority had been in breach of that duty from 1985 until August 1997. The contaminants included cadmium, chromium, nickel, polycyclic aromatic hydrocarbons and dioxins. They had been present in mud and dust disturbed at the reclamation sites which was spread either by the wind or by lorries and vehicles and deposited on public roads in the Corby area. The local authority had failed to carry out the reclamation safely and in accordance with best practices at the time for the management and disposal of contaminated waste;
- as a result of that breach of duty, Corby Group Litigation's mothers had been exposed to relevant teratogenic substances. Those contaminants had the ability to cause the limb defects suffered by all but two of the Corby Group Litigation members. That conclusion was supported by the evidence of a statistically significant cluster of birth defects to children born of mothers living in Corby in the period 1989 to 1998. It was reasonably foreseeable that the local population might be exposed to hazardous or contaminated substances as a result of the land reclamation programme and that pregnant mothers could inhale or ingest sufficient of the relevant contaminants that could lead to birth defects of the type complained of;
- the local authority was liable for public nuisance in causing, allowing or permitting the dispersal of dangerous or noxious contaminants. It was also in breach of its statutory duty under the Environmental Protection Act 1990, s 34 to the same extent as its breaches of its duty of care, as from April 1992;
- the local authority was therefore liable in public nuisance, negligence and breach of statutory duty, subject to it being established in later proceedings by individual claimants that their particular conditions were actually caused by the local authority's defaults.

## Derry v Peek (1889) 14 App Cas 337

In the prospectus released by the defendant company, it was stated that the company was permitted to use trams that were powered by steam, rather than by horses. In reality, the company did not possess such a right as this had to be approved by a Board of Trade. Gaining the approval for such a claim from the Board was considered a formality in such circumstances and the claim was put forward in the prospectus with this information in mind. However, the claim of the company for this right was later refused by the Board. The individuals who had purchased a stake in the business, relied on the statement, and brought a claim for deceit against the defendant's business after it became liquidated.

In this case, the court was required to assess the statement made by the defendant company in its prospectus to see whether the statement was fraudulent or simply incorrect. The claim of the shareholders was rejected by the House of Lords. The court held that it was not proven by the shareholders that the director of the company was dishonest in his belief. The court defined fraudulent misrepresentation as a statement known to be false or a statement made recklessly or carelessly as to the truth of the statement. On this basis, the plaintiff could not claim against the defendant company for deceit.

## DPP v Ara [2001] EWHC Admin 493

A decision of justices to stay proceedings as an abuse of process was justified in the light of a police refusal to disclose the terms of a police interview without which a defendant could not be given appropriate advice from his solicitor on whether to consent to a caution.

The Director of Public Prosecutions (DPP) appealed a decision by magistrates to stay proceedings against Ara, as an abuse of process. The police had decided to caution Ara following his alleged admission during a police interview, at which his solicitor had not been present, of an offence of assault occasioning actual bodily harm. Ara's solicitor had been unable to advise Ara to accept the caution because he was unable to assess the strength of the prosecution case in the face of a refusal by the police to release a record of the interview. Consequently, Ara had been charged with the offence. The DPP submitted that:

- if the police were to become subject to a duty of disclosure prior to charge, the caution process would be undermined since the police would simply proceed immediately to charge. It was further contended that the jurisprudence of the European Court of Human Rights concerning access to documents should not be directly applied to English jurisdiction procedure; and
- the lack of disclosure did not render the proceedings such an abuse as to necessitate a stay.

The appeal was dismissed:

- legal advice on the question of whether to agree to a caution could only be of use to a defendant if it was given with knowledge of the degree of guilt accepted by him. Acceptance of a caution was linked with entitlement to informed legal advice. It was neither in the public interest, nor that of the defendant, for the caution procedure to be ignored and proceedings instituted in circumstances where the police were minded to offer, and the defendant to accept, a caution; and
- although there could be no general duty on the police of disclosure prior to charge, the failure to disclose the terms of the interview in this case, followed by the commencement and pursuit of criminal proceedings, had provided sufficient justification for the magistrates' decision to stay the proceedings.

## Duchess of Argyll v Beuselinck [1972] 2 Lloyd's Rep 172

The Duchess of Argyll wanted to publish her life story and engaged a literary agent. She gave a retainer to a solicitor who had a reputation in the world of authorship. He found that a 'minor industry' was contemplated for the exploitation of her memoirs. The solicitor was sent a draft agreement with a newspaper group for the publication of a number of articles, which he was not allowed to keep, but which he authorised his articled clerk to approve. Because of this agreement the Duchess incurred a substantial tax liability which could have been avoided had the transaction been organised differently. The Duchess sued the solicitor for negligence in failing to give her advice on her tax liability. It was decided that the solicitor was not negligent. The court considered the question whether a higher standard of care should be expected of experts in a field than of general practitioners.

## Edwards v National Coal Board [1949] 1 All ER 743

Under the Coal Mines Act 1911, there is an absolute duty imposed on the mine owner to make the roof and sides of every travelling road secure, and civil liability can only be avoided for breach of this duty if the mine owner can prove, the onus being on them, that it was not 'reasonably practicable' to avoid or prevent the breach. 'Reasonably practicable' is a narrower term than 'physically possible', and implies that a computation must be made by the owner in which the level of risk is placed on one side of the scale and the sacrifice involved in the measures necessary for averting the risk (whether in money, time or trouble) is placed on the other. If it be shown that there is a gross disproportion between them – the risk is insignificant in relation to the sacrifice – then the owner can discharge the onus on them.

In this case a colliery timberman was killed as a result of a fall which occurred from the side of a travelling road. The accident was due to a latent defect, known as a glassy slant, in the side of the roadway. The evidence showed that the defendants' officials had never looked at whether it was reasonably practicable to provide artificial support for this roadway or not. Although more than half the existing roads were already artificially supported, it was held that the defendants had failed to discharge the burden which lay on them under the Coal Mines Act and there had been a clear breach of their statutory duty. Consequently, the claim of the deceased's widow for damages under the Fatal Accidents Acts 1846 succeeded.

## El-Ajou v Dollar Holdings Plc (No 1) [1994] 2 All ER 685

El-Ajou was the victim of fraud involving Dollar Holdings Plc, a company run by trustees. The question was whether a director described as a 'nominee director with non-executive responsibility' was the company's directing mind and will for the purpose of establishing the liability of a company under a constructive trust. El-Ajou appealed against the dismissal of the action against Dollar Holdings.

The appeal said that although the director may have had no general managerial responsibility in the company he did have management and control so far as the receipts of the fraud were concerned, having made all arrangements for the receipt and disposal of the money. The directing mind and will of the company was the individual who controlled its actions. Being the directing mind and will of the company in the fraudulent transaction, the director incurred liabilities on behalf of the company which meant that the company had the requisite knowledge for El-Ajou to enforce a constructive trust against it.

## Field v Leeds City Council [1999] EWCA Civ 3013

Field, a local authority tenant, brought a claim against Leeds City Council, the landlord, for damages for personal injury and for specific performance arising from disrepair in the property. The district judge held that Leeds City Council's choice of surveyor was inappropriate as he was employed in its housing department and therefore not independent as required by the Civil Procedure Rules 1998, Pt 35. The judge upheld the decision and Leeds City Council appealed, saying that the decision was a judicial error. Field argued that the decision was correct since it related solely to the individual expert concerned.

The appeal was dismissed. The fact that the expert was employed by Leeds City Council did not disqualify him as an expert, provided that he was suitably qualified. The judge in trying to ensure the independence of the expert so that it agreed with the overall requirements of Pt 35 had been wrong to exclude the evidence purely on the basis of the expert's employment with Leeds City Council. The fact that the hearing was due shortly, meant that there was insufficient time to decide on the appropriateness of the witness concerned, so that Leeds City Council would have to use another witness whose credentials were not in dispute. There was a need for a procedure whereby claimants could inform authorities of the expert they intended to use, thus allowing the use of more single experts in such cases.

## Goldscheider v Royal Opera House Covent Garden Foundation [2018] EWHC 687 (QB)

It was found that the opera house was liable to a viola player in its orchestra after he suffered acoustic shock due to noise levels during a rehearsal. The opera house had breached its duties under the Control of Noise at Work Regulations 2005 in that it had:

- failed to carry out an adequate risk assessment;
- failed to do everything reasonably practicable to eliminate the risk of noise exposure;
- failed to designate its orchestra pit as a mandatory hearing protection zone;
- failed to train orchestra members about the risks.

It could not compromise its standard of care for artistic considerations.

The viola player had been a professional musician employed by the opera house and he brought a personal injury claim against the opera house. The opera house's orchestra played in a pit, half-covered by a stage and they had duties under the Control of Noise at Work Regulations 2005. They had provided the claimant with custom 9dB earplugs, and 28dB earplugs were available in the orchestra pit. These caused difficulties in hearing other players, so players were told to wear them at their discretion. In 2012 the orchestra began rehearsals for Wagner's Ring Cycle and the conductor planned a different pit configuration for artistic reasons. The violas were immediately in front of the brass section and the claimant was immediately in front of the principal trumpet. The defendant's risk assessment anticipated that noise would exceed the EAV (upper exposure action values) provided in the regulations. The claimant wore his 9dB earplugs intermittently. He and the adjacent viola player complained about the noise at lunchtime. Noise dosimeters were attached to his shoulder for the afternoon but they did not provide live readings. After the afternoon rehearsal he felt ear pain and dizziness and was unable to return to work and was diagnosed with high frequency hearing loss.

## H (Stephen) v R [2014] EWCA Crim 1555

In a case where the defendant was accused of sexual offences against his daughter, the judge had been correct to refuse to admit the evidence of a retired psychiatrist and psychotherapist, her thesis of false memory syndrome lacked evidence to support it.

The applicant H, who had been convicted of cruelty by neglect to a person under 16, three specimen counts of cruelty to a person under 16, six specimen counts of rape of a child under 13 and three specimen counts of sexual assault of a child under 13, sought leave to appeal against his conviction and sentence.

The complainant X was H's daughter. In 2011, when she was 15, she made a complaint that H had sexually abused her over a period of two to two-and-a-half years, when she was aged 10 to 12/13. In the autumn of 2007, X had started to show signs of mental illness; the first counts of the indictment covered the later part of that year. H, a GP, seemed willing to take her for a Child and Adolescent Mental Health Service appointment so that a psychiatrist could assess her. In the event, she did not attend. H later cancelled three appointments, citing an unwillingness or refusal to attend on X's part and/or on the part of her mother. The prosecution alleged that H had cancelled the appointments to prevent X from reporting the sexual abuse she had suffered. That conduct formed the basis of the charge of cruelty by neglect. H had sought to rely on the evidence of a retired psychiatrist and psychotherapist B. Her view was that X was suffering from false memory syndrome in that she had a delusional belief as a result of 'recovered memories' and had filled in gaps in her memory to make a coherent narrative. According to B, such recovered memories could not be relied on in the absence of independent confirmatory information. The judge refused to admit her evidence. H was sentenced to 18 years' imprisonment.

*Cases*

Leave to appeal was granted and the appeals dismissed:

- the judge had not erred in refusing to admit B's evidence, having found that there was no evidence enabling the jury to find that X had 'recovered' or 'retrieved' memories during her treatment for her mental illness. B's evidence contained inadmissible comment and had the effect of usurping the function of the jury in assessing X's credibility as a witness. There was real concern about the use of unreliable or inappropriate expert evidence, which the Criminal Procedure Rules and a new Practice Direction would soon be addressing. Comment by an expert based only on analysis of the evidence, which effectively usurped the task of the jury, was to be avoided;
- as to the offence of cruelty by neglect, one ingredient of the offence was that the conduct had to be willful, meaning deliberate. The judge stated that if the jury were sure that H's motivation for deliberately cancelling the appointments was his concern that X might disclose ongoing abuse, they could decide that his conduct was willful and deliberate. That was an error. The word 'wilfully' did import any element of motive into the crime of child cruelty. However, that misdirection was not sufficient to render the jury's verdict unsafe;
- H's 18-year sentence was justified. The judge had concluded that there were a number of aggravating features which placed the offending in the most serious category:
    - the repeated nature of the offending over a period of two-and-a-half years;
    - X's age;
    - the gross breach of trust;
    - the deliberate and cynical decision not to treat her for a developing disorder for the purely selfish reason of preventing her from disclosing the abuse;
    - the very serious psychological harm caused to X;
    - H had made threats that he would use X's mental ill-health against her to discredit her;
    - further, he had at no time shown any remorse.
- H's five-year sentence for the offence of cruelty by neglect would be reduced to a term of three years, but that would not have the effect of reducing the overall sentence of 18 years.

## Hart v Lancashire & Yorkshire Railway Co (1869) 21 LT 261

Hart alleged negligence when injured by a runaway train. Their argument centred on the fact that the train company had recently changed the points on the track to avoid a repetition of the event that had occurred. The court decided that this change in practice occurred after the accident and was irrelevant to proving or disproving that the company was negligent – all it showed was they were improving safety standards.

## Herald of Free Enterprise

On 6 March 1987 the roll on/roll off passenger ferry Herald of Free Enterprise sailed form Zeebrugge. The Vessel capsized just outside Zeebrugge harbour where 150 passengers and 38 members of the crew lost their lives. The bow doors had been open when the ferry set sail. The details of the formal investigation can be found in the Department of Transport Report of Court No 8074 Formal Investigation: see https://assets.publishing.service.gov.uk/media/54c1704ce5274a15b6000025/FormalInvestigation_HeraldofFreeEnterprise-MSA1894.pdf.

## Hertfordshire Oil Storage Ltd v TAV Engineering Ltd, Motherwell Control Systems 2003 Ltd [2008] EWHC 1296 (Comm)

The court had no jurisdiction under the CPR Pt 18, to require disclosure of the third party's insurance position. Hertfordshire Oil Storage Ltd, applied for information and disclosure in respect of the insurance arrangements of the third party TAV Engineering Ltd. In their claim they sought a contribution in respect of any liability that they might incur to those interests damaged by the Buncefield oil storage depot explosion. It was their case that TAV Engineering Ltd were the designers, manufacturers or suppliers of the switch which failed to operate which allowed an overflow of fuel to occur leading to the explosion. The claims totalled over £700 million.

Hertfordshire Oil Storage Ltd contended that:

- the nature and scope of TAV's liability insurance cover was material to the issues and in particular the question of apportionment;
- the material was necessary from the perspective of efficient case management.

The application was refused:

- apportionment under the Civil Liability (Contribution) Act 1978 involved consideration of both the blameworthiness of the party and any fault on its part. The Act was not expressed exclusively in terms of causative responsibility but the circumstances in which non-causative factors could properly be taken into account would be exceptional and of limited impact. It was not arguable that the existence or scope of any insurance cover could be material to the issue of apportionment in this case. There was nothing exceptional in there being some form of insurance cover. It had no connection whatsoever with the alleged causative conduct;
- the court had no jurisdiction to require disclosure of the insurance position. The insurance policies were not disclosable under the CPR Pt 31 whether as part of standard disclosure or otherwise. They did not support or adversely affect any party's case, they were not relevant to the issues nor did they constitute documents which might lead to an inquiry enabling a party to advance their own case or damage their opponent's. Nor would

any information furnished relate to any matter which was in dispute in the proceedings under the CPR Pt 18. The insurance position was not a matter that enabled a party to prepare their case or understand the case they had to answer under the CPR Pt 18. Hertfordshire Oil Storage Ltd's submission required a rewriting of both the rule and the practice direction. The court had no jurisdiction to make the order sought.

## HM Inspector of Health and Safety v Chevron North Sea Ltd [2018] UKSC 7

On an appeal under the Health and Safety at Work etc Act 1974, s 24 against a prohibition notice, the employment tribunal was entitled to take into account all the available evidence relevant to the state of affairs at the time the notice was served, including information coming to light afterwards.

Following the inspection of an off-shore installation, the inspector served a prohibition notice for some stairways and staging as he considered that corrosion had caused a risk of serious personal injury. The company obtained an expert report that all the metalwork passed the British Standard strength test and there was no risk of injury from falling through it. The company appealed against the notice and sought to rely on the expert report. The employment tribunal considered that it was entitled to look at the expert evidence and, as a result, cancelled the notice. The inspector unsuccessfully appealed to the Inner House, which held that an appeal on the facts, was a wider concept than judicial review and this enabled an appellant to prove, using whatever competent information was available at the time of appeal hearing, that the factual content of the notice was wrong.

The appeal was dismissed.

When an inspector served a notice, he made it clear that what mattered was that he was of the opinion that the activities in question involved a risk of serious personal injury. However, on appeal the focus shifted. An appeal was not against the inspector's opinion but against the notice itself. The appeal involved the tribunal looking at the facts on which the notice was based. The inspector's opinion about the risk, and the reasons why he formed it and served the notice, could be relevant as part of the evidence as to whether the risk existed, but there was no good reason for confining the tribunal's consideration to the material that was, or should have been, available to the inspector. It was entitled to look at other evidence which assisted in assessing what the risk was.

It was not a criticism of an inspector when new material led to a different conclusion about risk, and inspectors should not be deterred from serving the notice. The effectiveness of a notice was in no way reduced by an appeal that enabled the situation to be examined by a tribunal with the benefit of additional information. The wider interpretation would not undermine the role that prohibition and improvement notices played in encouraging employers to have robust systems in place with a view to demonstrating easily, when an inspection took place, that no risk existed. If s 24 was given a narrow interpretation, a notice that an inspector agreed was unnecessary would remain in force and would have the capacity to damage the reputation of the employer and their ability to do business. It would not be right that an employer in such circumstances would continue to be exposed to the possibility of criminal proceedings, however improbable it was that proceedings would actually be taken.

## Huckerby v Elliot [1970] 1 All ER 189 (DC)

A director of a company cannot be said to be neglectful if he fails to enquire about certain matters which are dealt with by a fellow director. A company pleaded guilty to a charge of providing gaming premises without an appropriate licence contrary to the Finance Act 1966, whilst its secretary and a director, pleaded guilty to a charge under the Customs and Excise Act 1952 in that the offence was committed with his consent. The appellant, also a director, pleaded not guilty to a charge under the same Act in that the offence was attributed to her neglect. It was clear from the evidence that she knew little of the conduct of the premises, nor did she have any knowledge of whether or not a licence had been obtained.

The appeal said that they were entitled to leave certain matters to a fellow director or company official and that the prosecution had failed to show any neglect on the appellant's part.

## Hughes, Re [1943] 2 All ER 269

In a will dated 16 January 1858, a testator, who died in 1869, settled certain real estate in strict settlement. The will contained a name and arms clause under which it was directed that the interest of every person who should 'neglect' to comply with the conditions contained in it, within 12 months of becoming entitled in possession to the property, should cease and it would be as if he or she were dead without issue. A grandson of the testator, who became entitled in possession to the property in February 1940, did not become aware of the existence of the name and arms clause within 12 months from that date.

It was held, that, as he had been unable to comply with the condition contained in the name and arms clause through ignorance of its existence, he did not 'neglect' to comply with the condition, and, having executed a disentailing deed, was entitled to an assent in respect of the property.

## Hui-Chi-Ming v R [1992] 1 AC 34 (PC)

Hui-Chi-Ming appealed against his conviction for murder in Hong Kong. Hui-Chi-Ming had been one of a group of friends who had accompanied a man who had set out to injure his girlfriend's brother. An innocent man died of injuries inflicted during that attack. Hui-Chi-Ming was charged with murder although two years earlier the boyfriend had been convicted of manslaughter. Hui-Chi-Ming appealed on the grounds that:

- evidence of the boyfriend's acquittal of murder should have been adduced at his trial;
- the trial judge should have directed the jury that Hui-Chi-Ming, as an accomplice, could not be found guilty of murder unless the principal had been convicted of that offence;
- that he had been charged with murder to pressurise him to plead guilty to manslaughter and that was an abuse of process.

The appeal was dismissed. The evidence of the principal's acquittal of murder and conviction of manslaughter was correctly excluded from Hui-Chi-Ming's trial. There were no exceptional features which rendered that evidence admissible. Their Lordships concluded that it was not necessary for both the principal and the secondary party to have contemplated the material act for the secondary party to be proved guilty. The guilt of the secondary party did not require consideration of the principal's state of mind. Thus, the accomplice must have foreseen the offence which took place as one which the principal could commit as a potential consequence of the unlawful joint venture and also have taken part in that venture. There was strong evidence for a charge of murder and as there was no unfairness, deceit or procedural irregularity there was no abuse of process.

## Hunter v Canary Wharf Ltd [1997] AC 655

A person's right to build on their land was not restricted because their building might interfere with a neighbour's enjoyment of the land. A nuisance action based on interference due to noise, dirt or smell might succeed, whereas interference with a television signal would not.

Hunter and others brought an action in nuisance with regard to interference caused to their television reception as a result of the construction of the Canary Wharf Tower. Hunter appealed against a Court of Appeal ruling that no action lay in private nuisance for interference with a television signal caused by the mere presence of a building, and Canary Wharf cross-appealed against a ruling that the mere occupation of property as a home entitled an occupier to sue in private nuisance.

The appeal was dismissed and the cross-appeal allowed.

- As to the right to sue in private nuisance, it had for many years been regarded as settled law that a person who had no right in the affected land could not sue for private nuisance. Recently the Court of Appeal had departed from this line of authority in *Khorasandjian v Bush* [1993] QB 727, where the plaintiff had been held able to sue for harassing phone calls received at her parents' home. That case must be overruled in so far as it decided that a mere licensee could sue in private nuisance, *Khorasandjian* was overruled in part. The only exception for the plaintiff to have title in the affected land was if he was in exclusive possession of the land although he could not prove title to it. The decision of the Court of Appeal was overruled as to any extension of entitlement to sue for private nuisance. Occupation of the property as a home was an acceptable criteria for entitlement to sue in private nuisance.

- In relation to the interference with television reception, there was no reported case where an easement against the interruption of radio or television signals had yet been recognised. The closest was with interrupted prospect, which could not be acquired by prescription but only by agreement or express grant. Unless restricted by covenant the owner was entitled to put up whatever they choose on their own land even though their neighbour's view was interrupted. The interruption of view would carry with it various consequences. It might reduce amenity generally, or it might impede more particular things such as the transmission of visual signals to the land from other properties. That might be highly inconvenient and it might even diminish the value of the land which was affected. But the proprietor of the affected land had nevertheless no actionable ground of complaint. Radio and television signals fell into the same category. It would be difficult, if not impossible, for the developer to have become aware of their existence before they put up the new building. If they were to be restricted by an easement from putting up a building which interfered with these signals, they might not be able to put up any substantial structures at all. The interference with his freedom would be substantial. It would be inconsistent with principle for such a wide and novel restriction to be recognised.

## Kennedy v Cordia (Services) LLP Supreme Court (Scotland) [2016] UKSC 6

It was found that an employer was liable for injuries sustained by a home carer when she slipped and fell on an icy path during the course of her employment. There was a failure to carry out a suitable risk assessment and provide personal protective equipment and they had therefore breached the Management of Health and Safety at Work Regulations 1999, SI 1999/3242, reg 3(1) and the Personal Protective Equipment at Work Regulations 1992, SI 1992/2966, reg 4(1).

## Kings Cross Fire

On 18 November 1987 a fire broke out at the King's Cross St Pancras London Underground station. This killed 31 people and injured 100. The details of the investigation can be found in the Department of Transport report 'Investigation into the King's Cross Underground Fire' by Desmond Fennel QC, seehttp://www.railwaysarchive.co.uk/documents/DoT_KX1987.pdf.

*Cases*

## London Borough of Wandsworth v Covent Garden Market Authority [2011] EWHC 1245 (QB)

An employment judge had made a mistake in concluding that it was not reasonably practicable for a statutory authority to serve notices of appeal against ten improvement notices within time. The authority had taken expert legal advice, knew of the relevant time limits and would not have been prejudiced in respect of an impending criminal investigation into incidents arising out of the same subject-matter by issuing its appeal notices.

Covent Garden Market Authority was the body created by statute to operate the New Covent Garden Market in London. It had responsibility for the environmental services, health and safety and licensing for that part of London in which the market was located. The local authority served ten improvement notices on Covent Garden Market Authority under the Health and Safety at Work etc Act 1974, s 21 for its traffic management following several incidents where injuries were caused to pedestrians. The local authority also requested that Covent Garden Market Authority attend an interview under the Police and Criminal Evidence Act 1984 (PACE) in respect of those incidents. Covent Garden Market Authority sought to appeal, out of time, against the issue of the improvement notices. In extending time, the employment judge determined that although Covent Garden Market Authority had been capable of submitting the appeals within time, it had not been reasonably practical for it do so in light of the impending PACE interview.

The local authority submitted that it was clear that it was Covent Garden Market Authority's choice not to lodge its notices of appeal, it knew its rights, had expert legal advice and was capable of submitting the appeals within the time limit.

The appeal was allowed. Whether presentation of a claim was 'reasonably practicable' was an issue of fact for the consideration of the tribunal. Accepting the basis for delay Covent Garden Market Authority simply chose to give precedence to the PACE interview and to see if relevant material would be learned from it notwithstanding the fact that it was in receipt of expert legal advice and knew of the time limits for launching appeals against the improvement notices. It was difficult to see why appealing against the improvement notices could adversely affect the criminal proceedings. In those circumstances, no employment judge properly directing themselves could have concluded that it was not reasonably practicable to present the notices of appeal in time.

## Malcolm v DPP [2007] EWHC 363 (Admin)

Magistrates had been entitled to use their discretion to receive further evidence to remedy a deficiency in the prosecution case, notwithstanding the fact that they had already retired, returned to the court room and had been part way through giving their decision, as the most important issue was whether justice could be done.

Malcolm appealed against her conviction for driving whilst in excess of the prescribed alcohol limit contrary to the Road Traffic Act 1988, s 5(1)(a).

- Malcolm had been visiting her mother's house where her mother's boyfriend had also been in attendance. Malcolm had been drinking and her mother's boyfriend became aggressive and attacked her. Malcolm became frightened and drove to a telephone box, where she contacted the police. Malcolm was told to wait where she was for an officer to attend. Malcolm remained there frightened. As her mother's boyfriend knew her address, she decided to drive to another telephone box. In the course of her journey she was seen by the policeman who signalled her to stop. The policeman smelt alcohol on Malcolm's breath and she returned a positive breath test. Malcolm was arrested for driving whilst under the influence. At the police station, the policeman carried out the drink drive procedure and asked Malcolm to provide another breath sample. Malcolm initially failed to provide a specimen but eventually provided two further samples. At trial, Malcolm ran a defence of necessity and duress. The policeman was not cross-examined. During her final speech Malcolm's counsel submitted that the policeman had failed to provide an appropriate warning that Malcolm's failure to provide a sample could render her liable to prosecution. The magistrates retired to consider their verdict and returned to announce their decision to dismiss the case on the basis of a lack of admissible evidence of the proportion of alcohol that had been in Malcolm's breath. Part way through giving their decision, prosecuting counsel requested the magistrates' permission to recall the policeman to give further evidence to remedy a deficiency in the prosecution case. The prosecution submitted that since the policeman had not been cross-examined, there would be no injustice to Malcolm as a consequence. The policeman confirmed that he had followed the correct procedure methodically, including providing Malcolm with a copy of the printout from the breath analysis machine. The magistrates retired again and convicted Malcolm. The issues were whether:

    - the magistrates had been correct to exercise their discretion to admit further evidence after they had started to consider their verdict, and had returned to court and started to announce their decision on the point of law;
    - the magistrates had been correct to allow the prosecution to draw the policeman's attention to the fact that he had circled a pro-forma document saying that Malcolm had accepted a copy of the printout.

The appeal was dismissed as it was clear that magistrates' courts had a discretion to permit either party in a criminal case to adduce further evidence at any time before they retired, provided that no injustice was done. However, the position after they had returned to give their verdict was more restricted. The magistrates still had a discretion to receive further evidence but special circumstances were required if that discretion was to be exercised. Criminal trials were no longer to be run in which each move was final and any omission by the prosecution led to the trial's failure. It was the duty of the defence to make its defence clear to the prosecution and the court at an early stage. That duty was implicit in the Criminal Procedure Rules 2005. At no stage before their final speech did Malcolm's counsel raise any issue concerning the policeman's compliance with Road Traffic Act. If Malcolm wished to raise that issue, her counsel ought to have done so during cross-examination. In the circumstances, Malcolm's counsel should not have been permitted to raise the point in her final speech unless the prosecution had been given the opportunity to call evidence to deal with the point. To have taken the point during closing speeches had been a classic and improper defence ambush of the prosecution. Malcolm's failure to raise the point during a cross-examination of the policeman amounted to a special circumstance that justified the recall of the policeman, notwithstanding the fact that the magistrates had retired and partially announced their decision in the case. The most important question was whether justice could be done. Malcolm had been able to dispute the policeman's evidence concerning the printout but had not done so. There had been no injustice to Malcolm and in the circumstances the magistrates had been entitled to use their discretion.

## Manley v New Forest DC [2007] EWCH 3188 (Admin)

Where a business has resisted the service of an abatement notice, it was for the business to show that at the time of the abatement notice, the best practicable means were in use to prevent or counteract the noise. In this case the business appealed against a decision of the Crown Court that their dogs' howling constituted a nuisance. They owned and operated a dog kennels which housed 24 Siberian huskies. The local authority had served an abatement notice and suggested that they could line the kennels or build new kennels where the huskies could be kept during the night. The business appealed against the abatement notice to the district judge and then to the Crown Court. The Crown Court accepted that the kennels were business premises but found that the owners had not demonstrated that the best practicable means had been used to prevent or counteract the noise, and the notice was therefore justified.

The business said that they were not given a fair opportunity to demonstrate why the suggestion of boxing in or lining the existing kennels was not practicable. They argued that linings would create too small a space for the dogs, there was no space on the land for any new buildings and the business could not afford remedial building to abate the noise. The appeal was dismissed.

It was not disputed that the noise from the dogs fell within the descriptions of statutory nuisances in the Environmental Protection Act 1990, s 79(1). If the business sought to resist the service of an abatement notice pursuant to the Statutory Nuisance (Appeals) Regulations 1995, SI 1995/2644, the burden was upon them to demonstrate that at the time of the abatement notice the best practicable means were in use to prevent the noise. It was not for them to complain that the suggestions of the local authority were impracticable. It was for the business to demonstrate that they were doing something and that was the best practicable means. If the business had done nothing, the only way they could succeed in having the abatement notice set aside was to show that nothing could be done. In the context of dogs and noise that would be an almost impossible task. There was plenty of material to demonstrate that the question of boxing in or lining of the kennels was properly canvassed before the court and that the business had a fair opportunity to deal with it.

## Massar v DAS Nederlandse Rechtsbijstand Verzekeringsmaatschappij NV (Case C-460/14) [2016] Lloyd's Rep IR 463 and in Buyuktipi v Achmea Schadeverzekeringen NV and Stichting Achmea Rechtsbijstand (Case C-5/15) [2016] Lloyd's Rep IR 586

A procedure at the end of which a public body authorised the dismissal of an employee covered by legal expenses insurance fell within the scope of the term 'inquiry' in Directive 87/344, Art 4(1)(a).

The European Court of Justice (ECJ) considered a request for a preliminary ruling from a Dutch court concerning the interpretation of Directive 87/344, Art 4(1)(a). The request was made in proceedings between Mr Massar and DAS Nederlandse Rechtsbijstand Verzekeringsmaatschappij NV (DAS), an insurance company, concerning the refusal of the insurance company to bear the costs of legal assistance provided by the lawyer chosen by the insured person in a procedure before the Employee Insurance Agency that led to the termination of his employment contract. DAS informed Mr Massar that the procedure before the Employee Insurance Agency was not an 'inquiry' or proceedings within the meaning of the law on financial supervision and therefore the insured person had no right to choose a lawyer and the insurer would not bear the costs associated with representation by a lawyer. The Dutch court essentially asked whether Directive 87/844, Art 4(1)(a) must be interpreted as meaning that the term 'inquiry' referred to in that provision included a procedure at the end of which a public body authorised the employer to dismiss an employee, who was covered by legal expenses insurance.

A preliminary ruling was given.

Directive 87/344, Art 4(1)(a) must be interpreted as meaning that the term 'inquiry' referred to in that provision included a procedure at the end of which a public body authorised an employer to dismiss an employee who was covered by legal expenses insurance. An interpretation of the term 'inquiry' that sought to limit the scope of that term to legal proceedings in administrative matters only, would deprive the term of its meaning. The court recalled that the objective pursued by Directive 87/344 concerning the free choice of lawyer or representative was to protect, broadly, the interests of insured persons. Directive 87/344, Art 4(1)(a) was therefore not to be interpreted restrictively. In the case at issue, it was indisputable that the rights of the employee were affected by the decision of the Employee Insurance Agency and that his interests as an insured person required protection in the context of the procedure before that body.

## O'Brien v Chief Constable of South Wales Police [2005] UKHL 26

The chief constable appealed against a decision that similar fact evidence was admissible in a claim brought by the respondent for misfeasance in public office and malicious prosecution. The respondent alleged that he had been framed for a murder which he did not commit. He gave notice of his intention to adduce evidence designed to demonstrate that the investigating police officers had behaved with similar impropriety on other occasions. The Court of Appeal applied the test of admissibility in civil proceedings, the approach adopted in criminal proceedings. The judge had to decide whether the evidence was admissible and then whether as a matter of discretion he would permit the evidence to be led. Evidence of the similar incidents alleged by the respondent was admitted. The chief constable contended that there was a rule of law which prevented the admission of similar fact evidence unless it had an enhanced probative value.

The appeal was dismissed. It was incorrect that similar fact evidence was only admissible in a civil suit if it was likely to be reasonably conclusive of a primary issue in the proceedings or alternatively if it had enhanced relevance so as to have substantial probative value. Far from being too lenient a test of admissibility in civil proceedings, the test applied by the Court of Appeal was too restrictive. The test of admissibility of similar facts against a defendant in criminal proceedings required an enhanced relevance because, if the evidence was not cogent, the prejudice that it would cause to the defendant might render the proceedings unfair. If a defendant wished to have evidence of bad character against a police witness, the test of admissibility required an enhanced relevance in order to ensure that the trial remained manageable. There was no reason for the automatic application of either of those tests as a rule of law in a civil suit. To do so would build into civil procedure an inflexibility which was inappropriate and undesirable. The appropriate test for similar fact evidence in a civil suit was relevance. Such evidence was admissible if it was potentially probative of an issue in the action. Nevertheless, policy considerations would still have a part to play in the conduct of civil litigation and the court had the power to exclude evidence that would otherwise be admissible and to limit cross-examination. Furthermore, judges should be astute to see that the probative cogency of similar fact evidence justified the risk of prejudice in the interests of a fair trial. In this case the evidence was potentially probative and therefore admissible.

## Pan Atlantic Insurance Co Ltd v Pine Top Insurance Co Ltd [1995] 1 AC 501, [1994] 3 All ER 581

A circumstance may be material for the purposes of an insurance contract (whether marine or non-marine) even though it would not have had a decisive effect on the underwriter's decision whether to accept the risk. Pan Atlantic wrote a quantity of direct American liability insurance, much of it 'long-tail' business in which a long period of time may elapse before claims matured.

Pine Top became a reinsurer for excess of loss above a certain figure for the 1980 policy year and for two subsequent years. Disputes arose in relation to all three years. Judgment was given in favour of Pan Atlantic as regards the first two policy years but the judge found for Pine Top in respect of the third. It was common ground that, in respect of the contract of reinsurance for that year, the disclosed losses for the previous year were significantly lower than the true losses and that Pan Atlantic had had information about those additional losses before the slip had been signed. The judge held that the additional losses had been material to the contract and should have been disclosed and that Pine Top was entitled to avoid the contract. The Court of Appeal dismissed Pan Atlantic's appeal:

- a circumstance may be material for the purposes of an insurance contract (whether marine or non-marine) even though it would not have had a decisive effect on the prudent underwriter's decision whether to accept the risk or on the amount of premium demanded however, an underwriter who was not induced by the material non-disclosure to make the contract could not rely on the non-disclosure to avoid the contract;
- the additional losses for 1981 had been a material circumstance that ought to have been disclosed and the judge's conclusion that Pine Top were entitled to avoid the contract should stand.

## R (DPP) v Chorley Justices [2006] EWHC 1795 (Admin), [2002] EWHC 2162 (Admin)

The Crown Prosecution Service (CPS) sought to challenge by judicial review, a decision by the justices that they could not lawfully impose a doorstep condition on a defendant subject to a curfew condition. The CPS had sought to impose on the defendant a requirement that he present himself at the door of his home if requested to do so by a police officer during the hours of his curfew. Granting the application for judicial review, the justices had had the power under the Bail Act 1976, s 3(6) to impose a doorstep condition in addition to a curfew condition when granting bail. Whether in any particular case such a condition was necessary in order to protect the public would be a question of fact to be determined in the circumstances of the case.

## R (Ebrahim) v Feltham Magistrates' Court: Mouatt v DPP [2001] EWHC Admin 130

Where videotape evidence had been destroyed or was otherwise unavailable due to the default of the prosecution, the grant of a stay on the basis of abuse of process would only be considered where a defendant could demonstrate on the balance of probabilities that it was no longer possible to conduct a fair trial.

Ebrahim, who had been charged with common assault, sought judicial review of a refusal to grant a stay of proceedings for abuse of process following the destruction of video evidence which he maintained was relevant to his defence.

The application was refused. In such cases it was first necessary to establish the extent of the duty upon the prosecution to obtain or retain in its possession the videotaped material. If there was no such obligation, then there was no prospect that the loss or destruction of that material would result in the trial process being unfair. However, if such an obligation did exist then a stay would only be granted in circumstances where:

- the defendant was able to establish on the balance of probabilities that it was no longer possible to conduct a fair trial;
- there had been bad faith or other serious default on the part of the prosecution.

In circumstances where, on appeal from the magistrates' court, a complaint was made that the prosecution had acted in bad faith, an appellant should apply for an order allowing his appeal and quashing his conviction on the ground that the unfairness of the original trial was not capable of being remedied on the appeal. When ruling on an application for a stay, the lower court should provide reasons. An advocate was under a duty to take notes of any reasons provided. If an application for judicial review was made, the court would anticipate seeing a note of those reasons.

## R (for and on behalf of the Health and Safety Executive) v Paul Jukes [2018] EWCA Crim 176

The appellant had been a manager at a waste-recycling company at a time when an employee was killed after they came into contact with dangerous machinery. Jukes had not made out his challenges to his conviction for failing to take reasonable care for the health and safety of employees contrary to the Health and Safety at Work etc Act 1974, s 7.

The appellant appealed against his conviction for failing to take reasonable care for the health and safety of employees contrary to the Health and Safety at Work etc Act 1974, s 7.

He had been the transport and operations manager for a waste-recycling company and the employee had been killed after coming into contact with a baling machine. The door which provided access to the chamber in which the machine was located was fitted with an interlock which stopped the machine when the door was opened. The accident happened because the interlock had been bypassed. When interviewed, the appellant provided a prepared statement in which he said that another man had been the health and safety manager at the time of the accident and that he did not know that the interlock had been bypassed. In his defence statement, he repeated the assertion that he had not been responsible for health and safety. The prosecution case was that by the time of the accident he had taken over responsibility for health and safety and the maintenance of the baling machine and that he had been made aware that the interlock had been bypassed. The prosecution relied on a signed statement which he had provided to the company's solicitors in which he said that he had in fact been responsible for health and safety at the time of the accident. There were three co-accused, one of whom was the company's managing director. They pleaded guilty to offences under the 1974 Act and the trial proceeded against the appellant alone.

The appellant argued that the trial judge had been wrong to rule that the statement which he had provided to the company's solicitors was not a privileged document and to allow it to be adduced by the prosecution. He also argued that the judge had been wrong to refuse his application for permission to adduce bad-character evidence in the form a conviction of the managing director for conspiring to pervert the course of justice (he and others had prevailed upon an employee at the local magistrates' court to alter details on driving licences to avoid totting up or disqualification).

The appeal was dismissed.

Admissibility of his statement – a document would only attract litigation privilege if three conditions were met:

- litigation was in progress or reasonably in contemplation;
- the document was made or created with the sole or dominant purpose of conducting that litigation;
- the litigation was adversarial, not investigatory or inquisitorial.

At the time that the appellant provided his statement, matters were still at the investigatory stage and a criminal prosecution was not a reasonable contemplation. Sixteen months passed before he was interviewed by the police and the Health and Safety Executive. In any event, his submission that the privilege was his was misconceived. The privilege was that of the company or the managing director, being the solicitors' clients. Those solicitors never acted for the appellant. As the maker of a statement given to the party who was entitled to rely on litigation or legal-advice privilege, he was at best a potential witness who could not rely on the company or the managing director's privilege for his own benefit. The fact that the company or the managing director might have claimed privilege over the document was not in itself a reason for excluding it, if it was otherwise admissible and probative.

Admissibility of bad-character evidence – it was important to note that the reason why the appellant sought to adduce the evidence of the managing director's conviction was to support his case that the managing director was unreasonable, deceitful, untruthful and manipulative. Under the Criminal Justice Act 2003, s 104, such evidence would only have been admissible if any defence run by the managing director had sought to undermine the appellant's defence. The managing director did not run a defence at all but pleaded guilty. His conviction was evidence of the bad character of a non-defendant, but such evidence was at best of peripheral significance. Further, the appellant had been well able to make his point about the managing director's manipulative and difficult character in his own evidence. The judge had been right to exclude the evidence of the managing director's conviction.

## R (Inland Revenue Commissioners) v Kingston Crown Court [2001] EWCH Admin 581

In seeking to determine whether it could be inferred from documentary evidence that a tax adviser had played a part in a scheme to defraud HMRC, the court observed that the use of minutes of board and company meetings that had been prepared in advance was not improper provided that the meeting had dealt with the business indicated and the board had actually discussed and made the decisions that were indicated in the draft.

The Revenue applied for judicial review of the decision of a Crown Court judge dismissing charges brought against an accountant of conspiracy to defraud the Revenue. The accountant had advised L, who was resident in Switzerland, about a scheme which had involved the purchase by companies controlled by L of English registered companies whose assets consisted primarily of cash and which had substantial liabilities for corporation tax. He also advised of the steps subsequently required to be taken to eliminate those tax liabilities. The Revenue alleged that certain of the transactions subsequently relied on by L were fictitious and that the accountant had known this. The judge had dismissed the charges on the basis that it was not possible for the jury to infer the necessary knowledge on the part of the accountant. The Revenue contended that the judge had failed to properly consider the documentary evidence, and in particular, that minutes of board meetings showed the accountant's involvement in the alleged conspiracy.

In refusing the application, that the judge had adopted the correct approach to the documentary evidence and his decision could not be categorised as perverse, he court observed that the use of pre-prepared minutes of board and shareholder meetings was not improper provided that the meeting then dealt with the business indicated in the draft minutes.

## R v (on application of Dennis) v DPP [2006] EWHC 3211 (Admin)

It was appropriate for the Crown Prosecution Service (CPS) to reconsider its decision not to prosecute individuals for gross negligence manslaughter after an employee had fallen through a roof light to his death. It was arguable that a different decision might be reached if consideration was given to the seriousness of an employer's failure to give proper instruction to an employee as to the dangers of working at heights or on roofs.

The claimant applied for judicial review of a decision of the CPS not to bring prosecutions for gross negligence manslaughter arising out of the death of his son in an industrial accident.

The son, who was 17 years old, had fallen through a roof light to his death in his second week of work as a labourer with his employer. The father maintained that the employer had instructed his son to go onto the roof, even though he had had no previous experience of working at heights or on roofs. At the time of the accident, the son had offered to climb onto the roof in search of timber. One of his son's colleagues had told him not to bother but he had continued and had fallen to his death. At an inquest the jury returned a unanimous verdict of unlawful killing. The CPS considered whether various individuals should be prosecuted for gross negligence manslaughter but concluded that although individuals including the employer were in breach of duty of care to the son, the degree of negligence exhibited was not such as to amount to criminal negligence. The CPS had relied on various factors including:

- the suggestion that the son had some experience in the building trade;
- that the son's colleagues had told him not to go near roof lights;
- that there was no reason for him to have gone onto the roof;
- that he had been specifically told by a colleague not to go onto the roof.

The father submitted that the CPS had failed to appreciate that the employer had exposed his son to the risk of death by instructing him to work on the roof without any training, particularly without training in relation to the danger of roof lights, and had also totally failed to assess the seriousness of that risk.

The application was granted as the CPS had not dealt with the real thrust of any case that might be brought against the employer. There was evidence of why the son might have gone onto the roof as he had been instructed to do so as part of his duties as an employee, without any training or induction course, or any serious warning about roof lights and had not been told not to do so prior to receiving that induction course. By focusing on the particular moment before the accident, the CPS had failed to take account of the seriousness of a failure to give proper instruction not to go on the roof prior to induction or proper instruction in relation to working on a roof and particularly a roof with roof lights. It could not be said that the CPS had provided clear reasons as to why the verdict of the inquest jury should not have led to a prosecution. Consequently, it was appropriate to refer the matter back to the CPS.

## R v Adaway [2004] EWCA Crim 2831

Before criminal proceedings were started by a local authority in relation to strict liability offences under the Trade Descriptions Act 1968, consideration had to be given to the terms of the authority's own policy guidelines on the prosecution of offences.

Adaway appealed against his conviction for supplying goods with a false trade description contrary to the Trade Descriptions Act 1968, s 1(1)(b). Adaway had supplied and fitted a greenhouse for the complainant, B. B contended that the wrong sort of glass had been used and that no vents had been put in the roof. Adaway said he had made a mistake in ordering and offered to replace the glass or pay B compensation. B referred the matter to the local authority's trading standards department, which instigated a prosecution. Adaway applied for a stay of prosecution on the ground that it was an abuse of process, but the judge refused, although he criticised the local authority for bringing a prosecution that did not follow its own prosecuting policy criteria as there was no evidence of fraud or a deliberate breach of the Act. Adaway was convicted. On appeal, Adaway argued that the judge had been wrong to refuse the stay since it was clear even at the start of the trial that the case had no substance.

The appeal was allowed. The judge should have stayed the proceedings. It was clear, and indeed had been largely conceded by the prosecution, that there was no evidence capable of meeting the policy criteria. Adaway had needlessly been cross-examined on the basis of an alleged fraudulent act. The judge had wrongly exercised his discretion as it was apparent that the prosecution was oppressive. The local authority should have given better consideration to its prosecution policy before bringing the prosecution.

## R v Adomako [1995] 1 AC 171

In cases involving manslaughter by breach of a duty of care the questions are whether:

- there had existed a duty of care;
- there had been a breach of that duty;
- the breach had caused the death and, if so, whether the breach should be characterised as gross negligence and a crime?

It is for a jury to decide whether the accused's acts were so bad that in all the circumstances they amounted to a crime. It is not necessary for a judge to refer to the test of recklessness The defendant was acting as an anaesthetist during an operation when a tube from the ventilator came free, causing the death of the patient. He was convicted of manslaughter and his appeal dismissed by the Court of Appeal.

Dismissing the defendant's appeal, the question of whether the defendant's acts or omissions were so bad as to be criminal, having regard to the risk of death involved, was one for the jury and it was not appropriate to interfere with their decision.

## R v Argent [1996] EWCA Crim 1728

Argent appealed against conviction and a sentence of ten years' imprisonment for manslaughter having been indicted for murder. Following his arrest, after an anonymous call to the police, he declined to answer questions in police interviews on legal advice. The trial judge declined to admit police evidence of a first interview, but admitted the second on the grounds that it had been preceded by a positive identification. Argent contended that the judge had erred when directing the jury that it was open to them to draw an inference from Argent's silence.

The appeal was dismissed in that:
- before a jury could draw 'such inferences ... as appear proper', in terms of the Criminal Justice and Public Order Act 1994, s 34(2)(d), from an

accused's failure to mention during police questioning any fact which he subsequently relied on in his defence, six conditions had to be fulfilled. As well as the requirement for proceedings to have been started the alleged failure, which must have taken place before the defendant was charged, had to have occurred while the accused was undergoing questioning under caution, the objective of which was to establish whether or by whom the alleged offence was committed. Also, the alleged failure had to be to mention any fact which the defendant relied on in his defence, and it was for the jury to decide, as questions of fact, whether there was some fact so relied on and whether the defendant failed to mention such fact when being questioned. The relevant fact had to be one which the defendant could reasonably have been expected to mention, taking account of that particular defendant's characteristics, such as age, health and mental capacity, and legal advice, as relevant circumstances. Whilst the issue requires appropriate jury directions, the matter should then be left for the jury to decide and it would only rarely be the case that a judge should direct a jury that they should or should not draw the appropriate inference;

- with regard to sentence for an offence of manslaughter with use of a knife, seven blows with the knife were inflicted on the victim, there was no provocation, guilty plea or excuse, and in those circumstances the sentence was appropriate.

## R v Associated Octel Co Ltd [1996] 4 All ER 846

Associated Octel, a chemicals company, engaged a firm of independent contractors, RGP, to repair the lining of a tank, in the course of which RGP's employee suffered severe injury. RGP had worked under Associated Octel's 'permit to work' system, which required them to obtain approval from Associated Octel for every task undertaken and Associated Octel had to consider the safety precautions required and provide the safety equipment. Associated Octel was prosecuted under the Health and Safety at Work etc Act 1974, s 3(1) for failure to conduct its work, as far as practicable, so that persons not in its employment were not exposed to health and safety risks. Associated Octel submitted that there was no case to answer because repairing the tank was part of RGP's undertaking, and Associated Octel had no control over the way independent contractors carried out their work. The judge found that repair of the tank, whether by Associated Octel's employees or by contractors, was part of their undertaking as a chemicals firm and directed the jury accordingly, who subsequently convicted. The Court of Appeal dismissed Associated Octel's argument that the judge had wrongly rejected its submission of no case to answer. Associated Octel appealed.

The appeal was dismissed as there was a difference between an employer's vicarious liability, which in general required that an employee was acting under their contract of employment, and the duty imposed on the employer himself under s 3 of the Act. Where an employer engaged contractors to carry out work which was part of the employer's work, such as routine maintenance, the employer must take whatever steps were reasonably practicable to avoid risks to those contractors. Whether the tasks the contractor was engaged in formed part of the employer's undertaking was a question of fact for the jury. In this case, the judge in the Crown Court had directed the jury that RGP's task was part of Associated Octel's undertaking, the judge's finding was correct and, given the nature of the permit to work system and Associated Octel's provision of the safety equipment, a properly instructed jury would undoubtedly have convicted.

## R v Balfour Beatty Rail Infrastructure Services Ltd [2006] EWCA Crim 1586, [2007] Bus LR 77

It was appropriate in the interest of proportionality to reduce the fine imposed on a rail track maintenance contractor for its failure to discharge its duty as an employer under the Health and Safety at Work etc Act 1974, s 3, which had been a cause of the Hatfield rail disaster, where there was a huge disparity between the fine imposed on the contractor and the fine imposed on the co-defendant rail network owner.

The contractor had been responsible for carrying out regular visual and ultrasonic inspections of a rail track owned by Railtrack, which had primary responsibility for the safety of the track. A train had derailed after two sections of track disintegrated, causing multiple deaths and numerous injuries. Each company had been charged with corporate manslaughter and a count of a breach of s 3 of the 1974 Act. After the charges of corporate manslaughter had been dismissed, the contractor had entered a late guilty plea to the breach of s 3. Railtrack was found guilty of a breach of duty under s 3. The judge held that the contractor's failure to fulfil its duties under s 3 had been at the top of the scale. The judge found that the visual inspections were largely a useless formality as the inspectors had to walk along the outside of the track where it had been impossible to see anything of the head of the rail, the contractor had failed to consider any of the ultrasound reports and had failed to put a low emergency speed restriction on the track. The judge assessed the contractor's culpability at between two and three times that of Railtrack and fined the contractor £10 million and Railtrack £3.5 million. No discount was given for the contractor's guilty plea on the basis that it had been entered very late. The contractor submitted that:

- the judge had significantly overestimated the contractor's culpability;
- the level of the fine imposed against the contractor was excessive and the judge had erred in his assessment of the relative culpability of the two companies;
- the judge had erred in failing to make any reduction for the contractor's guilty plea as the contractor could not have reasonably been expected to plead guilty to a breach of s 3 at the time when the charges of manslaughter against itself and its employees were still being pursued.

The appeal was allowed:

- the severe terms in which the judge had castigated the contractor's breach of duty had been justified. The contractor had been contracted to carry out regular inspection of the track, visually and ultrasonically, against defects that could threaten its safety. The visual inspections had been carried out from a point that had rendered the inspection futile and the results of the ultrasonic inspections had not been considered. That situation constituted a systemic failure by the contractor of a very high order that had put large numbers of the travelling public at risk;
- the fine of £10 million imposed on the contractor was severe. There was no reason why the judge when sentencing could not properly have had regard, when considering Railtrack's culpability, to the fact that the seriousness of Railtrack's failure to ensure that the contractor had performed its duties was the greater. The differences between the sentences of the two defendants was not an automatic reason for reducing a sentence. However, in this case, the difference between the two fines was so great that there was scope for reduction in the interest of proportionality. Therefore, the fine was reduced to £7.5 million;
- the outstanding charges of manslaughter against the contractor had not precluded the contractor from pleading guilty to the s 3 offence at the outset. In the circumstances, the judge had been entitled to find that the contractor had not pleaded guilty at the first reasonable opportunity.

## R v Beckford [1996] 1 Cr App R 94

Beckford appealed against a conviction of causing death by driving without due care and attention while unfit through drink or drugs on the grounds that the proceedings ought to have been stayed as an abuse of process. Beckford had been unable to establish in his defence that a mechanical failure had caused the accident because the car was scrapped without first being examined.

The appeal was dismissed. In this case Beckford's trial had been fair despite the absence of evidence about his car. However, procedures should be established under which no car involved in an accident could be scrapped without express permission from the police. The police should not allow a car to be destroyed where serious criminal charges which might involve the possibility of a mechanical defect were pending.

## R v Beckles [2004] EWCA Crim 2766

A jury should be directed not to draw an adverse inference from a defendant's silence when interviewed by the police where they concluded that the defendant had genuinely and reasonably relied on the advice of his solicitor to remain silent.

The appellant appealed against his convictions for robbery and attempted murder, following a ruling by the European Court of Human Rights that the jury directions given by the trial judge in respect of the adverse inferences that could be drawn under the Criminal Justice and Public Order Act 1994, s 34 from his silence during a police interview had been flawed, and had contravened his right to a fair trial under the Human Rights Act 1998, Sch 1, Pt 1, Art 6.

When arrested, he had voluntarily made remarks to the police which foreshadowed the defence relied on at trial. However, in the police interview he had remained silent on the advice of his solicitor. At trial he had shown a willingness to waive legal professional privilege to enable examination of his motives for remaining silent, although this had not been pursued by the prosecution. Also, in the transcript of the police interview, the solicitor had given the reasons for her advice. The summing up had not referred to his willingness to waive privilege and had failed to specify the facts that it was alleged he relied on that he had not mentioned previously, had misdirected the jury as to the inferences which might be drawn in the light of his voluntary remarks on arrest, and did not inform the jury that they should not draw adverse inferences if they considered that his reliance on his solicitor's advice was genuine and reasonable. He submitted that in the light of these failures the trial had not been fair and the conviction was unsafe.

The appeal was allowed. Although the directions given by the judge had conformed to the Judicial Studies Board specimen direction applicable at the time, they had not met the standards laid down in *R v Hoare (Kevin)* [2004] EWCA Crim 784, [2005] 1 WLR 1804 as they had not directed the jury to consider whether he had genuinely and reasonably relied on the solicitor's advice. The proper procedure where there was a possibility of adverse inferences being drawn was for counsel and the judge to discuss the matter in the absence of the jury to see whether directions were necessary and, if so, what form they should take. In this case the defence relied on had been given in outline to the police on arrest and all the evidence suggested that his reliance on his solicitor's advice was genuine. In the circumstances a section 34 direction might not have been appropriate at all. The misdirection might have affected the jury's decision and it followed that the conviction was unsafe. A retrial was ordered.

## R v Beedie [1997] 2 Cr App R 167, CA

Beedie, a landlord, appealed against his conviction of manslaughter following the death of a tenant from carbon monoxide poisoning caused by a defective gas heater. Beedie had previously pleaded guilty to offences under the Health and Safety at Work etc Act 1974 and the Housing Act 1985 in respect of the same incident, but at trial his plea of autrefois convict (previously convicted), was rejected by the trial judge. Beedie argued that the judge had been wrong to reject his plea on the basis that it could only have been accepted if both offences bore the same legal characteristics, and had erred in exercising his discretion by refusing to stay the indictment.

The appeal was allowed and the conviction quashed. The majority of the House of Lords had identified the narrow principle of autrefois convict which applied only where the same offence was alleged in the second indictment as in the first and had ruled that it was for the judge to exercise discretion in other appropriate cases. Although the trial judge in this case had analysed the issues correctly, he had exercised his discretion wrongly by failing to consider whether any special circumstances existed, by carrying out a balancing exercise which was inappropriate and by taking into account the possibility of a fair trial. A stay of proceedings would have been the appropriate course as the manslaughter indictment arose from the same facts as the earlier prosecutions. Furthermore, the continuance of the trial offended the principle that there should be no sequential prosecutions for offences of greater gravity.

## R v Boal [1992] 3 All ER 177

The Fire Precautions Act 1971, s 23, is intended to fix with criminal liability persons who have real power to decide corporate policy. Boal was employed by a company as assistant manager of its bookshop and had responsibility for the day-to-day running of the shop. He had been given no training as to the health and safety aspects of his job. On a day when the general manager was away on holiday, serious breaches were found in the requirements of the fire certificate. The company and Boal were charged with offences under the 1971 Act. Boal was given legal advice that he was a 'manager' within s 23(1), and pleaded guilty.

Boal's appeal against conviction was allowed, as criminal liability was for those who were in positions of real authority, who had the power to decide policy. It was probable that Boal had a good defence in law, of which he had been deprived through no fault of his own. Despite Boal's unequivocal plea, the conviction was quashed.

## R v Chaaban [2003] EWCA Crim 1012

The defendant's right to a fair trial was not inconsistent with proper judicial control over the use of time. Chaaban appealed against a conviction for blackmail and against a sentence of six years' imprisonment for the offence. Chaaban had been employed by the victim, who was a wealthy widow, and had introduced her to M, his co-defendant. M and the victim had a sexual relationship, which was kept secret as the victim's family would not have approved. Chaaban and M set up a secret camera in a hotel room and made a video recording of M and the victim having sexual intercourse. The victim was sent a copy of the tape and a demand for £750,000. Chaaban contended that:

- the judge's handling of the case was unsatisfactory in that he did not allow a defence application for an adjournment;
- the judge had imposed a timetable for the trial, and there was an overall impression that the trial was being rushed with little regard for its fairness; and
- there was fresh evidence which undermined the safety of his conviction.

The appeals against conviction and sentence were dismissed as:

- the judge was responsible for the management of the trial, and had to strike a balance between the needs of everyone involved in the case and the need for justice to be done swiftly. A judge should refuse an adjournment unless satisfied that it was necessary and justified. In this case there was nothing to support the view that an adjournment was justified;
- the judge was also responsible for controlling the timetable of the trial and could exercise his powers to ensure that the trial ended by a certain date; and
- the fresh evidence was not capable of belief and did not serve to undermine the safety of Chaaban's conviction.

As to the appeal against sentence, the judge had taken into account Chaaban's good character and the impact that the sentence would have on his family. However, the blackmail was carefully planned and had targeted a vulnerable victim who trusted Chaaban. The victim had been severely affected by the ordeal. M had been entitled to receive a discounted sentence of four years' imprisonment because he gave evidence for the Crown. Chaaban's sentence was not excessive or wrong in principle and the distinction that the judge made between Chaaban and M was proper.

## R v Chandler [2015] EWCA Crim 1825

An order disqualifying a company director for five years following his guilty pleas to three regulatory offences was quashed as the judge had failed to identify the misconduct which was said to have made the director unfit.

Chandler appealed against an order disqualifying him from being a director for five years pursuant to the Company Directors Disqualification Act 1986, s 2. Chandler's company had acquired two motor vehicles in a car auction. The vehicles were later advertised for sale on eBay with mileage that was substantially less than the actual mileage. Chandler pleaded guilty to three regulatory offences of engaging in a commercial practice which was a misleading action, contrary to the Consumer Protection from Unfair Trading Regulations 2008, SI 2008/1277, reg 9. In his basis of plea, he indicated that a company employee had altered the mileage on the vehicle odometers without his knowledge, however he accepted liability as managing director for the misrepresentations even though he had no personal knowledge of them. The judge imposed fines of £1,250 for each offence with a period of ten weeks' imprisonment in default and a victim surcharge order. Without warning, the judge then made the disqualification order.

The appeal was allowed.

The judge had not identified the conduct which was said to have made Chandler unfit to be a company director for the purposes of s 6 of the Act. That problem was exacerbated because three offences of fraud which were also on the indictment, and which might have been evidence of such misconduct, were not pursued and were abandoned in favour of the regulatory offences. The regulatory offences were ones of strict liability incurred as a director and they did not suggest any personal misconduct by Chandler. It was always possible that there had been misconduct by Chandler's failure to supervise the commercial activities of the company for which he had responsibility. However, without any further investigation, there was nothing in the basis of plea that would have founded a factual basis of misconduct. The judge was not bound by the basis of plea, but if he was going to depart from it he should have indicated his intention and given Chandler an opportunity to give evidence and address the particular issues. That was not done. Furthermore, Chandler's previous conviction for fraudulent use of a vehicle licence registration document was disregarded by the judge and thus could not form the basis of the relevant misconduct. If he was going to pursue a director's disqualification, he needed to ensure that Chandler had proper notice of what allegations of misconduct within the meaning of the statute he faced and had an opportunity to make informed submissions about them. The disqualification was something of an afterthought, not anticipated when mitigation was addressed, and not something that had been sought by the prosecuting authority. Accordingly, the disqualification order was quashed.

## R v Chargot [2008] UKHL 73

In proceedings brought under the Health and Safety at Work etc Act 1974 the prosecution only had to prove that the result described in those sections had not been achieved or prevented. A prima facie case of breach had then been established, unless the defendant could make good the reasonable practicability defence. Prosecutors had to do more than simply assert that a state of affairs existed, but they did not have to identify and prove specific breaches of duty. The overriding test was whether or not defendants had been given fair notice of the claim against them.

Chargot appealed against the dismissal of their appeals against convictions for failure to comply with the duties laid down in the Health and Safety at Work etc Act 1974, ss 2(1), 3(1) and 37.

An employee of the company had died when the dumper truck he was driving fell onto its side and buried him in a load of spoil that was being transported at the time. The issues for determination were:

- the scope of the duties imposed on an employer by ss 2(1) and 3(1) of the Act;
- whether, in proceedings under those sections, it was sufficient for the prosecution merely to prove a risk of injury arising from a state of affairs at work or whether it needed to go on to identify and prove specific breaches of duty;
- whether the onus on employers was proportionate;
- the required standard of proof for a prosecution under s 37 of the Act.

The appeal was dismissed.

*Cases*

- An employer had to ensure the health and safety at work of all his employees and had to ensure that persons not employed by him were not exposed to risks to their health and safety. Sections 2(1) and 3(1) therefore described a result which an employer had to achieve or prevent; they did not prescribe a particular means of achieving that result. In order to establish a breach, the prosecution had to prove that the result had not been achieved or prevented. The onus then passed to the defendant to make good the defence provided by s 40 on the ground of reasonable practicability.
- Even where an injury had occurred, it may not be enough for a prosecutor simply to assert that the injury demonstrated a health and safety risk. It would often be necessary to identify and prove the respects in which there had been a breach of duty. That was likely to require evidence of the particular risk that had arisen rather than a simple assertion that a state of affairs existed. Identification of the risk required an analysis of the facts on a case-by-case basis. Prosecutors gave varying amounts of detail when formulating charges. In England and Wales, the prevailing practice was for the statement of offence to be accompanied by particulars in which the facts and circumstances were set out, but the overriding test was that of fair notice approved. It was not the case that prosecution allegations had to be specifically proved, nor should a jury be directed to convict only if they were unanimous as to which allegations had been made out. As long as the jury agreed about the result that the employer had to achieve or prevent, they did not need to agree on all the details of the evidence.
- Regarding proportionality, the law did not aim to create an environment that was entirely risk-free. The word 'risk' in the Act meant material risks to health and safety that any person would appreciate and take steps to guard against. Section 2 and s 3 imposed duties on employers who might reasonably be expected to accept the general principles on which those sections were based and to have the means of fulfilling that responsibility. The placing of a legal burden of proof on the employer was not disproportionate.
- In a prosecution under s 37 of the Act, there was no fixed rule as to what had to be proved to establish that an officer's state of mind amounted to consent, connivance or neglect. Where the officer's place of activity was remote from the work place or what was done there was not under his immediate direction or control, quite detailed evidence might be required, of which fair notice would have to be given. Where the officer was in day-to-day contact with the place of activity, little more than what was required to establish a breach under s 2 or s 3 might be needed. An officer had to be proved to know the material facts which constituted the offence by the body corporate and to have agreed to its conduct on the basis of those facts, but consent could be established by inference as well as by proof of an express agreement. The state of mind contemplated by the words 'connivance' and 'neglect' could also be established by inference. Where it was shown that a company had failed to achieve or prevent the result contemplated by s 2(1) and s 3(1), it would be a relatively short step for the inference to be drawn that there was connivance or neglect on his part if the circumstances under which the risk arose were under the direction or control of the officer.

## R v Cheshire [1991] 1 WLR 844

The victim had died following negligent medical treatment received for his injuries and the jury had to decide whether they were satisfied that the accused's acts made a significant contribution to the victim's death. The victim had been shot in the leg and stomach and was taken to hospital and placed in intensive care. He developed respiratory problems and a tracheotomy tube was placed in his windpipe to assist his breathing. More than two months after the shooting, he died of cardio-respiratory arrest due to obstruction of the windpipe due to the tracheotomy. The person who shot the victim was charged with murder. A consultant surgeon gave evidence for the defence at the trial that the leg and stomach wounds were no longer life-threatening at the time of actual death and that death had been caused by negligent medical treatment. The judge directed the jury that the person who shot the victim was responsible for the death unless the medical staff had been reckless in their treatment of the deceased. The person who shot the deceased was convicted and appealed.

The appeal was dismissed as the jury did not have to evaluate competing causes of the death or choose the dominant cause. The jury had to decide whether they were satisfied that the accused's acts could fairly be said to have made a significant contribution to the victim's death. The judge had to direct the jury that they had to be satisfied that the Crown had proved that the acts of the accused caused the death, and that the acts need not be the sole or even the main cause of death, it was sufficient that his acts contributed significantly to the death. Even though negligent medical treatment was the immediate cause of death, that should not exclude the accused's responsibility unless the negligent treatment was so independent of his acts and in itself so potent in causing death that the jury regarded the contribution made by his acts as insignificant. Although the trial judge erred, no miscarriage of justice had occurred, since the medical, and rare, complication was a direct consequence of the accused's acts which remained a significant cause of death.

## R v Cornish [2016] EWHC 779 (QB)

Although corporate manslaughter charges against an NHS trust had been dismissed on the basis of no case to answer, the trust was unsuccessful in seeking to recover the costs it incurred in defending the proceedings. Since the testimony of the Crown's expert, although unconvincing, was not plainly wrong in a way that should have been obvious to the Crown, the decision to prosecute could not be regarded as improper.

A patient died due to the mismanagement of her recovery from an anaesthetic. Corporate manslaughter proceedings were brought against the trust on the grounds that:

- the staff in question were not appropriately qualified for the posts they held and should not have been appointed;
- that their shortcomings would have been apparent to the trust if it had carried out a proper appraisal process;
- that the supervision on the day in question was inadequate.

*Cases*

The court held that, although there was evidence to support an allegation of breach of duty in relation to the supervisory structure, there were insurmountable problems as to the extent to which that failure caused the patient's death. The allegations of failure in respect of appointment and appraisal were strenuously supported by the Crown's expert who, according to the trust, was an unreliable witness.

The Crown submitted that the trust should have applied prior to the trial for the case against it to be dismissed.

The application was refused.

- According to the Prosecution of Offences Act 1985, s 19(1) and the Costs in Criminal Cases (General) Regulations 1986, reg 3(1), the court might award costs in favour of a party to criminal proceedings who had incurred such costs as a result of 'an unnecessary or improper act or omission' by another party. Improper conduct means an act or omission that would not have occurred if the party concerned had conducted his case properly. The test was one of impropriety, not merely unreasonableness. A failed prosecution, even where the defendant was found to have no case to answer, was not in itself sufficient to overcome the threshold criteria for a section 19 costs order. The conduct of the prosecution had to be so starkly improper that no great investigation into the facts or decision-making process was necessary to establish it. Even where a case failed as a matter of law, the charge was not necessarily improper since many legal points were properly arguable. It was important that section 19 applications were not used to attack decisions to prosecute by way of a collateral challenge: the courts had to be vigilant to avoid imposing too high a burden or standard on a public prosecuting authority in respect of prosecution decisions. Accordingly, a successful section 19 application would be very rare and would be restricted to those exceptional cases where the prosecution had made a clear and stark error as a result of which a defendant had incurred costs justifying compensation.
- The problems about how the supervisory deficiencies contributed to the patient's death were not necessarily apparent at the time of the decision to prosecute. So, on that basis alone the decision to prosecute the trust for corporate manslaughter could not be regarded as improper. A case such as this one depended heavily on expert evidence, since the facts were not in dispute. In accordance with the Code for Crown Prosecutors, the Crown had reviewed the prosecution between the issue of proceedings and the trial and there was nothing which should have led it to conclude that its expert was unreliable. There was a significant burden on the Crown's expert to identify and then convey his views in such a way as to give rise to a case to answer. In this case, the Crown's expert had formed his views too early and was at times cavalier in his attitude. His unconvincing responses in cross-examination were the main reason for the finding of no case to answer. However, it could not be said that his testimony was plainly wrong in a way that should have been obvious to the Crown. Justice had manifestly been done and it was not possible to say that the decision to prosecute, or the continuation of the prosecution, were improper.

- The trust's failure to apply for dismissal of the case was not relevant, as that was tantamount to an argument that the court should assess the reasonableness of the decision to prosecute by reference to the defendant's reaction to it.

## R v DPP, ex p Manning [2000] EWHC Admin 342

The sisters of AM, who had died of asphyxia whilst being restrained by prison officers, applied for judicial review of the decision of the DPP not to prosecute any of the officers involved. A coroner's inquest found that the asphyxia had been attributable to the way in which AM had been held by one of the prison officers and returned a verdict of unlawful killing. Following police investigations into the incident, the papers were passed on to a special casework lawyer of the Crown Prosecution Service (CPS), who concluded that there was insufficient evidence to create a realistic prospect of conviction. A senior CPS caseworker assigned to review the decision not to prosecute determined that the responses of the prison officers during cross-examination at the coroner's inquest tended to support the allegation that excessive force had been used. However, whilst able to establish which officer was responsible for causing the asphyxiation, the caseworker concluded that insufficient evidence existed to support a criminal prosecution and therefore the case did not have a realistic prospect of success. This decision was subsequently communicated to the solicitors acting for AM's sisters by a letter and a press release issued by the DPP the following day. It was contended that:

- while no general duty existed for the CPS to give reasons for a decision not to prosecute, the circumstances of this case imposed an obligation to supply coherent and sensible reasons for their decision;
- the caseworker had erred in his application of the Code for Crown Prosecutors.

The application was allowed:

- while the DPP was not under a general duty to give reasons for a decision not to prosecute, it was reasonable where no compelling grounds existed, that in circumstances where an individual had died whilst in the custody of the State and a properly directed inquest had reached a verdict that the killing had been unlawful, reasons should be given for a decision not to prosecute. The coroner's verdict had created an expectation that a prosecution would result. Therefore, it was desirable that the DPP in deciding to go against such an expectation should provide grounds for that decision;
- the caseworker had failed to take into account certain critical evidential matters and had applied, in considering the prospect of success, a higher test than was required under the provisions of the code. The code required that a prosecution, if brought would 'more likely than not', result in a conviction. The CPS was not required to establish an equivalent standard of proof as that of a jury or magistrates' court when considering whether or not to bring a conviction.

## R v Ensor [2009] EWCA Crim 2519

Where a psychiatrist's report stating that a defendant would have difficulty in giving evidence, had been requested by the defence two weeks before trial, its service one week into the trial and after the decision had been made that the defendant should not give evidence was a breach of the Criminal Procedure Rules 2005 (CPR).

Ensor appealed against convictions for robbery, possessing a firearm, and possessing, using or acquiring criminal property. Some two weeks before the start of his trial, Ensor was examined by a psychiatrist at the request of his solicitors. Five days later, the psychiatrist produced a report stating that Ensor would feel extreme difficulty in giving evidence at trial and that the stress of appearing in court could become counterproductive to his mental health. Ensor's solicitors received the report over the weekend before the start of the trial, and his counsel saw it on the first day of the trial. One week after the trial had begun, Ensor and his advisers decided that he should not give evidence. Ensor then served the report on the prosecution and applied for it to be admitted in evidence. The judge refused the application to adduce the report on the grounds that its service so late was a grave breach of the CPR and the decision to serve the report only after a decision had been made not to call Ensor had been a deliberate tactical ploy.

Ensor argued that the judge had been wrong to refuse the application, as it contained evidence that would have demonstrated to the court that his mental condition was such as to make it undesirable for him to give evidence, within the meaning of the Criminal Justice and Public Order Act 1994, s 35(1)(b), in which case the judge would have had to direct the jury not to draw any adverse inferences from his failure to give evidence.

The appeal was dismissed.

- The judge had been entitled to refuse to allow the report to go before the jury. The effect of CPR, r 1.2 and r 3.3 together was that it was incumbent on both prosecution and defence to alert the court and the other side at the earliest practical moment if it was or might be intending to adduce expert evidence. That should be done if possible at a plea and case management hearing, and if not then, as soon as the possibility became live. The nearer to the start of the trial, the greater the urgency, so that the court and the other side could take appropriate steps to manage the expert evidence in an efficient way. Ensor had failed totally to comply with either the spirit or the letter of the CPR. The psychiatrist must have been instructed well before he saw Ensor, but the prosecution and the court had not been informed. Even accepting that defence counsel had not received the report until the first day of trial, there was no excuse for the failure to inform the prosecution and the court for a week after that. The judge had been correct to find that Ensor was in grave breach of the CPR, and that the decision not to serve the report until after a decision had been made for Ensor not to give evidence had been a tactical ploy. It had been an attempt to ambush the prosecution.

- That a physical or mental condition might merely cause difficulty in giving evidence was not enough to satisfy s 35(1)(b). The psychiatrist's opinion did not demonstrate that Ensor's mental condition made it undesirable for him to give evidence. Although he said that Ensor would have had extreme difficulty in giving evidence, that was quite common among defendants and witnesses and did not in itself make it undesirable that he should do so. His opinion that the stress of appearing could become counterproductive to Ensor's mental health stated a possibility only: there was no certainty that it would adversely affect his mental health so that giving evidence was undesirable.

## R v F Howe & Son [1999] 2 All ER 249

There was an appeal against the imposition of a fine in respect of four offences under the Health and Safety at Work etc Act 1974 and related regulations. The Court of Appeal gave guidance on the factors to be taken into account by courts when imposing such penalties, in the light of concern that the level of fines currently being set for such offences was too low and increasing recognition of the seriousness of this type of offence.

The aim of the Act was to ensure a safe environment for workers and members of the public and fines needed to be large enough to convey that message to both management and shareholders but, in general, not so large as to put a company at risk of bankruptcy. In determining the seriousness of an offence, it was often useful to consider how far short of the appropriate standard the defendant had fallen, the standard of care being the same for small organisations as for large. Other relevant matters might be the degree of risk and extent of the danger involved, the defendant's resources and the effect of a fine on its business. Aggravating features included failure to pay attention to warnings, deliberate breach of the regulations for the purposes of profit or saving money, and loss of life. Mitigating features included an early admission of responsibility and plea of guilty, the taking of action to remedy any breach brought to the company's notice and a good safety record. It was for a defendant seeking to make representations about their financial position to provide copies of its accounts to the court and the prosecution in good time. There was no reason why a defendant in a position to pay the whole of the prosecution costs as well as the fine should not be made to do so.

## R v Friskies Petcare (UK) Ltd [2000] EWCA Crim 95

Friskies Petcare appealed against the sentence which had been imposed on them following their guilty plea to an offence under the Health and Safety at Work etc Act 1974. Having taken into account all relevant factors, the court reduced the fine imposed on Friskies Petcare from £600,000 to £250,000. The court also recommended that in the case of prosecutions under the 1974 Act, the Health and Safety Executive should, at the outset of proceedings, provide a document setting out not only the facts of the case but also any aggravating features of the offence, and that, in the event of a guilty plea, the defendant should submit a list of any mitigating circumstances to be taken into account.

Friskies Petcare had appealed against a fine of £600,000 imposed after pleading guilty before a magistrates' court for failing to discharge the duty imposed by the Health and Safety at Work etc Act 1974, s. 2(1) and contravening reg 3 of the Management of Health and Safety at Work Regulations 1992, SI 1992/2051. Friskies Petcare was a large manufacturing concern operating a factory manufacturing pet food. Two technicians went into a silo to repair a stirrer and, in the course of carrying out this process, one of the technicians apparently suffered an electric shock and died from electrocution. The inspector concluded that the electrocution was the result of the deceased coming into contact with the exposed and live parts of the welding electrode. The voltage in use was substantially above the threshold at which precautions were required to be taken to control risk of electrocution when work was carried out in a confined or conductive location, or in wet or damp conditions. There was no system in place which alerted the technicians to the risk inherent in their activities. The system had been in operation for three years before the factory came into the ownership of Friskies Petcare about three months before the accident. The underlying cause of death was that welding with a potentially lethal voltage was taking place in a confined, conductive and damp environment. No proper risk assessment of the activity had been done and no steps had been taken to avoid it.

The appeal was allowed. The aggravating features of the case were:

- the death of the technician;
- the inaccessible position of the off switch;
- the fact that the breaches had been going on for some time;
- the fact that no employee had been alerted to the relevant Health and Safety Executive pamphlets; and
- that Friskies Petcare conducted no assessment of the risk involved in repairing stirrers on site.

The mitigating factors were:

- Friskies Petcare's prompt admission and plea of guilty; and
- their good health and safety record.

The court took into account the financial position of Friskies Petcare who had a substantial business with a considerable turnover generating pre-tax profits of £40 million. Taking those factors into account the court considered that the appropriate fine was £250,000.

# R v Galbraith (1981) 73 Cr App R 124

On a submission of no case the judge ought to stop the case only when there is either no evidence, or the evidence is so tenuous that taken at its highest a jury could not properly convict. Galbraith was charged with affray. There were passages in the evidence of two witnesses which tended to show that Galbraith had taken part in the affray, though in his statement to the police Galbraith had made denials. A submission of no case was rejected. Galbraith made an exculpatory statement (ie favourable to him), from the dock, and was convicted.

The appeal was dismissed. Where the case turned on the credibility of witnesses or where on one possible view of the facts there was sufficient evidence to convict, then the matter must be left to the jury.

## R v Gateway Foodmarkets Ltd [1997] 3 All ER 78

Following the death of a duty manager at a supermarket who fell through a trap door in the lift control room, Gateway were convicted of a section 2(1) offence under the Health and Safety at Work etc Act 1974. Gateway appealed. The employee had entered the room to free the lift, which had become jammed, by hand. This was a regular, though unauthorised, practice of which head office was unaware. The duty manager failed to notice that the trap door had been left open by contractors. The judge ruled that s 2(1) established strict liability for breaches of duty by the company's servants. Gateway pleaded guilty in response to the ruling, but argued that the head office was remote from the local store and that the company's 'directing mind' was not responsible.

The appeal was dismissed. Under s 2(1) the company was responsible for a failure at store management level to ensure safety. Section 3(1) of the Act dealt with liability for the health and safety of those who were not employees. Both sections contained the wording 'the duty of every employer', and both were to be interpreted so as to impose liability in the event of a failure to ensure safety unless all reasonable precautions had been taken, not only by the company itself but by servants and agents on its behalf. The prosecution did not have to establish that the company's 'directing mind', ie the senior employees who embodied the company, had failed to take all reasonable precautions.

## R v Goodman [1993] 2 All ER 789

An indictable offence in connection with the management of a company was an offence with a relevant factual connection to the management of the company. Goodman pleaded guilty to an offence under the Company Securities (Insider Dealing) Act 1985 and was sentenced to a term of imprisonment and disqualified from being a company director for ten years. He appealed against the disqualification, contending that the court had no power to make such an order.

The appeal was dismissed. The Company Directors Disqualification Act 1986, s 2 gave the court power to disqualify where a person is convicted of an indictable offence 'in connection with the management of a company'. That meant that there had to be some relevant factual connection with the management of the company, but the test was not stricter than that. Such a connection did exist in Goodman's case.

## R (Health and Safety Executive) v ATE Truck and Trailer Sales Ltd [2018] EWCA Crim 752

The court emphasised that while a basis of plea and sensible agreement between parties was encouraged and expected to be weighed carefully by the court before departing from it, such agreement was not binding on the court as a matter of constitutional principle.

In the instant case, the sentencing judge had had insufficient justification for departing from the parties' agreement, and a fine of £475,000 following a company's guilty plea to an offence under the Management of Health and Safety at Work Regulations 1999, SI 1999/3242, reg 3(1)(a) was reduced to £200,000.

The company appealed against the imposition of a £475,000 fine following its guilty plea to failing to provide a suitable and sufficient risk assessment as required by the Management of Health and Safety at Work Regulations 1999, reg 3(1)(a) in relation to its employees.

The company dealt in trucks and trailers. A contractor worked independently from the company's employees in a designated area and died when the roof section of a trailer he was dismantling struck him. The Health and Safety Executive (HSE) concluded that his method of work was unsafe. The company's employees dismantled trailers using a different method. The company had health and safety procedures and systems in place, but no written risk assessments for the activity of dismantling trailers when conducted by employees. In relation to the Definitive Sentencing Guideline on Health and Safety Offences, Corporate Manslaughter and Food Safety and Hygiene Offences, the parties agreed that the offence was low culpability, level A harm, and had a more than minimal, negligible or trivial connection with the accident leading to the contractor's death, but that it was not a major cause. They disagreed as to the likelihood of harm. The HSE claimed that it was medium, the company claimed that it was low. The HSE did not criticise the company's dismantling method for its employees, other than the fact that there was no evidence of a written risk assessment. In calculating the fine, the sentencing judge found that culpability and the likelihood of harm were both high.

The appeal was allowed. The court outlined several steps to be taken when carrying out the sentencing exercise. It emphasised that it was not straitjacketed by the guideline and that a death substantially increased a sentence.

- Basis of plea: the agreement between the parties and the court's role – the judge had departed significantly from the agreement and views of the parties, particularly in relation to the level of culpability and the likelihood of harm arising. While sensible agreement between the parties was encouraged and expected to be weighed carefully by the court before departing from it, such agreement was not binding on the court as a matter of constitutional principle. Accordingly, the judge had been entitled not to concur with the agreement.
- Basis of plea: analysis and causation – the causal link to the contractor's death essential to the company's guilty plea involved a concession that

its failure to provide a suitable and sufficient risk assessment for its own employees had resulted in a failure to communicate that risk assessment to the contractor, therefore a 'more than minimal, negligible or trivial' connection with his death. The judge therefore had to concentrate on the method of work followed and the frequency of work undertaken by the company's own employees, not the contractor.
- Application of guideline: culpability – there was insufficient justification for categorising the case as high culpability. The judge had assessed culpability by reference to the method adopted by the contractor. That was not in accordance with the basis of plea and strayed into a separate count on which no evidence had been offered. While the absence of a risk assessment for its own employees was a failure on the company's part, no other criticism of its methods had been made by the HSE. Insofar as the judge had regard to the breach subsisting 'over a long period of time', he went outside the period of the indictment, focusing on the work done by the contractor rather than by employees.
- Application of guideline: harm – the seriousness of harm risked was death, and therefore level A. The judge had considered that there was a high likelihood of such harm arising. However, he seemed to have been influenced by consideration of the contractor's, rather than the company's, method of work. The fact that there was no risk assessment in place pointed to something other than a low likelihood of harm
- Application of guideline: paragraph 2(i) – The judge erred in holding that para 2(i) 'whether the offence exposed several workers or members of the public to harm', applied. He had been focused on the work undertaken by the contractor when the relevant activity was the work done by the company's employees. Even if that was wrong, the evidence fell short of showing that the contractor's activity had exposed several workers or members of the public to the risk of harm. With regard to para 2(ii), there had been a death and, on the company's basis of plea, the offence was a more than minimal, negligible or trivial cause of it. The fact of death was a significant aggravating factor that could justify a move to the top of the next category range.

The company was a medium organisation in turnover terms and the case was low culpability falling within harm category 2. The starting point was therefore £40,000, with a range of £14,000 to £100,000. To reflect the application of para 2(ii) and to have a real economic impact, the right course was to move harm to the top of the range for category 1 harm, namely £300,000. That was reduced by one-third to take account of the guilty plea. The original fine was quashed and replaced with one of £200,000.

# R v HM Coroner for Greater London, ex p Ridley [1985] 1 WLR 1347

Although a coroner has jurisdiction over a body while in their possession the power to order a post-mortem is not exclusive to the coroner, and they could be directed to give consent to one. On Saturday, 3 August 1985 the deceased was taken into police custody and about 10 pm found unconscious in his cell. He was taken to hospital and found to be dead on arrival. On the Monday, 5 August, the widow's solicitor learnt that a post-mortem was being held that morning but, there being insufficient time to attend, she arranged with the coroner's office for a second post-mortem. On 9 August she heard that the coroner had refused permission for a second post-mortem. She applied for judicial review to quash this decision and to order the coroner to give her consent to the holding of a second post-mortem.

Her application was granted. Although the coroner had jurisdiction over the body while it was in their possession and her consent to a second post-mortem was required, the power to order a post-mortem was not exclusively with them. There were insufficient grounds advanced by the coroner for their refusal to order a second post-mortem, and their decision was unsustainable and would be quashed. They would be directed to give consent for a second post-mortem as soon as practicable.

## R v Honey Rose [2017] EWCA Crim 1168

An optometrist was found not guilty of the gross negligence manslaughter of a young boy where she had breached her statutory duty of care to examine the internal structure of his eyes as part of a routine eye examination and consequently failed to identify an abnormality on the optic nerve which ultimately led to his death. That was not enough to find a case of gross negligence manslaughter as there had not been a 'serious and obvious risk of death' at the time of the breach.

In February 2012, she conducted a routine eye test and examination on a boy aged seven and recorded no issues of concern. Under the Opticians Act 1989, s 26(1), an optometrist had a statutory duty of care to examine the internal eye structure as part of a routine eye examination, to detect signs of abnormality or disease including life threatening problems evident from the optic nerve. Five months after the examination, while at school, the boy was taken ill. He died in hospital later the same day. Expert opinion was that the cause of his death was acute hydrocephalus, and that the obstruction in his brain had been a longstanding chronic problem, although he had not presented with many associated symptoms. His condition was said to have been treatable up to the point of acute deterioration and death. The appellant maintained that she had had problems with her examination of him as he had had poor fixation and slight photophobia. She accepted that her failure to examine the back of the eye without a good reason was a breach of her duty of care. Retinal images taken of his eyes during the sight test showed swelling of the optic nerve. The experts agreed that a competent optometrist would have known the significance of that swelling and would immediately have referred the case on to others. The judge rejected a submission of no case to answer, determining that the appellant had failed to conduct a full internal examination of the boy's eyes, there was no good reason for that failure, and thus she had breached her duty of care. He further found that the risk of death caused by the breach of duty was reasonably foreseeable. He directed the jury to consider whether that risk would have been obvious to a reasonably competent optometrist with the knowledge that the appellant would have had 'if she had not acted in breach of her duty to investigate the true position' and in addition, whether her conduct was so bad as to amount to a criminal omission.

The appellant submitted that the submission of no case to answer was wrongly rejected because the judge had applied the wrong test, and in addition that the judge had erred in his directions to the jury as to the elements of gross negligence manslaughter.

## R v HT-M Ltd [2006] EWCA Crim 1156, [2006] ICR 1383

The jury were asked to consider whether the defendant had done all that was reasonably practicable and could not be prevented from providing evidence in support of their case that it had taken all reasonable steps to eliminate the likelihood of the event occurring.

The Health and Safety Executive appealed against rulings given in a preparatory hearing of an action brought against the employer for the alleged failure to discharge its duty under the Health and Safety at Work etc Act 1974, s 2(1). The employer had provided traffic management services to contractors resurfacing a road. The traffic was subject to contraflow arrangements lit by mobile towers that extended to an operating height of 9.1m. Overhead power cables, that in places were as low as 7.5m above ground level, crossed the road. Following instructions from the contractors, two of the employees attempted to move one of the towers when fully extended, but it made contact with the cables and both were fatally injured. The employer wished to provide evidence at trial to establish that it had taken all reasonably practicable steps to:

- ensure the safety of the employees;
- that the accident was a result of the employees' own actions; and
- that it could not be foreseen that they would act in that way.

In a preparatory hearing, the judge ruled that evidence of foreseeability was admissible as it was relevant to the case alleged against the employer, particularly with regard to the reasonable practicability of it ensuring the health, safety and welfare of its employees, and that the Management of Health and Safety at Work Regulations 1999, SI 1999/3242, reg 21 and did not preclude the employer from relying upon any act or default of its employees in its defence. The Health and Safety Executive submitted that foreseeability played no part in the exercise of determining whether the duty under s 2 of the 1974 Act had been met, and where foreseeability was an element in any obligation in a health and safety context it was expressly provided for the employer was precluded from relying on any act or default of either of its employees in order to avoid liability, pursuant to reg 21 of the Regulations.

*Cases*

The appeal was dismissed in that:
- foreseeability was a tool with which to assess the likelihood of a risk causing injury or damage, it was not a means of permitting a defendant to bring concepts of fault appropriate to civil proceedings into the equation by the back door. However, a defendant to a charge under s 2 or indeed s 3 or s 4 of the 1974 Act, in asking the jury to consider whether it had established that it had done all that was reasonably practicable, could not be prevented from providing evidence as to the likelihood of the incidence of the relevant risk causing and injury in support of its case that it had taken all reasonable means to eliminate it. The phrase 'so far as [was] reasonably practicable' in s 2(1) qualified the word 'ensure' in that section;
- the employer would be entitled to put before the jury evidence to show that what had happened was purely the fault of one or both of its employees. If the jury was persuaded that everything had been done by or on behalf of the employer to prevent the accident from happening, it would be entitled to be acquitted.

## R v Ineos Chlorvinyls Ltd [2016] EWCA Crim 607

A fine of £166,650 imposed on a company following its guilty plea to an offence contrary to the Environmental Permitting (England and Wales) Regulations 2010, SI 2010/675, regs 12(1), 38(1)(a) and 39(1) was not excessive where the company had negligently failed to inspect a filter, the failure of which caused 500 litres of caustic soda to enter a canal. In setting the level of the fine, the judge had been entitled to take into account the turnover of the company and the available resources of its parent company.

Ineos Chlorvinyls Ltd appealed against a fine imposed following its guilty plea to an offence contrary to the Environmental Permitting (England and Wales) Regulations 2010, regs12(1), 38(1)(a) and 39(1).

In 2012, approximately 500 litres of caustic soda escaped into a canal whilst being pumped from the Ineos Chlorvinyls Ltd's premises onto a ship after a filter, through which the chemical was being pumped under pressure, failed. The company informed the Environment Agency, who assessed that the chemical would have sunk to the bottom of the canal. There were no signs of dead fish or other environmental harm. The company's own investigation found that the main caustic soda transfer system was regularly inspected, but that the filter had not been part of that relevant inspection regime as it had not been registered. The judge found that the offence fell within the negligence category in the sentencing guidelines and noted that the starting point for a large organisation within that category was a fine of £60,000. He stated that the company had not been intent on cost cutting to maximise profit and that the problem arose because it had failed to follow a proper system of inspection. Although that failure was negligent, it could not be said that there was a systematic problem or lax attitude. It was an isolated event and the company had a very good record in respect of health and safety and environmental matters. He noted the turnover of the company and stated that the fact that it was loss making was not significant as it was able to obtain finance from its parent company. The judge adopted a starting point of £250,000, to which he applied a one-third reduction for the guilty plea leading to a fine of £166,650.

The company argued that the judge wrongly:

- categorised the offence as negligent;
- focused on the question of turnover and had adopted a starting point associated with a more serious level of culpability.

The appeal was dismissed.

There were numerous features in the evidence which entitled the judge to find that the offence was properly categorised as negligent. Those features included the fact that:

- the filter had not been inspected on purchase;
- the filter was not registered so that it would be subject to periodic testing;
- none of the operatives noted or acted upon the fact that the filter was missing the relevant pressure valve number;
- the filter was an important piece of equipment whose failure could have had dramatic consequences;
- it was critical that such equipment was rigorously subject to inspection and maintenance;
- the filter had been in the possession of the company for a number of years and used on a number of occasions;
- there was a failure to enforce a proper system for avoiding the commission of the offence;
- it was not a case where the defect was of such a nature that reasonable steps could not have detected it.

The company's turnover was vastly larger than the indicative figure given in the guidelines for 'a large' organisation. The guideline stated that where a company's turnover greatly exceeded the threshold for large companies, it might be necessary to move outside the suggested range to achieve a proportionate sentence. Furthermore, although the company had had some losses, the judge had been entitled to take the resources of any linked organisation available to the company into account. The fine represented the company's turnover within an hour-and-a half. Accordingly, the fine was a mere pinprick in the company's finances. It was impossible to say that it was excessive in any respect.

## R v Mirza (Zulfiqar Baig) [2012] EWCA Crim 3074

A suspended custodial sentence was imposed in respect of multiple breaches of the Regulatory Reform (Fire Safety) Order 2005, SI 2005/1541 and this was not wrong in principle given the offender's history of failure to comply with previous assessments and enforcement notices, but the unpaid work requirement of 200 hours was excessive given the offender's circumstances and was reduced to 100 hours.

Mirza appealed against a suspended sentence of three months' imprisonment imposed following his pleas of guilty to nine offences of failing to comply with the Regulatory Reform (Fire Safety) Order 2005, arts 8–22 and art 38. He was also ordered to carry out 200 hours unpaid work and to pay £2,000 prosecution costs. He owned a small business selling furniture, household electrical goods and flooring. The business premises were inspected and:

- fire exit routes were found to be obstructed;
- a fire door was obstructed and deadlocked;
- there was inadequate signage and no emergency lighting.

Mirza had failed to fully comply with an enforcement notice despite two extensions of time. Although he was of previous good character, he had also failed to address similar issues identified in an earlier fire risk assessment. The judge noted that each breach was serious, putting one or more persons at risk of death or serious injury, and that the multiple breaches increased the seriousness of the offence. The judge found that the case was further aggravated by Mirza ignoring the previous assessment and his clear history of failure to comply could have had catastrophic consequences. The judge considered that the case crossed the custody threshold.

Mirza said that fire safety cases usually involved substantial financial penalties but, as he was in serious financial difficulty and therefore not in a position to pay such a financial penalty, a community punishment was appropriate.

The appeal was allowed in part. The judge had not made an error in imposing a custodial sentence, or in finding that the sentence did not need to be one of immediate custody. The sentence was not therefore wrong in principle. However, the unpaid work requirement of 200 hours was excessive given that Mirza, in the light of his financial difficulties, would need to spend considerable time saving his livelihood and paying the costs order. An order for 100 hours was more appropriate.

## R v Nelson Group Services (Maintenance) Ltd [1998] 4 All ER 331

Nelson Group Services (Maintenance) Ltd, a company involved in the installation and maintenance of gas appliances, appealed against two convictions of failing to discharge its duty under the Health and Safety at Work etc Act 1974, s 3(1). The second related to the removal of a gas fire by one of its employees which exposed the occupier of the premises to health or safety risks. Regarding the first conviction, Nelson Group Services (Maintenance) Ltd challenged the validity of its committal, which had been made in form 16 rather than form 19.

The appeal against the second conviction was allowed, but the appeal against the first was dismissed. The trial judge was wrong to direct the jury that, if they concluded that the gas fittings had been left in a manner exposing the occupier to danger, the defence of reasonable practicability was not available to Nelson

Group Services (Maintenance) Ltd. It was still open to Nelson Group Services (Maintenance) Ltd to show that everything reasonably practicable had been done to ensure a safe system of work, with the employee having received appropriate training and sufficient supervision to enable him to carry out the work properly. The provisions of the Magistrates' Courts Act 1980 relating to the required form of committal of a corporation were not mandatory and use of the wrong form did not render the committal or the subsequent indictment and trial invalid.

## R v New Look Ltd [2010] EWCA Crim 1268

The level of fines imposed for breaches of the Regulatory Reform (Fire Safety) Order 2005, SI 2005/1541, art 32 depended on the context and was to reflect the magnitude of risk to public safety regardless of whether the breaches were an influence in the fire or in death or serious injury.

New Look appealed against the assessment of a fine imposed for offences under the Regulatory Reform (Fire Safety) Order 2005. New Look is a large clothing retailer, with pre-tax profits of £200 million and annual turnover of approximately £1 billion. It was responsible for complying with all fire and safety precautions at the retail premises it leased on a shopping street in London. A serious fire broke out at the premises, with no known cause resulting in the evacuation of several visitors and disruption to the local area. New Look were prosecuted for breaches of art 32 of the order, which made it an offence to place persons at risk of death or serious injury in case of fire. They admitted to failing to carry out a suitable and sufficient assessment of the fire risks and failing to ensure that its employees were provided with adequate safety training. In imposing a fine of £400,000, the judge stated that he had considered all the relevant case law but that each case had to be considered on its own facts and merits.

New Look said that the judge had failed to give sufficient weight to the fact that the breaches of duty were not the cause of the fire, nor had they caused injury or death. They argued that the fine exceeded levels previously imposed for breaches of the Health and Safety at Work etc Act 1974, which for cases of fire precaution regulation appeared in part to mirror the order, where death had resulted, and that the judge had made an error if he had applied a higher presumed standard of seriousness to breaches of fire safety responsibilities than he would for breaches of duty under the Act.

The appeal was dismissed as the judge had neither intended nor purported to set a new standard for sentencing corporations for breaches of fire safety legislation, and he had followed the correct approach to sentencing. Article 32 specifically required breaches of a level that would put people at risk of death or serious injury in the case of fire, however caused. The terms did not imply that fines for breaches of art 32 should be on a different scale from those imposed under the Act, but, as in all cases of risk of death or serious injury in health and safety, assessment of culpability and harm depended upon the particular context. The judge had recognised the fact that the nature of the risk against which employees and others were to be protected was the risk of death or serious injury in a fire, and that in the case of an organisation taking responsibility for large numbers of visitors to its premises, breach of art 32 would be a very serious matter. The standard was no different from that owed by any organisation towards large numbers of people whom it was required to protect. The judge did not have to wait until death or serious injury had occurred to express his displeasure at the breaches of a defendant's responsibilities under the order. It did not follow that fines would be imposed at the same level for breaches that did and breaches that did not have a causative influence in the fire or in death or serious injury, but it was clear that the judge had imposed a fine that reflected the seriousness of the offence in its creation of the risk to its visitors. The magnitude of that risk was demonstrated, not by death or serious injury, but by a fire in which death and serious injury was fortuitously avoided. What the fire served to illustrate was the magnitude of the risk that New Look ran with public safety. It followed that the judge had made no error of principle or approach to the issues of seriousness and culpability, and although the fine was severe it was not manifestly excessive.

## R v Newell [2012] EWCA Crim 650

Whilst a statement by counsel in a plea and case management hearing form was admissible at trial, the judge should have excluded it using the discretion under the Police and Criminal Evidence Act 1984, s 78 as the Crown was seeking to use that statement to the detriment of the defendant.

Newell appealed against his conviction for possession of cocaine with intent to supply. Newell had been arrested following the discovery of cocaine and drugs paraphernalia in a flat where he lived. At the Plea and Case Management Hearing (PCMH), no defence case statement had been served. In response to a question in the PCMH form asking what were the real issues, Newell's advocate, who did not represent him at trial, had written 'no possession'. A defence statement was served on the first day of the trial which stated that he accepted possession of cocaine but denied intent to supply. A second count of simple possession was added to which Newell pleaded guilty. The Crown sought to cross-examine Newell on a statement within the PCMH form on the basis that it was inconsistent with his defence and plea to possession. The judge allowed the cross-examination.

The appeal was allowed.

- Counsel's statement, made in Newell's presence, which was relayed to the court at the PCMH was admissible. It did not matter that a defendant could call evidence to show that what was said was not said on instructions. The advocate had authority to make the statement. Accordingly, the trial judge was entitled to conclude that the statement in the form was, in principle as a matter of law, admissible at the trial.

- Given the statutory regime in the Crown Court under the Criminal Procedure and Investigations Act 1996 and the Criminal Procedure Rules, the requirements of a PCMH form should be seen primarily as a means for the provision of information to enable case management. The trial advocate at the PCMH should see it as part of his duty to help the court with the case management setting out information in the form without the risk of the information provided being used as a statement admissible in evidence against the defendant. Accordingly, the position should be, provided the case was conducted in accordance with the letter and spirit of the Criminal Procedure Rules, that information on a PCMH form should not be admitted in evidence as a statement that could be used against a defendant, in the exercise of the court's discretion under the Police and Criminal Evidence Act 1984, s 78.

Whilst there might be cases where it was right not to exercise discretion under s 78, those cases would be rare. In this case, the judge should have refused to admit the statement in the PCMH form as evidence against Newell under s 78. At the time of the trial Newell had produced a defence statement which made the case clear. The sanction, under s 11 of the 1996 Act, for the failure to serve the statement in time, was sufficient. There was no disadvantage to the Crown which was seeking to use the statement to Newell's detriment.

## R v Newton (1982) 4 Cr App R (S) 388

Where there is a sharp divergence on a question of fact which is relevant to sentence, there are three ways in which a court can approach the problem to determine the matter:

- it may be possible to obtain an answer from a jury, eg whether the conviction should be under the Offences Against the Person Act 1861, s 18 or s 20 where the jury's verdict will determine the matter; or
- the judge can hear evidence on one side or the other and come to a conclusion, acting as their own jury on the issue; or
- the judge can hear no evidence, and come to a conclusion on the basis of submissions of counsel, but in this instance, the judge must come down on the side of the defendant, where there is a substantial conflict between the two sides the version of the defendant must be accepted so far as possible.

Newton pleaded guilty to buggery of his wife. The prosecution alleged that he had buggered her against her will and inflicted various other sexual indignities upon her. Newton admitted the offence but claimed that his wife consented to the buggery and other acts alleged. He was sentenced to eight years' imprisonment.

The judge had failed to adopt one of the three courses set out above (only the last two of which were really open to him in the circumstances) and had sentenced Newton on the basis that the wife did not consent. The sentence would be varied to allow Newton's immediate release (having served about ten months).

*Cases*

## R v Northallerton Magistrates' Court, ex p Dove [1999] EWHC Admin 499

Dove was prosecuted by MAFF (Ministry of Agriculture Fisheries and Food – now DEFRA) and convicted of an offence under the Arable Area Payments Regulations 1996, SI 1996/3142, reg 19(3) and the European Communities Act 1972, s 2(2). He received a fine of £1,000, the maximum fine for that offence being £5,000, and the magistrates' made an order, under the Prosecution of Offenders Act 1985, s 18, that he pay prosecution costs in the sum of £4,642.86. Dove applied for judicial review of the decision to make the costs order.

The application was allowed. The amount of the fine indicated the level of criminality that the magistrates' had determined and the costs order was therefore grossly disproportionate. The costs order was quashed and remitted with a direction that Dove should provide the magistrates' with information about his means. It was clear from the authorities that the following guidelines applied:

- the defendant's means and his liability for any other financial order should be ascertained, so that a costs order did not exceed a reasonable sum that the defendant was able to pay;
- that sum should never be more than the costs incurred;
- it was clear from the fact that there was no right of appeal under the Magistrates' Courts Act 1980, s 108, that the policy was intended to compensate the prosecutor and not to further punish the defendant;
- a costs order should be proportionate to the level of fine and, if the total of fine and costs was excessive, then the latter should be reduced accordingly;
- the onus was on the defendant to provide details of his means and, in default, magistrates' would be entitled to deduce his financial circumstances from the available evidence;
- the defendant must be allowed the opportunity to produce information as to his means and should be put on notice of any unusual costs order that was intended.

## R v P Ltd and G [2007] EWCA Crim 1937, [2008] ICR 96, CA

The correct standard of proof to be established for the commission of an offence through neglect under the Health and Safety at Work etc Act 1974, s 37 was a state of fact that required action to be taken, of which the company officer ought to have been aware, and into which appropriate investigation ought to have been made.

The Crown appealed against a preliminary ruling at a hearing in the Crown Court which had determined the standard of proof necessary to establish the commission of an offence through neglect, under the Health and Safety at Work etc Act 1974, s 37(1).

The Health and Safety Executive had been prosecuting the first respondent company (P) for two offences contrary to s 33(1)(a), and the second respondent managing director (G) for two offences contrary to s 37(1). The prosecution arose out of the death of a six-year-old boy, who was thrown from a fork lift truck he was being carried on as a passenger when it collided with another truck which was 'riding reel'. The practice involved carrying a third unclamped newspaper reel on top of two other clamped reels. The Crown alleged that the practice was commonplace and dangerous and that G, as managing director of P and the chair of its Strategic Health and Safety Management Committee, was ultimately responsible for ensuring that P employed safe systems of work. The Crown asserted that G had been aware of the practice of riding reel and that through consent, connivance or neglect, had caused P to act in breach of ss 2 and 3. At a preliminary hearing the judge ruled that to prove the commission of an offence under s 37 through 'neglect' by an individual, it had to be established that, amongst other things, the individual had a duty to inform himself of the facts giving rise to the company's breach, and that he did know of the material facts.

The Crown said that the judge erred in his interpretation of 'neglect' in s 37 by requiring the Crown to establish that G 'knew of the material facts'. The Crown argued that the correct approach was to establish that there was a failure on the part of the company office holder to take a step which should have been taken, and that was to be determined from consideration of all the circumstances of the case including the office holder's knowledge of the need for action, or the existence of a state of fact that required action to be taken, and of which the office holder ought to have been aware.

The appeal was allowed. The judge had erred in his interpretation of neglect in s 37 and placed the burden of proof too high. The correct question in terms of neglect would always be whether, where there was no actual knowledge of a state of fact, nonetheless, the officer in question of that body corporate should have been, by reason of the surrounding circumstances, put on enquiry so as to require him to check that relevant safety procedures were in place (see *Wotherspoon (John Maxwell) v HM Advocate* 1978 JC 74). It was not whether the particular company officer ought to have been aware in the sense that he turned a blind eye. The latter approach taken by the judge equated to the test for connivance under s 37, whereas parliament had clearly intended there to be a distinction between consent, connivance and neglect. In this case, it might be that in order to establish that there was a case to go before a jury, the Crown had to prove that G did know of the riding reel practice and its dangers. However, the Crown would not have to prove that fact if it could prove that there were circumstances that ought to have put G on enquiry as to that practice. That may be sufficient to require an answer from G. Therefore, it was a question which could only be answered at the end of the prosecution case: the judge's ruling was too prescriptive.

# R v Pabon [2018] EWCA Crim 420

A conviction for conspiracy to defraud was safe despite the fact that one of the prosecution's expert witnesses had signally failed to comply with his basic duties to the court. While the expert had gone beyond his general knowledge of banking, there had been no causal link between his failings and the issue of dishonesty, which had been the key issue at trial.

Pabon appealed against his conviction for conspiracy to defraud in respect of dishonestly rigging the London Interbank Offered Rate (LIBOR). Pabon was a derivatives trader at a bank. The Serious Fraud Office (SFO) brought proceedings against him and five others, each of whom were either convicted or pleaded guilty. It was alleged that Pabon had defrauded counterparties to LIBOR referenced trades by agreeing to procure or make false or misleading LIBOR submissions. In Pabon's original grounds of appeal, he admitted seeking to move the LIBOR rate to suit his book and to favour the bank, but claimed that he had not acted dishonestly. The central issue for the jury had therefore been dishonesty. At the retrial of two of his co-defendants, in cross-examination on new material concerning one of the SFO's expert witnesses, it was revealed that the expert had gone beyond his general knowledge of banking into very specific areas which were at the edge of, or beyond, his knowledge, particularly in relation to short-term interest rate trades. The two co-defendants were acquitted.

Pabon argued that the fresh evidence concerning the expert's failings would have permitted devastating cross-examination at his trial, as it had done at the co-defendants' retrial, and therefore his conviction was unsafe.

The appeal was dismissed.

Expert evidence – experts' duties were enshrined in the Criminal Procedure Rules 2015, Pt 19. Expert evidence assisted the jury with matters likely to be outside their experience and knowledge. It could only be considered 'expert' if it was within the expert's area of expertise, otherwise it was of no use to the jury and detrimental to the trust placed in experts. In this case, the expert had signally failed to comply with his basic duties by signing declarations of truth and of understanding his disclosure duties, knowing that he had failed to comply with those obligations. Alternatively, he was reckless in his failure to comply with them by:

- obscuring a colleague's role in preparing sections of his report;
- failing to inform the SFO, or the court, of the limits of his expertise;
- straying into areas that were beyond, or at the outer edge of, his expertise;
- flouting the judge's admonition not to discuss his evidence when he was still in the witness box. However, as observed by the judge at the retrial, the expert had a general expertise in banking and finance and many of the issues he dealt with involved basic matters which were not disputed.

Safety of conviction – the word 'unsafe' suggested a risk of error or mistake or irregularity that exceeded a certain margin so as to justify the description 'unsafe'. It involved a risk assessment. The court was required only to answer the direct and simply stated question of whether it thought the conviction was unsafe. Based on Pabon's admissions in his original grounds of appeal, he had faced difficulty with the initial questions of the genuineness of the LIBOR submissions. All that had remained for the jury was the key issue concerning his alleged dishonesty, to which the SFO's strong case and Pabon's admissions were also damaging. There was also evidence of emails sent by Pabon to his co-defendants that were damaging to his case. Pabon's defence had not required or involved delving into the technical details of short-term interest rate trades or related matters. Notwithstanding the conclusions reached concerning the expert, there had been nothing in his evidence that impacted sufficiently on the dishonesty issue so as to render the conviction unsafe. That conclusion was fact sensitive and turned on a consideration of the expert's evidence in the round, evaluated in the context of the trial as a whole. The manner in which the fresh evidence had emerged at the retrial was very damaging, but there was no proper basis for assuming that that would have been replicated at Pabon's trial. If it had been available at the trial, it was likely that the expert would not have been called at all, or that his evidence would have been tightly circumscribed. It would be pure speculation to transpose the outcome of the retrial to the trial and to conclude that Pabon's conviction was unsafe. In any event, regardless of the events at the retrial, there was no causal link between the expert's failings and the issue of the appellant's dishonesty, which was the key focus of the trial. Further, whilst not determinative, the court was satisfied that, if the new material had been available at trial, it would not reasonably have affected the jury's decision to convict. This case highlighted the need for those instructing expert witnesses to be satisfied with the witness's expertise and to engage an expert of a suitable calibre.

## R v Pearce (1979) 69 Cr App 365, CA

A sentencer is not bound by the view of the facts of the offence put forward by the prosecution and may form their own view on the material before them. A sentencer should not however adopt a graver view of the facts than is put forward by the prosecution unless there is a substantial basis in evidence for doing so.

The appellant admitted 59 offences of handling part of the proceeds of a series of burglaries carried out by another person. Counsel for the prosecution accepted the police version of the offence, and in cross-examination the police officer agreed that the appellant was a naive person who had received very little profit from the offences. The sentencer did not accept this view and stated that the appellant had plenty of profit.

The prosecution had presented the case on a lower basis than had been adopted by the sentencer. Although the sentencer was not bound to accept the prosecution's version of the case, and the sentence of two years could not be considered excessive, the divergence in the view put forward by the prosecution and that adopted by the sentencer left the appellant with a grievance, and his sentence was reduced to 18 months.

## R v R and S Recycling Ltd [2014] EWCA Crim 2302

A fine of £65,000, in addition to an order to pay prosecution costs of almost £60,000, was appropriate following a company's late guilty plea to

*Cases*

contravention of health and safety regulations which resulted in the death of an employee, taking into account the resources of the company and the fact that it had no previous convictions and no reported history of disregarding health and safety matters.

R and S Recycling Ltd appealed against a £100,000 fine imposed following its plea of guilty to contravening health and safety regulations. R and S Recycling Ltd was a family business which collected large quantities of materials for recycling, stored in bales. An employee had died when a bale fell on him. A specialist mechanical engineer instructed by the Health and Safety Executive (HSE) considered the bales to have been poorly stacked. The prosecution case was that relatively simple and reasonably practical precautions could have prevented the accident and that R and S Recycling Ltd had failed to carry out a proper risk assessment. R and S Recycling Ltd indicated a few days before trial its intention to plead guilty to the charge under the Health and Safety at Work etc Act 1974, s 33(1). R and S Recycling Ltd was also ordered to pay prosecution costs of £57,927, the total amount to be paid at the rate of £25,000 per year. R and S Recycling Ltd had no previous convictions and there had been no previous reports to the HSE regarding its conduct. The judge had regard to the sentencing guidelines for corporate manslaughter and health and safety offences causing death, which stated that the court should consider turnover, profit and assets when gauging a defendant's resources. The guidelines indicated that the appropriate fine would seldom be less than £100,000. The judge acknowledged that there was no evidence of any ingrained culture of disregarding health and safety and that there had been some risk assessments in place. He also noted, however, that there had been a foreseeable risk of accident. He adopted a starting point of £125,000 before giving 20% credit for the late guilty plea.

R and S Recycling Ltd argued that the judge had failed to properly assess its financial status as, despite its sizable turnover, it had made losses in three of the previous four years and could not be said to be in a solid financial position.

The appeal was allowed.

The judge had correctly directed himself and was to be commended for the evident care he had given to the matter and the clearly structured nature of his remarks. It was clear that he realised he had discretion regarding the level of fine and had not considered himself bound by the guidelines to impose a fine of at least £100,000. It came down to a question of evaluation and judgment. The judge had taken all relevant matters into account and this court had to assess whether the total figure was too high in the circumstances. The costs figure was not challenged but had to be considered under the principles of totality. The judge had chosen significantly too high a starting point. R and S Recycling Ltd had a significant turnover, but the fact that its net profit and loss position was such that it could not be said to be financially secure could not be ignored. Any fine had to carry a sting; it was essential that a deterrent message was sent out to companies in the same position. However, the actual resources of a company, and its ability to pay, even allowing for payment over a significant period of time, had to be given due weight. A starting point of £80,000 for the fine would have been appropriate. Allowing credit for the guilty plea, the fine should be £65,000. There was no reason to interfere with the costs order properly made by the judge. The total amount of £122,927 was to be paid at the rate of £15,000 per year.

## R v Rimmington (Anthony); R v Goldstein (Harry Chaim) [2005] UKHL 63

The offence of public nuisance was clear, precise, adequately defined and based on a discernible rational principle, and was not therefore contrary to common law principles or incompatible with the Human Rights Act 1989, Sch 1, Pt I, Art 7.

The appeal by Rimmington and Goldstein was against a decision refusing their appeals against convictions of causing a public nuisance at common law. Rimmington sent a large number of separate postal packages containing racist material to individual members of the public based on their perceived ethnicity. He had been charged on indictment of a single count of public nuisance, contrary to common law. Goldstein had posted an envelope containing salt to the address of a friend as a practical joke. The envelope did not reach Goldstein's friend, as at a post sorting office some of the salt leaked onto a postal worker's hands. The postal worker raised the alarm believing that the salt was anthrax. The sorting office was evacuated, the second delivery was cancelled and the police were called. Rimmington and Goldstein said that:

- the conduct formerly chargeable as the crime of public nuisance had now become the subject of express statutory provision, that the offence should be charged under the appropriate statutory provision, and that the crime of public nuisance had therefore ceased to have any practical application or legal existence;
- the crime of causing a public nuisance, as currently interpreted and applied, lacked the certainty and predictability necessary to meet the requirements of the common law itself or the Human Rights Act 1998, Sch 1, Pt I, Art 7.

The appeals were allowed as:

- the most typical and obvious causes of public nuisance were the subject of express statutory prohibition. Where parliament had defined the offence, possible defences, a prescribed mode of trial and a maximum penalty it was right that conduct falling within that definition be prosecuted under the statutory offence and not a common law offence for which the potential penalty was unlimited. Good practice and respect for the primacy of a statute required that conduct falling within the terms of a specific statutory provision should be prosecuted under that provision unless there was good reason for doing otherwise. Although cases of common law public nuisance were relatively rare, it was not open to the court to conclude that the common law crime of causing a public nuisance no longer existed;
- the guiding principles of common law, is that no one should be punished under a law unless it was sufficiently clear and certain to enable them to

know what conduct was forbidden before they did it, and that no one should be punished for any act that was not clearly and ascertainably punishable when the act was done. The offence of public nuisance was clear, precise, adequately defined and based on a discernible rational.

In this case, Rimmington had not caused a common injury to a section of the public, so his conduct lacked the essential ingredient of common nuisance. To permit a conviction of causing a public nuisance to rest on an injury caused to separate individuals, rather than on an injury suffered to the community or a significant section of it as a whole, was to contradict the rationale of the offence, pervert its nature, and change the constituent elements of the offence to the detriment of the accused.

Rimmington's conviction was quashed. A defendant was responsible for a nuisance which he knew, or ought to have known, would be the consequence of what he did or omitted to do. In Goldstein's case it had not been proven that Goldstein knew or should reasonably have known that the salt would escape into the sorting office or in the course of the post. Goldstein's conviction was therefore quashed.

## R v Sadhu [2017] EWCA Crim 908

A sentence of eight months' imprisonment was not excessive where the owner of a hotel had pleaded guilty to five breaches of fire safety laws that had taken place over a long period of time. It was not appropriate to use newspaper reports in court as evidence of sentences for similar breaches as they were not the full or authorised reports of the cases.

Sadhu appealed against an eight-month sentence imposed following his guilty plea to five offences contrary to the Regulatory Reform (Fire Safety) Order 2005, SI 2005/1541 and the Regulatory Reform Act 2001. Sadhu's company owned a hotel. He accepted that he was responsible for the day-to-day running of the hotel. The local authority received a call from a hotel guest who had heard staff saying that neither the fire alarm nor the emergency lighting was working. The hotel was investigated and five breaches of the relevant legislation were found:

- the first breach was that the fire alarm did not work. The evidence was that Sadhu had been told that the alarm was in such poor condition that it needed replacing, and that there had been significant faults at least during August and September 2015;
- the second breach concerned a failure to conduct a suitable and sufficient fire safety risk assessment. A risk assessment had been carried out in 2010, but it should have been reviewed at least annually;
- the third breach concerned the procedures for evacuation: during a genuine emergency in 2014 the emergency lighting had failed;
- the fourth breach consisted of inadequate maintenance and testing of both the emergency lighting system and the fire alarm system;
- the fifth breach concerned staff training on fire safety procedures. No staff training had been provided.

There were no Sentencing Council guidelines applicable, but the recorder was assisted by two cases provided by the prosecution, and by the guidelines for health and safety offences. The recorder found that although no injury had been caused, a fire could have had catastrophic results and that staff and guests had been at significant risk of serious injury or death in case of fire. He took a starting point of 12 months' imprisonment and, giving Sadhu full credit for his guilty plea, imposed a total sentence of eight months' imprisonment.

Sadhu said that the sentence was manifestly excessive, it was not a high culpability case, nor was there a high level of harm. He argued that the sentence should have been suspended.

The appeal was dismissed. There were few reports of authorities dealing with fire safety offences. Cases had been cited to the recorder by reference to newspaper articles and the like. The practice of providing the court with newspaper and other reports of cases had to stop. Not only were they not guideline cases, they were not full or authorised reports of the cases. Material matters that were in the mind of the sentencing judge might well be absent and the court might be led into error in thinking it had the full picture of the case when it did not.

Where there were no relevant sentencing guidelines, the court had to apply the basic principles of sentencing. Under the Criminal Justice Act 2003, s 143, a sentencing judge had to consider the offender's culpability in committing the offence and any harm which the offence caused, was intended to cause, or might foreseeably have caused.

Sadhu's culpability was high. Although he had not ignored any enforcement notices, he had failed to respond to failures in the system over a long period of time and had shown no urgency addressing the issues. Although no harm had in fact been caused, the hotel had 45 rooms and a number of staff, serious harm could have occurred, including death and serious injury. The potential harm was at the very highest level therefore a point of 12 months' imprisonment was appropriate. The recorder had been entitled to aggregate the breaches and take a global view of culpability and potential harm. Although sentencing guidelines on breaches of health and safety law were not directly relevant, they could be used as a check. The recorder had been entitled to look at them and to conclude that the case was one of high culpability and harm. A suspended sentence would not have been appropriate. Fire precautions had to be adhered to. The breaches had been very serious, and the court was not persuaded that there was anything wrong in principle with the sentence, or that it was manifestly excessive.

## R v Sellafield Ltd and R v Network Rail Infrastructure Ltd [2014] EWCA Crim 49

Sellafield Ltd and Network Rail Infrastructure Ltd appealed against the level of fines imposed following their guilty pleas to breaches of environmental protection and health and safety legislation.

Sellafield Ltd, with turnover of £1.6 billion and an annual profit of £29 million, had been fined £700,000 for offences relating to the disposal of radioactive waste. Network Rail Infrastructure Ltd, with turnover of £6.2 billion, had been fined £500,000 following a collision at an unmanned level crossing which resulted in very serious injuries to a child.

The judge found that Sellafield's failure was systemic and potentially exposed the public and those who handled waste off-site to unnecessary risk. Sellafield had relevant previous convictions. The judge took into account the fact that the breaches were not deliberate or reckless, no harm had been done and the actual risk of harm was low.

Network Rail Infrastructure Ltd pleaded guilty, on a particular basis, to failing to discharge a duty under the Health and Safety at Work etc Act 1974, s 3(1). Network Rail Infrastructure Ltd had relevant previous convictions. The judge found that risk assessments had been poorly carried out and that there had been repeated failures to follow the correct guidance.

Sellafield submitted that the level of fine equated to a major public disaster or loss of life, a significant nuclear event or an unmitigated environmental pollution incident. Network Rail Infrastructure Ltd submitted that a starting point of £750,000 would only be appropriate where there was more than one fatality, a public disaster, or where the defendant was convicted of corporate manslaughter.

The appeals were dismissed.

The court had to have regard to the purposes of sentencing and the seriousness of the offences, and to take account of the criteria set out in the Criminal Justice Act 2003, s 164. The structure, turnover and profitability of companies with turnover in excess of £1 billion was carefully examined. It was important that any information necessary to enable the sentencing court to assess their financial circumstances was provided well in advance of the sentencing hearing. Sellafield Ltd and Network Rail Infrastructure Ltd discharged important public services that had from time to time been directly undertaken by the state, but differed considerably. Sellafield Ltd was an ordinary commercial company, which made profits for its large multinational company shareholders. Network Rail Infrastructure Ltd's parent company had no shareholders who received profits; it invested its profits in the rail infrastructure. Sellafield Ltd's offences were of medium culpability, extending to management but with no actual harm and a very low risk of harm. Guilty pleas had been entered at the first opportunity and Sellafield Ltd had co-operated considerably. Account was also taken of its previous offences. It was not appropriate to consider a fine of £1 million as apposite only to a major disaster. That would ignore the court's obligation under s 164 of the 2003 Act to have regard to the offender's financial circumstances and the sentencing guidelines. There was no ceiling on the amount of fine that could be imposed. It was clear that a fine of £700,000 after a guilty plea reflected moderate culpability, no actual harm and a very low risk of harm. It also had to be viewed against the requirement that directors or shareholders of companies involved in the nuclear industry had to give the highest priority to safety, as parliament had directed. The fine imposed would achieve the statutory purposes of sentencing by emphasising to those directors and professional shareholders the seriousness of the offences, and provide a real incentive to remedy the failures found to exist. In respect of Network Rail Infrastructure Ltd, the actual harm was serious and even greater harm had been foreseeable. The culpability of local management was serious and persistent, but there had been no specifically identified failure by senior management. The failures had to be judged in the context of Network Rail's poor previous record of similar offending, which did reflect on senior management, but also in the light of Network Rail Infrastructure Ltd's expenditure of £130 million on level crossing safety. Account was taken of Network Rail Infrastructure Ltd's guilty plea, its remedying of the safety failures at the crossing in question, and the other mitigating and aggravating factors. Network Rail Infrastructure Ltd's submission that a fine of £750,000 was only appropriate where there had been a fatality was rejected; it ignored the statutory obligation to consider the offender's means. However, a significant fine imposed on Network Rail would, unlike Sellafield, in effect inflict no direct punishment on anyone and could be said to harm the public, as Network Rail Infrastructure Ltd's profits were invested in the rail infrastructure for the public benefit. A fine would serve other sentencing purposes if it reduced such offending, reformed and rehabilitated Network Rail Infrastructure Ltd as an offender, and protected the public. It could be inferred from Network Rail Infrastructure Ltd's investment in level crossing safety and some minor adjustment downwards of its directors' bonuses that it was attempting to reduce its offending behaviour, was being reformed and rehabilitated, and was taking steps to protect the public. Nonetheless, the fine imposed on a company of Network Rail Infrastructure Ltd's size represented a very generous discount for the mitigation advanced, and a materially greater fine could not have been criticised.

## R v Squibb Group Ltd [2019] ECWA Crim 227

The defendant, a demolition contractor, was prosecuted for breaches of the Health and Safety at Work etc Act 1974, ss 2(1) and 3(1) following exposure of employees and others to asbestos during a construction project. In respect to the likelihood of harm, the sentencing judge was provided with a report from an independent expert which gave an estimate of the risk to employees and others of contracting an asbestos-related disease as a result of their likely exposure. This was based on statistical data derived from published studies. The expert estimated that if 100,000 people were exposed to a similar extent to the defendant's employees, about 90 deaths would occur. While acknowledging the limitation of such evidence and that the estimates were necessarily 'very rough', the Court of Appeal found that the judge was wrong to have assessed the likelihood of harm as medium concluding the appropriate assessment was low. Given the impact on sentence of this element of the sentencing process, the reliance upon expert statistical evidence may become more common in the future. The fine was reduced from £400,000 to £190,000.

## R v Stubbs [2006] EWCA Crim 2312

A bank employee's conviction for conspiracy to defraud was safe as the judge had been correct to allow a witness to give expert evidence on the online banking system that was in use when the passwords of accountholders were reset without their authority. The witness's limitations had been clearly put to the jury, and the fact that he was also an employee of the bank affected only the weight not the admissibility of his evidence.

Stubbs appealed against his conviction for conspiracy to defraud. Stubbs worked as a password reset clerk on a bank's online banking system. While he had been on duty attempts were made using his identification to reset the passwords of five corporate clients without their authorisation, two of which were successful. Stubbs accepted that he had carried out legitimate password resets moments before and after the unauthorised activity. On the following two days unauthorised transfers totalling about £11.8 million were made from one of the accounts. When Stubbs was arrested, he initially claimed that he had reset the passwords on the strength of supporting documentation, then later claimed that somebody else must have used his identification to reset them. Evidence concerning the operation of the system was given by an employee of the bank. At trial Stubbs objected to the admissibility of parts of the employee's evidence on the basis that he lacked the expertise and independence to give expert opinion. The judge ruled the employee's evidence to be admissible and declined to exclude it. Stubbs submitted that:

- the employee's detailed account of the actual activity carried out on the system amounted to inadmissible opinion evidence because he lacked both expertise and independence;
- the judge should have withdrawn the case from the jury as the employee's evidence was unsafe;
- the judge had erred by directing the jury that it should satisfy itself that the employee was an expert before relying on him;
- there was a real and lurking doubt as to the safety of the conviction.

The appeal was dismissed.

- The judge had been correct to find that the employee had sufficient knowledge of the subject to render his opinion of value in resolving issues concerning the operation of the banking system. His finding was based on an assessment properly made after hearing the employee's evidence. The employee's limitations were explored in depth in cross-examination and placed before the jury. It was accepted that the employee was not an information technology specialist in any wider sense and that his technical knowledge of the system was limited, but that did not preclude his being regarded as an expert to the extent indicated by the judge. The fact that the employee worked for the bank did not affect the admissibility of his evidence it went only to its weight, and it was for the jury to determine whether he displayed any bias or lack of objectivity.
- Once the employee's evidence was held to be admissible, the evaluation of it was a matter for the jury. It was capable of providing a proper framework

- for the other prosecution evidence, and the evidence as a whole plainly provided a case to answer.
- The judge had not erred in his direction to the jury: he had made it perfectly clear that the employee was an expert witness and that it was for the jury to decide whether to accept his evidence and what weight to place on it.
- There was no lurking doubt that justified interference by the court. There were points to be made in Stubbs's favour but there were also many points against him. These points were for the jury to evaluate and there was a solid evidential basis for their decision to convict.

## R v Takhar [2014] EWCA Crim 1619

In a case where a 61-year-old offender had pleaded guilty to multiple breaches of the Regulatory Reform (Fire Safety) Order 2005, SI 2005/1541, concurrent sentences of six months' imprisonment were appropriate as he was in poor health, presented a low risk of reoffending and there had been a long delay in bringing the case against him.

Takhar appealed against a sentence of 12 months' imprisonment imposed after pleading guilty to multiple breaches of the Regulatory Reform (Fire Safety) Order 2005.

Takhar had managed a hotel and, following a complaint, fire officers inspected the hotel and found a series of fire safety breaches. A later follow-up inspection occurred and Takhar had remedied some of the existing breaches but further breaches were found. There was a significant delay before the matter came to court, which was not attributable to Takhar. He pleaded to breaches of the order. He was of previous good character and a pre-sentence report indicated that there was a very low risk of reoffending but that there was not total acceptance of responsibility and that he had a tendency to minimise his culpability and blame others. The judge said that a sentence of two years' imprisonment after trial would have been appropriate. He found that Takhar's culpability was high, gave him credit for his guilty plea, noted various mitigating factors and had regard to the delay in bringing the case to court. The judge imposed a 12-month term of imprisonment. At the time of the appeal, Takhar was 61 years old and in poor health. He submitted that his sentence was manifestly excessive and that it should have been suspended.

The appeal was allowed. The judge was correct to find that the custodial threshold had been crossed. The scale of the offending and the length of time over which it had occurred justified a custodial sentence. However, no deaths had resulted but the order was directed at the potential for death or serious injury and the judge had not overstated the position by describing the hotel as a potential 'death trap'. The judge was entitled to decline to suspend the sentence as that was a matter for his discretion and there was no basis for interfering with his decision. An element of deterrence was appropriate; however, the immediate custodial sentence imposed on Takhar was as much a deterrent as the actual length of imprisonment. Taking into account his age, poor health, inability to engage in a hotel or any other similar business, low reoffending risk, and the long delay in the matter being brought to court, it was appropriate to reduce his sentence to six months' imprisonment to run concurrently on each count.

## R v Tangerine Confectionery Ltd [2011] EWCA Crim 2015

The Court of Appeal gave guidance on the effects of the Health and Safety at Work etc Act 1974, ss 2 and 3.

The companies had appealed against their convictions under the Health and Safety at Work etc Act 1974, ss 2 and 3. The appeals demonstrated that the terms of the Act had given rise to difficulties in the Crown Court. The issues to be determined were:

- the relationship between 'safety' under s 2 and 'risk to safety' under s 3;
- whether, where there had been an injury, the Crown was required to prove that the offence had caused it;
- the extent to which the Crown had to prove that the risk 'derived' from the defendant's activities;
- the relevance to offences under s 2 and s 3 of foreseeability of injury or of an accident which had in fact happened.

The appeals were dismissed.

- Ensuring safety under s 2 and ensuring an absence of risk to safety under s 3 were the same thing. Safety was not ensured, for the purposes of s 2, if there was a relevant risk to the safety of employees.
- The offences were not primarily concerned with ascribing responsibility for the cause of injury, but with avoiding injury.
- The risks towards which the offences were directed were those materially related to the activities of the defendant. Although s 3 required the risk to arise from the conduct of the defendant's undertaking, there could exist concurrent risks from both the undertaking and something independent. The existence of one risk did not mean that the defendant was not responsible for doing what was reasonably practicable to avoid the second risk. In s 2 cases it was not difficult to postulate circumstances in which the defendant could be responsible for failing to ensure that the employee was not exposed to a risk at work which derived from something else. Although it was sometimes necessary to address the source of a risk, a test of derivation was potentially confusing. It would be better to ask the jury to concentrate on the exposure to risk and whether it had been reasonably practicable to avoid it.
- Foreseeability of danger was relevant to whether a material risk to safety existed (see *Baker v Quantum Clothing Group Ltd* [2011] UKSC 17, [2011] 1 WLR 1003).
- The issues considered were largely marginal to T's cases, and in each case the decision had been correct.

# R v Tata Steel UK Ltd [2017] EWCA Crim 704

Fines of £1,315,000 and £185,000 were appropriate following the guilty pleas of a major steel-producer to two health and safety offences arising from incidents in which employees had got their hands caught in dangerous machinery.

Tata Steel UK Ltd appealed against fines totalling £1,985,000 which had been imposed on it following its pleas of guilty to two health and safety offences.

Tata Steel UK Ltd was a steel-producer with a turnover of some £4 billion. It was a 'very large organisation' for the purposes of the Definitive Guideline which covered health and safety offences. Both offences took place at Tata Steel UK Ltd's steel-manufacturing site in Corby:

- the first offence, an employee was working at a paint bay where cylindrical lengths of steel entered an enclosed painting area via an inlet table and transfer conveyor. The tubes exited the painting process from the transfer table, where they were 'kicked off' and then packed. The kicker was contained within a caged part of the line. It was not unusual for blockages to occur on the inlet side of the machine. When that happened, a practice had developed whereby a green tunnel guarding the tube conveyor was removed and the lengths of pipe manipulated by hand. That guard should not be removed without the power line being isolated. The employee was using his hand to move pipes when a fellow employee powered up the line. That caused the pipes suddenly to move, trapping and crushing two fingers of his left hand;
- the second offence occurred after the appellant had been served with an improvement notice requiring it to check all of its production lines to ensure that all identified preventative and protective devices were in place and effective. An employee's glove had got caught in the moving parts of a lathe, resulting in his hand being pulled in and in the amputation of part of one of his fingers. The lathe was inadequately guarded. The sentencing judge imposed a fine of £185,000 for the first offence and a fine of £1.8 million for the second. He placed the second offence in harm category 2, having concluded, among other things, that it involved a high likelihood of harm. That category had a starting point of £1.1 million. He increased the starting point to £2.4 million to reflect the fact that the appellant's turnover made it a very large organisation. He further increased the starting point to £2.75 million so that the fine would have a real impact on management and shareholders and in the light of his view that senior management had been inadequately focused on day-to-day safety. He then reduced the fine to £1.8 million to take into account the appellant's early guilty plea.

The issues were:

- whether the fine of £185,000 for the first offence was manifestly excessive;
- whether the judge had erred in concluding that the second offence involved a high likelihood of harm;
- whether he had been entitled to increase the starting point in the way that he had;

- whether he should have made a downwards adjustment of the fine to take into account the fact that the appellant had, despite its sizeable turnover, recorded a loss of £851 million in the relevant accounting year;
- the appropriate fine for the second offence.

The appeal was allowed.

- Had the first offence stood alone, the fine would have greatly exceeded £185,000. The judge had, very generously, reduced the initial fine he had arrived at (£465,000) by 65% to allow for totality. In those circumstances, a fine of £185,000 could not realistically be described as manifestly excessive (see para 63 of judgment).
- The judge should have characterised the second offence as one of medium likelihood. He had had regard to a previous similar incident, but it had occurred 15 years earlier. Further, as the judge himself noted, the lathe in question had been operated for some 150,000 man hours without incident.
- The judge had been entitled to increase the starting point in the way that he had. He was amply entitled to move up a harm category to reflect the fact that the appellant, judged by turnover, was a very large rather than a large organisation and so to impose a proportionate fine. At step three of the Guideline, the judge was specifically urged to pass a substantial fine so as to bring home to management and shareholders the need to comply with health and safety legislation. Having regard to that objective, the judge had not erred in further increasing the starting point to £2.75 million, given his conclusion that senior management had been inadequately focused on day-to-day safety.
- The judge had taken the resources of the appellant's parent company into account when deciding not to make a downwards adjustment of the fine to reflect the appellant's recorded losses. He was amply entitled to do so.
- Given the revised categorisation of the second offence as one of 'medium likelihood', the correct starting point was £2 million. Having regard to the appellant's early guilty plea and giving it a little leeway, the appropriate fine was £1,315,000.

# R v Thames Water Utilities Ltd [2015] EWCA Crim 960, [2015] 1 WLR 4411

Thames Water Utilities Ltd, who had pleaded guilty to an offence arising from the discharge of untreated sewage into a brook flowing through a nature reserve, appealed against the fine of £250,000 which had been imposed on it.

The discharge had occurred from a sewage pumping station operated by Thames Water Utilities Ltd. The function of the pumping station was to receive untreated sewage from the surrounding area and from another upstream pumping station and to pump it to a downstream pumping station and thence to a sewage treatment works. Sewage was pumped by two pumps. The cause of the discharge was the failure of both pumps. They failed after becoming clogged with 'rag' discarded into the sewage system by domestic and other users. In the five months before the incident, there had been at least 16 instances of failure of one or both of the pumps. Before the discharge, alarms signifying pump failure were triggered, but the appellant's staff did not respond to them. Once notified of the discharge, the Thames Water Utilities Ltd's staff attended and unblocked the pumps. Soon afterwards, the pumps were replaced by newer pumps better able to cope with the ingestion of rag. The recorder who imposed the fine found that the appellant had been negligent. They had had a number of warnings that the pumps were breaking down and they were close to a very special nature site and should have been replaced earlier.

The appeal was dismissed.

- This was the first case of its kind to come before a court since the Sentencing Council's Definitive Guideline on Environmental Offences came into effect. The council had made it clear that the starting points and range of fines in the guideline did not apply to very large organisations such as the appellant. It would be appropriate to give guidance on the approach to be adopted in the case of very large commercial organisations run for profit. The provisions in the Criminal Justice Act 2003, ss 142, 143 and 164 were a starting point. The aim of the sentence was to give an appropriate message to the directors and shareholders of the company in question. Sentences imposed before this had not been adequate to achieve that object. This court had on two occasions observed that it would not have interfered with fines 'very substantially greater' or 'significantly greater' than six-figure fines imposed for environmental offences. Environmental pollution cases would include prompt and effective measures to rectify the harm caused by the offence and to prevent its recurrence, frankness and co-operation with the authorities, the prompt payment of full compensation to those harmed by the offence and a prompt plea of guilty. In addition, significant expense voluntarily incurred in recognition of the public harm done should be taken into account. Clear and accepted evidence from the chief executive or chairman of the main board, that the board was taking effective steps to secure substantial overall improvement in the company's fulfilment of its environmental duties, would be a significant mitigating factor. The size of the company became much more important when harm was caused by negligence or greater fault. Even in the case of a large organisation with an impeccable record, the fine had to be large enough to bring the appropriate message home to the directors and shareholders and to punish them. In the case of repeat offenders, the fine should be far higher and should rise to the level necessary to ensure that the directors and shareholders took effective measures properly to reform themselves and ensure that they met their environmental obligations. In this case, the appellant's record over the years did not suggest a routine disregard of environmental obligations, but it did leave room for substantial improvement; its recent record suggested that the appropriate message had not fully struck home. On the other hand, a statement from one of the appellant's senior officers showed that the appellant was taking the issue of environmental pollution seriously and was spending substantial sums to modernise and improve its infrastructure. That represented significant mitigation. Nevertheless, the fine of £250,000

was lenient. This court would have had no hesitation in upholding a very substantially higher fine.
- Sentencing very large organisations involved complex issues. It was for that reason that special provision was made for such cases in Crim PD XIII, listing and classification. Such cases were categorised as class 2C cases and had therefore to be tried either by a High Court judge or by another judge only where, either the presiding judge had released the case, or the resident judge had allocated the case to that judge. It was essential that the terms of the practice direction were strictly observed.

## R v Thelwall [2016] EWCA Crim 1755

A sentence of 12 months' imprisonment following a guilty plea to a Health and Safety Act offence that caused the death of a worker, where the offender had a similar previous conviction, was not manifestly excessive. However, the Court of Appeal criticised the Health and Safety Executive (HSE) for seeking to claim excessive costs, for having submitted an 18-page skeleton argument and instructing a solicitor to attend an appeal in a straightforward case. A case brought by the HSE, was the same as any other criminal case prosecuted by the Crown Prosecution Service and should have been approached in the same way.

Thelwall appealed against a sentence of 12 months' imprisonment following a guilty plea to a breach of health and safety laws, that resulted in the death of a worker.

Thelwall had been the sole director of a company that hired out mobile equipment. One of the workers had been loading a mobile elevated work platform onto a flatbed truck when it toppled over, causing him fatal injuries. The company had pleaded guilty to a health and safety offence and was fined £166,000. T had a previous conviction for a similar offence. The judge put the offence in category 1A of the sentencing guidelines, which had a starting point of 26 weeks.

Relying on a bundle of unreported cases from newspaper cuttings, Thelwall submitted that the judge had put the offence in the wrong sentencing bracket and that the sentence had been too high. The respondent, the HSE, sought its costs of the appeal of around £9,000.

The appeal was dismissed.

There had been enough evidence for the judge to have concluded that there had been a high degree of culpability and a high risk of harm in Thelwall's behaviour. The judge had put the sentence in the appropriate bracket. Guidelines were only guidelines and other reported cases of the Court of Appeal (Criminal Division) were of no assistance in most appeals. Similarly, it was impermissible to have given the sentencing judge or the Court of Appeal a bundle of cases that were irrelevant to the sentencing exercise. There was no difference between this case, which was prosecuted by the HSE, and any criminal case prosecuted by the Crown Prosecution Service, and both types of cases should have been approached in the same way. It was a straightforward case and the attendance at court by a solicitor for the HSE had been unnecessary, as had the 18-page skeleton argument submitted by the HSE. The maximum length of a skeleton argument allowed in civil proceedings under the Criminal Procedure Rules was 25 pages. In relation to costs, it was disproportionate for the HSE to seek to claim a sum that was ten times the amount that a representative from the CPS would have been able to seek. There should have been a greater sense of proportionality exercised by the HSE.

## R v Underwood [2004] EWCA Crim 2256

This was an appeal against concurrent sentences of six months' imprisonment imposed at the Crown Court in 2004 in respect of guilty pleas to two counts of gross indecency with a child. The appeals were brought with leave of the single judge.

There were two incidents: the first, one of exposing himself naked at a window and fiddling with his penis in view of two girls; and the second, an incident of stroking a girl's leg and dropping her a suggestive note.

The appellant had a substantial record for sexual offending and there was a pessimistic pre-sentence report. Initially the sentences appeared to be unobjectionable, but the case had some background complications. In March of the previous year, the appellant had been sentenced by the same judge to an extended term of imprisonment. He had served the custodial element of that sentence with the extension left open. When he came before the judge in relation to these matters, it was evident from the transcripts that it was the intention of the judge that he should be immediately released. For understandable reasons everyone assumed that because he had spent time in custody that would count towards the sentence and the time that he had spent was the time that led the judge to believe he would be released immediately. This conclusion misunderstood the rules that govern time on remand. The actual position was that he was still in prison and not due to be released until the end of the month. That was clearly not what was intended. It seems that the court, without investigating the merits of the original approach, needed to give effect to what the judge had in mind and what the appellant was entitled to expect were the consequences of the sentence. The appropriate way of doing that was to quash the sentences of six months' imprisonment concurrent and substitute for them sentences of one day's imprisonment concurrent. That should not be taken as any reflection of the offences themselves. The appeal was allowed.

## R v Whirlpool UK Appliances Ltd [2017] EWCA Crim 2186

The court considered the Definitive Sentencing Guideline on Corporate Manslaughter, Health and Safety and Food and Safety Hygiene Offences when significantly reducing the fine imposed on a company following the death of a contractor on its premises. The company, a 'very large organisation' for the purposes of the guideline, had pleaded guilty to an offence under the Health and Safety at Work etc Act 1974, s 3(1) which occurred in unusual circumstances and involved low culpability and a low likelihood of harm.

Whirlpool appealed against a fine of £700,000 imposed following its guilty plea to an offence contrary to the Health and Safety at Work etc Act 1974, s 3(1).

A contractor had died following an accident at the company's premises. He fell from an elevated working platform when an overhead conveyor was activated by a separate maintenance team. Section 3(1) imposed a duty on an employer to conduct its undertaking in such a way as to ensure, so far as reasonably practicable, that persons not in its employment were not exposed to health and safety risks. The company had not required the contractor to prepare a job-specific risk assessment and method statement for the work he was going to carry out, and could have prepared a more detailed permit to work identifying the potential risk of the work to be carried out. The Definitive Guideline on Corporate Manslaughter, Health and Safety and Food and Safety Hygiene Offences required the court to consider the level of culpability and harm. The judge found that the breach involved low culpability and that it was a 'harm category 3' case. He referred to the company's turnover as £500 million and adopted a starting point of £1.2 million, before reducing it by £150,000 for good character and remorse, and then giving a further one-third credit for the guilty plea.

The issues were the impact of a death on the approach to the guideline; the identification and treatment of a 'very large organisation' for the purposes of the guideline; and the impact of relatively poor profitability in the context of an organisation with a substantial turnover.

The company submitted that the judge's starting point was too high when compared with the starting points and category ranges for large organisations. It further submitted that the judge had failed to examine the company's financial circumstances when considering whether the fine was proportionate to its overall means.

The appeal was allowed.

- Culpability had a marked impact on starting points. No other workers or members of the public had been exposed to harm, but the systemic failings involved were a significant cause of the death. That justified an upward movement within the appropriate category range or a move into the next harm category. A consistent feature of recent sentencing policy had been to treat death as a factor which substantially increased a sentence, as required by the second stage assessment of harm. The fact of death alone justified a move to the top of the next category range, suggesting a starting point of around £250,000. No upper limit of turnover was mentioned for a large organisation, but most organisations with a turnover which 'very greatly exceeds £50 million' would be treated as very large organisations. The company's turnover was approximately £700 million, not £500 million.

It was therefore a very large organisation and it was permissible to move outside the appropriate range in order to achieve a proportionate sentence. Having determined that an organisation was very large, the guideline did not dictate an arithmetic approach to calculation of the fine. The starting point of £250,000 had to be increased to reflect the company's turnover and its status as a very large organisation. The next range in the guideline extended from £180,000 to £700,000. The company's turnover moved the starting point to £500,000. The reduction to reflect its strong mitigation made it £450,000. The judge had not expressly considered the company's financial circumstances. There was a big difference between an organisation trading on wafer-thin margins and one where the profits shared between partners or shareholders was a substantial percentage of turnover. However, having regard to the company's overall means, the figure of £450,000 did not require adjustment. The company had an underlying profitability, notwithstanding recent losses, and directors' remuneration had not been affected. The £450,000 starting point ensured a real economic impact and emphasised the need for compliance with health and safety legislation, but was also proportionate to the company's overall means. With a one-third reduction to reflect the guilty plea, the appropriate fine was £300,000.
- The recent policy, consolidated by the Sentencing Council, of ensuring that organisations paid fines that were properly proportionate to their means did not relieve the court of a duty to enquire carefully into the facts of each case so as fairly to reflect different levels of harm and culpability. The circumstances of this case were unusual in that they flowed from an offence of low culpability and low likelihood of harm. The guideline was subtle enough to recognise that culpability, likelihood of harm and harm itself should be properly reflected in any fine, as well as turnover. Large commercial entities were vulnerable to very substantial fines for regulatory failings. The same was true for breaches of health and safety or environmental law in appropriate cases. However, the level of fine initially imposed in this case would only have been appropriate if the factors weighing in the balance for the purposes of the guideline had been different.

## Ready Mixed Concrete (South East) Ltd v Minister of Pensions and National Insurance [1968] 2 QB 497

A contract of service exists if the following three conditions are fulfilled:

- the servant agrees that in consideration of a wage or other remuneration he will provide his own work and skill in the performance of some service for his master;
- he agrees, expressly or impliedly, that in the performance of that service he will be subject to the other's control in a sufficient degree to make that other master; and
- the other provisions of the contract are consistent with its being a contract of service.

*Cases*

A person entered into a contract with the applicant company for the carriage of concrete. He contracted with an associated company for the hire purchase of a suitable lorry. His contract with the applicant described him as an independent contractor. By this contract it was provided that he was under an obligation:

- to provide the lorry painted in the applicant's colours and marked with a number given by the applicant;
- to wear the applicant's uniform;
- to carry on the lorry one of the applicant's mixing units;
- to make the lorry available to the applicant at all times and to use it for no other purpose;
- to carry out all reasonable orders from competent servants of the applicant; and
- to pay all running costs.

Provision was made in the contract for him to be paid remuneration based on load and mileage. He was permitted to employ substitute drivers, and there was provision for determination by either party on notice. No directions were given to him concerning the mode of transport of the concrete. On the question whether he was an employee or an independent contractor, the court held that in the circumstances he was an independent contractor.

## Registrar of Restrictive Trading Agreements v WH Smith & Son Ltd [1969] 3 All ER 1065

A branch manager of a company who were newspaper wholesalers is not an 'officer' of the company within the Restrictive Trade Practices Act 1956, s 15, for him to be examined under oath on alleged secret restrictive practices. The plaintiff, who lived and worked in Newport, Monmouthshire, wanted to commence business as a newspaper retailer. She was refused supplies by the three wholesalers who were the only wholesalers in Newport. She obtained supplies from a Cardiff wholesaler, but after a while these supplies were terminated, and she alleged that this was due to the influence of one of the Newport wholesalers. This wholesaler operated on his own account and in Newport alone. The other two Newport wholesalers were large companies with many branches in many parts of the country, including one each in Newport. The question arose as to whether this wholesaler and the Newport branch managers of the other Newport wholesalers were persons who could be examined on oath about the existence of secret restrictive trade agreements. It was decided that only the independent wholesaler could be so examined. The appeal was dismissed.

The branch managers were not persons as could be examined and even if they could, no order would be made since the wholesalers employing them had good economic reasons for refusing to supply the plaintiff and since the Registrar had been guilty of such delay (one year since serving notice) in seeking orders and in particular one manager had been subjected to a private cross-examination at the Registry.

## Rylands v Fletcher (1868) LR 3 HL 330

A person who, for their own purposes, brought onto their land and collected and kept there anything likely to do damage if it escaped, had to keep at their peril and if they did not do so, they were answerable for all the damage which was the natural consequence of its escape. This case is the basis for the term 'rule in *Rylands v Fletcher*'.

Rylands appealed against a decision that they were liable for damages to Fletcher for an escape of water from their reservoir into Fletcher's coal mines. In order to serve his mill, Rylands had built a reservoir on land adjacent to Fletcher's mines. Underneath the reservoir there were disused mine shafts with which Fletcher's mine shafts came into contact. When the reservoir was filled or partly filled with water, its weight broke through the disused shafts and the water penetrated Fletcher's mine and caused damage for which Fletcher claimed against Rylands. The Court of Exchequer decided that there was no cause of action. The Court of Exchequer Chamber reversed that decision, holding that there was a cause of action and awarding Fletcher damages.

The appeal was dismissed.

Rylands as the owners or occupiers of the land on which the reservoir was built, might lawfully have used that land for any purpose for which it might in the ordinary course of the enjoyment of land be used and if, in the natural user of that land, there had been any accumulation of water and if by the operation of nature that water had passed onto Fletcher's land, Fletcher could not have complained about it. On the other hand, if Rylands had desired to use the land for a non-natural purpose, for example by introducing water either above or below ground in quantities and in a manner not the result of any work or operation on or under the land, and if in consequence of their doing so, or of any imperfection in the mode of their doing so, the water came to escape onto Fletcher's land, then what Rylands were doing they were doing at their own peril and they were liable for any damage suffered. The Court of Exchequer Chamber had correctly stated the law in saying that a person who, for his own purposes, brought on his land and collected and kept there anything likely to do mischief if it escaped, had to keep it in at his peril and if he did not do so, he was prima facie answerable for all the damage which was the natural consequence of its escape.

## Scottish Power Generation Ltd v HM Advocate [2016] HCJAC 99

A fine of £1,750,000 imposed on an energy company following a guilty plea for failing to ensure the health and safety at work of its employees, contrary to the Health and Safety at Work etc Act 1974, ss 2(1) and 33(1)(a), was excessive and was quashed, and a fine of £1,200,000 substituted.

Scottish Power Generation Ltd who pleaded guilty to failing to ensure the health and safety at work of its employees, such that an employee severely injured

*Cases*

contrary to the Health and Safety at Work etc Act 1974, ss 2(1) and 33(1)(a), appealed as excessive the sheriff's imposition of a fine of £1,750,000.

The employee had sustained injury in October 2013 when he had been engulfed in pressurised steam from a faulty valve, identified in May 2009, due to Scottish Power Generation Ltd's failure to repair or replace it, and a short term safety measure had been removed without explanation and not replaced. The sheriff had determined that he ought to have regard to the Sentencing Council of England and Wales Guideline 2015 where there was no reason for the levels of fine to be different, the ratio of the Scottish cases did not restrict the court to considering only guidelines in force when those cases had been decided and the factors to be considered according to the 2015 Guideline did not differ, to any material extent, from those in the Scottish cases. The sheriff had considered that the circumstances of the offence demonstrated a breach of duty falling far short of the appropriate standard, Scottish Power Generation Ltd had no explanation for any of the failures regarding the valve, and those failures fell within the description of 'high culpability' in the 2015 Guideline and not within the medium category where there had been no proper system in place. In sentencing, the sheriff had found that Scottish Power Generation Ltd were able to pay any fine imposed, and that applying the 2015 Guideline, Scottish Power Generation Ltd fell within the description of 'very large', the starting point for a fine for an offence of high culpability with a harm category of 2 was £1.1 million, with a range between £550,000 to £2.9 million, having regard to Scottish Power Generation Ltd's size, together with the lack of any record and the steps which had been taken since to improve safety, he had selected a fine towards the upper end of the range, £2.5 million being an appropriate starting point, reduced to £1.75 million on account of the early guilty plea.

The appeal was allowed, the fine quashed and £1,200,000 fine substituted:

- recognising the significant difference between fatal and non-fatal cases, the court would have considered a starting point of approximately £1.5 million in the present case, which had regard to the serious nature of the breach, the mitigating circumstances, the employee's serious injury, the absence of a fatality and the fact that Scottish Power Generation Ltd were part of a multinational corporation;
- where the court had regard to the guidelines in England and Wales it meant such guidelines as were in current use and would be applied to such an offence in that jurisdiction, and the appropriate guideline to which to have regard as a cross check in the present case was the 2015 version;
- the sheriff had had regard to the 2015 Guideline, although the manner in which he had done so was unclear; his calculation, which might be seen as an attempt to follow the numbered steps in the guideline, might be flawed where a figure ought to have been reached and only then could the proportionality check relative to means have been carried out to adjust it, which was not the exercise described by the sheriff in his report; on the other hand, it might be that the sheriff had reached a figure and range which he had simply used as a cross check on the selection of his ultimate

starting point as that was understood in Scottish sentencing practice rather than a term of art in the guideline. However, there was no explanation as to the manner in which the sheriff had arrived at that figure with regard to pre-guideline Scottish decisions, and he had recognised that in so far as the guideline might be applied, it would produce a higher level of fine than in the cited Scottish cases;
- where the guideline is used as a method of calculating the appropriate fine the court would have reached the same figures as the sheriff by applying the high culpability factor and the harm category 2, however, the court would have proceeded to have regard to the low number of employees exposed, which would not have decreased the starting point, the fact that the offence had been a cause of actual harm might have increased it, possibly moving it into the level 1 category with a starting point of £2.4 million and a range commencing at £1.5 million but the mitigatory factors would have kept the figures to the lowest level of that range. Were that range not selected, although those factors would have reduced the figure from the starting point, the very large nature of the parent group would have prompted a significant increase equal to, and possibly greater than, the original starting point in order to meet the test of the being sufficiently substantial to have a real economic impact to reinforce the requirement to comply with health and safety legislation;
- using the 2015 Guideline as a cross check to the figure of £1.5 million, the sum selected as a starting point in terms of Scottish sentencing practice, prior to a discount for an early plea was reasonable, and approaching the matter in a similar manner to *HM Advocate v Svitzer Marine* (13 November 2013, unreported), High Court of Justiciary, a discount of 20% was reasonable, to produce a fine of £1.2 million, *Svitzer Marine*, applied.

## Serious Fraud Office v Eurasian Natural Resources Corp Ltd [2018] EWCA Civ 2006

The court considered the circumstances in which litigation privilege and legal advice privilege could arise against a background of potential criminal litigation. It was possible that documents prepared for the purpose of settling or avoiding a claim could be created for the dominant purpose of defending litigation. The court also considered the effect of *Three Rivers DC v Bank of England* [2003] EWCA Civ 474, [2003] QB 1556 in relation to legal advice privilege.

A multinational company appealed against a decision concerning the scope of legal professional privilege in relation to various categories of documents generated during internal investigations by its solicitors and forensic accountants. A whistleblower had alerted the company to allegations of corruption, fraud and bribery within its group and the company had undertaken investigations. The Serious Fraud Office (SFO) had investigated the company, with a view to pursuing a possible prosecution and issued notices compelling the production of documents including:

*Cases*

- statements and evidence provided by the company's employees and officers;
- reviews of books and records by forensic accountants;
- factual evidence;
- documents containing legal advice.

The company said that all documents were subject to litigation privilege. The SFO maintained that there was no generic entitlement to litigation privilege. The High Court found that the company could not claim litigation privilege because it could not establish that the relevant documents had been created for the dominant purpose of being used in the conduct of litigation. It said that a criminal investigation by the SFO was not 'litigation', but a preliminary step taken prior to a decision to prosecute. The judge found that in the case of a corporate client, legal advice privilege only attached to communications between a lawyer and those individuals authorised by the company to obtain the legal advice, but did not extend to other officers or employees of the company.

The appeal was allowed in part.

- Litigation privilege: reasonable contemplation of criminal proceedings – The judge had been wrong to conclude that a criminal prosecution had not reasonably been in prospect. Documents showed that the company was aware of circumstances which rendered litigation between itself and the SFO a real likelihood rather than a real possibility. Not every SFO concern would be regarded as adversarial litigation, but in this case the SFO had made it clear to the company that there was a prospect criminal prosecution, and legal advisers had been engaged to deal with the situation.
- Litigation privilege: dominant purpose of preparing documents – The fact that solicitors prepared a document with the ultimate intention of showing that document to the opposing party did not automatically deprive their preparatory legal work of litigation privilege. In both the civil and criminal contexts, legal advice given to head off, avoid or even settle reasonably contemplated proceedings was as much protected by litigation privilege as advice given for the purpose of resisting or defending such contemplated proceedings. In any event, the company had never agreed to disclose to the SFO the materials which it created in the course of its internal investigation. Even if litigation was not the dominant purpose of the investigation at its very inception, it was clear that it swiftly became the dominant purpose. It was obviously in the public interest that companies should be prepared to investigate allegations from whistleblowers or investigative journalists, prior to going to a prosecutor such as the SFO, without losing the benefit of legal professional privilege. The judge ought to have concluded that most of the documents had been brought into existence for the dominant purpose of resisting or avoiding contemplated criminal proceedings. The documents covered by litigation privilege were notes of interviews conducted by the company's lawyers with employees, former employees, officers of the company and its subsidiaries, suppliers and other third parties. They also included materials generated by a books and records review commissioned by the company.

- Legal advice privilege: effect of *Three Rivers* – The above conclusions in relation to litigation privilege meant that it was not necessary to determine the question of legal advice privilege. However, if it had been necessary to determine the issue, the court would have determined that *Three Rivers DC v Bank of England* [2003] EWCA Civ 474, [2003] QB 1556 determined that communications between an employee of a corporation and the corporation's lawyers could not attract legal advice privilege unless that employee was tasked with seeking and receiving such advice on behalf of the client. There was force in the submission that *Three Rivers* had been wrong in that respect. If it had been open to this court to depart from that decision it would have been in favour of doing so, but that issue could only be determined by the Supreme Court. If the documents had not been subject to litigation privilege, the judge would have been right to follow *Three Rivers* and decide that the relevant documents were not covered by legal advice privilege. The question of whether interviews with ex-employees would be covered by legal advice privilege was similarly a matter for the Supreme Court to determine, as was the question of whether lawyers' working papers were only protected by legal advice privilege if they would betray the tenor of the legal advice (see paras 81, 123–130, 133–134, 138–142).

## Sneller v DAS Nederlandse Rechtsbijstand Verzekeringsmaatschappij (Case C-442/12) [2014] Bus LR 180

A legal expenses insurer which stipulates in its insurance contracts that legal assistance will in principle be provided by its employees from also providing that the costs of legal assistance provided by a lawyer or legal representative chosen freely by the insured person should be covered only if the insurer takes the view that the handling of the case must be subcontracted to an external lawyer.

The European Court of Justice was asked to give a preliminary ruling on the interpretation of the Legal Expenses Directive 87/344/EEC, art 4(1). The insured person took out legal expenses insurance with the defendant, a Dutch insurance company. The contract of insurance provided that cases were to be dealt with by the insurer's own staff but if, according to the insurer's opinion, a case had to be delegated to external counsel, the insured person had the right to instruct a legal representative their own choosing. The insured person wished to bring an unfair dismissal claim against his former employer and he wished to be assisted by a lawyer of his own choosing and to have the costs covered by his insurer. Under national Dutch law, legal assistance was not compulsory for such proceedings. The insurer indicated that it was prepared to provide legal assistance to the insured only through one of its own lawyers and was not prepared to bear the costs of an external lawyer. Subsequently, the insured appealed to the Hoge Raad der Nederlanden (Supreme Court of the Netherlands), which referred to the Court of Justice of the European Union questions on the interpretation of art 4(1) of Directive 87/344/EEC which provided that any legal expenses insurance contract had to expressly recognise that where recourse was had to a lawyer in order to 'serve the interests of the insured person in any ... proceedings', that insured person was free to choose such a lawyer.

A preliminary ruling was given.

The freedom of choice, within the terms of Directive 87/344/EEC, art 4(1), did not mean that member states were obliged to require insurers, in all circumstances, to cover in full the costs incurred in connection with the defence of an insured person, on condition that that freedom was not rendered meaningless. However, the insured person's right to choose his lawyer could not be restricted to situations in which the insurer decided that recourse should be had to an external lawyer. Also, it made no difference whether legal assistance was compulsory under national law for the particular proceedings, since first, the right freely to choose a representative was obligatory and of general application, and second, Directive 87/344/EEC, did not make the right to choose a representative and the scope of that right subject to national rules on legal representation.

## Southall Train Crash

On 19 September 1997, an Intercity 125 passenger train failed to decelerate on entering within sight of two warning signals one of which was slightly misaligned and collided with a freight train causing seven deaths and 139 injuries. Full details of the investigation can be found in the HSE – The Southall Rail Accident Inquiry report by Professor Uff QC can be found at https://www.railwaysarchive.co.uk/documents/HSE_Southall1997.pdf.

## Stark v Post Office [2000] ICR 1013

Stark challenged a finding that the Post Office (PO) had not been negligent or in breach of the Provision and Use of Work Equipment Regulations 1992, SI 1992/2932, in supplying him with a defective bicycle which had resulted in personal injury. Stark contended that reg 6(1), when considered in the light of other regulations concerned with the safety of employees, imposed an absolute obligation on the PO to provide safe work equipment. The court held that reg 6(1) imposed an absolute obligation of which PO were in breach.

Stark, a postman, was injured when the stirrup on the front brake of his delivery bicycle broke. Stark's claim for damages for personal injuries was dismissed and he appealed, contending that there was an absolute obligation on the employer under the Provision and Use of Work Equipment Regulations 1992, reg 6(1) to ensure the safe and efficient operation of all equipment. Moreover, it was argued that Council Directive 89/655 was concerned to set a minimum standard and did not prevent member states from putting in place more stringent requirements.

The appeal was allowed as reg 6(1) imposed an absolute obligation and as the bicycle was not in an efficient working order when the brake broke, the PO was in breach of its absolute duty under the regulations. The Directive set a minimum standard in terms of the duty of employers to ensure the health and safety of workers but member states were free to adopt a stricter approach.

## Three Rivers DC v Governor and Company of the Bank of England (No 5) [2003] EWCA Civ 474

This judgment in an appeal from Tomlinson was in relation to disclosure of documents in a current litigation in which the appellants, liquidators and creditors of Bank of Credit and Commerce International (BCCI), were suing The Bank of England for misfeasance in public office. The Bank had claimed legal professional privilege for numerous documents which came into existence between the time when BCCI collapsed and the time when they made their final submissions to the Bingham Inquiry conducted by Lord Justice Bingham. The Bank did not claim that the documents were prepared in contemplation of litigation and were therefore protected by legal professional privilege which could be described as 'litigation privilege' rather the Bank claimed that the documents were protected from disclosure by reason of that category of legal professional privilege known as 'legal advice privilege'. That is privilege in relation to legal advice that was not founded on the existence or the contemplation of litigation.

Granting the application, that the Court of Appeal reaffirmed that the true rationale of legal advice privilege was that it was a privilege in aid of litigation. It covered the seeking or obtaining of advice concerning rights and obligations because it was rights and obligations which formed the subject matter of litigation. Furthermore, the Court of Appeal had stated that it was important to confine legal advice privilege to its proper limits and it was not open to the Court of Appeal to extend the ambit of the privilege, even if it thought it should. It was therefore unlikely that the Court of Appeal could have intended to decide that all communications or documents passing directly between the Bank and their solicitors concerning the judicial inquiry attracted legal advice privilege, because the subject matter of such communications and documents was not the rights and obligations of the Bank. The communications amounted to presentational assistance and advice and could not be categorised as legal advice of the sort which attracted legal advice privilege.

## Three Rivers DC v Governor and Company of the Bank of England (No 6) [2004] EWCA Civ 218

The provision of advice in relation to an inquiry did not involve the type of professional relationship between solicitor and client that attracted legal advice privilege regardless of whether any legal rights or liabilities were in issue.

The bank appealed against a decision that communications between itself and its solicitors concerning preparations for the Bingham Inquiry into the bank's regulation of Bank of Credit and Commerce International (BCCI) were not covered by legal advice privilege where those communications were solely to the manner in which the bank should present its evidence.

The appeal was dismissed as whilst solicitor and client communications were often what could be expected in the normal course of business, legal advice privilege only arose when such communications pertained to advice on liabilities and rights. Legal advice meant advice in law. However, where the initial relationship between the client and solicitor consisted of advising on rights and liabilities, legal advice privilege would cover a broad spectrum of communication and ancillary matters. In circumstances of this case, the purpose of the communications was not to obtain advice on rights and liabilities, but advice on presentation, and accordingly legal privilege did not arise.

## Transco plc v Stockport Metropolitan Borough Council [2003] UKHL 61, [2004] 2 AC 1

The court reviewed the rule of law laid down in *Rylands v Fletcher*, finding that the piping of a water supply from the mains to storage tanks within a property was a routine function that would not ordinarily raise a hazard and was therefore an ordinary use of the land.

Transco appealed against a ruling ([2001] EWCA Civ 212, [2001] Env LR 44) that the local authority was not liable for damage to Transco's property under the rule in *Rylands v Fletcher*. Water had escaped from a pipe belonging to the local authority and supplying a block of flats of which it was the owner. There was no negligence on the part of the local authority. The water caused the collapse of a nearby railway embankment which left a gas pipe belonging to Transco unsupported and at risk of damage. Transco claimed against the local authority the cost of remedial measures to protect the gas pipe, arguing that the local authority was liable for damage caused by the escape of the water without proof of negligence. The issues to be decided were whether the local authority had brought onto its land something likely to cause danger or mischief if it escaped, and that was an ordinary user of its land.

The appeal was dismissed. The test was whether the local authority had done something on its land which it:

- recognised, or ought reasonably to have recognised judged by the standards appropriate to the place and time, as giving rise to an exceptionally high risk of danger or mischief if there should be an escape; and
- recognised, or ought to have recognised, as being quite out of the ordinary for the place and time.

Piping of a water supply was a routine function which would not have struck anyone as raising any special hazard. The local authority had not accumulated any water but had merely arranged a supply adequate to meet the needs of the residents of the flats. The situation could not be compared with the substantial reservoir in *Rylands v Fletcher*. It was entirely normal and routine and could not be seen as in any way extraordinary or unusual. The conditions to be met before strict liability could be imposed on the local authority were far from being met on the facts of this case.

## West London Pipeline & Storage Ltd v Total UK Ltd [2008] EWHC 1296 (Comm)

The court's power to order the cross-examination of the person making an affidavit should be reserved for extreme cases where there was no alternative relief. The applicant TAV sought an order permitting it to cross-examine the managing director of Total UK Ltd in respect of affidavits which they had sworn in response to an application that TAV had issued for the specific disclosure of documents.

The litigation arose from an explosion and fire at an oil terminal. Total and another company had been sued as potential operators of the site. On the day after the incident, Total had set up an 'accident inspection team' (AIT). TAV, the third party in the action, was the engineering company which had designed and manufactured the switch which had been fitted to the tank from which the fuel spilled. TAV sought from Total factual material gathered by it in the course of its investigations into the incident. Total declined to disclose the relevant documents, stating that they were covered by litigation privilege. The managing director of Total UK Ltd swore affidavits stating that his primary objective in setting up the AIT enquiry was to gather the facts so that Total could secure legal advice in respect of any criminal and civil proceedings arising from the incident. TAV found the managing director's affidavits unsatisfactory and applied for him to be cross-examined.

TAV argued that it had to be possible to go behind an affidavit as to discovery because otherwise a party would be able conclusively to claim litigation privilege by his *ipse dixit* (dogmatic and unproven statement). It submitted that the Rules of the Supreme Court (RSC) did not make provision for cross-examination on affidavits before trial as the CPR r 32.7 did, and the effect of r 32.7, taken together with the procedure in r 31.19 for challenging a claim of privilege, meant that the old authorities did not survive. TAV submitted that, accordingly, there was jurisdiction under the CPR to order cross-examination on an affidavit as to discovery where the court, having carried out the necessary balancing exercise, considered that the overriding objective required it.

The law as it stood provided that, where the court was not satisfied on the basis of the affidavit and other evidence before it that the right to withhold inspection was established, it had four options, one of which was to order the cross-examination of the person who submitted the affidavit. However, the weight of authority was that cross-examination could not be ordered in the case of an affidavit of documents. Notwithstanding TAV's submissions, the old law could not be discarded in the way TAV argued it should be. The procedure under the CPR was, in substance, the same as that under the RSC although under the CPR the claim for privilege was made in a disclosure statement instead of an affidavit. The rationale of avoiding mini-trials at an interlocutory stage was still there. As to whether there was still a jurisdictional bar to ordering cross-examination of the deponent on his affidavit in this context, the need to avoid the party claiming privilege being judge in his own case, and the statements in the authorities that an assertion of privilege was not determinative and might require to be independently proved, were difficult to reconcile with an absolute bar. In the light of the overall approach in the CPR, in an extreme case where there was no alternative relief, it might be just to order such cross-examination rather than concluding, without such examination, that the evidence before the court did not establish a legal right to withhold inspection and ordering inspection. That in turn, however, should only be contemplated if it could be done without impinging to any material extent on the issues in the action, and only after the court had considered whether the position could be addressed by ordering further evidence to be produced on oath, or by inspecting the documents. Even at that stage, cross-examination was unlikely to be necessary. If the deponent was not able to deal with any gaps and inadequacies in a further affidavit, it was likely that the burden of proof that lay on the person claiming privilege would not have been satisfied. In this case, J's affidavits were unsatisfactory in a number of respects and they failed to establish a claim for privilege. In the circumstances, the managing director would be ordered to swear a further affidavit dealing with the deficiencies which had been identified.

## Wotherspoon (John Maxwell) v HM Advocate 1978 JC 74

The Health and Safety at Work etc Act 1974, s 37(1) provides:

> 'Where an offence under any of the relevant statutory provisions committed by a body corporate is proved to have been committed with the consent or connivance of, or to have been attributable to any neglect on the part of, any director, manager, secretary or other similar officer of the body corporate or a person who was purporting to act in any such capacity, he as well as the body corporate shall be guilty of that offence and shall be liable to be proceeded against and punished accordingly.'

A managing director of a company which had failed to guard machinery in contravention of statutory provisions was convicted of two charges under s 37(1) of the 1974 Act. He appealed against conviction on the ground that the Sheriff Principal had misdirected the jury in that he had failed to give them any direction as to the meaning of the words 'attributable to any neglect':

- the word 'neglect' presupposed the existence of some obligation on the part of the person charged with the neglect;
- that the issue was whether the applicant had failed to take some steps to prevent the commission of an offence by the company if the taking of those steps fell within the functions of the office which he held;
- that the functions of the office of the person charged under s 37(1) of the 1974 Act would be a highly relevant consideration;
- that any degree of attributability would suffice that the jury had been given sufficient direction and appeal refused.

# Index

*[all references are to paragraph number]*

**Abatement notices and orders**
  appeals, 6.35
  examples, 6.36
  generally, 6.32
  noise nuisance, and, 6.30
  notices, 6.33
  penalties, 6.34
**Abuse of process**
  criminal proceedings, 12.25
**Admissions**
  criminal proceedings, 12.31
**Alterations notices**
  content, 8.28
  generally, 8.29
  purposes, 8.29
**Ancillary orders**
  corporate manslaughter, 13.31
  environmental offences
    compensation, 7.18–7.19
    confiscation of assets, 7.12–7.13
    criminal behaviour orders, 7.14–7.15
    disqualification of directors, 7.10–7.11
    forfeiture of equipment, 7.16–7.17
    individuals, by, 13.98
    introduction, 7.9
    organisations, by, 13.82
    vehicle seizure, 7.20–7.21
  health and safety offences by individuals, 13.20
  health and safety offences by organisations, 13.11
**Animal by-products**
  environmental offences, 6.1
**Anti-pollution works notices**
  environmental sanctions, 7.5
**Appeals**
  abatement notices and orders, against, 6.35

**Appeals**–*contd*
  civil claims, in
    fatal accidents, 15.30
    generally, 15.5
  criminal proceedings
    Crown Court, from, 12.47
    introduction, 12.45
    magistrates' courts, from, 12.46
  Crown Court, from, 12.47
  enforcement, against
    costs, 5.5
    procedure, 5.4
    purpose, 5.6
  environmental offences
    abatement notices and orders, 6.35
  environmental sanctions
    appealable decisions, 7.44
    compliance notices, 7.48
    environment tribunal, 7.42–7.43
    fixed monetary penalties, 7.45
    grounds, 7.45–7.48
    introduction, 7.42
    powers of tribunal, 7.49
    restoration notices, 7.48
    stop notices, 7.47
    variable monetary penalties, 7.46
  fatal accident claims, 15.30
  fire safety
    England and Wales, 8.41
    Northern Ireland, 8.43–8.44
    Scotland, 8.42
  magistrates' courts, from, 12.46
**Arrest powers**
  criminal investigations, 11.22
**'As low as is reasonably practicable'**
  risk management, 2.4
**Assisting prosecution**
  sentencing
    environmental offences by individuals, 13.96

*Index*

**Assisting prosecution**–*contd*
  sentencing–*contd*
    environmental offences by organisations, 13.80
    health and safety offences by individuals, 13.18
    health and safety offences by organisations, 13.9
**Audit**
  UK Corporate Governance Code, 1.7
**Bad character**
  criminal proceedings, 12.23
**Bail**
  criminal proceedings, 12.14
**Batteries**
  environmental offences
    generally, 6.20
    penalties, 6.21
    prosecution example, 6.22
**Biological agents**
  RIDDOR reports, 10.18
**Board of directors**
  composition, 1.6
  division of responsibilities, 1.5
  duties, 1.7
  evaluation, 1.6
  key issues, 1.10
  leadership, 1.4
  remuneration, 1.8
  succession, 1.6
  UK Corporate Governance Code, 1.4–1.7
**Bodies corporate**
  environmental offences, 6.9
**Breathing apparatus**
  RIDDOR reports, 10.18
**Bundles**
  criminal proceedings, 12.28
**Burden of proof**
  criminal proceedings, 12.27
**Business continuity**
  after the event, 3.35
  communications
    after the incident, 3.34
    data protection, 3.31
    introduction, 3.28
    liaison with emergency services, 3.30
    personnel, 3.32
    public relations, 3.29
    security issues, 3.33
  critical activities, 3.8
  data protection, 3.31

**Business continuity**–*contd*
  fire, 3.12
  impact analysis
    critical activities, 3.8
    introduction, 3.4
    key products and services, 3.5
    quantifying the resources, 3.9
    recovery time, 3.7
    time the organisation can manage, 3.6
  insurance, 3.14
  introduction, 3.1
  key products and services, 3.5
  liaison with emergency services, 3.30
  management, 3.3
  personnel, 3.32
  plan
    assessment of current situation, 3.10
    creation, 3.10–3.27
    fire, 3.12
    insurance, 3.14
    introduction, 3.2
    planning, 3.16–3.27
    revision, 3.35
    salvage, 3.15
    security, 3.11
    services, 3.13
  planning
    back-up IT, 3.27
    call-out list, 3.24
    co-ordination of arrangements with neighbours, 3.20
    damage minimisation, 3.25
    elements of plan, 3.21
    evacuation of premises, 3.26
    implementation of plan, 3.23
    integration of departments, 3.19
    integration of emergency plans, 3.18
    introduction, 3.16
    relocation, 3.27
    response to incident, 3.17
    senior management involvement, 3.22
  public relations, 3.29
  quantifying the resources, 3.9
  recovery time, 3.7
  revision of plan, 3.35
  salvage, 3.15
  security issues
    communications, 3.33
    plan, 3.11
  services, 3.13
  time the organisation can manage, 3.6

# Index

**Business impact analysis**
 critical activities, 3.8
 introduction, 3.4
 key products and services, 3.5
 quantifying the resources, 3.9
 recovery time, 3.7
 time the organisation can manage, 3.6
**Case management**
 bail, 12.14
 entering a plea, 12.13
 generally, 12.9
 plea and trial preparation hearing, 12.11
 preparation for trial form, 12.10
 statements in forms, 12.12
**Cautions**
 criminal investigations, 11.24–11.30
 environmental sanctions
  civil, 7.4
  criminal, 7.7
 'simple', 5.13
**Central funds**
 criminal proceedings, 12.43
**Certification audits**
 external certification, 2.39
 generally, 2.38
 ISO 45001
  generally, 2.40
  relationship with other standards, 2.41
 stages of certification, 2.42
**Chair of the Board**
 UK Corporate Governance Code, 1.5
**Civil claims**
 appeals, 15.5
 common law business, 15.6
 costs, 15.4
 Court of Appeal, 15.5
 disclosure, 15.2
 environmental incidents
  breach of statutory duty, 15.40
  generally, 15.39
  negligence, 15.41
  public nuisance, 15.43
  statutory duty, 15.40
 expert evidence, 15.2
 fatal accidents
  appeals, 15.30
  assessment of dependency, 15.21–15.23
  benefits resulting from death, 15.27
  calculation, 15.25

**Civil claims**–*contd*
 fatal accidents–*contd*
  causation, 15.24
  cohabitees, 15.23
  date of assessment of dependency, 15.26
  defences, 15.32
  dependant, 15.20
  enforcement, 15.31
  insurance, 15.33
  introduction, 15.19
  multiplicand, 15.25
  multipliers, 15.26
  procedural defences, 15.32
  provisional damages, 15.29
  re-marriage, 15.22
  settlement approval, 15.28
 fire damage
  accidental, where, 15.38
  generally, 15.37
 hearing by judge, 15.2
 introduction, 15.1
 judgment, 15.3
 limitation period, 15.7
 permission to appeal, 15.5
 personal injuries
  alternative dispute resolution, 15.18
  claim, 15.15
  disclosure, 15.16
  dismissal of fraudulent claims, 15.10
  expert evidence, 15.17
  generally, 15.8
  letter of claim, 15.14
  letter of notification, 15.12
  pre-action protocol, 15.11–15.17
  rehabilitation, 15.13
  response, 15.15
  *Stark v Post Office*, 15.9
 property damage
  award of damages, 15.36
  generally, 15.34
  measure of damages, 15.35
 Queen's Bench Division, 15.6
 witness statements of fact, 15.2
**Climate change regime**
 environmental sanctions, 7.41
**Closing addresses**
 criminal proceedings, 12.37
**Code for Crown Prosecutors**
 evidential test, 11.5
 generally, 11.4
 public interest test, 11.6

*Index*

**Communications**
  business continuity
    after the incident, 3.34
    data protection, 3.31
    introduction, 3.28
    liaison with emergency services, 3.30
    personnel, 3.32
    public relations, 3.29
    security issues, 3.33

**Community orders**
  environmental offences by individuals, 13.104

**Compensation**
  corporate manslaughter, 13.31
  environmental offences
    example, 7.19
    generally, 7.18
    individuals, by, 13.86
    organisations, by, 13.64
  health and safety offences by individuals, 13.20
  health and safety offences by organisations, 13.11

**Compliance notices**
  environmental sanctions
    generally, 7.25
    non-compliance penalties, 7.35

**Confiscation of assets**
  environmental sanctions
    example, 7.13
    generally, 7.12
    individuals, by, 13.87
    organisations, by, 13.65
  generally, 12.42

**Conflicts of interest**
  criminal investigations
    interviews, 11.23
    response protocol, 11.11

**Coroners' inquests**
  adjournment, 14.21
  calling
    duty to hold, 14.8
    duty to investigate, 14.7
    introduction, 14.6
    timing, 14.9
  Chief Coroner, 14.2
  conclusions
    generally, 14.24
    narrative, 14.26
    short form, 14.25

**Coroners' inquests**–*contd*
  conflicts of interest
    inquest disclosure, 14.32
    insured and insurer attending, 14.31
  coroner areas, 14.3
  coroners' officer, 14.5
  determinations
    conclusions, 14.24–14.26
    introduction, 14.22
    standard of proof, 14.27
    summing up, 14.23
  disclosure
    charges and fees, 14.15
    generally, 14.11
    insured and insurer, 14.32
    interest persons, to, 14.12–14.13
    restrictions, 14.14
  duty to hold, 14.8
  duty to investigate, 14.7
  eligibility of coroners, 14.4
  evidence
    disclosure, 14.11–14.15
    powers of coroners, 14.10
    witness, 14.17
  finding of fact
    conclusions, 14.24–14.26
    introduction, 14.22
    standard of proof, 14.27
    summing up, 14.23
  generally, 14.2
  hearing
    introduction, 14.16
    self-incrimination, 14.18
    witness evidence, 14.17
  holding, 14.8
  insured and insurer
    attending, 14.31
    disclosure, 14.32
  introduction, 14.1
  investigations
    general duty, 14.8
    lasting more than a year, 14.28
  jury
    composition, 14.20
    purpose and use, 14.19
  meaning, 14.2
  post-mortem examinations, 14.30
  purpose, 14.2
  qualifications of coroners, 14.4
  reports to prevent further deaths, 14.29

Index

Coroners' inquests–*contd*
  self-incrimination, 14.18
  standard of proof, 14.27
  summing up, 14.23
  suspension, 14.21
  timing, 14.9
  witness evidence, 14.17
Corporate governance
  definition, 1.3
  FRC guidance, 1.11
  G20/OECD Principle, 1.12
  historical background, 1.2
  introduction, 1.1
  UK Code
    application, 1.9
    audit, 1.7
    company purpose, 1.4
    composition, 1.6
    division of responsibilities, 1.5
    evaluation, 1.6
    internal control, 1.7
    introduction, 1.3
    key issues, 1.10
    leadership, 1.4
    relevant companies, 1.9
    remuneration, 1.8
    succession, 1.6
Corporate manslaughter
  causation, 4.12
  charities, 4.11
  constabularies, 4.8
  corporations, 4.5
  Crown bodies, 4.7
  defendants
    charities, 4.10
    constabularies, 4.8
    corporations, 4.5
    departments, 4.7
    foreign companies, 4.10
    introduction, 4.4
    parent companies, 4.6
    partnerships, 4.9
    police forces, 4.8
    sub-contractors, 4.11
  departments, 4.7
  duty of care
    generally, 4.13
    gross breach, 4.14
  elements, 4.3
  exclusions, 4.18
  foreign companies, 4.10
  foreseeability, 4.15

Corporate manslaughter–*contd*
  generally, 4.2
  government departments, 4.7
  gross breach of duty of care, 4.14
  introduction, 4.1
  investigations, 4.19
  jurisdiction, 4.17
  offence
    causation, 4.12
    duty of care, 4.13
    elements, 4.3
    generally, 4.2
    gross breach of duty, 4.14
    qualifying organisation, 4.4–4.11
    senior management, 4.16
  parent companies, 4.6
  partnerships, 4.9
  police forces, 4.8
  senior management, 4.16
  sentencing
    adjustment, 13.28
    ancillary orders, 13.31
    category range, 13.26
    compensation, 13.31
    examples, 13.34–13.54
    guilty plea, 13.30
    introduction, 13.24
    proportionality of fine to means of offender, 13.27
    reasons, 13.33
    reduction of fine, 13.29–13.30
    seriousness of offence, 13.25
    starting point, 13.26
    totality principle, 13.32
  statutory background, 4.1
  sub-contractors, 4.11
  subsidiaries, 4.10
Costs
  civil claims, 15.4
  criminal proceedings
    central funds, from, 12.43
    defendant's costs, 12.43
    prosecution costs, 12.44
Criminal behaviour orders
  environmental sanctions
    example, 7.15
    generally, 7.14
Criminal investigations
  arrest powers, 11.22
  associated litigation, 11.18
  caution at interview, 11.24–11.30

459

*Index*

Criminal investigations–*contd*
  Code for Crown Prosecutors
    evidential test, 11.5
    generally, 11.4
    public interest test, 11.6
  collecting evidence from scene, 11.16
  compelled interviews of witnesses, 11.32
  conflicts of interest
    interviews, 11.23
    response protocol, 11.11
  contact point for investigating authority, 11.10
  deaths in the workplace
    Protocol for Liaison, 11.3
  disclosure of documents and evidence
    EA officers, 11.37
    HSE inspectors, 11.36
    police powers, 11.35
  Environment Agency officers' powers, 11.37
  environment investigations, 11.37
  evidential test, 11.5
  expert evidence, 11.20
  freedom of information, and, 11.38
  informing insurers, 11.8
  interim reporting, 11.17
  internal advisory team, 11.14
  investigation report
    generally, 11.34
    response protocol, 11.17
  interviews
    adverse inference, 11.25
    caution, under, 11.24–11.30
    conflicts of interest, 11.23
    'full' response, 11.28
    'no comment', 11.27
    prepared statement, 11.29
    representative of organisation, by, 11.30
    response options, 11.26–11.29
    rights of interviewees, 11.12
    SRA guidance, 11.23
    voluntary statements, and, 11.31
    witnesses, of, 11.32
  introduction, 11.2
  knowing powers and authority of agency, 11.15
  legal advice, 11.9
  legal professional privilege, 11.33
  media monitoring and response, 11.21

Criminal investigations–*contd*
  nominating person to speak for organisation, 11.13
  police powers, 11.35
  powers of arrest, 11.22
  powers of EA officers, 11.37
  powers of HSE inspector, 11.36
  powers of investigator, 11.2
  powers of police, 11.35
  prosecutions
    evidential test, 11.5
    generally, 11.4
    public interest test, 11.6
  Protocol for Liaison, 11.3
  public interest test, 11.6
  record of witnesses, 11.16
  reporting accidents, 11.19
  representation for individuals, 11.11
  response protocol
    assembling internal advisory team, 11.14
    associated litigation, 11.18
    collecting evidence from scene, 11.16
    conflicts of interest, 11.11
    contact point for investigating authority, 11.10
    expert evidence, 11.20
    informing insurers, 11.8
    interim reporting, 11.17
    interview rights, 11.12
    introduction, 11.7
    knowing powers of authority, 11.15
    legal advice, 11.9
    media monitoring and response, 11.21
    nominating person to speak for organisation, 11.13
    record of witnesses, 11.16
    reporting accidents, 11.19
    representation for individuals, 11.11
    social media, 11.21
  RIDDOR responsibilities, 11.19
  social media monitoring and response, 11.21
  voluntary witness statements, 11.31
**Criminal proceedings**
*see also* **Prosecutions**
  abuse of process, 12.25
  admissions, 12.31

*Index*

Criminal proceedings–*contd*
  appeals
    Crown Court, from, 12.47
    introduction, 12.45
    magistrates' courts, from, 12.46
  bad character, 12.23
  bail, 12.14
  bundles, 12.28
  burden of proof, 12.27
  case management
    bail, 12.14
    entering a plea, 12.13
    generally, 12.9
    plea and trial preparation hearing, 12.11
    preparation for trial form, 12.10
    statements in forms, 12.12
  central funds, 12.43
  closing addresses, 12.37
  commencing proceedings, 12.8
  costs orders
    central funds, from, 12.43
    defendant's costs, 12.43
    prosecution costs, 12.44
  courts
    Crown Court, 12.3
    magistrates' courts, 12.2
  criminal investigations
    evidential test, 11.5
    generally, 11.4
    public interest test, 11.6
  Criminal Procedure Rules, 12.1
  Crown Court
    appeals from, 12.47
    appeals to, 12.46
    generally, 12.3
  defence case, 12.36
  defence disclosure, 12.18
  defence statement
    generally, 12.19–12.20
    introduction, 12.18
  defendant's costs, 12.43
  delay in prosecution, 12.25
  disclosure
    defence, 12.18
    initial, 12.18
    investigator's duty, 12.16
    stages, 12.18
    test, 12.17
    unused material, 12.15
  disclosure officer, 12.16
  dismissal of charges, 12.24

Criminal proceedings–*contd*
  double jeopardy, 12.25
  either way offences, 12.6
  entering a plea, 12.13
  evidence
    bad character, 12.23
    expert, 12.21
    hearsay, 12.22
  evidential test, 11.5
  expert evidence, 12.21
  failure to disclose evidence, 12.25
  files of documents, 12.28
  hearsay evidence, 12.22
  indictable offences, 12.7
  initial disclosure, 12.18
  judge's summing up, 12.38
  loss of evidence, 12.25
  magistrates' court
    appeals from, 12.46
    generally, 12.2
  Newton hearing, 12.41
  no case to answer, 12.35
  plea
    case management, 12.13
    trial, at, 12.33
  plea and trial preparation hearing
    generally, 12.11
    introduction, 12.6
  points of law, 12.32
  preparation for trial form, 12.10
  process
    abuse of process, 12.25
    appeals, 12.45–12.47
    bad character, 12.23
    case management, 12.9–12.14
    commencing proceedings, 12.8
    costs, 12.43–12.44
    courts, 12.2–12.3
    defence statement, 12.19–12.20
    disclosure, 12.15–12.18
    dismissal of charges, 12.24
    expert evidence, 12.21
    hearsay evidence, 12.22
    Rules, 12.1
    sentencing, 12.40–12.42
    third party disclosure, 12.20
    trial, at, 12.26–12.39
    types of offence, 12.4–12.7
  prosecution case, 12.34
  prosecution costs, 12.44
  public interest test, 11.6

*Index*

**Criminal proceedings**–*contd*
  sentencing
    confiscation, 12.42
    costs, 12.43–12.44
    hearing, 12.40
    Newton hearing, 12.41
  start of the trial, 12.33
  statements in forms, 12.12
  summary offences, 12.5
  summing up, 12.38
  third party disclosure, 12.20
  trial procedure
    admissions, 12.31
    bundles, 12.28
    burden of proof, 12.27
    closing addresses, 12.37
    defence case, 12.36
    files of documents, 12.28
    introduction, 12.26
    judge's summing up, 12.38
    no case to answer, 12.35
    plea, 12.33
    points of law, 12.32
    prosecution case, 12.34
    start of the trial, 12.33
    summing up, 12.38
    verdict, 12.39
    witness evidence, 12.29
    witness statements, 12.30
  types of offence
    either way, 12.6
    indictable, 12.7
    introduction, 12.4
    summary, 12.5
  unused material
    failure to disclose, 12.25
    generally, 12.15
  verdict, 12.39
  witness evidence, 12.29
  witness statements, 12.30
**Criminal sanctions**
  environmental offences
    ancillary orders, 7.9–7.21
    cautions, 7.7
    fixed penalty notices, 7.6
    prosecution, 7.8
**Critical activities**
  business impact analysis, 3.8
**Crown Court**
  appeals from, 12.47
  appeals to, 12.46
  generally, 12.3

**Crown Fire Inspectors**
  generally, 8.22
**Dangerous occurrences**
  RIDDOR reports, 10.18
**Data protection**
  business continuity, 3.31
**Death of person**
  Protocol for Liaison, 11.3
  RIDDOR reports
    mandatory investigations, 10.28
    reportable events, 10.12
**Defence case**
  criminal proceedings, 12.36
**Defence disclosure**
  criminal proceedings, 12.18
**Defence statement**
  generally, 12.19–12.20
  introduction, 12.18
**Defendant's costs**
  criminal proceedings, 12.43
**Delay in prosecution**
  criminal proceedings, 12.25
**Director's duties**
  generally, 1.13
  statutory basis, 1.13
**Disclosure of documents and evidence**
  criminal investigations
    EA officers, 11.37
    HSE inspectors, 11.36
    police powers, 11.35
  defence, 12.18
  initial, 12.18
  investigator's duty, 12.16
  officer, 12.16
  stages, 12.18
  test, 12.17
  unused material, 12.15
**Dismissal of charges**
  criminal proceedings, 12.24
**Disqualification of directors**
  environmental sanctions
    example, 7.11
    generally, 7.10
**Diving operations**
  RIDDOR reports, 10.18
**Double jeopardy**
  criminal proceedings, 12.25
**Either way offences**
  criminal proceedings, 12.6
**Electrical incidents**
  RIDDOR reports, 10.18

# Index

**Emergency lighting**
fire safety, 8.13
**Emergency services liaison**
business continuity, 3.30
**Emissions**
environmental offences, 6.1
**Enforcement**
agencies
*see also* **Enforcement agencies**
Crown Fire Inspectors, 8.22
Environment Agency, 9.24–9.26
environmental, 9.24–9.33
fire safety, 8.15–8.22
Fire and Rescue Service, 8.16–8.19
health and safety, 9.3–9.23
HELA, 9.3
HSE, 8.21, 9.4–9.5
HSENI, 9.18–9.21
introduction, 9.1–9.2
local authorities (environment), 9.33
local authority (fire safety), 8.20
local authorities (health and safety), 9.6–9.9
Natural Resources Wales, 9.29–9.30
NIEA, 9.31–9.32
Office of Nuclear Regulation, 9.16–9.17
Office of the Rail Regulator, 9.10–9.15
SEPA, 9.27–9.28
appeals
costs, 5.5
procedure, 5.4
purpose, 5.6
cautions, 5.13
enforcement notices
*see also* **Environmental notices**
appeals, 5.4–5.6
fire safety, 8.30–8.31
generally, 5.1
environmental offences
*see also* **Environmental sanctions**
ancillary orders, 7.9–7.21
appeals, 7.42–7.49
cautions, 7.4
compensation, 7.18–7.19
compliance notices, 7.25
confiscation of assets, 7.12–7.13
criminal behaviour orders, 7.14–7.15
disqualification of directors, 7.10–7.11

**Enforcement**–*contd*
environmental offences–*contd*
enforcement cost recovery notices, 7.39
enforcement notices, 7.5
enforcement undertakings, 7.30
fixed monetary penalties, 7.23
forfeiture of equipment, 7.16–7.17
injunctions, 7.2
introduction, 7.1
non-compliance penalties, 7.31–7.38
other, 7.39–7.41
RESA 2008, under, 7.22–7.30
restoration notices, 7.26
stop notices, 7.27
suspension notices, 7.28–7.29
undertakings, 7.30
variable monetary penalties, 7.24
vehicle seizure, 7.20–7.21
warnings, 7.3
fatal accident claims, 15.31
fee for intervention (FFI)
background, 5.7
challenging an invoice, 5.8–5.12
disputing, 5.10
generally, 5.7
purpose of challenge, 5.12
querying, 5.9
recoverable time, 5.7
repayment, 5.11
fire safety
*see also* **Enforcement (fire safety)**
alterations notices, 8.29
appeals, 8.41–8.44
authorities, 8.15–8.22
Crown Fire Inspectors, 8.22
enforcement notices, 8.30–8.31
Fire and Rescue Service, 8.16–8.19
Health and Safety Executive, 8.21
inspections, 8.23
local authority, 8.20
notices, 8.30–8.31
procedures, 8.27–8.35
prohibition notices, 8.32–8.34
prosecutions, 8.36–8.40
public register, 8.24–8.26
health and safety agencies
agencies, 9.3–9.23
HELA, 9.3
HSE, 9.4–9.5
HSENI, 9.18–9.21
introduction, 9.1

*Index*

Enforcement–*contd*
  health and safety agencies–*contd*
    local authorities, 9.6–9.9
    Office of Nuclear Regulation, 9.16–9.17
    Office of the Rail Regulator, 9.10–9.15
    working together, 9.2
  improvement notices
    appeals, 5.4–5.6
    fee for intervention, 5.7–5.12
    generally, 5.2
  introduction, 9.1
  notices of contravention, 5.7
  prohibition notices
    appeals, 5.4–5.6
    fee for intervention, 5.7–5.12
    fire safety, 8.32–8.34
    generally, 5.3
  reporting injuries, diseases and occurrences
    *see also* **RIDDOR reports**
    discretionary investigations, 10.33
    duration of record keeping, 10.37
    exempt events, 10.36
    failure to report, 10.23
    insurance, 10.22
    internal investigations, 10.38–10.48
    investigations, 10.26–10.33
    legal requirement, 10.10
    maker of report, 10.2–10.9
    mandatory investigations, 10.27–10.32
    over reporting, 10.24
    procedure, 10.21
    purpose of report, 10.1
    records, 10.25, 10.34
    reportable events, 10.11–10.20
    timing of report, 10.35
  working together, 9.2

**Enforcement agencies**
  Crown Fire Inspectors, 8.22
  Environment Agency
    establishment, 9.24
    policy, 9.26
    responsibilities, 9.25
  environmental
    Environment Agency, 9.24–9.26
    local authorities, 9.33
    Natural Resources Wales, 9.29–9.30
    NIEA, 9.31–9.32
    SEPA, 9.27–9.28

Enforcement agencies–*contd*
  fire safety
    Crown Fire Inspectors, 8.22
    Fire and Rescue Service, 8.16–8.19
    Health and Safety Executive, 8.21
    introduction, 8.15
    local authority, 8.20
  Fire and Rescue Service
    England and Wales, 8.17–8.18
    introduction, 8.16
  health and safety
    HELA, 9.3
    HSE, 9.4–9.5
    HSENI, 9.18–9.22
    introduction, 9.1
    local authorities, 9.6–9.9
    Office of Nuclear Regulation, 9.16–9.17
    Office of the Rail Regulator, 9.10–9.15
    other authorities, 9.23
    working together, 9.2
  HELA, 9.3
  HSE
    fire safety, 8.21
    generally, 9.4
    introduction, 9.1
    policy statement, 9.5
    working with EA, 9.2
  HSENI
    generally, 9.18
    local councils, and, 9.20–9.22
    objectives, 9.19
    responsibilities, 9.21
  introduction, 9.1–9.2
  local authorities
    environment, 9.33
    fire safety, 8.20
    health and safety, 9.6–9.9
  local authorities (health and safety)
    generally, 9.6
    intervention and enforcement activity, 9.9
    introduction, 9.1
    national code, 9.8
    provision, 9.7
    working with HSE, 9.2
  Natural Resources Wales
    generally, 9.29
    policy, 9.30
  NIEA
    generally, 9.31
    policy, 9.32

*Index*

Enforcement agencies–*contd*
  Office of Nuclear Regulation
    generally, 9.16
    policy, 9.17
  Office of the Rail Regulator
    formal tools, 9.14
    generally, 9.10
    policy, 9.11
    powers, 9.12
    prosecutions, 9.15
    strategies, 9.13
  other authorities, 9.23
  SEPA
    generally, 9.27
    policy, 9.28
Enforcement (fire safety)
  alterations notices
    content, 8.28
    generally, 8.29
    purposes, 8.29
  appeals
    England and Wales, 8.41
    Northern Ireland, 8.43–8.44
    Scotland, 8.42
  Article 47 notices, 8.35
  authorities
    Crown Fire Inspectors, 8.22
    Fire and Rescue Service, 8.16–8.19
    Health and Safety Executive, 8.21
    introduction, 8.15
    local authority, 8.20
  Crown Fire Inspectors, 8.22
  enforcement notices
    content, 8.28
    example, 8.31
    generally, 8.30
    introduction, 8.27
    public register, 8.24–8.26
  Fire and Rescue Service
    England and Wales, 8.17–8.18
    introduction, 8.16
  fire fighters' cut-off switches for luminous tube sign
    content, 8.28
    generally, 8.35
    introduction, 8.27
  HSWA 1974 notices, 8.34
  Health and Safety Executive, 8.21
  improvement notices, 8.34
  local authority, 8.20

Enforcement (fire safety)–*contd*
  procedures
    alterations notices, 8.29
    content of notices, 8.28
    introduction, 8.27
    'relevant notice', 8.27
  prohibition notices
    content, 8.28
    example, 8.33
    generally, 8.32
    HSWA 1974, under, 8.34
    introduction, 8.27
  prosecutions
    companies, 8.38
    examples, 8.37–8.40
    factors affecting choice, 8.37
    generally, 8.36
    individual, 8.39
    responsible person, 8.40
  public register of notices
    duration, 8.25
    generally, 8.24
    viewing, 8.26
  'relevant notice', 8.27
  restriction notices
    content, 8.28
    example, 8.33
    generally, 8.32
Enforcement cost recovery notices
  environmental sanctions, 7.39
Enforcement notices
  appeals
    costs, 5.5
    procedure, 5.4
    purpose, 5.6
  environmental sanctions, 7.5
  fire safety
    content, 8.28
    example, 8.31
    generally, 8.30
    introduction, 8.27
    public register, 8.24–8.26
  generally, 5.1
Enforcement undertakings
  environmental sanctions
    generally, 7.30
    non-compliance penalties, 7.33
Environment Agency (EA)
  establishment, 9.24
  policy, 9.26
  powers of officers, 11.37
  responsibilities, 9.25

*Index*

**Environmental claims**
*see also* **Civil claims**
breach of statutory duty, 15.40
generally, 15.39
negligence, 15.41
private nuisance, 15.42
public nuisance, 15.43
statutory duty, 15.40
**Environmental enforcement**
*see also* **Environmental offences**
agencies
　Environment Agency, 9.24–9.26
　local authorities, 9.33
　Natural Resources Wales, 9.29–9.30
　NIEA, 9.31–9.32
　SEPA, 9.27–9.28
Environment Agency
　establishment, 9.24
　policy, 9.26
　responsibilities, 9.25
introduction, 9.1
local authorities, 9.33
Natural Resources Wales
　generally, 9.29
　policy, 9.30
NIEA
　generally, 9.31
　policy, 9.32
SEPA
　generally, 9.27
　policy, 9.28
**Environmental offences**
abatement notices and orders
　appeals, 6.35
　examples, 6.36
　generally, 6.32
　noise nuisance, and, 6.30
　notices, 6.33
　penalties, 6.34
animal by-products, 6.1
batteries
　generally, 6.20
　penalties, 6.21
　prosecution example, 6.22
bodies corporate, and, 6.9
civil sanctions
　*see also* **Environmental sanctions**
　ancillary orders, 7.9–7.21
　appeals, 7.42–7.49
　cautions, 7.4
　compensation, 7.18–7.19
　compliance notices, 7.25

**Environmental offences**–*contd*
civil sanctions–*contd*
　confiscation of assets, 7.12–7.13
　criminal behaviour orders, 7.14–7.15
　disqualification of directors, 7.10–7.11
　enforcement cost recovery notices, 7.39
　enforcement notices, 7.5
　enforcement undertakings, 7.30
　fixed monetary penalties, 7.23
　forfeiture of equipment, 7.16–7.17
　injunctions, 7.2
　introduction, 7.1
　non-compliance penalties, 7.31–7.38
　other, 7.39–7.41
　RESA 2008, under, 7.22–7.30
　restoration notices, 7.26
　stop notices, 7.27
　suspension notices, 7.28–7.29
　undertakings, 7.30
　variable monetary penalties, 7.24
　vehicle seizure, 7.20–7.21
　warnings, 7.3
criminal sanctions
　ancillary orders, 7.9–7.21
　cautions, 7.7
　fixed penalty notices, 7.6
　prosecution, 7.8
emissions, 6.1
EU law, 6.1
fly-tipping
　fixed penalty notices, 6.13
　generally, 6.10
　penalties, 6.11
　prosecution examples, 6.12
food waste, 6.1
illegal dumping of waste
　fixed penalty notices, 6.13
　generally, 6.10
　penalties, 6.11
　prosecution examples, 6.12
industrial emissions, 6.1
introduction, 6.1
landfill, 6.1
noise nuisance
　abatement notices, 6.30
　criminal behaviour orders, 6.31
　fixed penalty notices, 6.30
　generally, 6.29
　penalties, 6.30

Environmental offences–*contd*
  packaging waste
    activity list, 6.18
    definition of 'handling', 6.17
    definition of 'packaging', 6.15
    description, 6.18
    generally, 6.14
    legal background, 6.1
    obligated packing producer, 6.16
    registration, 6.19
  public sewers
    use restrictions, 6.37
  sentencing
    individuals, 13.85–13.104
    organisations, 13.63–13.84
  sentencing of organisations
    adjustment, 13.79
    ancillary orders, 13.82
    assisting prosecution, 13.80
    category range, 13.67
    combination of financial orders removes economic benefit derived, 13.77
    compensation, 13.64
    confiscation, 13.65
    determining offence category, 13.66
    financial information, 13.69–13.75
    fines, 13.68–13.75
    guidelines, 13.63–13.75
    guilty plea, 13.81
    introduction, 13.61
    proportionality of fine to means of offender, 13.78
    reasons, 13.84
    reduction, 13.80–13.81
    starting point, 13.62
    structure ranges, 13.62
    totality, 13.83
  statutory nuisance
    appeals, 6.35
    examples, 6.36
    generally, 6.32
    notices, 6.33
    penalties, 6.34
    public sewers, 6.37
  strict liability, 6.2
  UK law, 6.1
  waste
    batteries, 6.20–6.22
    carriers brokers registration, 6.7
    definition of 'waste', 6.3

Environmental offences–*contd*
  waste–*contd*
    electrical and electronic equipment, 6.23
    fly-tipping, 6.10–6.13
    generally, 6.5
    legal background, 6.1
    packaging, 6.14–6.19
    penalties, 6.8
    unlawful deposit of controlled waste, 6.6
  waste electrical and electronic equipment
    generally, 6.23
    legal background, 6.1
  water
    anti-pollution works, 6.26
    England and Wales, in, 6.25
    generally, 6.24
    Northern Ireland, in, 6.27
    penalties, 6.28
    Scotland, in, 6.27
  wildlife
    examples, 6.39
    generally, 6.38
    prosecution examples, 6.40
**Environmental sanctions**
  ancillary orders
    compensation, 7.18–7.19
    confiscation of assets, 7.12–7.13
    criminal behaviour orders, 7.14–7.15
    disqualification of directors, 7.10–7.11
    forfeiture of equipment, 7.16–7.17
    introduction, 7.9
    vehicle seizure, 7.20–7.21
  anti-pollution works notices, 7.5
  appeals
    appealable decisions, 7.44
    compliance notices, 7.48
    environment tribunal, 7.42–7.43
    fixed monetary penalties, 7.45
    grounds, 7.45–7.48
    introduction, 7.42
    powers of tribunal, 7.49
    restoration notices, 7.48
    stop notices, 7.47
    variable monetary penalties, 7.46
  cautions
    criminal sanctions, 7.7
    generally, 7.4
  climate change regime, under, 7.41

*Index*

**Environmental sanctions**–*contd*
  compensation
    example, 7.19
    generally, 7.18
  compliance notices
    generally, 7.25
    non-compliance penalties, 7.35
  confiscation of assets
    example, 7.13
    generally, 7.12
  criminal behaviour orders
    example, 7.15
    generally, 7.14
  criminal sanctions
    ancillary orders, 7.9–7.21
    cautions, 7.7
    fixed penalty notices, 7.6
    prosecution, 7.8
  disqualification of directors
    example, 7.11
    generally, 7.10
  enforcement cost recovery notices, 7.39
  enforcement notices, 7.5
  enforcement undertakings
    generally, 7.30
    non-compliance penalties, 7.33
  fixed monetary penalties
    generally, 7.23
    non-compliance penalties, 7.32
  fixed penalty notices, 7.6
  forfeiture of equipment
    example, 7.17
    generally, 7.16
  groundwater prohibition notices, 7.5
  injunctions, 7.2
  introduction, 7.1
  landfill, 7.41
  monetary penalties
    fixed, 7.23
    non-compliance penalties, , 7.32
    variable, 7.24
  non-compliance penalties
    application of, 7.40
    compliance notices, 7.35
    enforcement undertakings, 7.33
    fixed monetary penalties, 7.32
    introduction, 7.31
    restoration notices, 7.34
    stop notices, 7.36
    variable monetary penalties, 7.32
  other, 7.39–7.41
  remediation powers, 7.5

**Environmental sanctions**–*contd*
  RESA 2008, under
    background, 7.1
    compliance notices, 7.25
    enforcement undertakings, 7.30
    fixed monetary penalties, 7.23
    introduction, 7.22
    restoration notices, 7.26
    stop notices, 7.27
    suspension notices, 7.28–7.29
    variable monetary penalties, 7.24
  restoration notices
    generally, 7.26
    non-compliance penalties, 7.34
  revocation notices, 7.5
  stop notices
    generally, 7.27
    non-compliance penalties, 7.36
  suspension notices
    challenges, 7.29
    generally, 7.28
    introduction, 7.5
  undertakings
    generally, 7.30
    non-compliance penalties, 7.33
  variable monetary penalties
    generally, 7.24
    non-compliance penalties, 7.32
  variation notices, 7.5
  vehicle seizure
    example, 7.21
    generally, 7.20
  warnings, 7.3

**Environmental tribunal**
  appealable decisions, 7.44
  background, 7.42
  compliance notices, 7.48
  composition, 7.43
  establishment, 7.42
  fixed monetary penalties, 7.45
  grounds
    compliance notices, 7.48
    fixed monetary penalties, 7.45
    restoration notices, 7.48
    stop notices, 7.47
    variable monetary penalties, 7.46
  introduction, 7.42
  membership, 7.43
  powers of tribunal, 7.49
  restoration notices, 7.48
  stop notices, 7.47
  variable monetary penalties, 7.46

# Index

Evidence
  coroners' inquests
    disclosure, 14.11–14.15
    powers of coroners, 14.10
    witness, 14.17
  criminal proceedings
    bad character, 12.23
    expert, 12.21
    hearsay, 12.22
  public inquiries
    generally, 14.44
    privileged information, 14.48
    production, 14.47
Evidential test
  criminal proceedings, 11.5
Expert evidence
  criminal proceedings, 12.21
Explosions
  RIDDOR reports, 10.19
External audit
  safety auditing, 2.37
External certification
  certification audits, 2.39
Failure to disclose evidence
  criminal proceedings, 12.25
Fatal accident claims
  appeals, 15.30
  assessment of dependency
    cohabitees, 15.23
    date, 15.26
    generally, 15.21
    re-marriage, 15.22
  benefits resulting from death, 15.27
  calculation, 15.25
  causation, 15.24
  cohabitees, 15.23
  date of assessment of dependency, 15.26
  defences, 15.32
  dependant, 15.20
  enforcement, 15.31
  insurance, 15.33
  introduction, 15.19
  multiplicand, 15.25
  multipliers, 15.26
  procedural defences, 15.32
  provisional damages, 15.29
  re-marriage, 15.22
  settlement approval, 15.28
Fatalities
  RIDDOR reports
    mandatory investigations, 10.28
    reportable events, 10.12

Fee for intervention (FFI)
  background, 5.7
  challenging an invoice, 5.8–5.12
  disputing, 5.10
  generally, 5.7
  purpose of challenge, 5.12
  querying, 5.9
  recoverable time, 5.7
  repayment, 5.11
  use, 5.12
Financial information
  environmental offences by individuals, 13.90–13.91
  environmental offence by organisations, 13.69–13.75
Financial Reporting Council (FRC)
  corporate governance guidance, 1.11
Fines
  see also Sentencing
  corporate manslaughter, 13.24–13.54
  environmental offences, 13.61–13.104
  generally, 13.3
  health and safety offences, 13.4–13.23
  fire safety, 13.60
  reduction, 13.105
  totality, 13.106
Fire
  business continuity plan, 3.12
  RIDDOR reports, 10.1
Fire and Rescue Service
  England and Wales, 8.17–8.18
  introduction, 8.16
Fire damage claims
  accidental, where, 15.38
  generally, 15.37
Fire fighters' cut-off switch
  content, 8.28
  generally, 8.35
  introduction, 8.27
Fire safety
  alarm systems, 8.12
  alterations notices
    content, 8.28
    generally, 8.29
    introduction, 8.27
    purposes, 8.29
  appeals
    England and Wales, 8.41
    Northern Ireland, 8.43–8.44
    Scotland, 8.42

*Index*

Fire safety–*contd*
  Article 47 notices, 8.35
  certificates, 8.7
  company prosecutions, 8.38
  Crown Fire Inspectors, 8.22
  determinations
    England and Wales, 8.45–8.47
    Scotland, 8.48–8.50
  emergency lighting, 8.13
  enforcement
    authorities, 8.15–8.22
    notices, 8.30–8.31
    procedures, 8.27–8.37
    public register, 8.24–8.26
  enforcement authorities
    Crown Fire Inspectors, 8.22
    Fire and Rescue Service, 8.16–8.19
    Health and Safety Executive, 8.21
    introduction, 8.15
    local authority, 8.20
  enforcement notices
    content, 8.28
    example, 8.31
    generally, 8.30
    introduction, 8.27
    public register, 8.24–8.26
  enforcement procedures
    alterations notices, 8.29
    content of notices, 8.28
    introduction, 8.27
    'relevant notice', 8.27
  extinguishers, 8.10
  Fire and Rescue Service
    England and Wales, 8.17–8.18
    introduction, 8.16
  fire fighters' cut-off switch
    content, 8.28
    generally, 8.35
    introduction, 8.27
  HSWA 1974 notices, 8.34
  Health and Safety Executive, 8.21
  improvement notices, 8.34
  individual prosecutions, 8.39
  inspections, 8.23
  introduction, 8.1
  legislation
    England and Wales, 8.3–8.4
    introduction, 8.2–8.7
    Northern Ireland, 8.6
    Scotland, 8.5
  local authority, 8.20

Fire safety–*contd*
  luminous tube sign switches
    content, 8.28
    generally, 8.35
    introduction, 8.27
  Primary Authority Scheme
    elements, 8.18
    generally, 8.17
    persons entitled to enter, 8.19
  prohibition notices
    content, 8.28
    example, 8.33
    generally, 8.32
    HSWA 1974, under, 8.34
    introduction, 8.27
  prosecutions
    companies, 8.38
    examples, 8.37–8.40
    factors affecting choice, 8.37
    generally, 8.36
    individual, 8.39
    responsible person, 8.40
  public register of notices
    duration, 8.25
    generally, 8.24
    viewing, 8.26
  Regulatory Reform Order 2015
    alarm systems, 8.12
    emergency lighting, 8.13
    extinguishers, 8.10
    generally, 8.8
    risk assessment, 8.9
    signs, 8.11
    training, 8.14
  'relevant notice', 8.27
  responsible person
    generally, 8.3
    prosecutions, 8.40
    requirements, 8.4
  restriction notices
    content, 8.28
    example, 8.33
    generally, 8.32
  risk assessment, 8.9
  signs, 8.11
  training, 8.14
**Fixed monetary penalties**
  environmental sanctions
    generally, 7.23
    non-compliance penalties, 7.32
**Fixed penalty notices**
  criminal sanctions, 7.6

**Flammable liquids and gases**
  RIDDOR reports, 10.19
**Fly-tipping**
  fixed penalty notices, 6.13
  generally, 6.10
  penalties, 6.11
  prosecution examples, 6.12
**Food waste**
  environmental offences, 6.1
**Forfeiture of equipment**
  environmental sanctions
    example, 7.17
    generally, 7.16
**Freedom of information**
  criminal investigations, 11.38
**Gas incidents**
  RIDDOR reports, 10.20
**Gross negligence manslaughter**
  breach of duty of care
    generally, 4.23
    grossness, 4.26
  causation, 4.25
  directors, 4.22
  duty of care
    breach, 4.23
    directors, 4.22
    generally, 4.21
  elements of offence, 4.20
  foreseeability, 4.24
  generally, 4.20
  gross breach, 4.26
  offence, 4.20
  sentencing
    examples, 13.56–13.59
    generally, 13.55
**Groundwater prohibition notices**
  environmental sanctions, 7.5
**G20**
  corporate governance guidance, 1.12
**Guilty plea**
  sentencing
    corporate manslaughter, 13.30
    environmental offences by
      individuals, 13.97
    environmental offences by
      organisations, 13.81
    health and safety offences by
      individuals, 13.19
    health and safety offences by
      organisations, 13.10
**Hazardous escapes of substances**
  RIDDOR reports, 10.19

**Health and safety enforcement**
  *see also* **Health and safety offences**
  agencies
    HELA, 9.3
    HSE, 9.4–9.5
    HSENI, 9.18–9.22
    local authorities, 9.6–9.9
    Office of Nuclear Regulation,
      9.16–9.17
    Office of the Rail Regulator, 9.10–9.15
    other authorities, 9.23
  HELA, 9.3
  HSE
    fire safety, 8.21
    generally, 9.4
    introduction, 9.1
    policy statement, 9.5
    working with EA, 9.2
  HSENI
    generally, 9.18
    local councils, and, 9.20–9.22
    objectives, 9.19
    responsibilities, 9.21
  introduction, 9.1
  local authorities
    generally, 9.6
    intervention and enforcement
      activity, 9.9
    introduction, 9.1
    national code, 9.8
    policy, 9.11
    powers, 9.12
    provision, 9.7
    working with HSE, 9.2
  Office of Nuclear Regulation
    generally, 9.16
    policy, 9.17
  Office of the Rail Regulator
    formal tools, 9.14
    generally, 9.10
    prosecutions, 9.15
    strategies, 9.13
  other authorities, 9.23
**Health and safety enforcement notices**
  generally, 5.1
**Health and Safety Executive/Local Authorities Enforcement Liaison Committee (HELA)**
  generally, 9.3
**Health and Safety Executive (HSE)**
  corporate governance guidance, 1.12
  fire safety, 8.21

*Index*

**Health and Safety Executive (HSE)**–*contd*
  generally, 9.4
  introduction, 9.1
  policy statement, 9.5
  working with EA, 9.2
**Health and Safety Executive Northern Ireland (HSENI)**
  generally, 9.18
  local councils, and, 9.20–9.22
  objectives, 9.19
  responsibilities, 9.21
**Health and safety offences**
  bodies corporate, and, 4.35
  connivance, 4.38
  consent, 4.37
  delegation of duties, 4.31
  directors, 4.34–4.39
  employees' duties, 4.40–4.41
  employers' duties
    delegation, 4.31
    generally, 4.27
  exposure to material risk, 4.29
  failures of frontline employees, 4.32
  fire safety notices, 8.34
  general duties, 4.27
  neglect, 4.39
  post-accident changes to safe systems, 4.33
  prosecutions under ss 2 and 3, 4.28
  'reasonably practicable', 4.30
  risk management
    'as low as is reasonably practicable', 2.4
    generally, 2.3
  safe system changes, 4.32
  senior managers, 4.34–4.39
  sentencing
    individuals, 13.14–13.23
    organisations, 13.4–13.13
  sentencing of individuals
    ancillary orders, 13.20
    assisting prosecution, 13.18
    category range, 13.16
    compensation, 13.20
    determining offence category, 13.15
    guilty plea, 13.19
    introduction, 13.14
    reasons, 13.21
    reduction, 13.18–13.19
    review of financial element, 13.17

**Health and safety offences**–*contd*
  sentencing of individuals–*contd*
    starting point, 13.16
    time spent on bail, 13.23
    totality principle, 13.21
  sentencing of organisations
    adjustment, 13.8
    ancillary orders, 13.11
    assisting prosecution, 13.9
    category range, 13.6
    compensation, 13.11
    determining offence category, 13.5
    forfeiture, 13.11
    guilty plea, 13.10
    introduction, 13.4
    proportionality of fine to means of offender, 13.7
    reasons, 13.13
    reduction, 13.9–13.10
    remediation, 13.11
    starting point, 13.6
    totality principle, 13.12
**Hearsay evidence**
  criminal proceedings, 12.22
**Illegal dumping of waste**
  fixed penalty notices, 6.13
  generally, 6.10
  penalties, 6.11
  prosecution examples, 6.12
**Improvement notices**
  appeals
    costs, 5.5
    procedure, 5.4
    purpose, 5.6
  fee for intervention (FFI)
    background, 5.7
    challenging an invoice, 5.8–5.12
    disputing, 5.10
    generally, 5.7
    purpose of challenge, 5.12
    querying, 5.9
    recoverable time, 5.7
    repayment, 5.11
  fire safety, 8.34
  generally, 5.2
**Indictable offences**
  criminal proceedings, 12.7
**Industrial emissions**
  environmental offences, 6.1
**Injunctions**
  environmental sanctions, 7.2

*Index*

**Inquests**
  adjournment, 14.21
  calling
    duty to hold, 14.8
    duty to investigate, 14.7
    introduction, 14.6
    timing, 14.9
  Chief Coroner, 14.2
  conclusions
    generally, 14.24
    narrative, 14.26
    short form, 14.25
  conflicts of interest
    inquest disclosure, 14.32
    insured and insurer attending, 14.31
  coroner areas, 14.3
  coroners' officer, 14.5
  determinations
    conclusions, 14.24–14.26
    introduction, 14.22
    standard of proof, 14.27
    summing up, 14.23
  disclosure
    charges and fees, 14.15
    generally, 14.11
    insured and insurer, 14.32
    interest persons, to, 14.12–14.13
    restrictions, 14.14
  duty to hold, 14.8
  duty to investigate, 14.7
  eligibility of coroners, 14.4
  evidence
    disclosure, 14.11–14.15
    powers of coroners, 14.10
    witness, 14.17
  finding of fact
    conclusions, 14.24–14.26
    introduction, 14.22
    standard of proof, 14.27
    summing up, 14.23
  generally, 14.2
  hearing
    introduction, 14.16
    self-incrimination, 14.18
    witness evidence, 14.17
  holding, 14.8
  insured and insurer
    attending, 14.31
    disclosure, 14.32
  introduction, 14.1

**Inquests**–*contd*
  investigations
    general duty, 14.8
    lasting more than a year, 14.28
  jury
    composition, 14.20
    purpose and use, 14.19
  meaning, 14.2
  post-mortem examinations, 14.30
  purpose, 14.2
  qualifications of coroners, 14.4
  reports to prevent further deaths, 14.29
  self-incrimination, 14.18
  standard of proof, 14.27
  summing up, 14.23
  suspension, 14.21
  timing, 14.9
  witness evidence, 14.17

**Inquiries in public**
  access by public
    generally, 14.45
    restrictions, 14.46
  assessors, 14.40
  challenging by judicial review, 14.53
  closing, 14.42
  composition of panel, 14.37
  conversion into statutory inquiry, 14.43
  determination of liability, and, 14.36
  end, 14.42
  enforcement for non-compliance, 14.51
  establishment, 14.35
  evidence
    generally, 14.44
    privileged information, 14.48
    production, 14.47
  expenses of witnesses and participants, 14.54
  immunity from suit, 14.52
  impartiality, 14.39
  information, 14.45
  introduction, 14.33
  judicial review, and, 14.53
  non-compliance, 14.51
  offences, 14.50
  participants' expenses, 14.54
  power to establish 14.35
  powers to produce evidence, 14.47
  power to suspend, 14.41
  privileged information, 14.48
  procedure, 14.44

*Index*

**Inquiries in public**–*contd*
  production of evidence, 14.47
  public access
    generally, 14.45
    restrictions, 14.46
  public interest immunity, 14.49
  purpose, 14.33
  scope, 14.34
  setting-up date, 14.38
  suspension, 14.41
  terms of reference, 14.38
  witness expenses, 14.54
**Insurance**
  business continuity plan, 3.14
  business, 16.1
  business interruption, 16.9
  choice of solicitor
    generally, 16.22
    ICOBS, 16.26
    post-*Sneller* cases, 16.25
    *Sneller v DAS*, 16.23
    UK position, 16.24
  contract law, and, 16.11
  criminal investigations, 11.8
  directors' and officers' liability, 16.8
  disclosure, 16.21
  employers' liability, 16.3
  environmental liability, 16.4
  fatal accident claims, 15.33
  introduction, 16.1
  non-consumer contracts
    background, 16.11
    contracting out, 16.19
    definition, 16.10
    duty of pair presentation, 16.12–16.14
    fraudulent claims, 16.17
    generally, 16.11
    introduction, 16.10
    'knowledge', 16.15
    knowledge of insured, 16.13
    knowledge of insurer, 16.14
    remedies for breach, 16.18
    representations, 16.16
    third party rights against insurers, and, 16.20
    warranties, 16.16
  product liability, 16.5
  professional indemnity
    claims-made nature, 16.7
    generally, 16.6
  public liability, 16.2

**Insurance**–*contd*
  representations, 16.21
  RIDDOR reports, 10.22
  types, 16.1
**Internal audit**
  safety auditing, 2.36
**Internal control**
  UK Corporate Governance Code, 1.7
**Internal investigations**
  cause of incident, 10.45
  conduct, 10.44–10.45
  decision to investigate, 10.43
  gathering information, 10.46
  generally, 10.38
  immediate supervisor, and, 10.42
  incident, 10.39
  information analysis, 10.47
  investigators, 10.41
  reasons, 10.40
  recommendations, 10.48
  relevant events, 10.41
  root cause, 10.45
**Interviews**
  adverse inference, 11.25
  caution, under, 11.24–11.30
  conflicts of interest, 11.23
  'full' response, 11.28
  'no comment', 11.27
  prepared statement, 11.29
  representative of organisation, by, 11.30
  response options, 11.26–11.29
  rights of interviewees, 11.12
  SRA guidance, 11.23
  voluntary statements, and, 11.31
  witnesses, of, 11.32
**Investigations**
  *see also* **RIDDOR reports**
  criminal
    *see also* **Criminal investigations**
    caution at interview, 11.24–11.30
    Code for Crown Prosecutors, 11.4–11.6
    compelled interviews of witnesses, 11.32
    conflicts of interest, 11.23
    deaths in the workplace, 11.3
    disclosure of documents and evidence, 11.35–11.37
    environment investigations, 11.37
    freedom of information, and, 11.38
    internal investigation report, 11.34
    interviews, 11.23–11.32

# Index

Investigations–*contd*
  criminal–*contd*
    introduction, 11.2
    legal professional privilege, 11.33
    police powers, 11.35
    powers of arrest, 11.22
    powers of EA officers, 11.37
    powers of HSE inspector, 11.36
    powers of investigator, 11.2
    powers of police, 11.35
    Protocol for Liaison, 11.3
    response protocol, 11.7–11.21
    voluntary witness statements, 11.31
  discretionary, 10.33
  internal
    cause of incident, 10.45
    conduct, 10.44–10.45
    decision to investigate, 10.43
    gathering information, 10.46
    generally, 10.38
    immediate supervisor, and, 10.42
    incident, 10.39
    information analysis, 10.47
    investigators, 10.41
    reasons, 10.40
    recommendations, 10.48
    relevant events, 10.41
    root cause, 10.45
  introduction, 10.26
  mandatory
    death of any person, 10.28
    fatalities, 10.28
    introduction, 10.27
    likelihood of serious breach of health and safety law, 10.31
    major hazard precursor events, 10.32
    occupational diseases, 10.30
    specified injuries, 10.29
ISO 45001
  generally, 2.40
  relationship with other standards, 2.41
  stages of certification, 2.42
Landfill
  environmental offences, 6.1
  environmental sanctions, 7.41
'Leading Health and Safety at Work' (HSE/IOD guidance)
  generally, 1.14
Legal advice
  criminal investigations, 11.9
Legal professional privilege
  criminal investigations, 11.33

Lifting equipment
  RIDDOR reports, 10.18
Local authorities
  enforcement agencies, as
    environment, 9.33
    fire safety, 8.20
    health and safety, 9.6–9.9
  environmental enforcement, 9.33
  fire safety enforcement, 8.20
  health and safety enforcement
    generally, 9.6
    intervention and enforcement activity, 9.9
    introduction, 9.1
    national code, 9.8
    provision, 9.7
    working with HSE, 9.2
Luminous tube sign switches
  fire safety
    content, 8.28
    generally, 8.35
    introduction, 8.27
Major hazard precursor events
  RIDDOR reports, 10.32
Magistrates' court
  appeals from, 12.46
  generally, 12.2
Management
  business continuity, 3.3
Management of Health and Safety at Work Regulations 1999
  risk management, 2.5
Managing risk
  *see also* Risk management
  corporate governance
    definition, 1.3
    FRC guidance, 1.11
    G20/OECD Principle, 1.12
    historical background, 1.2
    introduction, 1.1
    UK Code, 1.4–1.10
  director's duties
    generally, 1.13
    statutory basis, 1.13
  introduction, 1.1
  'Leading Health and Safety at Work' (HSE/IOD guidance), 1.14
  UK Corporate Governance Code
    application, 1.9
    audit, 1.7
    company purpose, 1.4
    composition, 1.6

475

*Index*

**Managing risk**–*contd*
  UK Corporate Governance Code–*contd*
    'corporate governance', 1.3
    division of responsibilities, 1.5
    evaluation, 1.6
    internal control, 1.7
    introduction, 1.3
    key issues, 1.10
    leadership, 1.4
    purpose, 1.10
    relevant companies, 1.9
    remuneration, 1.8
    structure, 1.10
    succession, 1.6
**Mandatory investigations**
  *see also* **Investigations**
  death of any person, 10.28
  fatalities, 10.28
  introduction, 10.27
  likelihood of serious breach of health and safety law, 10.31
  major hazard precursor events, 10.32
  occupational diseases, 10.30
  specified injuries, 10.29
**Manslaughter**
  corporate
    causation, 4.12
    charities, 4.11
    constabularies, 4.8
    corporations, 4.5
    departments, 4.7
    duty of care, 4.13
    elements, 4.3
    exclusions, 4.18
    foreign companies, 4.10
    foreseeability, 4.15
    generally, 4.2
    gross breach, 4.14
    introduction, 4.1
    investigations, 4.19
    jurisdiction, 4.17
    parent companies, 4.6
    partnerships, 4.9
    police forces, 4.8
    senior management, 4.16
    sub-contractors, 4.11
    subsidiaries, 4.10
  gross negligence
    breach of duty of care, 4.23
    causation, 4.25
    directors, 4.22

**Manslaughter**–*contd*
  gross negligence–*contd*
    duty of care, 4.21–4.25
    foreseeability, 4.24
    generally, 4.20
    gross breach, 4.26
  sentencing
    corporate manslaughter, 13.24–13.54
    gross negligence manslaughter, 13.55–13.59
**Media monitoring and response**
  criminal investigations, 11.21
**Monetary penalties**
  environmental sanctions
    fixed, 7.23
    non-compliance penalties, , 7.32
    variable, 7.24
**Natural Resources Wales**
  generally, 9.29
  policy, 9.30
**Newton hearing**
  criminal proceedings, 12.41
**No case to answer**
  criminal proceedings, 12.35
**Noise nuisance**
  abatement notices, 6.30
  criminal behaviour orders, 6.31
  fixed penalty notices, 6.30
  generally, 6.29
  penalties, 6.30
**Non-compliance penalties**
  environmental sanctions
    application of, 7.40
    compliance notices, 7.35
    enforcement undertakings, 7.33
    fixed monetary penalties, 7.32
    introduction, 7.31
    restoration notices, 7.34
    stop notices, 7.36
    variable monetary penalties, 7.32
**Non-executive directors**
  UK Corporate Governance Code, 1.5
**Northern Ireland Environment Agency (NIEA)**
  generally, 9.31
  policy, 9.32
**Northern Ireland Health and Safety Executive (HSENI)**
  generally, 9.18
  local councils, and, 9.20–9.22
  objectives, 9.19
  responsibilities, 9.21

# Index

Notices of contravention
  see also Enforcement
  generally, 5.7
Nuisance
  environmental claims
    private nuisance, 15.42
    public nuisance, 15.43
  noise
    abatement notices, 6.30
    criminal behaviour orders, 6.31
    fixed penalty notices, 6.30
    generally, 6.29
    penalties, 6.30
  statutory
    appeals, 6.35
    examples, 6.36
    generally, 6.32
    notices, 6.33
    penalties, 6.34
    public sewers, 6.37
Occupational diseases
  RIDDOR reports
    mandatory investigations, , 10.30
    reportable events, 10.17
Offences
  abatement notices and orders
    appeals, 6.35
    examples, 6.36
    generally, 6.32
    noise nuisance, and, 6.30
    notices, 6.33
    penalties, 6.34
  animal by-products, 6.1
  batteries
    generally, 6.20
    penalties, 6.21
    prosecution example, 6.22
  bodies corporate, and
    corporate manslaughter, 4.1–4.19
    environmental offences, 6.9
  corporate manslaughter
    causation, 4.12
    charities, 4.11
    constabularies, 4.8
    corporations, 4.5
    departments, 4.7
    duty of care, 4.13
    elements, 4.3
    exclusions, 4.18
    foreign companies, 4.10
    foreseeability, 4.15
    generally, 4.2

Offences–*contd*
  corporate manslaughter–*contd*
    gross breach, 4.14
    introduction, 4.1
    investigations, 4.19
    jurisdiction, 4.17
    parent companies, 4.6
    partnerships, 4.9
    police forces, 4.8
    senior management, 4.16
    sub-contractors, 4.11
    subsidiaries, 4.10
  emissions, 6.1
  environmental
    batteries, 6.20–6.22
    bodies corporate, and, 6.9
    fly-tipping, 6.10–6.13
    introduction, 6.1
    noise nuisance, 6.29–6.31
    packaging waste, 6.14–6.19
    statutory nuisance, 6.32–6.37
    strict liability, 6.2
    waste electrical and electronic
      equipment, 6.23
    waste, 6.3–6.8
    water, 6.24–6.28
    wildlife, 6.38–6.40
  fire safety
    alarm systems, 8.12
    alterations notices, 8.29
    appeals, 8.41–8.44
    Article 47 notices, 8.35
    certificates, 8.7
    company prosecutions, 8.38
    Crown Fire Inspectors, 8.22
    determinations, 8.45–8.50
    emergency lighting, 8.13
    enforcement authorities, 8.15–8.22
    enforcement notices, 8.30–8.31
    enforcement procedures, 8.27–8.37
    extinguishers, 8.10
    Fire and Rescue Service, 8.16–8.19
    HSWA 1974 notices, 8.34
    Health and Safety Executive, 8.21
    improvement notices, 8.34
    individual prosecutions, 8.39
    inspections, 8.23
    introduction, 8.1
    legislation, 8.2–8.7
    local authority, 8.20
    luminous tube signs, 8.35
    Order 2015, 8.8–8.14

*Index*

Offences–*contd*
  fire safety–*contd*
    Primary Authority Scheme, 8.17–8.19
    prohibition notices, 8.32–8.33
    prosecutions, 8.36–8.40
    public register of notices, 8.24–8.26
    'relevant notice', 8.27
    responsible person, 8.3–8.4
    responsible person prosecutions, 8.40
    restriction notices, 8.32–8.33
    risk assessment, 8.9
    signs, 8.11
    training, 8.14
  fly-tipping
    fixed penalty notices, 6.13
    generally, 6.10
    penalties, 6.11
    prosecution examples, 6.12
  food waste, 6.1
  gross negligence manslaughter
    breach of duty of care, 4.23
    causation, 4.25
    directors, 4.22
    duty of care, 4.21–4.25
    foreseeability, 4.24
    generally, 4.20
    gross breach, 4.26
  HSWA 1974, under
    bodies corporate, and, 4.35
    connivance, 4.38
    consent, 4.37
    delegation of duties, 4.31
    directors, 4.34–4.39
    employees, 4.40–4.41
    employers, 4.27
    exposure to material risk, 4.29
    failures of frontline employees, 4.32
    general duties, 4.27
    neglect, 4.39
    post-accident changes to safe systems, 4.33
    prosecutions under ss 2 and 3, 4.28
    'reasonably practicable', 4.30
    safe system changes, 4.32
    senior managers, 4.34–4.39
  illegal dumping of waste
    fixed penalty notices, 6.13
    generally, 6.10
    penalties, 6.11
    prosecution examples, 6.12

Offences–*contd*
  industrial emissions, 6.1
  landfill, 6.1
  manslaughter
    corporate, 4.1–4.19
    gross negligence, 4.20–4.26
  noise nuisance
    abatement notices, 6.30
    criminal behaviour orders, 6.31
    fixed penalty notices, 6.30
    generally, 6.29
    penalties, 6.30
  packaging waste
    activity list, 6.18
    definition of 'handling', 6.17
    definition of 'packaging', 6.15
    description, 6.18
    generally, 6.14
    legal background, 6.1
    obligated packing producer, 6.16
    registration, 6.19
  public sewers
    use restrictions, 6.37
  statutory nuisance
    appeals, 6.35
    examples, 6.36
    generally, 6.32
    notices, 6.33
    penalties, 6.34
    public sewers, 6.37
  strict liability
    environmental offences, 6.2
  waste
    batteries, 6.20–6.22
    carriers brokers registration, 6.7
    definition of 'waste', 6.3
    electrical and electronic equipment, 6.23
    fly-tipping, 6.10–6.13
    generally, 6.5
    legal background, 6.1
    packaging, 6.14–6.19
    penalties, 6.8
    unlawful deposit of controlled waste, 6.6
  waste electrical and electronic equipment
    generally, 6.23
    legal background, 6.1
  water
    anti-pollution works, 6.26
    England and Wales, in, 6.25

*Index*

Offences–*contd*
  water–*contd*
    generally, 6.24
    Northern Ireland, in, 6.27
    penalties, 6.28
    Scotland, in, 6.27
  wildlife
    examples, 6.39
    generally, 6.38
    prosecution examples, 6.40
Office of Nuclear Regulation (ONR)
  generally, 9.16
  policy, 9.17
Office of the Rail Regulator (ORR)
  formal tools, 9.14
  generally, 9.10
  policy, 9.11
  powers, 9.12
  prosecutions, 9.15
  RIDDOR reports, 10.10
  strategies, 9.13
Overhead electric lines
  RIDDOR reports, 10.18
Packaging waste
  activity list, 6.18
  definition of 'handling', 6.17
  definition of 'packaging', 6.15
  description, 6.18
  generally, 6.14
  legal background, 6.1
  obligated packing producer, 6.16
  registration, 6.19
Personal injury claims
  alternative dispute resolution, 15.18
  claim, 15.15
  disclosure, 15.16
  dismissal of fraudulent claims, 15.10
  expert evidence, 15.17
  generally, 15.8
  letter of claim, 15.14
  letter of notification, 15.12
  pre-action protocol, 15.11–15.17
  rehabilitation, 15.13
  response, 15.15
  *Stark v Post Office*, 15.9
Personnel
  business continuity, 3.32
Pipeline works
  RIDDOR reports, 10.18
Plea
  case management, 12.13
  trial, at, 12.33

Plea and trial preparation hearing
  generally, 12.11
  introduction, 12.6
Points of law
  criminal proceedings, 12.32
Police powers
  criminal investigations, 11.35
Powers of arrest
  criminal investigations, 11.22
Pressure systems
  RIDDOR reports, 10.18
Prohibition notices
  appeals
    costs, 5.5
    procedure, 5.4
    purpose, 5.6
  fee for intervention (FFI)
    background, 5.7
    challenging an invoice, 5.8–5.12
    disputing, 5.10
    generally, 5.7
    purpose of challenge, 5.12
    querying, 5.9
    recoverable time, 5.7
    repayment, 5.11
  fire safety
    content, 8.28
    example, 8.33
    generally, 8.32
    HSWA 1974, under, 8.34
    introduction, 8.27
  generally, 5.3
Property damage claims
  award of damages, 15.36
  generally, 15.34
  measure of damages, 15.35
Proportionality
  fine to means of offender, of
    corporate manslaughter, 13.27
    environmental offences by organisations, 13.78
    health and safety offences by organisations, 13.7
Prosecution case
  criminal proceedings, 12.34
Prosecution costs
  criminal proceedings, 12.44
Prosecutions
  appeals
    Crown Court, from, 12.47
    introduction, 12.45
    magistrates' courts, from, 12.46

*Index*

**Prosecutions**–*contd*
  costs orders
    central funds, from, 12.43
    defendant's costs, 12.43
    prosecution costs, 12.44
  criminal investigations
    evidential test, 11.5
    generally, 11.4
    public interest test, 11.6
  Criminal Procedure Rules, 12.1
  environmental offences, 7.8
  evidential test, 11.5
  fire safety
    companies, 8.38
    examples, 8.37–8.40
    factors affecting choice, 8.37
    generally, 8.36
    individual, 8.39
    responsible person, 8.40
  Health and Safety at Work etc Act 1974 offences, 4.28
  lack of system, for
    *Cundall v Leeds City Council*, 2.10
    *Goldscheider v Royal Opera House*, 2.9
    *Kennedy v Cordia (Services) LLP*, 2.11
  Office of the Rail Regulator, 9.15
  process
    abuse of process, 12.25
    appeals, 12.45–12.47
    bad character, 12.23
    case management, 12.9–12.14
    commencing proceedings, 12.8
    costs, 12.43–12.44
    courts, 12.2–12.3
    defence statement, 12.19–12.20
    disclosure and defence statement, 12.15–12.18
    dismissal of charges, 12.24
    expert evidence, 12.21
    hearsay evidence, 12.22
    Rules, 12.1
    sentencing, 12.40–12.42
    third party disclosure, 12.20
    trial, at, 12.26–12.39
    types of offence, 12.4–12.7
  public interest test, 11.6
  sentencing
    confiscation, 12.42
    costs, 12.43–12.44

**Prosecutions**–*contd*
  sentencing–*contd*
    hearing, 12.40
    Newton hearing, 12.41
  trial procedure
    admissions, 12.31
    bundles, 12.28
    burden of proof, 12.27
    closing addresses, 12.37
    defence case, 12.36
    files of documents, 12.28
    introduction, 12.26
    judge's summing up, 12.38
    no case to answer, 12.35
    plea, 12.33
    points of law, 12.32
    prosecution case, 12.34
    start of the trial, 12.33
    summing up, 12.38
    verdict, 12.39
    witness evidence, 12.29
    witness statements, 12.30
  waste offences
    batteries, 6.22
    illegal dumping, 6.12
  wildlife offences, 6.40
**Protocol for Liaison**
  criminal investigations, 11.3
**Public inquiries**
  access by public
    generally, 14.45
    restrictions, 14.46
  assessors, 14.40
  challenging by judicial review, 14.53
  closing, 14.42
  composition of panel, 14.37
  conversion into statutory inquiry, 14.43
  determination of liability, and, 14.36
  end, 14.42
  enforcement for non-compliance, 14.51
  establishment, 14.35
  evidence
    generally, 14.44
    privileged information, 14.48
    production, 14.47
  expenses of witnesses and participants, 14.54
  immunity from suit, 14.52
  impartiality, 14.39
  information, 14.45

Public inquiries–*contd*
 introduction, 14.33
 judicial review, and, 14.53
 non-compliance, 14.51
 offences, 14.50
 participants' expenses, 14.54
 power to establish 14.35
 powers to produce evidence, 14.47
 power to suspend, 14.41
 privileged information, 14.48
 procedure, 14.44
 production of evidence, 14.47
 public access
  generally, 14.45
  restrictions, 14.46
 public interest immunity, 14.49
 purpose, 14.33
 scope, 14.34
 setting-up date, 14.38
 suspension, 14.41
 terms of reference, 14.38
 witness expenses, 14.54
Public interest test
 criminal investigations, 11.6
Public register
 fire safety notices
  duration, 8.25
  generally, 8.24
  viewing, 8.26
Public relations
 business continuity, 3.29
Public sewers
 use restrictions, 6.37
Radiation generators
 RIDDOR reports, 10.18
Recovery time
 business impact analysis, 3.7
Remediation
 environmental sanctions, 7.5
 health and safety offences by organisations, 13.11
Remuneration policies
 UK Corporate Governance Code
  generally, 1.8
  key issues, 1.10
Reporting
 UK Corporate Governance Code, 1.10
Reporting injuries, diseases and occurrences
 biological agents, 10.18
 breathing apparatus, 10.18
 criminal investigations, 11.19

Reporting injuries, diseases and occurrences–*contd*
 dangerous occurrences, 10.18
 death of person
  mandatory investigations, 10.28
  reportable events, 10.12
 discretionary investigations, 10.33
 diving operations, 10.18
 duration of record keeping, 10.37
 electrical incidents, 10.18
 exempt events, 10.36
 explosions, 10.19
 failure to report, 10.23
 fatalities
  mandatory investigations, 10.28
  reportable events, 10.12
 fires, 10.1
 flammable liquids and gases, 10.19
 gas incidents, 10.20
 hazardous escapes of substances, 10.19
 insurance, 10.22
 internal investigations
  cause of incident, 10.45
  conduct, 10.44–10.45
  decision to investigate, 10.43
  gathering information, 10.46
  generally, 10.38
  immediate supervisor, and, 10.42
  incident, 10.39
  information analysis, 10.47
  investigators, 10.41
  reasons, 10.40
  recommendations, 10.48
  relevant events, 10.41
  root cause, 10.45
 investigations
  discretionary, 10.33
  internal, 10.38–10.48
  introduction, 10.26
  mandatory, 10.27–10.32
 legal requirement, 10.10
 lifting equipment, 10.18
 likelihood of serious breach of health and safety law, 10.31
 major hazard precursor events, 10.32
 maker of report, 10.2–10.9
 mandatory investigations
  death of any person, 10.28
  fatalities, 10.28
  introduction, 10.27
  likelihood of serious breach of health and safety law, 10.31

*Index*

Reporting injuries, diseases and occurrences–*contd*
  mandatory investigations–*contd*
    major hazard precursor events, 10.32
    occupational diseases, 10.30
    specified injuries, 10.29
  non-fatal incidents to non-workers, 10.16
  occupational diseases
    mandatory investigations, , 10.30
    reportable events, 10.17
  Office of Rail Regulator, and, 10.10
  over reporting, 10.24
  overhead electric lines, 10.18
  over-seven-day incapacitation of worker, 10.14
  over-three-day incapacitation, 10.15
  pipeline works, 10.18
  pressure systems, 10.18
  procedure, 10.21
  purpose of report, 10.1
  radiation generators, 10.18
  records, 10.25, 10.34
  reportable events
    dangerous occurrences, 10.18
    death of any person, 10.12
    gas incidents, 10.20
    introduction, 10.11
    non-fatal incidents to non-workers, 10.16
    occupational diseases, 10.17
    other than offshore workplaces 10.19
    over-seven-day incapacitation of worker, 10.14
    over-three-day incapacitation, 10.15
    specified injuries to workers, 10.13
  'responsible person'
    control of premises, 10.4
    employers, 10.3
    employment agency, 10.7
    gas engineers, 10.9
    gas suppliers, 10.8
    injured persons, 10.6
    introduction, 10.2
    public, 10.6
    representatives, 10.6
    self-employed, 10.5
  scaffolding collapse, 10.18
  specified injuries
    mandatory investigations, 10.29
    reportable events, 10.13

Reporting injuries, diseases and occurrences–*contd*
  structural collapse, 10.19
  timing of report, 10.35
  train collisions, 10.18
  wells, 10.18
'Responsible person'
  control of premises, 10.4
  employers, 10.3
  employment agency, 10.7
  fire safety
    generally, 8.3
    prosecutions, 8.40
    requirements, 8.4
  gas engineers, 10.9
  gas suppliers, 10.8
  injured persons, 10.6
  introduction, 10.2
  public, 10.6
  representatives, 10.6
  self-employed, 10.5
**Restoration notices**
  environmental sanctions
    generally, 7.26
    non-compliance penalties, 7.34
**Restriction notices**
  fire safety
    content, 8.28
    example, 8.33
    generally, 8.32
**Revocation notices**
  environmental sanctions, 7.5
**RIDDOR reports**
  biological agents, 10.18
  breathing apparatus, 10.18
  criminal investigations, 11.19
  dangerous occurrences, 10.18
  death of person
    mandatory investigations, 10.28
    reportable events, 10.12
  discretionary investigations, 10.33
  diving operations, 10.18
  duration of record keeping, 10.37
  electrical incidents, 10.18
  exempt events, 10.36
  explosions, 10.19
  failure to report, 10.23
  fatalities
    mandatory investigations, 10.28
    reportable events, 10.12
  fires, 10.1
  flammable liquids and gases, 10.19

## Index

RIDDOR reports–*contd*
  gas incidents, 10.20
  hazardous escapes of substances, 10.19
  insurance, 10.22
  internal investigations
    cause of incident, 10.45
    conduct, 10.44–10.45
    decision to investigate, 10.43
    gathering information, 10.46
    generally, 10.38
    immediate supervisor, and, 10.42
    incident, 10.39
    information analysis, 10.47
    investigators, 10.41
    reasons, 10.40
    recommendations, 10.48
    relevant events, 10.41
    root cause, 10.45
  investigations
    discretionary, 10.33
    internal, 10.38–10.48
    introduction, 10.26
    mandatory, 10.27–10.32
  legal requirement, 10.10
  lifting equipment, 10.18
  likelihood of serious breach of health and safety law, 10.31
  major hazard precursor events, 10.32
  maker of report, 10.2–10.9
  mandatory investigations
    death of any person, 10.28
    fatalities, 10.28
    introduction, 10.27
    likelihood of serious breach of health and safety law, 10.31
    major hazard precursor events, 10.32
    occupational diseases, 10.30
    specified injuries, 10.29
  non-fatal incidents to non-workers, 10.16
  occupational diseases
    mandatory investigations, , 10.30
    reportable events, 10.17
  Office of Rail Regulator, and, 10.10
  over reporting, 10.24
  overhead electric lines, 10.18
  over-seven-day incapacitation of worker, 10.14
  over-three-day incapacitation, 10.15
  pipeline works, 10.18
  pressure systems, 10.18

RIDDOR reports–*contd*
  procedure, 10.21
  purpose of report, 10.1
  radiation generators, 10.18
  records, 10.25, 10.34
  reportable events
    dangerous occurrences, 10.18
    death of any person, 10.12
    gas incidents, 10.20
    incidents other than offshore workplace, 10.19
    introduction, 10.11
    non-fatal incidents to non-workers, 10.16
    occupational diseases, 10.17
    over-seven-day incapacitation of worker, 10.14
    over-three-day incapacitation, 10.15
    specified injuries to workers, 10.13
  'responsible person'
    control of premises, 10.4
    employers, 10.3
    employment agency, 10.7
    gas engineers, 10.9
    gas suppliers, 10.8
    injured persons, 10.6
    introduction, 10.2
    public, 10.6
    representatives, 10.6
    self-employed, 10.5
  scaffolding collapse, 10.18
  specified injuries
    mandatory investigations, 10.29
    reportable events, 10.13
  structural collapse, 10.19
  timing of report, 10.35
  train collisions, 10.18
  wells, 10.18

**Risk assessment**
  *see also* **Risk management**
  evaluating the risk
    generally, 2.18
    matrix, 2.19–2.32
  fire safety 8.9
  'hazard', 2.13
  identifying hazards, 2.16
  introduction, 2.12
  matrix
    consequences, 2.21
    impact, 2.21
    introducing risk controls, 2.24
    introduction, 2.19

*Index*

Risk assessment–*contd*
matrix–*contd*
likelihood, 2.20
likelihood × consequence, 2.22
probability, 2.20
reducing the consequence, 2.24
reducing the likelihood, 2.23
reducing the likelihood and consequence, 2.25–2.32
method of harm, 2.17
persons in danger of harm, 2.17
recording significant findings, 2.33
review, 2.34
'risk', 2.14
steps, 2.15–2.34
updating, 3.34
Risk management
*see also* Managing risk
'as low as is reasonably practicable', 2.4
assessment
evaluating the risk, 2.18–2.32
'hazard', 2.13
identifying hazards, 2.16
introduction, 2.12
matrix, 2.19–2.32
method of harm, 2.17
persons in danger of harm, 2.17
recording significant findings, 2.33
review, 2.34
'risk', 2.14
steps, 2.15–2.34
updating, 3.34
certification audits
external certification, 2.39
generally, 2.38
ISO 45001, 2.40–2.42
controls in the workplace, 2.2
external audit, 2.37
external certification, 2.39
Health and Safety at Work etc Act 1974
'as low as is reasonably practicable', 2.4
generally, 2.3
internal audit, 2.36
introduction, 2.1
ISO 45001
generally, 2.40
relationship with other standards, 2.41
stages of certification, 2.42

Risk management–*contd*
legislation
HSWA 1974, 2.3–2.4
MHSWR 1999, 2.5
other, 2.7
specific requirements, with, 2.8
W(HSW)R 1992, 2.6
Management of Health and Safety at Work Regulations 1999, 2.5
prosecution for lack of system
*Cundall v Leeds City Council*, 2.10
*Goldscheider v Royal Opera House*, 2.9
*Kennedy v Cordia (Services) LLP*, 2.11
risk matrix
consequences, 2.21
impact, 2.21
introducing risk controls, 2.24
introduction, 2.19
likelihood, 2.20
likelihood × consequence, 2.22
probability, 2.20
reducing the consequence, 2.24
reducing the likelihood, 2.23
reducing the likelihood and consequence, 2.25–2.32
safety auditing
external audit, 2.37
generally, 2.35
internal audit, 2.36
Workplace (Health, Safety and Welfare) Regulations 1992, 2.6
Risk matrix
consequences, 2.21
control, 2.30
deciding the risk control, 2.26
discipline, 2.32
elimination, 2.27
impact, 2.21
introducing risk controls, 2.24
introduction, 2.19
isolation, 2.29
likelihood, 2.20
likelihood × consequence, 2.22
personal protective equipment (PPE), 2.31
probability, 2.20
reducing the consequence, 2.24
reducing the likelihood, 2.23
reducing the likelihood and consequence, 2.25–2.32

Risk matrix–*contd*
  reduction, 2.28
  residual risk, 2.25
Safety auditing
  external audit, 2.37
  generally, 2.35
  internal audit, 2.36
Salvage
  business continuity plan, 3.15
Scaffolding collapse
  RIDDOR reports, 10.18
Scottish Environment Protection agency (SEPA)
  generally, 9.27
  policy, 9.28
Security issues
  business continuity
    communications, 3.33
    plan, 3.11
Sentencing
  adjustment
    corporate manslaughter, 13.28
    environmental offences by individuals, 13.95
    environmental offences by organisations, 13.79
    health and safety offences by organisations, 13.8
  ancillary orders
    corporate manslaughter, 13.31
    environmental offences by individuals, 13.98
    environmental offences by organisations, 13.82
    health and safety offences by individuals, 13.20
    health and safety offences by organisations, 13.11
  assisting prosecution
    environmental offences by individuals, 13.96
    environmental offences by organisations, 13.80
    health and safety offences by individuals, 13.18
    health and safety offences by organisations, 13.9
  category range
    corporate manslaughter, 13.26
    environmental offences by individuals, 13.89

Sentencing–*contd*
  category range–*contd*
    environmental offences by organisations, 13.67
    health and safety offences by individuals, 13.16
    health and safety offences by organisations, 13.6
  community orders
    environmental offences by individuals, 13.104
  compensation
    corporate manslaughter, 13.31
    environmental offences by individuals, 13.86
    environmental offences by organisations, 13.64
    health and safety offences by individuals, 13.20
    health and safety offences by organisations, 13.11
  confiscation
    environmental offences by individuals, 13.87
    environmental offences by organisations, 13.65
    generally, 12.42
  corporate manslaughter
    adjustment, 13.28
    ancillary orders, 13.31
    category range, 13.26
    compensation, 13.31
    examples, 13.34–13.54
    guilty plea, 13.30
    introduction, 13.24
    proportionality of fine to means of offender, 13.27
    reasons, 13.33
    reduction of fine, 13.29–13.30
    seriousness of offence, 13.25
    starting point, 13.26
    totality principle, 13.32
  costs, 12.43–12.44
  environmental offences
    individuals, 13.85–13.104
    organisations, 13.63–13.84
  environmental offences by individuals
    adjustment, 13.95
    ancillary orders, 13.98
    assisting prosecution, 13.96
    bands of fine, 13.103
    category range, 13.89

*Index*

**Sentencing**–*contd*
  environmental offences by individuals–*contd*
    combination of financial orders removes economic benefit derived, 13.94
    community orders, 13.104
    compensation, 13.86
    confiscation, 13.87
    determining offence category, 13.88
    financial information, 13.90–13.91
    general principles, 13.90–13.92
    guilty plea, 13.97
    introduction, 13.85
    reasons, 13.100
    reduction, 13.96–13.97
    seriousness of offence, 13.90
    starting point, 13.89
    time spent on bail, 13.101
    totality, 13.99
  environmental offences by organisations
    adjustment, 13.79
    ancillary orders, 13.82
    assisting prosecution, 13.80
    category range, 13.67
    combination of financial orders removes economic benefit derived, 13.77
    compensation, 13.64
    confiscation, 13.65
    determining offence category, 13.66
    financial information, 13.69–13.75
    fines, 13.68–13.75
    guidelines, 13.63–13.75
    guilty plea, 13.81
    introduction, 13.61
    proportionality of fine to means of offender, 13.78
    reasons, 13.84
    reduction, 13.80–13.81
    starting point, 13.62
    structure ranges, 13.62
    totality, 13.83
  financial information
    environmental offences by individuals, 13.90–13.91
    environmental offences for organisations, 13.69–13.75
  fines
    corporate manslaughter, 13.24–13.54

**Sentencing**–*contd*
  fines–*contd*
    environmental offences, 13.61–13.104
    generally, 13.3
    health and safety offences, 13.4–13.23
    fire safety, 13.60
    reduction, 13.105
    totality, 13.106
  fire safety, 13.60
  gross negligence manslaughter
    examples, 13.56–13.59
    generally, 13.55
  guidelines, 13.2
  guilty plea
    corporate manslaughter, 13.30
    environmental offences by individuals, 13.97
    environmental offences by organisations, 13.81
    guideline, 13.105
    health and safety offences by individuals, 13.19
    health and safety offences by organisations, 13.10
  health and safety offences
    individuals, 13.14–13.23
    organisations, 13.4–13.13
  health and safety offences by individuals
    ancillary orders, 13.20
    assisting prosecution, 13.18
    category range, 13.16
    compensation, 13.20
    determining offence category, 13.15
    guilty plea, 13.19
    introduction, 13.14
    reasons, 13.21
    reduction, 13.18–13.19
    review of financial element, 13.17
    starting point, 13.16
    time spent on bail, 13.23
    totality principle, 13.21
  health and safety offences by organisations
    adjustment, 13.8
    ancillary orders, 13.11
    assisting prosecution, 13.9
    category range, 13.6
    compensation, 13.11
    determining offence category, 13.5
    forfeiture, 13.11

*Index*

Sentencing–*contd*
  health and safety offences by organisations–*contd*
    guilty plea, 13.10
    introduction, 13.4
    proportionality of fine to means of offender, 13.7
    reasons, 13.13
    reduction, 13.9–13.10
    remediation, 13.11
    starting point, 13.6
    totality principle, 13.12
  hearing, 12.40
  introduction, 13.1–13.3
  manslaughter
    corporate manslaughter, 13.24–13.54
    gross negligence manslaughter, 13.55–13.59
  Newton hearing, 12.41
  proportionality of fine to means of offender
    corporate manslaughter, 13.27
    environmental offences by organisations, 13.78
    health and safety offences by organisations, 13.7
  purposes, 13.1
  reasons
    corporate manslaughter, 13.33
    environmental offences by individuals, 13.100
    environmental offences by organisations, 13.84
    health and safety offences by individuals, 13.21
    health and safety offences by organisations, 13.13
  reduction
    corporate manslaughter, 13.29–13.30
    environmental offences by individuals, 13.96–13.97
    environmental offences by organisations, 13.80–13.81
    health and safety offences by individuals, 13.18–13.19
    health and safety offences by organisations, 13.9–13.10
  remediation
    health and safety offences by organisations, 13.11

Sentencing–*contd*
  seriousness of offence
    corporate manslaughter, 13.25
    environmental offences by individuals, 13.90
  starting point
    corporate manslaughter, 13.26
    environmental offences by individuals, 13.89
    environmental offences by organisations, 13.62
    health and safety offences by individuals, 13.16
    health and safety offences by organisations, 13.6
  totality principle
    corporate manslaughter, 13.32
    environmental offences by individuals, 13.99
    environmental offences by organisations, 13.83
    guideline, 13.106
    health and safety offences by individuals, 13.21
    health and safety offences by organisations, 13.12
  trial procedure
    confiscation, 12.42
    costs, 12.43–12.44
    hearing, 12.40
    Newton hearing, 12.41
**Services**
  business continuity plan, 3.13
**Signs**
  fire safety, 8.11
**Social media monitoring and response**
  criminal investigations, 11.21
**Statutory nuisance**
  appeals, 6.35
  examples, 6.36
  generally, 6.32
  notices, 6.33
  penalties, 6.34
  public sewers, 6.37
**Stop notices**
  environmental sanctions
    generally, 7.27
    non-compliance penalties, 7.36
**Strict liability**
  environmental offences, 6.2

*Index*

**Structural collapse**
  RIDDOR reports, 10.19
**Summary offences**
  criminal proceedings, 12.5
**Summing up**
  criminal proceedings, 12.38
**Suspension notices**
  environmental sanctions
    challenges, 7.29
    generally, 7.28
    introduction, 7.5
**Third party disclosure**
  criminal proceedings, 12.20
**Totality in sentencing**
  corporate manslaughter, 13.32
  environmental offences by individuals, 13.99
  environmental offences by organisations, 13.83
  guideline, 13.106
  health and safety offences by individuals, 13.21
  health and safety offences by organisations, 13.12
**Train collisions**
  RIDDOR reports, 10.18
**Training**
  fire safety, 8.14
**Trial procedure**
  admissions, 12.31
  bundles, 12.28
  burden of proof, 12.27
  closing addresses, 12.37
  defence case, 12.36
  files of documents, 12.28
  introduction, 12.26
  judge's summing up, 12.38
  no case to answer, 12.35
  plea, 12.33
  points of law, 12.32
  prosecution case, 12.34
  start of the trial, 12.33
  summing up, 12.38
  verdict, 12.39
  witness evidence, 12.29
  witness statements, 12.30
**UK Corporate Governance Code**
  application, 1.9
  audit, 1.7
  Board of directors
    composition, 1.6
    division of responsibilities, 1.5

**UK Corporate Governance Code–**
    *contd*
  Board of directors–*contd*
    duties, 1.7
    evaluation, 1.6
    key issues, 1.10
    leadership, 1.4
    remuneration, 1.8
    succession, 1.6
  Chair of the Board, 1.5
  company purpose, 1.4
  composition, 1.6
  'corporate governance', 1.3
  division of responsibilities, 1.5
  evaluation, 1.6
  internal control, 1.7
  introduction, 1.3
  key issues, 1.10
  leadership, 1.4
  non-executive directors, 1.5
  purpose, 1.10
  relevant companies, 1.9
  remuneration policies
    generally, 1.8
    key issues, 1.10
  reporting, 1.10
  structure, 1.10
  succession, 1.6
**Undertakings**
  environmental sanctions
    generally, 7.30
    non-compliance penalties, 7.33
**Unused material**
  criminal proceedings
    failure to disclose, 12.25
    generally, 12.15
**Variable monetary penalties**
  environmental sanctions
    generally, 7.24
    non-compliance penalties, 7.32
**Variation notices**
  environmental sanctions, 7.5
**Vehicle seizure**
  environmental sanctions
    example, 7.21
    generally, 7.20
**Verdict**
  criminal proceedings, 12.39
**Voluntary witness statements**
  criminal investigations, 11.31
**Warnings**
  environmental sanctions, 7.3

## Index

Waste electrical and electronic equipment (WEEE)
  generally, 6.23
  legal background, 6.1
Waste offences
  batteries
    generally, 6.20
    penalties, 6.21
    prosecution example, 6.22
  bodies corporate, and, 6.9
  carriers brokers registration, 6.7
  definition of 'waste', 6.3
  electrical and electronic equipment
    generally, 6.23
    legal background, 6.1
  fly-tipping
    fixed penalty notices, 6.13
    generally, 6.10
    penalties, 6.11
    prosecution examples, 6.12
  food, 6.1
  generally, 6.5
  illegal dumping
    fixed penalty notices, 6.13
    generally, 6.10
    penalties, 6.11
    prosecution examples, 6.12
  legal background, 6.1
  packaging
    activity list, 6.18
    definition of 'handling', 6.17
    definition of 'packaging', 6.15

Waste offences–*contd*
  packaging–*contd*
    description, 6.18
    generally, 6.14
    legal background, 6.1
    obligated packing producer, 6.16
    registration, 6.19
  penalties, 6.8
  strict liability, 6.2
  unlawful deposit of controlled waste, 6.6
Water-related offences
  anti-pollution works, 6.26
  England and Wales, in, 6.25
  generally, 6.24
  Northern Ireland, in, 6.27
  penalties, 6.28
  Scotland, in, 6.27
Wells
  RIDDOR reports, 10.18
Wildlife
  environmental offences
    examples, 6.39
    generally, 6.38
  prosecution examples, 6.40
Witness evidence
  criminal proceedings, 12.29
Witness statements
  criminal proceedings, 12.30
Workplace (Health, Safety and Welfare) Regulations 1992
  risk management, 2.6